WAR AT SEA

·

A Naval History of World War II

·

NATHAN MILLER

A LISA DREW BOOK

SCRIBNER
NEW YORK LONDON TORONTO SYDNEY TOKYO SINGAPORE

SCRIBNER
1230 Avenue of the Americas
New York, NY 10020

SCRIBNER and design are trademarks of Simon & Schuster Inc.

DESIGNED BY ERICH HOBBING

Manufactured in the United States of America

1   2   3   4   5   6   7   8   9   10

Library of Congress Cataloging-in-Publication Data

Miller, Nathan, date.
War at sea : a naval history of World War II / Nathan Miller.
p.   cm.
Includes bibliographical references and index.
1. World War, 1939–1945—Naval operations. I. Title.
D770.M49   1995
940.54'5—dc20   95-8484
CIP

ISBN 0-684-80380-1

TO
ALL WHO SERVED
AT SEA
IN
WORLD WAR II

Contents

Preface

History records few more gripping dramas than the naval history of World War II. It was the last great sea war, but in the half century since the final battles of that struggle, the conflict has receded into the past. Narvik, the Battle of the Atlantic, Midway, and the Philippine Sea are to the current generation as remote as Waterloo and Gettysburg. The purpose of this book, then, is to bring the story of these monumental events—and the achievements, suffering, and heroism of those who served at sea in that war—to the attention of readers who have only a nodding acquaintance with it.

Too often today, war is viewed as a bloodless computer game complete with "smart" bombs, guided missiles, and "surgical strikes." In reality, war is about death. It is a mixture of boredom, exhaustion, and sudden and terrifying moments of horror. This is particularly true of war at sea. One minute a ship can be steaming peacefully on a calm ocean; in the next it can be ripped apart by torpedoes with its crew fighting for their lives in a cauldron of flaming oil or scalding steam.

The battle to secure the seas was the one campaign of World War II that raged from the beginning of the conflict to the end. Much of the early fighting in the European theater was at sea, as were the closing battles in the Pacific. Both sides used the oceans to their advantage. As an island nation, Britain depended for survival upon manpower and supplies brought from overseas. Unable to muster a conventional fleet, Germany employed submarines and surface raiders to try to impose a blockade upon Britain; to strike at the Arctic convoys carrying vital supplies to the Soviet Union; and to sever, with the help of the Italian Navy, British lifelines in the Mediterranean. These efforts failed by only the narrowest of margins.

In the Pacific, sea power determined the course of the struggle. Naval forces spearheaded the Japanese conquest of the Western Pacific and Southeast Asian waters. U.S. Navy ships and aircraft eventually blunted this offensive in the Coral Sea and at Midway, and then led the way to the Japanese home islands. On both fronts, the Allied navies carried armies to hostile shores, had a substantial role in isolating prospective beachheads, thrust aside enemy resistance to put the invaders ashore and kept them supplied.

World War II marked a decisive shift in naval warfare. At the beginning of the struggle, naval strength was measured by the battleship, and admirals still thought in terms of the decisive encounter between battle fleets articulated by Alfred Thayer Mahan, the high priest of sea power. Aircraft carriers and submarines were regarded as dubious auxiliaries to the battle line. The war changed all that. Carrier-based aircraft served first as an extension of the battleship's guns, and then, along with the submarine, took over the battleship's role. Together, the carrier and submarine became the supreme arbiters of naval warfare.

Numerous books deal with World War II naval operations in the Atlantic and Pacific as separate entities. Others are devoted to a single battle—Midway, for instance—or to limited episodes such as the epic pursuit of the German battleship *Bismarck*. Several of the participating nations have also produced their own multivolume official histories of events. One-volume histories of World War II at sea that treat the struggle as a conceptual whole are rare, however, perhaps because of the sheer magnitude of the conflict. This book is intended to fill this gap and to provide a study of the war at sea for general readers.

An effort has been made to cover the major operations of the British, German, Italian, American, Japanese, Canadian, and Russian navies. I have tried to supply a human face to these events by placing special emphasis upon the personal narratives of the men who manned the ships and aircraft. Unlike earlier writers, I had access to the recently released Ultra intelligence information the Allies procured from their deciphering of coded messages passed by their enemies.

This book is the fruit of my own service in the U.S. Navy during the closing months of World War II and years of reading and speculation. From this, I have concluded the underlying reason for the Allied victory in the war at sea was superior leadership in adversity. Usually, this triumph is credited to the overwhelming preponderance of manpower and materiel—which was certainly true after 1943. But what about the years in which the Allies lacked such superiority?

When the going was toughest—such as at Dunkirk in 1940, in the Mediterranean in 1941, and in the Atlantic in 1942—the Royal Navy produced such leaders as Bertram Ramsay, Andrew Cunningham, and Max Horton. In the Pacific in 1942, Chester Nimitz and Raymond Spruance brought the U.S. Navy back from the debacle at Pearl Harbor and won the decisive victory at Midway. Ernest King had the strategic vision to force through the Guadalcanal counteroffensive, which prevented the Japanese from consolidating their conquests, and began to march to victory. There were costly mistakes and blunders in the Allied conduct of the sea war, but the skill of the commanders, matched with the courage of the tactical leaders and enlisted men, denied the Axis powers a triumph. Once the tide had turned, overwhelming Allied resources made it impossible for them to recoup.

As befits its subject, this is a long book, and a book of such magnitude required much help. I am grateful for the assistance of the staffs of the Nimitz Library at the U.S. Naval Academy at Annapolis; the Public Records Office at Kew, outside London; the National Archives and the Naval Historical Center in Washington, especially Charles Haberlein and Edward Finney, Jr., of the photograph section; as well as Benis M. Frank, chief historian at the Marine Corps Historical Center. David Black, my literary agent, was generous with his time and advice. Lisa Drew, my editor, guided this book to completion with her usual skill, understanding, and enthusiasm. Her assistant, Katherine Boyle Ekrem, was helpful and supportive. Ernest B. Furgurson, the distinguished Civil War historian, provided encouragement throughout the entire project and, along with Kenneth J. Hagan, professor of history and museum director emeritus at the

Naval Academy, read the manuscript and made dozens of suggestions that improved it.

And, as always, it would have been impossible to complete the book without the support of my wife, Jeanette.

There are no flowers on a sailor's grave.
—*German sailors' song*

WAR AT SEA

Prologue

Rising and falling on the long Atlantic swells, *U-30*'s sharp bow knifed through the blue-black sea, sending whiplashes of spray hissing across her conning tower. Oberleutnant Fritz-Julius Lemp braced himself against her roll, and searched the horizon for prey. It was about 1730* on Sunday, September 3, 1939, and Germany had been at war with France and Britain since midday. An hour of light remained, and Lemp, a jaunty career officer of twenty-six, was eager to strike an early blow against the enemy. *U-30*'s four bow torpedo tubes were loaded and ready, but the North Atlantic shipping lanes, usually teeming with vessels, were disappointingly empty.

Over the previous sixteen days, *U-30* and fifteen other oceangoing submarines had secretly slipped to sea as Germany prepared for the invasion of Poland. Realizing that he could never hope to overtake the British lead in capital ships, Grand Admiral Erich Raeder, commander of the German navy—the Kriegsmarine—intended to rely on a war of attrition against Britain's maritime trade. Fanning out across the Western Approaches, where thousands of miles of sea routes converged on the United Kingdom, the U-boats were to be in

---

*Throughout this book, twenty-four-hour naval time will be used. Unless otherwise stated, all times and dates will be local. For a table of comparative American, British, and German naval ranks, see appendix 1.

a position to attack enemy shipping if Britain and France came to the
aid of their Polish ally. Two surface raiders, the pocket battleships
Admiral Graf Spee and *Deutschland*, were also sent to sea. *Graf
Spee*'s operational zone was south of the equator; *Deutschland* was to
hunt in the North Atlantic.

Under orders to avoid surveillance, the U-boats ran submerged
during daylight and surfaced only at night, to recharge their batteries. Lemp skirted the coast of Norway and turned westward into the
Atlantic, moving into his assigned station, a square designated by two
numbers on a chart, about 250 miles northwest of Ireland, without
being sighted by the patrols already mounted by the Royal Navy.

Shortly before dawn on September 1, the pre–World War I battleship *Schleswig-Holstein* opened up on the Polish fortress at the West-
erplatte, on the Vistula estuary, and German tanks slashed into
Poland with Stuka dive-bombers blasting the way. The Poles reeled
under this savage attack, and their handful of warships were almost
immediately bombed into wreckage.* The British and French, who
had previously attempted to appease Adolf Hitler, the German
Führer, issued an ultimatum demanding a withdrawal from Poland
by 1100 on September 3. Vessels in port were instructed to remain
there until convoys could be organized. As Big Ben solemnly tolled
out the hour without a reply from Hitler, the Admiralty sent a classically understated signal to its far-flung ships and shore stations:
TOTAL GERMANY.

The sun's last rays were casting a reddish light over the sea when
one of *U-30*'s lookouts sighted a plume of smoke to the east. Propping
up his elbows on the bridge rail to keep his binoculars steady, Lemp
carefully examined the oncoming vessel. She was a sizable ship and
steaming at about fifteen knots. In contrast to peacetime practice, he
noted, she was blacked out, her navigation lights dimmed, and was
steering a zigzag course, her wake twisting to starboard, then port.
Was she a passenger ship or an armed merchant cruiser?

By Hitler's direct order, U-boat skippers had been instructed to

---

*The Poles, realizing they would be unable to withstand a German attack, sent their
three most modern destroyers to Britain before the outbreak of the war. The naval base
at Hel was the last piece of Polish territory conquered by the Germans. It held out until
October 1, 1939, four days longer than Warsaw, despite intensive bombing and shelling.

conduct operations in accordance with the German naval-prize law and the London Submarine Treaty, to which Germany had adhered in 1936, which outlawed unrestricted submarine warfare. Although vessels sailing in convoy, troop transports, and merchant cruisers could be attacked without warning, other merchant ships were to be stopped and searched for war material. If it was necessary to sink them, passengers and crew were to be allowed to take to the boats and assisted to reach safety. U-boat captains complained that these rules deprived them of their major weapons—stealth and surprise— but Hitler had his reasons. Once Poland was beaten, he planned to offer the British and French a negotiated peace. Moreover, unrestricted submarine warfare, with its indiscriminate attacks on merchant ships, had brought the United States into World War I on the Allied side, and he had no intention of repeating the mistake.

Before leaving their base at Wilhelmshaven, Lemp and the other U-boat skippers had been briefed by Commodore Karl Dönitz, flag officer commanding U-boats, who told them the British were preparing to send armed passenger liners to sea and to be wary of them. With these instructions apparently in the forefront of his mind, and eager to make a kill, Lemp concluded from his quarry's conduct that she must be one of these merchant cruisers.

"Clear the bridge for dive!" Lemp ordered. As the crew hustled below, a Klaxon sounded diving stations. "Flood!" With a thundering roar, the air which gave the boat its buoyancy was forced from the ballast tanks, to be replaced by seawater, and *U-30* slid below the surface. The hydroplane operators held her at periscope depth. Through the eyepiece, Lemp saw at first only the green, translucent wash of the sea, but as the lens cleared, he took the bearing and range of the oncoming ship for a bow shot.

"Tube One! Fire!"

Rapidly, the boat's first watch officer called out the firing intervals for a spread of four torpedoes.

They sped toward the tall, black sides of 13,581-ton Donaldson liner *Athenia*. The last passenger ship out of Europe before the war began, she had sailed two days earlier from Glasgow with stops at Belfast and Liverpool, bound for Montreal. She was crammed with 1,417 passengers and crew, three-quarters of them women and children, including 311 Americans. One torpedo exploded on her port side, a little aft of midships, flinging up a huge geyser of water. The bulkhead between the boiler and engine rooms was shattered, and the ocean poured into the stricken vessel.

The war at sea had begun.

•

CHAPTER 1

"The Eerie and Sinister Sea"

Winston S. Churchill, the newly appointed First Lord of the Admiralty, needed no one to guide him to his office upon his arrival at the Admiralty on the first afternoon of the war: Having served in the post from 1911 to 1915, he raced up the stairs to his old "private lair" with an aide and secretary in his wake. Bursting into the room, he flung open a hidden wall panel that revealed a situation map on which he had plotted the daily positions of the Allied and German fleets during World War I. It was exactly as Churchill had left it twenty-four years before, when he had been driven from office following a bungled and costly attempt to force the Dardanelles and attack Germany through the back door.

With the abject failure of his attempts to appease Adolf Hitler, Prime Minister Neville Chamberlain had reluctantly offered the bitterest critic of that policy a place in the War Cabinet. For the sixty-four-year-old Churchill, the return to his old post as civilian head of the Royal Navy was doubly sweet. It not only salved the bitterness of his earlier defeat, but confirmed the validty of his warnings about Hitler. Although vilified as a warmonger, Churchill had stood almost alone during the late 1930s, issuing Cassandra-like prophesies of the menace of Nazism, condemnations of Chamberlain's efforts to mollify the German dictator with the territory of his neighbors, and vociferous demands for British rearmament.

In anticipation of Churchill's arrival, the Admiralty had flashed a signal to the fleet: WINSTON IS BACK. The Royal Navy's reaction to his return was mixed. "Bold," "brash," and "unpredictable" were words commonly used to describe Churchill. He was impetuous, imperious, fallible—and glorious. Like a human pinwheel, he threw off a kaleidoscopic variety of daring ideas—some good, others wildly impracticable—while wreathed in cigar smoke and primed with copious drafts of brandy and champagne. He considered himself a military genius, and bullied professional officers who thought otherwise. With a shudder, the admirals recalled his interference in strategic and technical matters during the previous war. Some, however, hailed his return, saying he would add a badly needed "zip" to the conduct of naval affairs.

That evening, as *U-30* stalked the *Athenia*,* Churchill met in the nobly proportioned Board Room with the men with whom he would work in a new effort to stem German aggression. In the middle of this paneled chamber where so much of Britain's history had been shaped was a long mahogany table ringed by chairs. Churchill plumped himself down in the high-backed First Lord's seat. Overseeing the proceedings was a portrait of Admiral Lord Nelson, whose victory over the combined fleets of France and Spain at Trafalgar in 1805 had given Britain unchallenged control of the oceans for a century. It was "a privilege and an honor" to be in that seat again, Churchill observed in reply to a few words of welcome from Admiral of the Fleet Sir Dudley Pound, the First Sea Lord and the navy's senior professional officer. The task ahead was great, Churchill said, but he was certain Britain would again prevail, and sent his listeners on their way with

---

Athenia sank with the loss of 112 lives, of whom eighty-five were women and children. Public opinion in the United States was aroused by the death of twenty-two American citizens. The sinking of the liner recalled the torpedoing of the British liner *Lusitania* by a U-boat in 1915, in which 1,198 people died, including 128 Americans, which contributed to the entry of the U.S. into World War I against Imperial Germany.

Lemp maintained radio silence after the attack, and the Germans steadfastly denied British charges that the ship had been sunk by one of their submarines. Dr. Joseph Goebbels, the Nazi propaganda chief, charged that the *Athenia* had been sunk at Churchill's orders in a diabolical plot to influence American public opinion against Germany. Upon his return to base at the end of September 1939, Lemp admitted sinking the ship by mistake. To hush up the affair, *U-30*'s crew was sworn to secrecy and the page of her log recording the sinking was removed. Another, placing the boat two hundred miles away from her actual position, was substituted. This forgery was not revealed until the Nuremberg war-crimes trials after the war.

a flourish: "Gentlemen, to your tasks and duties." Soon, the Naval Staff was being bombarded by a steady stream of memoranda demanding information on every aspect of the war at sea. These missives quickly became known as "daily prayers," because they usually began, "Pray inform me on one sheet of paper why . . ."

"A quarter of a century had passed, and still mortal peril threatened us at the hands of the same nation," Churchill later recalled, with his sense of history as drama. "Once again defense of the rights of a weak state, outraged and invaded by unprovoked aggression, forced us to draw the sword. Once again we must fight for life and honour against all the might and fury of the valiant, disciplined, and ruthless German race. Once again! So be it."

Churchill was not alone in sensing an ominous similarity between 1914 and 1939. With the first rumblings of war, the Royal Navy had mobilized, and many of the officers and enlisted men who had seen service in World War I had a feeling of *déjà-vu*. "It was as if time had stood still," observed one captain surveying the Royal Navy's battleships as they lay at bleak and windswept Scapa Flow—in the Orkneys, to the north of Scotland—the fleet's base in both wars. "A lot of the ships were even the same, too. Ruddy uncanny, I can tell you."

To a remarkable extent, World War II at sea was a continuation of World War I, and the naval strategies of both the British and the Germans were essentially unchanged from the previous war. Because it was an island nation, the United Kingdom's security rested upon the safe arrival of more than forty million tons of cargo annually in her ports, including all her oil,* most raw materials, and two-thirds of her food, as well as massive infusions of manpower from the Empire. There were seldom fewer than two thousand British merchant ships at sea, including coastal traffic. As Britain fought to keep open her lifelines, which ran eastward across the North Atlantic and northward from the Cape of Good Hope and the Straits of Gibraltar, the Germans tried to sever them with a relentless campaign of attacks by submarines, surface raiders, mines, and aircraft—tactics that had nearly proved successful in World War I.

The fundamental difference between 1914 and 1939 was the size of the opposing fleets. Twenty-five years before, Germany was sec-

---

*Britain received 90 percent of its oil from across the Atlantic—from the United States, Venezuela, and Trinidad.

ond only to Britain as a naval power and posed the most serious threat to her command of the seas since Trafalgar. Now the Kriegsmarine was far weaker than the Royal Navy, although its ships were newer than the aging British battle fleet. Paradoxically, neither nation was prepared to fight the kind of war that developed. Hitler had neglected submarines and planned a conventional surface fleet of battleships and cruisers. "A realistic policy would have given Germany a thousand U-boats at the beginning" of the conflict, Karl Dönitz bitterly told Allied interrogators after the war.

On the other hand, the British, despite their narrow escape from disaster at the hands of the U-boat in World War I, all but ignored antisubmarine warfare during the "Long Armistice" between the two wars. Policy errors, financial constraints, and strategic misconceptions were responsible for blunders on both sides.

Ten days after the Armistice that ended World War I, on November 21, 1918, the German High Seas Fleet loomed out of the North Sea mist, iron-gray ships against a sea of gray. They steamed silently between two columns of the Royal Navy's Grand Fleet—including five battleships of the U.S. Navy's Sixth Battle Squadron—into ignominious captivity at Scapa Flow, to await eventual distribution among the victors. "The German flag will be hauled down at sunset, and will not be hoisted again without permission," ordered Admiral Sir David Beatty, the Allied fleet commander. The following year, the rusting vessels were scuttled by their crews in a final act of defiance, a week before the signing of the Treaty of Versailles.

The war at sea had been fought in two phases. Britain had immediately imposed a blockade upon Germany to prevent food and military supplies from reaching her while preventing the German fleet from breaking out of the confines of the Baltic and North seas. This period was dominated by the battleship and the big gun, and was climaxed by the Battle of Jutland at the end of May 1916. Three British battle cruisers were lost,* and others sustained serious damage, while

---

*Although battle cruisers mounted heavy guns equal in power to those carried by battleships, they traded off armor protection for speed and could not stand up to the same punishment as battleships. For example, the battleship *Iron Duke*, the British flagship at Jutland, and the battle cruiser *Lion*, another Jutland veteran, both mounted 13.5-inch guns. *Lion* was seven knots faster than *Iron Duke*, but the latter was protected by a thirteen-inch armor belt, compared with a nine-inch belt on the battle cruiser.

German losses were less severe. Nevertheless, Jutland was a strategic victory for Britain, because the Germans never again seriously challenged the Royal Navy. With the exception of a few raids, the High Seas Fleet swung uselessly to anchor for the rest of the war while the fighting spirit of its crews was eroded by inaction, Prussian-style discipline, and finally by Bolshevik agitators and mutiny.

In its place, Germany unleashed a new and terrifying weapon against Britain's lifeline—unrestricted submarine warfare. The U-boats almost succeeded in driving Allied shipping from the seas. In April 1917, the same month in which the United States entered the war, German submarines sank an alarming 881,000 tons of shipping, far beyond the capacity of Allied shipyards to replace. With only a three-week supply of grain on hand, strict food rationing was introduced in Britain. But if the hemorrhage of shipping was not stemmed, she would be knocked out of the war by October.

Convoys were the traditional method of trade defense, but the Admiralty had resisted convoys with the argument that they were slow, inefficient, and purely defensive. Besides, destroyers could not be spared from the task of protecting the Grand Fleet. U-boats could only be defeated by offensive action: hunting them down, arming merchantmen, and mining the approaches to enemy naval bases. Faced with the question of national survival, the Admiralty belatedly overcame its prejudices and gave convoys a trial. These early convoys got through almost unscathed. Even if the U-boat was not entirely defeated, convoys substituted acceptable for unacceptable losses over the remaining eighteen months of World War I.

The eclipse of German sea power was expected to usher in a period of universal peace, yet, surprisingly, the world was plunged into a new naval race. American naval officers maintained that, as a result of the wartime expansion of the nation's merchant marine, the United States had become Britain's major commercial rival, a situation that could lead to war. Both British and American naval strategists were also alarmed about Japanese aggressiveness in the Pacific and Far East. While the rest of the world had been otherwise engaged, Japan had made demands upon China and the British worried about their empire east of Suez despite a long-standing alliance with Japan. The Americans were upset by Japanese seizure of the formerly German-held Caroline and Marshall island groups, which lay athwart the line of communications between Hawaii and the Philippines as well as the Anglo-Japanese treaty.

Even before the end of World War I, the United States and Japan had launched massive naval-building programs, with the Americans establishing the intended goal of a navy "second to none." In response to Japan's "eight-eight" program—eight battleships and eight battle cruisers in eight years—the U.S. Navy planned ten battleships and six battle cruisers to be built over five years. To maintain its naval superiority, Britain announced its own plans for four massive forty-eight-thousand-ton battleships and an equal number of battle cruisers with eighteen-inch guns, the biggest mounted on any warship.[*]

With the horror and waste of modern war fresh in the public mind, revolt flared against what was seen as a senseless new arms race. Britain put out diplomatic feelers to Washington for a disarmament conference and indicated that she would accept parity with the U.S. Navy—both a truly historic step and a recognition of existing reality. Although the Republicans had rejected the League of Nations proposed by Woodrow Wilson, a Democrat, his Republican successor, Warren G. Harding, was anxious to show that he, too, was for peace and disarmament, and adopted the British initiative as his own.

Secretary of State Charles Evans Hughes opened the Washington Conference for the Limitation of Naval Armaments, which convened on November 12, 1921, with a proposal that exploded among the delegates with the force of a sixteen-inch shell. He called for a moratorium on the building of new battleships and the scrapping of existing vessels, which would leave the navies of the United States, Britain, Japan, France, and Italy with a tonnage ratio of 5:5:3:1.7:1.7. Sixty-six battleships and battle cruisers were sent to the breakers under this proposal—"more than all the admirals of the world had sunk in a cycle of centuries," wryly noted a British observer.

Under the Washington Treaty, Britain was allowed to maintain twenty-two capital ships in commission; the United States could have eighteen and Japan ten.[†] The Japanese, though dissatisfied with their

---

[*]Most battleships of the period mounted guns ranging in size from thirteen to fifteen inches and averaged about twenty-five thousand tons' displacement.

[†]It was an article of faith among American naval officers that the Washington Treaty was an unmitigated disaster for the U.S. Navy. They charged that the United States scrapped modern vessels and newly laid-down hulls while other nations did little more

inferior position, were as yet unwilling to defy world opinion. Similar limitations were imposed on aircraft carriers, which were just entering the world's navies. No capital ships were to be built over the next ten years, and new vessels laid down after the expiration of this "holiday" were limited to sixteen-inch guns and thirty-five thousand tons' displacement. To mollify the United States, Britain abrogated its alliance with Japan.

The London Naval Treaty of 1930 extended the battleship moratorium to 1936. Budget slashes as a result of the Great Depression, and a vain hope for peace through collective security, contributed to further shrinkage of the battle fleets. Shipbuilding programs were punctuated by constant reductions and cancellations. Moreover, much of the Royal Navy's available funding was earmarked for a giant naval base at Singapore that was intended to serve the fleet that was to be sent from home waters to deal with any trouble that might arise with Japan.

This period of shaky equilibrium ended in 1936, when the Japanese renounced the treaty limitations. The 5:5:3 ratio "sounded to Japanese ears like Rolls-Royce:Rolls-Royce:Ford," confided one official. Shrouded in secrecy, the Japanese launched a massive program of warship construction that included the world's largest battleships, the seventy-two-thousand-ton *Yamato* and *Musashi*, each mounting nine 18.1-inch guns. Alarmed by the aggressions of Japan in China and those of Hitler and Fascist Italy, Britain and the United States also began to rearm. Britain, unaware of the size of the Japanese giants, replied with five battleships of the *King George V* class, which, designed within treaty limitations, displaced thirty-five thousand tons and were armed with ten fourteen-inch guns. The United States added two other thirty-five-thousand-tonners, *North Carolina* and *Washington*, which carried nine sixteen-inch guns.

When war came, however, only fifteen aging battleships and battle cruisers flew the Royal Navy's White Ensign. With the exception of

---

than junk worn-out vessels or tear up blueprints. Modern studies have shown that the U.S. Navy fared better at the conference table than was thought at the time, however. The battleships it retained were newer than most of those that remained in the British and Japanese fleets, and incorporated developments in firepower and protection that had resulted from wartime experience.

two—*Nelson* and *Rodney**—all had fought at Jutland or were laid down during the war. Only four had been extensively modernized, and the remainder, essentially unaltered over the last twenty years, were deficient in anti-aircraft protection. France had an additional seven capital ships, of which five were too old to be fully effective, and were, for the most part, stationed in the Mediterranean to keep an eye on the Italian fleet.

Naval thinking between the wars was dominated by Jutland and the controversies which surrounded it, and strategists still believed in the supremacy of the battleship and the big gun. Students at the U.S. Naval War College examined the battle with such intensity that one officer joked that it was "a major defeat for the U.S. Navy." Why was no attention paid to the submarine and antisubmarine warfare? Basically, armies and navies rarely learn from success—and the Royal Navy had been successful during World War I.

Britain had pioneered in the use of aircraft carriers, but the airplane was regarded as a weapon of dubious reliability, suitable only for scouting and patrol work. Should airplanes attack battleships, said the admirals, they would be immediately shot out of the skies by the ships' anti-aircraft guns. Churchill and Admiral Pound held this view. Only one of the Royal Navy's six aircraft carriers, the twenty-three-thousand-ton *Ark Royal*, which could carry sixty planes, was of modern design, and the Fleet Air Arm possessed only 232, mostly obsolescent, aircraft, including bi-wing Sea Gladiator fighters and Swordfish torpedo planes. The latter were known as "Stringbags."

Following World War I, the navy's air service had been yoked in a shotgun marriage to the newly established Royal Air Force, which was given responsibility for both land- and sea-based air operations. The Royal Navy did not regain control of seaborne aviation until 1937, and the Fleet Air Arm had fallen years behind the air units of the American and Japanese navies. The RAF's Coastal Command, which was to provide air cover for convoys, was grossly unprepared for the task before it, because the medium- and long-range aircraft needed to carry out prolonged patrols were never built.

---

*Nelson and *Rodney* were known as the "Cherry Tree Class," because, although originally intended to be larger, they were completed in accordance with the limits imposed by the Washington Treaty. They displaced 33,900 tons and mounted nine sixteen-inch guns but had a top speed of only twenty-three knots. They were unorthodox in appearance, their three main turrets all concentrated forward.

Convinced that the U-boat menace had died with the end of German sea power, the Admiralty also neglected antisubmarine warfare. Surface raiders, not U-boats, were seen as the major threat to seaborne trade in any future conflict. When war came, the Royal Navy had only 184 destroyers, compared with the 433 in service in 1918, and most of these were assigned to protect the battleships. Antisubmarine warfare was a backwater. The depth charge—an underwater bomb that could be set to explode at a certain depth—was still the only weapon for use against the submarine. With a killing radius of only seven yards, the depth charge was likened to catching fish by throwing stones at them. "Not one exercise in the protection of a slow mercantile convoy against submarine or air attack took place between 1919 and 1939," according to Captain Stephen W. Roskill, official historian of the Royal Navy's operations in World War II.

In the meantime, Germany was undergoing a modest naval revival. Under the Treaty of Versailles, the Weimar Republic was permitted only a few prewar vessels suitable for coastal defense, none larger than ten thousand tons or with a main armament greater than eleven-inch guns. Germany was allowed no aircraft, no aircraft carriers—and, above all, no submarines. Later, new vessels were authorized, and, cutting their cloak to the cloth available, the Germans produced a novel warship supposedly within treaty limitations: the *Panzerschiff*, popularly known as the "pocket battleship."

The first, *Deutschland*, was laid down in 1928 and was followed by two sisters, *Admiral Graf Spee* and *Admiral Scheer*. Intended as long-range commerce raiders, these ships were designed to outrun anything they could not outfight. They mounted six eleven-inch and eight 5.9-inch guns, were fitted with side armor 3.2 inches thick, and had a speed of twenty-six knots.[*] Other innovations included all-welded construction to save weight, and diesel engines, which gave them an operating range of some twenty thousand miles, but at a price in reliability. *Graf Spee* later became the first German warship fitted with radar. The Germans claimed these vessels were within the

---

[*]Although faster than the Royal Navy's older battleships, the pocket battleships were slower than the three remaining British battle cruisers, *Hood*, *Repulse*, and *Renown*, and the French *Dunkerque* and *Strasbourg*. The latter were specially built to counter the pocket battleships.

ten-thousand-ton limit set at Versailles, but in actuality they came in at twelve thousand tons, making them, in effect, supercruisers.

The navy oversaw the clandestine building of fast banana-freighters for eventual conversion to auxiliary cruisers, planned for the use of trawlers as minesweepers and arranged for private pilot training for naval officers. Efforts were also made to obtain submarine experience in defiance of the treaty. As early as 1922, a secret office was established in The Hague, using the cover of a Dutch firm, to develop improved U-boats for foreign sales. In 1928, German technicians directed construction of a 750-ton U-boat in Spain. Two years later, they built a 250-ton coastal submarine in Finland. Finally, in November 1932, two months before the accession of Hitler to power, the government openly approved a proposal for sixteen small U-boats.

Like the other branches of the Wehrmacht—the German armed forces—the navy was initially skeptical of Hitler. Conservative and determinedly monarchist in sympathies, it was contemptuous of the lower-class origins of Nazism.* The navy was less politicized than the other services, and officers were forbidden to engage in political activity. But it was also haunted by its failure in World War I and the mutinies which swept its ships at war's end. Hitler's stress upon German unity, patriotism, and nationalism, his denunciation of the Versailles *Diktat*, his promises to rebuild the armed services and to deal with the threat of communism appealed to naval officers.

Some officers were deeply disturbed by the Nazi attacks on the Jews and Hitler's expansionist foreign policy, but neither Grand Admiral Raeder, the navy's commander-in-chief since 1928, nor any of his senior officers opposed Hitler's will. Raeder was a mixture of conscientiousness, authoritarianism, and astonishing political naïveté. As a professional officer, he stood apart from the squalid infighting of Nazi court politics. But the High Seas Fleet's shame of 1918 had left a scar that never healed, and he was obsessed with building a fleet in the mold of the old Imperial Navy—not because he had developed a strategy for its use or wished a confrontation with Britain, but seemingly as an end in itself.

Hitler's reasons for supporting a large surface navy are something

---

*"I have a reactionary Army, an Imperial Navy and a National Socialist Air Force," Hitler was to say.

of a mystery. A continental strategist in the mold of Napoleon, he had as a goal the mastery of the Eurasian "heartland." He had no liking for what he called "the eerie and sinister sea," and was prone to seasickness when he visited the fleet. He regarded battleships as mere showpieces, manifestations of Germany's determination to be a world power. Moreover, he had a curious love-hate relationship with Britain and, as he made clear in *Mein Kampf*, believed Imperial Germany had committed a fatal error by challenging British command of the sea. France and the Soviet Union were Germany's rightful enemies, and he repeatedly told his admirals that he had no intention of going to war with Britain or the United States. In the event of a conflict with France or the Russians, his strategy was to keep the Anglo-Americans neutral until the "heartland" had been conquered; when faced with overwhelming force, they would have to accede to Germany hegemony over Europe.

With a pious show of goodwill, Hitler signed a treaty with Britain, the Anglo-German Naval Agreement of 1935, in which Germany accepted permanent naval inferiority in exchange for release from the Versailles limitations—limitations he had already renounced. The following year, Hitler acceded to the pact that outlawed unrestricted submarine warfare. Germany was permitted to build up to 35 percent of the tonnage possessed by Britain's surface navy and up to 45 percent of her submarine tonnage. With due notice, this could be raised to 100 percent. Winston Churchill opposed the agreement, because it would require the Royal Navy to keep a third of its strength in European waters to counter the Germans, thereby limiting the size of the force that could be sent to Singapore to deal with any Japanese threat that might arise.[*]

The green light given by Britain for the revival of Germany's U-boat flotillas was the height of folly in view of her disastrous World War I experience. The British rationalized this decision by saying that, inasmuch as their own submarine fleet was small, the limitations would be a brake on German construction. They also believed that, in case of war, Germany would abide by the accord outlawing unrestricted U-boat warfare. And if she didn't, the solution to the subma-

---

[*]Three years later, however, Churchill reversed himself, and discounted the possibility of a Japanese attack on Singapore. See Roskill, *Churchill and the Admirals*, p. 89.

rine menace lay at hand in convoys and Asdic, a system for detecting objects below the surface of the sea.* The Naval Staff reported in 1937 that "the submarine should never again be able to present us with the problem we were faced with in 1917."

The Kriegsmarine entered a period of mushroom growth after the London agreement. Admiral Raeder planned a small, balanced fleet which, when combined with that of Italy, Germany's ally, would assure naval superiority over France. Two 32,500-ton battle cruisers, *Scharnhorst* and *Gneisenau*, each mounting nine eleven-inch guns, were laid down.† They were followed by a pair of massive but elegant battleships—*Bismarck*, of 50,900 tons, and *Tirpitz*, of 52,600 tons— both carrying eight fifteen-inch guns, as well as two heavy cruisers, sixteen destroyers, and twenty-eight submarines. The harsh discipline that had prevailed in the Imperial Navy was replaced by a less rigid, more humane code. But Karl Dönitz protested that too much of the nation's limited shipbuilding capacity was taken up by surface ships at the expense of submarine construction. Such complaints were ignored, however, and when war came Germany was producing only four submarines a month.

Like the British, the Germans also neglected their naval air arm. Resources in the Third Reich were allocated on a political basis, and Reichsmarschall Hermann Göring, the World War I fighter ace who was chief of the Luftwaffe, the German air force, was second only to Hitler in the Nazi hierarchy. Göring blocked the navy's efforts to obtain its own air establishment with the declaration that "everything that flies belongs to me." Instead, he promised to supply the Kriegsmarine by 1942 with the seven hundred planes and air crews considered necessary to fulfill its tasks. But the sea was a foreign element to

---

*Asdic was known as "sonar" in the U.S. Navy. It sent out sound waves which bounced off underwater objects such as submarines. Originally developed in 1918, Asdic was shorthand for the "Allied Submarine Detection Committee," the group that developed it. The British were too optimistic about Asdic, however; the system had serious shortcomings. Operators might be confused by schools of fish, rough seas made detection difficult, and it was of little use in dealing with submarines operating on the surface at night, which in the last year of World War I had become the U-boats' favored tactic for attack.

†These guns were light for such large vessels, and Hitler later insisted that their armament be upgraded to fifteen-inch guns. No action was taken in the turmoil of events, however.

Göring and he never understood it. An aircraft carrier, the *Graf Zeppelin*, was laid down, and plans were discussed to convert the liners *Europa* and *Potsdam* to auxiliary carriers, but the proposal was scrapped, because Göring had no interest in developing aircraft suitable for carrier operations.

Hitler's increasing bellicosity and the Nazi seizure of Czechoslovakia in 1939 finally convinced the Allies of the futility of appeasement. Poland was the Führer's next likely target, and Hitler was warned that, if he attacked the Poles, Britain and France would come to their assistance—a warning accompanied by a belated program of rearmament. Hitler told Raeder that Britain must now be considered among Germany's enemies and ordered a naval buildup. Yet, repeating previous assurances, he said there would be no war with Britain until 1945 at the earliest.

A special committee of the Naval Staff, the Seekriegsleitung or SKL, headed by Korvettenkapitän Helmuth Heye, presented Raeder with the choice of a fleet of pocket battleships and submarines that could be built quickly for an attack on maritime trade, or an ambitious ten-year program of naval expansion that would give Germany a formidable balanced fleet of battleships, aircraft carriers, and submarines capable of contending with the Royal Navy for control of the seas.

Raeder and Hitler accepted the big-ship strategy—known as the Z-Plan—that would by 1948 have provided Germany with ten battleships of up to fifty-four thousand tons, four aircraft carriers, twelve battle cruisers, three pocket battleships, five heavy cruisers, forty-four light cruisers, sixty-eight destroyers, and 249 U-boats. This truly formidable force was to be divided into two units: a "Home Fleet," strong enough to tie down the Royal Navy in the North Sea, and a "Raiding Fleet," to attack British trade.

Hitler gave the Z-Plan the highest priority, but it was based upon two major fallacies. The British were unlikely to stand by passively and allow this crude challenge to their naval supremacy to pass without matching or exceeding it. And such a massive program of warship construction was well beyond German resources and the capacity of her shipyards. Work upon the fleet had barely started when war came, far swifter than anyone—probably including Hitler—had anticipated.

Having startled the world by signing a nonaggression pact with his old enemy, the Soviet Union, in August 1939, Hitler pressed ahead with his plans to deal with Poland. He was confident that, despite the tougher attitude of Britain and France, they would not defend the Poles. All available U-boats and the surface raiders *Deutschland* and *Admiral Graf Spee* were sent to sea to take up their positions as a precautionary measure. Similar steps had been adopted before in times of crisis, and Raeder was unworried. "In no circumstances would war with Britain come about," he told a group of U-boat officers after a meeting with the Führer on July 27. ". . . That would mean *finis Germaniae*."

Only a month later, Hitler attacked Poland. Much to his surprise, the British and French declarations of war followed three days later. Through a series of miscalculations, he had involved Germany in the major war he had promised to avoid, and without allies, for neither of his partners in the so-called Pact of Steel—Italy or Japan—showed any inclination to join the fight. Upon being handed a copy of the British "TOTAL GERMANY" signal, Dönitz was shocked. "My God!" he declared. "So it's war with England again!" Raeder, who was presiding at his daily staff conference when the news came in, was equally shaken.

The surface fleet consisted only of the battle cruisers *Scharnhorst* and *Gneisenau*, the three pocket battleships, one heavy cruiser,* six light cruisers, and thirty-four destroyers and torpedo boats. The U-boat arm was no better off, numbering only fifty-seven submarines, of which fewer than half were of Type VIIC, suitable for Atlantic operations.† Britain and France together had twenty-two battleships, seven carriers, twenty-two heavy cruisers, sixty-one light cruisers, 255 destroyers, and 135 submarines. "As far as the Kriegsmarine is concerned it is obvious that it is not remotely ready for the titanic struggle," Raeder gloomily concluded. "The only course open . . . is to show [it knows] how to die gallantly. . . ."

---

*The battleships *Bismarck* and *Tirpitz* were a long way from completion, but the heavy cruiser *Blücher* joined the fleet a few weeks after the beginning of hostilities. Another heavy cruiser, *Prinz Eugen*, was also close to completion, but construction was halted on the rest of the Z-Plan Fleet.

†The 750-ton Type VIIC submarine, which constituted the backbone of the U-boat fleet—some seven hundred saw service during the war—was hardly changed from the boats of World War I. Running on diesel engines, on the surface these boats could do seventeen knots, but when they were submerged their electric motors could only push them along at eight knots, and that for only a limited time before they had to surface to recharge batteries. They had five twenty-one-inch torpedo tubes, four in the bow and one in the stern, and carried twelve to fourteen torpedoes as well as an eighty-eight-millimeter deck gun and varying anti-aircraft armament.

*   *   *

Once Germany and the Soviet Union had divided a shattered Poland between them, the war in the West settled into an uneasy lull, known as the "Phony War." The two sides probed each other's defenses along the Maginot and Siegfried lines, while the Germans prepared for an attack upon France in the spring of 1940. Hitler held back the Luftwaffe, and the rain of bombs expected to fall on Allied cities failed to materialize; the British were equally anxious to avoid the blame of starting an air war against civilian populations. But there was nothing "phony" about the struggle at sea. Warships and merchantmen alike were assailed by shell, mine, torpedo, and bomb, and all claimed their deadly toll.

The Royal Navy promptly blockaded Germany by covering all exits from the North Sea with cruiser patrols, poising the Home Fleet at Scapa Flow to deal with any attempted breakout by the larger vessels. The British Expeditionary Force—some half-million men and eighty-nine thousand vehicles—was transported across the Channel to France, without the loss of a man or a gun. Canadian troops were brought to the United Kingdom for training, and Australians and New Zealanders were also being transported to the Middle East.

For his part, Raeder resolved to use the Kriegsmarine aggressively rather than repeat the World War I policy of inaction. The U-boats, pocket battleships, and auxiliary cruisers were assigned to a far-ranging war of attrition against Allied shipping, aimed at forcing the British to divert forces from home waters to trade protection. With British power divided, the remainder of the surface navy would make frequent forays into the North Sea and the Atlantic. Politics had as much to do with this strategy as military necessity. Having extolled the benefits of sea power to Hitler, Raeder was convinced the navy must take aggressive action to remain in the Führer's good graces.

On the other side of the Atlantic, Americans were shocked by the speed and ferocity of the German blitzkrieg against Poland, and, although sympathetic to the Allied cause, had no wish to become involved. To prevent war from spreading across the Atlantic, President Franklin D. Roosevelt drew a ring of defense around the Americas that extended three hundred miles out to sea and established a neutrality patrol to track belligerent ships approaching the area. On the other hand, the pro-Allied Roosevelt overcame strong isolationist feelings and persuaded Congress to repeal provisions of the Neutrality Act, which embargoed arms sales to the warring nations. Such cargoes were to be carried in their own ships—"cash and carry"—which meant that only Britain and France would have access to American supplies, because German commerce had been driven from the sea.

The sinking of the *Athenia* convinced the Admiralty that Hitler was going to ignore the London submarine accord. Convoys were immediately established and the first trans-Atlantic convoy was ready to sail for Halifax in Nova Scotia as early as September 8. Between September 1939 and May 1940, only twelve of the 229 British merchantmen sunk by U-boats were sailing in convoys. But there was a shortage of escorts. Convoys were escorted by a ragtag of Royal Canadian Navy vessels to fifty-six degrees west longitude. From there they were usually on their own except for a single armed merchant cruiser until picked up at fifteen degrees west longitude— about two hundred miles out in the Atlantic—by a trawler or two or perhaps a destroyer that had just bade farewell to an outward-bound convoy. When the convoy was twenty-four hours from Liverpool or Plymouth, it dispersed, and the ships made their way to port independently. Coastal Command aircraft flew patrols over convoys when possible, but inexperienced crews made appalling navigational errors. One fix placed a convoy in the Place de la Concorde in Paris.

The U-boats also had trouble with their torpedoes in the early months of the war. Although potential targets abounded, submarine skippers were chagrined to discover that the new G-7a trackless electrical torpedoes were prone to running too deep or running wild, and their magnetic pistols, or detonators, tended to go off prematurely and give away the boat's position. *U-56* hit *Nelson* with a pair of torpedoes, but both were duds. At least two submarines were sunk as a result of torpedo failure with a corresponding dip in morale. "It is my belief that never before in military history has a force been sent into battles with such a useless weapon," raged Dönitz, and he ordered a sweeping inquiry.*

---

*The contact pistol detonated when it hit its target; magnetic torpedoes were designed to be set off underneath the target by the victim's magnetic field and were likely to break its back. Postwar research indicates that 30 percent of torpedoes fired were duds because of defective pistols. Several ranking officers in the Torpedo Directorate were court-martialed and dismissed after the inquiry.

U-boat officers also complained that Hitler's reluctance to order unrestricted submarine warfare—reiterated after the sinking of the *Athenia*—not only made it difficult to operate at full efficiency but put their boats at risk. Kapitänleutnant Herbert Schultze of *U-48* reported that, when he ordered the cargo ship *Royal Sceptre* to heave to with a shot across her bow, the vessel tried to get away and flooded the airwaves with cries for help. The freighter *Clan McBean* tried to ram an attacking U-boat, which crash-dived before her gun crew could scramble below. As the submarine resurfaced to pick up the floundering men, the steamer escaped. Nevertheless, there were still instances of gentlemanly conduct. Once, Schultze risked his boat by radioing his position and reporting "to Mr. Churchill. Have sunk British S.S. *Firby*. . . . Please pick up crew."

With submarine operations limited by the fact that there were never more than ten U-boats available at a time during the first winter of the war, torpedo teething troubles, and a lull following the return of the boats from their first patrols, the Germans turned to an aggressive mining campaign. Pressing destroyers, minelayers, coastal submarines, and aircraft into service, they sowed the east coast of Britain and the tidal estuaries with hundreds of mines—including new magnetic models. Unlike contact mines, which had to be struck directly before they would explode, these devices were set off by magnetic effect as a ship steamed over them. Magnetic mines could not be swept by usual means, because the sweepers themselves detonated them as they passed overhead. Nothing could be done until a specimen could be found intact and examined.*

German mines accounted for the loss of 120 merchant vessels, or about four hundred thousand tons of shipping, during the first six months of the war, as well as at least fifteen minesweepers and two destroyers. *Nelson* and two cruisers were severely damaged; the former was put out of service until August 1940. The Port of London was almost shut down, and Churchill fumed about German "villainy."

---

*The magnetic mine was no novelty, however. The British had experimented with such mines in 1918, but had let the idea lapse. Experiments were conducted on methods to deal with them in the interwar years, but none had been perfected at the beginning of the conflict (Roskill, *War at Sea*, vol. I, pp. 98–99).

Fortunately for the British, the German navy's efforts to parachute all
its magnetic mines before countermeasures could be adopted were
hamstrung by Hermann Göring. He promised to provide sufficient
aircraft to accomplish this mission, but coordination with the navy
was all but nonexistent. In November, for example, the Luftwaffe
dropped a mere sixty-eight mines.

The break for which the British had been praying finally occurred
on November 23, when a magnetic mine was discovered in a tidal
marsh in the Thames estuary. The ticklish process of dissecting it was
undertaken by Lieutenant Commander John G. D. Ouvry, a mine
expert. Ouvry told the members of his party how he intended to disarm the device and ordered them to take cover. If it exploded, they
would not repeat his mistake. Gingerly, Ouvry opened the mine,
drew out the metal primer, unscrewed the detonator (which was
about half the size of a man's thumb), and put it in a place of safety.
Now the mine was safe for stripping.

With the secret of the magnetic mine in hand, British experts
quickly devised a method to deal with it. Electric degaussing* cables
were passed around a ship's hull and connected to its generators.
When a current of sufficient intensity was passed through the cable,
the magnetic field created canceled out the magnetic field of the
ship, and she was immune from magnetic mines. The toll of shipping
exacted by them declined.

Convoys and minesweeping were not enough for the pugnacious
Winston Churchill. Obsessed with the offensive, he urged the Royal
Navy to go on the attack rather than to devote its efforts to the defensive strategy of convoy and escort. World War I had taught that the
best time to find and kill enemy submarines was while they were trying to close in on their prey—convoys. But Churchill insisted on
establishing antisubmarine "hunter" groups, which went blindly racing about the ocean looking for U-boats, like seagoing cavalry.
Churchill, a onetime cavalry officer, actually compared these tactics to
those of a cavalry division. In reality, random sweeping of the seas for
a tiny sliver of steel such as a submarine was like searching for the

---

*Named after Carl Friedrich Gauss (1777–1855), the German scientist who invented
the gauss, a unit used to measure the intensity of a magnetic field.

proverbial needle in a haystack and took destroyers away from convoy-escort duty.

Nevertheless, the Naval Staff was unable to resist pressure from the First Lord, and two "search-and-destroy" groups were established around the carriers *Ark Royal* and *Courageous*.* These ships were ill-equipped for the task, their air crews poorly prepared. They were hurried to sea with little time for training and inadequate equipment, and the results were disappointing. For openers, a pair of Skua bombers from *Ark Royal* caught Fritz Lemp's *U-30* on the surface as he was examining a trawler and dropped several bombs on the submarine. They missed, but the inexperienced pilots were flying so low that the geysers thrown up by the explosions brought down their planes. The airmen were ignominiously fished from the sea by their intended victims and taken back to Germany as prisoners of war.

The hunters swiftly became the hunted. On September 14, *Ark Royal* was operating west of the Hebrides when she was tracked by *U-39*, which fired three torpedoes at her. The torpedoes exploded prematurely because of defective magnetic detonators, and the carrier escaped harm. Three escorting destroyers promptly counterattacked the U-boat. Blown to the surface by a heavy barrage of depth charges and reeking of deadly chlorine gas, she was abandoned by her crew, the first submarine lost to enemy action during the war.

Three days later, on September 17, Kapitänleutnant Otto Schuhart of *U-29* was searching for a convoy reported to be about 350 miles west of Ireland with the hope of adding to the three ships he had already bagged. He hardly believed his eyes as *Courageous* suddenly appeared in his periscope. She was steaming at high speed, and Schuhart had despaired of making an attack when, unexpectedly, the carrier reduced speed to recover aircraft. Exploiting his luck to the full, Schuhart maneuvered to within three thousand yards of *Courageous* without being detected. Two of her four screening destroyers had been dispatched to assist a merchant vessel under attack, and

---

**Courageous and her sister ship, *Glorious*, were originally 22,500-ton shallow-draft battle cruisers intended for service in the Baltic, and each mounted four fifteen-inch guns. Within the fleet, they were lampooned as *Outrageous* and *Uproarious*. In the late 1920s, they were rebuilt as aircraft carriers. Their guns were placed in storage and fifteen years later were taken out and fitted to *Vanguard*, the Royal Navy's last battleship. She went to the breakers in 1960.

there was no antisubmarine patrol in the air. Worried about the lack of experience of the air crews, the carrier's captain had opted against keeping too many planes aloft.

Schuhart, having previously had a bad experience with magnetic pistols, fired three torpedoes fitted with contact exploders at *Courageous* and dived deep. The U-boat's crew counted off the seconds, listening intently for the sound of a successful strike. It came after what seemed an eternity. "We can clearly hear the explosions from two torpedo hits," Schuhart reported. "Immediately after the second hit an enormous explosion followed by a few smaller ones. The noise is so loud that I have the impression that we ourselves have been damaged."

Ripped by internal explosions, *Courageous* heeled over to port and sank in only about twenty minutes. Although the sea was calm, 518 of her complement of twelve hundred officers and men were lost. The carrier had been rushed to sea before lifebelts were issued, and the life rafts were stuck to the ship's side by generations of paint. *U-29* survived a heavy depth-charge attack and returned safely to Germany to be credited with the first notable naval victory of the war. Winston Churchill, having almost lost *Ark Royal* and thrown away *Courageous*, finally ordered an end to the use of carriers in antisubmarine operations.*

Scarcely had Schuhart's feat been recorded in the annals of submarine warfare when it was followed by another, even more spectacular exploit—the sinking of the battleship *Royal Oak* by a U-boat in the lion's den of Scapa Flow. From the very beginning of the war, Karl Dönitz had cast a coolly appraising eye upon the base. Guarded by air and sea patrols, booms, blockships, nets, and minefields, and washed by fast currents and perplexing tides, the anchorage was supposedly impregnable. Two U-boats had been lost during the previous war while attempting to penetrate it. In truth, Scapa Flow was far

---

*An unrepentant Churchill later claimed that the success of "hunter-killer" groups of destroyers and small carriers that began operations in late 1942 and early 1943 proved the validity of his earlier plan (*History of the Second World War*, vol. I, p. 669n.). In fact, this statement reveals his ignorance of the nature of the operations of these units. Rather than blindly sweeping the seas in search of U-boats, these "hunter-killer" groups reinforced convoy escorts, and broke off to seek out enemy submarines only when they had accurate intelligence of their locations. They were successful because they *knew* where U-boats were lurking.

from invulnerable—a fact known to Churchill, who, soon after taking office, ordered new blockships to be sunk in a partially obstructed channel known as Kirk Sound.

German military intelligence—the Abwehr—informed Dönitz that a merchant skipper, who called at Kirkwall, near Scapa Flow, just before the war, had learned that the underwater defenses blocking Kirk Sound were badly deteriorated. Reconnaissance planes also provided detailed aerial photographs. After closely examining them, Dönitz concluded that indeed there was a passage about 550 feet wide between a sunken blockship and the shore which could be negotiated by a surfaced U-boat after high tide. Further inquiry revealed that, on the night of Friday, October 13–14, both periods of high tide would come during the dark hours, and there would be a new moon, reducing the chances for discovery.

To carry out this, "the boldest of bold enterprises," Dönitz selected Kapitänleutnant Günther Prien of *U-47*. Prien, a daring, hard-driving officer of thirty, accepted with alacrity. The boat's crew were not told of their mission until they were at sea, and as Herbert Herrmann, a torpedoman, later recalled, "everyone more or less [gave] up hope of coming back alive." Running on the surface, *U-47*, which bore a raging bull painted on its conning tower, ghosted into Kirk Sound at about 2330 on the night of October 13. The current pushed the boat along at considerable speed, amid a dazzling display of the northern lights. At 0027, Prien told his crew, "We are in Scapa Flow!"

Much to Prien's surprise, the anchorage appeared almost empty. The Home Fleet had gone to sea a few days earlier, in a vain attempt to prevent *Gneisenau* from breaking out on a raid, and, except for *Royal Oak*,* which had returned to Scapa Flow, all the battleships had dispersed to other ports. The seaplane tender *Pegasus* was anchored slightly to the north of the battleship, and Prien seems to have mistaken her for the battle cruiser *Repulse*. *U-47*'s log provides a vivid account of the operation:

> 0055 . . . We proceed north by coast. Two battleships are lying there. . . . [A]ttack on the two fat fellows. Distance apart 3000 meters. Estimated depth 7.5 meters. Impact firing.

---

*Launched in 1914, the 29,150-ton *Royal Oak* carried eight fifteen-inch guns and had joined the Grand Fleet just in time for Jutland.

0116. One torpedo fixed on the northern ship, two on the southern. After a good 3½ minutes, a torpedo detonates on the northern ship; of the other two nothing to be seen. About!

0121. Torpedo fired from stern; in the bow two tubes are loaded; three torpedoes from the bow. After three tense minutes comes the detonations on the nearer ship. There is a loud explosion, roar and rumbling. Then come columns of water, followed by columns of fire, and splinters fly through the air. . . .

Prien was mistaken on several points. In actuality, *U-47*'s first torpedo had hit the bow of *Royal Oak*, rather than the "northern ship" (*Pegasus*). The explosion inflicted only light damage, which was attributed to spontaneous combustion in a paint locker, and, incredibly, the ship was not placed on alert. Safe in Scapa Flow, no one seems to have considered the possibility of a U-boat attack, and most of the crew returned to their hammocks. The torpedo fired from the boat's stern tube missed completely. Thirteen minutes after the first hit, the final spread of torpedoes smashed into the starboard side of the battleship.

The explosions lifted *Royal Oak* out of the water and shook her from stem to stern. Cordite in one of the magazines ignited, and a bright-orange fireball swept through compartment after compartment, cremating everyone in its path. Water cascaded into the ship, and she rapidly heeled over to starboard. Shouting and struggling, men clawed their way topside in the darkness, and slipped down the slanting deck into the water. Within fifteen minutes, *Royal Oak* rolled over and sank. Of the ship's company of more than twelve hundred men, only 424 survived.*

Many were saved by a civilian trawler, *Daisy II*, commanded by John G. Gatt, which had been moored nearby. As she barely made way, her crew pulled in so many oil-coated survivors that the trawler herself was in danger of sinking. She finally moved off, but the voices of men still in the water could be heard calling out in the darkness, "Don't go *Daisy*! Don't go!"

Prien later claimed that the anchorage exploded into action and destroyers dashed about and depth-charged his boat. In reality, the British believed *Royal Oak* had been sunk by an internal explosion.

---

*Thus, the combined losses from *Courageous* and *Royal Oak* totaled 1,351 officers and men.

A hunt for a submarine was not launched for some time, and *U-47* escaped undetected from Scapa Flow. Upon his return to Germany, Prien was given a hero's welcome and personally decorated by Hitler with the Knight's Cross. The Kriegsmarine, having scored two astounding victories in a month, now ranked high in the Führer's favor. Another tribute came from across the Channel, where, in the House of Commons, Churchill described the penetration of Scapa Flow as "a remarkable exploit of professional skill and daring." For the Royal Navy, the sinking of *Royal Oak* in a supposedly impregnable harbor was a humiliating defeat. Even though *Royal Oak* was outmoded, the loss of a battleship—any battleship—was a blow. With Scapa Flow now considered unsafe, the Home Fleet moved to Rosyth, in the Firth of Forth, and Loch Ewe, on the west coast of Scotland. Ironically, a blockship intended to seal Kirk Sound arrived at Scapa Flow the day after *Royal Oak* was sunk.

Raeder and Dönitz, newly promoted to rear admiral, wasted no time in using the reflected glory of the "Bull of Scapa Flow" to press Hitler for an end to limitations on submarine warfare. As early as October 16, Raeder presented the Führer with an "Economic Warfare Plan" drafted by the Naval Staff that argued for an intensified attack on British shipping. "No threat by other countries, especially the United States, to come into the war—which can certainly be expected if the conflict continues for a long time—must lead to a relaxation of economic warfare once it is begun," the memorandum declared. "The more ruthlessly economic warfare is waged, the earlier it will show results and the sooner the war will end."

The peeling away of the limitations on submarine warfare over the next several weeks resembled the Dance of the Seven Veils. The first dropped when Hitler gave permission to sink any vessel that radioed it was under attack by a U-boat. Next, any vessel sailing without lights could be sunk without warning. And then it was decreed that prize law was not to apply in the North Sea, and after that in a large area to the west of the British Isles. Finally, at the end of November 1939, Dönitz issued orders that, in effect, marked the commencement of unrestricted submarine warfare. "Rescue no one and take no one on board," he told his captains. "Care only for your own boat and strive to achieve the next success as soon as possible! We must be hard in this war."

Raeder also prevailed upon Hitler to unleash the pocket battle-ships *Deutschland* and *Admiral Graf Spee*, which had been sent to sea with their supply vessels, *Westerwald* and *Altmark*, before the war. They began operations on September 26, after Britain and France had rejected the Führer's peace offers. Commerce raiding, however, was only a by-product of their real mission—to keep the Royal Navy off balance. As long as the raiders remained at large, eluding enemy warships and pouncing upon enemy merchantmen where least expected, heavy surface forces had to accompany every convoy, thereby dissipating the Royal Navy's strength and making it easier for German ships to get out.

In confirmation of German strategy, the Allies formed no fewer than eight hunting groups—British and French—consisting of battle cruisers, cruisers, and carriers, which fanned out over the Atlantic in search of the raiders. These dispositions were hampered, however, by uncertainty as to the actual number of raiders at large and their identities. Such uncertainty was enthusiastically encouraged by the Germans, who used every trick from adding false turrets and funnels to the vessels to change their appearance to the transmittal of fake signals. The time factor also worked in their favor. Reports of sinkings took days to reach the nearest port, and by then the raiders were operating in another area of the ocean.

Every two weeks or so, the pocket battleships rendezvoused with their auxiliaries to refuel, resupply, and transfer prisoners. They also had the support of B-Dienst, the Kriegsmarine's intelligence service, which was reading the British naval codes and could forecast enemy naval movements. Moreover, they could count upon assistance from the Ettapendienst, or Secret Naval Supply Service, organized before the war. German steamship companies operating in neutral ports around the globe equipped merchant vessels that met with the raiders at designated points with critically needed supplies. The organization also equipped blockade runners, and in some instances supplied U-boats with fuel.

On the other hand, the state of British naval intelligence was such that it was unable to confirm that two pocket battleships were at sea until early November, and one was misidentified as *Admiral Scheer*. By then, *Graf Spee* had poked her way around the Cape of Good Hope to operate in the Indian Ocean, and *Deutschland* was on her way home. With convoys already established in the North Atlantic, she had found slim pickings and had sunk only two ships.* Hitler, fearing that the loss of a ship bearing the name of the Fatherland would be catastrophic to German morale, had ordered her to return, and as soon as the vessel arrived in port she was renamed *Lützow*. This incident illustrates one of the most vexing command problems facing Raeder—Hitler's fear of losing a large ship and his consequent interference with naval operations. "On land, I am a hero," he told the Grand Admiral. "At sea, I am a coward."

Gneisenau and *Scharnhorst* were sent to sea on November 21, to relieve pressure on the *Graf Spee* by disrupting shipping and naval movements. In thick weather, they slipped through the Iceland-Faroes passage into the North Atlantic. Shortly before dusk on November 23, *Scharnhorst* spotted a sizable ship that answered a command to heave to by trying to escape. She was the armed merchant cruiser *Rawalpindi*, a P. & O. liner of 16,700 tons, deployed on the Northern Patrol. Captain Edward V. Kennedy barely had time to flash the signal ENEMY BATTLE CRUISER IN SIGHT before his vessel was hit by *Scharnhorst*'s eleven-inch shells. He gamely tried to put up a fight with his half-dozen old six-inch guns, scoring one minor hit, but within fourteen minutes his ship was a flaming pyre against the sub-Arctic sky. The Germans attempted to pick up survivors, but the appearance of a British cruiser caused them to break off operations after only twenty-seven men were saved. Kennedy and 270 members of *Rawalpindi*'s crew perished.

Having spread alarm in the Indian Ocean, *Graf Spee*'s captain, Hans Langsdorff, doubled back into the South Atlantic. Such frequent shifts of hunting grounds enabled the raider to elude the numerous warships seeking her. Although he had taken nine vessels totaling about fifty thousand tons, Langsdorff, a forty-five-year-old veteran of

---

Deutschland touched off a diplomatic row with the nominally neutral United States by seizing the American freighter *City of Flint*. The Germans charged she was carrying contraband in the form of supplies for Britain, and a prize crew attempted to take her to Germany by way of the Russian port of Murmansk and Norwegian waters. The Norwegian authorities interned the prize crew and returned the ship to her captain. The affair caused a furor in the United States, and British propagandists capitalized on it to arouse public opinion further against Germany.

Jutland, prided himself on the fact that there had been no loss of life. On December 6, he transferred a batch of prisoners to the *Altmark*, bringing the total on board the tanker to 299, and headed for the east coast of South America.

Graf Spee's engines badly needed an overhaul, but before she returned home Langsdorff intended to increase his bag by taking a rich harvest off the River Plate estuary. And there, at 0608 on December 13, a clear and sunny morning with excellent visibility, German lookouts sighted three ships—one large, two smaller—some seventeen miles away. Langsdorff took these vessels for a light cruiser and two destroyers shepherding a convoy that lay over the horizon. Although his orders required him to avoid engagements with enemy fighting ships, he disregarded them. Battle stations were sounded, speed increased, and battle ensigns hoisted.

The ships were Force G, composed of the heavy cruiser *Exeter* and the light cruisers *Ajax*, which flew the broad pendant of Commodore Harry Harwood, and *Achilles* of the Royal New Zealand Navy. A fourth ship, the heavy cruiser *Cumberland*, was refitting in the Falkland Islands. Harwood was convinced that sooner or later the *Graf Spee* would be attracted by the rich River Plate trade, and had concentrated his force there. Sighting a smudge of smoke, he ordered *Exeter* to investigate. Within minutes, she signaled the flagship: I THINK IT IS A POCKET BATTLESHIP. Harwood had been right, but now he faced the problem of dealing with a powerful enemy vessel.

Graf Spee's six eleven-inch guns outranged the *Exeter*'s six eight-inch guns and the eight six-inch guns carried by each of the other vessels. They would be on the receiving end of her radar-guided salvos long before they could get into range to fire their own guns. Harwood had, however, already worked out the tactics to be followed should he encounter the pocket battleship. He would harry her on both flanks, thereby forcing *Graf Spee* to divide her fire. "I remember a rather sickening feeling in the pit of my tummy as I realized we were in for an action in which the odds were hardly on our side," recalled Captain W. E. Parry of *Achilles*. "Luckily there wasn't much time to think of that."

Hindsight makes it clear that Langsdorff should have put the safety of his ship first and immediately retreated before being sighted by the British. Failing this, he should have stood off and battered his adversaries with his eleven-inch guns while they were unable to fight back. Instead, obviously still believing he was dealing only with an inferior force, he closed with the oncoming ships. By the time he discovered his mistake, Harwood would not allow him to break off the action.

Langsdorff's error allowed Harwood to conduct the fight on his terms. *Exeter* engaged the raider from the south, *Ajax* and *Achilles* from the east. The Germans concentrated their big guns on *Exeter* while their secondary battery of eight 5.9-inch guns dealt with the smaller vessels. Up in the pocket battleship's director-control tower, rangefinders were lining twin images together, automatically sending their observations down to the transmitting station to be averaged and passed on to the guns, which deliberately sought out their targets.

Graf Spee opened the battle at 0617 at a range of seventeen miles. The three guns of her forward turret were elevated for maximum range, and the 670-pound shells sent columns of water mushrooming about *Exeter*. The German gunnery was fast and accurate, and the cruiser was straddled by a hail of shells. Six minutes after *Graf Spee* opened fire, a German shell wrecked the turret forward of *Exeter*'s bridge, and a shower of metal splinters cut down almost everyone there. The men standing on either side of Captain F. S. Bell were killed, and he suffered a face wound. The gyrocompasses and communication with the engine room and steering position were put out of commission.

With his ship out of control, Bell disregarded his wound and made his way through the carnage to the after conning position, the vessel's secondary command station. Using a boat's compass, he conned the ship by giving commands which were passed by a chain of sailors to the after steering control and the engine room. Bell soon had the badly battered *Exeter* back in action, and launched her port and then her starboard torpedoes in an effort to gain a respite. *Graf Spee* turned away under the cover of a thick, black smoke screen. But she continued to pound the cruiser, knocking out her remaining forward turret and fire-control apparatus. *Exeter* now had only one turret left, which was being manually trained. Damage-control parties fought fires in several areas of the ship, wrestled smoldering cordite charges over the side, and plugged holes below the waterline.

By 0645, *Exeter* was ablaze amidships and listing badly; her last remaining turret was put out of action when seawater flooded its controls. Langsdorff moved in to finish off his shattered opponent, but *Ajax* and *Achilles* hung on to his ship like a pair of terriers. In the beginning, their gunnery was erratic, because the pilot of *Ajax*'s floatplane confused the fall of her shells with those of *Achilles*, but they avoided damage by masterful ship-handling. Harwood ordered the cruisers to close the range—a hazardous move, because only their forward guns would bear as they steamed toward *Graf Spee*. This gamble paid off: the Germans shifted the fire of one of their eleven-inch turrets to the smaller ships from *Exeter*, which limped away.

The range was now down to eight hundred yards, and clouds of smoke lay on the sea like a shroud. A German shell burst on the waterline below the bridge of *Achilles*, killing or wounding four men and stunning her gunnery officer. The British cruisers also lost their radio link, but soon got back on target and kept up a steady fire. *Graf Spee*'s upperworks were hit repeatedly, causing chaos in the secondary batteries, where the gun crews were only partially protected by shields.

Graf Spee was still a dangerous opponent, however. A German shell tore into *Ajax* and knocked out her two after turrets. Harwood quickly turned away and, with his ship heeling over sharply, fired four torpedoes. But the moment they hit the water, the torpedoes leaped into the air like porpoises, and the Germans easily avoided them. Having received an erroneous report that 80 percent of *Ajax*'s ammunition had been expended, Harwood drew off at 0740 to the east, under cover of smoke, to conserve ammunition with the expectation of renewing the battle after nightfall. "The prospects of continuing a successful daylight action were anything but rosy," concluded a British Naval Staff report. Instead of pressing his advantage, however, Langsdorff turned away toward the Uruguayan coast. The Battle of the River Plate, as it became known, had lasted about ninety minutes.

Throughout the remainder of the day, the two cruisers dogged *Graf Spee*, while the Germans periodically turned to fire salvos to keep them at arm's length. As darkness fell, it was clear that the raider was making for the neutral harbor of Montevideo, and Harwood called off the pursuit. Scorched and blackened by shell blasts, *Graf Spee* had lost thirty-seven men killed and fifty-seven wounded. She was short of ammunition and fuel and was so battered that Langsdorff, who had been slightly wounded, doubted whether she was sea-worthy enough to return to Germany. He hoped to refuel and make repairs before venturing out to sea again. In the meantime, *Ajax* and *Achilles* took up station in international waters at the mouth of the Plate, while the crippled *Exeter* steamed away to the Falklands. Fifty-three of her crew had been killed and another fifty-nine wounded; the two light cruisers together had casualties of eleven killed and five wounded.

The diplomats now took over from the sailors. International law allows a belligerent warship only twenty-four hours in a neutral port to make repairs, but the Germans claimed this was not enough time for *Graf Spee* to be made ready for sea. The British played a double game. They demanded that the vessel be limited to a twenty-four-hour stay or be interned, while actually trying to hold her in port until a powerful force could be concentrated off Montevideo.* The Uruguayans gave *Graf Spee* permission to remain for seventy-two hours. In the meantime, false radio reports planted by the British convinced Langsdorff that *Ark Royal* and the battle cruiser *Renown* were waiting for his ship when she came out. Actually, they were several thousand miles away, and *Cumberland* was the only reinforcement to reach Harwood, who had been knighted and promoted to rear admiral.

Unwilling to sacrifice his crew in the face of what he believed were overwhelming odds, the exhausted Langsdorff asked Berlin whether he should accept internment or scuttle his ship. "*No* internment in Uruguay," Raeder replied, following a meeting with Hitler. Sanctuary in Buenos Aires, capital of pro-German Argentina, was also ruled out. Shortly after 1800 on December 17, *Graf Spee* weighed anchor and, followed a mile astern by the tanker *Tacoma* and several launches, proceeded slowly down the estuary as an immense crowd watched from the shore. Word that the pocket battleship had left its mooring was flashed to the three British cruisers, and they closed in from the sea.

---

*International law provided that a merchant ship leaving port be given a twenty-four-hour start over an enemy warship. To keep *Graf Spee* in port until reinforcements arrived, the British ordered their merchant ships at Montevideo to put to sea at the rate of one a day.

Four miles out, *Graf Spee* stopped. Langsdorff and a skeleton crew were seen disembarking in the launches and making for the *Tacoma*. Just as the sun was setting, a tongue of fire leaped up the pocket battleship's massive control tower, followed by the roar of an explosion. Flames engulfed the vessel, and her twisted hulk gradually settled into the mud of the Plate.* Ensigns and jacks snapping in the breeze, the victorious *Ajax* and *Achilles* swept by, their crews lining the rails and wildly cheering. Three days later, in a coda to this Wagnerian drama, Hans Langsdorff wrapped himself in the ensign of the old Imperial Navy and shot himself. Hitler sourly commented: "He should have sunk the *Exeter*."

Compared with the massive sea fights of the later years of the war, the Battle of the River Plate was a minor affair, yet it had wide ramifications. The destruction of *Graf Spee* not only ended the first challenge to Allied control of the sea, but also provided a badly needed boost to British morale. Amid such disasters as the sinking of *Courageous* and *Royal Oak*, it was, as Churchill said, "like a flash of light and color" against a dark sky. The attention of both the British and the Germans was already turning, however, from the blue South Atlantic to the frigid waters of the Norwegian Sea.

---

*British technicians later rowed out to *Graf Spee*'s hulk to dismantle her radar.

•

CHAPTER 2

"The Navy's Here!"

Two Coastal Command Hudson bombers, engines droning steadily, rolled in over the rugged southern coast of Norway shortly after noon on February 16, 1940. Pilot Officer C. W. McNeill spotted a large, gray-painted tanker moving slowly amid the drifting ice south of Bergen, and dropped down to get a closer look at her. Easing back on the throttle of his plane, McNeill made a sweeping turn over the vessel as he tried to make out the name on her stern. "The letters seemed to dance in a jumble," the airman later recalled, and he expected they would spell out a Norwegian name. "I could not suppress a whoop of joy when I saw they read *Altmark*."

The British had been searching for the *Altmark*, with its unhappy cargo of 299 merchant-seaman prisoners, ever since *Graf Spee* had been brought to bay. Keeping well to the north of the regular shipping lanes and assisted by dirty weather, Captain Heinrich Dau had crossed the Atlantic without being detected and had taken shelter in a narrow passage between the Norwegian mainland and a line of offshore islands known as the Inner Leads, before attempting the run across the North Sea to Germany. Word of the sighting of the prison ship was immediately flashed to a squadron consisting of a light cruiser and several destroyers under the command of Captain Philip L. Vian which was steaming to seaward.

Vian sent two of his destroyers to board the *Altmark* even though she was in neutral waters, but Dau refused to stop, and a pair of Norwegian torpedo boats interposed themselves between the British ships and the German vessel. The Norwegians, who had chartered 90 percent of their tanker fleet to the British, were fearful of Hitler's anger, and bent over backward to assist the *Altmark*. They accepted Dau's assurances that his ship was not carrying prisoners and false statements that she was unarmed, and protested against British violation of Norway's neutrality. The destroyers withdrew, and Dau sought asylum in the nearby Jossingfjord, where he thought he would be safe from enemy attack.

Vian informed the Admiralty of the situation, and, as First Lord, Churchill took personal charge. He instructed Vian to offer to escort the *Altmark* back to Bergen jointly with the Norwegian torpedo boats, for an inspection. If the Norwegians refused, he was to board the tanker and rescue the prisoners. That evening, Vian took the destroyer *Cossack* into the fjord. When the Norwegians rejected his compromise offer, he wasted no time in boldly laying his ship alongside the tanker. The *Altmark* attempted to ram the destroyer with her stern, but the British ship turned faster. Like a band of Nelson's tars, a boarding party of some thirty officers and men armed with pistols and rifles swarmed on board the tanker and made fast a hawser from *Cossack*'s foredeck. Several German seamen were killed or wounded in a brief struggle before the British won control of the *Altmark*.*

Breaking open a hatch, an officer called down into the darkness below: "Any British down there?"

"Yes," replied a chorus of voices. "We're all British!"

"Come on up, then," the officer called out. "Come on up, then. The Navy's here!"

In itself, the *Altmark* affair was of no great importance except as a British propaganda victory, but it focused attention on Norway. With her small population, long and vulnerable coastline, and economic dependence on shipping, war between Britain and Germany threatened her security. During World War I, the Norwegians suffered from the British blockade and German submarine attacks on their ships, but had managed to keep out of the struggle. Like most Western democracies, Norway deplored Nazi brutality, but with her

---

*The tanker was not seized by the British, and eventually made her way back to Germany.

southern territory exposed to Germany, she felt it was impossible to do anything but try to preserve her neutrality.

Churchill was drawn to Norway by his urge for action. In the early months of 1940, the war at sea appeared to have stabilized. German merchant shipping had been driven from the oceans, the surface raiders neutralized for the moment, the U-boats seemingly stymied by the convoy system, and improved fighter protection had taken much of the sting out of the Luftwaffe's attacks on coastal shipping. The situation was strikingly similar to 1915, when the seas had been cleared of the enemy, and Churchill had searched feverishly for an offensive role for the Royal Navy. Then he had found it in the Dardanelles operation. Now the First Lord's roving eye turned northward.

Reviving an aborted World War I proposal, Churchill suggested that three old battleships, a carrier, and a number of cruisers, destroyers, and submarines be sent into the Baltic as soon as the ice broke. Operation Catherine—named for Catherine the Great—was intended to establish a second front on the northern coast of Germany while shutting off vital shipments of high-grade Swedish iron ore to Germany. Churchill believed it might also induce the neutral Scandinavian countries to enter the war on the Allied side, or even influence the Soviet Union, Germany's nominal ally, to switch sides. Realizing the operation was hopelessly impractical because the ships would have been sitting ducks for German U-boats, bombers, mines, and coastal guns, Admiral Pound, the First Sea Lord, discreetly stalled until it was too late to mobilize shipping in time for the spring thaw.[*]

Unfazed, Churchill set out to deny Swedish iron ore shipments to

---

[*]It is useful at this point to examine briefly the relations between Churchill and Pound. Critics such as Captain Roskill charge that Churchill, both as First Lord and later as prime minister, dominated naval policy and strategy, while Pound knuckled under to his dictatorial behavior. Others, especially the American naval historian Arthur Marder, take an opposite view. Pound, Marder argues, kept a firm grip on the Admiralty and knew exactly how to manage Churchill. Realizing that a head-on collision would merely increase Churchill's obstinacy, the admiral avoided direct clashes. Instead, he referred Churchill's wilder schemes to the staff, which, with a groan, would produce an "appreciation" that pointed out its flaws. Usually, as in Operation Catherine, it died a quiet death. Only once did Churchill override Pound on a vital issue—the disastrous decision to send *Prince of Wales* and *Repulse* to Singapore in 1941 without an accompanying aircraft carrier. See Marder, *From the Dardanelles to Oran*, pp. 109–11, 173–78.

the Germans. In the summer, ore ships passed directly from the port of Luleå down the Gulf of Bothnia and across the Skagerrak to Germany. But from December to April, these waters were frozen, and the only outlet was through the northern-Norwegian port of Narvik, which was kept open by the Gulf Stream and linked to the Swedish ore fields by rail. Using the Leads, German ore carriers could remain in Norwegian waters during almost the whole voyage southward. Churchill proposed that the passage, which he called "the covered way," be mined in order to force German ore ships out onto the high seas, where they could legally be intercepted by the British navy. The War Cabinet declined, however, to violate international law and Norwegian neutrality.

A new dimension was added to Churchill's obsession with Norway when the Russians attacked Finland at the end of November 1939. The Soviet dictator, Joseph Stalin, worried about the possibility of an eventual assault by his German ally, tried to pressure the Finns into ceding a buffer zone along the frontier to protect Leningrad. When they refused, he launched a massive attack. Successive purges had weakened the officer corps of the Red Army, and, to the surprise and admiration of the world, the Finns, although vastly outgunned and outnumbered, fought the Russian invaders to a standstill.

For the moment, Russia, with whom the Allies were not at war, took the place of Germany as the enemy. With the French eager to draw the war away from their own territory, Britain and France organized an expeditionary force to go to the assistance of the Finns. This force was also to occupy Narvik and the southern ports of Stavanger, Bergen, and Trondheim for use as bases through which to pass Allied troops to the Finnish front. To "kill two birds with one stone," as Churchill put it, the Swedish ore port of Luleå would be seized as well. With little except wishful thinking to go on, the British believed resistance from the Norwegians and Swedes would be minimal. These schemes failed to take into account the likelihood of a violent German reaction. If the Allies occupied northern Norway, the Germans were certain to seize the southern part, and possibly Denmark and Sweden as well.

The Allied plan collapsed in mid-March 1940, when, after three months of war in the snows and Arctic darkness, the Russians crushed Finnish resistance. Churchill now urged the mining of the

Vestfjord, the outer approach to Narvik, and Stadlandet, to the south, to block the ore ships. On March 28, the Cabinet gave its approval not only to the minelaying expedition—dubbed Operation Wilfred—but also to an associated operation, known as Plan R-4. This called for the seizure of Narvik and other key ports if the Germans tried to take them in retaliation for the mining.

From this point on, both the Allies and the Germans were in a race for Norway. The British were hampered, however, by a concern for a show of legality. Under Plan R-4, troops were to be embarked on four cruisers and two converted passenger liners, but were to be held in readiness at Rosyth. They were not to be dispatched unless the Germans actually violated Norwegian neutrality. Had the mining begun as scheduled on April 5, the plan might have succeeded, but the mines were not laid until the early hours of April 8, with *Renown* and eight destroyers under the command of Vice-Admiral William Whitworth providing cover. As a result of the delay, the Allies lost the race for Norway. While the British were still embarking their troops, Hitler had already ordered a lightning attack upon Norway—and the "peaceful" occupation of Denmark as well.

Hitler's attention was first drawn to Norway by Admiral Raeder, and he became as obsessed with the country as Churchill. Raeder had been influenced by Vice-Admiral Wolfgang Wegener's 1929 treatise, *The Maritime Strategy of the Great War*, which argued that Imperial Germany had made a fatal mistake by failing to occupy Norway. Had the High Seas Fleet possessed bases on the Norwegian coast, it could not have been bottled up by the Royal Navy. Raeder pointed out at a Führer Naval Conference on October 10, 1939,[*] that the Abwehr had intelligence that the British were planning to occupy Norway, and stressed to Hitler the advantages of air and submarine bases on the Norwegian coast.

Raeder was equally concerned about the results of inaction. The Allies might again sow a barrier of mines across the North Sea from

---

[*]These meetings, held every two weeks or so, were attended by Hitler, Raeder, the Führer's naval adjutant Captain Karl Jesko von Puttkamer, and the leaders of the Oberkommando der Wehrmacht (OKW) or High Command, as well as others concerned with the specific problems under discussion.

the Orkneys to the territorial waters of Norway as they had in 1918,* which would block egress for the German fleet. They might try to mine the Leads or move into northern Norway and Sweden to cut off the ore supply; a British move into southern Norway would threaten German access to the North Sea. On the other hand, he realized that the risks of a German attack on Norway would be sizable and an occupied Norway would be difficult to defend. Hitler approved staff discussion of a possible Norwegian invasion, but was as yet unwilling to violate the nation's neutrality.

Two months later, on December 12, Raeder again brought up the question of Norway during a meeting with the Führer. Since their last discussion of the Norwegian question, he had met with Vidkun Quisling, a former Norwegian army officer and chief of the nation's small Nazi-type National Party, who assured the admiral that with German support he could seize control of the government and ally Norway with Germany. Impressed, Raeder had passed Quisling along to Hitler and asked for permission to begin immediate planning for the occupation of Norway. Two contingency plans were prepared. The first was mainly political, and called for a coup by Quisling and his "Fifth Columnists,"† who would ask for German support. The second was purely military and envisioned all-out assault on Norway. It was code-named Weserübung (Exercise Weser).

The *Altmark* affair tipped Hitler in favor of an invasion of Norway. It convinced him that henceforth Norwegian territorial waters would not assure certain protection for German shipping, nor would the Norwegians defend their neutrality against Allied transgressions. He resolved upon a military resolution of the Norwegian question, and on March 1, 1940, issued orders for a simultaneous invasion of both Norway and Denmark. Six divisions were diverted from a planned

---

*The North Sea Barrage, as it was called, was the brainchild of then U.S. Assistant Secretary of the Navy Franklin D. Roosevelt and consisted of seventy thousand mines. World War I ended before its effectiveness was fully tested, although it is believed that six U-boats were lost in the minefield. Some authorities also credit fear of the barrage with contributing to the decline of morale among German submarine crews. See Miller, *F.D.R.*, pp. 142–44.

†The term "Fifth Column" was first used for civilians engaged in treasonable conduct against their own governments during the Spanish Civil War, when the Nationalist General Emilio Mola stated: "We have four columns advancing upon Madrid. The fifth column will rise at the proper time." After the German invasion of Norway, such forces became known as "Quislings."

attack on France and the Low Countries scheduled for that spring, and General Nikolaus von Falkenhorst was named overall commander. Von Falkenhorst, faced with the need to produce plans for the invasion of a country of which he knew absolutely nothing, adopted a very unmilitary solution. "I went out and bought a Baedeker travel guide," he later declared.

Boldness, speed, and ruthlessness were the key elements of Weserübung. Involving almost the entire German surface navy, it was the first great combined operation involving sea, air, and ground forces in the history of warfare. For reasons of speed and safety, the initial striking force consisted of six groups of warships carrying small numbers of troops that were to slip into Norway's major harbors from Narvik to Oslo under the cover of darkness, and launch operations simultaneously at 0515 on April 9.

Scharnhorst and *Gneisenau* would provide cover for ten destroyers that would land two thousand Alpine troops at Narvik and would then make a diversionary sweep into the Arctic to decoy the British from the scene of action. The heavy cruiser *Admiral Hipper*, with four destroyers, would land seventeen hundred men at Trondheim. The light cruisers *Köln* and *Königsberg*, along with the gunnery-training ship *Bremse*, would land nineteen hundred troops at Bergen. The light cruiser *Karlsruhe* would land eleven hundred troops at Kristiansand and Arendal. Oslo was to be seized by two thousand men supported by *Hipper*'s sister ship, *Blücher*, and the pocket battleship *Lützow* and three torpedo boats. Four minesweepers would land 150 men at Egersund and capture the cable station. Three thousand troops would also be landed in Denmark, to support those that marched across the frontier.[*]

The Luftwaffe was to provide massive air cover for the operation, and drop paratroopers to assist in the capture of Oslo and to seize the airport at Stavanger. Twenty-eight U-boats were recalled from commerce raiding and took up station in a great arc stretching from Narvik to the Shetlands in preparation for the invasion. Some eighteen thousand troops to support the initial landing were embarked on fifteen steamships known as "Trojan Horses," which were to sail singly and inconspicuously and arrive at their objectives *before* the warships. An

---

[*]Unlike Allied amphibious operations later in the war, the Germans did not need special landing craft, because all the landings in Norway were to take place in fully equipped harbors rather than on beaches.

additional forty thousand men with heavy weapons were to follow and complete the occupation of the country. Fuel for the army, the Luftwaffe, and the return voyages of the warships was to be carried in three tankers, two from Wilhelmshaven and one from Murmansk in Russia.

"The operation in itself is contrary to all principles in the theory of naval warfare," Raeder told Hitler. "According to this theory, it could be carried out by us only if we have naval supremacy. We do *not* have this; on the contrary we are carrying out the operation in the face of a vastly superior British Fleet." But he assured the Führer that, "provided surprise is complete, our troops can and will successfully be transported to Norway."

Tankers and supply vessels began slipping to sea as early as April 3. In spite of elaborate efforts to mask these preparations, intelligence reports of increased activity in Heligoland Bight and the Skagerrak reached London, indicating an imminent attack on Norway. Allied submarines reported an unusual number of ships moving north under neutral flags, but they were forbidden to sink these vessels unless they could positively identify them as German troopships. But the Admiralty ignored these warnings. Indeed, on April 7, Admiral Sir Charles Forbes, commander-in-chief of the Home Fleet, was told, "All these reports are of doubtful value and may well be only a further move in the war of nerves."

The basic miscalculation, concludes Major General J. L. Moulton in his excellent study of the Norwegian campaign, was the conviction that the Germans would be unable to land a significant force on the Norwegian coast in the face of British command of the sea. This estimate was made by the Naval Staff, and accepted by the army and RAF because they wished to avoid commitments in Scandinavia. As a result, it was never effectively challenged by those who might have produced counterarguments.

On the evening of April 7, Admiral Forbes, acting on his own initiative after receiving continued air reports of enemy movements, took elements of the Home Fleet, including the battleships *Rodney* and *Valiant* and the battle cruiser *Repulse*, to sea.* Although he did not completely ignore the possibility of a German attack on Norway,

---

*No aircraft carriers were available. *Furious*, the nearest carrier, was fitting out in the Clyde. *Ark Royal* and *Glorious* were on training operations in the Mediterranean; *Eagle* was at Singapore; *Hermes* was in the South Atlantic.

his attention—as well as that of the Admiralty—was fixed on the threat of an Atlantic breakout by *Scharnhorst* and *Gneisenau,* and he steered northeast. This would put his force in position to deal with the German heavy ships, but it left the central North Sea area uncovered. From then on, he was known as "Wrong Way Forbes." Even as the British were steaming away from the Norwegian coast, advance elements of the German invasion force were thrusting their way through heavy seas and a snow squall toward their objectives.

Vice-Admiral Günther Lütjens, flying his flag in *Gneisenau,* led *Scharnhorst, Hipper,* and the destroyers of the Narvik and Trondheim forces to sea on April 7. The troops embarked on the destroyers were mostly from the mountains of the Tyrol and Styria, in the heart of Europe, and, as strangers to ships and the sea, looked upon the voyage as something of a lark. To the alarm of their hosts, they fiddled like children with unfamiliar valves and switches and raced up and down ladders. They had not been told their destination, and some thought they were going to Scotland.

This picnic atmosphere quickly vanished as darkness closed in and the destroyers ran into heavy weather. Terrified and seasick, the men were thrown from one unyielding steel bulkhead to another, only to be catapulted back as the ships pitched and rolled. Cascades of water swirled down companionways, soaking everyone and everything. Overcome by nausea, some soldiers disobeyed orders and sought fresh air on deck, where tumultuous waves were wrenching boats, supplies, motorcycles, and depth charges from their lashings. Ten men were washed overboard in the wild confusion.

The storm showed no sign of abating when, about 0900 on the morning of April 8, the skippers of two destroyers attached to the Trondheim group, *Hans Ludemann* and *Bernd von Arnim* sighted an unidentified ship which scudded in and out of view in the mountainous seas. Lieutenant Commander Gerard B. Roope, of the British destroyer *Glowworm,* was equally startled to see them. *Glowworm* had been part of *Renown's* screen in the minelaying operation but, having lost a man overboard, had left the formation to make a search. The missing seaman was recovered despite the wretched weather, but contact had been lost with the main British force. Radar and electronic navigational aids had not yet been installed on destroyers, and radio silence was all-important. Although both German vessels were considerably larger and more powerfully armed than *Glowworm*, her guns flashed out—the first shots of the Norwegian campaign.

A running fight developed, but, with the ships rolling and pitching and spray clouding gunsights and binoculars, accurate shooting was impossible. *Glowworm*'s fate was sealed, however, by *Hipper*'s arrival on the scene. Roope barely had time to break radio silence and signal the presence of the enemy cruiser before his ship was battered by her eight-inch shells. He launched his torpedoes and then dodged behind a smoke screen, but the cruiser adroitly avoided them and charged into the smoke to finish off her foe—whereupon the Germans were shocked to see the blazing *Glowworm* speeding straight toward them at her full speed of thirty-eight knots.

The destroyer struck *Hipper* near her starboard bow, grinding along her hull and ripping away 130 feet of armor belt. *Glowworm* drifted off and exploded. Thirty-eight survivors were rescued by the Germans despite the raging seas, but the exhausted Roope fell back into the water as he was being hoisted on board the cruiser. When the story of *Glowworm*'s epic last fight became known, he was posthumously awarded the Victoria Cross, the first won by a member of the Royal Navy in World War II. Though *Hipper* took on a list, her vital machinery was undamaged, and she continued on to Trondheim.

Admiral Forbes responded to *Glowworm*'s signals by dispatching *Repulse*, a cruiser, and four destroyers to intercept the enemy force, which was believed to be part of an Atlantic breakout. At the same time, *Renown* headed south on the same mission. Then the Admiralty ordered her to put about to rendezvous with the eight destroyers that had been guarding the newly laid minefield off the Vestfjord, which had been told to join her. These maneuvers left the entrance to the fjord unguarded at a critical moment. Confusion was compounded by report from a Coastal Command flying boat that a German battle cruiser and two cruisers were steering *west*—away from Trondheim—which added to the evidence of a German breakout. In reality, the ships were *Hipper* and her accompanying destroyers, which were merely passing time to seaward until dawn of the next day, when they would launch their attack. Forbes altered course to the north-northwest to intercept, and consequently missed the Germans when they turned to make their run into the Trondheimfjord.

By now, the admiral was leaning to the view that the Germans were about to invade Norway, but he had to keep up a guard against a possible Atlantic breakout. He was in the unenviable position of making decisions on the basis of imprecise information and trying to interpret the wishes of seniors who were not at all certain what they wanted. Forbes's task was made no easier by the mass of often conflicting signals sent him by the Admiralty, and he had to contend with interference not only from Churchill, but also from Admiral Pound. Having recently commanded the Mediterranean Fleet, he found it difficult to keep his hands off Forbes's ships. The Home Fleet was also being battered by a severe gale, making it even more difficult to make critical decisions. Visibility was bad, air search impossible and the destroyers were unable to maintain fleet speed.

While the Home Fleet pounded through stormy seas in pursuit of the phantom German squadron, events to the south that same afternoon, April 8, provided strong evidence of the enemy's real intentions. The Polish submarine *Orzel** sighted the German transport *Rio*

Orzel had an interesting history. At the outbreak of the war, she went on patrol in the Gulf of Danzig and survived numerous bombing and depth-charge attacks by the Germans. Within a week or so, her captain took sick and was landed at Tallinn, Estonia. Under German pressure, the Estonians interned the boat, and she was placed under guard. Fifteen of her twenty torpedoes had been removed when the hoisting cable snapped. This was not so providential as it appeared, because the cable had been secretly filed by her new skipper, Lieutenant Jan Grudzinski, while the Estonians were not looking.

About midnight on September 21, 1939, the Estonian guards were overpowered and the mooring lines cut, and *Orzel* got under way. Watchmen on the piers gave the alarm, and the submarine's conning tower was splattered by machine-gun bullets. Running half submerged, she ran aground on a bar at the mouth of the harbor. Searchlights played on her, and artillery fire damaged her radio. Grudzinski managed to get his command clear by blowing her tanks, and she proceeded out into the Gulf of Finland bound for a British port.

Since the Estonians had removed *Orzel*'s charts, Grudzinski decided to stop a German ship and seize her charts. Unfortunately, the only German ships sighted were warships, not merchantmen. The submarine's sole navigational aid was a list of lighthouses, and with these as a reference, Grudzinski followed a course along the Baltic coast, around Denmark out into the North Sea. In those waters, however, *Orzel* was subject to attack not only by the Germans but also by the British, because she had no means of identifying herself. Forty days after leaving Gdynia, the boat made a landfall off the east coast of Scotland.

Orzel lay on the bottom until the Poles managed to make emergency radio repairs, and then surfaced to transmit a message in pidgin English. Much of it was incomprehensible, but the British made out the last part: "Beg permission entrance and pilot. Have no chart. *Orzel*." A destroyer came out, inspected the boat, and escorted her into port, much to the surprise of the British, who thought she had been sunk long before (Cant, *The War at Sea*, pp. 4–6).

de Janeiro off Norway's southern coast and fired a warning shot across her bow. The steamer refused to stop and was torpedoed. A Norwegian destroyer and several fishing trawlers picked up survivors. To the amazement and alarm of the rescuers, they proved to be German soldiers in uniform, who frankly admitted they were on the way to "protect" Bergen from a British invasion. Incredibly, the Norwegian authorities took no steps except to alert their coast-defense forces—a general mobilization was not considered—while the Admiralty was still hypnotized by the prospects of a German breakout into the Atlantic.

In fact, Churchill personally ordered the four cruisers being held at Rosyth for Plan R-4 to disembark their troops, and sent the ships to join Forbes's flag. The men were hurriedly put ashore in considerable disorder and without their equipment. As a result, the British deprived themselves of the only military force available for a quick counterstroke against a German invasion of Norway at the precise moment it was most needed.*

Shortly after 0330 on April 9, a snow-covered signalman literally blew into Admiral Whitworth's chart room in *Renown* and asked Commander Robert Currie, the operations officer, to step outside for a moment. "Look, Sir!" he said, pointing to port.

Currie stared through a break in the intermittent snow squalls and shouted: "Call the Admiral—press the alarm!"

He had caught a momentary glimpse of two large German ships, which he identified as *Scharnhorst* and *Hipper*. In fact, the ships were *Scharnhorst* and *Gneisenau*. It was an easy mistake, because the German heavy cruisers and battle cruisers were similar in profile and visibility was poor.

Having escorted the ten destroyers bound for Narvik to the entrance to the Vestfjord, Admiral Lütjens had headed his ships west on his decoy mission. Running into a rising wind and heavy seas, he reduced speed to twelve knots. The Germans, hindered by tricks of

---

*Churchill claimed (in *History of the Second World War*, vol. I, p. 533) that this decision had been "concerted" with Forbes, but the admiral was not informed of it until after the orders had been given (Roskill, *The War at Sea*, vol. I, p. 161; Roskill, *Churchill and the Admirals*, pp. 98–99).

sea and light, failed to see *Renown* until her fifteen-inch shells began falling around *Gneisenau*. Lütjens immediately ordered full speed ahead while returning *Renown*'s fire at a range of 18,600 yards. A short, sharp duel developed while the ships ran at high speed through boiling seas on parallel courses.

Within ten minutes, *Renown* had scored three hits on *Gneisenau*, knocking out her forward fire-control position, and Lütjens broke off the action. The two modern German vessels, each mounting nine eleven-inch guns, were far more formidable than an old battle cruiser with her six fifteen-inch guns. But Lütjens's task was not to fight; it was to lure the British away from the Norwegian coast. Moreover, he was confused by the gun flashes from *Renown*'s accompanying destroyers. In the semidarkness he thought the firing came from *Repulse*, which in fact had not yet joined *Renown*, and decided against risking Germany's only two capital ships against a supposedly equivalent enemy force.

Whitworth gave chase in the teeth of a gale, with *Renown* working up to a speed of twenty-nine knots. Disregarding the damage inflicted on his ships by the heavy seas—the forward turrets of both were put out of action—Lütjens managed to draw away and was lost in the Atlantic mists. The British had won a tactical victory over stronger German forces, but Lütjens had fulfilled his mission of drawing *Renown* and its destroyer screen away from the Vestfjord and Narvik. The damage to *Gneisenau* was a modest price to pay for this success.

The British were still blindly searching for the Germans when the German invasion of Norway began in the predawn hours of April 9. Covered by darkness and falling snow, Commodore Friedrich Bonte entered the unguarded Vestfjord and led his ten destroyers up the hundred-mile-long, narrow passage to Narvik. The unsuspecting Norwegians had left the navigation lights and beacons on shore burning. Bonte's ships entered the crowded harbor exactly at 0515, as scheduled. A signal lamp winked agitatedly from the forty-year-old guardship *Eidsvold*. The Germans were ordered to stop, and a shot was fired across the bow of *Wilhelm Heidkamp*, the German flagship.

Bonte sent an officer across to *Eidsvold* with instructions to demand free passage. Taking Admiral Raeder's orders literally— "Resistance is to be broken ruthlessly"—he told the officer that if passage was denied he was to fire a signal from a red Very pistol as soon as he had left the Norwegian vessel. While waiting, Bonte trained his torpedo tubes on the guardship. As soon as the red signal light flashed in the sky, two torpedoes leaped from *Heidkamp*'s tubes and raced toward her. Before the Norwegians even realized their peril, a tremendous explosion shattered *Eidsvold*. *Norge*, her sister ship, opened fire on the Germans, but she was quickly put out of action. The commandant of the garrison, a Colonel Sundlo, was a follower of Vidkun Quisling and offered no resistance to the German troops scrambling off the destroyers.

At Trondheim, *Hipper* and her four destroyers confused the defenders by flashing Morse code in English as they steamed into the fjord. Only the innermost battery opened fire, and it was quickly silenced. The other batteries were taken from the rear by German troops and then manned by coastal artillerymen in expectation of a British counterattack. Bergen fell after the shore batteries damaged the gunnery-training ship *Bremse* and the light cruiser *Königsberg*. The cable station at Egersund was captured without difficulty, and paratroopers seized the airfield at Stavanger. Fog delayed the invaders at Kristiansand, and surprise was lost. The coast-defense guns forced the ships back out to sea under cover of a smoke screen, but the Luftwaffe sent in dive-bombers that smashed the fortifications holding up the ships.

The Germans encountered the most serious trouble at Oslo. A Norwegian patrol boat, *Pol III*, challenged the invaders and rammed a torpedo boat before being sunk. *Blücher* and *Lützow* pressed ahead at low speed through the moonless and hazy night toward the Drøbak Narrows, where the fjord is only about five hundred yards wide and dominated by the Oscarborg fortress. Holding their fire until the ships were at point-blank range, the Norwegians opened up on them with their eight- and eleven-inch guns. *Lützow* was hit three times, and *Blücher* was reduced to a flaming hulk by heavy shells and torpedoes. Wrapped in smoke and flame, she capsized and sank in deep water at 0630 with the loss of more than a thousand officers and men, including the expedition's Gestapo detachment.

Reversing course, the Germans steamed back down the fjord to disembark the troops below the narrows. They captured the fortifications and worked their way back to Oslo overland while the Luftwaffe bombed the city. Airborne troops finally occupied the capital and its airport, but the delay bought time for King Haakon VII and most of the Norwegian government to escape by train to Hamar, in the north. In their place, the Germans established a puppet regime headed by Vidkun Quisling.

The first phase of the Norwegian campaign had been a brilliant success. In spite of its superior strength, the Royal Navy had failed to prevent German naval forces from capturing all their objectives. Even though there were setbacks, such as the loss of *Blücher*, German troops were firmly established ashore, reinforcements were pouring in, and the Luftwaffe was moving bomber squadrons to the Norwegian airfields with remarkable speed. Denmark had also been overrun the same morning without resistance.[*] Norwegian fumbling and British blunders played a significant role in the outcome, but the German victory was primarily due to the boldness and determination with which the operation was carried out.

Although reports that the Germans were invading Norway poured in upon the Admiralty on the morning of April 9, the British reaction was confused. The Home Fleet was reinforced by the battleship *Warspite* and the carrier *Furious*, but the latter put to sea so hurriedly that she sailed without her fighter squadron, rendering her all but useless in the ensuing operations. Forbes, who was now about ninety miles west of Bergen, ordered an attack upon the port by a force of four cruisers and seven destroyers, but the Admiralty countermanded his orders. Had the attack gone forward, the British would have caught *Köln* coming down the fjord on its way back to Germany while the damaged *Königsberg* and *Bremse* were still at their moorings.

The Royal Navy quickly learned the cost of bringing its ships within range of land-based bombers without fighter cover or effective anti-aircraft guns. By the afternoon of April 9, the gale had moderated, and for three hours nearly ninety bombers lashed at the Home Fleet as it steamed off the Norwegian coast. The destroyer *Gurkha* was sunk, and two cruisers were lightly damaged; so was *Rodney*, hit

---

[*]The German occupation of Denmark provided an excuse for the Allied occupation of Iceland, a Danish possession with a strategic location that was to prove of immense value during the Battle of the Atlantic.

by a heavy bomb which failed to explode but splintered her armored deck. Forbes, now convinced it would be suicidal to remain within range of German bombers without fighter support, moved the Home Fleet away from the coast. Thus, it was unable to interfere with German sea communications with Norway during a critical phase of the campaign.*

The Kriegsmarine still faced the difficult task of bringing its ships back to Germany before they were bottled up or destroyed. Some vessels made their move that night. *Köln* and *Hipper* reached home safely. *Karlsruhe*, however, was torpedoed by the British submarine *Truant* off Kristiansand, and after a three-hour struggle to keep her afloat, she was scuttled. *Lützow* fell victim to another submarine, *Spearfish*. With her rudder and propellers wrecked, the pocket battleship almost drifted ashore on the Danish coast. Three days later, she barely limped into Kiel, so severely mauled that it took a full year to make her ready for sea again.

British submarines also took a toll of the supply ships and transports carrying reinforcements for the German army. *Trident* accounted for four enemy vessels; *Triad, Sea Lion,* and *Snapper* sank one each; *Orzel* added a tanker to her bag. *Triton* accounted for a pair of transports carrying nine hundred troops. Three British boats were lost. The U-boats sank no enemy ships, however, primarily because of continued torpedo failures. Günther Prien returned from a patrol in which his torpedoes had repeatedly failed to explode or gone off prematurely, and angrily told Dönitz he "could hardly be expected to fight with a dummy rifle."

Königsberg, which lay immobilized at Bergen, was a temptation to the British. Twenty-four high-level RAF bombers attacked her on the evening of April 9, without result. Then it was the turn of the Fleet Air Arm. Sixteen Skua dive-bombers took off from Hatson, in the Orkneys, in the early-morning darkness of the following day, bound for Bergen. The planes lumbered into the air, each carrying a five-

---

*British anti-aircraft defenses were inadequate for several reasons. The ships lacked high-angle guns, their fire-control systems were of little use against high-performance aircraft and the multiple pom-poms—known as "Chicago pianos"—and heavy machine guns intended for use against low-flying planes were unreliable, clumsy, and few in number. Modern forty-millimeter Swedish Bofors and twenty-millimeter Swiss Oerlikons were not ordered until war was imminent.

hundred-pound bomb and so heavily loaded with fuel they barely managed to clear the runway.

Two hours later, they crossed the Norwegian coastline as the sun was coming up, and climbed to eight thousand feet. On reaching Bergen, the Skuas screamed down on the surprised Germans and smothered the cruiser in direct hits and near misses. Turned into a blazing wreck, she exploded and sank, the first major warship to be sunk by aerial bombing in actual warfare. Flying low through heavy anti-aircraft fire, the planes zigzagged down the fjord, all but one making good their escape. The margin of safety was so fine that, upon landing at Hatson, the engines of several planes sputtered and died for lack of fuel before they taxied off the runway. A BBC broadcast that night credited the exploit to the RAF—which had failed to hit the ship the previous day.

Having quickly captured Narvik, Commodore Bonte was anxious to return to Germany before the British sealed the fjord, but he had difficulty in refueling his ten destroyers. Only one of the two allotted tankers had arrived—the other was sunk—and her pumping equipment was inadequate. This meant that only two of the destroyers could be refueled at a time, and the process took seven or eight hours. Bonte expected to make his dash the morning of April 10. As he waited, he put one vessel to patrolling the entrance to the Ofotfjord, leading to Narvik, and deployed the nine others about the adjacent waterways. Having made these arrangements, and lulled by a report from *U-51* that it had sighted five British destroyers in the Vestfjord at 2022 steering *away* from the entrance to the Ofotfjord, he turned in for the night.

These ships were the Second Destroyer Flotilla, under the command of Captain Bernard A. W. Warburton-Lee in *Hardy*, and had been sent in by Admiral Forbes to prevent a German landing at Narvik. The other vessels were *Hotspur, Havock, Hunter*, and *Hostile*. On the way up the fjord, Warburton-Lee learned from the Norwegian lighthouse-keepers that a German force of six destroyers, all larger and more powerful than his ships, was at Narvik. INTEND ATTACKING AT DAWN AT HIGH WATER,[*] he signaled Forbes. This would

---

[*]Note Warburton-Lee's use of the word "intend." In Royal Navy parlance, this meant "I will take action unless ordered not to do so." If he had used the word "propose," it would have meant "I await instructions before taking action."

give him the advantage of surprise and enable his vessels to pass over any mines laid in the fjord.

As Warburton-Lee's ships slowly groped through the tortuous passage in line ahead, there were several anxious moments. Visibility was limited to a few hundred feet because of a heavy snowfall, and they almost ran aground at one point and then narrowly averted a collision with a local passenger steamer that had somehow gotten in among the darkened destroyers. Undetected, the British flotilla reached Narvik at 0430, just as the curtain of snow and mist parted at first light. A seaman in *Hardy* described what occurred next:

> We saw two ships. One was a German whaling factory, and the other a British ship. Behind them were some German destroyers, bigger than we were. There were plenty of other ships, but we did not have time to count them. We opened up with our torpedoes at the enemy destroyers, the destroyers all releasing 'tin fish' one after the other. Two German destroyers were hit the first time. When our torpedoes hit we saw a flash, and it was just as if some huge hand had torn the German ship in half. It just split in two. With all those torpedoes going into the harbor, nearly every ship there seemed to be sunk. It was like a shambles.

Bonte's flagship, *Wilhelm Heidkamp*, was the first casualty. The alarm had barely been sounded when a torpedo exploded in her after magazine. She blew up with most of her complement, including the commodore. Another destroyer was sunk and three were damaged in the first chaotic minutes. Six German supply vessels were also accounted for. Warburton-Lee, having dealt with all but one of the six warships he had expected to meet, withdrew down the fjord at fifteen knots. But his ships were ambushed by the five undamaged German destroyers, which had been lying in nearby fjords. *Hunter* was sunk in a short, savage fight; *Hotspur* was seriously damaged; *Hardy* was shattered and set on fire, Warburton-Lee was killed, and the ship was beached in sinking condition.

Fortunately for the British, the German vessels were too battle-damaged or short of fuel to pursue them. On their way out to the open sea, they encountered the German supply ship *Rauenfels* and shelled her. She was carrying most of the landing force's ammunition and exploded with a shattering roar that sent a column of flame and debris soaring three thousand feet into the air. So ended the First Battle of Narvik. Warburton-Lee had either sunk or immobilized ten enemy destroyers with only five of his own. The daring attack earned him a posthumous Victoria Cross.

Fuel and ammunition shortages and battle damage held the five remaining German destroyers at Narvik. Their fate was sealed with the arrival of *Warspite* off the Vestfjord. Forewarned by B-Dienst, which was reading the British signals, Fregattenkapitän Erich Bey, who had succeeded to command after Bonte's death, resolved to inflict as much damage on the enemy as possible before being overwhelmed. He laid ambushes in the various fjords and deployed two submarines that were on hand in positions to attack the British force.

The Second Battle of Narvik began on the morning of April 13. Brushing off the U-boat threat, Admiral Whitworth, who had transferred his flag to *Warspite*, stood into the fjord with a force of nine destroyers and the battleship's Swordfish floatplanes leading the way. The German destroyer *Hermann Künne* was on patrol outside the Ofotfjord. It was a gray day with low clouds and patches of mist. Out of the general grayness to the southwest, a lookout saw the darker-gray forms of several British destroyers with the towering bulk of a capital ship looming over them. *Künne* radioed an alarm, and in the face of this overwhelming force fled toward Bey's other ships.

At 1300, *Warspite* fired her big guns in earnest for the first time since Jutland, nearly a quarter-century before. Petty Officer Daniel Reardon, a gunner's mate in one of the turrets, reported:

> The Turret Officer tells me I can load. We hear the order repeated to the men down below, the cages come up with a thud and out go the rammers. We can feel that we have increased speed as the ship has begun to vibrate. Heavy explosions shake the ship. . . . Suddenly comes the order 'Salvos,' and the right gun comes to the ready. Then 'Enemy in Sight' and the sight-setters chant the ranges. It is just like a practice shoot. Our guns are nearly horizontal, so the range must be short. Then the 'ding ding' of the fire gong, the right gun moves a little, comes steady and there is a 'Woof' which rocks the turret. . . .

The roar of the battleship's fifteen-inch guns reverberated from the steep, snow-covered sides of the fjord, and the water boiled and erupted with shell splashes. Bey's ships tried to dodge the fusillade

of shells and torpedoes, but tall columns of oily black smoke soon
marked their positions. *Warspite* and her destroyers moved relent-
lessly past one beached or burning wreck after another, and the gun
crews were given permission to climb on top the turrets to inspect
their handiwork. "It is a sight," reported Reardon, "burning and sinking enemy ships all around us, and our own destroyers search into
every little corner that might hide something." *U-64* was discovered
on the surface by a Swordfish. Putting his clumsy craft into the semblance of a dive, Petty Officer F. R. Price released two 350-pound
bombs. A direct hit sent the submarine to the bottom.

The destroyers *Cossack* and *Eskimo* were severely mauled, but the
entire German force was annihilated. Some twenty-five hundred
crewmen from the sunken ships made their way ashore and joined the
troops defending Narvik. Norwegian sources reported that the invaders,
cut off from the outside world and short of ammunition and supplies,
were completely demoralized. Whitworth urgently sought permission
to put a landing force ashore, but the Admiralty rejected his request. He
was told to await the arrival of two brigades of British and French troops
that had been embarked from the Clyde on April 11. But this force did
not arrive until April 15, and went ashore at Harstad, on an island thirty
miles northwest of Narvik. They landed in considerable disorder, and
valuable time was lost in sorting out equipment and supplies. In the
interval, bad weather set in, and the Germans recovered their fighting
spirit. Had Narvik been attacked immediately, many observers believe
it could have been captured. It was at this juncture, as Captain Roskill
has noted, that the troops earmarked for Plan R-4, but put ashore so
hastily, could have been used to advantage.

Trondheim was regarded as the key to control of central Norway. If it
could be retaken, the Allies reasoned, the Germans might be held to
the south while they established themselves in the northern areas. At
Churchill's urging, part of the expeditionary force earmarked for
Narvik was diverted while still at sea and put ashore at Namsos, a
small port to the north of Trondheim.* Troops were also landed at

---

*In an incident typical of the entire Norwegian campaign, the officer commanding
the troops landed at Namsos was on a different ship from his men and was carried away
willy-nilly to Narvik.

Åndalsnes, to the south, and the two forces, totaling some eleven thousand men, formed the arms of a pincers that was to converge on Trondheim. Although the Allies were now ashore in three places, the operation was a fiasco. They were unable to overcome the initial advantage of surprise won by the Germans, and their countermeasures were hurriedly improvised and ill-planned, and lacked clearcut objectives.

To add to the confusion, Major General P. J. Mackesey, the land commander, refused even to speak to his opposite number, Admiral Lord Cork and Orrery. And both the fleet and the expeditionary force lacked adequate air cover. The Luftwaffe controlled the skies over Norway, and the troops were subjected to savage attacks by German dive-bombers. Åndalsnes was repeatedly bombed, and the British troops took cover in the nearby forests during the day. Namsos also received its share of battering. "The whole place was a mass of flames from end to end," one officer wrote following a particularly devastating raid.

Because the RAF's Hurricane and Spitfire fighters based in Scotland lacked the range to reach Norway, the army relied upon the ships for protection against the incessant raids on its supply bases. With the fjords offering little room for maneuvering, losses among the anti-aircraft cruisers and destroyers and merchantmen mounted alarmingly. Under repeated attack by Stukas, these ships suffered from ammunition shortages, gun wear, and the exhaustion of their crews.

The cruiser *Suffolk* bombarded the Stavanger airfield on April 17 in an attempt to deny it to the Germans, but she limped away so badly damaged by dive-bombers that her quarterdeck was awash. Planes from *Furious* and *Ark Royal* attempted to defend the Allied forces, but, fearing German air attacks, the ships remained more than a hundred miles from the coast, a situation that placed their aircraft at a disadvantage. *Furious* was soon damaged by a German bomber and withdrawn.

British pilots quickly found their aircraft inferior to those of the Germans. When a flight of Skuas tried to break up a bombing raid by twin-engined Ju-88s, they were unable to catch the Germans. "Our Fleet Air Arm aircraft are hopelessly outclassed by everything that flies in the air," observed Admiral Forbes, "and the sooner we get some different aircraft the better." Poor flying conditions, sudden snow squalls, and mountains that suddenly appeared out of the mists all made the campaign an airman's nightmare.* By the time the Norwegian campaign was over, the Fleet Air Arm lost a third of its total flying strength. In an effort to provide land-based fighter cover, eighteen obsolescent RAF Gladiators were flown off *Glorious* and used a frozen lake as an airfield. The old biplanes quickly shot down six German planes, but most were destroyed by enemy bombers when caught on the ground with frozen engines.

The evacuation of Namsos and Åndalsnes was inevitable. German air attacks on the supply route were devastating, and it was becoming increasingly difficult to unload men and equipment. Without sufficient air cover and artillery, the campaign became, in Churchill's words, "a muddy waddle forward and back." Crises were also brewing elsewhere. Benito Mussolini, the Italian dictator, was showing signs of taking advantage of Britain's difficulties in Norway, and heavy ships were moved to the Mediterranean in case he made the plunge into war. And with the Germans menacing the Low Countries, consideration was given to cutting losses in Norway and concentrating Allied forces where they were most needed.

Åndalsnes and Namsos were evacuated between April 30 and May 3. The soldiers trudged down from the mountains to the sea, silent, fatigued, and dazed by unceasing air attack. They were taken off at Åndalsnes without loss under cover of darkness. At Namsos, however, waves of dive-bombers attacked the ships crowded into the fjord. Several were damaged, but only one of these stationary targets, the sloop *Bittern*, was a total loss. The full fury of the Luftwaffe fell upon the destroyers carrying the rearguard to sea. Two ships were lost, but the evacuation was so skillfully handled that General Sir Adrian Carton de Wiart observed: "In the course of that last end-

---

*The experience of Captain Richard Partridge, who had led the raid on *Königsberg* and was flying Skuas off *Ark Royal*, was not untypical. He shot down a German bomber, and then was shot down himself. Having crash-landed on a frozen lake, he and his observer struggled through the snow to a nearby cabin. The British airmen had just settled down when the crew of the German bomber they had shot down came through the door. An uneasy truce prevailed through the night. At dawn they were all arrested by a Norwegian ski patrol, which provided the Englishmen with skis and directions to the coast. "We made a very comprehensive tour of a large portion of Norway on foot, by car and by boat," Partridge commented dryly upon his return to *Ark Royal*. "We both agreed it was a very lovely country" (Cameron, *Wings of Morning*, p. 34).

less day I got a message from the Navy to say that they would evacuate the whole of my force that night. I thought it was impossible, but learned a few hours later that the Navy did not know the word."

In the meantime, the ill-starred Norwegian adventure was under fire in Parliament, and after a vote of "No Confidence," power slipped from Chamberlain's faltering hands. Ironically, Winston Churchill, who had more to do with the Norwegian fiasco than anyone, succeeded him as prime minister on May 10. But the eyes of the world were shifting elsewhere. That same morning, Hitler launched his long-feared blitzkrieg in the West, as some 135 German divisions struck neutral Holland and Belgium; at the other end of the Western Front, German armor smashed through the supposedly impenetrable Ardennes Forest. Outflanking the Maginot Line, these units raced toward the Channel ports to cut off the British army.

With every soldier and gun needed to stem the onrushing German tanks, the Norwegian operation was hastily closed down. The British took Narvik on May 28, but held it only long enough to destroy the railroad and ore loading piers. *Ark Royal* and *Glorious* provided air cover for the withdrawal, which began on June 7. The troops were embarked in two large convoys, and the Norwegian royal family was taken off in the cruiser *Devonshire* with the nation's gold reserve.

Prudence dictates that such vital convoys be heavily defended, but Forbes lacked the ships for an adequate escort. *Repulse* and *Renown* had been sent to find some German heavy ships falsely reported to be breaking out into the Atlantic, and the bulk of the Home Fleet had steamed south in case the Germans attempted to disrupt the vital cross-Channel link during the massive evacuation of British forces from France under way at the same time. As a result, Forbes had only the battleship *Valiant* and a handful of smaller vessels to protect the large number of ships at sea between Narvik and Scapa Flow. Tragedy lay just over the horizon—for, unknown to the British, *Scharnhorst, Gneisenau, Hipper*, and four destroyers were steaming toward the convoys.

Earlier damage repaired, the German squadron had sailed from Kiel on June 4 under the command of Admiral Wilhelm Marschall, who flew his flag on *Gneisenau*. Unaware of the Allied evacuation of Narvik, Admiral Raeder had ordered Marschall to attack enemy ships in the anchorage at nearby Harstad to relieve pressure on the defenders and to assist a German army advancing up the coast. Favored by misty weather, the squadron's movements were undetected. Three days out, Marschall received reports from the Luftwaffe of the presence of large convoys in the area. Suspecting that Narvik was being evacuated, he abandoned the attack on Harstad to go after the nearest convoy.

Early on the morning of June 8, the Germans intercepted a tanker, an escort trawler, and the empty troopship *Orama*, all of which were sunk. Their attempts to get off an enemy-sighting report were jammed. The hospital ship *Atlantis* was spared when, in accordance with the Geneva Convention, she did not attempt to make a radio report. *Hipper* and the destroyers were short of fuel, and were ordered into Trondheim while the battle cruisers pressed on to the north in pursuit of the convoy.

Shortly before 1600, Midshipman Siegfried Goss, on watch in *Gneisenau's* foretop, saw a wisp of smoke a long way off on the eastern horizon. At first he thought it was his imagination; then it was confirmed by the powerful lens of a rangefinder. Admiral Marschall ordered his crews to action stations and waited to see what ship would take shape as the distance closed. "Thick funnel, and mast with turret," a gunnery officer reported from the foretop. "Probably also a flight deck." The Germans had run into *Glorious* and a pair of escorting destroyers, *Ardent* and *Acasta*.

Glorious had just participated in an unprecedented naval operation. She had remained behind at Narvik to pick up a squadron of shore-based Gladiators, but ten Hurricanes operating with them were to be destroyed, because it was thought impossible to land them on a carrier without arresting gear. But their pilots had managed to put down safely on the ship—disposing of the old argument that modern high-performance aircraft could not operate from carriers. Without waiting for a strong escort, Captain Guy D'Oyly-Hughes, the carrier's skipper, sailed immediately for Scapa Flow with only two destroyers.[*]

---

[*]Originally, it was believed *Glorious* had sailed with such a small escort because she was short of fuel and needed to return to base immediately. The evidence indicates that D'Oyly-Hughes was mentally unbalanced and raced off to Scapa Flow to expedite a court-martial of one of his officers, against whom he was nursing a grudge. See Winton, *Carrier Glorious*; Roskill, *Churchill and the Admirals*, pp. 107–8.

Scharnhorst opened up at a range of twenty-eight thousand yards, and her radar-directed salvos were extremely accurate. *Glorious* had neither kept her planes at the ready nor mounted the air patrols which were her only defense, and D'Oyly-Hughes was taken completely by surprise by the unexpected appearance of the German vessels. Leading Seaman C. G. Carter, in charge of *Acasta*'s after torpedo tubes, saw "a great column of water shoot up astern" and thought the ship was under air attack. "Whilst looking at *Glorious*, I heard a whistling noise pass over me, and it was a shell which hit *Glorious*."

Eleven-inch shells plunged into the carrier's flight deck, breaking up a frantic, last-minute effort to launch four Swordfish armed with torpedoes. Large sections of the deck were flipped up "like the lid of a box," according to Admiral Marschall. With fires raging in her crowded hangar deck, the carrier tried to flee under cover of smoke laid down by *Acasta* and *Ardent*. Handled with skill and gallantry, the destroyers raced in to launch their torpedoes, forcing the battle cruisers to turn away. *Glorious* had only a brief respite, however, for the German gunners again found the range.

There was no hope of assistance. At 1720, *Devonshire* picked up a cryptic message, barely intelligible, from *Glorious*; since it made no sense, she did not break radio silence to pass it on. None of the other ships in the area received the signal. Hit repeatedly, the carrier burned out of control as ammunition and fuel fed the holocaust. A shell struck her bridge, killing D'Oyly-Hughes and everyone there. "Slowly the giant began to turn on her side," relates a German report. "Pouring out flames and smoke . . . a moment later she sank." Not long before, *Ardent*, under Lieutenant Commander J. F. Barker, which had fired all her torpedoes, was overwhelmed by enemy gunfire and sank, leaving only *Acasta*, under Commander C. E. Glasfurd, to carry on the fight. Seaman Carter later described her last sortie:

> We . . . altered course into our own smoke screen. When we came out of it I had my first glimpse of the enemy. I fired two torpedoes, the foremost tubes fired theirs. From one of the ships a yellow flash and a great column of smoke and water shot up. We knew we had hit. After we had fired our torpedoes we went back into our smoke screen. "Stand by to fire remaining torpedoes." This time, as soon as we poked our nose out the enemy let us have it. A shell hit the engine room. I was blown to the after end of the tubes. The ship stopped with a list to

port. I fired the remaining torpedoes. . . . The enemy hit us several
times and one big explosion took place right aft. The captain gave
orders to abandon ship. . . .

The tracks of *Acasta*'s last torpedoes, fired at the extreme range of thirteen thousand yards, could not be readily seen, and *Scharnhorst*'s
captain misjudged their run. He turned his ship to evade for three minutes and then—too soon—turned back on course. A torpedo struck
Scharnhorst near her after turret, and the explosion not only flooded two
of her engine rooms but put the turret out of action. With *Scharnhorst*'s
speed cut to twenty knots, Marschall abandoned further attempts to
attack the Allied convoys and set a course for Trondheim. Through her
dying gesture, *Acasta* had saved a troop convoy that was only a hundred
miles away and could hardly have escaped destruction. Upon the
scene of the battle itself, silence descended. Of the 1,561 men in *Glorious* and the two destroyers, only forty-six survived.*

After his arrival at Trondheim, Marschall was involved in a dispute
with the Naval Staff. Raeder was critical of his decision to abandon
the plan to bombard Harstad and blamed him for the crippling of
Scharnhorst. He was replaced by Admiral Lütjens, but Lütjens had
no better luck than Marschall. *Gneisenau* was severely damaged by
the British submarine *Clyde* on June 23, during a feint toward Iceland to distract enemy attention while *Scharnhorst* limped home.
Both battle cruisers were thus out of action for months to come.

For the Allies, the only bright aspect of the Norwegian campaign
was the bravery of those who did the fighting—and the dying. "The
unswerving constancy of purpose of the young men who bore the
brunt of the sea and air fighting during these unhappy weeks shines
in strong contrast to the indecision and mismanagement at home
which marred the whole campaign," observes Captain Roskill. For
the Germans, Norway was a resounding military success. Although
much of the Kriegsmarine had been either sunk or damaged, the

*The Germans believed the torpedo that struck *Scharnhorst* had been fired by a submarine that was still in the area, rather than *Acasta*, and steamed away without stopping
to pick up survivors. Hundreds of men survived the sinking of the ships, but most died in
the frigid Arctic waters before the remnants were found two days later. Although questions
were raised in Parliament as to why the Admiralty had allowed so valuable a ship to be at
sea with an escort of only two destroyers, the Admiralty hid its blunders behind the cloak
of national security, and no formal explanation was ever forthcoming.

losses were no more severe than Raeder had expected.* In exchange, they had succeeded in all their objectives. The Swedish ore supply was assured, and the short sea passages across the Baltic were under tight German control. Most important of all, they had won valuable bases and airfields on the Norwegian coast for a fresh onslaught by the U-boats, surface raiders, and Luftwaffe against Britain's maritime lifeline—bases which were soon to be augmented by even more advantageous sites on the coast of France.

---

*Only *Hipper*, the light cruisers *Emden, Köln, Leipzig*, and *Nürnberg*, and ten modern destroyers were ready for sea. Work was halted on the aircraft carrier *Graf Zeppelin*.

•

CHAPTER 3

"Sailing Against England"

The telephone at the prime minister's bedside rang at 0730 on May 15, 1940. Winston Churchill, who habitually worked into the early-morning hours, was a late sleeper, but he was awake in an instant. Paul Reynaud, the French premier, was on the line. "We have been defeated," Reynaud quickly declared in English. French counterattacks had failed to stem the German breakthrough in the Ardennes, and the Allies faced disaster. When the shocked Churchill did not immediately respond, he said again, "We are beaten; we have lost the battle."

Churchill tried to calm the distraught Frenchman by pointing out that in March 1918 the Germans had broken through the Allied lines but the onslaught was stemmed. He was, however, under no illusions about the gravity of the situation. In the five days he had held office, German armored columns had, in a whirlwind of fire and movement, swept across the Low Countries and northern France, and appeared unstoppable. Rotterdam had been bombed into ruins, and Antwerp had fallen. SS units were shooting prisoners. The Luftwaffe was dumping cargoes of death on ragged columns of troops and terrified, fleeing civilians. Holland was on the verge of surrender, and the Allies were falling back in Belgium. "The small countries are simply smashed up, one by one, like matchwood," Churchill told President Roosevelt, with whom he was conducting an almost daily correspondence. "We expect to be attacked here ourselves, both from the air and by parachute and airborne troops in the near future, and are getting ready for them."

The success of the German assault was as big a surprise to Hitler's generals as it was to the Allies. When the Führer unveiled the plan for Fall Gelb (Operation Yellow), the attack in the West, many of his senior commanders doubted whether they could repeat the triumph won in Poland. Only part of the explanation for the Allied catastrophe can be found on the field of battle, however. Equal weight must be given to events preceding the German offensive. Traumatized by the savage bloodletting of World War I, a declining birthrate, and a decade of political and social upheaval, the French had resolved to fight any new conflict with as little cost as possible. France put its faith in barbed wire and concrete—as exemplified by the Maginot Line—while the Germans dealt with these obstacles with imagination, firepower, and rapid movement.

Except for hit-and-run raids by fast motor-torpedo craft known as *Schnellboote*, or S-boats, and a few coastal submarines, the Kriegsmarine, tied down by the Norwegian operation and with its larger ships undergoing repairs, played no role in the dramatic German victories in the West. Had Hitler and his commanders had a better understanding of the sea, they could have used the available light naval forces to promptly seize harbors on the French and Belgian coasts, which would have prevented the Allies from later establishing a temporary haven at Dunkirk, and the British Expeditionary Force from slipping through their fingers.

For the Royal Navy, however, this was one of the most intensive periods of operations of the war. Holland's coastal waters were mined, and teams destroyed harbor facilities and brought out merchant vessels. Following the Dutch surrender on May 15, the royal family, the nation's bullion reserves, and the diamond stocks at Amsterdam, the world's diamond-cutting center, were brought to England.* Oil tanks, lock gates, and other vital installations were demolished. The French Navy blocked Antwerp and had responsibility for operations off the Belgian coast. With German bombers operating from their newly won bases, ships engaged in these tasks were under constant attack by the Luftwaffe.

---

*Most of the ships of the Royal Dutch Navy were in the East Indies, but the handful of destroyers and gunboats in home waters at the time of the invasion fought gallantly until put out of action. The survivors made their way to Britain to continue the struggle after Holland surrendered.

On May 21—after only eleven days of fighting—the German tanks that had outflanked the Maginot Line by breaking through the Ardennes reached the English Channel near Abbeville. Having cut off the British Expeditionary Force (BEF), they wheeled north to trap it in a shrinking perimeter between Boulogne and Ostend, where it huddled like some wounded animal with its back to the sea. In the face of this disaster, Churchill ordered the Admiralty to begin assembling small vessels "in readiness to proceed to ports and inlets on the French coast" for the evacuation of what was left of the army. The French were kept in the dark about the plan.

The task of organizing the evacuation was in the hands of Vice-Admiral Bertram H. Ramsay, flag officer, Dover. Although Ramsay had a distinguished record, he had retired four years before, after a disagreement with a superior, and had been recalled to duty only because of the outbreak of war. He made his headquarters deep within the fabled "white cliffs," in rooms and galleries that had been hollowed out of the chalk by prisoners during the Napoleonic Wars. From a windowed embrasure, he could see towering columns of black smoke rising only twenty-one miles away, across the Channel, and plainly hear the rumble of bombs and heavy guns. The operations center was in a large chamber which had housed an electric-power plant during World War I, known as the Dynamo Room. As a result, the task of rescuing the troops trapped on the French coast was dubbed Operation Dynamo.

Ramsay secured the Straits of Dover against submarines, S-boats, and enemy air attack while gathering whatever vessels were on hand—destroyers, gunboats, minesweepers, cross-Channel ferry-boats, coasters, and trawlers—for an improvised rescue service. One by one, the Channel ports fell, and some four hundred thousand battle-weary soldiers, British and French, fell back upon Dunkirk, the only usable harbor left, and about forty-five minutes from Dover by destroyer. They were short of food and supplies, and demoralized after a disastrous retreat. "The situation is really grave and I just fail to visualize where it will be in 4 or 5 days' time," Ramsay wrote his wife.

The pattern for Dunkirk was already being established at Boulogne and Calais, where British troops had landed on May 21 to bolster attempts by the French to delay the German drive toward Dunkirk. Working dangerously close inshore and under heavy air attack, British and French destroyers shelled motorized columns advancing along the coastal road. Street-by-street fighting raged in the outskirts of Boulogne while stragglers, who had broken into cafés and wineshops, reeled about drunkenly. Explosions rocked the town as demolition parties blew up bridges, cranes, and other facilities, and a thick pall of smoke covered everything. The situation quickly deteriorated and the troops retreated toward the port.

The evacuation of Boulogne began on May 23, when German tanks rumbled toward the main quay, where three destroyers were loading elements of the 20th Guards Brigade. As the enemy came in sight, the ships laid down an intense barrage that knocked out several tanks and machine-gun positions. Then they backed out stern-first, because there was no room to maneuver. Other destroyers came in, loaded under Stuka attack and severe shelling, and made their way back to sea through channels congested with wrecks and mines. The last fourteen hundred men were snatched from the jaws of the enemy by the destroyer *Vimiera*, which was so crowded there was only standing room on her narrow deck. By the evening of May 25, some forty-three hundred men had been taken off, but about three hundred were left behind.

At Calais, there was no evacuation. Bitter at the abandonment of Boulogne, the French protested that the BEF had done nothing except prepare for its own escape to England while the French army protected the evacuation. As a result, the three thousand British and eight hundred French troops in Calais were ordered to hold on at all costs. Ramsay dispatched several destroyers to assist the doomed garrison, which was commanded by Brigadier Claude Nicholson,* by shelling German movements on the coastal road. These ships, like the troops, were subjected to remorseless Stuka attacks; one was sunk and two were damaged. Calais was an inferno. Out of ammunition and water, the garrison was overrun on the night of May 25, but the survivors of a Royal Marine demolition party held out. They were

---

*When he was called upon by the Germans to surrender, Nicholson's reply was recorded by the admiring enemy: "The answer is no, as it is the British Army's duty to fight as well as it is the German's."

rescued the following day by motor-torpedo boats which braved the dive-bombers to go in after the trapped men.

The delaying actions at Boulogne and Calais provided time for the beaten British and what was left of the French northern army to fall back to a defense line based upon the network of canals crisscrossing the area about Dunkirk. Two German-army groups were closing in for the kill and were only ten miles southwest of Dunkirk when, on May 24, Hitler unexpectedly ordered his armored spearheads to halt for three days. It has been suggested that the Führer allowed the British to escape so they could honorably make peace once they realized the magnitude of their defeat; in reality his motives were less benevolent.

Hitler had his eye on Paris, not Flanders. With the bulk of the French army still undefeated, he wished to save his armor, which had already suffered considerable wear and tear, for the climactic drive on the French capital. Moreover, the Germans were unaware of the size of the force trapped inside the pocket; their estimates on May 23 were of only one hundred thousand men—less than a quarter of the actual total. Nor did they believe it possible that the British troops could be evacuated by sea before the tanks dealt with them. Hermann Göring assured Hitler that the Luftwaffe would prevent any escape. "Let's hope the Tommies are good swimmers," he declared.

Because of strict censorship, the full magnitude of the catastrophe unfolding across the Channel was unknown to the public, but the mood in Britain was grim. On May 26—a Sunday—there was a service of prayer and intercession in Westminster Abbey attended by King George VI and Prime Minister Churchill; throughout the country churchgoers gathered to pray for a miraculous deliverance. Fields in eastern England were ordered plowed up and obstacles strewn about to make parachute landings more difficult. Churchill warned the House of Commons that afternoon that it "should prepare itself for hard and heavy tidings." Shortly before 1900, the Admiralty signaled Admiral Ramsay at Dover: OPERATION DYNAMO IS TO COMMENCE.

Ramsay had already jumped the gun. Four hours before, he had dispatched the first flotilla of rescue vessels to Dunkirk. The most optimistic expectation was that perhaps forty-five thousand men might be plucked from Dunkirk over the next two days, which was regarded as the maximum window of opportunity before the perimeter was overrun by the Germans. Legend has it that a ragtag armada of yachts, motorboats, and skiffs manned by yachtsmen and weekend sailors spontaneously emerged from every harbor, estuary, and creek and crossed the Channel to bring the British army home to fight another day. In reality, the bulk of the BEF was evacuated by Royal Navy destroyers and a flotilla of cross-Channel steamers and Irish Sea packets.

The shortest route from Dover to Dunkirk was only thirty-nine miles long, but it brought the vessels close to the enemy-held coast east of Calais, where German long-range guns and bombers harassed them. "Immediately hell was let loose on our ship," reported Captain R. Duggan of the Isle of Man packet *Mona's Queen* during the first crossing. "We were shelled from the shore by single guns and by salvos from shore batteries. Shells were flying all round us and . . . the ship was riddled with shrapnel." Some turned back, but most steamed on. Dunkirk was ablaze, the quays were in ruins, and the harbor was strewn with wrecks. The ships tied up to piers only recently used by holiday trippers and embarked as many soldiers as they could carry. *Mona's Queen*, packed with 1,420 men, survived a strafing by German planes in which twenty-three soldiers and crewmen were killed. Early the next morning, the first batch of exhausted men disembarked at Dover. All their equipment except their rifles had been left behind.

Upon being informed that the British were trying to escape by sea, Hitler realized he had made a mistake in halting his armor and ordered the destruction of the Dunkirk pocket. German artillery and bombers pounded the town and any ship entering the port, making life a living hell for men who had already been under attack for weeks. Captain W. G. Tennant, dispatched by Ramsay with a small staff to take direct charge of the embarkation, toured the port on May 27 and found it a bedlam of exploding bombs and shells and falling masonry, and a graveyard of wrecked ships. Flames and a thick cloud of black smoke darkened the sky, and the stench of burning oil was everywhere. Tennant, convinced the harbor was untenable, ordered the troops out of the town to the open beaches of Malo, Bray, and La Panne, which stretched seven miles to the northeast of Dunkirk.

By afternoon, a vast multitude was sprawled across the dunes. To the men on the ships arriving to take them home, the beaches looked "like some mighty antheap upturned by a giant's foot . . . some standing in black clusters at the water's edge, waiting for the boats . . . while others, whose turn had not yet come, or were too tired to care whether it was their turn or not, lay huddled together in a disorderly and exhausted multitude."

Large steamers were unable to approach the shore because of sandbars and shallow water, so small boats—lifeboats, navy whaleboats, motor launches, and similar craft—were pressed into service. Boats were requisitioned from liners in London's docks, and the Royal National Life-Boat Institution volunteered its craft and men. Enduring strafing and bombing attacks, the boat crews snatched men off the beaches, ferried them out to the larger vessels, and then, with a courage that rapidly became routine, returned for another cargo. There was considerable disorder among the troops. Some units still maintained discipline, but most had been shattered on the retreat. As a boat came in, men rushed out and tried to clamber in, threatening to capsize it. In such cases, officers had to use their pistols to restore order. It was agonizingly slow work, and only about seventy-six hundred men were landed in England that day. If this remained the only means of rescue, a major part of the BEF would not escape.

The Allies were in desperate straits as the second day of Dynamo ended. Belgium's surrender that afternoon freed more German troops for attacks upon the ever-shrinking defense perimeter. The men on the beaches were suffering from shortages of food and water, as well as the cold and alternating terror and boredom. Rescue ships passing Calais came under increasingly heavy fire from the German batteries, and some turned back as heavy shells churned up the sea about them. Moreover, operations would have to be suspended if there was only the slightest surf, for it was impossible for a man in a wet uniform to climb into a small boat with a two-foot swell running.

Long columns of troops waiting to be evacuated snaked out across the beaches, scattering among the dunes when German aircraft swarmed over. They raged against the RAF for its seeming failure to drive off the Stukas and low-level bombers. Fighter Command did its best to provide air cover, but it had too few aircraft for the job, and its Spitfires and Hurricanes were able to remain over the area for only about twenty minutes because they were so far from their bases. And most of its battles took place above the clouds and out of sight. Even so, RAF claims of German aircraft shot down were wildly inaccurate. For example, on May 27 the RAF reported shooting down thirty-seven enemy planes against a loss of fourteen planes. Postwar examinations of the Luftwaffe's records reveal, however, that German losses over Dunkirk that day totaled ten aircraft.

In desperation, Captain Tennant took another look at the harbor and discovered that ships could be tied up to the East Mole, a breakwater that extended a mile out to sea from the beach at Malo. Maneuvering large vessels alongside the structure was a risky business because of the tidal race, but Tennant was convinced it was the only way that significant numbers of troops could be embarked.As dusk fell on May 27, the first ship edged up to the mole and tied up bow-first; under the direction of navy beachmasters, men were moved in more or less disciplined groups of fifty or so from the beach and along the mole to the ship. Others followed—and Operation Dynamo had reached its turning point.

Fortunately for the men on the beaches, rain and fog set in the following day and, along with the pall of smoke which hung over the town, forced the curtailment of German air operations for two days. Under cover of the smoke and lowering clouds, Tennant ordered every available destroyer to the East Mole. The decks of the vessels were well below the top of the mole, so ladders were erected to allow men to scramble down to the ships. Once loaded, a ship backed off, picked its way through the tortuous Channel to avoid the wrecks and mines, and then sped off to Dover, its decks crowded with soldiers. And then it set off for another excursion to hell. In all, 65,114 men were evacuated over the next two days.

In the small hours of May 29, the destroyer *Wakeful* was proceeding to Dover at twenty knots over a new but longer (eighty-seven miles) evacuation route designed to avoid the German batteries at Calais. She was carrying 640 exhausted soldiers, who had bedded down wherever they could find space. Suddenly, an officer on the bridge spotted the tracks of a pair of torpedoes—fired by a lurking German S-boat or submarine—and shouted an order for evasive action. *Wakeful* avoided one torpedo, but the other struck amidships. Broken in half, she sank almost immediately, and everyone on board was lost except those on deck at the time of the impact. The worst day of the evacuation had begun.

Several other vessels immediately came to the aid of the survivors, which made them easy targets. Two torpedoes struck the destroyer *Grafton*, with eight hundred evacuees on board.[*] The force of the blast knocked the nearby trawler *Comfort* almost on her beam's end, pitching some survivors of *Wakeful* back into the sea. After righting herself, the craft raced about in a circle to avoid further torpedoes. In the confusion, gunners on the sinking *Grafton* took *Comfort* for an S-boat and opened fire on her, and the minesweeper *Lydd* rammed her amidships. The sinking trawler's crew tried to climb on board *Lydd* but were mistaken for a German boarding party and shot down. In less than an hour, more than a thousand British sailors and soldiers were lost, and the operation threatened to dissolve into panic.

Traffic was shifted back to the old evacuation route, but the troop-laden destroyer *Montrose* had her bow blown off by the German shore batteries at Calais and had to be towed into Dover. A new route—this one fifty-five miles long—was cleared by minesweepers, and it carried the ships away from the guns and inshore from the S-boat hunting grounds. The ships had a brief respite, because the Germans did not immediately detect the change.

In the meantime, a brisk wind had blown up, dispersing the cloud cover over the Channel. German bombers pounded the ships moving in and out of Dunkirk. Plainly marked hospital ships were among those callously attacked.[†] The destroyer *Grenade* and five passenger ships—including *Mona's Queen*, the first vessel to run the gauntlet to Dunkirk—were sunk, and five other destroyers, a sloop, and several civilian vessels were damaged. While the offshore ships were being pounded, the East Mole was almost free of air attacks, and the evacuation continued. In spite of the unpropitious start of the day, a total of 47,310 men reached Britain on May 29.

Operation Dynamo hit full stride over the next three days. On May 30, the total number of men rescued was 53,823. The following day, a record 68,014 men were lifted off in operations that continued around the clock. And on June 1, another 64,429 were brought to

---

[*]German records show that *U-62* was in the area and may have sunk either *Wakeful* or *Grafton* (Roskill, *White Ensign*, p. 76).

[†]Most of the wounded were left behind in France because of the German failure to respect hospital ships.

England. These included the first French soldiers evacuated from Dunkirk. Men were packed on deck, between decks, into any cranny where they would fit. By midnight, only twenty thousand British and sixty thousand French troops were still waiting to be taken off.

That same day also saw the most intensive German air attacks of the campaign. The first RAF patrol arrived over Dunkirk at 0500 and was heavily engaged by enemy fighters. Another patrol, an hour later, also met strong opposition. No more British aircraft were due until 0900, and the Luftwaffe pounced during this interval. Peeling off at ten thousand feet, wave after wave of Stukas came down upon the ships with a terrifying snarl of engines. Under attack for days, and with no time to resupply, the destroyers were short of anti-aircraft shells; some had only thirty rounds on hand. Within little more than an hour, four destroyers, three British and one French, were sunk; four more were severely damaged, and one of the large passenger ships was also sent to the bottom. Other vessels were on fire or sinking. Had Reichsmarschall Göring launched such a savage attack earlier in the operation, it might have been decisive.

Remarkable rescues took place amid this havoc of bombs and exploding ships. The cross-Channel steamer *Prague*, coming away from Dunkirk with nearly three thousand French troops, was attacked by dive-bombers. Although she was not hit, her plates had been weakened by near misses, and, with water pouring in, she was in danger of foundering. As the *Prague* raced shoreward to beach herself, the destroyer *Shikari* came alongside, at considerable peril, and five hundred men were transferred to her as the two ships sped ahead. A minesweeper and then a corvette repeated this risky maneuver and took off most of the soldiers still on board. Relieved of her burden, the *Prague* made it safely to port. The Irish mail packet *Scotia*, with two thousand Frenchmen on board, sailed directly out of Dunkirk into an air attack. A bomb went down her after funnel, and she began to sink. The destroyer *Esk* found *Scotia* heeling over with her starboard boat deck already underwater. *Esk* nosed her bow against the stricken packet's side and held it there while keeping up a steady fire against the German bombers, until every surviving French soldier had scrambled on board.

The RAF claimed seventy-eight "kills" on June 1, but analysis reduced the tally to forty-three to cover duplications. Luftwaffe records placed actual German losses at ten fighters and nineteen bombers, some of which were accounted for by anti-aircraft fire from the ships. On the other hand, thirty-one British fighters were lost. Later, the RAF claimed to have won "qualitative superiority" over Dunkirk, but the unadorned fact was that it never dominated the Luftwaffe.* Nevertheless, the jolting baptism of fire at Dunkirk gave the British pilots the experience to permit them to face the Germans on roughly equal terms during the Battle of Britain.

Thirty-one vessels of various types were lost on June 1, and another eleven were seriously damaged. As a result, Admiral Ramsay ordered an end to daylight operations. He believed the perimeter could not be held much longer—German units were pressing near enough to bombard the beaches with their artillery—and called for the small boats to be placed on alert back on May 21, to join in a final attempt to lift as many men as possible before Dunkirk fell. Yachts, motor launches, and other small craft crept out of Ramsgate, Folkestone, Dover, Deal, Margate, and Sheerness—all the ports of southeastern England—and proceeded, sometimes in convoy, sometimes alone, to Dunkirk.

Among these ill-assorted craft was the sixty-ton yacht *Sundowner*, belonging to Charles H. Lightoller, a retired Naval Reserve commander and senior surviving officer of the *Titanic*. He took her across the Channel with a crew consisting of a youthful Sea Scout and his son, who was detailed to pack in the men below as tight as possible. Lightoller later provided this account:

> At fifty I called below. 'How are you getting on?' getting the cheerful reply, 'Oh plenty of room yet.' At seventy-five my son admitted they were getting pretty tight. . . . I now started to pack them on deck, having passed word below for every man to lie down and keep down; the same applied on deck. By the time we had fifty on deck, I could feel her getting distinctly tender, so took no more. Actually, we had 130 on board. . . . Whilst entering [harbor at Ramsgate] the impression ashore was that the fifty-odd lying on my deck . . . was the full load. After I got rid of those on deck I gave the order 'Come up from below,' and the look on the official's face was amusing to behold as troops vomited

*In the period from May 26 to June 3, the Luftwaffe lost 240 aircraft to the RAF's 177.

up from the forward companionway, the after companionway, and the doors either side of the wheelhouse. As a stoker Petty Officer, helping them over the bulwarks, said, 'God's truth, mate! Where did you put them?' He might well ask. . . .

The massive aerial assault of June 1 was Hitler's final attempt to block the evacuation. Once the last of the BEF had gotten clear, he lost interest in Dunkirk and withdrew his troops for the major assault on France, although harassing attacks on the beachhead continued. Some Scottish troops left amid the swirling of a bagpipe, but Frenchmen made up the bulk of the approximately fifty thousand soldiers taken off on the nights of June 2 and 3.* With his crews at the limit of human endurance and his ships battered, Ramsay was now anxious to close down Dynamo. But Churchill, to maintain a semblance of harmony among the Allies, insisted that a last attempt be made to bring out the remaining thirty thousand Frenchmen of the rearguard, whose stout defense of the perimeter had permitted the British to escape.

At about 2015 on June 3, nine destroyers as well as a host of other vessels, including sixty-three French-manned craft, crossed the English Channel on their final mission. A strong easterly wind and fast-running tide made attempts to come alongside the East Mole hazardous, and German machine guns could be heard rattling close at hand. Rather than the expected thirty thousand troops, an equal number of stragglers who had been hiding out in the ruins of Dunkirk during the fighting suddenly appeared, jamming the approaches to the mole and blocking the rearguard from embarkation. Amid considerable disorder, 26,175 men were evacuated during the night, but the rest had to be left behind, much to the anger of the French. In the dawn's early light of June 4, *Shikari* cast off with six hundred soldiers—the last British warship to leave Dunkirk. Not long afterward, the victorious Germans entered the shattered town.†

---

*The French were reluctant to entrust themselves to the small boats, and one yachtsman reported receiving a note from a French officer that he had just eaten and could not venture into the water (Divine, *The Nine Days of Dunkirk*, p. 211).

†Between the end of Dynamo (on June 4) and June 25, the Royal Navy carried out a whole series of evacuations, known collectively as Operations Aerial and Cycle. They started at Le Havre, included the Channel Islands, then worked their way around the Bay of Biscay to St.-Nazaire and down to the Bayonne and St.-Jean-de-Luz, short of the

The final tally showed that 338,226 Allied soldiers had been lifted from the mole and the beaches—about 220,000 British and the remainder French and a few Belgians. Had these troops been captured, Britain would have been unable to create a new army, and the course of the war would have been altered. As it was, the BEF lost some 68,000 men killed, wounded, captured, and missing during the campaign in France. In all, 222 naval vessels and 665 civilian craft took part in Dynamo, of which no fewer than 226 were lost. Nine of 41 destroyers assigned to the operation—6 British and 3 French— were sunk, and 19 others were put out of action, losses which were to be felt during the struggle to keep ocean communications open. Eight Channel packets were also sunk, and 9 so badly damaged they had to be written off.

Much has been written of the "miracle" of Dunkirk. Hitler's decision to halt his troops outside Dunkirk, the calm seas and foggy weather over the Channel coast, and the RAF's efforts to contest the air over the beaches were all significant factors in the evacuation. But in the final analysis, the success of this mass rescue was largely due to the efforts of the Royal Navy. The navy carried the vast majority of those who were taken off, provided protection against German bombers and fighters, and suffered the greatest losses. Once again, sea power had performed one of its classic roles: saving a defeated army so it could fight another day. But in a speech before the House of Commons on June 4, in which he announced the return of the BEF from France, Churchill cautioned, "Wars are not won by evacuations."

Britain was in dire straits. European ports from North Cape to the Pyrenees were now open to the U-boats and surface raiders. For the first times since Napoleon the nation faced the threat of invasion. There was no reserve to replace the weapons left behind across the

Spanish frontier, and on to the French Mediterranean coast. Nearly two hundred thousand fighting men and as many as forty thousand civilians reached the safety of Britain.

Most of the these evacuations were carried out without significant loss, although six thousand men of the 51st (Highland) Division were trapped at St.-Valéry, between Dieppe and Le Havre, by dense fog and the premature surrender of the French commander. It was the only incident in which troops made it to the seacoast but were not taken off. At St.-Nazaire, the troopship *Lancastria* was sunk by German bombers, with the loss of about half the fifty-eight hundred men on board. Churchill ordered the report suppressed, saying, "The newspapers have got quite enough disaster for today at least" (Churchill, *The Second World War*, vol. II, p. 194).

Channel; only five hundred heavy guns were left on British soil, some of them museum pieces. Only thirty-nine Spitfires were produced during the last twelve days of May, while seventy-five were lost. If the Germans mounted an immediate air attack, Air Chief Marshal Sir Hugh Dowding, head of Fighter Command, declared that he "could not guarantee air superiority for more than forty-eight hours."

To add to the anxiety of the British, they were unable to persuade the most powerful units of the French navy to sail to Britain to continue the war, and feared the French navy would fall into German hands.* Only two old battleships, four destroyers, seven submarines, and some minesweepers had joined the British. The nearly completed *Richelieu*, one of the world's most powerful battleships, and the uncompleted *Jean Bart* sailed for French bases in Africa, the former to Dakar and the latter to Casablanca.

Some high officials, particularly Lord Halifax, the foreign secretary, urged that efforts be made to secure "honorable" peace terms from Hitler. In this hour of doubt and anxiety, Churchill rejected defeatism and exhibited a bulldog tenacity that inspired the British people. "We shall defend our island, whatever the cost may be," he told the Commons. "We shall fight on the beaches, we shall fight on the landing grounds, we shall fight in the fields and in the streets, we shall fight in the hills; we shall never surrender." Even if Britain was finally subjugated, "our Empire beyond the seas, armed and guarded by the British Fleet, would carry on the struggle, until in God's good time, the New World, with all its power and might, steps forth to the rescue and liberation of the Old."

Would the United States respond?

"All bad, all bad," muttered President Roosevelt as he looked over the latest dispatches from Europe. The fury and rapidity of the German victory stunned the American people, shattering the comfortable sense of distance from Europe's dangers they had enjoyed. Sooner than many Americans, Roosevelt understood the danger the

---

*The French navy had a long history of antipathy to the British. During a visit to England in 1939, Admiral Jean Darlan, the French naval chief, pointedly reminded his hosts that his great-grandfather had been killed at Trafalgar. (See Churchill, *The Second World War*, vol. II, p. 229.) These sentiments were aggravated by what the French regarded as the British betrayal at Dunkirk.

United States would face should Britain fall. With the Royal Navy in control of the Atlantic, the U.S. Navy was free to deploy its strongest units to the Pacific in readiness to deal with any threat from the Japanese. If Britain went under, the United States would be forced either to fight a two-ocean war without allies or to kowtow to the Nazis and the Japanese.

Though Roosevelt wished to support the beleaguered Allies with all aid short of war, isolationist sentiment was strong, and his election to an unprecedented third term not at all certain. Moving cautiously, he coupled support for the Allies with a massive buildup of American military and naval forces, while assuring the isolationists that "we will not send our men to take part in European wars." The "ready" military force of the United States consisted at that time of an army of three hundred thousand men, a navy overly burdened with obsolescent ships, and an air service with only a handful of modern aircraft. General George C. Marshall, the army's chief of staff, frankly described the United States as "a third rate power."

France, already reeling from the German attack, was dealt another crippling blow on June 10, when Mussolini took Italy into the war on Hitler's side. With cold contempt, Roosevelt bitingly observed that "the hand that held the dagger has struck it into the back of its neighbor." He also made the pledge to the Allies that "we will extend to the opponents of force, the material resources of this country. We will not slow down or detour. Signs and signals call for speed—full speed ahead."

Frantic appeals for "clouds of warplanes" and then for American troops poured in upon Roosevelt from the desperate French, but the United States did not have the aircraft, nor did the American people want any part of the war. With northern France and Paris overrun, the French surrendered on June 22. Hitler had accomplished in six weeks what the Kaiser had been unable to do in four years. France was carved up between the Germans and a collaborationist government located at Vichy headed by the doddering Marshal Henri Pétain, a hero of World War I.

Pessimists, including Joseph P. Kennedy, the U.S. envoy to London, doubted Britain's ability to survive and were convinced that any assistance to the British would be wasted. Roosevelt himself privately thought the chances of an eventual British victory only one in three. Nevertheless, when asked by Henry Morgenthau, the secretary of the Treasury, if he would continue to help the British, the president promptly replied: "Absolutely."

To meet the urgent requests for arms to bolster Britain's home defenses against invasion, the Neutrality Act was stretched to enable rifles, artillery, and ammunition in the U.S. Army's reserve stocks to be declared "surplus" and made available to the British. Within a week, a cargo ship carrying the first installment of American aid— forty-eight field guns, twelve thousand rifles, 15,270 machine guns, and thirty-seven million rounds of ammunition, most of it left over from World War I—had cleared for England.

And three days after the Germans entered Paris, Admiral Harold R. Stark, the chief of naval operations, went up to Capitol Hill to seek $4 billion for a "two-ocean" navy. These funds were to provide for a 70-percent increase in the size of the fleet, or 257 ships, including several large, fast battleships and twenty-seven *Essex*-class carriers. But it would take time to build them—"[D]ollars cannot buy yesterday," as Admiral Stark put it. In the meantime, Britain teetered on the brink of disaster.

Throughout the summer of 1940, while the British peered anxiously across the Channel for signs of an expected invasion, fortune had provided them with a unique insight into German planning and intentions. Since late May, the code breakers at the Government Code and Cypher School (the name was a disguise) at Bletchley Park, near Oxford, had been reading the Luftwaffe version of the Enigma machine, used by the Germans to encipher their most secret messages.* This provided the British with information not only on air operations but also on preparations for an invasion of Britain. Much

---

*The Enigma machine was originally a commercial enciphering device, first put on the market in 1923. Its name was derived from Sir Edward Elgar's *Enigma Variations*. Messages were typed in plaintext into a battery-powered device which resembled a portable typewriter, and automatically enciphered by setting the rotors of the machine. The message could only be unscrambled if the recipient had set the rotors of his machine to the same key or setting as the sender. Enigma was adopted by the German armed forces, which modified and improved the machine by adding plugs to vary the circuits. The operators changed the circuits and rotor settings every twenty-four hours according to a dated instruction book of keys. This gave an astronomical number of alternatives for each letter. The Poles made the first breakthrough by constructing a reproduction of the German version. Over the years, the Germans made the Enigma machine more complex, and the Poles, lacking the resources to continue, turned their discoveries over to their allies, the French and the British.

to their relief, they learned that the Germans had no plans to attempt a Channel crossing immediately. As Count Ciano, Mussolini's son-in-law, remarked, "Hitler is now the gambler who has made a big scoop and would like to get up from the table risking nothing more."

In fact, Hitler was ambivalent about an invasion. He believed that the British would soon see the futility of continuing the struggle alone. Indeed, he hoped to make Britain an ally as he turned eastward to settle scores with Stalin and Bolshevism. The original operational plan for the attack on France had not even mentioned the possibility of an invasion of Britain. Admiral Raeder had, however, in November 1939 ordered his staff to prepare a feasibility study of a landing, primarily to have it in hand should the Führer ask for it. Raeder mentioned this study in a meeting with Hitler on May 21, 1940, but the Führer, jubilant over the defeat of the French, spoke instead of a plan to settle European Jews in Madagascar. The admiral did not pursue the matter. Some analysts contend that if an immediate invasion had been launched while Britain was nearly prostrate it could have succeeded. In reality, however, such an operation was impossible, because no landing craft were available.

Hitler briefly discussed the possibility of a landing in Britain with his top commanders for the first time a month later. Raeder emphasized the difficulties of the operation in view of the crippled state of the Kriegsmarine and the Royal Navy's command of the Channel. Instead he argued that Germany should rely upon stepped-up submarine and air attacks to defeat Britain. Hitler was inclined to accept these arguments. Regarding the war as all but over, he toured the old Western Front with some World War I comrades and visited Paris. Except for a triumphal return to Berlin, he spent the early part of July in seclusion in the Black Forest, allowing a political and military vacuum to develop. This providential lull provided the British with time to prepare for the inevitable onslaught.

With a resolve born of desperation, the British underscored their determination to continue the fight by moving to prevent the French fleet from falling into German hands. Admiral Darlan, now navy minister in the Vichy government, pledged that under no circumstances would the ships be turned over to the Germans, but the British were unconvinced. The largest single concentration of French warships— the modern battle cruisers *Strasbourg* and *Dunkerque* and old battleships *Bretagne* and *Provence*—was at Mers el-Kébir, near Oran in

North Africa. Force H, consisting of the battle cruiser *Hood*, the battleships *Resolution* and *Valiant*, and the carrier *Ark Royal*, under the command of Vice-Admiral Sir James Somerville, was assigned to deal with them. Somerville had, in Churchill's words, "one of the most disagreeable and difficult tasks that a British admiral has ever been faced with. . . ."

On July 3, under direct orders from the prime minister, Somerville trained his guns on the French ships and offered Admiral Marcel Gensoul a choice of options: to sail his ships to British ports and "fight with us"; to hand the ships over to the Royal Navy; or to disarm or scuttle them within six hours. Tension in both fleets was high as the French considered the ultimatum. For some unexplained reason, Gensoul informed his superiors that the only option he had been offered was to scuttle his ships within six hours or be sunk. Under these circumstances, Darlan confirmed the admiral's intention to resist.

When Gensoul rejected his demands, Somerville, reluctant to open fire on the French, offered him another choice—to take his ships to the French West Indies with reduced crews and remain there until the end of the war. Again Gensoul refused. Somerville wished to continue the negotiations, which he thought might prove successful given additional time, but the day was wearing on, and Churchill was pressing him to conclude the affair by nightfall. With the French ships getting up steam and their crews at action stations, time was running out.

At 1754, Somerville ordered his ships to open fire. The French vessels tried to clear the harbor but were sitting ducks. Fifteen-inch shells ripped into *Bretagne*, and, aflame from stem to stern, she heeled over and sank with a roar and a hissing of steam. *Dunkerque* and *Provence* were also crippled. The French used various-colored dyes in their shells to make it easier to spot their fall, and the sea about the British ships was churned up by brightly colored blue, red, and yellow splashes, but they sustained no serious hits. It was all over in ten minutes. Casualties were heavy; 1,297 French sailors were killed. *Strasbourg* and five destroyers escaped the holocaust, and made their way across the Mediterranean to Toulon despite an attack by *Ark Royal*'s torpedo planes.

That same day, the French squadron at Alexandria—a battleship, four cruisers, and three destroyers—disarmed itself following negotiations with Admiral Sir Andrew B. Cunningham, commander of the Mediterranean Fleet. Cunningham ignored several deadlines set by Churchill. The British also partially immobilized the battleship *Richelieu* at Dakar.* Catapult, as the Oran operation was called, had gained most of its objectives, but it also stirred animosities between the former allies unhealed a half-century later. On the other hand, Harry Hopkins, President Roosevelt's personal emissary, later informed Churchill that the ruthless attack on the French had convinced Roosevelt that Britain meant to go on fighting, no matter what.

What Churchill called the "deadly stroke" against the French also turned Hitler's thoughts toward an invasion of Britain. On July 16, he signed Directive No. 16: "Since England, in spite of her hopeless military situation, shows no signs of being ready to come to a compromise, I have decided to prepare a landing operation against England, and, if necessary to carry it out." Did Hitler actually intend to carry out Sea Lion, as the operation was called? Or was it a bluff designed to keep the British off balance? Strategists still debate these questions, but the evidence indicates the Führer was skeptical from the start about the feasibility—or necessity—of an invasion. Russia was his main enemy and he harbored no fear that Britain, even though unconquered, was able to do him any real harm.

Admiral Raeder attempted to interest Hitler in another approach to ending the war. Upon several occasions he suggested a Mediterranean alternative to both Sea Lion and the invasion of Russia. German, Italian, Spanish, and possibly Vichy French forces should seize Gibraltar and Suez and drive the British from the area. The Canary Islands, the Azores, and the Cape Verde Islands should be seized and used as bases for a final campaign against British shipping—and against the United States, if the Americans intervened. Hitler was impressed and for a time toyed with this *Mittelmeer* or "Middle Sea" strategy, but eventually ruled it out, and continued planning for the invasion of Russia and Sea Lion.

---

*Under cover of darkness, Lieutenant Commander Richard H. Bristowe and a team of six volunteers ran a motor launch up beside the battleship and set off four depth charges under her stern, which damaged her rudder and propellers. Her guns were unaffected, however.

The Luftwaffe was to knock out the RAF, the army was to provide the troops, and the navy was to wall off the English Channel with mines and transport the soldiers safely to the beaches of southern England. Bombers and U-boats were to assail the Home Fleet to keep it from blocking the operation, while the Italians were to tie down the British fleet in the Mediterranean. With the optimism of ignorance, Hitler decreed that all was to be ready to proceed by mid-August. Viewing the Channel merely as a river too wide for a pontoon bridge, the army produced a plan calling for an initial landing by 260,000 men and thirty thousand vehicles on a broad front extending two hundred miles, from Ramsgate to the Lyme Bay.* Getting them there was the navy's problem.

Raeder was appalled by this unrealistic proposal. He hastened to Hitler's mountain retreat and emphasized the risks involved in ferrying such a huge force across stormy, tide-swept waters savagely contested by the British. Patiently, he explained that a simultaneous landing could not be made on such a wide front because of the differences in the tides at the ends of the bridgehead, and the large amount of shipping required could not be assembled in time to meet the deadline. Sea Lion should be delayed until at least mid-September. Better yet, Raeder argued, it should be shelved until May 1941. Hitler postponed the landing until September 15, reduced the initial invasion force to ten divisions, and concentrated the landings at four points between Dover and Beachy Head. Air operations against Britain would begin on August 5—Adlertag, or Eagle Day.

Amphibious operations are among the most complex in war, and the Germans never overcame the daunting problem of transporting large numbers of troops and equipment across the deceptively narrow Channel. No specialized landing craft were available, so Rhine River barges—1,722 of them—were rounded up along with 1,161 motorboats and 155 small transports. The barges were to be towed by 471 tugboats at a speed of only three knots.† Soon, ports from Delfz-

---

*In contrast, when the Allies landed in Normandy in June 1944, they established only a fifty-mile front.

†The historically minded noted that this was slower than Julius Caesar's legions had sailed across the English Channel to invade Britain in 55 B.C. These units were sardonically labeled the *Himmelfahrtskommando* (the heaven-bound command).

ijl in Holland to Le Havre were crowded with improvised landing craft while troops were moving into the staging areas. The song "Wir fahren gegen Engelland" ("We're Sailing Against England") boomed from loudspeakers and radios all over Germany.* Not everyone was confident of success, however.

"Tell me your opinion," Admiral Raeder asked Korvettenkapitän Heinrich Bartels, who was in charge of the preparations at Dunkirk. "Do you think we shall make it across to England? Are you optimistic about it?"

"Without optimism," Bartels unhesitatingly replied. "The thing will be a flop from the start."

Nevertheless, the British braced for the worst. Plans were laid to set the Channel ablaze with burning oil, and Bomber Command was secretly training its crews in the use of poison gas. Concrete pill-boxes and fortifications were hastily thrown up along such natural defenses as hills, rivers, and canals. Tank traps, minefields, and barbed wire were strewn about the beaches. The army, reinforced by troops pouring in from the Empire, was concentrated in southeastern England. War veterans were organized into a ragged Home Guard armed with shotguns and hunting rifles. Fighter Command moved all available Spit-fires and Hurricanes into position. The Home Fleet was transferred to Rosyth to be in a position to speed south if required. Destroyers and other escort vessels were stripped from the Atlantic convoys and held in readiness at the Channel ports to deal with the invasion peril.

Göring was supremely confident that his bombers and fighters could accomplish the twin tasks of driving the RAF from the sky and preventing the Royal Navy from interfering with the landings. Like all air-power enthusiasts, he was convinced that the bombers would always get through. Both the army and navy chiefs were happy to shift the burden of responsibility to the Luftwaffe. The massive aer-ial attack was pushed back for eight days to allow additional time for preparation; meantime, the Stukas attacked coastal shipping in the Channel in an effort to draw the RAF's fighters into a premature struggle. But Fighter Command, taking the position that its job was

---

*With typical German thoroughness, a mansion on the brow of Richmond Hill with a fine view of the Thames Valley was hand-picked for the Führer's personal use once the invasion had succeeded.

to defend Britain not to protect shipping, refused to rise to the bait.

Nine destroyers were savaged in Channel operations, and one merchantman in three venturing passage through those waters was sunk or badly damaged. Bombing raids, shelling by long-range guns mounted by the Germans at Cape Gris-Nez, and hit-and-run attacks by S-boats closed the Straits of Dover to all but the smallest coasters and forced the British into a highly disruptive reorganization of shipping and convoys. The destroyer flotillas based at Dover were compelled to abandon the immediate area of the planned German landings. Wave after wave of bombers and fighters crossed the Channel on the morning of August 13, the new Eagle Day, to begin the massive attack on Britain with raids on the airfields, command centers, and radar stations in southeastern England.

While the eye of the British people was fixed on the duel between the Luftwaffe and the RAF, the Battle of the Atlantic entered an even more dangerous stage. Admiral Dönitz seized the opportunity presented by the shortage of escorts to wreak havoc on British shipping. Only two days after the end of the fighting in France, he transferred the U-Boat Command from Wilhelmshaven to Lorient, on the Bay of Biscay, where he made his headquarters in a handsome château. The first boat to put in was Fritz Lemp's *U-30*, which had sunk the *Athenia* on the opening day of the war.

The new base brought the U-boats some 450 miles closer, in sailing terms, to the enemy's vital sea lanes, almost doubling their effectiveness by extending their range of operations and time on patrol. Lorient was soon followed by Brest, Bordeaux, La Pallice, and St.-Nazaire as operating bases. On August 17, recognizing an existing fact, Hitler proclaimed a total blockade of Britain.[*]

---

[*]By late summer, all ships bound to British ports from across the Atlantic whose speeds were less than fifteen knots were making the trip in convoys, both fast and slow. The fast convoys, consisting of vessels with a maximum speed of nine to 14.9 knots, assembled at Halifax, Nova Scotia. The slow convoys, in which the lowest speed was 7.5 knots, began their voyage from Sydney, Cape Breton. The former were designated HX, the latter SC. Outward-bound convoys were designated by the port of origin. OA convoys were gathered from ships sailing from the east coast of Britain; OB convoys comprised ships from Liverpool, the Clyde, South Wales, and Belfast. WS convoys were military transports from the United Kingdom to the Middle East.

U-boat skippers called this period the "Happy Time." With the convoys all but denuded of escorts and the torpedo crisis resolved by a switch from the erratic magnetic pistols to contact detonators, morale among the submarine crews soared in proportion to the tonnage they were sending to the bottom. Over the three-month period from July to September, 153 ships were sunk, for a monthly average of 252,926 tons, while only five submarines were lost. In October, 352,407 tons, or sixty-three ships, were sunk, including the forty-two-thousand-ton *Empress of Canada*, the only one of Britain's great liners sunk by a U-boat during the war. With sinkings by the Luftwaffe, mines, surface raiders, and S-boats added, the toll exceeded Britain's capacity to replace the lost vessels.

Dönitz was still plagued, however, by the perennial shortage of boats, of which there were never more than fifteen at sea at a given time. As Jürgen Rohwer, a leading German historian of the Battle of the Atlantic, has written, "[T]he high tonnage losses sustained by the British . . . are quite sufficient to give some idea of what could have been done . . . with effective long-range reconnaissance and more U-boats."

The second half of 1940 was the heyday of the individual U-boat "aces"—the "gray wolves," as they were dubbed by Dr. Goebbels's propaganda machine, which treated them like movie stars. Bands played, champagne flowed, and wild parties were held when they returned in triumph to the French bases. For their crews, there was plenty of wine, available women, and raucous song as they spent their accumulated pay. "Living like a god in France" became the byword in the U-boat service.

Günther Prien, the "Bull of Scapa Flow," was among the first to earn the designation of ace, won for sinking fifty thousand tons of merchant shipping. He sank eight ships during a two-week period late in June, bringing his total bag of merchant shipping to 66,600 tons, including the liner *Arandora Star*, which was carrying 1,250 German and Italian aliens from Britain to internment in Canada. Nearly half those on board were lost. Prien was awarded the Knight's Cross with Oak Leaves.

Otto Kretschmer of *U-99* was the most successful of Dönitz's aces. On July 24, his boat put to sea with a golden horseshoe riveted to her conning tower, and over a two-week period Kretschmer set a record for a single patrol by accounting for seven ships totaling 65,137 tons. "We all felt like schoolchildren at Christmas time," Kretschmer declared. Admiral Raeder came to Lorient to offer his personal congratulations, and was startled to find the crew of *U-99* braced to attention in British-army battle dress. Their uniforms had worn out while they were at sea and had been replaced from captured stocks. Kapitänleutnant Joachim Schepke of *U-100* was equally aggressive and ranked behind only Kretschmer and Prien in tonnage sunk.

The "gray wolves" took their toll not only from stragglers and vessels sailing independently, but from the poorly defended convoys as well. They were assisted by the ability of B-Dienst to read the British naval codes, which it had been doing since the crisis over the Italian invasion of Ethiopia. In fact, German intelligence was reading upward of 50 percent of the Royal Navy's signal traffic, which contained information about routings and timings of convoys and independent sailings. In a battlefield as large as the North Atlantic, any information about the location of enemy merchant shipping was of inestimable value. The Germans eavesdropped on this traffic until July 1943, when the British finally realized what was happening.[*]

Taking advantage of their low profiles and the speed of their boats, U-boat captains got in among the convoys at night with their decks awash—where Asdic could not pick them up—and their targets so close their torpedoes could not miss. If sighted, they dived and hoped to get clear, knowing that the escorts could not afford to indulge in a long hunt while the convoy steamed away. Once the escort had broken off the search, they resumed stalking the convoy and awaited another opportunity to strike. Some boats attacked the same convoy again and again, like a shark taking repeated thrusts at its prey.

Dönitz, who had commanded U-boats during World War I, had observed that the introduction of convoys in 1917 had saved Britain from almost certain defeat. In the years between the wars, he had experimented with tactics designed to overcome convoys and had devised a system of pack attacks by several submarines—or *Rudeltaktik*—aimed at swamping the escort and then annihilating

---

[*]Lord Louis Mountbatten, then a lieutenant commander, drew the Admiralty's attention to the weakness of the Royal Navy's codes and ciphers before the war, only to be told to mind his own business.

the convoy. Rather than searching the sea for targets of opportunity, the U-boats homed in on convoys. The first boat to make a contact did not attack immediately, but trailed the convoy on the surface, staying well to the rear, while reporting its position, speed, and composition by radio to Dönitz's headquarters, which ordered other boats to join the one shadowing the convoy.

Originally, the senior commander on the scene assumed tactical control, but he sometimes had to submerge and so lost contact with the other boats. As a result, Dönitz decided that control should be exercised by U-boat headquarters—which required constant radio communication, all enciphered by the Enigma machine—which eventually became the system's Achilles' heel. "Hitler may make me an Admiral," observed Dönitz, "but communications can put me in command."

In his operational orders to his commanders, Dönitz established his rules for success:

1. Obtain a sighting.
2. Report your sighting.
3. Keep in touch until other U-boats arrive.
4. Attack together.

The first effective "wolf-pack" attack, which began on September 6, contained all the elements that were soon to become lethally familiar. B-Dienst picked up a British signal reporting that Convoy SC 2, composed of fifty-three ships inbound to Britain from Nova Scotia, was to meet its escort off Rockall Bank, near Ireland. Dönitz detailed four submarines to the attack, and over the next four days they sank five ships—Prien accounting for four—despite a heavy gale.

On September 21, Prien sighted HX 72, a convoy of forty-one ships, in mid-Atlantic. He signaled its position and course to Dönitz, who dispatched six additional U-boats. "As darkness came it was attack after attack," reported A. M. Kellar, a gunner on one of the ships in the convoy. "The sea was lit up with giant fires dotted over the ocean. The escorts seemed to be racing about in panic trying to protect the tankers which were the number one target of the U-boats." Eleven merchantmen were sunk within seven hours as the U-boats engaged in a feeding frenzy. Only one depth-charge attack was made during the entire battle. As they approached port, the remnants of the hapless convoy were bombed by four-engine, long-range Focke-Wulf 2000 Condor bombers based in France and Norway.*

Convoy SC 7 fared even worse. Its thirty-four ships were repeatedly attacked by no fewer than seven U-boats, including those of Kretschmer and Schepke, on the nights of October 17 and 18. Fifteen ships were sunk from the convoy, and five stragglers were picked off in what the Germans called "The Night of the Long Knives." The escorts were completely ineffective, breaking station to rescue survivors and thus making it easier for the Germans to sink even more ships. In his log, Kretschmer presented a vivid picture of events:

> I make off at full speed to the south-west and again make contact with the convoy. Torpedoes from other boats are constantly heard exploding. The destroyers do not know how to help and occupy themselves by constantly firing star shells, which are of little effect in the bright moonlight. I now start to attack the convoy from astern. . . .

The Admiralty was completely taken by surprise by the intensity of the U-boat offensive. Shipping losses were running at two or three times the replacement building rate, and rationing grew more severe. Despite new construction, the number of destroyers available to the Royal Navy had dropped from 184 in 1939 to 171. Escorts were in such short supply that convoys from the United States and Canada were unprotected until they were nearly in the Western Approaches. Even then, the handful of ships available, supported by a few Sunderland flying boats operated by Coastal Command, were hard pressed to protect flocks of forty or fifty ships scattered over a large patch of sea.

To make up for the shortage of escorts, the Admiralty had belatedly in 1938, placed orders for a patrol vessel that became known as the *Flower*-class corvette. Based on a whale-catcher design, these 950-ton craft were sturdy and simple to build—"cheap and nasties," Churchill called them—and were intended for coastal work. The first

---

*The Condor was originally designed as a transport plane; in August 1938, one had flown nonstop from Berlin to New York. With its long range, it could venture hundreds of miles out to sea to sight and shadow convoys and report their positions and course to Dönitz's headquarters. A convoy tracked by a Condor could count on an eventual U-boat attack as well as a bombing by the aircraft itself. In two months, Condors accounted for thirty merchantmen, totaling 110,000 tons.

trickle of corvettes, appearing in the summer of 1940, bore such names as *Crocus, Pansy, Tulip*, and *Periwinkle.** They were armed with a single 4.1-inch gun and depth charges. Although extremely handy—corvettes were said to be able to "turn on a dime"—they had a maximum speed of only sixteen knots, less than that of a surfaced submarine. And they "rolled on wet grass," which made them a purgatory when pressed into service as ocean escorts, a task for which they were not designed.†

Churchill also appealed to President Roosevelt for the loan of forty or fifty of the World War I–vintage destroyers being refurbished by the U.S. Navy for the Neutrality Patrol. He also wished to establish a precedent for transferring American weapons to Britain without cost. Roosevelt was reluctant to provide fresh ammunition to the isolationists, who were accusing him of trying to drag the United States into the war, and was certain Congress would not approve such an unneutral act. Churchill was insistent. At the end of July, he told Roosevelt that Britain's survival might turn on the loan of the old destroyers. "Mr. President, with great respect," he declared, "I must tell you . . . this is a thing to do."

One of the points in dispute was the future of the British fleet if Britain were successfully invaded. Roosevelt demanded a pledge that the ships would cross the Atlantic to continue the fight. Churchill would not agree to any public disclosure of such an agreement, because it would be seen as defeatist. Finally, a successful formula was worked out, and, to sweeten the deal for the American public, the fifty ships were exchanged for ninety-nine-year leases on a chain of eight sea and air bases ranging from Canada to the Caribbean.

---

*Upon joining her first convoy at Plymouth, *Periwinkle* had the following exchange with a destroyer:

"What are you?"
"*Periwinkle*."
"Can I stick a pin in you?"
"No. I am a pale blue flower—not a shellfish."
"Then I will come over and fertilize you."

Later, *Periwinkle* had the satisfaction of sinking a U-boat.

†In all, 288 corvettes were built in Britain and Canada—they formed the bulk of the Royal Canadian Navy—and accounted for some fifty U-boats, despite their limitations. Later in the war, they were joined by improved "supercorvettes," or frigates.

Unable to round up congressional support for the deal, Roosevelt exhibited considerable courage in an election year by cutting through political and legal restraints and transferring the vessels to the Royal Navy by executive order on September 2. The gesture was costly to the U.S. Navy, however, for it had only seventy-five modern destroyers and needed the old ships as a reserve.

Four days later, U.S. Navy crews arrived at Halifax, Nova Scotia, with the first eight "four-pipers"—so called because they had four funnels—which were turned over to the Royal Navy in a curious ceremony. The Americans hauled down their flags and then marched off to waiting trains, which took them home. British crews then boarded and raised the White Ensign, while the small group of American officers and men detailed to instruct them in the operation of the vessels remained discreetly below. The ships were a somewhat dubious gift, because they were cantankerous and outmoded. The British appreciated the full stocks of food and other luxuries left behind, but had difficulty in getting accustomed to such touches as enclosed bridges and bunks. "It's like lying on a bloody sack of jelly," complained a sailor used to a hammock. Only a handful of the ships were ready for convoy-escort duty before the end of the year, but they upped Britain's destroyer strength by 30 percent—more than compensating for the losses incurred at Dunkirk and in the narrow seas.*

Throughout that summer, river barges and other vessels proceeded to the Channel ports from all over Germany in preparation for Sea Lion. British bombers struck every night, and warships, including the fifteen-inch-gunned monitor *Erebus*, shelled them, disrupting preparations and sinking or damaging about 10 percent of these craft. Enigma decrypts told the British that Hitler had made no final decision for an invasion, nor would one be made "pending the result of the present struggle for air superiority." Fortunately for the British, that "struggle" was not going at all as Göring had expected.

The Reichsmarschall had expected to destroy Fighter Command,

---

*Six were given to the Royal Canadian Navy, the rest to the Royal Navy. To commemorate their American origin, they were called the "Town" class and named after towns common in both the British Commonwealth and the United States, such as *Annapolis* and *Campbeltown*.

its airfields, and its early-warning network in southern England in four days, with another four weeks allotted to mopping up the rest of the RAF and British aircraft factories. But the British, outnumbered by the Luftwaffe by more than two to one, shot down nearly two German aircraft for every British plane lost.* As a result, the Germans lost tactical flexibility by being forced to use fighters to protect their bombers rather than engaging the British fighters. Thus, the proportion of bombers to fighters in the attacking forces fell to less than one in four. The slow, ungainly Stukas were particularly vulnerable and were withdrawn from the struggle. But after three weeks of intense action, the pressures upon Fighter Command's pilots were at the breaking point. Some were so exhausted after flying four or five sorties a day that they fell asleep in their cockpits after landing.

Three-and-a-half weeks after Eagle Day—on September 7—Göring committed a fatal blunder. Mistakenly convinced that Fighter Command was on its last legs, he switched his bruising attacks from the RAF and British aircraft factories to the terror bombing of London. The East End docklands and the surrounding slums were set ablaze. Flames engulfed huge warehouses full of rum, sugar, wood, and pepper; a towering, apocalyptic white cloud of smoke, which turned an angry red as night drew on, rose over the city. It was spectacular, yet, by diverting his planes to the capital, Göring gave Fighter Command the time to regroup it so desperately needed. Great air battles were fought in the skies over London in which the Luftwaffe was repeatedly bloodied. On September 15 alone, the British shot down fifty German aircraft at the cost of twenty-six of their own.

Increased activity was observed in the Channel ports at the height of these battles, mine barrages were being laid along the edges of the proposed invasion routes, and under interrogation captured German spies revealed they had come to prepare the way for a landing. The code word "Cromwell" was flashed to all military units: a German invasion was imminent. Church bells pealed the alarm, and the Home Guard turned out. But no invasion materialized—nor was one planned. In reality, on September 6, large numbers of German troops

*In the course of the Battle of Britain, from mid-August to the end of September 1940, the Germans lost over 1,100 aircraft—not the 2,698 claimed by the British—while Fighter Command lost about 650 planes, not the 3,058 claimed by the Luftwaffe.

were transferred from France to Poland, where thirty-five divisions were already massing for an attack on the Soviet Union. And Raeder, following a meeting with Hitler three days later to discuss the timetable for Sea Lion, told his staff the Führer had "no thought of executing the landing if the risk of the operation is too high."

Bad weather was settling in over the Channel, and with the Luftwaffe unable to win air superiority over Britain, Hitler repeatedly put off a decision on Sea Lion. Finally, on September 17, he postponed the invasion indefinitely. The following year, it was canceled for good. "We have conquered France at the cost of 30,000 men," he told his naval aide Captain Karl Jesko von Puttkammer. "During one night of crossing the Channel we could lose many times that—and success is not certain." The nighttime "blitz" against London and other cities continued, but the Führer had turned his attention eastward, to the invasion of the Soviet Union. The road to the conquest of Britain now led through the steppes of Russia.

Hitler did not regard his failure to subjugate Britain as vital. Yet his inability to drive the Royal Navy and RAF from the sea and sky ultimately proved fatal to the Third Reich. The escape of the BEF from Dunkirk, the Battle of Britain, and the abandonment of Sea Lion were the beginning of the end for Germany. An unconquered Britain kept Germany off balance, lent support to the Russians after Hitler invaded the Soviet Union, and served as an unsinkable base for the eventual return of the Allies to the European continent.

•

CHAPTER 4

"A Caged Tiger"

Trailing tatters of smoke, the Mediterranean Fleet slipped out of Alexandria Harbor on the evening of July 7, 1940, and headed for the open sea. Admiral Sir Andrew B. Cunningham, flying his flag in *Warspite*, intended to sweep into the central Mediterranean to cover the passage of two convoys from Malta to Alexandria, and to challenge directly Italian attempts to control those waters. With him were the old battleships *Royal Sovereign* and *Malaya* and the small aircraft-carrier *Eagle*, as well as five six-inch gun cruisers and a screen of seventeen destroyers.* "You may be sure that all of us are imbued with a burning desire to get at the Italian Fleet," Cunningham told Prime Minister Churchill.

Shortly after 0800 the following day, as the fleet steamed westward at twenty knots, a submarine reported that it had sighted two Italian battleships and four destroyers steaming southward roughly two hundred miles to the east of Malta. The sighting report was received with considerable satisfaction on the admiral's bridge of *Warspite*. Cunningham surmised that the enemy ships were covering a convoy carrying supplies to the Italian army in Libya, and instructed the naval base at Malta to dispatch flying boats to keep tabs on the enemy while he pressed ahead with his fleet. The stage was being set for the

---

*Force H, built around the battle cruiser *Hood* and the battleships *Valiant* and *Resolution* and *Ark Royal*, had also sortied from Gibraltar to launch an air attack on the Cagliari airfield on Sardinia as a diversion.

first major fleet action in the Mediterranean since the Battle of Lissa in 1866.

Ever since the rise of Fascism in Italy in the 1920s, the prospect of a clash between Britain and the Italians over control of the Mediterranean had become increasingly likely. Mussolini had made it abundantly clear that his goal was the re-establishment of the Roman Empire in what he called "Mare Nostrum." The *duce* had conquered Ethiopia in 1936 while the Western powers stood by wringing their hands. Now his eyes were fixed upon Corsica, Tunisia, and Nice, and his Adriatic ambitions were reflected in the names of three of the Italian navy's newest cruisers, *Fiume, Trieste,* and *Pola.* In the Balkans, he had occupied Albania in 1939, and was plotting against Greece and Yugoslavia.

Until the collapse of France, the French had had responsibility for the western basin of the Mediterranean, and the Royal Navy's Mediterranean Fleet, which operated from Alexandria, covered the eastern area. British ships passed unhindered through the Suez Canal to and from India and the East.* Mussolini's decision to take Italy into the war on the side of Germany as France was reeling to defeat tipped the balance of naval power in favor of the Axis, forcing these convoys to take the long voyage around the Cape of Good Hope.

With the elimination of France, the Italians had the most powerful navy in the Mediterranean. The core of their battle fleet included six battleships, two of the powerful new thirty-five-thousand-ton *Littorio* class, mounting nine fifteen-inch guns; two modernized World War I–era ships of the *Cavour* class with ten 12.6-inch guns; and two sister ships in the process of modernization. They also had nineteen cruisers, seven of them of the eight-inch-gun type, some 120 destroyers and torpedo boats, and about a hundred submarines, twice the number with which the Germans were wreaking havoc in the Atlantic.† The navy had no aircraft carriers, and relied upon the shore-based air force, the Regia Aeronautica, to cover the fleet. But

---

*Most of Britain's fuel came across the North Atlantic; the Allied forces in the Middle East received their oil from the Persian Gulf.

†Following the declaration of war, some two dozen Italian submarines entered the Atlantic and served under German command. For details, see chapter 6.

the air force lacked dive-bombers and torpedo planes, the most effective weapons against ships, and the level of cooperation between the two services was low.

In the early months of the war, the British Mediterranean Fleet was milked of ships to meet other commitments, but after the entry of Italy into the conflict, the fleet was reconstituted. Cunningham had four battleships based upon Alexandria, of which only *Warspite* had been modernized; seven six-inch-gun cruisers; twenty-two destroyers; twelve submarines; and the carrier *Eagle*, with her seventeen antiquated Swordfish and a pair of Sea Gladiator fighters.* Except for a handful of flying boats, the British had no land-based aircraft. In the face of the overwhelming strength of the Italian fleet and air force, the Admiralty contemplated withdrawal of its ships from the eastern Mediterranean and the concentration of British forces at Gibraltar, about two thousand miles from Alexandria. Churchill vetoed this proposal, because it would mean writing off Malta and Egypt, and men and ships were scraped together for the Mediterranean Fleet.†

The Italian fleet was more impressive on paper than in actuality, however. Basically, its problem was that it was defensive- rather than offensive-minded and its ships and tactics reflected this outlook. Although sleek and graceful, the major vessels sacrificed armor protection for speed—to give and avoid battle except on their own terms—for Italian admirals usually fought only when they held an overwhelming advantage. This strategy was reminiscent of the "fleet-in-being" doctrine adopted by the German High Seas Fleet following the Battle of Jutland in World War I. The Italians were also handicapped by abysmal communications; a lack of radar, sonar, or

*Like *Courageous* and *Glorious*, the 22,600-ton *Eagle* was a makeshift carrier. She had been under construction as the Chilean battleship *Almirante Cochrane*, but her uncompleted hull was commandeered by the Royal Navy during World War I. Following the war, she was converted into a carrier, and joined the fleet in 1923. In the absence of trained fighter pilots, *Eagle*'s air-operations officer, Commander Charles L. Keighly-Peach, and two other Swordfish pilots volunteered to fly the Gladiators.

†Churchill's decision to stand firm in the Mediterranean though hard pressed at home impressed the Germans. "That Great Britain was ready, despite her difficult position, to station half her capital ships and thirty-three of her irreplaceable destroyers in the Mediterranean . . . showed she was confident of the failure of any German attempt to invade England," states Admiral Friedrich Ruge (*Der Seekrieg*, p. 135).

reliable torpedoes; poor gunnery; and little training in night fighting. Moreover, Mussolini, who believed the war would last only three months, had not stockpiled adequate fuel-oil supplies. Perhaps the Italian navy's greatest handicap, however, was an inferiority complex when dealing with the Royal Navy.*

This might have been remedied had the Italians achieved some initial success against the British, but they never won such laurels— and Admiral Cunningham was determined they would never win them. In Cunningham, an acerbic Scot, the Royal Navy found a second Nelson.† Like Nelson, he combined professional competence with the ability to stir the admiration of his officers and men. Having won the Distinguished Service Order—second only to the Victoria Cross—three times in World War I, he was guided by the basic principle that the enemy was there to be beaten, and this could happen only if the fleets met, preferably at close range.

Within hours of Italy's declaration of war, Cunningham went to sea with his fleet, hoping to encounter enemy naval units and to "try out the Italian air at the earliest possible moment." Unable to draw his reluctant opponents out of their base at Taranto, on the heel of the Italian boot, Cunningham led an Anglo-French force in bombarding the Libyan port of Bardia. The old cruiser *Calypso* was sunk by an Italian submarine, but the British, assisted by Bletchley Park's ability to read the Italian naval version of Enigma, sank or captured ten enemy submarines in the first month of Italy's participation in the war.

France's defeat emboldened the Italian navy to greater action, and it began running convoys to the army in Libya, which was expected to soon advance against the pitifully small British Army of the Nile in Egypt. These convoys operated within striking distance of Malta, but

---

*The most recent study of the Italian navy's wartime performance disputes the idea that it had a inferiority complex when dealing with the Royal Navy. James J. Sadkovich argues that material deficiencies and poor command decisions were the major causes of its failures. Despite these handicaps, he points out, the Italian navy forced the British to keep considerable resources in the Mediterranean until Italy left the war in 1943. See Sadkovich, *The Italian Navy in World War II*.

†Upon learning that his friend Admiral Somerville, already a Knight Commander of the Bath, had been made a knight of the British Empire, Cunningham signalled him: "Congratulations. Fancy twice a knight at your age" (Pack, *Cunningham*, p. 120).

prewar strategists had written off the island—a mere fifty-six miles from the Sicilian coast—as vulnerable to blockade by submarine and bombers. But as the war developed, Malta became the focal point of British strategy in the Mediterranean. It was the staging area for British light forces, submarines, and aircraft which harried Italian convoys to North Africa, and considerable effort was expended on keeping the besieged island supplied.

The first surface action between British and Italian forces grew out of these Libyan convoy operations. Three Italian destroyers carrying troops and supplies were sighted on June 28 in the Sicilian Channel by a British reconnaissance plane which passed the report on to a cruiser squadron. Unable to escape this force, Commander Baroni of the destroyer *Espero* elected to sacrifice his ship to save the others. While he fought an unequal battle, the two remaining ships escaped. *Espero* went down with colors flying; forty-seven of her complement were picked up, but Baroni was not among them.

"Action Stations!"

"Hostile aircraft bearing Red Three Oh!"

"Open fire!"

Such commands repeatedly swept through Cunningham's fleet on the afternoon of July 8, as it passed south of Crete into what was soon to become known as "Bomb Alley." Upon learning that a pair of enemy battleships were at sea, Cunningham had temporarily abandoned his rendezvous with the two Alexandria-bound convoys. He turned his ships toward Taranto to get between the Italians and their base, despite prolonged attacks by wave after wave of Savoia-Marchetti trimotor bombers.

Unlike the dive-bombers favored by the Germans, Italian aircraft operated in formations at high altitudes, usually at twelve thousand feet, and dropped their bombloads together. Here was the supreme test of the air-power theorists' claim that massed heavy bombers could sink battleships. The fast-moving ships proved to be difficult targets, however. Captains waited until the bombers released their sticks of bombs and in the remaining seconds took evasive action. Hundreds of bombs were dropped, but there was only one hit—on the bridge of the cruiser *Gloucester*. Everyone there was wiped out, but the ship remained in action. Nevertheless, "it was most frightening," acknowledged Cunningham, a man not given to overstatement, and an exhausting ordeal for the crews who were at action stations for hours on end. As one observer noted:

> How a ship shakes and thunders when all her anti-aircraft guns are firing! The noise was tremendous; the pom-pom-pom of the 'Chicago pianos'; the sharp rattle of the multiple machine guns; and the bark of the 4-inch. Under the hot sun the sweat trickled down the sailors' bodies. They wore clean overalls with the trouser ends tucked into their socks and antiflash gear covering their faces and hands. Before action of any kind every man was supposed to change into clean underwear, so that if he were hit there would be no dirty material driven into the wound. This precaution could not be taken against aircraft attacks, which might develop at any hour of the day. . . .

Finally, darkness brought release from these incessant assaults, and the fleet pressed on in silence through the night in search of the Italians. The berth decks were hot and humid, and many sailors slept on deck with their clothes rolled up for pillows. Others, just coming off watch, had their tea amid the dull blue or red light of the emergency lamps and awaited the coming of morning.

Eagle flew off three Swordfish at first light on July 9. Along with flying boats from Malta, they confirmed the presence of an Italian fleet of at least two battleships, twelve cruisers, and numerous destroyers about ninety miles from the British fleet. *Giulio Cesare*, the flagship of Admiral Inigo Campioni, and her sister, *Cavour*, were returning home after covering the passage of a convoy of five supply ships for Benghazi in Libya. The Regia Aeronautica had failed to find the British fleet, and Campioni learned that it was closing in only after the ships were spotted by a floatplane catapulted off his ship. Although outnumbered three battleships to two, Campioni decided to offer battle, because he had the advantage of speed, the air force claimed considerable damage to the British vessels, and he expected Italian bombers and submarines to tip the scale in his favor. Much to his chagrin, he would discover that the reports of damage had been wildly exaggerated by the excited pilots.

Shortly before noon, and then again about four hours later, Cunningham ordered torpedo attacks on the Italians by *Eagle*'s Swordfish, with the hope of slowing down the speedier Italian ships and bringing them within range of his big guns. It was the first time an aircraft carrier participated directly in a fleet action. Because of the inexperience of the air crews, these attacks were ineffective. The weather was clear, with a light breeze flecking the sea, when, just before 1500, *Neptune*, which had been scouting ten miles ahead with the three other light cruisers of Vice-Admiral John C. Tovey's force, flashed the eagerly awaited signal: ENEMY BATTLE FLEET IN SIGHT.

The western horizon was soon alive with ships. Leaving the slower *Royal Sovereign* and *Malaya* behind, Cunningham dashed ahead at *Warspite*'s top speed of twenty-four knots to lend support to his embattled cruisers. "ABC felt that with the Italian battle fleet at sea any risks were justified in order to get at it," Rear Admiral Algernon Willis, the admiral's chief of staff, later related. "This was when he first showed himself a master of the calculated risk." A half-hour later, the Italian heavy cruisers opened fire on Tovey's ships with their eight-inch guns. "The Italians' shooting was very good and our cruisers and *Warspite* were continually straddled," Willis said. The six-inch guns of the British cruisers were unable to reply to this fire, but the enemy scored no hits. As soon as *Warspite*'s fifteen-inch shells began falling among them, the Italian cruisers turned away and took cover in a smoke screen. Two of the enemy cruisers tried to circle back to get at *Eagle*, but salvos from the battleship gave them second thoughts.

A short lull followed until 1553, when the British caught sight of *Giulio Cesare*. Elevating her main battery to maximum elevation, *Warspite* opened fire on the enemy flagship at a range of twenty-six thousand yards and straddled her with the first salvo. The Italians also opened up with their 12.6-inch guns, but the salvos fell about a thousand yards short of *Warspite*. At 1559, one of the British battleship's fifteen-inch shells struck her opponent amidships. "I saw the great orange-coloured flash of a heavy explosion at the base of the enemy flagship's funnels," reported Cunningham. "It was followed by an upheaval of smoke, and I knew that she had been heavily hit. . . ."

This single shell decided the encounter. Four of *Giulio Cesare*'s boilers were put out of action, and she suffered 115 casualties. Campioni's brief display of offensive spirit also faded. With his flagship's speed reduced to eighteen knots, he feared she might fall behind to become a victim of the onrushing British battleships. Both the *Giulio*

Cesare and *Cavour* turned away and soon disappeared in a smoke screen laid down by the rest of the fleet. From then on, the horizon was obscured by smoke, broken intermittently by the gun flashes of a confused fight between cruisers and destroyers. Torpedo attacks were launched by both sides, but, with the ships dodging in and out of the smoke, little damage was done.

By 1700, all firing had ceased. British aircraft reported that *Giulio Cesare* had been repaired and the Italians were heading at high speed for the Strait of Messina. Now, within sight of the mountainous coast of Calabria, Cunningham called off the pursuit and headed south for Malta. Campioni's only success was drawing the British within range of Italian shore-based aircraft, so that for nearly three hours the fleet was subjected to massed attacks by high-level bombers.

"At times a ship would disappear behind the great splashes," Cunningham reported. "I was seriously alarmed for the old ships *Royal Sovereign* and *Eagle*, which were not well protected. A clutch of those eggs hitting either must have sent her to the bottom." The bombers failed to score any hits but distributed their bombs with fine impartiality: they attacked their own ships as well as those of the enemy, and the angry signals of the Italian admiral were read on the British flagship with amusement. Six days later, the Mediterranean Fleet and the convoys from Malta were back at Alexandria, having survived no fewer than twenty air attacks without damage. One of *Warspite*'s officers described the return passage as "Bombs, bombs, and bombs!" *Eagle*'s Gladiators claimed to have shot down five of the raiders.

So ended what the British called the Action off Calabria and the Italians the Encounter off Punta Stilo. The Italians put the best face upon the episode by calling it a draw, but the laurels had clearly gone to the Royal Navy.* The encounter reinforced the moral ascendancy of the British, for the Italians resolved never again to risk their battleships in a stand-up fight, and rarely ventured from their haven at

---

*The Italian Naval Staff was particularly impressed by the advantages conferred upon the British by the presence of an aircraft carrier. "Besides permitting them to fight off the activities of our aircraft . . . [it] allowed the enemy to carry out attacks with torpedo aircraft, which, although frustrated by ships maneuvering, interfered with the formations attacked and so delayed their rejoining the remainder of our forces" (Bragadin, *The Italian Navy in World War II*, p. 33).

Taranto. On the other hand, the ineffectiveness of the Regia Aeronautica's bombing of Cunningham's ships bred a complacency among
the British that turned out to be sadly misplaced—especially after the
Luftwaffe entered the fray.

Never content to remain on the defensive, Winston Churchill let his
ever-roving eye now fall upon Dakar, on the westernmost point of
Africa, which was under control of the Vichy regime. With the
Mediterranean all but closed, the main north-south Atlantic shipping
route over which British troops and supplies for Egypt traveled lay
within striking distance of Dakar, and the prime minister was
alarmed by the possibility that Vichy might turn the naval base over
to the Germans or place the damaged but still-dangerous battleship
Richelieu at their disposal. Although the Vichy regime denied any
such intentions—and it is now clear that there was never any possibility of German control—Churchill decided to "liberate" Dakar.

Operation Menace, as it was called, was not expected to be seriously contested. The landing, scheduled for late September 1940,
was to be carried out by twenty-seven hundred Free French, under
the direct command of General Charles de Gaulle, supported by
forty-two hundred British troops and a naval force of two battleships,
a carrier, and several cruisers and destroyers. But the plan miscar-
ried, because it was based more upon wishful thinking than anything
else. Churchill convinced himself that most Frenchmen supported
de Gaulle rather than the Vichy regime despite considerable evidence to the contrary. In fact, the Free French leader had only marginal support,[*] and the French navy, smarting from the destruction of
its ships at Mers el-Kébir, was determined to resist the British intervention.

As luck would have it, while the invasion force was plodding down
the coast of Africa, three large French cruisers and three "superde-
stroyers" sailed from Toulon for Libreville in French Equatorial
Africa. Admiral Sir Dudley North, the commander at Gibraltar, and
Admiral Sir James Somerville, commander of Force H, both had

---

[*]For example, only a handful of the French soldiers rescued from Dunkirk and still
in England at the time of France's surrender opted to join the Free French forces. The
rest chose to go home, despite the German occupation.

ambiguous orders, and each thought the other would deal with these ships. By the time the Admiralty realized the situation, the French squadron had gotten clear and was far down the coast of Africa. Two of the cruisers put into Dakar, adding to the defense force.

The Allied force arrived off Dakar on September 23, and a dense mist veiled the scene, adding a physical murkiness to the political and military uncertainties. De Gaulle's efforts to persuade French officials to join him were rejected, and a landing by his troops was repelled. A bombardment of the port by the Royal Navy over the next two days achieved little. The immobilized *Richelieu* and the two cruisers scored several hits on the attacking vessels, and the battleship *Resolution* was seriously damaged by a Vichy submarine. Now realizing that the capture of Dakar would require the diversion of substantial forces, the British withdrew—and Menace became a symbol of undue political interference in military operations and muddled planning.*

In the Mediterranean, however, the tide for the moment flowed strongly in favor of the British, and those waters became known as "Cunningham's Pond." Repeatedly in the summer of 1940, the Mediterranean Fleet sortied from Alexandria and Force H from Gibraltar to cover convoys to Malta, to support the British army in North Africa by shelling targets on the Libyan coast, and to try— unsuccessfully—to lure the Italian fleet into battle. Italian reaction, including the usual bombing attacks, was limited and ineffective.

British confidence was further buoyed by the outcome of an encounter on July 19 between the light cruiser *Sydney* of the Royal Australian Navy and a pair of Italian light cruisers, *Bartolomeo Colleoni* and *Banda Nere* off Cape Spada, northwest of Crete. Mistaking one of *Sydney's* five accompanying destroyers for a cruiser, the Italians, who had the advantage of speed, fled. In the running fight

*In the wake of the Dakar fiasco, the Admiralty removed Sir Dudley North from the Gibraltar command amid accusations that amounted to dereliction of duty for permitting the French squadron to pass through the straits. Earlier, North had been critical of the decision to attack the French fleet at Mers el-Kébir, and many officers viewed his dismissal as an effort to get rid of a critic and to establish a scapegoat for Dakar. Following a long fight to vindicate himself, North was finally cleared in 1957 after an inquiry ordered by Prime Minister Harold Macmillan.

which ensued, *Sydney* scored a disabling hit on the thin-skinned *Colleoni*, which stopped dead in the water. *Sydney* poured six-inch shells into the stricken vessel and, leaving her to be finished off by the destroyers, pursued *Banda Nere*. Hit repeatedly, the Italians escaped only because *Sydney* ran short of ammunition and Captain John A. Collins called off the pursuit.[*]

Unhappy with the lack of speed of his old battleships, Cunningham bombarded the Admiralty with demands for a modernized ship to replace *Malaya* and *Royal Sovereign*, plus a modern carrier. "Our principal trouble is that we cannot move without our movements being known," he told Admiral Pound. The Italians "send planes over Alexandria every day, and no force in the last three weeks has been at sea without being discovered and bombed, in some cases very heavily."

Despite the demands of the Battle of Britain and the threat of invasion, the Admiralty found reinforcements for the Mediterranean Fleet in the form of the modernized battleship *Valiant*, the anti-aircraft cruisers *Calcutta* and *Coventry*, both fitted with an early form of radar which could give warning of the approach of attacking enemy aircraft from fifty miles away, and the new twenty-three-thousand-ton carrier *Illustrious*. She had not only an armored flight deck, a revolutionary feature for carriers at the time, but a squadron of Fulmar fighters. A significant improvement over the Skua and the Gladiator, these planes mounted eight machine guns, like the Spitfire and the Hurricane, but were not so fast.

Cunningham received this sorely needed transfusion of resources just in time for the opening of the long-expected Italian offensive against the British Army of the Nile. The attack bogged down, however, in a welter of inefficiency and a general lack of aggressiveness at Sidi Barrâni after a mere forty-five-mile advance. The left flank of the Italian army was exposed to the Mediterranean Fleet's shallow-draft ships, and they made the lot of the troops wretched, with almost nightly bombardments. Gunboats that had served on the Yangzte and

[*]With submarines reported in the area, Collins left without picking up survivors from *Colleoni*, but dropped a boat along with the course to be steered to reach land. Many years later, on a NATO exercise, he found himself with a group of Italian naval officers who grew animated when they learned he was an Australian. One of them remarked, " 'We love the Australian Navy. When they had to steam away, they gave us a boat and we got back to Italy' " (R. Hough, *The Longest Battle*, p. 209).

other Chinese rivers in the years between the wars made up the bulk of this force and were joined by the fifteen-inch-gun monitor *Terror*.

Mussolini chose this moment to expand the war in the Mediterranean. On October 28, he declared war on Greece, a step taken against the advice of the Italian Naval Staff. For the Royal Navy, the entrance of Greece into the war was a mixed blessing. The Italian thrust toward Suez was weakened, and the British fleet was provided a refueling-and-supply base at Suda Bay, off Crete, that was valuable for sustaining operations in the central Mediterranean. On the other hand, the fleet had to stretch its resources to protect convoys carrying materiel—and then troops—to Greece.

Eager to get at the Italian fleet, Cunningham repeatedly tried to entice it out of its base at Taranto by dangling convoys bound to and from Malta and Alexandria before the Italians, but they refused to rise to the bait. Early in October, however, a flotilla of Italian destroyers delivered a night attack on a convoy, and a spirited action followed. The New Zealand cruiser *Ajax*, one of the victors over *Admiral Graf Spee*, sank three of the vessels and damaged a fourth.

The Royal Navy also dusted off a plan of attack originally conceived by Admiral Sir David Beatty during the closing months of the previous war. Frustrated by the refusal of the German fleet to give battle after Jutland, Beatty had proposed a strike by two hundred torpedo planes against the German battleships as they lay in port, but the war ended before the technical obstacles to such an operation could be overcome. During the 1930s, the plan had been revised by Captain A. L. St. G. Lyster for use against the Italians. Lyster, now a rear admiral and commander of Mediterranean Fleet's carriers, called it to Cunningham's attention, who ordered a strike against the Italian Fleet at Taranto.

The attack was originally to be made by Swordfish from *Illustrious* and *Eagle* on October 21—Trafalgar Day—but was postponed because of a fire in the hangar deck of *Illustrious*. Early in November, American-built Maryland reconnaissance planes spotted all six Italian battleships moored in Mar Grande, the semicircular outer harbor of Taranto, and several cruisers and destroyers were anchored in the inner Mar Piccolo. Cunningham camouflaged his movements with considerable convoy traffic and set the air attack for the night of

November 11. But the day before the ships were to sail, it was discovered that *Eagle* had been weakened by the repeated bombings she had undergone, and seawater had seeped into her fuel tanks. Five of her Swordfish were transferred to *Illustrious*, and the carrier, taking leave of the rest of the fleet, steamed to the launch position, about 170 miles southeast of Taranto.

Taking off into bright moonlight shortly before 2100, the first wave of twelve heavily laden Swordfish—half with eighteen-inch torpedoes* slung below them and the rest carrying flares and six 250-pound armor-piercing bombs each—lumbered down the carrier's flight deck and droned off toward Taranto. Half the rear cockpits of the torpedo planes were taken up with sixty-gallon gasoline tanks, to add to the discomfort of the observer, and the bombers had an extra fuel tank strapped on the outside of the fuselage. One lucky hit and a plane would explode into a fiery ball from which there would be no escape.

The torpedo planes were led by Lieutenant Commander Kenneth Williamson, with Lieutenant N. J. Scarlet as his observer. Making little more than a hundred miles an hour, they were like an undirected school of fish, rising and falling as they were caught in the sudden blast of a wingmate's slipstream. Although the Italians had lost track of the Mediterranean Fleet and assumed it was on its way back to Alexandria, there was little chance of surprise. Listening devices on the ground picked up the formation while it was still well offshore. Taranto was defended by some three hundred anti-aircraft guns, plus those on the ships, plus torpedo nets, galaxies of searchlights, and ninety barrage balloons—a special hazard for low-flying torpedo planes. Scarlet sighted the red twinkling of anti-aircraft fire while the planes were thirty miles from their target.

"That's Taranto," he told Williamson.

"Yes," replied the pilot. "They seem to be expecting us."

Flares were dropped as a signal for the Swordfish to begin their dives into a volcano of gunfire. Wind whistling in the wing wires, they dropped to 7,500 feet . . . 5,000 feet . . . 3,000 feet . . . buffeted by flak and pilots nearly blinded by explosions. Less than 2,000 feet above

---

*These torpedoes were set to run at a depth of thirty-three feet and fitted with newly developed twin-Duplex pistols. One would explode on contact while the other would be set off by the target vessel's magnetic field if the torpedo passed under it.

the dark waters of the Mar Grande, they slipped through the balloon barrage, the wingtips of Williamson's aircraft barely missing one of the cables. At less than 30 feet, he released his torpedo at the first warship that appeared before him. It missed a destroyer and ran on to explode against a much more important target, the battleship *Cavour*. Water poured into a gaping hole just aft of her forward turrets, and she slowly sank into the Mar Grande until her deck was awash. Before Williamson could get away, however, his plane was shot down, and he and Scarlet were taken prisoner.

Two other Swordfish made their way through the hail of antiaircraft fire and, having sent their tin fish into the Italian flagship *Littorio*, got away unscathed. Another pair almost hit *Andrea Doria*, their torpedoes exploding against a nearby quay with such force that the pressure caused the battleship's hull plates to buckle. The bombers attacked vessels and installations in the Mar Piccolo, and even though many of the bombs failed to explode, they destroyed fuel-storage tanks, set a seaplane depot afire, and provided a diversion for the torpedo attack.

The eight Swordfish of the second wave—five carrying torpedoes and three serving as bombers—flew into a hellish crossfire from battleships, cruisers, and shore batteries. Miraculously, only one plane was shot down. Lieutenant A. F. Sutton, whose plane attacked the stricken *Littorio*, reported: "She saw us and opened fire. The flash of her close-range weapons stabbed at us, first one then another, along her whole length. . . . They fired everything they had."

Sutton pressed the torpedo-release grip at seven hundred yards. Nothing happened! By now the immense bulk of the battleship seemed to fill his vision. Feverishly, he banged on the release grip. At the last moment, the torpedo dropped away, speeding on a true course for the tall sides of *Littorio*. Moments later, another torpedo hit *Caio Duilio*. With all torpedoes expended, the Swordfish, dodging wildly from side to side, escaped through the bursting shells and acrid smoke.

Next morning, when *Illustrious* rejoined the fleet, all the ships were flying the classically understated tribute: "Maneuver well executed." Three battleships—half of Italy's battle line—had been sunk at their moorings. *Littorio* and *Caio Duilio* were out of action for nearly six months, and *Cavour* was damaged beyond repair. In a few minutes, twenty obsolete aircraft had done more damage than the entire British Grand Fleet had inflicted upon the Germans at Jutland. The attack on Taranto, made with a remarkable economy of force, demonstrated that carrier aircraft was becoming the dominant weapon of war at sea. Half a world away, it was a lesson not lost on Admiral Isoroku Yamamoto, commander-in-chief of the Japanese Combined Fleet, who was planning an attack on the U.S. Navy's Pacific Fleet as it lay at its base at Pearl Harbor in the Hawaiian Islands.[*]

The beleaguered Army of the Nile needed reinforcements, and, to save time, the British ran a troop convoy directly through the Mediterranean instead of around the tip of Africa. This convoy was under the protection of Force H—now reduced to *Renown* and *Ark Royal* and a handful of cruisers and destroyers—which was to hand it over to the Mediterranean Fleet in the Sicilian narrows. Having learned of the British plan, an Italian force consisting of the two remaining battleships, *Vittorio Veneto* and *Giulio Cesare*, seven heavy cruisers, and sixteen destroyers attacked on November 27, about 120 miles off Cape Spartivento, at the tip of Sicily.

The action began at 1220 and lasted about an hour, during which a British cruiser and an Italian destroyer were damaged. In the meantime, Force H had been reinforced by the old battleship *Ramillies*, which had been detached earlier by Admiral Cunningham. Upon sighting the battleship, the Italians realized they had lost the opportunity to exploit their earlier superiority, and broke off the action. Several air strikes were launched by *Ark Royal* against the retreating enemy without result. Admiral Somerville, who saw his primary duty as the protection of the transports, abandoned the chase and rejoined the convoy. The results of the encounter were disappointing, and Somerville was unjustly criticized by the Admiralty for failing to continue the pursuit.

With these reinforcements in hand and their seaward flank secure,

[*]Lieutenant Commander Takeshi Naito, the assistant Japanese naval attaché in Berlin, quickly flew to Taranto to make a personal inspection of the Italian ships and to pick up details of the raid. Upon his return to Japan, he was interviewed by several of the officers engaged in the secret planning of the Pearl Harbor attack. Naito was not let in on the operation, however (Prange, *At Dawn We Slept*, p. 320).

the British Army surprised the Italians at Sidi Barrâni with a devastating counterattack on December 6. The operation was successful beyond anyone's wildest expectations. Within little more than a week, the Italians were expelled from Egypt and 130,000 prisoners were captured and four hundred tanks were destroyed. The Mediterranean Fleet took an active role in support of this offensive. Inshore squadrons supplied bombardments as needed, delivered food, water, and ammunition to the advancing troops, and took off the wounded and Italian prisoners. "The Army owes much to the Royal Navy . . . for its support," reported General Sir Archibald Wavell, the British commander in the Middle East.

On the north shore of the Mediterranean, *Warspite* and *Valiant* shelled Valona, the Albanian port through which passed the bulk of supplies and reinforcements for the Italian army, now in full retreat from the aroused Greeks. Surprise was complete, and about twenty enemy Italian aircraft were wrecked on the ground. The small Greek navy was also active in these waters; its destroyers bombarded Italian positions along the Albanian coast, and submarines harried the Italian convoys.

By the beginning of January 1941, British convoys were passing through the Mediterranean and across to Greece almost without interference, while an increasing toll was being taken of enemy convoys to Tripoli. But Mussolini's fiascoes in Greece and North Africa led to German intervention in the Mediterranean. Hitler took full control of operations in the Balkans to protect his flank in preparation for the planned attack on Russia, and also dispatched to North Africa a small but highly mobile force under the command of Major General Erwin Rommel, to reinforce the shattered Italian army.

The Luftwaffe also soon made its appearance in the Mediterranean skies. Fliegerkorps X, a unit of about three hundred dive-bombers and fighters that had been especially trained to attack ships, was transferred to the Mediterranean with direct orders from the Führer to "attack the British Navy . . . in Alexandria . . . the Suez Canal . . . and in the straits between Sicily and the north coast of Africa." It struck for the first time on January 10, 1941. The Admiralty had dispatched a large convoy with supplies for British forces in Greece and the Middle East, and, following the usual practice, Force H escorted it as far as Sicily, where it was handed over to the Mediterranean Fleet for the remainder of the voyage.

The day began with a torpedo attack on the convoy by the Italians. They were driven off by anti-aircraft fire and Fulmar fighters from *Illustrious*. While the British were distracted by this low-level attack, the carrier's radar picked up a swarm of some three dozen planes boring in from the north at twelve thousand feet. Veterans of the bitter fighting in the Norwegian fjords and the English Channel readily identified the snarl of Ju-87s and 88s. Peeling off in flights of three, the dive-bombers screamed down on *Illustrious*.

Twisting and turning and throwing up a wall of fire, the carrier heeled violently to port and then to starboard as she tried to evade the attackers. Five enemy aircraft were shot down, but she was hit by six eleven-hundred-pound bombs that set her ablaze fore and aft. After limping into Malta, *Illustrious* was patched up and sent to the United States for a refit that required almost a year to complete. The heavy cruiser *Southampton* was lost to dive-bomber attack the following day, and another cruiser was severely damaged.

For the next two months, the Mediterranean Fleet was without a carrier, and the British position in the Middle East was threatened by the combination of German air superiority and the growing strength of Rommel's Afrika Korps. Thus, the Mediterranean campaign, which had begun as something of a sideshow, became a major struggle between the Germans and the British. Without air cover, the British battle fleet was unable to operate safely in the central Mediterranean, and operations against German and Italian convoys devolved upon the Malta Striking Force, a handful of light cruisers, destroyers, and submarines based on the island.

As the German menace to Greece mounted, the British stripped the Army of the Nile of some fifty-eight thousand troops and sent them to Greece. It was one of Churchill's worst mistakes of the war. The decision to go to the aid of the Greeks owed as much to his fascination with peripheral strategy—the perennial search for the enemy's soft underbelly—as it did with military strategy or the political necessity of assisting an ally. The Allied defeats in Norway and France made it abundantly clear that control of the air was vital to such operations, and there was no hope of winning it with the inadequate squadrons available. Had the North African army not been

denuded of men and equipment, Tripoli might well have been captured, forestalling German attempts to reinforce the shattered Italian
army in North Africa. Instead, the British were driven from Greece
and Crete—and Libya as well.

Prodded by German promises of strong air cover and an erroneous
Luftwaffe report of heavy damage to the British fleet—only *Warspite*
was supposedly still operational—the Italians reluctantly sent their
fleet to sea to attack the Greece-bound convoys. On March 26, *Vittorio Veneto*, flying the flag of Admiral Angelo Iachino, six eight-inch-
gun cruisers, two six-inch-gun cruisers, and thirteen destroyers
sailed from Naples and other ports for the Aegean Sea. The next day,
Admiral Cunningham departed Alexandria with a fleet consisting of
Warspite, Valiant, and *Barham* and nine destroyers. They were joined
at sea by the carrier *Formidable*, which had come through the Suez
Canal only a few weeks before and was still working up to peak efficiency.* Convoys bound to and from Greece were ordered out of
harm's way. Force B, the six-inch-gun cruisers *Orion, Ajax, Perth,* and
Gloucester and four destroyers under Vice-Admiral Sir Henry D.
Pridham-Wippell, which was operating in the Aegean, were ordered
to rendezvous with Cunningham at 0630 on March 28, near Gavdos
Island, to the south of Crete.

The intelligence that led to these dispositions had been provided by
Bletchley Park from its reading of the Luftwaffe and Italian-naval
versions of Enigma.† The enemy moves were confirmed by a Sunderland flying boat from Malta, which spotted part of the Italian force.
Although surprise had been lost, Admiral Iachino decided to continue
the operation, because the plane's radio report, picked up by the flagship, stated it had sighted only four light ships. For his part, Cunningham, devoutly wishing to bring about a decisive action, resorted to
subterfuge so as not to alarm the enemy about his intentions.

To mask his movements, the admiral presented a picture of serene

---

*Among her aircraft, *Formidable* carried a squadron of Albacore torpedo planes, an
updated version of the Swordfish, but still a slow and ungainly biplane, obsolescent by
American and Japanese standards.
†The Code and Cypher School had enlisted several women as cryptanalysts as well
as clerks, and one, Mavis Lever, was a member of the team that broke into the Italian
naval cipher. See Kahn, *Seizing the Enigma*, p. 139.

inactivity. The Japanese consul general in Alexandria was suspected of spying for his Axis partners and was a keen golfer, so Cunningham went ashore that afternoon to play golf, conspicuously carrying a suitcase, as if he intended to remain away from his ship overnight. Awnings were spread on *Warspite*'s deck, and invitations were sent out to a supper party to be held that evening. The party was quietly canceled, the awnings were struck, and Cunningham secretly returned to the flagship just before she slipped her moorings and vanished into the covering darkness.

First light on March 28 found the Italians steaming to the south of Crete in three groups with a pair of cruiser forces running ahead of *Vittorio Veneto*. Much to the anger of Admiral Iachino, he had not received the air support promised by the Germans and was unaware of the enemy's position. "I felt pretty well deceived by the lack of cooperation," he later declared. Iachino launched a floatplane to reconnoiter the area, and it reported four British cruisers and four destroyers sailing in a southerly direction off Gavdos, about fifty miles away. The British fleet was supposedly still at Alexandria, so Iachino sniffed the presence of a convoy. Three heavy cruisers and a trio of destroyers were detailed to deal with the enemy ships.

Iachino's targets belonged to Force B, under Admiral Pridham-Wippell. Unexpectedly faced by enemy ships faster and more heavily armed than his own, he was in a perilous position. Reversing course, he sped away at twenty-eight knots toward the expected position of Cunningham's fleet, with the Italians in pursuit. The tactical situation was unfolding in a fashion remarkably similar to the opening moves of Jutland. In that battle, scouting forces on both sides had sighted each other but each was unaware that the other side had battleships over the horizon. Like the British battle cruisers of a quarter-century before, Pridham-Wippell tried to lure the unsuspecting Italians within range of Cunningham's big guns.

The Italians opened fire with their eight-inch guns at the extreme range of nearly fourteen miles, a distance at which the British cruisers could not reply. Huge waterspouts blossomed about them as the distance between the two forces narrowed uncomfortably. "We were shot at for quite a long time and lots of salvos came close—close enough for us to get some splashes on deck—but nobody was hit," Commander R. L. Fisher, the squadron's Operations officer, later recalled. With the range down to twelve miles, *Gloucester*, at the end of the British line, fired back, but her six-inch shells fell short. To Pridham-Wippell's alarm, more Italian cruisers were spotted pounding down at top speed with the intention of sandwiching his ships between them and the other cruisers. "It began to look as if we were going to be trapped between the devil and the deep blue sea," Fisher observed.

Cunningham was deliberately using the cruisers as bait, and held off sending *Formidable*'s aircraft to their rescue to avoid alerting the Italians to the presence of his carrier and battleships. Shortly before 0900, Iachino broke off the running fight and ordered his cruisers to return. With the vessels now within range of British land-based bombers at Tobruk in North Africa and no convoys sighted, he thought it wise to call off the operation. As the Italians retreated, Pridham-Wippell also put about and began shadowing them as they steered to the northwest.

As soon as the horizon cleared of enemy ships, bully-beef sandwiches were passed out on the British cruisers, and the gun crews sunned themselves under cobalt skies atop their turrets. A staff officer came on the bridge of *Orion* and, as Fisher later recalled, "with his mouth full of sandwich, nudged me and said, 'What battleship is that over on the starboard beam? I thought ours were miles to the east?'" Just as the startled Fisher put his binoculars to his eyes to examine a large ship hull down to the northward, there was a whistling sound and *Veneto*'s first fifteen-inch salvo exploded among the British cruisers.

Eighty miles away, Cunningham was electrified to receive three intercepted emergency signals from Pridham-Wippell to his ships:

"Make smoke by all available means."

"Turn together to 180 degrees."

"Proceed at your utmost speed."

Obviously, Force B had sighted the enemy battle fleet, and the admiral immediately ordered full speed ahead. Flinging off bow waves, and with ensigns streaming out, the battleships steamed off in line ahead. But the fleet was limited to twenty-two knots, the most that could be coaxed out of the old *Barham*, and *Warspite* was having trouble with her condensers. Once again, Cunningham had to endure the teeth-grinding frustration of trying to bring an enemy fleet of modern battleships to action with old and slow ships. He paced the admiral's bridge of *Warspite* like "a caged tiger," reported one officer, on "the side nearest the enemy; the speed of advance . . . never fast enough for him. . . ."

Making thick smoke, Pridham-Wippell's cruisers were racing south toward the British fleet, but this time they were being pressed by a powerful battleship as well as numerous heavy cruisers. The range was soon down to twelve miles, and the Italian fire was intense and accurate. *Orion* sustained some damage from a near miss, and it was only a matter of time before one of the vessels would be hit. To take the pressure off them, Cunningham ordered a strike at 0939 by six Albacore torpedo planes escorted by a pair of Fulmar fighters.

As they passed over Pridham-Wippell's cruisers on their way north, the Albacores were mistaken by the excited gunners for enemy aircraft. In spite of repeated attempts to identify themselves, they were bounced about by heavy anti-aircraft fire. The planes finally found their target, but at almost the same moment the Luftwaffe made a belated appearance in the form of two Ju-88s. One was shot down by the accompanying Fulmars and the others driven off. Braving a barrage of anti-aircraft fire, the Albacores dropped their torpedoes, but *Vittorio Veneto*, steaming at thirty knots, evaded them. Nevertheless, the sortie saved Pridham-Wippell's beleaguered cruisers. Reasoning that the presence of a carrier meant that British battleships were nearby as well, Admiral Iachino broke off the action and headed home at his best speed.

With Cunningham's fleet still forty-five miles astern, the operation appeared doomed to be chalked up as another abortive effort to force the Italians into battle. Cunningham could barely keep from expressing his fury. "No prudent staff officer approached the 'caged tiger' without good reason," reported Commander Fisher. In one last try at damaging *Vittorio Veneto* enough to bring her within range of his guns, the admiral ordered another torpedo-plane attack.

Three Albacores and a pair of Swordfish led by Lieutenant Commander J. Dalyell-Stead zoomed down on the battleship at 1519. Fortunately for the British flyers, the Italians had just been bombed by RAF Blenheims from Greece, and although no hits were made, the attention of the gunners was focused on a high-level attack. The British leveled off only a few feet above the sea, then attacked from both the port and starboard sides in the face of withering fire. Just before his plane was hit and smashed into the sea, Dalyell-Stead released his torpedo. It found its mark, blowing a gaping hole near *Vittorio Veneto*'s stern and jamming her rudder. She was soon wallowing dead in the water. Dalyell-Stead and his crew were killed.

Spurred on by the realization that the British battle fleet was less than three hours' steaming away, *Vittorio Veneto*'s engineers feverishly made repairs and gradually won control of their vessel. Surrounded by a tight screen of cruisers and destroyers, she worked up to seventeen knots, but the British now had a chance to catch her, if not in daylight, then during the night. Cunningham launched another torpedo attack at 1925, which was carried out in the face of heavy fire from the massed Italian fleet. The battleship was unscathed, but the heavy cruiser *Pola* was hit amidships by a torpedo and immobilized. Unobserved by both the British and the Italians, she drifted out of line while Iachino pressed on ahead. Informed of *Pola*'s situation an hour later, he dispatched the cruisers *Zara* and *Fiume* and four destroyers to lend assistance to the stricken vessel. It was a fatal decision.

Cunningham was also making key decisions. Although uncertain of what lay ahead in the unscouted darkness, he decided to rely upon radar and his fleet's expertise in night fighting and to press on in pursuit of the crippled Italian flagship. The admiral's staff expressed strong misgivings, however. Cunningham later said he "paid respectful attention to this opinion" and decided to think it over during supper. Commander Geoffrey Bernard, the fleet gunnery officer, recalled Cunningham's actual words as more pungent: " 'You're a pack of yellow-livered skunks. I'll go and have my supper now and see after supper if my morale isn't higher than yours.' "

No matter what the correct version, at 2037 Cunningham ordered eight destroyers forward to "fix" the enemy battle fleet with a torpedo attack, while the rest of his fleet came up at full speed. At 2220, *Valiant*'s radar picked up the "blip" of a stopped ship about 4.5 miles to port. The destroyer *Stuart* followed up with a report of two large darkened ships and four smaller ones proceeding in line off the starboard bow. Cunningham swung his fleet in line ahead on a course almost parallel but opposite to this force. Slowly, the fifteen-inch turrets of *Warspite*, *Valiant*, and *Barham* were brought to bear on the unsuspecting Italians. Cunningham later wrote:

One heard the 'ting-ting-ting' of the firing gongs. Then came the great orange flash and the violent shudder as the six big guns bearing were fired simultaneously. . . . Our searchlights shone out with the first salvo, and provided full illumination for what was a ghastly sight. Full on the beam, I saw our six great projectiles flying through the air. Five out of the six hit a few feet below the level of the cruiser's upper deck and burst with splashes of brilliant flame. The Italians were quite unprepared. Their guns were trained fore and aft. They were helplessly shattered before they could put up any resistance. . . .

Zara and *Fiume* were torn apart by the rain of heavy shells. *Pola* escaped the massacre, only to be sunk later by British destroyers, which took off 257 survivors of the crew of 800, many of them drunk.* Two of the four Italian destroyers were also sunk. Unfortunately, Captain Philip J. Mack, the commander of the destroyer flotilla sent in pursuit of *Vittorio Veneto,* underestimated her speed by at least four knots and made his turn to intercept too soon, allowing the battleship to escape in the darkness. So ended what became known as the Battle of Cape Matapan. In addition to the ships sunk and damaged, approximately twenty-four hundred Italian officers and sailors were lost. It was, as a British admiral had said in an earlier day, "a victory . . . very necessary to England at this time."

Matapan ushered in a new era in naval warfare. It was the first battle fought on the open sea in which an aircraft carrier played the decisive role. Had it not been for the hits scored by *Formidable*'s torpedo planes, none of the Italian ships would have come under the fire of the British battleships. The carrier and its aircraft were now an extension of the battle fleet, projecting its power hundreds of miles beyond the range of its guns.† What was left of the Italian navy's fighting spirit was also consumed in the holocaust that lit up the Mediterranean night.

---

*The British picked up a total of 905 Italian survivors before daylight, but under the threat of a bombing attack by the Luftwaffe the fleet shaped course for Alexandria. Cunningham broke radio silence to inform the Italian Admiralty of the position of the survivors as he left the scene of the action.

†Pressured by his admirals after Matapan, Mussolini agreed to build up his naval air capability and ordered the conversion of two liners, *Aquila* and *Sparviero*, to aircraft carriers. Work on the vessels proceeded slowly, however, and they were still in the dockyards when Italy left the war in 1943.

*   *   *

Paralyzed by the shock of defeat, the Italians now failed even to provide adequate escorts for the vital cross-Mediterranean convoys. On April 15, 1941, a British patrol plane spotted five ships off Tunisia carrying ammunition, fuel, and stores for Rommel under escort by three destroyers. Italian intelligence knew the ships had been spotted but made no effort to reinforce the escort. Four British destroyers from Malta attacked and, in a violent night action, sank the entire convoy and the escort as well. Only one British ship was lost.

The complete absence of Italian reaction encouraged Cunningham to steam 850 miles through the Mediterranean to shell Tripoli. Originally, Churchill, pulling one of his most bizarre rabbits from his hat, ordered that the harbor be blocked by sinking *Barham* and an old cruiser in the narrowest part of the channel, to cut Rommel's supply line.* These ships were to enter the harbor firing their guns and then to scuttle themselves. Cunningham was appalled at the idea of sacrificing a fully operational battleship—even an old one—on such a project, and, choosing the lesser of two evils, substituted the bombardment for it. For three-quarters of an hour, the ships stood offshore and blasted the port installations and shipping with little effect. There was no resistance, and the return voyage was completed without an air attack.

These, however, were the few bright spots in one of the gloomiest periods of the war for the British. In North Africa, the Army of the Nile, stripped of men and equipment for the Greek adventure, fell back upon Egypt in the face of a counterattack by the Afrika Korps. With the exception of Tobruk, all of Libya was soon in Rommel's hands. And on April 6, 1941, Hitler invaded Greece and Yugoslavia. Both countries were rapidly overrun, and within two weeks the fifty-eight thousand British, Commonwealth, and Polish troops so laboriously transported to Greece had to be withdrawn under intense enemy fire.

The evacuation—code-named Operation Demon—began on April 24. Although the number of troops to be rescued totaled only one-

---

*Churchill had a perverse fascination with the suicidal use of battleships. During the Normandy invasion, he proposed that one be run aground on the beaches, for use as a fort. Cunningham, then First Sea Lord, vetoed the venture.

fifth of those taken off at Dunkirk, vexing problems confronted Admiral Pridham-Wippell, who was in charge of the operation. The Luftwaffe controlled the skies over Greece and the adjacent seas; the sea passage was longer, and there were no well-equipped bases nearby where the ships could replenish ammunition and supplies or be repaired. German bombing had wrecked the main Greek port of Piraeus, and the troops had to be lifted from six beaches scattered about the deeply indented southern coast. For the task, Pridham-Wippell flung together a force of seven cruisers, twenty destroyers, twenty-one transports, and sundry small craft.

The operation continued over six nights without air cover. Troops due for evacuation would be assembled in the vicinity of the appointed beach, keeping well out of sight during daylight. After dark, they waded out from the open beaches to small boats, which carried them to the transports and destroyers lying offshore. To avoid air attack, the rescue ships were ordered not to approach the beaches until after dark and to be away from the coast by 0300. Nevertheless, casualties among the ships, especially the transports, were heavy. The Luftwaffe sank or damaged twenty-six ships during the evacuation, including five hospital ships.

The Dutch steamer *Slamat* was caught by Stukas in daylight and promptly sunk. Two British destroyers took off seven hundred troops, but they were also bombed and sent to the bottom. Only a single officer, forty-one sailors, and eight soldiers survived from all three ships. Some units were cut off by the rapidity of the German advance; seven thousand men were captured at Kalamata, to the north of Cape Matapan, before they could be taken off. Yet the soldiers had a blind faith that the navy would come to their rescue. One young New Zealander vividly recalled his feelings when, after crossing the mountains, his unit reached the sea. "With a torch we flashed an S.O.S., and to our tremendous relief, we received an answer. It was the Navy on the job—the Navy for which we had been hoping and praying all along the route."

The embarkation beaches were unmolested during the night, because the Italian fleet, still paralyzed by Matapan, failed to intervene. In all, over fifty thousand troops were evacuated from Greece, although their tanks, trucks, and artillery were left behind. The remnants of the Greek navy—a cruiser, six destroyers, and four submarines—escaped to join the British at Alexandria. "I feel the episode is one for which the Royal Navy and Merchant Navy can look with pride," Cunningham said. Most of the troops were taken to Egypt, but an unlucky sixteen thousand soldiers of a half-dozen nationalities were diverted to Crete, only forty miles from southern Greece—and the next Axis target. Hitler decided to attack the island because he was worried the RAF would use it as a base to strike the Romanian oil fields, source of nearly half Germany's oil supply.

Following the Greek debacle,* the British land, sea, and air commanders in the eastern Mediterranean unanimously recommended the abandonment of Crete, yet Churchill insisted that Crete must be stubbornly defended. In view of the Luftwaffe's control of the air, the inability to re-equip the beaten and disorganized troops landed from Greece, and the failure during six months of British occupation to improve the island's defenses, the decision smacked of the purest folly.

The Germans began the campaign for Crete with five days of ferocious bombing in which the handful of British planes based at Máleme, the island's airfield, were wiped out. Once again, the troops were condemned to endure the agony of relentless dive-bombing by seemingly inexhaustible numbers of German aircraft. On May 20, this softening-up process was followed by history's first airborne invasion.

Shortly before dawn, nearly five hundred Ju-52 transports dropped stick after stick of paratroopers on Crete from an altitude of four hundred feet. The sky was filled with green, yellow, red, and white parachutes, lending a macabre festivity to the scene. Other planes towed huge troop-carrying gliders, which were cut loose to swoop silently

---

*In the interlude between the Greek and Cretan campaigns, Churchill, responding to a plea from General Wavell for more tanks, unhesitatingly stripped the army in Britain of its armor, and, despite grave misgivings by the Admiralty, pushed a fast convoy of five ships (Operation Tiger) through the Mediterranean. No such effort had been made since the Luftwaffe had disabled *Illustrious*. Despite mines and German bombers, four of the ships arrived safely in Alexandria, with an infusion of 238 tanks and forty-three crated Hurricanes. Under Churchill's prodding, however, Wavell sent the tanks into battle before his army was ready to take the offensive, and ninety-nine of them were lost in an abortive offensive in June 1941. See Roskill, *The War at Sea*, vol. I, p. 437; Churchill, *The Second World War*, vol. III, pp. 218–20.

down on the island. Following a bitter struggle the Máleme airfield was captured by the Germans, and more Ju-52s began landing, one every minute, each disgorging forty fully armed soldiers. Some twenty-two thousand German troops were brought in by air, and although many were killed and injured in crashes on landing, they secured a foothold on the island.

To bar seaborne reinforcements from reaching the island, Cunningham deployed his cruisers and destroyers to sweep the waters between Greece and Crete at night. They shelled enemy positions and broke up convoys carrying troops and the invasion force's tanks and artillery. *Formidable* and the remainder of the battle fleet provided general support from south of the island, with the battleships being used as floating anti-aircraft batteries. Captain Lord Louis Mountbatten, whose destroyer flotilla participated in these night operations, later recalled: "After pouring a barrage of 4.7-inch shells on German-held positions, we turned our guns on some Greek fishing vessels packed solid with supplies and German troops. . . . It was an absolute massacre. None of that group of vessels survived, and not one German soldier arrived by sea of the thousands who embarked from the Greek mainland."

But the Luftwaffe exacted its revenge. Cunningham's ships were savagely attacked by dive- and high-level bombers for hours on end. Only darkness offered respite from this unrelenting assault, but the early-summer days were long and the skies dazzlingly bright. Lacking air cover, the ships had to depend upon concentrated anti-aircraft fire for protection and quickly ran low on ammunition and fuel. Some were reduced to firing practice shells. The crews were exhausted, and the toll of vessels sunk or severely damaged mounted ominously. "I shall never forget the sight of those ships coming up harbor, the guns of their fore-turrets awry, one or two broken off and pointing forlornly skyward," Cunningham noted with dismay as one flotilla limped back to Alexandria.

Crete recalled the Norwegian fiasco. In both cases, the navy had been pressed at short notice, as a result of Churchill's grandiose strategy, to carry ill-prepared military forces to theaters far removed from its bases, and then to bring back the survivors. In both cases, cruisers and destroyers operating close inshore in support of the troops bore the brunt of the German air attack. But in sheer magnitude, the weight of fire directed against the ships off Crete dwarfed the Norwegian episode. Norway clearly showed that a fleet could not operate within range of a powerful land-based air force unless protected by its own aircraft. Greece and Crete confirmed it. Admiral Cunningham later observed that three squadrons of fighters would have been enough to save Crete.

On the island itself, British defenses crumbled and an evacuation began on the evening of May 28. Some 16,500 of the 22,000-man garrison were lifted off over the next three nights, but on the way back to Egypt the ships were prime targets for the Stukas. One bomb exploded on the crowded mess deck of *Orion* and killed or wounded 562 crewmen and soldiers. Other ships suffered equally severe casualties. When his staff bemoaned the heavy cost entailed in the rescue mission, Cunningham bluntly told them: "It takes the Navy three years to build a ship. It would take three hundred years to rebuild a tradition."

Tradition was maintained, but the cost of defending Crete and the rescue operation equaled that of a great sea battle. Three cruisers and six destroyers* were sunk; *Formidable*, three battleships, six cruisers, and seven destroyers were put out of action. Some two thousand officers and sailors lost their lives, and another six hundred were wounded.

So the first year of the war in the Mediterranean ended with the tide running strongly in favor of the Axis. Rommel's tanks were advancing across the Western Desert toward the Suez Canal; the Mediterranean Fleet had been crippled and deprived of its only carrier; German airfields on Crete now outflanked the thousand-mile-long British supply line from Alexandria to Malta—and as Malta staggered under a German and Italian bombing, the Axis supply line to North Africa became more secure. Yet the Royal Navy's sacrifices off Greece and Crete had not been in vain. Hitler's timetable for the invasion of the Soviet Union was upset; Operation Barbarossa did not begin until June 22, 1941—and five weeks of good weather had been lost.

---

*Including Mountbatten's *Kelly*, which was the model for the destroyer in Noël Coward's wartime film on the Royal Navy, *In Which We Serve*.

•

CHAPTER 5

"A Triple *Sieg Heil* to Our *Bismarck!*"

Captain Theodor Krancke leaned over the wing of the bridge of the pocket battleship *Admiral Scheer* to watch as her Arado floatplane was catapulted into the lowering North Atlantic sky. It was 0940 on November 5, 1940, and his ship had just slipped unseen through the Denmark Strait, between Iceland and Greenland, crashing into seas so violent that two crewmen had been washed overboard. *Scheer* had undergone an intensive refit since the Norwegian operation, including the removal of the heavily armored fighting mast that had been a distinctive feature. Her silhouette now resembled that of most German warships, which made accurate identification more difficult, a plus for a raider. She had also been fitted with the latest radar. B-Dienst had informed Krancke of the sailing of Convoy HX 84 of thirty-seven ships from Halifax on October 27, and the pilot had been ordered to search for it.

Three hours later, the Arado returned, touched down on the rough sea beside the raider, and was quickly hoisted on board. Hastening to the bridge, the pilot reported that he had found the convoy about eighty-eight sea miles to the southwest, in almost the center of the main North Atlantic route between Newfoundland and Ireland. There was no sign of a heavy escort. The pocket battleship leaped ahead at full speed, her eight sets of diesels humming and her bow throwing off a huge wave.

The extensive damage suffered by the Kriegsmarine during the Norwegian campaign had been repaired, and Admiral Raeder and the Naval Staff seized the opportunity to strike at Britain's lifeline with their surface warships as well as the U-boats. With bases on the Norwegian and French coasts in German hands, the strategic position in the Atlantic offered "exceptionally favorable possibilities for waging war against the enemy's ocean communications," Raeder declared. Moreover, Hitler was thinking of occupying Gibraltar, and there was talk of bases in the Azores, the Canaries, and the Cape Verde Islands.

Admiral Scheer had been preceded to sea by several armed merchant raiders that had already sunk considerable enemy tonnage, and other heavy warships were being readied to join in the struggle. *Admiral Hipper*, in fact, had made an attempt to get to sea the previous month, but had developed engine trouble. *Gneisenau* and *Scharnhorst* were being prepared to break out, and the powerful new battleship *Bismarck* and the heavy cruiser *Prinz Eugen*, which were working up in the Baltic, were to join them as soon as they were ready. Work had begun again on the aircraft carrier *Graf Zeppelin*, and *Tirpitz*, Germany's other battleship, was nearing completion.

Little more than an hour after retrieving her aircraft, *Scheer* encountered a British steamer, the *Mopan*, sailing independently of the convoy. Wary that she might be a decoy, Krancke ordered his gunners to sink her before she could get off "RRR"—the signal for an attack by a surface raider. *Scheer* pressed on after stopping only long enough to pick up survivors, and at 1630 lookouts sighted the masts of a convoy. Then, one by one, the hulls of the merchantmen rose over the horizon, huddling together for protection. As the pocket battleship approached, bow-on at high speed, a signal light flickered anxiously from a large vessel with the towering superstructure of a passenger liner that hauled out of line and interposed herself between the oncoming *Scheer* and the convoy: "What ship?"

Krancke, certain this vessel was an armed merchant cruiser, stood in toward her in silence with the intention of closing the range, then about fifteen miles, so he could make quick work of her and then pounce on the convoy. On the other side, Captain Edward S. F. Fegen, skipper of the onetime liner *Jervis Bay*, realized that the oncoming vessel was an enemy and fired a sheaf of red rockets—the signal for his flock to make smoke and scatter. Having radioed an alarm, he moved with doomed gallantry toward the enemy ship so his handful of six-inch guns would have some effect. Because of the shortage of escorts, *Jervis Bay* was the convoy's sole defense. When the two vessels were about ten miles apart, Krancke turned to port to bring all six of his eleven-inch guns to bear and opened fire.

Outgunned and outclassed, *Jervis Bay* was methodically shot to pieces while the raider's 5.9-inch secondary battery concentrated on a nearby tanker. Salvo after salvo cut down men at their posts, shattered steel bulkheads, and started numerous fires that blazed out of control. Nevertheless, Fegen did his best to keep his ship between *Scheer* and the fleeing convoy. The first German shell tore off one of his legs and smashed the other. A surgeon bandaged the stump, and Fegen remained on the bridge until it was destroyed and the midships guns knocked out. He dragged himself aft to the stern gun and directed its fire until *Jervis Bay* sank under the relentless German bombardment, with her ensign still flying. Captain Fegen and two hundred crewmen went down with their ship, and he was awarded a posthumous Victoria Cross.

This hopeless struggle lasted only twenty-two minutes but won invaluable time for the convoy. It scattered in the smoke and fading light, and Krancke was able to overtake and sink only five ships and damage three others before nightfall ended the chase.* Heavy units of the British fleet drawn by *Jervis Bay*'s signals were likely to converge on the area soon, and he decided to put as much distance as possible between himself and any pursuers.

Krancke had achieved his goal, however. The presence of a German pocket battleship in the North Atlantic created chaos in the British convoy system. It was shut down for twelve days, and for an entire week not a single convoy reached Britain—a far more serious affair than the sinking of a few merchantmen. All major convoys had to be held up until protection by a battleship had been arranged,

---

*One of the damaged ships, the tanker *San Demetrio*, provided an epic of its own. Set afire by *Scheer*'s gunfire, she was abandoned, but was found again the next day by part of her crew, still burning but afloat. They reboarded the ship, put out the flames, and sailed her to England, with much of her precious cargo of oil still intact, even though they had no compass, charts, or navigational instruments. The incident was later the subject of a book and a movie.

which meant valuable shipping days were lost. Five capital ships were deployed to block the passages to and from the North Atlantic— all to deal with a single raider.

As for *Scheer*, apprised by B-Dienst of enemy movements, she steamed southward, making for the shipping lane between the Azores and the West Indies. She sank two ships before moving into the South Atlantic, where she captured the refrigerator ship *Duquesa*, which was crammed with meat, eggs, and tons of tinned provisions. Krancke took her along with him as a floating larder, and steamed into the Indian Ocean at the turn of the year. Wearing British-style warpaint, *Scheer* pretended to be a Royal Navy cruiser and approached her prey bows-on with two of her three guns raised and the other depressed, to give the impression of dual turrets.

Once, *Scheer* sighted two ships simultaneously, one Dutch and the other British, which provided Krancke with a dilemma. He decided to take the Dutchman first. Having bluffed the crew into believing the pocket battleship was a British cruiser, he dispatched a boarding party which took her without a single shot. The captain of the other vessel also thought she was British, and not until his ship was boarded did they realize that their visitors wore German-navy uniforms. Not long after, in February 1941, *Scheer* turned homeward.[*] She had been at sea for 161 days and accounted for sixteen ships totaling ninety-nine thousand tons. This was the most successful cruise by a regular warship of the modern German navy, and showed what excellent high-seas commerce raiders the pocket battleships could be—if handled properly, and kept beyond the range of enemy land-based aircraft.

The half-dozen disguised auxiliary cruisers—the "ghost ships"— which preceded *Admiral Scheer* to sea, broke out between the end of March and mid-July 1940.[†] Averaging about seven to eight thousand tons each, although some were smaller, these marauders were ex–fruit

---

[*]When *Scheer*'s crew learned that the Führer had awarded Krancke the Knight's Cross of the Iron Cross, the machine shop made a replica of the decoration, which he wore proudly.

[†]The Italians sent one raider to sea, *Ramb I*, which was sunk by a British cruiser shortly after departing Massowa, on the Horn of Africa, without taking a single prize.

steamers or similar craft and were chosen for their wartime assignments because of their endurance, speed, and a nondescript appearance which allowed them to play the role of innocent cargo vessel while approaching intended victims. Each, however, was a floating Pandora's box of nasty tricks. They were armed with six to eight modern 5.9-inch guns hidden behind hinged steel plates, machine guns, two to six torpedo tubes, a stock of mines, and one or two fold-up spotter aircraft. Two raiders carried small motor-torpedo boats.

Back in 1914, Winston Churchill had described Admiral Graf von Spee's Pacific raiding squadron as "a cut flower in a vase, fair to see yet bound to die," because it had no resources to fall back upon, but this did not apply to the armed merchant raiders of 1940–41. They drew upon the Etappendienst network of supply ships, tankers, and captured supplies.* They made use of remote Japanese-held islands in the Pacific to refit, even before Japan entered the war. To disguise themselves, they often were repainted, sported dummy funnels, telescoping masts, and fake deck houses, flew false flags, and broadcast bogus "attacked-by-pocket battleship" signals to confuse the British. A raider captain lured unsuspecting victims within range of his guns by dressing part of his crew as female passengers; one wheeled a baby carriage along the boat deck.

With their ships at sea for extremely long periods—*Atlantis*, for example, was at sea for nine months, during which her crew did not set foot on land—raider captains made a major effort to maintain morale. Food was of the best quality, and the same fare was served both officers and men. Luxuries found on prizes were shared out equally among them. Sometimes there was a ship's newspaper which printed radio reports, and word of promotions and other good news for crewmen was played up. Courses in mathematics, history, and English were taught by more or less qualified officers and enlisted men. There were amateur theatricals, band concerts, and sing-alongs. One skipper established a system of "leave-on-board" in which crew members had eight or twelve days off with no duties unless the ship went into action.

The first evidence the British had of this new element in the naval

---

*The tanker *Nordmark* remained in an isolated area of ocean some 600 miles to the north of Tristan da Cunha where she made her services available to the raiders.

war was the arrival on July 18, 1940, at a West Indian island of the survivors of two merchant ships, who reported their vessels had been sunk by a disguised German raider. Because of its commitments to the U-boat war and the struggle in the Mediterranean, the Royal Navy was unable to reintroduce the powerful hunting groups formed to search for *Graf Spee* the previous year. All that could be done was to establish convoys for troop ships and to patrol the focal points of shipping with a grab bag of light cruisers and merchant cruisers.

British intelligence about the raiders was woefully vague and contradictory, and losses caused by them were often attributed to U-boats or the normal hazards of the sea. When one of these vessels finally assumed an identity, it was given a letter designation ("Raider A," etc.) in the order in which it was discovered rather than in which it had sailed. To add to the confusion, the Germans gave them ship numbers as well as names. Thus, *Atlantis*, which was known to the British as Raider C, was *Schiff 16* to the Germans. The raiders did not attack convoys but targeted ships sailing independently, often springing upon them at night or in poor visibility. As soon as one area became too dangerous, they changed disguise and shifted to new hunting grounds. Before their heyday had passed at the end of 1941, these ships sent almost six hundred thousand tons of shipping to the bottom. Although not intended to engage in stand-up fights, one raider sank an Australian light cruiser. Another sent an armed merchant cruiser to the bottom and put two others out of action.

Atlantis, the first and most successful raider, left Germany the last day of March 1940, under the command of Captain Bernhard Rogge, who had previously been in charge of the Kriegsmarine's two sail-training ships. She was followed by *Orion, Widder, Thor, Pinguin,* and *Komet. Komet* made the most remarkable debut of all. Unlike the other marauders, which had scudded through the Denmark Strait and other passages into the Atlantic, she passed around the North Cape of Norway. With a pair of Russian icebreakers, *Lenin* and *Stalin,* opening the way, she made a two-month voyage along the coast of Siberia into the Bering Sea and the Pacific.*

Once out on the open sea, Rogge headed immediately for the busy

---

*The German government paid the Russians about $300,000 for this service.

Freetown-Capetown shipping route, where in the guise of a Japanese freighter he sank his first victim on May 3. After laying mines off Cape Agulhas, at the southernmost tip of Africa, Rogge, who believed a raider's best defense was unexpected appearances at widely separated places, steamed into the Indian Ocean. Now pretending to be a Dutch cargo steamer, *Atlantis* captured a Norwegian tanker on June 10, and sent her in as a prize to a port in western France with all the prisoners captured up to that time. The tanker was torpedoed by a British submarine off the French coast.

Orion (Raider A), which followed *Atlantis* to sea, rounded Cape Horn in mid-June and after crossing the South Pacific laid 228 mines off Auckland, New Zealand. Three ships fell victim to these mines, one of them the steamer *Niagara*, which was carrying ten tons of gold ingots valued at £2.5 million.* Steaming north to the Japanese-held Marshall Islands, *Orion* rendezvoused with *Komet* (Raider B). Together, the two ships attacked the phosphate island of Nauru on December 7–8. The sea was running too high for them to put a landing party ashore, so the Germans sank five ships lying off the island and steamed away. Returning to Japanese territory, they landed about five hundred prisoners on a remote island, from which they were soon rescued.

Orion, which had been at sea for 268 days, was badly in need of a refit, so she shifted to the Marianas, where, with two supply ships in attendance, she underwent repairs. *Komet* returned to Nauru and on December 27 carried out the postponed attack. A phosphate plant and some oil tanks were destroyed, and a loading pier was put out of commission, thus interrupting British fertilizer production for several months. *Komet* next headed south, operated in New Zealand waters, and then steamed into the Indian Ocean to meet *Pinguin* (Raider F), which had sailed from Germany in mid-June.†

Unlike the raiders that had preceded her to sea, *Widder* (Raider D) operated mostly in the Central Atlantic and adjacent areas. From the

---

*The *Niagara* sank in 438 feet of water, but a large part of her valuable cargo was recovered by divers despite strong currents and the fact that the salvage operation took place in the middle of a minefield. The story is a classic tale of its kind. For a full account, see R. J. Dunn, *Niagara Gold*.

†*Pinguin* later ventured into the Antarctic, the home of her namesake, and destroyed the Allied whaling fleet in those waters.

time of her breakout in mid-May and return to Brest at the end of October, she sank or captured ten ships totaling 58,645 tons. Most were tankers being independently routed between the Caribbean oil ports and West Africa or Gibraltar. In contrast to most of the raider captains, who were ruthless in ensuring the safety of their ships without being brutal, Captain Helmuth von Rucktescell, *Widder*'s skipper and later skipper of *Michel* (Raider H), was convicted of war crimes by a British tribunal in 1947. He was accused of continuing to shell enemy ships after they had heaved to, and was less than scrupulous in attempting to pick up survivors. One witness testified that *Widder* had shelled a lifeboat as it pulled away from a sinking ship.

The fourth raider out, *Thor*, worked continuously in the Atlantic. A onetime banana boat, she was, at 3,144 tons, among the smallest of the raiders, but lived up to her name. Under the command of Captain Otto Kahler (who, like Rogge, had captained sail-training ships), *Thor* quickly bagged six victims in the Central and South Atlantic. On July 28, while some six hundred miles off the coast of Brazil, she sighted what appeared to be a large passenger vessel and investigated her. Kahler was alarmed, however, when the ship swung toward *Thor*. Suspecting she was an armed merchant cruiser, he turned away at full speed.

Thor had a lead of ten miles, but her pursuer, which proved to be the auxiliary cruiser *Alcantara*, gained steadily upon the raider. Realizing that he could not outrun her, Kahler accepted the inevitable and, as soon as the range had dropped to seven miles, swung his ship across the bow of the enemy vessel, raised his gun flaps, broke out a battle flag, and opened fire. *Thor* fired rapidly and well; the British gunners, facing into the sun, had difficulty in finding the target. A German shell severed one of *Alcantara*'s steam lines, and she slowly lost way, eventually stopping dead in the water. Kahler later reported that he would have liked to have finished off the enemy vessel, but, wary of receiving a crippling hit, he steamed away.

Four months later, on December 5, *Thor* sighted another large vessel, off the River Plate. Kahler correctly suspected that she was *Carnarvon Castle*, also an auxiliary cruiser. Heavy fog lay on the sea, and the Germans tried to slip back into the mists, but once again the British overhauled them. Kahler fired two torpedoes, which missed, and then opened fire at a range of less than four miles. *Thor* fired so rapidly that some salvos were only six seconds apart, and her guns got so hot they jammed. Badly mauled, listing, and on fire, *Carnarvon Castle* broke off the action without having scored a single hit on the German vessel and headed for Montevideo for repairs. Ironically, the patches to her hull were made from plates salvaged from the wreck of *Graf Spee*.

Thor needed to replenish her bunkers and stores of ammunition, so Kahler headed for a prearranged South Atlantic rendezvous with a supply ship, and on Christmas morning they were joined by *Admiral Scheer* in company with *Duquesa*. Captain Krancke shared out his loot with the grateful Kahler. While the pocket battleship's floatplane kept watch against the approach of the enemy, they discussed plans for the two raiders to operate together. But it was agreed that the twenty-six-knot *Scheer* would be severely handicapped if she had to tailor her speed to that of the much slower *Thor*. The ships parted and independently continued their depredations against British commerce.

On April 4, 1941, *Thor* was off the Cape Verde Islands when she encountered *Voltaire*, another British merchant cruiser. "We hit with our first salvo," Kahler reported in his war diary. ". . . Within three minutes of our opening fire . . . the enemy was heavily on fire amidships and from time to time she was completely covered in flames." With her steering gear damaged, she began steaming in circles as the German gunners hit her again and again. Less than a hour after the action began, *Voltaire* raised a white flag, and Kahler came as close as he dared to the burning ship to pick up survivors. In all, 197 men, including her captain, were rescued. Two weeks later, *Thor* turned homeward, and arrived at Hamburg on April 30, ending a voyage of 329 days in which she had sunk twelve ships totaling 96,547 tons.

Elated by the success of *Admiral Scheer* and the armed merchant raiders, Admiral Raeder decided to escalate surface operations against enemy commerce. He used these successes to obtain approval from Hitler, who since the loss of *Graf Spee* was reluctant to risk his heavy ships as commerce raiders. The Grand Admiral envisioned a powerful battle squadron that could annihilate any convoy, no matter what the escort. Until it was assembled, the Kriegsmarine would have to send its warships to sea as they became ready while the raiders continued to harry Britain's seaborne trade.

Balky engines repaired,* *Hipper* put out to sea on November 30, 1940, and passed unseen through the Denmark Strait. She was followed a few days later by *Kormoran* (Raider G), the first of what the Germans called the "second wave" of six merchant raiders.† On Christmas Day, *Hipper* made contact with Troop Convoy WS 5A, twenty ships carrying reinforcements to the Middle East, about seven hundred miles west of Cape Finisterre. She moved in to attack but was surprised to find the convoy defended by three cruisers as well as the carrier *Furious*. The Germans were driven off after a brisk gun duel in which the heavy cruiser *Berwick* and two transports were slightly damaged. While *Hipper* sustained only light injury, her erratic machinery failed again, and she made for Brest, the first major German warship to use a French port.

Scharnhorst and *Gneisenau*—"Salmon" and "Gluckstein" to the Royal Navy—had also sortied out, on January 23, 1941, again under the command of Vice-Admiral Günther Lütjens, who had participated in the Norwegian operation. Forbidding in manner and with a permanent frown, the fifty-one-year-old Lütjens seldom showed emotion. With the example before him of his predecessor, Admiral Wilhelm Marschall, who had been dismissed as fleet commander for exercising his own discretion off Norway, he was rigorous in his attention to orders. Raeder, no longer content with merely dislocating the enemy's supply-and-convoy system, ordered him to concentrate on "the destruction of the shipping bound for Britain," but Lütjens's hands were tied by instructions not to risk his ships under any circumstances.

The battle cruisers headed for the Iceland-Faeroes passage but were detected by a picket line thrown out by the new commander-in-chief of the Home Fleet, Admiral Sir John Tovey, who had been warned to expect such a breakout. Superior radar enabled the Germans to avoid being brought to action by Tovey's battleships, and they steamed into the fog and ice floes of the Arctic to await an opportune moment to escape. As soon as the British returned to Scapa Flow to refuel, Lütjens slipped through the Denmark Strait and

---

**Hipper was far from ideally suited for work as a commerce raider. She was fitted with steam turbines that were constantly malfunctioning, rather than the reliable diesels propelling the pocket battleships. Moreover, she consumed fuel at an enormous rate, which gave her a short radius of operation.

†Including *Michel*, *Stier*, *Togo*, and second cruises by *Thor* and *Komet*.

turned south in search of Convoy HX 106, which, reported B-Dienst, had left Halifax at the end of January.

Balky engines repaired, *Hipper* had also gotten out again. On February 9, 1941, she was summoned by *U-37* to join in an attack on Gibraltar Convoy HG 53 along with five Focke-Wulf Condors. The U-boat and the planes had already sunk eight of the convoy's sixteen ships before the cruiser arrived to snap up a straggler. It was the first instance in which a U-boat, aircraft, and a surface warship mounted a combined attack on enemy shipping. Three days later, *Hipper* was working the convoy route from Sierra Leone to Britain when she sighted Convoy SLS 64, east of the Azores, and attacked with guns and torpedoes. Seven Allied ships totaling 32,806 tons were sunk, according to the Admiralty. Captain Wilhelm Meisel purposely left one vessel undamaged and flashed his parting instructions to it: "Save the crews." Fuel was running low, so the notoriously short-legged *Hipper* immediately returned to Brest, arriving with her bunkers almost empty.

Scharnhorst and *Gneisenau* sighted the smoke of HX 106 on February 8, and Lütjens maneuvered his ships to attack from the north and south. But the vague outline of what appeared to be a capital ship loomed out of the mist. She was identified as the veteran battleship *Ramillies*, the convoy's sole escort. Captain Kurt Hoffman of *Scharnhorst* suggested that he use his superior speed to draw off the enemy while *Gneisenau* dealt with the convoy, but Lütjens dared not engage; indeed, his orders forbade him to risk damage to his ships. Breaking off contact, he slipped away. Raeder's plan to force the British to use battleships to escort their convoys was working only too well, as far as Lütjens was concerned.

The battle cruisers moved on to westward and on February 22, only five hundred miles east of Newfoundland, fell upon several merchantmen which had recently dispersed from a westbound convoy. Five ships totaling 25,784 tons were sunk, but the Germans were unable to jam their reports of being under attack. Realizing the British would now be hot on his trail, Lütjens headed into the South Atlantic to try his luck off the bulge of Africa. On March 8, Convoy SL 67 was sighted about 350 miles to the north of the Cape Verde Islands, but Lütjens forbore to attack when he discovered it was covered by the battleship *Malaya*. Navy Group West, in Paris, was informed of the convoy's position, and two nearby U-boats were ordered to the scene. They sank five ships the next day. Lütjens returned to the Halifax route, sinking a lone merchantman on the way.

Using two of his supply ships to help in the search for targets, he covered a broad swath of ocean and encountered Convoy HX 114 on March 15 as it was dispersing. Over the next two days, the Germans sunk thirteen ships and captured three tankers, which were sent to German-held ports with prize crews. With the air thick with raider reports and appeals for help, Lütjens decided to make for home before he was found by the British. His worst nightmare was confirmed when he caught a fleeting glimpse of *Rodney*, but he eluded her. For his part, Admiral Tovey expected the Germans to try to get home through one or the other of the northern passages, and deployed the Home Fleet to block their triumphant return. But Lütjens shaped a course for Brest arriving there on March 22. He had bagged 115,622 tons of Allied shipping and completely disrupted the British convoy system.

Admiral Raeder hastened to congratulate the vessels' captains and crews, but Admiral Dönitz, the U-boat chief, was less impressed by the effectiveness of these operations. *Scharnhorst, Gneisenau,* and *Hipper* had accounted for forty-eight ships totaling some 270,000 tons. Did this match the toll inflicted upon the enemy month after month by his handful of submarines, at far less cost in materiel and manpower resources? Raeder, however, brushed off questions about skewed priorities and cost-effectiveness. He was planning an even bolder stroke against Allied commerce.

Toward midday on May 18, 1941, the gray bulk of *Bismarck* eased away from her pier at the Baltic naval base of Gydnia as her band played "Muss i denn," the traditional German military song of parting. This was clear evidence to the astute observer that the battleship, the very spirit of grace and power, was sailing on more than another training exercise. Launched in February 1939, *Bismarck* displaced fifty-two thousand tons, and her armor ranged from five to fourteen inches thick. She was 820 feet long and exceptionally broad, with a beam of 118 feet, which made her a very steady gun platform. On trials, she had made thirty knots. She carried eight fifteen-inch guns in four turrets and a secondary battery of twelve 5.9-inch guns as well as numerous anti-aircraft weapons.

For a few hours, she lay in the roadstead taking on last-minute supplies and topping off her bunkers, which carried eighty-seven hundred tons of fuel. Unfortunately, a fueling pipe ruptured and prevented the task from being completed—with dire consequences for the future. At 0200 the following morning, she weighed anchor, in company with several destroyers, and rendezvoused in the North Sea with *Prinz Eugen*. Four U-boats, two supply ships, and five tankers assigned to the operation had preceded her to sea. Operation Rheinübung (Exercise Rhine) had begun.

Originally, Raeder had planned to send *Scharnhorst* and *Gneisenau* to sea from Brest at the same time *Bismarck* and *Prinz Eugen* escaped from the Baltic. Each squadron would create opportunities for the other. *Bismarck* would distract the British capital ships, which would allow the battle cruisers to wreak havoc on the convoys. But *Gneisenau* and *Scharnhorst* were unavailable. Upon reaching Brest, they came under repeated attack by the RAF; the former was severely damaged by a torpedo strike by Coastal Command while the latter required a major engine-refit.[*] There was another setback when *Prinz Eugen* struck a magnetic mine on April 23, and two weeks of repairs were needed to make her shipshape.

Lütjens, appointed to command the operation, was pessimistic about its chances of success, because he thought the force too weak and *Bismarck* and *Prinz Eugen* grossly mismatched. Like her sister ship, *Admiral Hipper*, the cruiser lacked endurance and would be a drain on her consort. Lütjens urged that the breakout be delayed at least until *Scharnhorst* was operational again, or, even better, until *Tirpitz* was ready to sail. Raeder, however, wanted immediate action to keep the momentum of the Atlantic battle going. With the convoy system well established and more escorts available to the Royal Navy—including the fifty old American destroyers—the "Happy Time" of the U-boats was long over. The surface raiders would supply fresh impetus for the campaign against British trade.

Even more important, with the invasion of Russia about to begin, Raeder believed the army and the Luftwaffe would have top priority for resources unless the Kriegsmarine could produce some spectac-

---

[*]While in drydock undergoing repairs, *Gneisenau* took four bomb hits, adding to the damage.

ular victories of its own. Thus, Raeder's insistence on sending *Bismarck* to sea may have rested less upon strategic considerations than upon his wish to improve the navy's position in the bureaucratic struggle with the other services. Lütjens obviously thought so.

"I'd like to make my farewells, I'll never come back," the admiral gloomily told a friend. When the friend looked at him questioningly, he added: "Given the superiority of the British, survival is improbable."

Raeder found Hitler's reluctance to use heavy ships as commerce raiders more difficult to overcome. Skeptical of the successes claimed by Raeder for the surface warships, and with the Taranto raid in mind, he was worried about an attack upon the ships by carrier-based torpedo planes. After *Gneisenau* was torpedoed at Brest, he told his naval aide he had "seen it coming." Thus, the admiral did not inform the Führer of Rheinübung, and instructed Lütjens to say nothing about *Bismarck*'s impending departure when Hitler visited the ship on May 5. He appeared impressed by the vessel's formidable concentration of power and the dedication of her officers and men. But his misgivings were confirmed when Lütjens pointed out that, though *Bismarck* needed fear no other capital ship, there was a threat from enemy carriers and their torpedo planes.

Secrecy was essential to the success of the operation. Once the Royal Navy knew *Bismarck* was at sea, the far superior forces of the Home Fleet would be concentrated against her. The British were unaware that the battleship and her consort had sailed, although the Bletchley Park code breakers had detected increased Luftwaffe activity that pointed to a major naval operation. If a breakout was actually under way, it could not have come at a worse time. The British army had just been expelled from Greece, and the Royal Navy was bracing against an attack upon Crete. The Admiralty considered dispatching Force H from Gibraltar to support Admiral Cunningham's fleet in the eastern Mediterranean, but if *Bismarck* got out into the Atlantic that would be impossible.

Whatever doubt remained about her presence at sea was settled shortly after noon on May 20, when *Bismarck* was spotted in the Kattegat by the Swedish cruiser *Gotland*. By evening, word of the sighting had reached the British naval attaché in neutral Stockholm, who promptly relayed the news to London. The Admiralty surmised that the Germans were either on a raiding expedition against Iceland, which had been in British hands since Denmark had fallen under Nazi control, or, more likely a breakout into the Atlantic to prey upon ocean convoys.

Early the next day, the German task force anchored in Grimstadt-fjord, just to the south of Bergen, so *Prinz Eugen* could refuel. This stop was not part of the operational plan—the ships had been scheduled to refuel from a tanker already waiting to the north, in the Norwegian Sea—but Lütjens apparently decided that refueling now would give him flexibility of action. It was a major mistake. The ships remained all day in the fjord, bathed in bright sunshine, as if waiting to be discovered by the RAF—and about 1315 a photo-reconnaissance Spitfire snapped their picture. To compound this error, *Prinz Eugen* took on fuel but Lutjens, for some unexplained reason, failed to order *Bismarck* to top off her bunkers. She had sailed two hundred tons short of oil and had already used up eleven hundred tons. Considering the uncertainties of war at sea, Lütjens blundered first by stopping, and then by not taking the opportunity to refuel his flagship.

The next move in this deadly chess game was up to Admiral Tovey. At fifty-six, he had been in the Royal Navy since his appointment as a naval cadet at fifteen, and had commanded a destroyer at Jutland. Unlike Lütjens, he was brimming with self-confidence, was popular with subordinates and did not brook interference by superiors—which did not endear him to Prime Minister Churchill. Upon receiving word that *Bismarck* was in Norwegian waters, Tovey deduced that the Germans were breaking out and deployed his ships to watch the passages into the Atlantic. Once this was done, he could only wait and rely upon the RAF to keep him posted on the movements of the enemy task force.

The radar-fitted heavy cruiser *Norfolk*, flying the flag of Rear Admiral W. F. Wake-Walker, was placed on alert in the Denmark Strait, and *Suffolk*, which was fitted with more advanced surface-warning radar, was ordered to join her as soon as she had refueled.[*] Two light cruisers, *Birmingham* and *Manchester*, were guarding the

[*]Rheinübung had been launched under the supposition that British radar was primitive, and the Germans were unaware that the British picket ships were equipped with efficient search radar. See *Fuehrer Conferences on Naval Affairs*, p. 201.

Iceland-Faeroes gap. A squadron consisting of the battle cruiser *Hood* (flying the flag of Vice-Admiral Lancelot E. Holland), the newly commissioned battleship *Prince of Wales*, and six destroyers was sent to Hvalfjord, in Iceland, where they could cover both likely escape routes. Tovey remained at Scapa with his flagship, *King George V*, five cruisers and five destroyers with steam up, ready to move as soon as *Bismarck*'s movements became clearer. He received last-minute reinforcements when the Admiralty withdrew the battle cruiser *Repulse* and carrier *Victorious* from convoy-escort duty and ordered them to join him.

And then the worst happened, as far as the British were concerned. Foul weather closed in, and at 2300 on May 21, Lütjens slipped out to sea. Behind them, the Germans saw the fiery explosions of bombs dropped by the RAF on their former anchorage, welcome assurance that their departure had not been discovered. *Bismarck* and *Prinz Eugen* hurried northward at twenty-five knots toward the Denmark Strait as haze and overcast turned to fog and rain. Lütjens, hoping to clear the passage before the enemy learned his ships had left Bergen, passed up the opportunity to refuel from the tanker in the Norwegian Sea.

The vessels were steaming northward when Raeder finally informed the Führer of the sortie. Hitler "expressed lively misgivings" when he heard of the operation, the admiral wrote in his memoirs. These rather guarded words suggest Hitler was more than a little angered by Raeder's conspiracy of silence, for the admiral added: "I did my best to soothe his anxiety and explained that Naval Operations Command had the highest expectations of the operation, whereupon he agreed that it should continue." Nevertheless, relations between the Führer and his navy chief soured over this lack of frankness.

In the meantime, dirty weather had settled in, and both Tovey and Lütjens were let down by their aerial reconnaissance. Throughout most of May 22, British pilots were unable to determine whether or not the German ships were still in the fjord. On the other side, a Luftwaffe pilot who flew over Scapa Flow mistakenly reported that the Home Fleet had not left its base, when, in reality, *Hood* and *Prince of Wales* had already sailed for Iceland. For Tovey it was a day of tortured anxiety, and his customary good humor was put to the test.

Where were the German ships? Were they at sea or holed up in the fjord? Or were they on the way back to Germany?

These questions were not resolved until that evening, when a Fleet Air Arm reconnaissance plane, flying at little more than wave-top altitude above the North Sea, penetrated the fjord to discover that the birds had flown the coop. Within three hours of receiving this report, Tovey was heading westward in *King George V* toward the passages into the Atlantic, while the Germans were preparing to turn west to round Iceland and steer into the Denmark Strait. With *Bismarck* now definitely known to be at sea, frantic steps also had to be taken to protect the eleven convoys either in the Atlantic or preparing to sail, including a Clyde-to-Cape troop convoy carrying twenty thousand men. Force H was ordered up from Gibraltar to escort it.

The Denmark Strait is only about thirty to forty miles wide during that time of year, and bounded by the Greenland ice-edge on one side and a British-laid minefield on the other. Hugging the pack-ice throughout May 23, Lütjens hoped rain and heavy mist would cover his ships. But *Suffolk* was on the alert, her radar and lookouts cease-lessly scanning the horizon. At 1922, Able Seaman Newall, the star-board after lookout, sighted a great black shape looming out of a snow squall, no more than seven miles away. "Ship bearing green one-four-oh!" he reported. Then a second vessel appeared, only to vanish like the first. One of *Suffolk*'s officers observed:

> The enemy ships were moving fast in a southwesterly direction, parallel to our own. 'Action Stations' was immediately piped, full-speed rung to the engine room, and a sharp alteration of course made away into the enveloping mist as the first of a stream of sighting reports was sent out. . . . About an hour later HMS *Norfolk* joined us and began to shadow too. The pursuit was roughly parallel to the coast of Greenland.

Unpleasantly surprised to discover that the British cruisers had sophisticated surface-warning radar, Lütjens tried to shake them off in the murk by firing several salvos, which damaged his own forward radar. The cruisers scuttled away and maintained their flickering radar contacts. *Suffolk*'s sighting signal was picked up by Admiral Holland, three hundred miles due south of the German ships, but Tovey, some six hundred miles to the southeast, was unaware of these dramatic events until he received a report from Admiral Wake-Walker in *Norfolk* an hour later. Holland sped south through the night at twenty-four knots, which would put *Hood* and *Prince of Wales* in position to intercept the Germans early on the morning of May 24.

Unfortunately, these were the ships of Tovey's fleet least suited to challenge *Bismarck*. Although *Hood* and *Bismarck* each mounted eight fifteen-inch guns, and *Prince of Wales* had ten fourteen-inch, the British vessels were outclassed. *Hood* was the Royal Navy's most famous ship, but she was more than twenty years old and had not been modernized. Like all British battle cruisers, she had sacrificed protection for speed, and her lightly armored decks were particularly vulnerable to long-range plunging fire. *Bismarck*, on the other hand, was one of the best-protected battleships afloat, and was at peak efficiency.* As some writers have observed, an encounter between the two ships was like a duel between a modern jet fighter and a World War I fabric-and-wood biplane. For her part, *Prince of Wales* was still suffering from teething troubles. Numerous dockyard workers were on board, trying to adjust her guns and turret machinery, which frequently jammed.

The two task forces hurtled toward each other on a converging course at a combined speed of sixty miles an hour when, at 0537, *Prince of Wales* flashed the signal ENEMY IN SIGHT DISTANCE 17 MILES. Holland had made a perfect intercept, but he quickly lost his advantage. He led his line with *Hood*, rather than placing the better-armored *Prince of Wales* in the van, where she would have drawn the brunt of enemy fire. And, in defiance of a lesson learned at Jutland, he kept his two ships clustered close together (six hundred yards apart) and maneuvered them as a single unit, which made it easier for the German gunners to target them, rather than calling for open order (one thousand yards).

Holland swung the vessels toward the Germans, racing in bows-on, fine on the enemy's port bow, in an effort to shorten the range quickly so the flat trajectory of the German shells would strike *Hood*'s heavier, side armor instead of plunging through her inadequately protected decks. But this meant that only the forward turrets of his ships would

Bismarck's main deck armor was 7¾ inch, *Hood*'s only 3¾.

bear, reducing the guns in action to four fifteen-inch on *Hood* and six fourteen-inch on *Prince of Wales*—and one of these was malfunctioning—while they faced a full enemy broadside. Nor was this all. *Prinz Eugen* was leading *Bismarck*, and Holland, because of the similarity in the profiles of the German vessels, mistook her for the battleship and ordered his ships to concentrate their fire on the cruiser.[*]

Prince of Wales's gunnery officer recognized the mistake and on his own initiative shifted his fourteen-inch guns to *Bismarck*. Although Holland quickly realized his error and ordered both ships to "Shift target right," his fire-control officer apparently did not receive the order, and *Hood*'s guns remained targeted on *Prinz Eugen*. Holland gave the order to open fire at 0553, at a range of 26,500 yards; *Prince of Wales* followed a half-minute later.

"The *Hood*—it's the *Hood!*"

Lütjens was surprised by the unexpected appearance of the enemy vessels, and thought the dim shapes on the horizon were the shadowing cruisers until an officer in the foretop fire-control station identified the closest of the onrushing ships as the famous battle cruiser. Tension rippled through *Bismarck*, for she had been their paper adversary in countless training exercises. The other ship was thought to be *King George V.*[†] *Bismarck*'s turrets swung around, and the muzzles of her guns lifted. Except for the sound of the breaking sea and the crackle of orders and reports, a great silence engulfed the ship.

"The clock showed 0553," Kapitänleutnant Burkard Baron von Mullenheim-Rechberg, whose station was in *Bismarck*'s after fire-control center, later recalled. "The range, I figured, was less than 20,000 meters. There were flashes like lightning out there! Still approaching nearly bow-on, the enemy had opened fire. *Donnerwetter!* . . . Certain that we would immediately return the fire, I braced myself for 'Permission to fire' and the thunder of our guns that would follow. Nothing happened. We in the after station looked at one another in bewilderment. Why weren't we doing something?"

---

[*]Earlier, Holland had planned to have *Norfolk* and *Suffolk* engage *Prinz Eugen*, but once the battle started he failed to issue such orders and the two cruisers took no part in the action.

[†]The Germans believed *Prince of Wales* was not yet operational.

For some unknown reason, Lütjens hesitated to open fire, and the tension-laden seconds seemed to stretch into minutes. There was no response, as the first British shells fell about the German ships. *Bismarck*'s captain, Ernst Lindemann, anxiously awaited the signal, and finally could restrain himself no longer. "I will not let my ship be shot out from under my ass," he muttered as he went to the intercom and commanded: "Permission to fire!"

Both German ships concentrated on *Hood*, and their shooting was remarkably good. *Bismarck*'s first salvo exploded in the water ahead of *Hood*, the second fell astern, and the third straddled her, engulfing the vessel in leaping columns of seawater as the fifteen-inch shells exploded about her. At about this time, an eight-inch round from *Prinz Eugen* hit her at the base of the foremast, touching off some UP (unrotated projectile) anti-aircraft rockets.* A spectacular fire spread rapidly along the deck to the thin steel ready-use four-inch ammunition lockers, which exploded, adding to the conflagration.

In contrast, the British ships had trouble finding the range. *Prince of Wales* was dogged by machinery failures; her first salvo was well wide of *Bismarck*, and she did not get a straddle until the sixth salvo. *Hood*, her fire-control stations handicapped by antiquated equipment and the spray thrown up by the ship's high-speed approach, and apparently still mistakenly aiming at *Prinz Eugen*, scored no hits. Undeterred, Holland pressed ahead, and at 0600, with the range reduced to some eighteen thousand yards, ordered a course change to unmask his full broadside. At the same moment, *Bismarck* fired her fourth salvo.

"We started turning round to port [and] were hit somewhere and the ship shook all over and lot of debris and bodies began falling all over the decks," reported Able Seaman Robert Tilburn. One or more German shells had hit forward of *Hood*'s after turrets, penetrated the thinly armored deck, and exploded somewhere inside the ship, probably in the four-inch magazine, which set off a flash that spread in

---

*UP rockets were the brainchild of Professor Frederick Lindemann (later Lord Cherwell), one of Churchill's favorites. They were mortar-type weapons that fired a seventy-six-millimeter rocket into the air that, once it reached a certain altitude, released a parachute with a mine attached. The mine was supposed to explode among groups of attacking aircraft. The weapon proved to be useless in combat and, following the loss of *Hood*, was removed from all Royal Navy warships.

seconds down to the after fifteen-inch magazine. The battle cruiser erupted with a tremendous roar, and a huge black mushroom cloud, tinged with orange and red, shot upward into the sky.*

"She's blowing up!" shouted someone in *Bismarck*'s after fire-control station, and Mullenheim-Rechberg rushed over to the port director. He never forgot the sight that met his eyes:

> At first the *Hood* was nowhere to be seen; in her place was a colossal pillar of black smoke. . . . Gradually, at the foot of the pillar, I made out the bow of the battle cruiser projecting upwards at an angle, a sure sign that she had broken in two. Then I saw something I could hardly believe: a flash of orange coming from her forward guns! Although her fighting days had ended, *Hood* was firing a last salvo!

Lieutenant Esmond Knight, who observed the battle from *Prince of Wales*'s anti-aircraft fire-control station, recalled that "there had been a rushing sound which had ominously ceased, and then, as I looked a great spouting explosion issued from the center of *Hood*, enormous reaching tongues of pale-red flame shot into the air, while dense clouds of whitish-yellow smoke burst upwards, gigantic pieces of brightly burning debris being hurled hundreds of feet into the air. I just did not believe what I saw—*Hood* had literally been blown to pieces."

When the smoke had somewhat cleared, it became evident that the forty-two-thousand-ton *Hood* had split in two, and both bow and stern sections pointed almost vertically into the sky like tombstones before sinking. The horrified Admiral Wake-Walker sent a laconic message to the Admiralty: HOOD HAS BLOWN UP. Only three of her crew of 1,419 officers and men survived—a midshipman and two seamen—to be picked up from the sea of floating wreckage several

---

*Some analysts believe the UP rockets caused *Hood*'s loss, and Arthur Marder accepted that view (see *From the Dardanelles to Oran*, p. 116 n.). Another theory holds that torpedoes for the battle cruiser's above-water torpedo tubes may have exploded after the hit and touched off the fifteen-inch magazine (see Eric Grove, "*Hood*'s Achilles Heel?," *Naval History*, Summer 1993). Two boards of inquiry concluded, however, that the ship was lost because of penetration of the lightly armored deck and the consequent magazine explosion. Three battle cruisers had been lost at Jutland when German shells penetrated their turrets and sent fires flashing straight down into the magazine. *Hood*'s turrets were of a post-Jutland design intended to correct such a threat.

hours later by a destroyer. From *Hood*'s opening salvo to her destruction, the battle lasted about six minutes.

Prince of Wales swung sharply to starboard to avoid *Hood*'s funeral pyre. Both German ships now concentrated their fire upon her, at a range of 14,500 yards. Almost at once, at 0602, she took a direct hit on the bridge, and everyone there was thrown to the deck. Captain John Leach groggily pulled himself to his feet to discover that he and the chief yeoman of signals were the only persons still alive and unwounded. Other German shells put both fire-control directors out of commission and damaged the battleship below the waterline. Turrets jammed, big guns misfired, and she never had all ten fully operational.

At 0613, with only two guns still firing, Leach broke off the action.[*] Retiring under cover of smoke, he joined Wake-Walker's cruisers, with the intention of maintaining contact with the enemy until reinforcements could arrive on the scene. Much to the surprise of the British, the Germans did not give chase and complete the destruction of the ships. Instead, they resumed their former speed and course to the south.

The destruction of *Hood* was greeted on *Bismarck* first with shock and then with jubilation. "Overwhelmed with joy and pride in the victory," reported Mullenheim-Rechberg, officers and men "slapped one another on the back and shook hands. . . . A triple *Sieg Heil* to our *Bismarck!*" shouted one crewman. Upon being informed of Germany's greatest naval victory, Hitler lavished praise on the Kriegsmarine, and the German people were elated.

But on *Bismarck*'s bridge, a battle of wills raged between Lütjens and Captain Lindemann. Buoyed by the euphoria generated by the sudden victory over *Hood*, Lindemann pressed Lütjens to pursue and destroy the hard-hit *Prince of Wales*. But Lütjens rejected the proposal. Several factors probably influenced his decision. Believing his opponent was the efficient *King George V*, he was undoubtedly worried that she would draw him in the direction of the heavy British

---

[*]Later, Admiral Pound proposed a court-martial for Leach and Wake-Walker for not re-engaging *Bismarck*, despite the serious damage sustained by *Prince of Wales*. Upon learning of the proposal, Tovey announced that if it were carried out he would haul down his flag and appear at the trial as "Prisoner's Friend"—which effectively killed the plan.

units coming up to avenge *Hood*. Lütjens also had orders from Admiral Raeder to attack British trade, not to seek out British battleships. And as damage-control reports came in, it became clear that *Bismarck* had not emerged unscathed from the battle.

Three of *Prince of Wales*'s fourteen-inch shells had hit her, two of them doing serious damage. One had penetrated the armor belt below the waterline and put a boiler room out of action, reducing her maximum speed to twenty-eight knots. The other passed through the port bow, rupturing two fuel tanks, flooding a pump room, and effectively making a thousand tons of fuel inaccessible. Although *Bismarck*'s fighting ability was unimpaired and she was completely seaworthy, Lütjens informed Navy Group West in Paris, his shore authority, that he had decided to abandon the sortie because the loss of fuel would restrain operations. *Prinz Eugen* would be released to continue the raid on commerce, and *Bismarck*, trailing a large oil slick and down by the bow because of the water taken on, set a course for St. Nazaire, the only port on the French coast with a drydock large enough to accommodate her. Lütjens's critical decision not to refuel off Bergen or from the waiting tanker in the Norwegian Sea was now bearing bitter fruit.

For the British, it was one of the most difficult moments of the war. Admiral Cunningham's ships were being mercilessly pounded by the Luftwaffe off Crete, and May had been another terrible month for British shipping, with 511,042 more tons lost to the U-boats. But the destruction of *Hood*, the symbol of the Royal Navy's domination of the seas, was an even deeper psychological blow. "For most Englishmen the news of *Hood*'s death was traumatic, as though Buckingham Palace had been leveled or the Prime Minister assassinated," noted Sublieutenant Ludovic Kennedy* of the destroyer *Tartar*.

Winston Churchill was at Chequers, his country home, when he learned the awful news. "The *Hood* has blown up, but we've got the *Bismarck*," he told W. Averell Harriman, President Roosevelt's personal representative. This was a typical piece of Churchillian bravado, for he was anything but confident of the outcome. Churchill buried

---

*The son of Captain Edward Kennedy, who had commanded *Rawalpindi* in her unequal fight with *Scharnhorst*.

himself among his papers and dispatches for most of the day, but *Bismarck* was never out of his mind, and as he later wrote:

> Only one scene riveted my background thoughts; this tremendous *Bismarck*, forty-five thousand tons, perhaps invulnerable to gunfire, rushing southward towards our convoys, with the *Prinz Eugen* as her scout. . . . As long as we held fast to the *Bismarck* we could dog her to her doom. But what if we lost touch with her in the night? Which way would she go? She had a wide choice, and we were vulnerable everywhere.

Wasting no time in mourning, Admiral Tovey, 330 miles to the southeast, pounded along behind the retreating *Bismarck* in *King George V*, along with *Repulse*, the carrier *Victorious*, and five cruisers. *Renown* and *Ark Royal* of Force H, *Rodney*, and the old battleships *Ramillies* and *Revenge* were ordered to break off their current duties and steer to converge with *Bismarck*'s course. But the German giant was still making twenty-four knots and could escape. Tovey, hoping to slow the German vessel down and bring her within the range of his big guns, sent *Victorious* ahead with an escort of cruisers.

In those latitudes, daylight lasted until midnight, and at 2210 on May 24, *Victorious* launched an air strike against *Bismarck*, which was about 120 miles away. As new and as unready as *Prince of Wales*, the carrier had put to sea hurriedly, and only nine Swordfish had been embarked. Taking off from a pitching deck in the teeth of a near gale, the planes, led by Lieutenant Commander Eugene Esmonde, a survivor of the sinking of *Courageous* in 1939, pushed on through rain squalls toward their quarry. Most of the air crews had little operational experience, and visibility was poor; still, they were able to find *Bismarck* through radar.[*]

Esmonde tried to hide in the lowering clouds, but surprise was impossible. "It was incredible to see such obsolete-looking planes having the nerve to attack a fire-spitting mountain like *Bismarck*," noted Mullenheim-Rechberg. In the face of an unbroken stream of orange and yellow flak—the battleship had eighty-four anti-aircraft

---

[*]The U.S. Coast Guard cutter *Modoc* was an amazed witness to the attack. She had been searching for survivors of a convoy previously attacked by U-boats when *Bismarck* and then the Swordfish suddenly appeared. The planes almost attacked the cutter, but Esmonde realized the mistake in time.

guns of various types—the Swordfish flew to within a half-mile of the target before dropping their torpedoes. The din of anti-aircraft fire was so heavy that Captain Lindemann's orders could not be heard and *Bismarck*'s helmsmen, Seaman Hans Hansen, steered on his own and evaded all but one—which exploded against her heavily armored starboard side, doing little damage.

Nevertheless, the British expected to bring *Bismarck* to bay next morning, and *Suffolk*'s radar was relied upon to keep track of her throughout the night. As the cruiser zigzagged from port to starboard, she intermittently lost contact on the outward legs and then regained it when she turned and closed the range. But at about 0115 on May 25—Lütjens's fifty-second birthday—the usual contact failed to materialize at the expected moment. With his ship short of fuel and her crew near exhaustion, Lütjens had decided to change course to the southeast and make for Brest. After detaching *Prinz Eugen*, *Bismarck* made a complete circle that took her across *Suffolk*'s wake and dropped off the cruiser's radar screen, because the British radar was ineffective directly astern of the ship.

Gloom settled in on the British ships, and it was feared the German vessel would soon be in the safe embrace of a protective screen of U-boats and land-based aircraft. For a night and a day, suspense mounted. Where was *Bismarck*? Force H was thrown across her likely course—but no one knew her actual position. Some of the larger ships were running short of fuel, which meant the chase would soon have to be called off.[*] In addition, Tovey and his staff were bombarded with instructions and inquiries—"back-seat driving"—from Admiral Pound, which really meant Winston Churchill.

Help arrived from the Admiralty's intelligence sources. Bletchley Park was just beginning to read the naval version of Enigma and *Bismarck*'s position was determined largely from radio-direction[†] and signals analysis. Making a blunder equal to his failure to refuel, Lüt-

---

[*]With a plethora of overseas bases, the British were not expert at refueling at sea.

[†]Direction finding consisted of rotating an antenna until an enemy signal had been heard most loudly. The direction from which the signal came was its line of bearing. Two or more antennas took bearings on a signal from different places, the lines were drawn on a map, and the point at which they intersected gave the location of the transmitter. The direction finders of this period were not precise; the margin of error averaged twenty-five miles and could be more.

jens had sent out a lengthy situation report to Navy Group West. Curiously, Lütjens reported that, because of the effectiveness of enemy radar, he was unable to rid himself of his pursuers. In fact, he was "free" but did not know it. British radar superiority had been fixed in his mind and he could not shake it. The Admiralty's Operational Intelligence Center made a fix, and it was transmitted to Tovey at 0854 on May 25. But the plotters on *King George V* mistakenly placed *Bismarck* two hundred miles north of her actual position, which suggested she was heading for the Iceland-Faeroes gap and back to Germany. At 1047, Tovey altered course to the northeast, while the Germans were actually steaming southeast.

Nearly six hours were required to rectify this error; Tovey did not get his ships back on the correct course until 1610. In the meantime, additional confirmation of *Bismarck*'s destination was gleaned from other sources. From its reading of the Luftwaffe Enigma, Bletchley Park learned she was heading for Brest,* and a French naval officer secretly reported that preparations were being made to receive her there. At the end of all this confusion, *Bismarck* and *King George V* were both steering roughly the same course to the southwest, with the Germans about 150 miles ahead but still a thousand miles from the safety of Brest. Fuel shortages had forced *Prince of Wales* and *Victorious* to break off the chase, and the fleet was running short of destroyers.

Throughout that night, the weather continued vile, but at 1015 on the morning of May 26, a Coastal Command Catalina flying boat† piloted by Ensign Leonard B. Smith of the U.S. Navy, one of nine Americans secretly assigned to the RAF as "special observers," sighted *Bismarck*. For three hours the crew had flown over the sea at five hundred feet without sighting anything. Suddenly, Smith saw a dull-black object; he gradually recognized it as a large warship. "What's that?" he asked Flying Officer Dennis Briggs. Before Briggs had time to reply, *Bismarck* disclosed her identity. Shells burst all about the Catalina, which vibrated as if she were going to break apart

---

*General Hans Jeschonnek, the Luftwaffe's deputy chief of staff, who was in Athens for the Crete operation, had a son serving in *Bismarck* as a midshipman; he had asked for her destination and was given his answer in the Luftwaffe's Enigma code, which was being read by Bletchley Park.

†The American PBY.

in midair, before Smith took evasive action. "Never been so scared in my life," he said later.

Bismarck had been found 690 miles from Brest—only thirty hours' steaming from safety. Although the British heaved a sigh of relief now that they knew the location of the enemy ship, she could still escape unless slowed down. *Ark Royal* of Force H was little more than fifty miles away, and her torpedo planes were ordered to make a strike. In getting into position, the carrier was sighted by *U-556*, which had a perfect shot, but the submarine had expended all her torpedoes and could only watch as this rich target steamed by. Fifteen Swordfish were launched at 1450, despite a gale that sent mountains of seawater pouring over the flight deck, which rose and plunged as much as sixty feet.

Forty minutes after launch, the air crews spotted a ship a few miles west of *Bismarck's* expected position. She had to be their target, because they had been told there was no other ship in the area. More than half the planes had dropped their torpedoes before it was discovered they were attacking the British cruiser *Sheffield!* She had been detached to shadow *Bismarck*. What could have been a major tragedy was averted when the torpedoes, armed with magnetic pistols, either exploded prematurely or were evaded by the cruiser's exasperated crew. "Sorry about the kipper," signaled one of the Swordfish.

Time and torpedoes wasted, the crestfallen airmen returned to *Ark Royal*. Tovey must have felt as if he had played his last card. *King George V* had only 32 percent of her fuel remaining, and *Rodney* reported she would have to break off the chase at 0800 the next morning because of near-empty bunkers. Within an hour, the Swordfish were rearmed, this time with torpedoes fitted with contact pistols, and were again airborne in search of *Bismarck*. In the fading light and intermittent rain squalls, they had some difficulty in finding the target and split up into subflights of two or three aircraft. From below, *Sheffield* signaled, "The enemy is twelve miles ahead."

The attack began at 2047, with small groups of Swordfish striking from several quarters. There was little coordination, however, because of the heavy flak and poor visibility. Some pilots found their target only because they saw the red-orange flash of *Bismarck's* guns. The decks of the wildly maneuvering ship seemed "to explode into crackling flame and the sea was lashed with shot and fragments," reported one airman.

At least two hits were scored on *Bismarck*. One torpedo struck her amidships, doing little damage, but the other exploded near her stern, the Achilles' heel of all battleships, jamming her twin rudders fifteen degrees to port and putting the steering gear out of commission. It was the crucial blow of the long-drawn-out struggle. As the last Swordfish left the scene, *Bismarck* was circling aimlessly. Despite heroic efforts by Captain Lindemann and his crew, repairs proved impossible in the heavy seas, and she refused to steer on any course except to north—wallowing straight into the guns of Tovey's fleet. At 2140, Lütjens signaled Navy Group West: "Ship no longer maneuverable. We fight to the last shell. Long live the Führer."

The Royal Navy now began to crowd in on its stricken quarry. *Bismarck* was still capable of snarling defiance, however, as the shadowing *Sheffield* found when she ventured too close. Three of her men were killed by German shells, and the cruiser was forced to turn away under cover of smoke, losing contact again. Five destroyers—four British and one Polish—under the command of the dashing Captain Philip Vian, who had liberated the *Altmark*'s prisoners, found the battleship and harassed her with repeated torpedo attacks during the early-morning hours of May 27. *Bismarck* was now reduced to a funereal ten knots and listing to port.

This sporadic night battle had one blessing for the exhausted Germans: it kept their minds off what lay ahead, with the coming of daylight. Reassuring reports from Navy Group West that U-boats and massed waves of Luftwaffe bombers were on the way to help were passed throughout the ship, but morale plunged after a coldly formal message was received from the Führer: "All Germany is with you. What can be done, will be done. Your performance of duty will strengthen our people in the struggle for its destiny." It was as if they were hearing their own eulogies before they were dead.

In contrast to the usual bleak grayness of the North Atlantic, the next morning was bright. "The sun appeared for the first time in days, shining from a blue sky between white racing clouds," reported Sublieutenant Kennedy. These reveries were broken as *Rodney*'s sixteen-inch guns flashed out at 0847 at a range of about sixteen thousand yards; *King George V* followed up with her fourteen-inch batteries at 0848. Two minutes later, *Bismarck* returned fire. She straddled *Rodney* with early salvos, but Tovey, having resolved not to repeat Holland's error, kept his ships in open order. *Bismarck*'s fire-control system was knocked out early in the action, and the quality of her gunnery quickly deteriorated. At 0859, *King George V* swung to starboard to bring all her guns into action, and *Rodney* followed. Unable to maneuver, *Bismarck* quickly became a sitting duck. "Get closer, get closer, I can't see enough hits!" Tovey urged the flagship's captain.

In little more than an hour, *Bismarck* was a bloody shambles. Her guns had been battered into silence, fires burned out of control in several places, her internal spaces were littered with the dead and maimed, and all communications had broken down. "Some men were trapped below," reported Mullenheim-Rechberg. "The hatches leading to the main deck . . . were either jammed shut or there was heavy wreckage lying on top of them. . . . In Compartment XV . . . two hundred men were imprisoned behind jammed hatches. . . . Flames cut off the whole forward part of the ship. . . . Further aft, two men who had managed to reach the main deck were blinded by the dense smoke and fell through holes in this deck back into the fire below. . . ."

The range had closed to three thousand yards, and the British battleships were now methodically pumping shell after shell into *Bismarck*. But she would not surrender; nor would she sink—a tribute to the German skill in building stout ships. With fuel running low, Tovey broke off the action at 1015, and *Rodney* and *King George V* left the hulk to be finished off by torpedoes from the cruisers and destroyers.* Hit by two torpedoes fired by the cruiser *Dorsetshire*, and flooded as a result of scuttling charges set off by her crew, *Bismarck* rolled over to port and at 1036 sank stern-first with her colors still flying. Lütjens, Lindemann, and her crew of 2,206 officers and men were lost, except for 117 who were subsequently rescued. Only nine days had passed

---

*As he was steaming home after *Bismarck* had sunk, Tovey received a message from Admiral Pound that had been drafted by Churchill which Captain Roskill has called "the most extraordinary signal of the war." "We cannot visualize situation from your signal. *Bismarck* must be sunk at all costs and if to do this it is necessary for *King George V* to remain on the scene she must do so even if it subsequently means towing *King George V*." Had this order been executed, both *King George V* and the ship towing her would probably have been lost to either the U-boats or Luftwaffe. Later, Pound apologized to Tovey for permitting it to be sent. Tovey said that if he had received this signal before the action, he would have ignored it (Roskill, *Churchill and the Admirals*, p. 125).

since the graceful battleship had slowly steamed out of Gdynia with her band playing "Muss i denn."*

Now that the killer shark had been put out of action, the British systematically hunted down the piranhas—the armed merchant raiders and the logistical network of tankers and supply ships that supported them. With the assistance of some of the first naval Enigma decrypts, most of these vessels were rounded up.† *Pinguin*, in fact, was sunk in the Indian Ocean on May 8, before the *Bismarck* episode, by the heavy cruiser *Cornwall*. She was sighted by the cruiser's floatplane and identified herself as a Norwegian freighter. The pilot almost accepted this disguise but became suspicious when no one on deck waved to him. *Pinguin* was ordered to heave to, and Captain Felix Krüder realized the game was up. He raised the German ensign and opened fire on *Cornwall*. Within minutes, the raider blew up, with heavy loss of life. In eleven months at sea, she had sunk or captured twenty-eight ships totaling 136,551 tons—second only to the score racked up by *Atlantis*.

Kormoran made the most spectacular exit of all the raiders. She was caught off Western Australia on November 19, 1941, by the Australian cruiser *Sydney*, which had performed valiant service in the Mediterranean. Having incautiously approached to within two thousand yards of this strange vessel to check her out, the cruiser's captain found himself on the receiving end of an unexpected broadside. Within minutes, *Sydney*'s bridge was a wreck, her forward turrets were knocked out, and she had been hit by one of *Kormoran*'s torpedoes, while the raider had also suffered crippling damage. Both ships were blazing fiercely as they drifted apart. *Sydney* disappeared over the horizon and was never seen again. It is believed she blew up with all hands. *Kormoran* was also sinking and was abandoned by her crew. Some 315 men were picked up and became prisoners of war. In her eleven months at sea, *Kormoran* had accounted for 68,274 tons of enemy shipping.

Three days later, *Atlantis*, the first and most successful of the

---

**Prinz Eugen escaped the British and refueled at sea, but was forced to return home because of engine trouble and slipped into Brest on June 1, without having sunk a single enemy ship.

†For the breaking of the naval Enigma, see chapter 6.

raiders, met her end off Ascension Island, in the South Atlantic. Captain Rogge, in 622 days at sea, had bagged twenty-two ships totaling 145,697 tons, but his ship's engines were worn out, and he had decided to return to Germany. *Atlantis* was lying to with one of her engines dismantled to replace a damaged piston while *U-126* refueled astern. The submarine commander and some of his crew were enjoying the luxury of hot showers and breakfast on the raider when a lookout sighted the cruiser *Devonshire*, which had administered the *coup de grâce* to *Bismarck*. She had been alerted by Enigma decrypts of signals instructing U-boats to rendezvous with *Atlantis* to refuel. *U-126* cut the fuel line and crash-dived, while Rogge conducted a charade with the cruiser, pretending to be a British freighter, so the submarine could get a shot at her.

But the British were wary and kept well out of range. Having finally ascertained the raider's real identity, *Devonshire* opened fire with her eight-inch guns.[*] Escape was impossible, and Rogge ordered *Atlantis* scuttled. Worried about the presence of U-boats, the cruiser steamed away without stopping to pick up survivors. Now Rogge and this crew experienced the fate of their victims—in boats and on rafts on the open sea. Once the British had left the scene, *U-126* surfaced and lent a hand. The survivors were arranged in three groups: one on the submarine's deck with their life jackets inflated and ready to swim for it if she had to submerge, one belowdecks, and the last being towed in the boats. The men were periodically rotated until they were picked up two days later by the supply ship *Python*.

Not long afterward, *Python* herself was caught off St. Helena by *Devonshire* while resupplying several U-boats. The submarines got away after making an unsuccessful attack on the cruiser, but the supply ship was scuttled. Once again, the crew of *Atlantis* found themselves in the sea. Another rescue was organized by the U-boats, and Admiral Dönitz ordered additional boats to the South Atlantic to help—eight in all. Rogge and his men eventually returned safely to Germany to bring an end to one of the great raiding voyages in maritime history. He was awarded the Oak Leaves to the Knight's Cross.

---

[*]One conclusive piece of evidence was a photograph of the raider secretly made by a former prisoner that had been published in *Life* magazine and distributed to the ships searching for *Atlantis*.

The sinking of *Bismarck* marked the end of Germany's effort to use surfaces forces to war on Britain's Atlantic supply line.* Hitler regarded her loss as confirmation of his misgivings about such operations and saw no purpose in further risking these vessels on the high seas.† In hunting down *Bismarck*, the Royal Navy had done more than sink a battleship; Admiral Raeder's strategy of using heavy surface ships to harry the enemy's sea communications also sank with her. Although several merchant raiders managed to sneak out to sea in 1942, the heavy ships swung idly at anchor in French ports or the Baltic. As Admiral Raeder ruefully acknowledged, "The loss of the *Bismarck* had a decisive effect on the conduct of the war at sea."

Now it was the turn of Admiral Dönitz and his U-boats.

---

*The pocket battleship *Lützow* tried to break out on June 13, 1941, but was seriously damaged by torpedo planes off Norway. See Roskill, *The War at Sea*, vol. I, p. 484.

†Work was also halted on the on-again, off-again carrier *Graf Zeppelin*. At the end of the war, she was blown up in the Oder River, near Stettin. Later, she was refloated by the Russians but, overloaded with loot, capsized while under tow.

•

CHAPTER 6

"I Shall Run Wild"

"Heil U-38!"

"Heil, Herr Admiral!" came the reply from the men in grease-stained work uniforms drawn up at attention on the submarine's slippery deck. Pale, bearded, and exhausted, they reeked of diesel oil after several weeks at sea. Handmade pennants flew from *U-38*'s conning tower, denoting the tonnage of her victims. A band played military marches, and well-wishers waved and cheered. As soon as the submarine nosed up to an old wooden hulk in the harbor of Lorient on the Bay of Biscay, where incoming U-boats moored upon their return, Admiral Karl Dönitz quickly stepped on board.

Having served as a U-boat skipper during World War I, Dönitz knew what a dockside welcome meant to weary sailors returning from a war patrol, and tried to greet his crews personally when they came in from the sea. The admiral quickly surveyed *U-38* with an experienced eye. Streaks of protective red undercoat showed through the gray paint on her conning tower, and her hull was battered and flecked with patches of rust. Obviously, the boat and her crew had seen rough service.

Each crewman felt the admiral's searching gaze as he made an inspection. Unlike the stiffly formal Admiral Raeder and other officers of the old school, Dönitz espoused a less rigid, less harsh discipline than that which had prevailed in the Imperial Navy. Although usually reserved and taciturn, he had a human touch and stopped for a brief exchange of words here and a nod to a familiar face there.

"Men! Your boat has sunk over one hundred thousand tons in only three patrols," he declared when the inspection had been completed. "The credit for this splendid performance goes chiefly to your gallant captain." Turning to Kapitänleutnant Heinrich Liebe, he announced that the Führer had conferred upon him the Knight's Cross, and the bright-red ribbon gleamed as the admiral draped it around the young officer's neck.

Dönitz's commitment to the U-Boat Command and those who served in it communicated itself to officers and men alike. He inspired them with his enthusiasm and confidence, encouraged them to believe they belonged to an elite corps, and saw to it that they received the best pay and finest rations available. They, in turn, were devoted to the man they called "Onkel Karl" and "the Lion." From the earliest days of the Atlantic war, Dönitz believed the ultimate victor would be the side that remained steadfast, and he strived to make certain the morale of his men survived all shocks and setbacks. "Dönitz seldom 'ordered,' " said an aide. "He convinced."

The U-boat crews at this stage of the war were all volunteers, mostly in their early twenties, and projected an air of swaggering arrogance. Many, like Dönitz—whose speeches usually included lavish praise of Hitler—were fervent supporters of the Führer, but their highest loyalty was to their shipmates. They shared a comradeship built upon the strains of wartime patrols—an eternity of semidarkness, cramped quarters, the ever-present stench of unwashed bodies, fuel oil, and fetid air—capped by the sheer terror of waiting, gray-faced and silent, as the thunder of depth charges approached nearer and nearer.

U-boats were spare, functional fighting machines containing a spaghettilike tangle of pipes and valves, handwheels, levers, and other operating controls. Living space was at a premium. The crew ate and slept in the same place; there was only one toilet for forty-four officers and men, which could not be used when the boat dived; and there were no bathing facilities, heat, or air conditioning. "We were the captives of our own smells," said one U-boat officer. Food often spoiled or ran out. Bunks were so few they were in constant use day and night—"hot bunks," the crew called them. Nevertheless, during a Christmas visit to a U-boat at Kiel, the American radio correspondent William L. Shirer was impressed by the crew's spirit and the "absolute lack of Prussian caste discipline. Around our table, the officers and men seemed to be on an equal footing and to like it."

At the beginning of 1941, Dönitz faced a crisis. Bad weather in the North Atlantic, more and better-trained escorts, beefed-up air patrols, convoy rerouting, and, most important, a shortage of operational U-boats had blunted German attacks on convoys in the Western Approaches. With only four to six submarines active from November 1940 to January 1941, there were wide gaps in the patrol line, and Allied shipping losses fell to half those of the "Happy Time." The number of sinkings per submarine deployed dropped from eight to two, and some convoys were slipping through unscathed. New construction had barely replaced the thirty-one boats lost since the beginning of the war—a far cry from the three hundred operational boats Dönitz had deemed necessary to strangle Britain—and more were not expected until later in the year.* And enemy destroyers were starting to sprout strange-looking metal structures on their mastheads that looked like large wire mattresses—radar aerials, which enabled them to search for surfaced U-boats at night.

Italian-submarine reinforcements had not been helpful. Soon after Italy's entry into the war, Mussolini sent a flotilla of twenty-seven boats to join the Germans at Bordeaux. The Italian boats were larger and less maneuverable than the German craft, their methods outdated—they believed in individual patrols, and submerged attacks in daylight. They found few convoys, attacked none, guided no German submarines to any, and were credited with sinking only one ship, of 4,886 tons, before the end of 1940. "I am not at all certain that their presence in the German U-boats' area, their inability to remain undetected, their use of radio and their clumsy attacks do not prejudice more than they help our operations," Dönitz confided to his war diary. Eventually, the Italians removed themselves to the West African coast, where they scored some successes before returning to the Mediterranean.

Dönitz was also unhappy about the lack of air support. If he were not forced to use his boats for reconnaissance, more would be available for war patrols. But in the raucous free-for-all that passed for military coordination in Nazi Germany, he was frustrated by Hermann Göring's refusal to permit the long-range Focke-Wulf Condors

---

*The shortage of U-boats was partially due to Dönitz's decision to hold some back for training the officers and men that would be needed to man the new boats when they were ready. It was like a farmer saving his seed corn.

to pass from under his control. Waiting until Göring was away on a hunting trip, Dönitz flew to Berlin early in January 1941, to join Admiral Raeder in persuading Hitler to place KG 40, a Condor squadron of twelve planes based at Bordeaux, under his operational control. Upon his return, Göring tried to persuade Dönitz to relinquish the Führer's "gift" and, when the admiral refused, made it clear that little cooperation could be expected from the Luftwaffe. Fortunately for Dönitz, the commander of KG 40 was a former naval officer who voluntarily cooperated with the U-Boat Command.

If seven hundred thousand tons of shipping could be sunk each month, the admiral reckoned, it would mean shipping was being destroyed faster than it could be replaced by Anglo-American shipyards, and Britain would be brought to its knees. Probing for weak spots in Allied maritime defenses where he could wage the "tonnage war" with greater facility, Dönitz pushed his U-boats farther out into the Atlantic. Until then, the focal point of his operations had been between ten and fifteen degrees west; now he moved to the south of Iceland. In February, the toll of sunken ships began to move upward, reaching nearly two hundred thousand tons, while aircraft, surface raiders, and mines accounted for an equal sum.

The British measured the peaks and valleys of the Battle of the Atlantic on a large graph on a wall of the underground Submarine Tracking Room in the concrete bunker formally known as the Citadel,* hard by the Admiralty, that housed the supersecret Operational Intelligence Center (OIC), the nerve center of the war against the U-boats. The graph was divided by a thin red line. As long as the number of ships sunk by the enemy stayed below this line, Britain could survive. As the weather improved and more U-boats were at sea, the number edged upward, providing a cold, mathematical mirror of the battle raging on the heaving waters of the Atlantic.

Winston Churchill kept a wary eye on this graph—what ships had been sunk, what cargoes had gone down, what was still on the way, what escorts had been lost. "How willingly would I have exchanged a full-scale invasion for this shapeless, measureless peril, expressed in charts, curves and statistics," he later declared. "This mortal dan-

---

*It was informally, derisively called "Lenin's Tomb." The structure is now, mercifully, covered by ivy.

ger to our life-line gnawed at my bowels." The dismaying February figures spurred him into issuing a "Battle of the Atlantic directive" on March 6, which warned that the enemy was attempting "to strangle our food supplies and connection with the United States. . . . We must take the offensive against the U-boat and the Focke-Wulf. . . ." The headquarters of the Western Approaches Command was transferred from Plymouth to Liverpool, to be nearer the scene of action, and Coastal Command was placed under control of the Royal Navy.

Churchill got results faster than even he had expected. On the same day he issued his Battle of the Atlantic directive, Günther Prien, still in command of *U-47*, the boat in which he had penetrated Scapa Flow to sink *Royal Oak*, sighted westbound Convoy OB 293 about two hundred miles to the south of Iceland. Dönitz ordered Prien's fellow "aces"—Otto Kretschmer in *U-99*, Joachim Matz in *U-70*, and Hans Eckermann in the experimental boat *UA*—to join him. As *U-99* maneuvered for a surface attack the next night, the boat's conning tower was suddenly bathed in St. Elmo's fire, a spontaneous discharge of accumulated static electricity regarded by superstitious sailors as a bad omen. Kretschmer torpedoed a tanker which exploded into flames and a large Norwegian whaling factory ship that was crippled but remained afloat. Matz sank a freighter and damaged a Dutch tanker. The latter rounded on *U-70* and rammed her before she could complete a crash dive.

The escort, led by Commander J. M. Rowland in the destroyer *Wolverine*, supported by another destroyer and two corvettes, reacted swiftly. Kretschmer dived deep, and silently sat out a five-hour depth charge attack as his boat was rattled by near-misses. Matz was not so lucky. As a result of either the ramming or the depth charges, *U-70* was shipping water and it was difficult to maintain trim. She went out of control, rising and falling below the surface. When her bow reared up, the crew frantically raced forward; as it went down, they ran aft. The lights went out, rivets popped and lockers spilled their contents as the boat reeled from the well-placed depth charges. Finally, *U-70* shot to the surface and Matz had just enough time to surrender with most of his crew before she foundered. *U-99* and *UA*, which were also damaged, slipped away.

Prien continued to dog the convoy and about 0030 on March 8, his boat was sighted on the surface by *Wolverine*. In fact, Commander Rowland had smelled diesel exhaust fumes only moments before. *U-47* crash-dived just before the destroyer ran over her and dropped a full pattern of depth charges. Prien attempted to slip away but the attack had damaged his boat's propeller shafts which emitted a rattle picked up by *Wolverine*'s Asdic. Over the next four hours, the U-boat and the destroyer played a deadly game of cat-and-mouse.

Shortly after 0500, *Wolverine*'s hydrophone operator picked up loud clattering sounds "like crockery breaking," and *U-47* suddenly broke the surface within yards of the destroyer, only to dive again instantly. *Wolverine* charged over the bubbling waters where the U-boat had been and dropped a pattern of ten depth charges set for shallow detonation. As they exploded, the sea was momentarily lit by an eerie orange glow; not long after, the debris of a shattered submarine floated to the surface. "The hero of Scapa Flow has made his last voyage," Admiral Dönitz declared in his final tribute to Prien. "We of the U-boat Service proudly mourn and salute him and his men. . . ."

A week later, *U-110*, one of a new class of long-range boats designated as Type IXA*—skippered by Fritz Lemp, who had opened the U-boat war with the sinking of the *Athenia*—sighted the forty-one ships of HX 122 inbound from Halifax about three hundred miles north of Scotland. The convoy included several valuable tankers, so the escort, under Commander Donald Macintyre in the destroyer *Walker*, was unusually strong—five destroyers and two corvettes. Macintyre had no inkling of the proximity of a U-boat until early on the morning of March 16, when a tanker "burst into a blinding flame casting a ghastly glare over the heaving waters. . . . I had never seen this most appalling of all night disasters and . . . we were shocked into silence by the horror of it. . . ."

Macintyre was relieved when there were no further attacks that night, but *U-110* continued to trail the convoy. Four more boats—including Kretschmer in *U-99*, and *U-100* commanded by Joachim Schepke, his rival for first place in the tonnage race—went on the attack the following night. *U-100* was sighted, and three destroyers raced away to hunt her. In the meantime, Kretschmer got in among

---

*The Type IX boat was, at twelve hundred tons, larger than the familiar Type VII, had a longer range, mounted six torpedo tubes instead of five, and carried nineteen torpedoes.

the convoy and, in a brilliant maneuver, torpedoed five ships in rapid succession. The night was filled with explosions, rockets, and the glare of burning tankers.

"I racked my brains to find some way to stop the holocaust," Macintyre recalled. "Our one hope was to sight a U-boat's telltale wake, give chase to force her to dive and so give the Asdics chance to bring our depth charges into action." Shortly before 0100, the destroyer *Vanoc* picked up a firm Asdic echo and, working with *Walker*, plastered the contact with depth charges. A half-hour later, *U-100* broke the surface. Schepke tried to get away in the pitch darkness but was spotted by *Vanoc*, one of the first escort vessels to be fitted with radar. The destroyer rammed *U-100* at high speed, her bow slamming into the boat's conning tower, crushing Schepke as he stood on the bridge, and running over her with a grinding, scraping roar of metal.

Survivors were still being pulled from the sea when *Walker*'s Asdic operator heard the steady "ping" of another contact. Macintyre was skeptical, but the operator insisted his contact was firm. *Walker* attacked again with a pattern of a half-dozen depth charges, and Macintyre was about to drop more when *Vanoc* signaled that a submarine had surfaced astern of her. The badly battered boat was Otto Kretschmer's *U-99*. With all his torpedoes expended, he had been circling the convoy on his way home when he was ensnared by *Walker*'s Asdic. Badly damaged by the depth charges and out of control, the boat plummeted down to seven hundred feet, where she was in danger of being crushed by the water pressure. To save himself and his crew, Kretschmer surfaced and surrendered.* All but three of the crew were rescued by the British destroyers before *U-99* followed

---

*The British were surprised to find that Kretschmer was not a raving Nazi. An interrogator reported that he said he had become weary of the war well before his capture and "his political views were less extreme Nazi than had been assumed" (quoted in Padfield, *Dönitz*, p. 226).

Kretschmer spent the remainder of the war in a Canadian prisoner-of-war camp, where, despite strict censorship, he organized a system for the transmission of intelligence to Germany. This line of communication worked so well that he was able to arrange for a U-boat to rendezvous with some escaping German prisoners at the mouth of the St. Lawrence. The submarine duly arrived, but the escapees had previously been recaptured. When West Germany founded a navy, Kretschmer joined the Bundesmarine, held several important NATO commands, and retired in 1970 with the rank of admiral.

her victims to the bottom. In eighteen months, Kretschmer had sunk nearly 270,000 tons of Allied shipping—the highest score achieved by any U-boat captain.

Prien . . . Schepke . . . Kretschmer . . . Matz—but still the toll was not complete. On March 23, a British trawler sank *U-551* between Iceland and the Faeroes, making it the fifth boat lost in just two weeks. Coming after a three-month period in which no submarines had failed to return, the loss of so many boats—and of three invincible "aces" in particular—stunned and baffled the German people and the U-Boat Command. Dönitz wondered whether the enemy might have developed some devastating new antisubmarine weapon. In reality, this reversal of fortune had resulted from improvements in escort training and tactics, and the increasing number of escort vessels available to stiffen convoy defenses.

For their part, the British were elated by their success, and Churchill believed a turning point had been reached in the war against the U-boats. Nevertheless, March 1941 was a difficult month for Britain as well as the Germans—the most difficult since the previous June. Forty-three ships totaling 236,000 tons were sunk by U-boats, and with the shipping accounted for by the Luftwaffe, surface raiders, and mines added, the total loss for the month reached over a half-million tons, a setback for Britain of ominous proportions.

With the convoys suddenly having developed a sting of their own, Dönitz again shifted his boats in search of "soft" targets, this time to the south of Greenland. There the U-boats would be working in mist-shrouded seas beyond the range of air and sea escorts based in the British Isles. This move brought immediate results. On April 3, seven U-boats attacked eastbound SC 26 two days before it was to be joined by its Western Approaches escort. Ten of the twenty-two ships were sunk, and an armed merchant cruiser was damaged at the cost of a single submarine, sunk by the ubiquitous *Wolverine*, after it arrived to join the escort. Toward the end of April, U-boats attacking in daylight while submerged picked off four ships from HX 121 south of Iceland, again losing only one submarine.

In response to Dönitz's alteration of the killing ground, the Royal Navy also turned its attention westward, establishing bases for escort groups and aircraft on Iceland, occupied the previous year in a pre-emptive strike to prevent German occupation. Over the next four years, the bleak, cheerless island became a familiar landfall for weary Allied sailors and airmen. Escort vessels based there took over the protection of convoys out to thirty-five degrees west, and brought in convoys from that point to a rendezvous with Western Approaches escorts based at Londonderry in Northern Ireland and Greenock in southwestern Scotland.

Efforts were also made to provide air escorts for the convoys, which had been found to be the best way to deter U-boat attacks. Coastal Command twin-engine Hudson bombers, which had a five-hundred-mile patrol radius, based upon Iceland, along with Sunderland flying boats operating from Northern Ireland, provided air cover for nearly half the Atlantic crossing. They lacked effective bombs and depth charges and were not yet good U-boat killers, but their presence forced the submarines to remain submerged.

Nevertheless, in spite of Allied countermeasures, the U-boats accounted for forty-five ships totaling some 260,000 tons in the North Atlantic in April, and another fifty-eight ships of 325,000 tons in May. In June, the delivery rate of U-boats reached fifteen a month. These developments had an impact in Britain. Meat rations were cut; cheese rationing was ordered; butter and sugar were scarce; eggs and fresh fruit merely a memory. Churchill had estimated that thirty-one million tons a year of imports, exclusive of petroleum stocks, were necessary to keep Britain's people healthy, her industry running, and her armed forces fed, equipped, and fighting. In the first four months of 1941, imports were running at a rate of under twenty-eight million tons.

With the U-boats reaching farther and farther out into the Atlantic, the Admiralty realized, continuous escort would have to be provided all the way across the ocean. British destroyers lacked the endurance to remain with a convoy for an entire crossing, nor had the Royal Navy practiced the technique of refueling at sea, so the Royal Canadian Navy was called upon to fill the last surface "gap," the patch of sea between Newfoundland and Iceland, some six to seven hundred miles wide.

The Canadians were ill-prepared to meet the emergency. They had begun World War II with a token force of seven destroyers and five minesweepers divided between the Atlantic and the Pacific. Like the Royal Navy, Canada's professional naval officers had dismissed the submarine threat at the war's beginning and placed orders for a dozen large destroyers designed to deal with surface raiders. But these vessels took years to complete, and in the meantime the U-boat threat created a rush demand for convoy escorts. The lowly corvette filled the breach and became the backbone of Canada's seagoing forces.* In all, Canadian yards turned out more than 130 corvettes, manned by a mixture of ex–merchant mariners and barely trained reservists forced to learn their trade by trial and error in the grim school of the Atlantic war.

By the end of May 1941, there were enough Canadian corvettes in commission to establish the Newfoundland Escort Force and provide an escort from St. John's, Newfoundland, to thirty-five degrees west. There a Mid-Ocean Meeting Point (MOMP) was established, where a group based on Iceland would take over the escort while the Canadians assumed protection of a westbound convoy on its final leg. The Iceland group was relieved at an Eastern Ocean Meeting Point (EOMP), at about eighteen degrees west, by a Western Approaches escort. HX 129, the first convoy to sail to Britain under end-to-end escort, completed the crossing in safety.

Canadian corvettes were rushed to sea without the modifications that experience had taught the Royal Navy were necessary to prepare them for a role as ocean escorts. Living conditions on these ships, notoriously poor under the best of circumstances, were abominable. One sailor recalled:

> The mess decks of a corvette in bad weather are indescribable. . . . There is absolutely no fresh air. . . . Dim emergency lights, red or blue, provide the only illumination in the dark hours, and around the clock there is always at least one watch trying to catch a few hours of oblivion, while all about them the life of the mess goes on. . . . Plunging into a head sea, the noise and motion of the fo'c'sle must be experienced to be believed; a constant roar of turbulence, wind, and water, punctuated by a crashing thud as the bow bites into another great sea, while the whole little world is uplifted—up, up, up—only to come crashing down. . . .

Though the rust-stained corvettes of the Newfoundland Escort Force had closed the "surface gap," there still remained an "air gap," a sec-

---

*The Canadians also received the dubious gift of seven of the American "four-pipers."

tion of the North Atlantic that was uncovered by aircraft. Nine Catalina patrol planes supplied to the Royal Canadian Air Force made it possible to provide the convoys with air cover until they were five hundred miles out from Newfoundland, but this left a patch of sea about six hundred miles wide south of Greenland where no air escort could yet be provided. Soon, it would be given the sinister name of "The Black Pit."

"You have only to kick down the door and the whole rotten edifice will come crashing down." So said Adolf Hitler as German troops plunged across the 2000-mile Soviet frontier from the Baltic to the Black Sea on June 22, 1941. Stalin had been given ample warning, by the British as well as by his own spies, of the impending invasion, yet he stubbornly refused to believe them. The massing of German troops on the border and the presence of minelayers in the Gulf of Finland and near the lonely islands at its mouth had no effect. Thus, the German attack caught the Red Army completely by surprise, the Russian air force was destroyed on the ground and the navy was bottled up in its bases by German mines. Entire units surrendered without a fight, seeming to confirm the Führer's comments.

Landbound as ever in his thinking, Hitler failed to see the usefulness of the Baltic as a highway for attacks on the Russians and to supply his own forces. Moscow, the main objective of the invasion, was only about 375 miles from the inner part of the Gulf of Finland compared to 625 miles from the Polish border. But in Directive No. 21, in which Hitler outlined his plans for Operation Barbarossa, he stated that the main effort of the Kriegsmarine would remain "unequivocally directed against England even during the eastern campaign." For the most part, German naval activity was to consist of air attacks on Russian ports, aggressive mining to seal the Russians into the Gulf of Finland, and S-boat operations. The progress of the German army was expected to eliminate Russian naval forces by depriving them of their bases in the Baltic and Black Sea.

There was a cretain resemblance between the Russian and German fleets at the outbreak of the war. Each was subordinate to the land forces and had developed during the previous decade. Until a few years before the war, most of the Russian navy's ships were relics of the tsarist era. Beginning in 1935, however, large numbers of submarines and tor-

pedo boats suitable for coastal defense were built and efforts were made
to obtain battleships in the United States and cruisers and destroyers
in Italy. At the beginning of the war, the Soviet navy consisted of
three battleships, two of pre–World War I vintage, seven cruisers, fifty-
nine destroyers, and 218 submarines. It was divided into four widely
separated commands: the Baltic Red Banner Fleet based on Tallinn in
Estonia; the Black Sea Fleet at Sevastopol; the Pacific Fleet at Vladi-
vostok; and the smallest unit, the Northern Fleet, at the ice-free port
of Murmansk. The Russians were handicapped by obsolescent ships,
a lack of modern equipment such as radar and sonar, poor training, a
bloody Stalinist purge that had decimated its officer corps, and heavy-
handed political interference at every level of operations.

The major naval operation of the first weeks of the war was the
Russian defense of Tallinn, as the Germans and their Finnish allies
advanced toward Leningrad. By August 28, the port, main base for
Soviet destroyers, submarines, and minesweepers in the Gulf of Finland, was surrounded on land by German troops and at sea by four
thousand German mines, some only twenty-five or thirty feet apart.
When the enemy reached the outskirts of the city, the Russians
hastily gathered a rag-tag fleet of 170 vessels and undertook a massive evacuation of the remnants of three infantry divisions and thousands of refugees. These ships, under the command of Vice-Admiral
V. P. Drozhd in the destroyer *Stoiki*, were preceded by minesweepers
and *Sperrbrechers*—merchantmen fitted to go ahead of convoys and
detonate any mines in the way.

As soon as the explosions began, German artillery ashore and the
Luftwaffe attacked the escaping ships. They were defended by the modern cruiser *Kirov*, which although damaged was under tow by three
destroyers, and hidden by clouds of smoke that were being blown out
to sea from huge forest fires. When gaps were blown in the minefields,
the rest of the convoy followed. There were continuous attacks throughout the night and into the next day by aircraft and torpedo boats, and
altogether about fifty vessels were lost. Nevertheless, disregarding heavy
casualties, the Russians sailed on and saved two-thirds of the ships.

The Soviet navy had ninety-four submarines available for use in
the Baltic, but only about twenty-five were operational. Five were
immediately sunk and the rest accomplished little because of the
poor training of the crews. Once Tallinn had been captured by the

Germans, naval activity in the Baltic consisted primarily of mining and countermining, and commando raids by the Russians and Germans on each other's coastal and island positions.

Winter and the freezing of the Gulf of Finland brought an end to conventional naval warfare—but the mining went on. The Germans dragged mines across the ice on sleds, cut holes in the ice and dropped the mines through them, ready for spring. By the time the weather warmed, however, the main thrust of the German attack was directed to the southeast toward the Ukraine, and the advance on Leningrad was transformed into a bitter siege. Thanks to a flotilla of small craft on Lake Ladoga, the Russians ferried enough supplies into the city to enable it to hold out until relieved in January 1944, but not enough to save thousands of Leningrad's people from starvation. Big guns from the Russian ships blockaded at the naval base at Kronstadt and their crews played a conspicuous role in the defense of the city.

In the Black Sea, the Soviets were surprised by a massive, well-planned minelaying campaign by the Luftwaffe that sealed much of the Soviet Black Sea Fleet in harbor until channels could be swept. The Russians had fifty-one submarines in various stages of operational readiness, the old battleship *Sevastopol*, six cruisers, two of them modern, and twenty-seven destroyers and torpedo boats. The Germans had no ships in those waters, but the Kriegsmarine met the challenge by quickly moving 428 vessels into the Black Sea. They included six 250-ton U-boats, six Italian midget submarines, as well as S-boats, Italian torpedo boats, and ferries that had been designed for the invasion of Britain. Some came down the Danube; others were knocked down and transported overland by rail to Constansa, the Rumanian naval base on the Black Sea, where they were reassembled.

For the most part, the Black Sea Fleet, despite its superiority over the Germans, played only a defensive role in the opening operations of the war. One of the few exceptions was a naval bombardment of Constansa on June 26, 1941, by a pair of large destroyers. In dodging the fire of the shore batteries, which were manned by German gunners, one Russian ship was sunk by a mine, with the loss of all but sixty-six of her crew.

Odessa was the first target of German operations in the area. For political reasons, the Rumanians were given responsibility for leading the attack, but they were beaten back by the Russian defenders led by Rear Admiral Sergei G. Gorshkov, later commander of the Soviet fleet. Odessa was soon surrounded on three sides but, supplied by surface ships and submarines, held out until mid-October, 1941. The seventy-three-day siege was capped by a skillful operation in which the Russian navy evacuated the garrison to Sevastopol, the main Russian base in the Black Sea, leaving behind a thoroughly sabotaged and booby-trapped port that was not operational again for several months.

Sevastopol itself was besieged for 209 days. The heavy guns of the battleship *Sevastopol* and the cruisers supplied supporting fire for the garrison, but the bulk of their support came from smaller vessels and submarines, which brought in a steady stream of supplies. The destroyer *Tashkent* made more than forty such runs and was attacked by German aircraft ninety-six times before being sunk by a dive bomber. Bad weather grounded the Luftwaffe at the end of 1941, and the Russians seized the opportunity to launch their largest amphibious operation of the war in an attempt to relieve beleagured Sevastopol. Troops were landed at several points behind the German lines, and the time required to wipe them out delayed by many months the final German assault on the base. Sevastopol finally fell on July 1, 1942 and the Germans took some ninety-seven thousand prisoners.

Following the fall of Sevastopol, it appeared as if the Germans would make a clean sweep of the Black Sea coast as far as the Turkish frontier and deprive the Russians of all their bases. But the German advance stalled and the Black Sea was divided into German and Russian sectors, with the former holding the western end and the latter the eastern part. Numerous small craft actions and commando raids on shore points followed, along with a war of attrition against each other's coastal supply lanes. This lasted through the end of 1942, when the German reverses at Stalingrad began, with neither side getting the upper hand.

The Germans, in their certainty that the Russian campaign would be concluded quickly, had made no plans for naval operations in the Arctic Sea or to interdict communications between the Soviet Union and the outside world via the North Cape. But these waters soon became one of the most important areas in the whole war, as Allied convoys came to play an increasingly vital role in the stiffening of

Russian resistance. Britain's prospects for survival were immediately transformed by the Soviet Union's entry into the war, and Churchill promptly offered all possible assistance to the embattled Russians, and was joined by the United States.

There was little the British could do in the beginning, but by taking advantage of their one great asset—command of the sea—they tried to supply the Russians with tanks and aircraft, the weapons of which they were in greatest need. Originally, it was expected that these cargoes would be carried by Russian merchant shipping, but that proved inadequate, and the task fell upon Britain's merchant navy, already under the strain of the Battle of the Atlantic. Operations in the waters above Norway and Finland were particularly hazardous, because the area had some of the most violent weather in the world, and because of the presence of German air, sea, and submarine bases along the Norwegian coast.

The first delivery was made in September 1941, when a convoy defended by the carriers *Victorious* and *Argus* successfully transported thirty-nine Hurricane fighters to Russia. Seven other convoys—designated "PQ" when outward bound, loaded, and "QP" on their return, empty—followed during the remainder of the year, all lightly escorted. The first six reached Archangel or Murmansk unscathed; the seventh lost one ship to a U-boat. The Germans were slow to react, because they expected Russia to be defeated before Allied assistance would have any effect, but the vastness of their territory gave the Russians a resiliancy denied to Hitler's previous victims. Although the Germans tried desperately to score a knockout blow before the coming of the savage Russian winter, they failed. As the war dragged on, they began to appreciate the importance of the "Murmansk Run" and mounted a determined effort to halt it, with a heavy toll in men, ships, and cargoes.

In the Atlantic, the British were struggling to maintain their temporary edge over the U-boats by detouring convoys around Dönitz's patrol lines. These operations depended upon U-boat sightings, reports of ships sunk, and the bearings on U-boat radio transmissions obtained by shore-based direction finders. This information was analyzed and plotted on a huge map of the North Atlantic, in the Submarine Tracking Room of the OIC, dotted with pins and markers that

showed the position of convoys and U-boats at sea. Commander
Rodger Winn, an odd figure with a limp and twisted back as a result
of childhood polio, presided over the operation. A thirty-year-old
attorney with degrees from both Cambridge and Harvard, Winn possessed an uncanny ability to forecast the movements of U-boats after
gathering all the facts. Many of his decisions were based on hunches
and guesswork, for there was only one source that could provide an
absolute key to Dönitz's intentions—a break in the seemingly
impregnable Enigma cipher, in which submarines communicated
with U-boat headquarters in France.

Bletchley Park were reading both army and Luftwaffe versions of
Enigma, but the cryptologists had not gotten beyond the fringes of the
naval cipher. The Kriegsmarine's machine was far more complex than
those of the other services—with eight rotors to choose from instead
of five—and the settings were changed every twenty-four hours, a
practice requiring decrypters to break a new cipher every day. Low-
level cipher material had been scooped up from captured German
weather ships and a raid on the German-occupied Loften Islands, but
a genuine breakthrough awaited the capture of a U-boat Enigma
machine. Dönitz, however, regarded Enigma as the most important
secret in the German arsenal and carefully instructed his crews to
destroy the machines and scuttle their boats if they faced capture.

On May 9, 1941, the British received a surprise gift from the sea.
Convoy OB 318 was lumbering toward North America when it was
attacked by Fritz Lemp in *U-110* about three hundred miles off
Greenland. Lemp torpedoed two ships but was spotted by the
corvette *Aubretia*, which depth-charged the U-boat. The destroyer
Bulldog skippered by Commander A. J. Barker-Cresswell, the escort
group commander, and the sloop *Broadway* joined in the attack, and
the submarine was badly damaged by concentrated depth-charging.
Out of control, *U-110* plunged toward the bottom of the ocean. Lemp
ordered the tanks blown, and the submarine suddenly shot to the surface amid the enemy ships.

Barker-Cresswell tried to ram the U-boat, but when he realized
her crew was jumping into the sea, he saw a chance to capture her
before she sank. *Bulldog* narrowly sheered off without striking the
boat, and a boarding party led by twenty-year-old Sublieutenant
David Balme was sent over to the wallowing *U-110* in a small boat

while efforts were made to pick up the Germans struggling in the water. They were quickly hustled below, so they would be unable to see what occurred next. Lemp, apparently realizing to his horror that the scuttling charges had not exploded, desperately tried to swim back to his boat to complete the job before the British got on board. Before he could pull himself up the submarine's sides, he either drowned or was shot to death by the boarding party.

Led by Balme with revolver in hand, the British sailors warily descended into the conning tower in the eerie blue light of the emergency lamps, expecting the U-boat to blow up or sink under them at any moment. They were surprised to find that the Germans had made no attempt to destroy the submarine's confidential codebooks and secret papers. Upon inspecting the closet-sized radio room, Allen O. Long, a radioman, noticed a long, slim hardwood box that looked like a typewriter. Out of curiosity, he pressed the "A" key, but the results seemed "peculiar." Rather than an "A" lighting up on the illuminated panel, another letter appeared. Long, recognizing it as a cipher device, unscrewed the bolts holding it to a table. The Enigma machine, its rotors and settings, and two packing cases of codebooks and documents were passed over to *Bulldog*.* "Hearty congratulations," signaled Admiral Pound upon learning of the capture. "The petals of your flower are of rare beauty."

The Bletchley Park decrypters were overjoyed to have secured a U-boat Enigma machine complete with rotor settings correct through the end of June. With great speed, they penetrated Hydra,† the operational cipher for all U-boats, and were now able to plot the positions of individual boats and wolf packs through their radio traffic and take steps to avoid them. Dönitz's insistence on "hands-on" control of operations was the Achilles' heel of his system, because it required constant contact between his headquarters and the U-boats on patrol.

Positions, weather reports, convoy sightings, and reports on fuel and torpedo consumption flowed back and forth. The Enigma decrypts—

**U-110 was taken under tow by *Bulldog* but sank before reaching a safe harbor. To prevent the Germans from suspecting that the boat had fallen into British hands along with an Enigma machine, the Admiralty announced that it had been sunk in action with all hands.

†Hydra was only one of thirteen ciphers used by the Kriegsmarine, and not all were penetrated during the war.

designated "Ultra" as a security measure—that clattered into the Submarine Tracking Room over a secure teletype line from Bletchley enabled Winn and his staff to read the cards in Dönitz's hands with only a twenty-six-hour delay. To prevent the Germans from realizing that Enigma had been penetrated, it was decreed that operations were to be based upon information resulting from Ultra only where it could be attributed to some other source, such as aerial reconnaissance, radio direction finding, or traffic analysis. Naval history is written in terms of Trafalgars and Jutlands, but by any standard the seizure of *U-110* should rate as a major victory.

The value of Ultra to British naval operations quickly became apparent. On June 13, *Lützow* was attacked by torpedo bombers on the strength of Enigma decrypts as she steamed from Germany to Norway. The pocket battleship was put out of commission for seven months. Ten days later, the Tracking Room received advance warning from Bletchley that ten U-boats were gathering to attack Convoy HX 133 south of Greenland. The escort was reinforced, and although five steamers were sunk during the ensuing five-day battle, two U-boats were also accounted for.

U-boat operations in the North Atlantic dropped during the summer of 1941 to the lowest level of effectiveness. It appeared, says a German commentator, "almost as though the defense had won the race against the attack."[*] Even though there were now twenty-five U-boats at sea—more than ever before—the rate of success had declined to less than one sinking per boat per month, a new low. To add to Dönitz's problems, he was ordered to detach eight operational boats to the Baltic in conjunction with the German invasion of Russia, and, later, another half-dozen to the Arctic. As a result, the toll of ships sunk by the U-boats dropped from 310,000 tons in June to little more than ninety thousand in July, and even less in August.[†]

---

[*] Jürgen Rohwer, "The U-Boat War Against the Allied Supply Lines," in Jacobsen and Rohwer, *Decisive Battles of World War II*, p. 267.

[†] One boat, *U-570*, surfaced directly under one of the Coastal Command Hudsons based on Iceland and had the dubious distinction of being the first submarine to surrender to an airplane. The Hudson depth-charged the boat, badly damaging her, and with a fusillade of machine-gun fire convinced the captain to raise the white flag. A Catalina relieved the Hudson when it ran short of fuel, and stood by until a trawler came out to tow the U-boat to Iceland.

Frustrated and perplexed, Dönitz sought an explanation for this reduced effectiveness. "Coincidence alone it cannot be—coincidence cannot always work on one side," he observed. "A likely explanation would be that the British from one source or another gained knowledge of our concentrated dispositions and avoid them. . . ." There were three ways, Dönitz reasoned, in which the enemy could obtain this information—by deciphering radio signals, espionage, or radio direction. Cryptographic specialists assured Dönitz that Enigma was impregnable. U-boat headquarters, naval bases, and construction yards were combed for spies, to no avail. The admiral therefore concluded that direction finding was the most likely culprit. To prevent the British from getting fixes on his boats, he ordered a reduction in radio traffic, but because of his insistence on directing operations it remained substantially the same—and in any case Bletchley continued to read Enigma undetected.*

Turning southward in search of lightly defended convoys and vessels sailing independently, Dönitz shifted some of his long-range Type IX boats to the Gibraltar and West African runs, where they would have the assistance of the Condors of KG 40. In order to extend their time on patrol, the boats carried eight torpedoes in pressure-tight containers between their decks and pressure hulls, in addition to those below, and, to economize on fuel, cruised at only seven knots. Working with Condors, which hovered over targets sending out homing signals—which made it impossible to route convoys around the patrol lines—eight boats sank no fewer than eighty-one unescorted ships in a few months. *U-107*, commanded by Dönitz's son-in-law, Kapitänleutnant Günther Hessler, sank 86,699 tons, the highest toll achieved by any U-boat on a single patrol. These sinkings forced the Admiralty to divert convoys well to the west of the Canary Islands.

In an effort to combat the intrusion of marauding Condors over convoys, the Admiralty ordered catapults fitted to fifty ships, each of which carried a solitary Hurricane. These Catapult Aircraft Merchantmen were merely a one-shot measure; there was no way to

---

*A staff officer pointed the finger at a Paris nightclub run by White Russians, the Schéhérazade, which featured a number of attractive "hostesses" who spoke good German and was popular with the most dashing U-boat officers. One girl, a singer named Tania, was suspected of engaging in espionage, but the Germans, in spite of their best efforts, could never trap her.

recover the plane once it was launched. At the end of the mission, the pilot had to "ditch" in the sea near a ship if one were in sight, or bail out and hope to be picked up. "Their sorties demanded a cold-blooded gallantry," as Captain Roskill has written. The CAM ships scored their first victory in August 1941, when a Condor was shot down four hundred miles out in the Atlantic.

The CAM ship was only a stopgap; the next step was the small escort-aircraft carrier. These vessels, with flight decks built on merchant-ship hulls, would provide convoys with a continuing air umbrella. The first, *Audacity*, was right out of the bargain basement—improvised from the captured German liner *Hannover*—and carried six Grumman Martlets (the American F4F Wildcat). She entered service in September 1941, and achieved instant success. Two of her fighters shot down a Condor that was harassing a Gibraltar convoy and drove off others. The operation was clear evidence of the value of escort carriers, but it would be some time before such vessels were generally available. *Audacity* herself was lost in December 1941, when she was torpedoed while defending HG 76, a Gibraltar-England convoy. It was one of the most protracted convoy battles of the war, and the escort led by Commander Frederick J. Walker, soon to be one of Britain's ace submarine-killers, accounted for four U-boats and several Condors.* In the meantime, the war at sea entered a new and decisive phase, as the United States was drawn closer and closer into the struggle against Hitler and Nazism.

In the year since Franklin Roosevelt had won his bid for a third term in November 1940, American neutrality had become a fiction. Emboldened by his victory, the president took step after step to aid bombed, besieged, and nearly bankrupt Britain—and the Soviet

---

*"Johnny" Walker was one of the few British naval officers to show an interest in anti-submarine warfare in the years between the wars. Outspoken comments on the uselessness of battleships undoubtedly caused him to be passed over for promotion to captain, and he probably would have been retired had not the war intervened. As an escort commander, he devised aggressive tactics for the protection of convoys and other techniques later used throughout the Western Approaches Command. Perhaps his greatest quality was an ability to influence men of different backgrounds to work together as a team. He was the only Royal Navy officer to be awarded the Distinguished Service Order four times and was promoted to captain. Worn out by his exertions, he died of a stroke on July 9, 1944.

Union, after the German invasion—while laying down a two-ocean navy to deal with any threat that might develop in the Pacific as well as the Atlantic. In March 1941, the Lend-Lease Act was approved by Congress after bitter opposition by those who feared Roosevelt's intention was to embroil the nation in the war by easy stages. Ending the "cash-and-carry" provisions of the Neutrality Act, it permitted countries "whose defense the President deems vital to the defense of the United States" to obtain military supplies and equipment without paying for them. Ten Coast Guard cutters, all excellent sea-keeping vessels, were immediately made available to the Royal Navy for escort work.

Lend-Lease marked the beginning of an undeclared war on Germany. A triumphant Churchill hailed it as the "most unsordid act in the history of any nation," but Hitler was infuriated. Nevertheless, deeply involved in his Russian adventure, he chose to ignore this and other unneutral acts. The mistake made by the rulers of Imperial Germany in antagonizing the United States, and the decisive effect American participation had had on the outcome of the previous war, were in the front of his mind, and he postponed a showdown to a time of his own choosing.

Not long after the approval of Lend-Lease, the military and naval staffs of the United States and Britain, who had been meeting secretly in Washington to work out the details of potential American participation in the war should such a step be necessary, produced the "ABC-1 Staff Agreement." Fundamentally, it established a "Europe First" strategy. If the United States became involved in a two-ocean war, the Japanese were to be held in check through defensive operations until Hitler had been defeated and the Allies were ready to deal with Japan. Germany was considered more dangerous than Japan, because of her industrial capacity and the Führer's successful European conquests. It was also agreed that the U.S. Navy would begin escorting convoys in the North Atlantic as soon as it was ready.

In preparation for these new responsibilities, the old Neutrality Patrol, which had been patrolling the American Defense Zone, was transformed into the Atlantic Fleet, and Admiral Ernest J. King raised his flag as its commander. Roosevelt, who had been assistant secretary of the navy during World War I and maintained a proprietary interest in the service, had a hand in the choice of the sixty-three-year-old King as CINCLANT. Tough, brilliant, and short-tempered—Roosevelt said "he shaved with a blow torch"—King was an aviator, a submariner, and a staff officer, and the president's idea of a fighting sailor.* Only a short time before, the admiral had been passed over for a top command and was headed for retirement, because, it was said, he drank too much, chased other men's wives, and had too many enemies. "When they get into trouble they send for the sons-of-bitches," was his explanation of this reversal of fortune.

"We cannot allow our goods to be sunk," declared Navy Secretary Frank Knox, and on April 10 it was announced that, despite increasing tension with Japan, the Atlantic Fleet would be reinforced by transferring several ships from the Pacific. These included the battleships *Idaho, Mississippi*, and *New Mexico*, the carrier *Yorktown*, four light cruisers, and two destroyer squadrons. Greenland, and then Iceland, were occupied by American troops—in the name of hemispheric defense—and patrol aircraft were based there. The Defense Zone was extended more than halfway across the Atlantic to twenty-five degrees west, and the U.S. Navy established convoys to and from Iceland—declared to be independent of the British-Canadian convoy system—which the merchant ships of any nation were free to join. But Roosevelt stopped short of supplying U.S. Navy escorts for trans-Atlantic convoys, because he felt the determinedly isolationist American public was not yet ready for such drastic action.

To prevent American warships from becoming involved in a shooting war, they were ordered not to attack U-boats but to report their location to the British. On June 20, *U-203* turned the tables by pursuing the American battleship *Texas* for 140 miles in the waters between Greenland and Iceland while trying to get into position for a shot. In reply to her captain's sighting report, Dönitz sent an urgent signal to all U-boats "by order the Führer" forbidding attacks on American ships. The last thing Hitler wanted was an incident with the United States.

In this twilight period between peace and war, the U.S. Navy underwent rapid expansion. The Naval Academy class of 1941 was graduated in January rather than June, reserves were called to active

---

*King won his wings at the age of forty-seven.

duty, and "boot" camps were absorbing five thousand men a month, but American ships were shorthanded and the crews unskilled. Elaborate plans were drawn for escort vessels and a "bridge of ships" to carry supplies to Britain, but the work proceeded slowly because of shortages of steel plate and machinery. Like the Royal Navy in the interwar years, the U.S. Navy also had been afflicted with the Jutland "big-gun, big-ship" syndrome and neglected antisubmarine warfare. Both officers and men, many of them younger than their ships, picked up whatever training they got while at sea. Wirt Williams, a novelist who served on convoy duty, later wrote:

> The days ground you with dull and unvarying cruelty. The watches on the bridge struck as inexorably as the bells of a clock. Half your life you spent on the bridge; no night passed but that the hard hand on your shoulder and the malevolent light in your face jerked you from sleep made more troubled and uneasy by the tossing of that steel shell that encased you and with whose destiny yours was so irrevocably welded. And the clanging call of the general alarm rasped you to battle stations, night and day, from sleep and from meals, always with the same emptyhandedness of failure in the end. . . .

Early in August, Roosevelt cheerfully announced to the White House press corps that he was going fishing. The presidential yacht *Potomac* cruised idly near Martha's Vineyard for several days, and then disappeared as completely as if she had been torpedoed. It was not until August 14 that the world learned that Roosevelt and Churchill had rendezvoused for three days in Placentia Bay, off Argentia, Newfoundland, one of the bases transferred to the United States as part of the destroyer deal. Roosevelt arrived first, in the cruiser *Augusta*; the prime minister sailed into the misty harbor the next day in *Prince of Wales*, still bearing the scars of her encounter with *Bismarck*.

At this meeting, the two leaders discussed the problem of supplying the Russians, and Churchill tried to persuade Roosevelt to issue orders for the U.S. Navy to begin escorting trans-Atlantic convoys. The British were disappointed to find the ever-cautious president reluctant to make any commitment that would involve the United States in a shooting war, a wariness underscored by the news that Congress had approved extension of the draft by only a single vote.

Roosevelt assured Churchill that, as soon as an "incident" occurred that would stir American opinion, naval action would be stepped up. The major result of the meeting was the Atlantic Charter, in which the two countries expressed their war aims.

The emotional highpoint occurred on Sunday, August 10, when Roosevelt and several hundred members of *Augusta*'s crew attended church services on *Prince of Wales*. British and American sailors intermingled under the battleship's guns, shared the same prayer books, and joined together in the familiar old hymns, "Onward Christian Soldiers" and "For Those in Peril on the Sea." Tears flowed down Churchill's cheeks. "Every word seemed to stir the heart," he recalled in later years. "It was a great hour to live. Nearly half those who sang were soon to die."

The long-awaited "incident" sought by Roosevelt to permit the U.S. Navy to assume a major role in the Atlantic war occurred on September 4. While on a mail run to Iceland, the four-piper *Greer* received word from a Coastal Command Hudson that a German submarine, *U-652*, had been sighted about ten miles ahead. The destroyer raced to the scene and, with her sonar (the American term for Asdic) "locked" on the U-boat, tracked her for about three hours. The Hudson pilot, low on fuel and having ascertained that the Americans were not planning an attack, dropped three depth charges on the U-boat's suspected position and flew away. Unaware that an airplane had been responsible for the shaking up endured by his boat, *U-652*'s captain fired a torpedo at the destroyer that had been tormenting him. It missed, and *Greer* dropped a pattern of depth charges. A second torpedo was evaded, and, having lost contact with the U-boat, the destroyer resumed course to Iceland.

Roosevelt exploited the *Greer* incident, calling it "piracy," and branded the U-boats "the rattlesnakes of the Atlantic." The Defense Zone was extended to ten degrees west, only four hundred miles from Scotland. U.S. Navy warships now took over HX convoys from Canadian escorts south of Newfoundland and covered them to the MOMP off Iceland, where they were handed over to the Royal Navy. Having refueled, the American vessels would then shepherd convoys back to Newfoundland waters, where the Canadians had responsibility for their safety. Churchill hailed the move, saying it would relieve fifty destroyers and corvettes for duty in home waters. The first American-escorted convoy—HX 150, of fifty-one ships—arrived without loss.

Both Raeder and Dönitz pressed Hitler to remove the restrictions on attacking American shipping in the wake of these developments. "German forces must expect offensive war measures by these U.S. forces in every case of an encounter," the Grand Admiral declared. "There is no longer any difference between British and American ships." The Führer refused to act, however—a severe blow to Dönitz, who had once again shifted his boats to the westward. With his fleet growing larger, he set up patrol lines of ten or fifteen U-boats which combed the convoy routes in the Greenland-Iceland area like a giant rake. In mid-September, the U-boats sank sixteen ships of SC 42 in two nights of horror south of Greenland, and the convoy escaped additional losses only because fog set in. Two U-boats were sunk.

Not long afterward, the U.S. Navy engaged in its first convoy battle, and the inadequacy of its training and tactics became abundantly clear. Five American destroyers were sent to reinforce the escort of SC 48, a fifty-ship convoy that had lost three ships to a wolf pack on October 15, about four hundred miles south of Iceland. By sunset the following day, the division of American destroyers arrived, and they took up station close to the convoy, a tactic that, as the Royal Navy had discovered, allowed the U-boats to launch long-range attacks with relative impunity.

Three more ships were torpedoed that night, and the inexperienced Americans panicked. They dropped depth charges indiscriminately and fired star shells, which blinded the lookouts and added to the confusion. Swinging out to avoid a Canadian corvette in the melee, the U.S. destroyer *Kearny* was silhouetted against a flaming tanker. *U-568* fired a spread of torpedoes at her. One struck amidships on the starboard side, but *Kearny* was only a year old and survived to limp into port with eleven dead within her hull—the first American naval fatalities of the war. "Whether the country knows it or not," said Admiral Harold R. Stark, the chief of naval operations, "we are at war." Nevertheless, Hitler, still unwilling to precipitate a war with the United States, reiterated his order against attacks on American ships.

Four days later, on October 20, 1941, the four-piper *Reuben James* was torpedoed by *U-552* while serving as part of the four-ship escort of HX 156 about six hundred miles west of Ireland. Hit just ahead of her forward stack, the old ship broke in two. Fireman 1/c Norman Hingula scrambled topside and found "the lifeboats blown up, the number three stack toppled forward and just no ship at all forward of that." The bow section sank immediately, and the after part followed five minutes later. Only forty-five men of her complement of 160 were pulled from the icy, oil-covered sea. With no time to mourn its dead, the U.S. Navy girded for war in the Atlantic—but instead the blow fell in the Pacific.

Bogged down and being drained of resources by their long-running war in China, the Japanese looked to the oil-and-mineral wealth of Southeast Asia and the Dutch East Indies to keep their war machine running. The summer of 1941 seemed favorable for action. Britain was fighting desperately to defend the Suez Canal against Rommel's advancing troops, German armies were rolling across the plains of Russia, and the attention of the United States was fixed on the drama unfolding in the Atlantic. Japan began its drive to the south by occupying French Indochina in July 1941, with the acquiescence of the feeble Vichy regime.

The U.S. demanded that Japan immediately withdraw from the area, and when this was rejected, Washington delivered a body blow to the Japanese economy. Japanese assets in the United States were frozen, and an embargo on the shipment of oil and other vital supplies was tightened. The United States had supplied Japan with 90 percent of its aviation fuel, 75 percent of its scrap steel, and two-thirds of its machine tools. Without oil, Japan would be "like a fish in a pond from which the water is gradually being drained out," Admiral Osami Nagano, the chief of the Naval Staff, told Emperor Hirohito. The Japanese military, true rulers of the nation, responded to this threat by resolving upon war.[*]

Japanese naval strategists had planned for war with the United States since the naval limitations treaties of the 1920s. They were intox-

---

[*]Roosevelt had no desire to strangle Japan, however, and not long afterward Washington indicated that export licenses would be issued for low-grade petroleum products. Fearing that a complete embargo would trigger a Japanese invasion of the East Indies, "the President was still unwilling to draw the noose tight," observed Secretary of the Interior Harold L. Ickes. Lower-level bureaucrats blocked the Japanese from getting these export licenses, however. See Jonathan Utley, *Going to War With Japan*.

icated by the writings of Alfred Thayer Mahan and had adopted his idea of the "decisive battle," in which the two opposing fleets would eventually meet in a winner-take-all struggle that would determine the course of a war. Like the Americans and British, they had prepared for the next war in terms of the previous one, with the battleship and big gun the ultimate weapon. In case of war with the United States and the other Western nations, Japan planned to strike for the Dutch East Indies, taking the Philippines to protect their flank. When the U.S. Pacific Fleet counterattacked, submarines and aircraft would harass the Americans as they steamed through the Japanese-held Marshalls and Carolines, and the survivors would be destroyed in a climactic Jutland-style battle. It was the mirror image of War Plan Orange, the American plan for war with Japan, which called for an advance by the U.S. Pacific Fleet upon Japan through the Central Pacific.*

But Admiral Isoroku Yamamoto, commander-in-chief of the Combined Fleet since 1939, conceived a much more daring plan. Vigorous and outspoken, he attracted the friendship of both Japanese and foreigners and had a taste for Scotch, gambling, and women. Unlike most Japanese army officers, who had a limited world-view, Yamamoto had seen America's industrial might at first hand—as a language student at Harvard, and then as naval attaché in Washington—and regarded war with the United States as suicidal. Moreover, the training and traditions of the Imperial Navy were based on Britain's Royal Navy, which gave Japanese naval officers of Yamamoto's generation a pro-western view. He had opposed the Tripartite Treaty with Germany and Italy and at one time was earmarked for assassination by pro-Axis forces. "If I am told to fight [the Americans] regardless of consequences, I shall run wild . . . for the first six months or a year," he declared, "but I have utterly no confidence for the second and third years."

Once war became national policy, however, Yamamoto saw it as his duty to put Japan in the best position to win—and to win quickly. Urging a break with Japan's strategy of lying in wait in the Central Pacific to ambush the U.S. fleet, he called for a surprise aircraft-

---

*Orange was superseded in May 1941 by Rainbow Five, which became the U.S. Navy's governing war plan and reflected the "Europe First" strategy established by the ABC-1 Agreement. See Edward S. Miller, *War Plan Orange*, pp. 314–15.

carrier strike against the American battleships and carriers as they lay at anchor at Pearl Harbor, on the Hawaiian island of Oahu.

Such a bold stroke would take full advantage of the Imperial Navy's superior naval power in the Pacific—ten battleships to nine, and ten carriers to three. Japanese ships were powerful and battle-worthy; the superb oxygen-driven Long Lance torpedoes came as a terrible surprise to the Allies; the Imperial Navy's planes were superior to most American naval aircraft, with the Mitsubishi A6M Zero fighter soon becoming legendary. Unlike the U.S. Navy, the Imperial Navy had, in addition to carrier-based aircraft, a substantial land-based force. Japanese officers and men were skilled, especially in night fighting, and imbued with the fierce centuries-old samurai tradition. Moreover, Japanese strategists had only one ocean to think about, whereas the U.S. Navy had to consider the Atlantic as well as the Pacific. The Japanese also had the advantage of being closer to their objectives than the Americans.*

With the U.S. Pacific Fleet out of action, Yamamoto argued, Japan would be able to conquer the Philippines, Singapore, and the East Indies without interference. It could then retire behind a strong defense line running from the Kurile Islands, through the Marshalls, and along the fringes of Australia. Using interior lines of communication and supply, the Imperial Navy could beat off attacks on this barrier until the exhausted Allies accepted Japan's domination of the Greater East-Asian Co-Prosperity Sphere, as the Japanese called their new empire.

There was ample precedent for a surprise attack. Japan had launched victorious wars against both China and Russia with similar pre-emptive strikes. As early as 1928, Rear Admiral William A. Moffett, chief of the Bureau of Aeronautics, had predicted a carrier attack against Pearl Harbor. The only effective means of warding off such a strike was, he said, to maintain a continuous air patrol offshore to prevent enemy carriers from getting within range. The danger was dramatized when carrier aircraft coming in from the northeast

---

*On the other hand, the Japanese neglected antisubmarine warfare and radar, there was a shortage of small escorts to defend convoys, and, despite the nation's dependence on maritime trade, freighters and tankers were in short supply. There was also a rivalry between the navy and the army even more bitter than that prevailing among the American armed forces.

successfully "attacked" Pearl Harbor during U.S. Navy fleet exercises in 1932, 1933, and 1938.

In view of the exposed position of Pearl Harbor, Admiral James O. Richardson, commander-in-chief of the Pacific Fleet, sought permission from President Roosevelt to withdraw to California. Pearl Harbor, said Richardson, was a "God-damned mousetrap." Regarding the Pacific Fleet as a deterrent rather than a target, Roosevelt refused, saying such a move would convince the Japanese that the United States was abandoning the Pacific to them. Richardson continued to grumble and was relieved in February 1941 by Admiral Husband E. Kimmel, who had served as Roosevelt's aide when the president had been assistant secretary of the navy.

Yamamoto had no easy time selling his proposal for a strike by a fleet of carriers, however. A fleet of carriers? It was an idea unheard of at the time, and was called too risky, too unconventional by the Naval General Staff. Yamamoto overcame these objections by the force of his personality, even threatening to resign. Planning for the operation—known as Plan Z—began in February 1941 under the direction of Commanders Minoru Genda, Mitsuo Fuchida, and Kosei Maeda, and proceeded behind a thick veil of secrecy, with the actual training of the hand-picked air crews beginning in September on Kagoshima Bay, which resembled Pearl Harbor.

Technicians modified sixteen-inch armor-piercing shells into bombs and fitted wooden fins to the aerial torpedoes to enable them to run true in the shallow waters (about thirty-nine feet) of Pearl Harbor.[*] Every pilot had his designated target—with special attention being paid to the carriers. Japanese intelligence kept close watch on the Pacific Fleet's comings and goings, and the consulate in Honolulu sent in weekly summaries of ships at anchor in Pearl Harbor and at sea.

The go-ahead for the attack was given on November 3. The *Kido Butai*, the Pearl Harbor Strike Force, consisting of two fast battleships and six carriers—*Akagi, Kaga, Hiryu, Soryu, Shokaku,* and *Zuikaku*—crammed with 425 planes under the command of Vice-Admiral Chuichi Nagumo began to assemble in the Kuriles. One would have expected that an air admiral would be chosen to lead such an important operation, but Nagumo was without aviation expe-

---

[*]Japanese aerial torpedoes were standard models rather than the Long Lance type.

rience. The Pearl Harbor command fell to him because of seniority, even though he regarded Yamamoto's plan as a gambler's venture. Under such circumstances, he believed his primary duty was to preserve his fleet. To mask this massive gathering of warships, the Japanese generated false radio traffic aimed at convincing the U.S. Navy that the carriers were still in home waters. In reality, American intelligence had lost track of them.

Flying his flag in *Akagi*, Nagumo led the Pearl Harbor Strike Force to sea at 0600 on November 26, and it headed into the thick fog of the North Pacific to a previously arranged standby point to await the final decision for war. It was the strongest carrier force yet seen. Twenty-seven submarines, eleven of which carried planes while five had midget submarines, had gone ahead. Several factors contributed to the timing of the attack. The Japanese knew that the Pacific Fleet usually returned to Pearl Harbor during weekends, and the ships would not be fully manned at that time, making a Sunday the ideal choice for the raid. Further, after mid-December, the weather was likely to be unfavorable for landings in Malaya and the Philippines, since the monsoon would be at its peak.

As the Japanese ships headed ghostlike over a circuitous route toward Hawaii, avoiding the shipping lanes and maintaining strict radio silence, the final scenes in a diplomatic shadow play were being acted out in Washington, where Admiral Saburo Kurusu, a special envoy, was engaged in trying to negotiate a last-minute settlement with the United States. Unknown to the Japanese, the Americans were reading their "mail." A joint army-navy code-breaking operation known as MAGIC had broken the Japanese diplomatic, or Purple, code (an American designation). MAGIC provided no clues to the Pearl Harbor operation, however, because it was never discussed in the diplomatic code and the code breakers were just beginning to break into JN25, the Japanese fleet's operational cipher.*

---

*Unlike Enigma, which used rotors in its ciphering system, Purple worked like a telephone switchboard, using switches to shuffle arrangements of letters and numbers. William Friedman, the army's brilliant chief cryptanalyst, succeeded in the seemingly impossible task of cloning the Purple machine in August 1940 without ever having seen the original. MAGIC was limited to the president, the secretaries of state, war, and navy, and top-ranking army and navy officers. Despite several scares, the Japanese never discovered that Purple had been penetrated.

On November 26, the United States handed the Japanese emissary a note demanding the end of the war in China. No one expected Japan to accept this ultimatum, but Kurusu was instructed by Tokyo to continue the talks. Ominous reports of Japanese troop and naval movements along the coast of Southeast Asia were filtering into Washington, and on November 27 a "war warning" was sent to Admiral Kimmel and Lieutenant General Walter C. Short, the army commander in Hawaii, as well as Admiral Thomas C. Hart, commander of the small Asiatic Fleet, based at Manila. Negotiations with the Japanese had broken down, and an "aggressive move by Japan is expected within the next few days," against the Philippines or Thailand or Borneo, the message read. There was no mention of a possible attack on Pearl Harbor, but the two commanders were instructed to "execute defensive deployment."

Short, who was responsible for the defense of the islands, took no action except to mass his aircraft to prevent sabotage. Kimmel ordered the lowest condition of readiness. Rear Admiral Patrick N. L. Bellinger, his air chief, had warned in March 1941 that the most likely method of attack on Pearl Harbor was a surprise early morning air raid launched by carriers, but there were not enough planes available for around-the-compass patrols.* Kimmel considered sending the fleet to sea but decided against it, because the carriers Lexington and Enterprise were ferrying planes to Wake and Midway islands and Saratoga was undergoing repair on the West Coast. Torpedo nets were unavailable; Pearl Harbor was thought to be too shallow for torpedoes to be employed effectively, and there were no barrage balloons.

Winter gales buffeted Nagumo's eastward-moving ships, making it difficult for them to maintain formation, but it was excellent weather for escaping detection.† Radio silence was maintained by the strike

---

*One of the myths surrounding Pearl Harbor is that Bellinger warned Kimmel that it was most likely an enemy attack would come from the north because of the prevailing winds and Kimmel was derelict in not following up this warning. In point of fact, Bellinger made no mention of this in his recommendations to Kimmel.

†The Japanese were sighted on December 5 by a Russian freighter which supposedly did not make the usual sighting report. The incident raises speculation on the possibility that the ship did transmit a message but the Soviets deliberately withheld knowledge of the forthcoming attack in exchange for a Japanese promise not to attack Russia. Stalin was certainly capable of such double-dealing—and worse.

force, but it continued to receive instructions and intelligence reports from Admiral Yamamoto, who had remained behind in Japan. The decision for war was made on December 1, and on the following day a prearranged signal was flashed to Nagumo: CLIMB MOUNT NIITAKA 1208. The attack was set for December 8 (Sunday, December 7, U.S. time).

By December 6, it was evident in Washington that war with Japan was only hours away. "Gentlemen, are they going to hit us?" asked Navy Secretary Frank Knox at a staff meeting.

"No, Mr. Secretary," replied Rear Admiral Richmond Kelley Turner, head of the navy's War Plans Division. "They are going to hit the British. They are not ready for us yet."

The Japanese had sent their embassy a reply to the American ultimatum, which was read by American cryptanalysts. It broke off relations between the two countries; such a move had in times past been followed by a surprise attack. Japanese diplomats in various world capitals were reported to be burning secret documents—also usually a clue that war is imminent. Between 0400 and 0600 on December 7, MAGIC cryptanalysts deciphered instructions to Kurusu and Kichisaburo Nomura, the Japanese ambassador, to deliver their message to the State Department at 1300 Washington time—0730 at Pearl Harbor. As a result of a mix-up at the Japanese Embassy, the message was not delivered until the raid was under way.[*]

Picking up speed, the task force turned south toward Oahu at twenty-four knots. *Akagi* hoisted the "Z flag," which had been flown by the Japanese fleet at its overwhelming victory over the Russians at Tsushima in 1905. Last-minute intelligence reports reaching Nagumo caused concern, because they stated no American carriers were at Pearl Harbor. Yamamoto had made these his top priority and counted on the ships' being in port. But there was a full complement of battleships, and some carriers might return to Pearl Harbor by the time of the raid. So the task force sped on toward its target, every officer and man tense and ready for battle.

_____

[*]There is no evidence to indicate that the Japanese envoys knew of the Pearl Harbor attack beforehand.

•

CHAPTER 7

"Air Raid!
This Is No Drill!"

Ensign Joseph K. Taussig was nervous as the hands of the clock swept toward 0800 on Sunday morning, December 7, 1941. As officer of the deck in the battleship *Nevada*, moored on Battleship Row at Pearl Harbor, he was responsible for raising the colors, but he had never performed this duty before and was uncertain as to what size flag should be used. He sent a man over to *Arizona*, the next ship in line, to find out what size she was using. As *Nevada*'s band and marine guard lined up on the fantail at 0755, they idly noted a line of aircraft coming in from over the blue-green hills behind the base. Suddenly, the planes swooped down on the air station on nearby Ford Island, and the morning peace was ripped apart by bomb explosions.

Exactly at 0800, the band automatically crashed into the national anthem. Midway through the ceremony, one of the attacking planes, having let go a torpedo, pulled away over *Nevada*, spraying her after-deck with machine-gun fire. The color party could plainly see the Rising Sun emblem on its wings. The flag that had just been raised was slashed to ribbons, but the men, evidently in shock, remained rooted to the deck until the bandsmen had sounded the last note. "Air Raid! This is no drill!" Taussig repeatedly shouted into the public-address system. "Air Raid! This is no drill!"

Only two hours before, the six carriers of the Pearl Harbor Strike Force, bows flinging off white clouds of spray, had turned into the wind to launch their deadly brood. Their decks were pitching and heaving in the heavy sea, and the aircraft got off with some difficulty. As the plane of Commander Mitsuo Fuchida, the attack leader, roared down the deck of *Akagi* into the dawning sky, the crew sped him on his way with three ceremonial "*Banzai*'s." Within a quarter-hour, 183 aircraft—Nakajima B5N Kate* torpedo and high-level bombers, Aichi D3A Val dive-bombers, and Zero fighters—were speeding southwest toward Pearl Harbor, about 230 miles away. Undetected, the Japanese planes droned in on Oahu, as the clouds broke and the sun slanted down on an empty sea.

Shortly before 0700, the destroyer *Ward* reported that she had sunk an unidentified submarine that appeared to have been trying to sneak past the swinging gate at the entrance to Pearl Harbor. The report was delayed in transit to Admiral Kimmel's headquarters. Not long afterward, Privates Joseph Lockhard and George Elliott, army radar operators at the northern tip of Oahu, picked up a large "blip" on their screen, indicating a swarm of aircraft coming in from the northeast. Without checking, their superiors took these to be the dozen B-17 bombers expected in from the West Coast, and dismissed the report.

"Pearl Harbor was still asleep in the morning mist," one of the Japanese pilots later reported. "It was calm and serene inside the harbor, not even a trace of smoke rising from the ships at Oahu. The orderly groups of barracks, the wiggling white line of automobiles climbing up the mountaintop; fine objectives of attack lay in all directions." Despite the hours of drill at a mock-up table of Pearl Harbor, the flyers were awed by the sight that met their eyes. Seven battleships were moored with awnings spread on Battleship Row; the flagship *Pennsylvania* was in drydock.† None of the carriers had returned to Pearl Harbor, however. Surprise was complete. Commander Fuchida flashed a coded signal back to Admiral Nagumo at 0753: TORA . . . TORA . . . TORA ("Tiger . . . Tiger . . . Tiger").

The ninety-four ships in harbor and the shore stations were just

---

*The "Kate" and "Val" designations were applied by the U.S. Navy to simplify identification. Zeros were called "Zekes."

†*Colorado*, the Pacific Fleet's ninth battleship, was undergoing overhaul on the West Coast.

beginning to come to life. Many of the officers and men were enjoying weekend liberty ashore, and others were having a late breakfast. Some had found a quiet place to read the Sunday comics, or to write Christmas cards to the folks back home. A Honolulu radio station was broadcasting light music, and the sound of church bells in Pearl City drifted across the gently rippling waters of the anchorage. Only a few of the fleet's anti-aircraft guns were manned, and most of the ready boxes of ammunition were locked, the keys taken ashore by the officers.

The airfields scattered about Oahu—Hickam, Wheeler, Ewa, and Kaneohe—were hit first by the Japanese dive-bombers and fighters, to prevent U.S. planes from getting into the air. Some of the bombers plunged within a few hundred feet of the ground before releasing, to ensure the highest accuracy. Lined up wing to wing as if for inspection—it was easier to guard them from sabotage that way—dozens of army, navy, and marine aircraft were blasted into twisted and burning piles of scrap metal. Only a few of the defenders were able to get into the air,* and most were quickly shot down by the Zeros. Pilots and ground crews tried to fight back with machine guns wrenched from wrecked planes, but to little avail. Within minutes, the Japanese had completely knocked out the island's air defenses.

On the ships, men raced to their battle stations. Zeros ripped them with gunfire, trying to wipe out the gun crews before they could get into action. The decks were strewn with dead and wounded and slippery with blood. An eternity seemed to pass before the locks on the ready boxes were broken and the fleet began to put up an irregular fire. In a rage, Boatswain's Mate Thomas Donahue of the destroyer *Monaghan* threw several monkey wrenches at low-flying planes as he waited for ammunition for his five-inch gun. "Powder! I need powder!" he cried. "I can't keep throwing things at them."

Kate torpedo planes and Val dive-bombers now swept in from several directions to concentrate on the battleships. Zooming in at little more than forty feet above the water, the Kates dropped their torpedoes with deadly precision. Chief Flight Petty Officer Juzo Mori suddenly found a battleship looming up "directly in front of my speeding

---

*Two army P-40 fighters managed to get aloft, and shot down five planes. One of the pilots, Lieutenant George Welch, was recommended for the Medal of Honor, but it was denied because he had taken off without orders.

plane; it towered ahead of the bomber like a great mountain peak."
Oblivious to everything else, he continued to bore in. "Prepare for
release. . . . Stand by. . . . Release torpedo!" Mori jerked with all his
strength at the torpedo release and felt his plane pitch upward as it
was freed of its burden. Defensive fire was intensifying with every
second, so he turned away and headed for the open sea. "I was so
frightened," Mori said, "that before I left the target area my clothes
were soaking with perspiration."

Every one of the outboard ships on Battleship Row was hit several
times by torpedoes, and Pearl Harbor was dotted with towering
waterspouts. Black puffs of anti-aircraft fire exploded about Fuchida's
plane as he led his high-level bombers over the battleships to complete the task of destruction. He felt his craft "bounce as if struck by
a club." As he made his bombing run, he observed the fall of the
bombs through a hole in the plane's floor. "I watched four bombs
plummet toward the earth. The target—two battleships moored side
by side—lay ahead. The bombs became smaller and smaller and
finally disappeared. I held my breath until two tiny puffs of smoke
flashed suddenly on the ship to the left, and I shouted, 'Two hits!' "

Suddenly, the Japanese planes were rocked by the force of a
tremendous explosion as *Arizona* blew up. An armor-piercing bomb
had smashed through the battleship's steel deck—she had already
been hit by a torpedo—and touched off the forward magazine. Huge
pieces of the vessel were hurled hundreds of feet into the air, and a
dark-red cloud of smoke billowed into the sky. Torn in half and swept
by flames, *Arizona* became a tomb for nearly eleven hundred of the
roughly fourteen hundred officers and men on board. Fuel spewed
from her ruptured tanks and ignited, transforming the waters about
her into an inferno.

West Virginia was struck by six or seven torpedoes, which ripped
a gash 120 feet long and fifteen feet wide in her port side. She was
listing badly and only counterflooding kept her from capsizing. Two
torpedoes hit *California*, and she settled into the mud with her main
deck nearly awash. *Maryland, Tennessee,* and the flagship *Pennsylvania* escaped serious damage but were unable to get to sea—the first
two wedged in by sinking ships, and *Pennsylvania* because she was
drydocked. Hit by a spread of three torpedoes, *Oklahoma* began to
list to port almost immediately, and turned turtle after being struck

again and again. Stephen B. Young, a seaman assigned to Turret No. 4, later recalled:

> Those of us who were left behind down in the powder handling room during those final seconds when the ship capsized were not aware at first that she was turning turtle. The darkness there was wild and confusing with objects of all descriptions being tumbled and thrown about. As we frantically fought to save ourselves, we became disoriented. . . . I felt the ship lurch. The deck slipped out from under me and my hands snatched at empty air. I was tossed and spun around, pitched into a great nothingness, suspended in air. . . . All of us—the living, dying and the dead—were whirled about. . . . Then the dark waters closed in over me as the ship came to rest—upside down on the bottom of the harbor. . . . I was surprised to find myself alive. . . .

At 0854, a second wave, of 170 Japanese planes, continued the onslaught against the airfields and ships, now almost hidden by billowing clouds of black, oily smoke. Some concentrated on *Nevada*, which had steam up in two of her boilers at the time of the attack and got under way despite a gaping torpedo hole in her port bow. With her topsides a shambles and taking on water, she backed out of the flaming oil surrounding the shattered *Arizona* and made her way toward the harbor's mouth. Wave after wave of dive-bombers attacked *Nevada*, trying to sink her in the channel, but the battleship survived by throwing up a heavy barrage of anti-aircraft fire. She was too badly damaged to maintain way, however, and was run aground off Hospital Point.

Eighteen SBD Dauntless dive-bombers flying in from *Enterprise*, and the B-17s expected in from the mainland, were unlucky enough to arrive in the midst of the Japanese attack and were pounced upon by the Zeros. Several were shot down before they could defend themselves. Others fell victim to the anti-aircraft gunners, who were firing at anything in the air. "Please don't shoot!" radioed one pilot. "This is an American plane!" And then his radio went dead.

For nearly two hours, until about 0945, the Japanese dominated the skies over Pearl Harbor, strafing and bombing targets at will. By the time the planes returned to their carriers, the anchorage was dotted with the wreckage of nineteen ships, including almost the entire battle line of the Pacific Fleet. An estimated 265 American planes had

been destroyed, and American casualties totaled 2,403 sailors, soldiers, and airmen dead and 1,178 wounded. The Japanese lost
twenty-nine planes and fifty-five airman, one submarine with its
crew of sixty-five men, and all five midget submarines. It was the
worst disaster in American military history. A spent bullet struck
Admiral Kimmel in the chest during the attack, and he murmured,
"Too bad it didn't kill me."

Upon his return to *Akagi*, the elated Fuchida informed Admiral
Nagumo that the enemy's air-and-sea defense had been virtually
destroyed and, along with Commander Genda, pressed for another
strike, this time against the repair facilities and fuel-storage tanks. If
these were destroyed, Pearl Harbor would be useless, and Americans
would be forced back to the West Coast, two thousand miles away. But
Nagumo, a reluctant warrior who believed he had accomplished his mission, saw no reason to endanger the fleet any longer. Once all the aircraft of the second attack wave had been recovered, the Japanese
withdrew at top speed,slipping away as swiftly and silently as they had
come.*

"Yesterday, December 7, 1941—a date which will live in infamy—the
United States was suddenly and deliberately attacked by naval and
air forces of Japan." With these grim words, President Roosevelt
asked a joint session of Congress for a declaration of war against
Japan. Thick, black smoke was still rising from the shattered ships of
the Pacific Fleet as Congress promptly complied with the president's
request. But Pearl Harbor was merely one small part of a Japanese
master plan of conquest in Southeast Asia and the Pacific. Guam and
Wake Island, the Philippines, Malaya, Hong Kong, Burma, and the
Dutch East Indies were also attacked. War rapidly spread through six
time zones and across the International Date Line. Three days later,
the Pacific battle and the Atlantic conflict became a single global
struggle, after Hitler declared war on the United States.

---

*Intelligence documents turned over to the National Archives by the National Secu-
rity Agency in 1981 indicate that the Japanese planned a submarine attack on U.S. ships
operating from Pearl harbor on New Year's Eve 1941, a little more than three weeks after
the Pearl Harbor raid. The attack was not carried out, however. Washington *Post*, January 1, 1982.

Yet, despite their success in crippling the Pacific Fleet, the Japanese had won only a temporary victory. Except for *Arizona*, all the stricken battleships were raised from the mud of Pearl Harbor, and all but *Oklahoma* would see action. The Japanese failure to knock out the American carriers brought about a naval revolution, and the fast-carrier task force eventually became the spearhead of the U.S. Navy's offensive against Japan. Moreover, the attack united the American people, who, in their rage at what was perceived as a dastardly sneak attack, were determined to defeat Japan at any cost. If the Japanese had hoped for a negotiated settlement which would allow them to keep their spoils after the Americans had been exhausted by a series of defeats, they forfeited it by the way in which they had begun the war. This was the true importance of Pearl Harbor.

The last Japanese plane had hardly left the skies over Hawaii before there were angry demands to know why Pearl Harbor had been caught napping and who was responsible for the disaster. Admiral Kimmel and General Short were precipitously relieved of their commands. Yet, in vivid contrast, General Douglas MacArthur escaped censure, even through his forces in the Philippines were caught by surprise nearly nine hours *after* word had reached him of the attack on Pearl Harbor. As commanders, Short and Kimmel were responsible for what happened on their "watch," but it is also obvious that they were singled out as convenient scapegoats.

There was plenty of blame to go around. Pearl Harbor was more than an intelligence failure or the disastrous result of an inability to read an opponent's intentions; it was a failure of command from the top down. Roosevelt and the nation's ranking civilian and military leadership bore direct responsibility because of errors of commission and omission. Yet to place all the blame on the American side is to operate in a vacuum—to ignore the role of the Japanese at Pearl Harbor. The attack succeeded not because of American shortcomings but because it was brilliantly conceived, skillfully planned, and carried out with courage and daring. Surprise or no surprise, there was no Allied naval force that could have stopped the fleet that hit Pearl Harbor—and if the Pacific Fleet had tried it would have been destroyed.

Conspiracy theorists have built a cottage industry on attempts to prove that President Roosevelt had foreknowledge of the Japanese attack and deliberately sacrificed the Pacific Fleet to bring the United

States into the war against Nazi Germany through the back door. Having ignored clear signals of an impending raid on Hawaii, the master plotter in the White House then had the files "sanitized" to remove all traces of the conspiracy—or so goes this line of thinking. Some writers contend that the British had advance knowledge of the Japanese attack on Pearl Harbor, which Churchill intentionally withheld from Roosevelt to embroil the United States in the war. A study of British intelligence produced in 1945 and released in 1994 states that Britain did not have advance warning of Japanese intentions.

Pearl Harbor certainly rescued Roosevelt from an impossible situation, but it is hardly likely that he would have offered up the entire Pacific Fleet as a sacrifice when those same ships would be needed to win the war. Moreover, as far as Roosevelt was concerned, a war in the Pacific was the wrong war at the wrong time in the wrong ocean. The basic thrust of his policy was to keep Britain afloat; war with Japan would drain off men and materiel from operations against Germany, which he saw as the main enemy. The conspiracy theory is also undermined by the lack of any assurance that, even if Japan was provoked into an attack upon the United States, war with Germany would result. Nothing in the Tripartite Treaty, which Japan had signed with Hitler and Mussolini, required the signatories to come to the aid of the others in case of war. Japan used this loophole to escape joining in the Axis attack on the Soviet Union, so why should Hitler assist his less-than-faithful ally?

The Germans were unaware of the planned attack on Pearl Harbor and were just as surprised as the Americans. If Hitler had not declared war on the United States, it would have been a masterstroke. There was no certainty that, in their rage against Japan, the American people would also have demanded a declaration of war against Germany. Thus, the Americans and the British would have been trapped in a war in the Far East which would have diverted American arms and supplies from the European front—hardly the goal of Roosevelt's policy.

Paradoxically, there was no shortage of intelligence about the imminence of war with Japan. The problem lay in the fact that there was so much information that policymakers found it impossible to determine Japanese intentions. Conventional wisdom held that the Japanese would move south to seize Southeast Asia and the Philippines. Other analysts predicted a move north to attack the reeling Soviet Union. General George C. Marshall, the army chief of staff, thought the Panama Canal was in greater danger than Hawaii. Everyone ruled out an attack on Pearl Harbor, because it was believed Japan lacked the capacity to mount such an operation.

Racism had as much to do with this blindness as lack of foresight. Most Americans regarded the Japanese as bucktoothed, bespectacled little men, constantly photographing things so they could copy them. Japanese planes and ships were said to be inferior copies of American models, myopic Japanese pilots would be unable to hit their targets, and Japan's teahouse economy would quickly collapse under wartime strains. The New York tabloid *PM* ran an article on "How We Can Lick Japan in Sixty Days."

Information poured in upon Washington from a variety of sources. In addition to the MAGIC decrypts, the policymakers had access to messages in the lower-priority J-19 code, the tracking of Japanese naval vessels by their radio call signs, reports from American and foreign diplomats, and the observed movements of troops and vessels. Random clues pointing to an attack on Pearl Harbor were embedded in this mass of information, but the volume was overwhelming, and no one was vested with the task of weeding the significant from the irrelevant. Only in the brilliant light of 20/20 hindsight were these seemingly irrelevant hints seen as heralds of the Japanese attack.

MAGIC was a double-edged sword, for one of the major hazards of intelligence is the tendency to rely too heavily on a single source. Roosevelt and his advisers believed MAGIC provided them with an infallible guide to Japanese intentions. Other sources were downgraded or ignored. The fetish for secrecy surrounding the operation also proved to be self-defeating. Neither Kimmel nor Short was privy to MAGIC, which would have allowed them to monitor the progress of the talks under way in Washington. A Purple machine was to have been sent to Pearl Harbor in the summer of 1941 but went to Britain instead.

Although MAGIC was silent on the subject of Pearl Harbor, messages in J 19 displayed an abnormal interest in the base. On September 21, the Japanese consulate in Honolulu was instructed to divide the naval anchorage into five alphabetically coded zones and to report the exact positions of the ships of the Pacific Fleet. But

MAGIC had a higher priority than J 19; little importance was placed upon this message in Washington, and it was not even passed on to the commanders in Hawaii. "Had we seen messages that had to do with Pearl Harbor, then there would have been a different evaluation of those items," stated Lieutenant Commander Edwin T. Layton, the Pacific Fleet's top intelligence officer.

Having failed to provide Kimmel and Short with access to MAGIC, Washington blundered by not keeping them informed of changing conditions. General Marshall and Admiral Stark, the chief of naval operations, should both have made certain the military commanders in Hawaii were on the alert. Sound military doctrine holds that the commander on the scene should be given all pertinent information upon which to base his decisions. Failing that, he should be given explicit orders. Kimmel and Short received neither.*

Fanning out from the home islands like the rays of the rising sun, the Japanese won control of East Asia and the Pacific with a rapidity that surprised even themselves. While Nagumo's carriers were making the final approach to the Hawaiian Islands, a Southern Force under Vice-Admiral Nobutake Kondo was heading for targets in what the Japanese called the Southern Resource Area. Only hours after the attack on Pearl Harbor, pre-positioned Japanese troops were ashore in Malaya; Thailand was under Japanese control; and the Philippines, Singapore, and the all-important Dutch East Indies with their vital oil fields were being threatened. Guam and Hong Kong were captured. Once again, the Japanese proved, as the Germans had in Norway, that relatively modest units can achieve almost impossible goals through the bold use of sea-and-air power.

The Japanese conquest went off without a hitch except at Wake

---

*Early on the morning of December 7, Admiral Stark, worried about the deteriorating situation in the Far East, went to his office, read the latest intercepted messages, and tried to confer by telephone with General Marshall. Marshall, he was told, was out horseback riding, and Stark did not hear from him for at least two hours. Marshall agreed the situation was indeed ominous after reading the messages, and told the admiral he would send a warning to the Pacific commanders. There were further delays, and then— because atmospheric conditions interfered with army radio—the alert was sent by commercial cable. It arrived, delivered by a messenger boy of Japanese ancestry on a bicycle, just as the attack was beginning.

Island, which was defended by a tiny garrison of marines, supported by a few F4F Wildcat fighters and a half-dozen five-inch guns. Wake was under the overall command of Commander Winfield S. Cunningham; the marine detachment was led by Major James P. S. Devereux. They beat off an initial assault on December 11, sinking two destroyers—the first Japanese surface ships lost in the war—and damaged a light cruiser and several other vessels. Having lost at least five hundred men, the Japanese withdrew for the moment, although they subjected the atoll to daily bombing.

Reinforced by two carriers homeward bound from Pearl Harbor, the Japanese returned on December 23. "Enemy has landed," Cunningham radioed Pearl Harbor. "The issue is still in doubt." The marines fought hand to hand on the beaches for five hours but, outnumbered and exhausted, they were finally forced to surrender. The capture of Wake and Guam gave the Japanese full control of the line of communications running across the Central Pacific from Hawaii to the Philippines. Admiral Kimmel had dispatched Task Force 14, built around the carrier *Saratoga*, commanded by Rear Admiral Frank Jack Fletcher, and two other carrier groups to relieve the garrison and to try to entice the Japanese into a fleet action off Wake. But after Kimmel's removal, his temporary successor, Vice-Admiral William S. Pye, was unwilling to risk carriers and called off the operation.* Tragically, they put about for Pearl Harbor just as the ships were coming within range of the atoll. The order to withdraw was received with rage bordering on mutiny on *Saratoga*.

In the Philippines, there was an unhappy rerun of the Pearl Harbor debacle. With the rise of Japanese power in the Pacific, American

---

*Although Pye was at fault, Fletcher became the scapegoat for the failure of the operation. No American admiral has had a worst press in postwar histories than Fletcher, and even though he had won the Medal of Honor during the Vera Cruz expedition of 1914, he has been accused of cowardice. Fletcher's basic problem was that he was a battleship sailor rather than an aviator, and the flyers resented the idea of a nonaviator commanding a carrier task force. When the Wake Island operation failed, he rather than Pye became the fall guy. Fletcher's partisans state that Samuel Eliot Morison picked up these criticisms and repeated them in his semiofficial history of World War II naval operations. For a full discussion, see Lundstrom, "Frank Jack Fletcher Got a Bum Rap," pt. I, *Naval History*, Summer 1992.

strategists had written off the archipelago as indefensible. If there was a Japanese invasion, the skeleton American forces on Luzon were to retreat to the Bataan Peninsula on Manila Bay, establish a defense line, and hold out until the Pacific Fleet fought its way, island by island, to their rescue. But General Douglas MacArthur, the bombastic former army chief of staff who had been plucked from retirement and sent to the Philippines in the mid-1930s, was unhappy with the prospect of commanding a doomed army, and came up with a new plan.

MacArthur argued that an expanded Philippine army of two hundred thousand men backed up by a large concentration of American air power could meet the invaders on the beaches and drive them back into the sea. This proposal fell upon ready ears in Washington, which had been uncomfortable with the abandonment of the Philippines, and 128 of the nation's long-range B-17 bombers were earmarked for MacArthur's command. There was talk of using the bombers in pre-emptive strikes against Japan, and MacArthur was given a list of 250 industrial targets in the Tokyo area. But at the end of 1941, only the first B-17s had arrived, and the Filipino troops were raw and poorly supplied. Nevertheless, a few days before Pearl Harbor, MacArthur told the president he could hold the Philippines in the event of a Japanese attack, adding that his appraisal was based on the "inability of our enemy to launch his air attacks on the islands."

The Asiatic Fleet was commanded by the highly regarded Admiral Thomas C. Hart, who had been kept at his post beyond normal retirement age. Based at Cavite, on Manila Bay, the finest harbor in the Far East, this fleet consisted of the modern heavy cruiser *Houston*; two light cruisers, the modern *Boise* and the veteran *Marblehead*; thirteen "four-pipers"; and twenty-nine submarines—almost equal to the number of operational boats that Karl Dönitz had had when the European war began.

Manila received word of the Pearl Harbor attack at about 0300 on December 8, just as the last Japanese planes were leaving Pearl Harbor. General Lewis H. Brereton, MacArthur's air commander, immediately pressed headquarters for permission to send his thirty-four operational B-17s—based at Clark Field, about sixty miles from the capital—against Japanese bases on Formosa, to the north, from which an attack was likely to develop. Hours went by and, as Brereton told the story, he was unable to penetrate MacArthur's sycophantic Prae-torian guard despite several attempts to see him. Barricaded in his luxurious penthouse suite atop a Manila hotel, MacArthur was appar-ently undergoing a crisis of nerves. Some of Brereton's aircraft flew reconnaissance missions but found nothing. Finally, at 1120, about eight hours after the Pearl Harbor attack, he received orders to attack the Formosan airfields. But the B-17s were still on the ground when, at 1220, Japanese twin-engine bombers and Zeros struck Clark Field and other air bases.*

"Instead of encountering a swarm of enemy fighters," recalled Flight Petty Office Saburo Sakai, one of Japan's top fighter aces, "we looked down and saw some 60 enemy bombers and fighters neatly parked. They squatted there like sitting ducks. Our accuracy was phenomenal. The entire air base seemed to be rising into the air with the explosions. Great fires erupted, and smoke boiled upward." Within minutes, the U.S. Army Air Force, Far East, was eliminated as an effective combat unit—"on the *ground*, on the *ground!*," as a furi-ous President Roosevelt declared. Only four American fighters man-aged to take off, and all were shot down. With the destruction of American air power in the Philippines, any real hope of repelling a Japanese landing vanished. The Japanese returned on December 10, after a spell of bad weather, to attack the Cavite naval base.

For nearly two hours, bombers crisscrossed the sky high over the base, well out of range of its outmoded anti-aircraft guns. The few American planes that got into the sky were swept aside. "The entire Yard and about a third of the city of Cavite were ablaze from end to end," reported Admiral Hart. Fortunately, he had dispatched most of his ships to the Dutch East Indies. Only the submarines remained to contest the invasion of the islands.

Like the B-17s, the Asiatic Fleet submarines had been expected to play a key role in preventing Japanese landings, but they failed to

---

*There were eight separate investigations of the Pearl Harbor debacle, but not a sin-gle inquiry was even launched into the Philippine catastrophe. Instead, MacArthur, who managed to shift the blame to the shoulders of others, was elevated by a drumbeat of pro-paganda, much of it created by his own publicity machine, into the "Lion of Luzon." Once he was safe on his pedestal, it was impossible to dislodge him, because the Amer-ican people, shocked by a steady stream of defeats, needed heroes in this time of psy-chological stress.

impede or even threaten them. Forty-five attacks were made on enemy shipping and ninety-six torpedoes expended—yet only three freighters were sunk. The submarine *Sargo* made eight attacks on Japanese convoys bound for the Philippines and fired thirteen torpedoes without scoring a single hit. American training was inadequate, and some of submarine skippers were overcautious, if not actually timid. Unnerved by a depth charge attack, one captain turned over command of his boat to his executive officer and had himself locked in his cabin. The torpedoes themselves were also defective. Like the German torpedoes at the start of the war, the U.S. Navy's Mark XIV torpedoes tended to run deeper than set, and when a target was hit often failed to explode because of defective detonators.[*]

Unhindered by aircraft or submarines, the Japanese landed some forty thousand men at Lingayen Gulf on December 22. Instead of "meeting them on the beaches," as General MacArthur had avowed, he retreated with his ill-trained army of sixty-five thousand Filipino and twenty thousand American troops to the jungles of Bataan, and established his headquarters in the tunnels of Corregidor, a fortified island in Manila Bay—the plan he had originally called "defeatist." Expecting to prevent Japanese landings, MacArthur had failed to stockpile ammunition and supplies on Bataan and Corregidor, and his men were on short rations from the beginning. Nevertheless, despite disease and near starvation, Bataan held out until April 9, while Corregidor withstood siege for another month. MacArthur, however, had gone. In March, at the orders of President Roosevelt, he had left the Philippines by PT-boat to take charge of the defense of Australia.

On the evening of December 10, Winston Churchill, veering between gloating over the American entry into the war—"So we had won after all!"—and anguish over the endless string of defeats inflicted upon the Allies by the Japanese, received a telephone call from Admiral Pound, the First Sea Lord. Pound's voice was constricted, hesitant, a little indistinct. "Prime Minister, I have to report to you that *Prince of Wales* and *Repulse* have been sunk by the Japanese—we think by aircraft. . . ."

---

[*]Further details are in chapter 19.

"In all the war I never received a more direct shock," Churchill later confessed. "As I turned and twisted in bed the full horror of the news sank in upon me. There were no British or American capital ships in the Indian Ocean or the Pacific. . . . Over all this vast expanse of waters Japan was supreme, and we everywhere were weak and naked." Churchill's shock was understandable, for he was the person most responsible for the decision that had led to the Royal Navy's worst defeat in World War II.

Prewar British strategy in the Far East called for a strong battle fleet to be sent to Singapore, the main British base in East Asian waters, to deter Japanese aggression. Over the years, huge sums of money had been spent on its defenses. As late as August 1941, the Admiralty considered sending six capital ships and an aircraft carrier to the Far East. But the demands of the war in the Atlantic and the Mediterranean made such a transfer impossible, especially after *Tirpitz*, sister ship of *Bismarck*, had become operational. Churchill had his own plans, however. Despite the evidence of two years' war at sea, he had an exaggerated belief in the power of the battleship and, overcoming the objections of Admiral Pound, insisted that a squadron be dispatched to the Far East.

Pound, in poor health, acquiesced, and put together Force Z, as it was designated, consisting of *Prince of Wales*, the veteran battle cruiser *Repulse*, and the carrier *Indomitable*. It was obvious, however, that these ships would have no effect upon a Japanese regime already committed to war. Imperial politics had almost as much to do with Churchill's decision to dispatch the ships as military imperatives. Australia, which had sent thousands of troops to the Middle East, was restive about the Japanese threat; the squadron was to underline Britain's commitment to her defense. In the final analysis, however, the sinking of the two capital ships cruelly confirmed the fact that the Australians would have to turn elsewhere—to the United States—for security.

Several factors weighed against Force Z. *Repulse*—under the command of Captain W. G. Tennant, who had been in charge on the beaches of Dunkirk—had not been completely modernized, and her anti-aircraft armament was inadequate; *Prince of Wales* had never had time to work out some of the technical problems that had surfaced in its fight with *Bismarck*. Moreover, *Indomitable* ran aground in the West Indies while engaging in training exercises and did not accompany the squadron—the point at which the operation should have been called off. And Admiral Sir Tom Phillips, who was named to command Force Z, was less than an ideal choice. Known as "Tom Thumb" because of his diminutive stature, Phillips had been vice-chief of the Naval Staff since the beginning of the war and, not having held a command at sea under wartime conditions, stubbornly believed battleships had little to fear from attacking aircraft. "Tom, when the first bomb hits, you'll say, 'My God, what a hell of a mine!' " observed one friend as Phillips prepared to take up his new post.

Force Z's mission was quickly overtaken by events. Japanese landings on the Malay coast, even before the Pearl Harbor attack, meant that deterrence had failed, and Phillips decided to lend a hand to the embattled land forces. Under cover of darkness, he steamed northward on the evening of December 8 with his two big ships and four destroyers, to attack a Japanese force reported to be putting troops ashore at Singora, in the Gulf of Siam. The RAF was asked to provide reconnaissance in advance of his force, and fighter protection if it went into action. But the hard-pressed airmen, who had already lost many of their aircraft and airfields to the Japanese, were unable to supply such support.

The ships were not left completely without air cover, however. Phillips was informed that a squadron of outmoded Brewster Buffalo fighters would be kept in readiness at Sembawang, near Singapore, to answer any call for help. He was also warned that the Japanese were assembling a sizable force of torpedo bombers near Saigon. Perhaps basing his judgment on the limited range of the familiar Swordfish, Phillips assumed that no torpedo plane could cover the four hundred miles from Indochina to the invasion beaches. Lacking air cover, he would rely upon surprise and the anti-aircraft batteries of his ships.

Force Z, evading Japanese submarine patrols and minefields, steamed northward through the damp and clammy tropical night and into the next day, December 9, without incident. Fortune seemed to favor the British. A Japanese reconnaissance plane that flew over Singapore that morning mistakenly reported that *Prince of Wales* and *Repulse* had not left the harbor. And in midafternoon, a submarine sighted the ships at sea, but its signal was delayed in reaching Japanese headquarters. Believing the false report that the British were still in port, the Imperial Navy's 22nd Air Flotilla prepared aircraft at its air-fields near Saigon to attack the ships as they lay at anchor. "Everyone was busy investigating the water depth of the Singapore Naval Base, the best directions from which to attack, and the most advantageous flight information to utilize," Lieutenant Sadoa Takai later recalled.

The 22nd Air Flotilla was one of the most highly rated units in the navy. Most of its pilots and air crews had seen service in China, and it had a strength of 141 aircraft: twin-engine, pencillike G3M Nells and deep-bellied, high-tailed G4M Bettys, which could be employed as both high-level bombers and torpedo planes, as well as thirty-eight Zero fighters. When the delayed sighting report from the submarine was finally received at Saigon, the Japanese were startled and con-fused. If the British ships were actually at sea, the fate of the landing force hung in the balance, because the big guns of *Prince of Wales* and *Repulse* would make short work of the transports and supply ves-sels.

Intelligence officers pored over the pictures taken that morning showing the two ships in port and resolved the mystery. Because of the great height from which the photographs were made, two large cargo vessels had been mistaken for the warships. Orders were immediately given for the landing force—which had already put most of its men ashore at Singora—to disperse. Even though night was falling, every available ship and plane was ordered to search for the British vessels. Fifty-three bombers, most carrying torpedoes, took off from Saigon and headed south. Visibility was poor, and the planes almost attacked *Chokai*, the flagship of Rear Admiral Jisaburo Ozawa's cruiser force. Badly shaken by this narrow escape, the Japanese called off the search until daylight. The weary air crews returned to their base, but, because of a shortage of torpedoes, they could not dump them into the sea and had to make a harrowing night landing with live torpedoes.

In the meantime, Force Z had again been sighted. Just as darkness was falling, *Prince of Wales*'s radar picked up three floatplanes launched by Ozawa's cruisers. Remaining well out of range of British guns, the planes reported the squadron's position. Phillips now real-ized that all chance of surprising the Japanese invasion fleet had been lost, and reluctantly ordered his ships to return to Singapore. Neither side knew it, but Force Z and the Japanese cruisers missed each other by only five miles—and what might well have been one of the decisive sea battles of World War II.

The last of the Japanese torpedo planes and their exhausted crews had landed at Saigon well after midnight, but at dawn on December 10, ninety-four bombers were ready for takeoff, including fifty-one fitted with torpedoes, thirty-four armed with bombs, and nine for reconnaissance. But where were the British ships? Phillips's change in course to the south had been detected during the night by the submarine *I-58*, which fired a spread of five torpedoes at the speeding vessels; all missed, but the boat passed on a sighting report.

At dawn, the Japanese launched search planes, which headed south toward Singapore with the hope of finding the two ships. The bombers would follow later. Although almost all the air crews were veterans, none had participated in a torpedo strike. One young pilot asked Lieutenant Takai about the angle of attack to be followed and was told that if he became confused it was best to "fly very low and aim your torpedo directly at the bow of the vessel under attack." Having stowed their flight rations in their planes—rice cake coated with bean paste, and flasks of thick, sweetened coffee—the pilots began taking off at 0625. Visibility was good, and the Nells and Bettys climbed to ten thousand feet, where in formations of eight or nine they settled in a southerly course.

Prince of Wales and *Repulse* were no longer headed back to Singapore, however. During the night, Phillips had received a signal from Singapore that the Japanese were landing at Kuantan, about 180 miles north of the city. Seizing the opportunity to retrieve something from his sortie, the admiral ordered a detour to Kuantan. Radio silence was maintained, and no attempt was made to inform Singapore of his decision. Apparently, Phillips assumed that the staff would anticipate his reaction to the signal warning of the landing and would automatically send the Buffalo fighters to cover his ships. If so, he was wrong, for the planes remained on the ground. Arriving off Kuantan that morning, the British found no sign of a landing, but instead of immediately pressing on to Singapore, Phillips spent several hours investigating the situation.

Meanwhile, the Japanese planes had flown almost as far south as Singapore without sighting their quarry. "What is the matter with our reconnaissance planes?" Lieutenant Takai angrily asked himself.

"Still no signs of the enemy." With fuel dwindling, several planes were forced to return to Saigon, and the remainder would soon have to follow. One squadron found a target, the destroyer *Tenedos*, returning to Singapore because she was short of fuel. By skillful maneuvering, she avoided major damage, and at 1030 flashed a radio report that she was under attack to Phillips, who was still dawdling off Kuantan. He immediately headed back to Singapore at twenty-five knots, but once again failed to call for his air cover.

Not long after, a Japanese search plane flashed the long-awaited signal: "SIGHTED TWO ENEMY BATTLESHIPS, SEVENTY NAUTICAL MILES SOUTHEAST OF KUANTAN." Turning northward on the new bearing, the bombers raced to the reported position. As he strained for a sight of *Prince of Wales* and *Repulse*, Takai became "nervous and shaky. . . . It was exactly like the sensation one feels before entering a contest in an athletic meet. At exactly 1:03 P.M. [1133 Singapore time] a black spot was sighted directly beneath the cloud ahead of us. . . . Yes—it was the enemy!"

Eight Nells swept over *Repulse*, low enough so the men on deck could see the bombs fall. It was a harrowing moment, but, despite several near misses, the battle cruiser sustained only one hit, amidships, which did not reduce her speed. Ten minutes later, two squadrons of torpedo planes bored in on *Prince of Wales*. Used to the lumbering Swordfish, the flagship's gunners were amazed at the speed of their approach. "The air was filled with white smoke, bursting shells and tracers," Takai declared. "As if pushed down by the fierce barrage thrown up by the enemy, I descended to just above the water's surface. . . . I do not remember at all how I was flying the airplane, how I was aiming, and at what distance we were from the ship when I dropped the torpedo. . . ."

In all, nine torpedoes sped toward the battleship, the white trails of bubbles clearly visible in the mirrorlike sea. "Suddenly, there was a most terrific jolt accompanied by a loud explosion," reported a Royal Marine officer. "A vast column of water and smoke shot up into the air to a height of about 200 feet. . . . At least one torpedo had hit us." The torpedo had exploded on *Prince of Wales*'s port side near the stern, snapping one of her propeller shafts and tearing open the shaft passage. Water poured into her hull with a tremendous rush. The battleship immediately began to lose way, her speed dropping from twenty-five knots to fifteen, and took on a strong list. The electric generators failed, and soon there was no power for the guns, no lights, and no forced ventilation belowdecks. A single torpedo had transformed an efficient and powerful fighting machine into a crippled hulk.

Two formations of torpedo planes now attacked *Repulse*. Undeterred by the barrage thrown up by the old ship's outmoded anti-aircraft guns, the Japanese pressed in to drop their torpedoes at point-blank range. Only the magnificent ship-handling of Captain Tennant saved her from immediate destruction. Twisting and turning as if she were a destroyer, the battle cruiser managed to evade every one of the torpedoes. In the meantime, Tennant was shocked to learn from his signals officer that Phillips had not asked Singapore for air cover. Acting on his own initiative, he broke radio silence and reported that Force Z was under attack. The squadron of Buffaloes kept in readiness at Sembawang was ordered into the air, but they were almost an hour's flying time away from the scene of the struggle.

Just as the fighters were taking off, twenty-six Bettys armed with torpedoes attacked the ships. Six approached *Prince of Wales* from various directions. A few guns opened fire, trained by crews that frantically hauled the barrels around with ropes or chains in the absence of power. With the vessel's steering gear out of action, there was little her crew could do except watch in horrified fascination as the planes approached. Four torpedoes struck the battleship on her starboard side in quick succession, one passing through both sides of the bow.

The Japanese now turned their full attention to *Repulse*, about four miles away. Eight Bettys attacked her starboard side, and once again Tennant managed to avoid their torpedoes, but one launched by a plane that unexpectedly appeared on her port side struck her amidships. *Repulse*'s luck had run out. Although she shot down two of the attacking aircraft, she was struck by four more torpedoes. Only eleven minutes after being first hit, the gallant old ship rolled over and sank, leaving the water covered with struggling men, debris, and great globs of oil.

Prince of Wales took longer to die, which allowed the destroyers, working unhindered by the Japanese, to take off survivors. She floated upside down, with her flat bottom exposed, before her bow reared into the air and she plunged stern-first to the bottom. Three minutes before the battleship sank, the Buffaloes reached the disaster scene. The victorious Japanese, their fuel low, had already departed, and the fighters, which might have made a difference if summoned earlier by Phillips, could do nothing except circle aimlessly over the desolate scene. Casualties were heavy—840 dead out of 2,921 men on both ships—including Phillips.* The Japanese lost three planes.

Following on the heels of Pearl Harbor, the destruction of Force Z had far-reaching tactical and strategic effects. With both the British and American Far Eastern battle fleets having fallen victim to Japanese air power, the Japanese were now free to proceed with the conquest of Southeast Asia and the East Indies without interference from the western Allies. The loss of *Prince of Wales* and *Repulse* also marked an end to the dominance of the battleship and the big gun. For the first time, capital ships had been sunk by aircraft while under way on the high seas. Surface fleets now operated without air cover at their peril.

Without a fleet to defend it, the supposedly impregnable fortress of Singapore, upon which the British had lavished so much time and money, was useless. The Japanese advanced with ruthless efficiency down the Malay Peninsula toward the island. Time and again they leapfrogged over the defenders with amphibious landings, and under the protection of land- and carrier-based planes covered some five hundred miles of jungle in two weeks. The British hastily dredged up another forty-five thousand troops, mostly raw recruits, and, along with their remaining fighter planes, threw them into a vain attempt to halt the Japanese drive. Singapore's famous guns were of no help, because they were short of ammunition.

Like the tentacles of an octopus, Japanese amphibious forces reached out toward Java, richest of the East Indies, even before Singapore's fall. One tentacle crept along the Malay coast toward Sumatra. Another reached down past eastern Borneo. A third thrust also developed, farther to the east, aimed at New Guinea, the Bismarck Archipelago, and the Solomons. To meet these threats, General Sir Archibald P. Wavell was brought in from India and named supreme commander of a patchwork American, British, Dutch, and Australian (ABDA) force; Admiral Hart commanded the naval side with a force that included nine cruisers, twenty-six destroyers (some of World

---

*Captain Tennant was picked up.

War I vintage), and thirty-nine submarines. Before the fleet had time to do much about coordinating differences of language, communications, fire control, and tactics, it was forced to fight for its life.*

First blood was drawn by the four-pipers *John D. Ford, Pope, Parrott*, and *Paul Jones*, which attacked a large Japanese convoy at anchor off Balikpapan, Borneo, in the Makassar Strait, on the night of January 24, 1942. Oil tanks set afire by the retreating Dutch illuminated the Japanese vessels, and the blacked-out American destroyers dashed in at high speed firing their guns and torpedoes—the first surface action fought by the U.S. Navy since 1898. Although handicapped by defective torpedoes, they left five sinking ships behind them, four transports and a patrol boat, without damage to themselves. Yet, though Balikpapan helped buoy Allied morale, it had no effect on Japan's southward progress.

Houston and *Marblehead*; two Dutch light cruisers, *Tromp* and *De Ruyter*; and seven destroyers tried to repeat this operation by smashing a convoy heading for the southern Celebes on February 4, but came under heavy air attack near the southern end of Makassar Strait. *Marblehead* was badly damaged, and *Houston*'s after eight-inch gun turret was knocked out. A few days later, Japanese bombers—some from the carriers of Admiral Nagumo's First Air Fleet, which had taken part in the Pearl Harbor raid—roared over the airfields of Java and destroyed most of the remaining Allied planes on the ground. Port Darwin, on the north coast of Australia, the main staging area for supplying Allied forces in Java, was also attacked. Eight ships including an American destroyer were sunk, eighteen planes were shot down, and the base was put out of action—all at the cost of two aircraft.

Following Singapore's fall on February 15, Wavell concluded that the Allied position in the East Indies was untenable and he and Admiral Hart relinquished command to the Dutch. The Dutch heatedly disagreed with this pessimistic view, however, and Rear Admi-

---

*Despite the threat of war with Japan, the Western nations conducted no serious discussions of mutual defense in the Far East until the end of April 1941. Nothing was done about crucial tactical considerations until November, and war intervened before further talks could be held in December in Manila. The ABDA Command itself was established at the meeting between Roosevelt and Churchill, known as the Arcadia Conference, held in Washington from late December 1941 through mid-January 1942.

ral Karel W. F. M. Doorman, although in poor health, prepared to deal with the coming Japanese assault on Java. Rear Admiral Jisaburo Ozawa was steaming in from the west with fifty-six transports, Rear Admiral Shoji Nishimura coming in from the east with forty-one ships. The threat from the east appeared likely to develop first, so Doorman targeted it.

Superficially, the two sides seemed roughly equal. Besides his flagship, the light cruiser *De Ruyter*, Doorman's Combined Striking Force had four other cruisers: *Houston* and *Exeter*, a veteran of the *Graf Spee* action; and the Australian *Perth* and the Dutch *Java*, both light cruisers. They were screened by nine destroyers, including four four-pipers, which had to strain to keep up with the much faster cruisers. The Japanese convoy was defended by two heavy cruisers, *Nachi* and *Haguro*; two light cruisers; and sixteen destroyers—all led by Rear Admiral Takeo Takagi.

But the Japanese also had control of the air, their ships were in good repair, and their crews comparatively fresh, whereas Doorman's vessels were badly in need of overhaul—only two of *Houston*'s three eight-inch turrets were workable—and his crews were frazzled by frequent bombing. Moreover, Doorman's ships had never before worked together as a unit. The Allies suffered a serious blow even before the operation began, when the old seaplane tender *Langley*, ferrying a load of P-40 fighters to Java, was sunk by Japanese bombers only fifty miles from its destination.*

The Battle of the Java Sea began late in the afternoon of February 27, with a salvo of eight-inch shells fired by one of the Japanese heavy cruisers at the extreme range of twenty-eight thousand yards. This was answered by the guns of *Houston* and *Exeter*. *Houston* was using red dye in her shells so the fall of her salvos could be spotted, and some junior Japanese officers were startled by the blood-red geysers spouting about them. Commander Walter G. Winslow, one of *Houston*'s officers, provides a graphic account of what happened next:

> The sound of our guns bellowing defiance is terrific, the gun blast tears the steel helmet from my head and sends it rolling on the deck.

---

*Langley, a former collier, had been converted into the U.S. Navy's first aircraft carrier in 1922.

The range closes rapidly and soon all the cruisers are in on the fight. Salvos of shells splash in the water ever closer to us. Now one falls close to the starboard followed by another close to port. . . . Shells from our guns are observed bursting close to the last Jap heavy cruiser. We have her range and suddenly one of our 8-inch bricks strikes home. There is an explosion on board her. Black smoke and debris flies in the air and a fire breaks out forward of her bridge. We draw blood first as she turns out of the battle line making dense smoke.[*]

For an hour, the two squadrons exchanged fire while Doorman, worried that the Japanese were about to cross his "T," maneuvered to prevent them from passing across the bows of his ships. The Japanese had the advantage of spotting by floatplanes, and their fire was more accurate than that of the Allied squadron. One of *Nachi*'s eight-inch armor-piercing shells penetrated the boiler room of *Exeter*, and with her speed suddenly cut to half the British cruiser turned away from the enemy, exuding clouds of steam. The Allied battle line was turned into a shambles. Taking advantage of the confusion, the Japanese launched a shoal of Long Lance torpedoes, which sank a Dutch destroyer. Unprepared for the effectiveness of the Japanese torpedoes at such ranges, the surprised Allies thought they were under submarine attack and dropped depth charges.

Three British destroyers counterattacked. One was sunk, but two Japanese destroyers were damaged by their torpedoes. *Houston*, Doorman's only remaining big-gun cruiser, zigzagged so that her forward turrets would bear. When she ran out of shells for these guns, ammunition was manhandled from the after magazine. *Exeter*, her speed now restored to fifteen knots, withdrew under escort of a Dutch destroyer, and Doorman ordered the American four-pipers to make smoke while he reorganized his squadron. Having laid down a screen, they charged through it to launch a torpedo attack on the Japanese heavy cruisers, but scored no hits.

Night was falling, and Doorman set about trying to work his way around the escort with his four remaining cruisers to attack the troop transports. Japanese night-fighting skills now paid off. The Allied ships were fended off, and the floatplanes dropped flares that bathed

---

[*]Winslow was mistaken: *Houston* scored no hits.

them in an eerie white light, betraying all their movements to the Japanese gunners. Doorman's poor luck continued when one of his two remaining destroyers ran into a newly laid Dutch minefield and was lost. The remaining vessel was detached to pick up survivors.

Shortly before midnight, Doorman sighted *Nachi* and *Haguro* to port in bright moonlight and prepared to engage. Suddenly, *Java* was wracked by an explosion, and flames engulfed her. As the crews of the other ships looked on in horror, more torpedoes slashed through the sea and struck *De Ruyter*. Ordered by Doorman not to risk themselves by stopping to pick up survivors, the two remaining cruisers, *Houston* and *Perth*, escaped into the darkness. The Allies had lost two cruisers and four destroyers, and managed to delay the Japanese invasion of Java by only twenty-four hours.

The following night, as *Perth* and *Houston* steamed into the Sunda Strait, they ran into Admiral Ozawa's western group. Sweeping into Bantam Bay, they caught the Japanese flatfooted. In the wild melee that followed, the Japanese fired torpedoes indiscriminately, some striking their own ships, and the cruisers sank or damaged more than a half-dozen vessels. *Houston*, short of ammunition, was soon reduced to firing illumination shells at the enemy. A torpedo struck *Perth* in her forward engine room, and, lying dead in the water, she was finished off by Japanese gunners. *Houston*, caught in the white glare of searchlights that stabbed through the darkness, shuddered under the impact of hit after hit. Let Commander Winslow finish the story:

> A torpedo penetrated our after engine room, where it exploded, killing every man there and reducing our speed to fifteen knots. . . . Power went out for the shell hoists. . . . Number Two Turret, smashed by a direct hit, blew up, sending wild flames flashing up over the bridge. . . . Slowly we listed to starboard and the grand old ship gradually lost steerageway and stopped. The few guns still in commission continued to fire, although it was obvious that the end was near. . . .*

---

*Of *Houston*'s 1,064 officers and men, only 368 survived. Captain Albert H. Rooks, who went down with his ship, was posthumously awarded the Medal of Honor. The Presidential Unit Citation given his ship tells its own story: "Often damaged but self maintaining, *Houston* kept the sea and went down gallantly fighting to the last against overwhelming odds."

With the destruction of the ABDA fleet, the fate of the East Indies was a foregone conclusion. The mopping up was brief and brutal. *Exeter*, emergency repairs made, and a pair of accompanying destroyers were steaming to Ceylon (now Sri Lanka), when they were sunk in a battle with four heavy cruisers. Other vessels trying to extricate themselves fell prey to the Japanese or, like the Australian cruiser *Hobart* and a handful of surviving destroyers, made their way to Ceylon or Australia. Java surrendered on March 8, and Rangoon in Burma fell the same day. The Japanese army pushed up the Irawaddy Valley, and on May 1 took Mandalay, anchor of the Burma Road, over which China received most of the supplies that kept her in the war.

The tale of defeat and disaster in the Far East had not yet played itself out, however. From their newly won bases at Singapore and Java, the Japanese were now in a position to threaten Britain's lifelines in the Indian Ocean. Ceylon and the coast of India lay open to invasion, and the Japanese could interfere with the supply route for the British army in Egypt, which ran along the coast of East Africa. To restore a naval presence in these waters, the Royal Navy—despite heavy commitments in the Atlantic, Mediterranean, and Arctic—hastily cobbled together a new Eastern Fleet built around the ubiquitous *Warspite*, the carriers *Indomitable* and *Formidable* and the smaller *Hermes*, and four superannuated R-class battleships. Admiral Sir James Somerville, who had done yeoman service with Force H in the Mediterranean, was placed in command.

Two days after Somerville raised his flag at Colombo on the west coast of Ceylon, at the end of March, signals intelligence reported that Admiral Nagumo had led a Japanese force of five carriers and four fast battleships into the Indian Ocean with the intention of destroying or cowing the Eastern Fleet. Nagumo hoped to catch the British at anchor at Colombo—just as he had caught the Americans at Pearl Harbor. Realizing that his ships were inferior to the Japanese force, and vastly outnumbered in aircraft, Somerville prudently retreated to an emergency base at Addu Atoll, the southernmost of the Maldive Islands, some six hundred miles south of Ceylon.

Three hundred and fifty Japanese planes struck Colombo on Easter Sunday, April 5. When he found that most of the shipping had been sent to sea, Nagumo, profiting by the lesson he had learned at

Pearl Harbor, plastered the shops, harbor installations, and oil-tank farms. Another force, consisting of a small carrier and six cruisers under Admiral Ozawa, rampaged through the Bay of Bengal, sinking nearly a hundred thousand tons of shipping in five days. Japanese submarines accounted for another thirty-two thousand tons. Having left his weakest ships at Addu, Somerville came north with *Warspite*, *Indomitable*, and *Formidable*, with the hope of launching a night torpedo attack against Nagumo.

Nagumo struck first, however. The cruisers *Cornwall* and *Dorsetshire* were spotted at sea while on the way to rendezvous with Somerville, and they were attacked by eighty Japanese dive-bombers. On his bridge, Nagumo and his staff could hear the exchange of radio messages between the flight commander and his pilots:

"Sighted enemy vessels."

"Get ready to go in."

"Air Group, 1st Cardiv, take the first ship; Air Group, 2nd Cardiv, take the second ship."

There was a brief period in which no messages were heard. Then:

"Ship Number One has stopped. Dead in the water. Listing heavily."

"Ship Number Two is aflame."

"Ship Number One has sunk."

"Ship Number Two has sunk."

Only nineteen minutes separated the sighting report from the sinking of the second ship.

Unable to locate the Japanese carriers, Somerville decided to rejoin the rest of his fleet. It was just as well, because his Swordfish and Albacores were no match for the flocks of Zeros that would have awaited them. In the meantime, Nagumo attacked the naval base at Trincomalee, on the east coast of Ceylon. As at Colombo, the harbor had been cleared of shipping, but the Japanese did considerable damage to port installations. *Hermes*, which had been hustled to sea without its fighters and was returning to harbor, was caught by Japanese dive-bombers, which made quick work of her and an escorting destroyer.

Happily for the British, the Japanese had not planned an extended foray into the Indian Ocean. Running low on fuel, and having been at sea since November 26, when he had sailed on the Pearl Harbor raid, Nagumo retired through the Straits of Malacca and returned in triumph to Japan. The Admiralty, unaware of the Japanese withdrawal, ordered Somerville to pull his fleet back some three thousand miles to the East African coast for safety's sake. The Imperial Japanese Navy now commanded the seas from Hawaii to Ceylon. In little more than a hundred days, virtually the whole of Southeast Asia and its resources had fallen into Japanese hands in exchange for the loss of four destroyers and a half-dozen submarines. No navy in history had accomplished so much in so little time—but Japan was soon to overreach herself.

•

CHAPTER 8

"Scratch One Flat-Top!"

Turning into the wind at daybreak on April 18, 1942, the carrier *Hornet* prepared to unleash a strange and ungainly brood. Sixteen twin-engine army B-25 bombers lumbered down her spray-swept flight deck and, after groping their way into the air, headed for Tokyo, 668 miles away. No one was certain if all the planes would make it. "One pilot hung on the brink of a stall until we nearly catalogued his effects," observed Vice-Admiral William F. Halsey, Jr., commander of Task Force 16. Four months after Pearl Harbor, the United States was about to carry the war to the Japanese home islands.

The surprise raid on Tokyo and other Japanese cities was part of a "defensive-offensive" strategy devised by Admiral Ernest J. King, who had been named commander-in-chief, U.S. Fleet (COMINCH) and chief of naval operations in the wake of Pearl Harbor.* King defined the "defensive-offensive" as "hold what you got and hit them where you can." This strategy was aimed at keeping the Japanese off balance to prevent them from consolidating their conquests, and at buoying American morale. As part of it, Admiral Chester W. Nimitz, who replaced Admiral Kimmel as commander of the Pacific Fleet (CINCPAC) at year's end, began 1942 by preparing—in response to King's urging—several strikes against Japanese advanced bases in

---

*King was first designated CINCUS, but that was quickly dropped, for obvious reasons. Admiral Stark, tainted by Pearl Harbor, was sent to London as commander of U.S. Naval Forces in Europe.

the Gilbert and Marshall islands. He hoped this would relieve enemy pressure upon the battered ABDA fleet in the East Indies.

Two more dissimilar men could hardly have been chosen for their billets than King and Nimitz. King was irascible and intolerant; Nimitz—at fifty-six, seven years his junior—was, as Samuel Eliot Morison has observed, "the most successful, considerate and beloved of fleet commanders."* With flaxen hair just turning white and a pink complexion, Nimitz had a commanding presence. He was an authority on submarines and diesel engines, and introduced into the U.S. Navy such technological innovations as the refueling of ships while underway and the circular formation for defending aircraft carriers. He was handpicked for this new post by President Roosevelt and Navy secretary Knox. Despite the vivid contrast in their personalities and King's attempts to run the Pacific Fleet from Washington, King and Nimitz complemented each other and successfully conducted a naval war that brought Imperial Japan to her knees.

No American military leader doubted America's ability to win the war ultimately, despite the skein of early Japanese victories, but considerable controversy raged over how this was to be accomplished. In accordance with the old Orange plan and the Rainbow Five plan, the U.S. Navy was to commence an immediate thrust across the Central Pacific, to be climaxed by a great Mahanian sea battle. Rainbow Five had to be abandoned, because eight battleships of the Pacific Fleet rested on the mud of Pearl Harbor. But naval strategists knew that sooner or later operations would have to be undertaken in the Central Pacific, despite the ABC-1 plan, which established a "Europe First" strategy.

As one of the principal executors of this "Europe First" strategy, Admiral King faced a dilemma. Although he was incapable of accepting the concept of a "holding" war in the Pacific, he had to support this grand design. In fact, had he not, he would have been quickly dismissed by President Roosevelt. General Alan Brooke, chief of Britain's Imperial General Staff, fervently hoped the president would

---

*In one story that made the rounds of the U.S. Navy, King had gone to his heavenly reward and an officer who followed him was told by St. Peter that heaven had been reorganized and placed on "combat readiness" since the admiral's arrival. "I'm not surprised," replied the officer. "Ernie King always thought he was God Almighty." St. Peter shook his head. "That's not the problem. God Almighty thinks He's Ernie King."

do just that.* No one "had much effect in weaning King away from the Pacific," Brooke later wrote. "This is where his heart was, and the bulk of his Naval Forces. The European war was just a great nuisance that kept him from waging his Pacific war undisturbed."

King had a strong strategic rationale for his views. It would be enormously costly to allow the Japanese to dig in behind the defensive perimeter they had seized in the first weeks of the war. Only an immediate counterattack could prevent the Japanese from consolidating their gains, and making a later American offensive extremely costly. Moreover, forcing the Japanese to fight would begin the long process of wearing down their strength, particularly in the area of trained pilots.

Without openly challenging ABC-1, King resolved to fight the Pacific war as best he could. Hawaii and Midway would be held, the shipping lanes between the U.S., Australia, and New Zealand kept open, and a defense line established from Midway to Samoa to Fiji to Australia. From these "strong points," he told Nimitz, "we can drive northwest from the New Hebrides into the Solomons and the Bismarck Archipelago after the same fashion of step-by-step advances that the Japanese used in the South China Sea." Thus, King anticipated the entire course of the war in the South Pacific to the middle of 1944.

Early in 1942, Roosevelt and Churchill divided the world into three general areas. The United States alone possessed the resources to mount a counteroffensive against the Japanese, so the Americans were given operational responsibility for the Pacific area. Britain had similar authority in a "middle area" stretching from Singapore across the Indian Ocean and then over the Mediterranean. In the Atlantic, Britain and the United States would exercise joint responsibility.

No one was more delighted than Admiral King that the Pacific war was to be an American show. There would be no need to coordinate strategy with troublesome allies or sooth bruised feelings. The Pacific basin was divided into two commands: the Southwest Pacific, under General MacArthur, which included Australia, New Guinea, the Bis-

---

*Like many American naval officers, King was suspicious of the British, not only because the Royal Navy had been viewed as a rival in prewar days, but in his case because his family were working-class Scots and English immigrants and he was angered by what he saw as the aristocratic pretensions of some British officers.

marcks, the East Indies, and the Philippines, and the Pacific Ocean Areas Command, under Nimitz. The dividing line was called the "Pope's Line" after the line drawn by Pope Alexander IV in 1494 splitting the New World between Spain and Portugal. The Pacific Ocean Command was, in turn, subdivided into North, Central, and South Pacific areas. Nimitz retained direct command of the first two; Vice-Admiral Robert L. Ghormley was named to head the third as Nimitz's subordinate. King had known MacArthur in Washington— and distrusted him thoroughly—so he stipulated that, even if the Pacific Fleet entered MacArthur's zone of command, it would remain under Nimitz's control. The result of this arrangement was that the war against Japan became two wars—MacArthur's war and the U.S. Navy's war.

Nimitz's first act was to boost morale by keeping Admiral Kimmel's staff. Then he set about reorganizing the Pacific Fleet in keeping with post–Pearl Harbor realities. Before the raid, it had been divided into a Battle Force and a Scouting Force. With most of the Battle Force out of commission, the remaining ships, plus reinforcements from the Atlantic, were divided into four task forces, each built around a carrier with an accompanying screen of cruisers and destroyers. Submarines and aircraft took care of scouting. The half-dozen operational battleships were a full ten knots slower than the carriers, so they were relegated to patrol-and-escort duty between the West Coast and Hawaii. Thus, the battle fleet, which had for thirty years dominated American naval thinking, passed quietly from the scene, and its place was taken by the carrier task force.

In the early stages of the war, American planes and readiness levels were inferior to those of the Japanese. The standard navy fighter, the F4F Wildcat, was slower and less nimble than the Zero and no match for it in single combat.* The TBD Devastator, the navy's torpedo bomber, was slow and ungainly. The SBD Dauntless dive-bomber—

---

*The F4F-3, the model in use in early 1942, had a top speed of 329 miles per hour at 21,100 feet and took 4.6 minutes to climb to 10,000 feet. It was armed with 4 wing-mounted .50-caliber machine guns and had self-sealing fuel tanks and armor to protect the pilot. As a result of this additional weight, the F4F was less maneuverable than the Zero (more formally, the Mitsubishi A6M2 Type O), although it was better able to stand up to punishment. The Zero had a top speed of 331 miles per hour at 15,000 feet and an exceptional climb rate, requiring slightly less than 6 minutes to reach 16,400 feet. It was known as "Slow But Deadly"—was the navy's only effective air weapon, accounting for most of the damage inflicted upon Japanese ships in the early years of the war. Japanese flyers had far more experience than the Americans. The pilots who attacked Pearl Harbor averaged eight hundred hours of flight time, more than triple the American norm. But as the war went on, this advantage became moot, because the Imperial Navy refused to withdraw its most experienced air crews to train others, and they were lost, while the United States was training thousands of airmen.[*]

Admiral Nimitz's plan for carrier raids against the Gilberts and Marshalls generated considerable opposition. The carrier was still regarded by many senior officers as a weapon of dubious reliability. Unless surprise could be achieved, as at Pearl Harbor, some strategists thought carriers were too vulnerable to be sent against objectives protected by land-based aircraft. The pugnacious Admiral Halsey, who commanded the Pacific Fleet's handful of carriers, came to Nimitz's rescue, not only to support him but to volunteer to lead the first of the series of hit-and-run raids against Japanese targets in the Central Pacific. Halsey, a favorite of President Roosevelt, was a strong apostle of naval air power even though he had not won his wings until he was 53.[†]

On February 1, 1942, Halsey, flying his flag in *Enterprise* and accompanied by cruisers under command of Rear Admiral Raymond A. Spruance, raided Kwajalein, Wotje, and Taroa in the northern Marshalls. The ship's plan for the day was headed by a verse:

---

armed with 2 7.7-millimeter machine guns firing through the propeller and 2 wing-mounted 20-millimeter cannon. Lacking self-sealing tanks and armor, the Zero was highly vulnerable to gunfire. In May 1942, U.S. Navy pilots began using incendiary bullets, and, if hit, Zeros tended to catch fire or explode. The mixed armament of the Zero was inferior to the heavy machine guns of the F4F, because 7.7-millimeter bullets could not pierce th F4F's armor and the rate of fire of the cannon was slow. Japanese aircraft radios were also inefficient.

[*]Fighter ace Saburo Sakai noted that, although most pilots were enlisted men rather than officers, the navy accepted only seventy of the fifteen hundred enlisted men who volunteered in 1937 for flight training. Only twenty-five of these were awarded their wings (Sakai, *Samurai!*, p. 12).

[†]Halsey and Roosevelt became friends when FDR was assistant Secretary of the Navy and he allowed the "white-flanneled yachtsman" to pilot his destroyer through dangerous water off the coast of Maine.

> An eye for an eye,
> A tooth for a tooth,
> This Sunday, it's our turn to shoot.
> —Remember Pearl Harbor

Yorktown, under Admiral Frank Jack Fletcher, attacked targets in the southern Marshalls, and similar strikes were launched against Wake and Marcus islands and other points. Although these attacks did little damage, they were morale builders. Three weeks later, *Lexington*, flying Rear Admiral Wilson Brown's flag, steamed three thousand miles from Pearl Harbor to raid Rabaul, on New Britain, to the northeast of New Guinea, which had recently been seized by the Japanese to become the hub of Japanese air power in the Southwest Pacific.

The Japanese discovered the task force about 350 miles from its objective, and land-based Japanese bombers attacked without fighter escort. The first large air battle between U.S. and Japanese planes took place within full view of the crew of "Lady Lex," who waved and yelled encouragement to the pilots. The Japanese force was almost wiped out. Lieutenant Edward H. "Butch" O'Hare was credited with five Kate torpedo planes, to become the navy's first ace of the war, and win the Medal of Honor.[*]

On March 10, Brown returned with *Lexington*, accompanied by *Yorktown*, to attack Rabaul as well as newly established Japanese bases at Lae and Salamaua. To avoid land-based aircraft, the task force steamed into the Gulf of Papua, on the opposite side of the island, and sent 104 planes over the seventy-five-hundred-foot-high Owen Stanley Range. Loaded with heavy torpedoes, the obsolete Devastators could not climb as fast as the terrain rose beneath them. Lieutenant Commander James H. Brett, the squadron leader and a onetime glider pilot, recalled that sunlight reflecting on mountains often led to thermal updrafts. Having signaled his squadron to follow, Brett circled his plane in search of an updraft and, once he found it, was lifted along with the others over the mountains. Unhappily for the Devastator pilots, their torpedoes proved, like those of the submariners, to be defective. "You could see streaks of torpedoes going right to the side of these cruisers

---

[*]In actuality, he shot down three bombers and damaged two others. See Lundstrom, *The First Team*, p. 104. Chicago's O'Hare Airport is named for him.

and nothing happened," reported one pilot. The dive-bombers were more successful, sinking four vessels and damaging nine others, including a light cruiser and two destroyers.

Admiral Yamamoto and his staff were concerned about these attacks. "At this pace the enemy carriers are likely to appear next off Tokyo Bay," Rear Admiral Matome Ugaki, Yamamoto's chief of staff, confided to his diary in disgust. Not long after, Ugaki's appraisal became a frightening reality for the Japanese, when Doolittle's raiders appeared over the city in the most spectacular of these early attacks.

The Tokyo raid originated with President Roosevelt's repeatedly expressed desire for retaliation against the Japanese home islands. In mid-January 1942, Captain Francis S. Low of the COMINCH staff prepared a plan for a carrier strike. Admiral King thought it impracticable, because the short range of carrier aircraft meant the planes would have to be launched within the area covered by Japanese patrol planes. Low suggested that the Army's medium bombers, which had a longer range, be launched from a carrier on a one-way mission in which they would bomb Tokyo and then fly on eleven hundred miles to airfields in China. King accepted the plan and persuaded Lieutenant General H. H. Arnold, head of the air force, to approve the mission.

Lieutenant Colonel James H. Doolittle, a daredevil speed- and test-pilot, was placed in charge, and he selected the B-25 as the most suitable aircraft.* The air crews, all volunteers, practiced short take-offs at a Florida air base for a month, without knowing their target, before flying out to California, where the planes were loaded on board *Hornet*. They had never made even one practice takeoff from a carrier. Once Vice-Admiral Halsey's TF16, which also included the carrier *Enterprise*, had proceeded to sea, the airmen were told their destination was Tokyo, and wild cheering greeted the announcement.

The raid was to be made at night, but when the task force was spotted by a Japanese patrol boat on the morning of April 18, the planes were launched immediately. The first bomber rolled down the carrier's flight deck at 0725. "The wind and the sea were so strong that morning that green water was breaking over the carrier's ramps,"

---

*Ironically, the B-25 was designated the Mitchell bomber, after General Billy Mitchell, the air-power prophet who had derided the effectiveness of the aircraft carrier.

reported "Bull" Halsey. "Jimmy led his squadron. When his plane buzzed down . . . the *Hornet*'s deck . . . there wasn't a man topside who didn't sweat him into the air. . . ." All the planes were launched in fifty-nine minutes.

The Doolittle raiders achieved such complete surprise that Japanese schoolchildren waved cheerily at the bombers. They approached Tokyo from various quarters, skimmed in at rooftop level, and climbed just before releasing their bombs, to avoid the explosions. Thirteen planes hit the capital; the others struck Nagoya and Osaka. None were lost over Japan. Buffeted by head winds, the planes ran out of gas, and most of the men bailed out over China; eight who landed in Japanese-occupied territory were taken prisoner. Of these, three were executed for bombing civilian targets. As in the hit-and-run raids on the Pacific islands, the damage was slight, but these strikes lifted sagging American morale, kept the enemy guessing, and provided a valuable test of fast-carrier tactics.

Having completed the conquest of the Greater East Asian Co-Prosperity Sphere in half the time allotted, and with far fewer casualties than anticipated, Japanese leaders were heatedly debating what to do next. Some cautious strategists argued that now was the time to consolidate Japanese conquests and to strengthen their defense perimeter against the Allied assault that was certain to come. But others, infected with "Victory Disease," indulged in an orgy of strategic greed. The Western Allies were even weaker than thought, and the expansionists saw no need to halt or to consolidate Japanese gains. Why not expand the defense perimeter to an even greater distance from the home islands when the going was good?

Several possible campaigns of conquest presented themselves. The Naval General Staff suggested a move westward against Ceylon and India, and perhaps a link-up with their German allies in the Middle East, or a push south to isolate Australia. Fierce rivalry existed between Japan's military forces. The army, with its eyes firmly fixed on the war in China, and worried about Russia, flatly refused to commit the large numbers of troops required by these proposals. As a result, the Naval General Staff turned to a scaled-down version of the Australia option.

Operation MO, as it was dubbed, called for a sweep southeast to safeguard Rabaul by capturing Port Moresby on the southwest tip of New Guinea. Also, a seaplane base would be established on Tulagi, in the Solomons, a chain of islands stretching to the southeast, to protect the east flank of the Japanese advance and as a jumping-off point for operations against New Caledonia, Fiji, and Samoa. Once Port Moresby was secured, northern Australia would be in range of Japanese bombers. Thus, Japan's defense perimeter would be extended outward, and communications between Australia and the U.S. endangered. The Japanese ignored a basic military maxim: the farther a defense line is extended from its base, the weaker it becomes. Nonetheless, preparations for MO began in March.

Admiral Yamamoto was obsessed, however, with the need to finish the work of Pearl Harbor and destroy the U.S. Pacific Fleet—especially its carriers—before Japan was ground down by steadily growing American military power. Working independently of the Naval Staff, he produced an elaborate plan for an attack on Midway Island, which consisted of two tiny atolls about eleven hundred miles to the northwest of Pearl Harbor, and the westernmost U.S. base now that the Philippines, Wake, and Guam had been lost. The U.S. Navy would have to defend Midway, Yamamoto reasoned, which would draw the Americans into the long-sought high-seas confrontation. Early in April, while units were being gathered for MO, the Naval General Staff gave reluctant approval to the Midway operation—only after Yamamoto again threatened to quit—but without setting a date for it. The Doolittle raid a few days later, which seemed to underscore the validity of Yamamoto's arguments, shocked the General Staff, and the Midway operation was set for early June.

The Port Moresby operation was typical of Japanese naval planning in that it relied upon the convergence of several widely separated groups of ships. Vice-Admiral Shigeyoshi Inouye, commander-in-chief of the Fourth Fleet, at Rabaul, was in overall command. Rear Admiral Aritomo Goto was to come down to the Coral Sea from Truk, in the Carolines, with the light carrier *Shoho* and four heavy cruisers to cover the Tulagi landing and then turn west to protect the Port Moresby invasion force proceeding from Rabaul. Two large carriers, *Shokaku* and *Zuikaku*; two heavy cruisers; and six destroyers—all under Vice-Admiral Takeo Takagi—would sweep around the Solomons chain and approach from the east to support the Port Moresby landing.

This plan assumed that the Americans had only one carrier available, and that complete surprise could be achieved, as at Pearl Harbor. Unknown to the Japanese, however, Admiral Nimitz had been fore-warned of the approach of the enemy by American cryptanalysts who had broken the Japanese naval code.

Hidden away behind locked steel doors in the windowless basement of the Administration Building of the Fourteenth Naval District at Pearl Harbor, the Combat Intelligence Unit had been trying for months to read JN25b, the latest edition of the code used by the Imperial Navy. This unit, commonly called Station Hypo, was one of three cryptanalytic stations operated by the navy. The others were Station Negat, in Washington, and Station Cast, which had been at Cavite but had been evacuated by submarine to Melbourne, Australia.

Hypo was under the command of Lieutenant Commander Joseph J. Rochefort, a veteran navy cryptanalyst and onetime language student in Japan. A rather prickly character given to speaking his mind, he was regarded with suspicion in some quarters. Rochefort berated himself for not having kept track of the Japanese carriers before Pearl Harbor and personally assumed blame for the attack. Believing it was the duty of an intelligence officer to keep his chief informed of enemy intentions, he felt he had failed Admiral Kimmel.

To make up for it, he drove himself and his staff of cryptanalysts, translators, and clerks unmercifully. For the better part of three months, they worked around the clock amid an ever-rising tide of paper and the deafening clatter of IBM calculators and sorters. Lieutenant Commander Thomas H. Dyer, Rochefort's deputy, had pioneered in the use of this equipment to take over some of the mind-numbing drudgery of cryptanalysis. When more manpower was needed, the bandsmen of the crippled battleship *California* were pressed into service; the musicians proved particularly adept at cryptanalysis.

Rarely leaving his underground office, Rochefort stood sixteen- and twenty-hour watches and had a cot installed so he could be on call at all times. The air conditioning was erratic, so he sometimes wore an old smoking jacket belted over his uniform to ward off the chill while he padded about in felt slippers. All the staff worked closely together, sharing their findings and hunches. It was "not necessary to be crazy to be a cryptanalyst," Rochefort later declared, "but it always helps."

Unlike the Purple diplomatic cipher or Enigma, JN25 did not involve the use of a machine to encipher messages. To save money, the Imperial Navy relied instead upon printed codebooks and cipher tables that were distributed throughout the fleet.* The flaw in the Japanese system was that these materials were changed only after they had been in use for some months. This practice enabled the cryptanalysts at Pearl Harbor and the other stations to note that the same numbers were often used in the same sequence.

Little by little, Hypo broke into JN25. By the spring of 1942, about 30 percent of this traffic was being read. As the isolated fragments of information grew denser, enlarged, and touched each other, the analysts began to make educated guesses about Japanese fleet operations from them. If a small ship usually operated with carriers, there was a strong possibility that she was a tanker. Each time the carriers summoned the tanker, cipher groupings appeared that could mean "refuel" and "rendezvous" along with the names of favored locations for refueling. Not every message could be read—as in baseball, it was the batting average that counted—but the cryptanalysts were making giant strides in creating their own versions of the Japanese codebooks. Hypo also profited from the Japanese navy's failure to distribute the new codebooks and cipher tables that had been scheduled for April 1.

Toward the middle of April, Admiral King requested Station Hypo to provide a long-range estimate of Japanese intentions. Rochefort predicted that the enemy would soon launch a campaign aimed at capturing Port Moresby, and that later that summer a larger operation would be mounted in the Central Pacific. Nimitz mobilized his available ships accordingly. To deal with the Port Moresby operation, two carriers— *Yorktown* and *Lexington*, with 141 aircraft—one light and seven heavy

---

*The cipher consisted of some forty-five thousand five-digit numbers representing words and phrases. Before sending a message, a communications officer would encipher it by randomly choosing a five-digit number from the cipher table and subtracting it from the number of the first word of the message. The next cipher number would then be subtracted from the next number, and so on until the message was completed. To enable the recipient to decipher the message, the page, column, and line at which the sender had begun picking the cipher numbers from the table were included in the message.

cruisers (including two Australian ships), fifteen destroyers, and several submarines were concentrated in the Coral Sea under the command of Admiral Fletcher, who was flying his flag in *Yorktown*. Admiral Halsey was also ordered to join him with *Enterprise* and *Hornet* as soon as he returned from the Tokyo raid, but arrived too late for the action.

The curtain rose on the Battle of the Coral Sea on May 3, 1942, as the Japanese made an unopposed landing on Tulagi, which had been evacuated by the Australians, and rapidly set about establishing a sea-plane base. Upon learning of the landing, Fletcher left *Lexington* to complete refueling, and raced his force toward Tulagi at twenty-seven knots. Early the next morning, *Yorktown* launched three successive waves of dive-bombers and torpedo planes that blasted the island. Taken by surprise, the Japanese offered little resistance. The inexperienced American air crews claimed several hits, but the actual results were disappointing. Most of the Japanese ships had already departed, although a destroyer was badly damaged and later sank, and some small craft and five seaplanes were destroyed. The raid also alerted the Japanese to the presence of an enemy carrier in the area and put them on guard.

For the next two days, the Japanese and American carrier groups vainly groped about for each other amid rain squalls and poor visibility. Elsewhere in the Pacific, Corregidor, the last American stronghold in the Philippines, surrendered on May 6. At one point, the carrier forces were only about seventy miles apart but failed to sight each other. Poor weather was only partially responsible for this failure; the fragmented American command structure in the Pacific also played a key role. Long-range reconnaissance was the responsibility of General MacArthur's command, but he did not have enough aircraft to accomplish this mission, and Nimitz was forbidden to send patrol planes into MacArthur's zone of operations to make up for the deficiency.

Based on intelligence from Station Hypo and sighting reports, Fletcher surmised that the invasion force would advance on Port Moresby through the Jomard Passage. Rear Admiral John G. Crace of the Royal Navy was ordered to block the southern exit with Task Group 17—the heavy cruiser *Chicago* and two Australian ships, the heavy cruiser *Australia* and light cruiser *Hobart*. Fletcher was later to be criticized for depriving the carriers of the anti-aircraft protection of the cruisers' guns,[*] but he apparently believed the impending carrier battle might result in heavy damage on both sides and wished to have another force available to bar the door to Port Moresby if needed.

The pace of action picked up on May 7, when, at 0815, a Japanese patrol plane sighted an enemy carrier and cruiser. In actuality, they were the U.S. fleet oiler *Neosho* and the destroyer *Sims*, which had been ordered by Fletcher to a supposedly safe rendezvous to the south. Rear Admiral Chuichi Hara, the carrier commander, sent seventy-eight planes from *Shokaku* and *Zuikaku* roaring off to the attack. Only minutes after the strike force had been launched, Hara received a sighting report which correctly located TF 17. Unable to recall his planes, he ordered them to deal with the two ships and then to attack the American carrier. Instead of a carrier and a cruiser, the planes found *Neosho* and *Sims* and began searching the area for the reported carrier. Running low on fuel, they finally settled for the hapless tanker and destroyer.

The Americans also made their share of mistakes. That same morning, a scout plane reported sighting two Japanese carriers and four heavy cruisers. Believing that this was the main enemy force, Fletcher ordered a strike by ninety-three aircraft from *Lexington* and *Yorktown*. These planes had almost reached the target when it was discovered that the report was garbled—the plane had sighted only two cruisers and two destroyers. Gambling that the invasion fleet must be in the vicinity, Fletcher allowed the strike to proceed.

One mistake canceled another. *Lexington*'s leading SBD wandered off course and discovered Admiral Goto's force, which included *Shoho*, bathed in sunshine. Most of the carrier's planes were protecting the Port Moresby invasion force as it moved south, and the attackers were almost unopposed. *Shoho*, smothered by thirteen bomb hits and ripped by seven torpedoes, quickly went to the bottom. Only about a hundred of her some nine hundred crewmen sur-

---

[*]Morison, taking his usual negative view of Fletcher, ridiculed the move as "Crace's Chase" in vol. IV of his *History* (pp. 37–39), but Crace later declared that he agreed with Fletcher's decision. See Lundstrom, "Frank Jack Fletcher Got a Bum Rap," pt. II, *Naval History*, Summer 1992.

vived. "Scratch one flat-top!" an exuberant Lieutenant Commander Robert E. Dixon radioed *Lexington*.

In the meantime, Crace's TG 17, which was blocking the invasion route, served as a honeypot and attracted swarms of Japanese shore-based bombers that might have gone after Fletcher's carriers. Handling his ships with skill, Crace successfully avoided damage while shooting down five enemy aircraft. He also had to dodge an attack by three B-17s that took his ships for Japanese vessels. Learning of the loss of *Shoho* and of the presence of Crace's ships near the Jomard Passage, Admiral Takagi ordered the invasion force to turn back until the enemy had been cleared from the area.

Late in the day, the Japanese spotted *Lexington* and *Yorktown* and attacked with twenty-seven planes. They failed to find the ships, because of poor visibility and approaching darkness. Nine were shot down by the American combat air patrols. Following this fight, several Japanese pilots mistook *Yorktown* for their own ship in the darkness, and tried to land on her flight deck. One fell victim to the carrier's guns, and the others veered off. Eleven crashed into the sea as they tried to make night landings on their carriers. Thus, only six of the twenty-seven planes returned safely.

Dawn on May 8 found the two carrier forces—now evenly matched in number of ships and planes—about 175 miles apart. The ensuing battle consisted primarily of an exchange of aerial strikes. With torpedo planes and dive-bombers from *Yorktown* leading the attack, the Americans struck the first blow. *Zuikaku* had disappeared into a sudden rain squall, so they concentrated on *Shokaku*. Nine TBDs went in, but American torpedoes were notoriously slow and tended to misfire, so the carrier escaped unharmed. SBDs, joined by late arrivals from *Lexington*, had better luck and hit *Shokaku* with at least two five-hundred-pound bombs.

"The area on the port side from the bow aft for about 50 to 100 feet was one mass of flames from the waterline to the flight deck," reported Lieutenant Commander Joe Taylor of Torpedo Squadron 5. "The flame was exceptionally intense. It looked like that from an acetylene torch, and appeared to be coming from inside the ship." The blaze was brought under control, but although *Shokaku* could recover her planes she could not launch them, and she was ordered back to Truk.

In the meantime, an attack group of sixty-nine Japanese planes located *Yorktown* and *Lexington*. Flight Warrant Officer Kenzo Kanno had shadowed the carriers and then led the raiders to them, even though this meant he would not have sufficient fuel to return to his own ship. *Yorktown* was attacked at about 1120, while most of her combat air patrol was refueling. She evaded eight torpedoes, some running as close as ten yards of her hull, but a heavy bomb penetrated the flight deck near the island and exploded in the bowels of the ship. Although seventy men were either killed or wounded, she continued to operate her planes.

"Lady Lex" was not so lucky. "Never in all my years in combat had I ever imagined a battle like this!" reported Lieutenant Commander Shigekazu Shimazaki, leader of *Zuikaku*'s air group. "Our fighters and American Wildcats dived and climbed in the middle of formations. Burning and shattered planes of both sides plunged from the skies. Amidst this fantastic rainfall of anti-aircraft shells and spinning planes, I dived almost to the water's surface and sent my torpedo into *Lexington*."

Because of her great size, *Lexington* was unable to avoid the torpedoes in the same manner as the smaller *Yorktown*. Caught in the familiar "anvil" position between two groups of torpedo planes, she was hit on the port side forward and then on the starboard side under the bridge. Fires broke out in three places, some boiler spaces were flooded, and she began listing to port. Working frantically, her damage-control crews brought the flames under control, and by 1240 *Lexington* was making twenty-four knots and had resumed air operations.

"We have stopped up the holes made by the torpedoes, the fires are out and the vessel will be almost back on an even keel in a few minutes," *Lexington*'s damage-control officer, Lieutenant Commander H. H. Healy, told her skipper, Frederick C. Sherman, "but may I suggest, Captain, that if you intend to be hit by any other torpedoes, it would be as well to take them on the starboard side."

Not long afterward, *Lexington* was suddenly rocked by a massive explosion. Fumes from her aviation-fuel supply lines, ruptured by the bombing, had been ignited by a chance spark. Flames engulfed the vessel, and she was rocked by repeated secondary explosions. In spite of strenuous efforts to save her, there was nothing more to be done, and at 1707 Captain Sherman gave the order to abandon ship.

Most of the crew of three thousand men were saved before the blazing hulk was torpedoed by one of her escorts, to keep it from falling into enemy hands.

Although sporadic action continued into the next day, the Battle of the Coral Sea was over. As the first naval action in which surface ships did not exchange a single shot—or, indeed, even catch sight of one another—it was a turning point in history. Coral Sea was a tactical victory for the Japanese, but a strategic victory for the U.S. Navy. The Americans lost three ships, including *Lexington*, and sixty-six planes; the Japanese lost the less important *Shoho* and several smaller ships, as well as seventy-seven aircraft. But, as at Jutland, the losses do not tell the whole story. The attempt to capture Port Moresby was turned back, the first time a Japanese thrust had been blunted. *Yorktown* was soon in action again, but *Zuikaku*'s lost planes and experienced air crews could not be readily replaced, and *Shokaku* required long months of repair. Thus, neither carrier was available for Midway, the most crucial battle of the Pacific war.

Four weeks later, on the morning of June 3, 1942, a lone PBY droned over the endless Pacific some seven hundred miles west of Midway, on the lookout for an advancing Japanese fleet. When the clouds parted momentarily, Ensign Jack Reid spotted a large formation of vessels spread out on the horizon that looked like miniature ships on a pond. They were the transports of the Japanese force being sent to occupy Midway.

"Do you see what I see?" he asked his copilot.

"You're damn right I do!" was the vigorous response.

Rapidly ducking back into the cloud cover, Reid radioed the sighting report to Pearl Harbor, where Admiral Nimitz was anxiously awaiting some word of the Japanese. He greeted the report with "a bright, white smile," according to Lieutenant Commander Elmer T. Layton, his intelligence officer. Nimitz had staked everything on finding the enemy without his own ships' being discovered first, and he had won a desperate gamble. The Battle of Midway, turning point of the war in the Pacific, was about to begin.

A week before, on May 27, Admiral Nagumo's First Carrier Striking Force—*Akagi, Kaga, Soryu,* and *Hiryu,* the cutting edge of the Imperial Navy—had steamed out of the fleet anchorage at Hashirajima, in the Inland Sea, on its way to Midway. It was a special day in Japan, Navy Day, the thirty-seventh anniversary of the crushing defeat of the Russians at Tsushima, and Japan's leaders hoped this was an omen of another great victory. Prudent strategy dictated a delay in the Midway operation following the loss of most of the air groups of *Shokaku* and *Zuikaku* and damage to the former ship in the Coral Sea, but Admiral Yamamoto refused to await their return to readiness.

To the Japanese, the Coral Sea battle had been merely a diversion, one they thought they had won, whereas Midway was the main event. Intelligence reports reaching Yamamoto observed that the Americans "lacked the will to fight." Captain Mitsuo Fuchida, who had led the planes that attacked Pearl Harbor, was exhilarated. "As we steamed out of the anchorage the ships of the other forces, which would sortie two days later, gave us a roaring send-off. . . . Every man was convinced that he was about to participate in yet another brilliant victory."

Yamamoto's planning for the Midway operation was a complex blend of stealth, ruse, and division of forces intended to keep the enemy off balance. Unlike Pearl Harbor, when he had remained in Japan, he took personal command, flying his flag in the world's largest battleship, the seventy-two-thousand-ton *Yamato*, armed with 18.1-inch guns which could hurl a shell twenty-five miles. He divided his fleet into three major units: a striking force of Nagumo's four carriers with two battleships; a dozen transports carrying five thousand troops to occupy the atoll, escorted by another pair of fast battleships and the light carrier *Zuiho*; and the main body, consisting of seven battleships and the carrier *Hosho*.

This armada was preceded by a diversionary force—including the light carriers *Ryujo* and *Junyo*, two heavy cruisers, and some transports—that was to bombard Dutch Harbor in the Aleutians and to seize Adak, Attu, and Kiska. The Aleutians raid was intended to lure the enemy fleet to the north while Midway was being attacked and occupied. When the Americans learned of the ruse and hastened south, they would be intercepted by the carriers and battleships.

Yamamoto's plan smacked more of the war-gaming table than reality, however. The Combined Fleet was divided into no fewer than sixteen different groups of warships spread all over the North Pacific. Except for the three formations assigned to the Midway invasion, they were too far apart to provide mutual support to each other. And even though the Aleutians operation was a feint, it still had to be strong enough to deal with any opposition, thereby depriving the main attack force of the two light carriers and their planes. Thus, of the eight carriers available, only the four assigned to Nagumo's Striking Force would come into immediate contact with the enemy, giving the Japanese a superiority of only four ships to three. The two sides had parity in carrier aircraft, 234 for the Americans to 229 Japanese, but if Midway-based aircraft* and Japanese seaplanes are included, the Japanese were actually outnumbered by 344 to 246. Yamamoto's greatest weakness, however, was his assumption of total surprise.

The Japanese had already lost that advantage. Station Hypo was reading 85 percent of JN25, because the Japanese navy had not begun using a new version of their codebook and tables until May 24. Rochefort had pinpointed Midway as the target of the massive Japanese operation and passed his findings on to Nimitz. Few admirals have been confronted by a deeper strategic dilemma. The Japanese movements could be a cover for another attack on Pearl Harbor, or even on the West Coast. In fact, Admiral King's staff in Washington was convinced these were Yamamoto's objectives. But Layton and Rochefort argued forcefully that there was a mountain of evidence pointing to Midway. Nimitz, staking all his chips on Rochefort's analysis, committed his forces to the defense of the island. On May 25, Rochefort personally delivered the most important intelligence yet—a long intercept that contained much of the battle order of the Japanese fleet and the date and positions from which the attacks would be launched.

Nevertheless, there were skeptics in Washington, and Rochefort and his staff searched for means of convincing doubters. They noted that enemy radio traffic made numerous references to "AF," which was believed to be Midway. To nail down the identity of "AF," Lieutenant Commander W. J. Holmes, a sometime novelist,† suggested that Midway be instructed to send a message in plain English that its freshwater-distilling plant had broken down. Two days later, Hypo

---

*It should be noted that many of the aircraft based on the atoll were outmoded planes discarded from carriers that had received new equipment.

†Under the pseudonym of Alec Hudson.

intercepted a Japanese message reporting that "AF" was short of water.[*]

Knowledge of an opponent's intentions is of immense value to a commander, but does not always ensure that he can win a battle. That requires men, ships, and aircraft, and Nimitz was short of all three, though he redoubled efforts to strengthen the defenses of Midway and brought every available ship and plane to the Central Pacific. Laboring around the clock, fifteen hundred workers at Pearl Harbor patched up the damaged *Yorktown* in three days, a task that would have required three months in peacetime. Admiral Halsey brought *Enterprise* and *Hornet* back from the Southwest Pacific. By June 1, Nimitz had a fleet of three carriers, eight cruisers, fourteen destroyers, and about twenty submarines—about half the size of the Japanese force. But he had two advantages that the enemy lacked—radar and Midway itself, an unsinkable aircraft carrier. And he also knew enough to ignore the forthcoming assault on the Aleutians, although he sent Task Force 8—of five cruisers, four destroyers, and six submarines, under Rear Admiral Robert A. Theobald—to harass it.

The bulk of the American fleet was divided into two task forces. Nimitz wanted Halsey in overall command as well as in charge of TF 16, which was composed of *Enterprise* and *Hornet*. TF 17 was commanded by Admiral Fletcher, who once again flew his flag in *Yorktown*. But Halsey was hospitalized with a skin disease, and tactical command was given to Fletcher. Admiral King had misgivings, but

---

[*]The navy's treatment of Rochefort and his staff was shabby in the extreme following the Midway battle. Nimitz recommended Rochefort for the Distinguished Service Medal and asked for decorations for other code breakers as well, but the recommendation was turned down by Admiral King as a result of internal navy politics. Following the battle, Rochefort vigorously protested an attempt by the Office of Naval Communications to take over Station Hypo and angrily talked of "seceding" from it. Rochefort's rising prominence—and fierce independence—had aroused ill-feelings in Washington even before Midway, and his enemies now portrayed his conduct as verging on insubordination. Resenting the awards to the Pearl Harbor shop, they persuaded King that Station Negat, which had predicted an attack on Hawaii or the West Coast, had played the key role in breaking JN25 and deserved the bulk of the credit for Midway. Rochefort angrily requested sea duty—and spent most of the remainder of the war in command of a floating drydock. He received the Legion of Merit, which was finally upgraded to the Distinguished Service Medal in 1985, nine years after his death. But an effort to have a destroyer named for him was turned down.

Nimitz assured him that Fletcher "did a fine job and exercised superior judgment" in the Coral Sea action. He recommended that Fletcher be promoted to vice-admiral and awarded the Distinguished Service Medal; King chose to delay action on these requests. Halsey recommended that Raymond Spruance, his friend and cruiser commander, head TF 16, and Nimitz agreed. The fifty-six-year-old Spruance was surprised. Although a brilliant staff officer, he was like Fletcher, a nonavaitor with no carrier experience. He was, however, the only officer in the navy whom Admiral King regarded as his intellectual equal.

Nimitz ordered Fletcher to take up a position to the northeast of Midway, where he would be able to launch a surprise attack on the left flank of the Japanese carrier force coming in from the northwest. The *Hornet* and *Enterprise* air groups were designated as the main striking force once the Japanese carriers had been sighted, and *Yorktown* was to provide reconnaissance and act as a strike reserve. "You will be governed," Nimitz told Fletcher, "by the principles of calculated risk, which you shall interpret to mean avoidance of exposure of your forces to attack by superior enemy forces without good prospect of inflicting, as a result of such exposure, greater damage on the enemy." In plain language, this meant "Sink the enemy and don't get sunk yourself." These orders may have lacked eloquence, but there was little else to be said.

The Battle of Midway began at 0300 on June 3, 1942, in the fog-shrouded Aleutians. Nimitz had warned Admiral Theobald that the Japanese were expected to try to occupy Adak, Attu, and Kiska, in the western Aleutians, but Theobald, something of a maverick, was convinced this was merely a feint designed to lure Task Force 8 away from Dutch Harbor, his main base, which he believed was the real enemy target. Instead of trying to defend the threatened islands, Theobald, flying his flag in the light cruiser *Nashville*, concentrated his five cruisers and four destroyers far to the east, about four hundred miles south of Kodiak.

In the fog and darkness, Rear Admiral Kakuji Kakuta, commander of the Aleutian Strike Force, eluded the few American pickets and slipped in from the south-southwest with the carriers *Ryujo* and *Junyo*. On the morning of June 3, he launched a forty-five-plane strike against Dutch Harbor, designed to lure the Pacific Fleet to the north. Unable to find the target because of poor visibility, *Junyo*'s twenty-eight planes returned to their carrier, while *Ryujo*'s aircraft pressed on. Although a considerable number of Army P-40 fighters were based in the Dutch Harbor area, the Japanese achieved complete surprise. An oil-tank farm, with its twenty-two thousand barrels of fuel and other installations, was severely damaged, and all but two of the raiders escaped. While TF 8 groped about in the fog, the Japanese occupied bleak Attu and Kiska, without meeting any opposition. The occupation of Adak was canceled when they discovered that the U.S. had a heretofore secret air base nearby. Nimitz, confident of the accuracy of his intellegence regarding enemy intentions, refused to be diverted by the muddled events in the Aleutians.

The struggle in the Central Pacific began the same day, when nine B-17s based upon Midway launched an attack against the transports sighted by Jack Reid, under the impression that they were the main enemy fleet. With majestic splendor, the bombers attacked from between eight and twelve thousand feet but scored no hits. This was one more instance of the failure of high-level bombing against mobile ships; it did not, however, prevent the pilots from claiming damage to two battleships or heavy cruisers and other vessels. Before the battle was over, there were several more incidents in which the B-17s bombed the enemy fleet and made wild claims of damage done, when in reality they hit nothing.

Not long afterward, Fletcher turned his three carriers to the south and headed for a position about two hundred miles north of Midway, where he would be able to launch strikes against Nagumo's carriers the next morning. That night was one of worry, waiting, and work on both sides. Last-minute checks were made of aircraft, and final orders were given, as the ships plowed steadily ahead into the darkness. Sleep was fitful and there was a general feeling of uneasiness, marked by endless shifting in the bunks and constant journeyings back and forth to the head.

The carrier battle began in the predawn darkness of June 4, when, at 0430, Nagumo hurled 108 planes, half his force, at Midway's defenses from a position about 240 miles to the northwest of the atoll. Captain Fuchida, who was to have led the attack, was down with appendicitis, but managed to pull himself up to the *Akagi*'s bridge to

watch the takeoff. "A Zero fighter, leading the flock of impatient war
birds, revved up its engine, gathered speed along the flight deck, and
rose into the air to the accompaniment of a thunderous cheer," he
recalled. "Caps and hands wave wildly in the bright glare of the deck
lights."

Once this wave had been launched, the deck crews began arming
a second strike force. Worried about the possibility of an attack by
enemy surface ships, Admiral Nagumo had these aircraft fitted with
torpedoes and armor-piercing bombs. Once they were ready, they
were brought up on deck for launching at short notice. Seven floatplanes had also been catapulted off, to search the surrounding area
and make certain there were no U.S. carriers about. The last, from the
cruiser *Tone*, which was to search three hundred miles to the east, did
not get off until 0500, a half-hour late, because of catapult trouble.
Unhappily for the Japanese, this was the direction from which the
Americans were coming.

Shortly after 0600, a PBY spotted Nagumo's carriers about two
hundred miles to the northwest of Midway. Eager to get at the Japanese before they got at him, Fletcher ordered Spruance to proceed
southwesterly with *Enterprise* and *Hornet* and attack the enemy vessels as soon as their positions had been fixed. He would follow after
Yorktown's own search planes had been recovered. Thus, crucial
decisions regarding the battle would be made by Spruance rather
than Fletcher. Every serviceable plane on Midway was also scrambled to attack the Japanese carriers. As they flew out over the Pacific
in search of the enemy, swarms of Japanese bombers and fighters
bored in on the atoll.

Twenty-six marine fighters, eighteen outmoded Buffaloes and
eight Wildcats, rose to break up the attack. Outclassed and overwhelmed by the Zeros, fifteen were quickly shot down. But Midway's
defenders put up a firestorm of anti-aircraft fire; thirty-eight Japanese planes were lost during the raid, mostly to ground fire, and
another twenty-nine had to be written off—a loss of over 60 percent.
Nagumo, who now had substantially fewer planes than the Americans, had good cause to lament Yamamoto's decision to assign four
carriers and their air groups to other parts of the operation.

Lieutenant Joichi Tomonaga, leader of the Midway attack, surveyed the atoll from his bomber and found the strike had failed to

knock out the airfield. He radioed Nagumo at 0700: "There is need for a second attack." Having just beaten off the first wave of Midway-based aircraft—with heavy losses to the Americans*—the admiral needed no convincing about the continued threat from Midway. But for the next fifteen minutes, he agonized over what he should do. He had ninety-three aircraft loaded with torpedoes and bombs for an attack on enemy ships spotted on his flight decks; if he ordered a switch to pay loads suitable for another attack on Midway, it would take an hour to make the changeover. But, then again, the scout planes, which had been airborne for two hours, had reported no signs of enemy ships. An hour's delay seemed reasonable, and at 0715 Nagumo ordered the torpedo planes struck below and reloaded.

The plane handlers had just begun wrestling the bombers down to the hangar deck when *Tone*'s floatplane, which had been late getting off, reported at 0728 the sighting of ten enemy ships about three hundred miles away. Nagumo was shocked; this was the first indication he had of American ships in the area. If the enemy fleet had a carrier, his ships would be in serious danger, caught as they were with their decks cluttered with planes in the process of rearming. Had the scout plane gotten off on time, it might have sighted the Americans a half-hour before, giving Nagumo time to attack the U.S. carriers.

Frantic signals were sent to the pilot instructing him to identify the American ships. To add to Nagumo's discomfort, his vessels were under repeated attack by aircraft from Midway, which were beaten off by his Combat Air Patrols (CAPs). At 0809, *Tone*'s plane signaled that the enemy force was composed of five cruisers and five destroyers. Vastly relieved, the admiral resumed preparations for a ground strike. Once he had launched these planes, the aircraft returning from Midway could be recovered. Some of them were badly shot up, and all were short of fuel.

Ten minutes later, the scout plane flashed a new message: "Enemy force accompanied by what appears to be an aircraft carrier." Consternation reigned on *Akagi*'s bridge. Nagumo conferred with Commander Minoru Genda, his air officer, and decided to attack the newly sighted carrier. Once again, the second-strike planes were

---

*One Japanese officer noted that the enemy torpedoes "didn't have any speed at all," and one was exploded by machine-gun fire as it porpoised.

ordered reloaded, this time with torpedoes and armor-piercing bombs. But before they could be brought back to the flight deck and flown off, the returning Midway strike force had to be recovered, rearmed, and refueled. For the next hour, the flight decks of the Japanese carriers were crisscrossed by fuel lines; ammunition, bombs, and torpedoes were haphazardly strewn about as the deck crews struggled frantically to get their charges back into the air.

In the ready rooms of *Enterprise* and *Hornet*, pilots joked nervously as they awaited word that the Japanese carriers had been sighted. They tried to brush aside the sobering thought that there would be empty chairs in the wardrooms that night. "Pilots, man your planes!" ordered the metallic voice on the squawk box at 0702. The order to scramble brought a jumble of sensations—noise, confusion, and unstated fear. While Nagumo hesitated over sending a second strike against Midway, Admiral Spruance had decided to launch his air groups against the Japanese carriers. It was the most momentous decision of the battle—and perhaps of the entire Pacific war.

The normally prudent Spruance calculated that, though his ships would not reach the ideal flying-off position until 0900, or for another two hours, if he launched now, at the extreme range of 175 miles, TF 16's planes might reach the enemy carriers at their moment of supreme vulnerability, when they were landing and refueling the Midway strike force. Some of his aircraft would run out of fuel before they made it back to their carriers, but if lucky they would be able to land at Midway. Taking an immense risk, he sent every possible plane to attack, rather than holding back half to defend his ships.

Hornet launched thirty-five Dauntless dive-bombers, each with a five-hundred-pound bomb; fifteen Devastator torpedo planes; and ten Wildcats. *Enterprise* launched thirty-two dive-bombers, fifteen carrying thousand-pound bombs; fourteen torpedo planes; and ten fighters. *Yorktown* also put seventeen SBDs, a dozen TBDs, and six fighters into the air. It took over a half-hour to launch this armada, and the planes started toward the reported position of the enemy carriers in four unorganized groups. Worst of all, the torpedo squadrons, which were most in need of fighter cover, lost their escort early on.

Nagumo had withdrawn to the northeast to open the range between his ships and the enemy carriers while his planes were being rearmed and refueled, so the Americans saw only empty sea where they had expected to find the Japanese. But a squadron of fifteen Devastators from *Hornet*—Torpedo 8—found the carriers. Without fighter cover, they courageously pressed home an attack. Before taking off, the squadron leader, Lieutenant Commander John C. Waldron, had told his pilots: "I want each of us to do his utmost to destroy our enemies. If there is only one plane left to make a final run in, I want that man to go in and get a hit. May God be with us all."

Zeros and a heavy barrage of anti-aircraft fire met the ungainly TBDs as they came in just above the surface, and sent them splashing into the sea as if they were scraps dropped into a meat grinder. Few of them got close enough to drop their torpedoes, and only one of the thirty pilots and gunners survived. Ensign George Gay was shot down and, although wounded in the arm and leg, fought his way to the surface after his plane sank, and spent the next thirty hours in the water, where he had a fish-eye view of the battle. He was picked up by a PBY the next day. Two other squadrons of torpedo planes— one from *Enterprise*, the other from *Yorktown*—also attacked the carriers, only to be slaughtered by the fifty or more Zeros of the CAP. In all, only six of the forty-one torpedo planes returned from this mission—and not a single Japanese ship was hit.

So far the honors had gone to the Japanese, but just as Nagumo was breathing a sigh of relief, American dive-bombers arrived over his carriers. Lieutenant Commander Clarence W. McClusky, Jr., had difficulty in finding Nagumo's force but finally spotted a Japanese destroyer and trailed it to the carriers. *Enterprise*'s thirty-seven Dauntlesses came in from the southeast, while Lieutenant Commander Maxwell F. Leslie led thirteen of *Yorktown*'s planes in from the southwest. McClusky divided his planes into two groups, and at 1026 they nosed over to begin their dives on *Kaga* and *Akagi* from fourteen thousand feet; Leslie's squadron took on *Soryu*.

The SBDs were unopposed as they swept down on the carriers. The massacre of the torpedo planes is usually credited with diverting the attention of the defending fighters and anti-aircraft gunners from the dive-bombers. Although the sacrifice of the torpedo squadrons was important, another reason for the success of this attack is hardly ever touched upon. The Imperial Navy lacked a good fighter-direction system, its radar was primitive, and the radios in its planes were inadequate. The dive-bombers came in at high altitudes and from out of the clouds faster than the defending CAPs could be vectored to intercept them.

Lieutenant Clarence E. Dickinson, one of *Enterprise*'s pilots, reported:

> As I put my nose down I picked up our carrier target in front of me. I was making the best dive I have ever made. . . . We were coming down in all directions on the port side of the carrier, beautifully spaced. . . . I recognized her as the *Kaga*; and she was enormous. . . . The target was utterly satisfying. . . . I saw a bomb hit just behind where I was aiming. . . . I saw the deck rippling and curling back in all directions exposing a great section of the hangar below. . . . I dropped a few seconds after the previous explosion. . . . I saw the 500-pound bomb hit right abreast of the island. The two 110-pound bombs struck in the forward area of the parked planes. . . . Then I began thinking it was time to get myself away from there. . . .

Four bombs struck *Kaga*, and the fire fed on ruptured fuel lines, touching off secondary explosions among her parked planes. Everyone on the bridge was killed. Unlike the U.S. Navy, which emphasized damage control in its training, the Japanese were less thorough, and the attempts to put out the fires were unsuccessful. Engulfed in soaring flames, *Kaga* sank that evening.[*] *Akagi* was hit by a bomb that ripped open her flight deck; another fell among her planes. "The terrifying scream of the dive bombers reached me first, followed by the crashing explosion of a direct hit," Captain Fuchida recalled. The flagship was transformed into a flaming pyre, but Admiral Nagumo stubbornly refused to leave her. Finally, when she lost radio communication with the rest of the fleet, he shifted his flag to the light cruiser *Nagura*, and *Akagi* was sunk by her destroyers. The entire engine-room crew, trapped below, went down with the ship. *Soryu* was hit by three thousand-pound bombs and was soon blazing out of control. It was the most successful carrier air strike in history—and took only about six minutes from beginning to end.

Sixteen of the Dauntlesses were lost, although it is unlikely that

---

[*]The submarine *Nautilus* found the burning *Kaga* and fired three torpedoes at her. Typical of American torpedoes, two went awry and the third struck the hulk and bounced off.

many of them were shot down; most probably ditched into the sea after running out of fuel. The rest straggled back to their carriers, but those headed for *Yorktown* had unwelcome followers. *Hiryu*, the fourth Japanese carrier, had not been spotted by the Americans, because of poor visibility, and she hastily mounted a strike against *Yorktown*, the only American carrier sighted by the Japanese. In the meantime, Admiral Nobutake Kondo with his two battleships and Yamamoto's seven battleships was steaming at flank speed to Nagumo's assistance. It was already too late; the admiral should have concentrated the elements of his fleet far earlier in the engagement.

"Bogeys, 32 miles closing!" called out *Yorktown*'s radar officer as *Hiryu*'s strike force was sighted.

"Well, I've got on my tin hat," said Admiral Fletcher. "I can't do anything else now."

Fourteen of *Hiryu*'s bombers were shot down, one exploding in a huge orange flash. Three bombs hit the carrier, starting several serious fires, and the ship was stopped dead in the water. Fletcher transferred his flag to the cruiser *Astoria*, and he passed control of air operations to Spruance, who still had two carriers. Damage-control parties brought the fires under control and got *Yorktown* under way again, but just as her CAP was being refueled, *Hiryu*'s second wave of bombers and torpedo planes bored in. Two torpedoes struck the crippled carrier on the port side. Listing badly and without power, she was abandoned, but refused to sink.

No sooner had *Hiryu*'s surviving planes returned to their ship than they were ordered out again. Many of the flyers were exhausted, and a break was ordered before the next launch. Rice balls and tea were being passed around when, at about 1700, *Enterprise*'s dive-bombers appeared overhead. *Hiryu* had a CAP of fourteen Zeros aloft—most from the three carriers already put out of action—but they were brushed aside, and the ship was hit four times in succession, starting fires that would destroy her. Within a few hours, four of the carriers that had wreaked havoc upon the Allies from Pearl Harbor to the Bay of Bengal had been lost, along with some 250 aircraft and their crack air groups.

Nagumo discreetly refrained for several hours from reporting the loss of *Akagi, Kaga*, and *Soryu* to Yamamoto. Upon learning of the disaster, the admiral sank stunned into a chair and sat staring into space, as stupefied as General MacArthur had been in his penthouse in Manila. Hope was temporarily restored when Yamamoto was told that *Yorktown* had been sunk and *Hiryu* was undamaged and fighting back. He was led to believe that the Americans had only one carrier left, so that *Hiryu* faced even odds. Moreover, the battleships and two light carriers of Kondo's force and the main fleet would soon be on the scene; all was not yet lost.

Breaking radio silence, the admiral ordered the Aleutians Screening Force, with its two carriers, to join him by noon the next day; the transports carrying the troops that were to occupy Midway were ordered to retire temporarily to the northwest. Shortly after these orders were given, Yamamoto learned of the loss of *Hiryu*, last of Nagumo's carriers. "The members of the staff, their mouths shut, looked at one another . . . [with] indescribable emptiness, cheerlessness and chagrin . . ." the admiral's yeoman later wrote.

Nevertheless, at 1915, Yamamoto sent one of the most remarkable signals of the war. "The enemy fleet, which has practically been destroyed . . . is retiring eastward," he claimed in words of MacArthurian unreality. "Immediately contact and destroy the enemy." Four heavy cruisers under command of Rear Admiral Takeo Kurita were assigned to a dawn bombardment of Midway as a prelude to the seizure of the atoll. Nagumo added his own touch of surrealism to this scene by reporting that the enemy had five carriers left, later amending it to four. Convinced that Nagumo had lost his nerve, Yamamoto replaced him with Admiral Kondo, who was racing ahead to bring the American carriers within range of his battleships.

Bold in the morning, Spruance exercised caution in the evening. The Japanese expected him to continue pressing ahead into reach of their big guns, but Spruance refused to be drawn into this snare. With darkness falling, he skillfully withdrew to the east. Although there was some criticism of this "failure to pursue," to have done anything else would have been folly. Spruance reasoned that his air groups were bruised and battered, his pilots were untrained in night operations, and from intelligence he knew powerful Japanese forces were closing in. So he continued due east until midnight, which put him in a position to cover Midway or to launch a strike with the coming of daylight.

Shortly after midnight, Yamamoto began reining in his forces. If he continued to pursue Spruance, he was likely to face a dawn attack by American planes without air cover. Some of his staff wished to continue with the planned bombardment of Midway, but at 0255 the admiral bowed to reality and issued orders for a general withdrawal. "But how can we apologize to the Emperor for this defeat?" asked one officer. Yamamoto, who had remained silent during these discussions, now spoke up. "Leave that to me," he abruptly declared. "I am the only one who must apologize to His Majesty."

When the order to withdraw came, Admiral Kurita's four heavy cruisers, which had been steaming through the night toward Midway, were only about eighty miles from their target. They withdrew as ordered, but not long afterward they sighted the American submarine *Tambor*. In the confusion *Mogami* crashed into *Mikuma* and both ships were damaged. The two cripples limped away and were caught the following day, June 6, by American dive-bombers. *Mikuma* was sunk; *Mogami*, although so savagely pounded that she looked more like a wreck than a warship, managed to make it to Truk. Earlier that day, the Japanese submarine *I-168* had picked off *Yorktown* and one of her accompanying destroyers. The next morning, with lowered colors and all hands at attention, the escort vessels paid final tribute to her as she slipped beneath the waves. The Battle of Midway was over.*

Midway confirmed the supremacy of the aircraft carrier in modern naval warfare. With a single thrust, Spruance and Fletcher had destroyed the offensive capability of a fleet with far stronger gunpower than their own—and inflicted upon the Imperial Japanese Navy its first decisive defeat since 1592. The Japanese had lost four of their carriers, a heavy cruiser, three hundred twenty-two aircraft and thirty-five hundred men, including many experienced air crews that

---

*Midway had a bizarre aftermath. To protect the security of its code-breaking operations, the navy assigned credit for its successes to information supplied by patrol planes and submarines. But a few days after the battle, Washington was stunned by a front-page story in the Chicago *Tribune* stating that the U.S. Navy had known in advance of the strength and dispositions of the Japanese fleet. The navy wished to prosecute the paper for espionage but later thought better about such a step. It also had as much to fear from its friends in Congress. "Somehow our navy has secured and broken the secret code of the Japanese navy," Representative Elmer J. Holland announced on the floor of the House. Luckily, the Japanese did not read the *Tribune* or the *Congressional Record*.

could not be replaced. U.S. Navy losses included a carrier, a destroyer, one hundred forty-seven planes and three hundred seven men. The flood tide of Japanese conquest had been halted, first in the Coral Sea and then in the Central Pacific, and Japan now faced the prolonged war that Admiral Yamamoto had warned against. Now the time had come for the U.S. Navy to shift to the offensive. The place chosen was a malaria-ridden island in the Solomons called Guadalcanal.

•

CHAPTER 9

"Warning! Strange Ships Entering Harbor!"

"Land the landing force!"

With the coming of light on August 7, 1942, Task Force 61, fifty ships strong, plodded into Savo Sound and ranged itself off Guadalcanal, in the Solomons chain. The first wave of some nineteen thousand men of the First Marine Division clambered down the cargo nets draped over the sides of the transports and dropped into the landing craft bobbing alongside. Over the ships' loudspeakers had come a command to be heard often in coming years: "Land the landing force!"

Planes from *Saratoga*, *Wasp*, and *Enterprise* outlined the limits of Beach Red with colored smoke as the landing craft headed for shore. Three heavy cruisers, *Quincy*, *Vincennes*, and *Astoria*, and four destroyers blanketed the sixteen-hundred-yard sand strip between these two pillars and the jungle behind it with a barrage of five- and eight-inch shells. At 0910, the First Battalion, Fifth Marines, scrambled over the sides of their landing craft—most lacked ramps—and waded through the gentle surf, weapons held high. Within minutes, a flare signaled that the landing on Guadalcanal had been accomplished without resistance. The two thousand laborers working on an uncompleted airstrip, key to control of the Solomons and the adjacent seas, and about fifteen hundred Japanese troops simply vanished into the jungle. For the first time in the Pacific war, captured territory had been wrested from the enemy.

The Solomons stretch for six hundred miles from the tip of New Guinea in a double string toward New Caledonia, Fiji, and Samoa. Bougainville, at the north end, is followed by Choiseul, Santa Isabel, Florida, with tiny Tulagi nestled in its bight, and Malaita. Running parallel is a scattering of smaller islands—Shortland, Treasury, Vella Lavella, Kolombangara, New Georgia—and then, forming a rough southeast-pointing arrowhead with Malaita, lie Guadalcanal and San Cristóbal. The channel through the islands was called the Slot. Heat, humidity, and endless torrential rains ruled the islands. To the invaders, the high, dark mass of Guadalcanal, at ninety miles long and twenty-five miles wide the largest of the southern Solomons, appeared gloom-shrouded and sinister. "It gave you the creeps," remarked one sailor. The offshore smell evoked mud, slime, and rotting jungle. Soon, this dreary speck of land became the scene of one of the fiercest struggles in American military annals, and Savo Sound, between Guadalcanal and Florida, was so littered with sunken ships it became known as Ironbottom Sound.

Operation Watchtower, as the Solomons invasion was formally designated, was Admiral King's brainchild. It marked the shift of the fighting front thirty-five hundred miles across the Pacific from Pearl Harbor, and the switch by the United States from the "defensive-offensive" to the "offensive-defensive." Two months before the landing, on June 10, King had gone to the White House with confirmation in hand of the devastating losses suffered by the Japanese at Midway, and persuaded President Roosevelt to approve an immediate counteroffensive in the Southwest Pacific while the enemy was in disarray. "Since the Japanese have gotten a rude shock at the Battle of Midway," he wrote later, "here was a good chance to get the enemy off balance and *keep* him off balance."

The operation was designed to breach the Bismarck barrier, which stretched some 560 nautical miles, from Rabaul to Tulagi, blocking the Allied southern advance toward Japan. Following the American success at Midway, General MacArthur had proposed a lightning campaign in New Guinea calling for the capture of Rabaul in less than three weeks. This feat of magic was to be accomplished with the help of a task force with two aircraft carriers. Although the navy agreed with MacArthur that Rabaul should be seized, it had no intention of sending two of its precious carriers into the poorly charted

Solomon Sea, within range of Japanese land-based aircraft—and definitely not under MacArthur's command.

King favored a gradual advance upon Rabaul, through the Solomons and New Guinea. Taking a leaf from the Japanese, he planned to leapfrog up the island chain, building airfields along the way so land-based aircraft could cover the advance. Inasmuch as such an operation was amphibious in nature, it should be under the command of Nimitz, not MacArthur. Following a week of argument, the Joint Chiefs of Staff divided the operation into three separate offensives, or "tasks." Task One called for the occupation of the Santa Cruz Islands (to the south of the Solomons), Tulagi, and "adjacent positions" on August 1. Task Two called for an advance along the northeast coast of New Guinea and a simultaneous advance up the central Solomons. Task Three was the final assault on Rabaul by the two Allied pincers. Guadalcanal was not mentioned in this early version of Watchtower.

The Japanese Naval General Staff was also eyeing the heretofore obscure Solomons chain. The shocking loss of Admiral Nagumo's four first-line carriers at Midway had stunned the nation's leaders, and for several weeks after the battle there were fears of an American attack in home waters. "Victory Fever" was superseded by the cold sweat of despair. To counter the threat to Rabaul from MacArthur's growing American and Australian force, new efforts were mounted to take Port Moresby—this time from the rear, by sending troops over the supposedly impassable Owen Stanley Range. But the security of Rabaul depended on maintaining control of the Solomons. The islands are close to one another, and the surrounding waters could be dominated by land-based aircraft. So the Japanese, who already had a seaplane base at Tulagi, began bulldozing a thirty-six-hundred-foot airstrip out of the jungle near Lunga Point, on the north side of Guadalcanal, about twenty miles across Savo Sound.

U.S. cryptanalysts and radio-traffic analysts reported that the Japanese were preparing for a major new operation in the Southwest Pacific, and word of a new enemy airfield on Guadalcanal set off alarms. If the Japanese controlled the Solomons, they could take the New Hebrides, New Caledonia, the Fijis, and Samoa, which would cut the lifeline from America to Australia and New Zealand. Watchtower was hastily modified to make Guadalcanal and its airstrip the main objective.* Yet, in spite of the substantial expansion of the operation, King and Nimitz allowed only an additional week for preparation. D-Day was set for August 7.

Overall responsibility was assigned to Vice-Admiral Robert L. Ghormley, who had recently arrived at Nouméa, in New Caledonia, to take up his post as commander of the South Pacific area. Frank Jack Fletcher, finally promoted to vice-admiral in recognition of his efforts at Midway, was named to the command of Task Force 61—*Saratoga, Wasp,* and *Enterprise,* the new battleship *North Carolina,* and six cruisers. Rear Admiral Richmond Kelly Turner, who had just left King's staff, where he headed the War Plans Division, was in charge of the Amphibious Force (TF 62). The marines were under the command of Major General Alexander A. Vandegrift, a veteran of jungle fighting in Nicaragua. Rear Admiral Victor A. C. Crutchley of the Royal Navy† commanded TF 44—five American and three Australian cruisers, plus fifteen destroyers—assigned to cover the landing force. Turner would also have the support of American and Australian search planes based near Port Moresby, and land-based patrol planes and bombers under Rear Admiral John R. McCain at Espiritu Santo.

Few major military expeditions have been as hastily cobbled together as the Solomons operation. The controlling element was time. King and Nimitz were worried about the Japanese buildup in the Solomons. Less than two months passed from the date when King first broached his plan and the time when the marines landed on Guadalcanal and Tulagi. Plagued by shortages of equipment and supplies, the expedition was dubbed "Operation Shoestring." Landing craft were scrounged from wherever they could be found. The troops, mostly youthful post–Pearl Harbor volunteers leavened by the "Old Breed," the U.S. Marine Corps's professional cadre, were in only a partial state of combat readiness. Much of their equipment was

---

*Also about this time, U.S. Navy cryptanalysts decoded a message from Tokyo to Berlin in which the Japanese stated that they did not intend to open a second front against the Soviet Union unless forced to by extraordinary circumstances. This permitted Stalin to withdraw troops from the Far East for use against the German invaders, but it also left no doubt that the Japanese would pursue the Pacific war with undiminished intensity.

†Crutchley had won the Victoria Cross as a young officer during World War I.

old, if not obsolete.* Intelligence about the Solomons was rudimentary, and most of the charts, which dated back to the early years of the century, were distressingly vague. "Seldom has an operation been begun under more disadvantageous circumstances," states the official Marine Corps history.

Several of the top American commanders were also skeptical of the operation. Admiral Ghormley and General MacArthur sought a postponement, because Japanese air strength was too strong. "The initiation of the operation at this time without reasonable assurance of adequate air coverage would be attended with the gravest risk," they stated. But King and Nimitz dismissed all pleas for delay. Once his advice had been rejected, Ghormley seems to have distanced himself from the operation and, having decided to command from afar, sent a deputy to planning sessions rather than attending in person. Fletcher was also wary, because he did not relish the idea of tying his carriers down to Guadalcanal and operating within range of land-based aircraft from Rabaul.

Worse was yet to come. The first—and only—meeting of the expedition's principal commanders—held on July 26, as *Saratoga*, Fletcher's flagship, lay off Koro, in the Fijis—flared into an open fight between Turner and Fletcher.† Captain Thomas Peyton, a member of Turner's staff, called it "one long, bitter argument." Outspokenly critical of the operation, Fletcher implied that Turner, and the rest of King's armchair strategists in Washington who had drafted the plan, knew nothing about the realities of combat. Turner, an intellectual bully with a sharp temper and razor tongue, gave as good as he got. "I was amazed and disturbed by the way these two admirals talked to each other," recalled Peyton. "I had never heard anything like it."

The key issue was, how long would the carriers provide air cover for the operation?

Turner reported that the troop transports, along with an occupation force for the Santa Cruz Islands, would be ready to leave the

---

*For example, the marines were armed with the bolt-action Springfield rifle, used in World War I, though the army was issuing the new Garand semi-automatic M-1 rifle to its troops.

†As Admiral McCain was climbing up a Jacob's ladder on *Saratoga*'s side, someone on the carrier opened a garbage chute and doused him with sour milk.

island by the night of D+1. But he estimated he would need from three to six days to unload the five cargo ships—the AKAs—carrying the marines' supplies, ammunition, and heavy equipment and requested air cover for this entire period. Turner and Vandegrift were shocked when Fletcher announced that he would withdraw his carriers after two days because of the threat of Japanese submarines and a counterattack from Rabaul. Having already lost two carriers to Japanese air attacks, and with little faith in the ability of the B-17s to interdict enemy airfields, he obviously had no wish to risk three of the Pacific Fleet's four remaining carriers, particularly since no replacements could be expected for another nine months.

Vandegrift angrily interjected that the days of putting small detachments of marines ashore were over and the Guadalcanal operation required the landing of a full division and its equipment. Relenting, Fletcher promised to keep the carriers on station for three days, or till D+2, with the AKAs remaining behind to be protected by Crutchley's cruisers. Rear Admiral Daniel J. Callaghan, Ghormley's deputy, remained silent. Ghormley made no effort to deal with the tensions among his commanders and merely suggested that, if the carriers had to be withdrawn, fighters could operate from the airstrip on Guadalcanal as soon as it was ready. If not, F4Fs fitted with belly tanks could be flown up from Efate, in the New Hebrides. A practice landing was made on Koro to instill a sense of teamwork in the various units, but it was "a fiasco," according to Vandegrift.

On this unsettling note, TF 61 and the transports, cargo vessels, and auxiliary vessels sailed on the last day of July. Taking up antisubmarine cruising dispositions, they set a course for Guadalcanal—and the U.S.Navy's first opposed amphibious landing since 1898. Over the next week, the armada steamed north by west under the Southern Cross; for the marines it was anything but a pleasure cruise. Overcrowded holds, heat, the smell of vomit, body rashes, the constant threat of submarine attack, and the omnipresent uncertainty about what lay ahead—all these made the voyage a purgatory. Kelly Turner had plenty of time to ponder the observations of Captain B. H. Liddell Hart, the British military commentator, whose book on strategy he was reading: "A landing on a foreign shore in the face of hostile troops has always been one of the most difficult operations of war. It has now become almost impossible. . . ."

*   *   *

Although the Guadalcanal landing was accomplished without difficulty, Tulagi and the neighboring spits of Gavutu and Tanambogo
proved to be much tougher. For the first time, the Americans ran up
against the suicidal Japanese determination to resist that became
common during the rest of the war. The 750 Japanese troops were
well dug in and fought to the bitter end rather than surrender. General Vandegrift had to commit his reserves to this struggle, with some
units suffering 20 to 50 percent casualties, so the Santa Cruz invasion
was ordered postponed, and then abandoned.

Once the Japanese overcame their initial surprise at the Guadalcanal landing, they hit the invasion fleet with a whiplash of air strikes.
Even though Rabaul was bombed by B-17s on the morning of D-Day,
twenty-seven Betty bombers escorted by eighteen Zeros headed
south in an effort to catch the enemy fleet while it was most vulnerable. Two of the fighters were piloted by the Imperial Navy's top
aces—Flight Petty Officer Saburo Sakai and Warrant Officer
Hiroyoshi Nishazawa. The land-locked radars on the screening ships
functioned poorly, and the enemy planes slipped in without being
detected.

Nearing Guadalcanal, the fighters split up into two groups. One
flight of nine, including Nishizawa, tangled with the Wildcats of the
CAP, which had flown off Fletcher's carriers, lying about a hundred
miles to the southwest. After withholding his fire until he was at
point-blank range, Nishizawa shot down five planes, then made his
getaway. The other nine Zeros, including a section led by Sakai,
accompanied the bombers over the massed transports and warships
in Savo Sound, where they dropped their bombs without scoring any
hits. Turning for home, the Japanese were attacked by Wildcats, and
in the melee five bombers and two Zeros were shot down.* Later,
nine Val dive-bombers that were on a one-way mission because they
did not have enough fuel to return to their base, also attacked the
invasion fleet, damaging the destroyer *Mugford*.

Chaos reigned on the beaches. In the haste to get Watchtower
under way on schedule, the AKAs had not been combat-loaded, and

---

*Sakai accounted for a Wildcat, but his own plane was badly shot up, he was blinded
in one eye, and he barely made it back to Rabaul.

low-priority gear was stowed on top of ammunition.* Boat crews
dumped rations at points marked for fuel; medical supplies were
tossed in with ammunition. Working parties were inadequate, and supplies piled up on the beach creating a logistics nightmare. Landing craft
circled offshore for hours, waiting for a clear spot to land their cargoes.
Unloading continued into the night but finally had to be called off
because of congestion on the beach. None of the cargo ships was
even a quarter unloaded during the first night of the operation—a serious problem in view of Fletcher's skittishness about his carriers.

Twenty-three Bettys carrying torpedoes, as well as nine more Vals
and a fighter escort, returned to the attack next day. Forewarned of the
enemy's approach by an Australian coast watcher on Bougainville,†
Turner ordered a halt to unloading and had his transports and screening vessels in cruising formation. Massed anti-aircraft fire and the
Wildcats brought down eighteen Japanese planes. The destroyer
Jarvis was damaged, and a transport was set ablaze and later sank after
being hit by a Japanese pilot who deliberately smashed into the vessel. A destroyer tried to rescue a downed enemy air crew from the
waters of Savo Sound, but the flyers fired their pistols at the ship and
then shot themselves.

U.S. forces had suffered remarkably light casualties during the first
two days of Watchtower—one transport sunk, a pair of destroyers
damaged, and twenty-one fighters lost—and were beginning to
breathe easier. Yet, as the sun dropped behind Cape Esperance, on
the north shore of Guadalcanal, on August 8, the stage was being set
for what Morison called "one of the worst defeats ever inflicted on
the United States Navy in a fair fight."

In the late afternoon, Turner was on the flag bridge of *McCawley*, his
command ship, off Lunga Point, when an orderly handed him a radio
message. The admiral took a glance at the paper and unleashed one

---

*"The essence of combat loading is not to put the toilet paper on top of the ammuni-
tion," explained one marine officer.

†The coast watchers performed a vital task during the Solomons campaign. Operating under control of the Royal Australian Navy, they manned a network of portable radio
stations and, assisted by loyal natives, reported on the movements of Japanese ships and
aircraft. Some were captured and killed. New Zealand also had coast watchers in the
Gilbert and Marshall islands.

of the floods of profanity for which he was justly famous. It was an intercept of a priority dispatch from Fletcher to Ghormley:

> Total fighter strength reduced from 99 to 78. In view of large number of enemy torpedo planes and bombers in this area, I recommend the immediate withdrawal of my carriers. Request tankers be sent forward immediately as fuel running low.

Increasingly anxious about the threat to the carriers and worried about the whereabouts of the four Japanese flattops that had survived Midway, Fletcher weighed the value of the AKAs in the balance against his ships and decided he could no longer remain pinned down near Guadalcanal. Signals intelligence at Pearl Harbor had also warned him of a Japanese naval buildup in the area. Although his carriers had not yet been detected by the Japanese, he could not be certain this would continue. Both Turner and Vandegrift were amazed and angered by his decision; Vandegrift later accused Fletcher of "running away." Nevertheless, Ghormley approved the withdrawal, saying Fletcher "knew the situation in detail; I did not." Long before receiving Ghormley's signal to withdraw, Fletcher was already heading south, leaving the transports, the screen, and the marines to fend for themselves.[*]

Historians have almost uniformly condemned what they regard as

---

[*]It should be noted, however, that John Lundstrom, who has delved deeply into Fletcher's role in Watchtower, argues that he did not know he was leaving Turner in the lurch because he thought Turner was going to pull out that night (D+1), as originally scheduled. Turner had, however, radically altered his plans, because of the heavy casualties taken by the marines in the fighting on Tulagi and the delay in landing supplies, and had decided that none of his ships would withdraw until all had been unloaded. Neither Ghormley nor Fletcher was informed of this development, however, thanks to the poor state of communications among the various elements of the fleet. Lundstrom also argues that Fletcher was hardly "running away," because the carriers remained southeast of Guadalcanal and still in position on August 9 (D+2) to support the transports and the screen if needed.

Lundstrom states that Fletcher's critics have devoted considerable effort to discrediting him by proving that the fuel shortage was a myth, although "Fletcher himself never claimed that it was the primary reason he recommended withdrawing the carriers." They "eagerly consulted deck logs and counted up the gallons of fuel oil available on the various ships. That was a luxury not permitted Fletcher on 8 August." Lundstrom notes that two of Fletcher's task-group commanders—Rear Admirals Thomas C. Kinkaid and Leigh Noyes—reported drastic fuel shortages. See Lundstrom, "Frank Jack Fletcher Got a Bum Rap," pt. II, *Naval History*, Fall 1992.

Fletcher's ill-founded decision to leave the waters off Guadalcanal. Morison set the tone by stating that inasmuch as the enemy had not found his carriers, Fletcher risked little more than "sunburn" if he had remained to the southeast of Guadalcanal for another day. Moreover, says Morison, his ships had plenty of fuel, and despite his losses, Fletcher still possessed more fighters than Nimitz had at the start of Midway. One cannot but agree with a Naval War College analysis which stated the fact that "such a precipitous departure might seriously jeopardize the success of the entire operation at Tulagi-Guadalcanal . . . does not appear to have been given the serious consideration it deserved."

Both Ghormley and Fletcher apparently assumed that the beachhead and transports were in no danger because they had not received an alarm from Admiral McCain, who had the task of carrying out aerial sweeps of the likely area of the Japanese approach. But one sector was poorly covered by air patrols on August 8 because of bad weather: and it was the very one most likely to be used by a counterattacking fleet—the "Slot," the U.S. Navy's name for the channel through the central Solomons.

And just such an attack was hell-bent on its way. Only hours after the Marines had gone ashore, a strike force under Vice Admiral Gunichi Mikawa, commander of the Eighth Fleet, had left Rabaul and was steaming toward Guadalcanal. Mikawa had seen much of the Pacific War. He had been second in command of the Pearl Harbor Strike Force and had taken part in the raid on Ceylon and participated in the Midway operation. With the final radio message from Tulagi ringing in his ears—"The garrison will fight bravely to the last man!"—he stood out from Rabaul with a task force that included his flagship, *Chokai*, and four other heavy cruisers, *Aoba*, *Kako*, *Kinugasa*, and *Furutaka*, as well as two light cruisers and a destroyer. Hoping to surprise the enemy, he raced down the Slot in broad daylight, to reach Guadalcanal in the early-morning darkness of August 9—a Sunday—when the superior night-fighting skills of his crews and their Long Lance torpedoes would decide the battle.

Previous warnings of Japanese naval movements were reinforced by visual sightings; the Japanese ships were spotted at least three times as they raced down from Rabaul. The B-17s that raided the base on the morning of August 7 saw what they took to be a heavy cruiser, three light cruisers, and a destroyer at sea. S-38, an American submarine, sighted the Japanese off Cape St. George, at the southern tip of New Ireland, at about 1930 that evening, proceeding at high speed on a southeasterly course. Forced to dive hurriedly, the boat's captain identified the ships as two small and three large vessels. Turner received this report at 0738 on August 8, and apparently decided to await further information from air reconnaissance to determine whether they were combatants or auxiliary vessels.

Some three hours later, at 1026, a Royal Australian Air Force Hudson spotted a Japanese force east of Bougainville as it approached the entrance to the Slot. In his haste to escape a pair of floatplanes launched by one of the enemy ships, the pilot misidentified the vessels as three heavy cruisers, two destroyers, and two seaplane tenders or gunboats. What happened next is subject to debate. "Instead of breaking radio silence, as he had orders to do in an urgent case," writes Morison, the pilot "spent most of the afternoon completing his search mission, came down at Milne Bay, had his tea, and then reported the contact." Taking their cue from Morison, later writers have embroidered this tale with further damning details. As a result of the Australian pilot's failure to get off a signal immediately, it is charged, Turner did not receive the sighting report until nearly 1900, too late to track or attack the Japanese force.

But Denis and Peggy Warner, an Australian husband-and-wife team of researchers,[*] recently discovered that the pilot *did* break radio silence to send the crucial information immediately in the clear, *did* return quickly to base, and *did not* wait to have his tea before being debriefed. Proof was provided by the records of Mikawa's flagship, *Chokai*, which reported picking up the Hudson's signal. In fact, the admiral considered calling off the raid, since he had been discovered. Several officers in the Allied ships off Guadalcanal also reported receiving the message in the early afternoon, and calculated that the enemy force would arrive in the area at about 0100 on August 9.

Why did Turner disregard this warning? With more than seven hours of daylight remaining, there was ample time not only to go on the alert but to request a carrier strike against the Japanese force. The answer seems to be that he sensed no real danger. First, little cre-

[*] See *Disaster in the Pacific: New Light on the Battle of Savo Island.*

dence was placed in reconnaissance reports from the RAAF; second, he concluded that the ships were en route to set up a seaplane base at Rekata Bay, on Santa Isabel Island, about 155 miles from Guadalcanal. Admiral McCain's bombers were requested to attack them in the morning. To reach the combat zone, he reasoned, the Japanese would have had to pass through the area covered by McCain's patrols, and no sighting had been reported. (Unknown to Turner, these missions had not been flown that day.) Furthermore, the admiral was far more concerned about Fletcher's decision to withdraw the carriers than about the sighting of a nondescript enemy force. With his fleet about to be stripped of air support, he felt he had no choice but to withdraw the transports the next day. General Vandegrift and Admiral Crutchley, commander of the cruiser-destroyer screen, were summoned to his command ship at 2045 to discuss the situation.

Unworried about the possibility of a surface attack, Crutchley sped off to the rendezvous in *Australia*, his flagship, rather than taking a destroyer. This reduced the screen guarding the southern entrance into Ironbottom Sound (between Savo Island and Guadalcanal) to the Australian cruiser *Canberra* and *Chicago*. Three other U.S. cruisers—*Vincennes*, *Quincy*, and *Astoria*—steamed in a square between Savo and Florida at a torpid twelve knots. Twenty miles to the south, a pair of light cruisers, the American *San Juan* and the Australian *Hobart*, were patrolling to prevent Japanese submarines from entering the sound and attacking the transports. Two destroyers, *Blue* and *Ralph Talbot*, were posted as radar pickets on either side of Savo.[*]

Although approved by Turner, Crutchley's arrangements left much to be desired. Captain Howard D. Bode of *Chicago* was notified that he was in command of the southern group, but the admiral failed to inform Captain Frederick Riefkohl of *Vincennes* (who was also commander of the northern group) that, since he was senior officer present, overall command had passed to him. The various units of the task force were too widely dispersed to support each other in case of emergency. Too much reliance was placed upon the radars of the picket destroyers, which proved to be masked by the nearby islands.

---

[*]The patrols mounted by the picket ships were unsynchronized, and if both were at the extreme ends of their search legs there would be a hole as much as twenty-five miles wide in the screen.

Everyone was exhausted by the tensions of the past two days, and all the ships were in Condition Two, with half the watch off duty. Several planes were heard droning overhead in the darkness—they had been catapulted off by Admiral Mikawa—but were thought to be "friendlies." Expecting Crutchley back by midnight, the captains of the various cruisers turned in, leaving the screen widely dispersed, unready for combat, and without a tactical commander.

"WARNING! WARNING! STRANGE SHIPS ENTERING HARBOR!"

Commander Frank R. Walker was on the bridge of the destroyer *Patterson*, peering into darkness of August 9. Rain squalls had done nothing to relieve the sticky oppressiveness of the tropic night, and a mist hung low over Savo Sound. *Patterson* was about five miles south of the western tip of Savo Island when, at 0143, an unidentified ship loomed up unexpectedly before her. And then there was another! Walker immediately sounded general quarters and broadcast an alarm to *Canberra* and *Chicago*. But it was already too late.

Mikawa's cruisers had slipped unseen into the channel between Savo and Guadalcanal, with *Chokai* in the van and every man braced by the admiral's message: "Let us attack with certain victory in the traditional night attack of the Imperial Navy. May each one calmly do his utmost." For a moment, everyone had held his breath as, shortly before 0100, a darkened ship was sighted. It was *Blue*, one of the radar pickets. With every gun and torpedo tube in the task force fixed on her, she continued unruffled on her way. *Talbot* did no better. Hardly able to believe his luck, Mikawa increased speed to twenty-six knots and closed with the unsuspecting Allied cruisers.

Suddenly, the entire area was bathed in a harsh white light cast by parachute flares released by the floatplanes. *Canberra* and *Chicago* were silhouetted for the Japanese gunners, whose own ships remained all but invisible against the dark bulk of Savo. Within seconds, an avalanche of eight-inch shells and a pair of torpedoes ripped into the Australian vessel while her crew was still scrambling to battle stations. Within two minutes, *Canberra* was a blazing wreck, dead in the water and sinking—out of the battle even before anyone on board realized there was one. *Chicago* was under fire for several minutes before Captain Bode reached the bridge. Part of her bow was blown away by a torpedo, and in the confusion Bode steamed about blindly, then mistakenly turned his ship away from the action. Worse yet, he failed to alert the northern group that his ship was under fire. He subsequently committed suicide.

Unaware of the fighting to the south because of a rain squall, but puzzled by the flares and *Patterson*'s warning, *Vincennes*, *Quincy*, and *Astoria* had just turned a corner of their leisurely box patrol when they were fixed by searchlights that stabbed out of the darkness. Less than a minute later, the Japanese, who had swung to port and rounded Savo, fired a salvo, which struck *Astoria*, last in the line. Both of her forward turrets were knocked out, nearly everyone on the bridge was killed or wounded, and she lost way. Flames leaped from her, lighting up the sky and making the other cruisers easy targets for the Japanese gunners.

Quincy was caught in a deadly crossfire between Mikawa's ships, which were now in two lines on either side of her. Hit by both shells and torpedoes, she was soon burning so ferociously that the Japanese searchlights snapped shut, no longer needed for aiming their guns. The sick bay, crowded with wounded, was wiped out by a shell. One minute the surgeons, mates, and patients were alive; then there was only blood and mangled flesh. Nevertheless, she managed to get off several salvos. Two of her shells struck *Chokai*, one of them destroying Mikawa's chart room. *Quincy*'s communications were knocked out, and Lieutenant Commander J. D. Andrew, the assistant gunnery officer, sent to the bridge for instructions, reported:

> When I reached the bridge level, I found it a shambles of dead bodies with only three or four people still standing. In the pilothouse itself the only person standing was the signalman at the wheel. . . . On questioning him I found out that the Captain, who was at that time lying near the wheel, had instructed him to beach the ship and he was trying to head the ship for Savo Island, distant some four miles on the port quarter. . . . The ship was heeling rapidly to port, sinking by the bow. At that instant the Captain straightened up and fell back, apparently dead, without having uttered any sound other than a moan.

Vincennes was the last ship in the line. Captain Riefkohl had seen gun flashes through the rain squall, but assumed it was the *Chicago* group firing at enemy planes. When his ship was caught by a searchlight, he thought it came from the southern group and requested it be turned off. The reply came in the form of a salvo from the Japanese cruisers. *Vincennes* was ready for action, and her second salvo hit *Kinugasa*, but she was quickly smothered by shells. Riefkohl, still believing he was being fired upon by friendly ships, ordered an outsized ensign hoisted to the foremast. This convinced the Japanese that they were firing at an admiral's flagship, and they intensified their efforts to sink her. By 0215, *Vincennes* was listing badly to port, and the Japanese ceased fire.

Mikawa now considered his next move. In thirty frenzied minutes, he had sunk or left sinking four enemy cruisers and severely damaged a fifth. Turner's transports and AKAs, huddling off Lunga Point, lay completely bare to attack—but Mikawa abruptly ordered a withdrawal. With the benefit of hindsight, it is easy to fault him for losing a golden opportunity to wipe out the invasion fleet, but from his viewpoint the decision was a prudent one. All his torpedoes had been expended, his charts had gone up in smoke, and his ships had scattered in the confusion and turmoil of night battle. Two hours would be needed to reorganize for a fresh attack, which would leave him totally exposed to air assault at first light. Unaware of the retirement of Fletcher's carriers, and uncertain of the enemy's remaining strength, Mikawa chose the safest course and turned back up the Slot at thirty knots. The Japanese did not escape completely unscathed, however: *Kako* was torpedoed and sunk by *S-44* as she headed home—the first major Japanese warship to be sunk by a submarine in the Pacific war.

The Allies did not realize the full extent of the disaster until daylight. *Quincy* and *Vincennes* sank shortly after the battle; *Canberra* and *Astoria* lingered a bit longer, with huge columns of smoke pouring from their hulks. Hundreds of oil-covered sailors clung desperately to empty shell cases and bits of debris—anything that would keep them afloat. Blood attracted the sharks that abounded in Savo Sound, and throughout the night men vanished with screams and a horrible swiftness. In all, nearly two thousand sailors went down with their ships or were wounded, some so badly burned that rescuers could find no place to insert hypodermic needles.

Frantic efforts were made to unload the transports and AKAs, but by midday only about half the cargo had been taken off. Lacking air cover, and with his protective screen battered, Turner abandoned the beachhead on the evening of August 9, producing bitter comments from the sixteen thousand marines left behind to face a precarious future on Guadalcanal. As General Vandegrift put it, they were "bare ass," with only enough ammunition for four days of combat, and short rations. America's first Pacific offensive was in danger of collapse, and there was much talk of another Bataan. Coming on top of revelations of the inferiority of American fighters to the Zero, and the ineffectiveness of American torpedoes, the Battle of Savo Island was another rude shock.

Full details of the debacle were withheld from the public; the navy's own inquiry covered up the command failures and, blamed inadequate communications and a lack of "battle-mindedness," finding no one at fault. Turner was the major beneficiary of the cover-up. He had made the basic mistake of assuming what an enemy would do rather than preparing for what he could do. Had he not been a personal favorite of Admiral King, he probably would have been relieved. Once more, proof had been provided—as if it were needed—that war is the provenance of chance: enemies do not behave as expected, orders are misunderstood or not given, equipment breaks down, the weather does not obey forecasts.[*]

For nearly a week, Guadalcanal remained in limbo. The Japanese limited themselves to a few small air raids and nighttime shelling by submarines, while the marines hurried to finish the airstrip with construction equipment left behind by the enemy. They named it Henderson Field, in memory of Major Lofton Henderson, who had led the marine dive-bombers at Midway. Soon, however, both sides began slipping in supplies and reinforcements, and the island, of no importance itself, became a symbol. For the Americans, Guadalcanal represented their determination to remain on the offensive; to the Japanese, its loss threatened the security of their newly conquered

---

[*]It was felt that a thorough public airing of the deficiencies uncovered would strain relations between Australia, Britain, and the United States. It would be better to absorb the bitter lessons of defeat and learn from them, rather than give comfort to the enemy. The fable of the none-too-bright Australian airman was created to meet the needs of the time. The U.S. Navy subsequently named a new cruiser *Canberra*, and the British gave the Australians the eight-inch-gun cruiser *Shropshire* to replace the lost vessel.

empire. Neither side was willing to give up, yet neither could drive the other off the island.*

The U.S. Navy acted first. On August 15, four destroyer-transports (APDs) slipped in with a cargo of aviation gasoline, bombs, and ammunition for an air group to be sent to newly completed Henderson Field. Five days later, the first planes landed—nineteen marine Wildcats and twelve SBDs that had flown in from the escort carrier *Long Island*, the navy's first ship of this type. Planes flying from the strip made their first kill the next day. The Japanese brought in a thousand troops in six destroyers under the command of Rear Admiral Raizo Tanaka—the first of the high-speed troop-and-supply runs soon known as the Tokyo Express.

Henderson Field gave the Americans daytime air superiority over the lower Solomons, but life on the airstrip was grim. It was either a sea of mud or a bowl of black dust that fouled engines and guns. Fuel was short and was fed into the planes by primitive hand pumps. Spare parts were scarce. Radio communications were difficult to maintain. The pilots of the Cactus Air Force—"Cactus" was the code name for Henderson Field—existed on a diet of Spam, dehydrated potatoes, and captured rice. They flew all day, and efforts to sleep were interrupted by shelling by the Tokyo Express, which ran unchecked at night, or by floatplanes—"Louie the Louse" and "Washing Machine Charley"—that dropped a few random bombs.

Malaria and dysentery were rampant. The maximum time a fighter pilot could be expected to spend on Guadalcanal and still be physically and psychologically fit to fly was thirty days. Planes were used up even faster, and at times there were merely a dozen or so operational aircraft. Only a steady flow of replacements—as well as navy planes and some from the Army Air Force—kept the Cactus Air Force flying and fighting.

Wildcat pilots tried to avoid dogfights with the faster and more

---

*In an effort to divert Japanese attention from Guadalcanal, some two hundred marines of Carlson's Raiders were landed from two submarines at Makin Island, in the Gilberts, where they destroyed an airfield and set a large gasoline dump afire. James Roosevelt, the president's oldest son, was Carlson's second in command. The raid was to have unforeseen consequences, however. The alarmed Japanese began building strong fortifications in the Gilberts, which were later to cost the marines dearly. See Morison, *History*, vol. IV, pp. 235–41.

maneuverable Zeros and targeted the Bettys. Diving out of the sun, they aimed at the bombers' unprotected wing tanks in an effort to turn them into globs of fuel-fired flame. If a Zero got on a Wildcat's tail, the pilot could only hope that someone would pick it off. The marines adopted a defensive tactic known as the Thach Weave, developed by Lieutenant Commander John S. Thach, a leading navy fighter pilot. Pairs of Wildcats would cover each other by flying a synchronized crisscross pattern, so that if one came under attack his wingmate would swing in and counterattack.*

The emerging importance of Guadalcanal to both sides persuaded Admiral Yamamoto, who had moved his headquarters to Truk, that he might succeed in luring the American fleet into a decisive battle. On August 23, he sent a Tokyo Express with fifteen hundred troops along the eastern rim of the Solomons, under the cover of a massive force. The light carrier *Ryujo*, in the van of this formation, was to neutralize Henderson Field; in the center, some fifty miles away, were the fleet carriers *Zuikaku* and *Shokaku*—under the command of Admiral Nagumo, in somewhat reduced circumstances since Midway. The battleships *Hiei* and *Kirishima* brought up the rear, in case their big guns were needed. Vice-Admiral Nobutake Kondo was in overall charge of the naval side of the operation.

Signals intelligence alerted Admiral Ghormley to the Japanese advance, and he ordered Frank Fletcher to bring *Saratoga, Enterprise*, and *Wasp* up from the south along with *North Carolina*. Early patrols sighted no enemy ships, and intelligence reports placed the Japanese carriers north of Truk, so Fletcher, always concerned about fuel, detached *Wasp* for refueling. Thus, the American fleet was deprived of one-third of its carrier strength, and the enemy held a margin of 177 to 153 carrier planes, when the Battle of the Eastern Solomons erupted unexpectedly on the morning of August 24.

The Japanese opened up with an attack on Henderson Field by planes launched by *Ryujo*, joined over Guadalcanal by bombers from Rabaul. They were jumped by the Cactus Air Force, which downed twenty-one of the attacking aircraft. In the meantime, *Ryujo* was sighted, and at 1345 Fletcher ordered *Saratoga* to launch a strike by

---

*Captain Joseph E. Foss was the high scorer among the Cactus marines, with twenty-six victories.

thirty SBDs and eight TBF Avengers, the navy's new torpedo plane. Penetrating heavy flak and evading the defending Zeros, they hit the carrier with several bombs and a torpedo. With her rudder jammed, *Ryujo* began turning helplessly in circles while burning along her entire length, and after several hours she was abandoned. None of the American planes was lost.

Enterprise and *Saratoga* were also spotted by the Japanese, and Nagumo must have congratulated himself on the opportunity to hit them while their planes were attacking the unlucky *Ryujo*. But Fletcher was ready for him. Having learned the lessons of Midway, he had increased his CAPs until there were fifty-three Wildcats in the air and the flight decks of his ships had been cleared. The carriers separated into two defensive groups, ten miles apart. Two dozen Vals cut their way through to *Enterprise*, and as they dived upon her, they were met by heavy flak. Bursts of black smoke from exploding shells and tracers filled the sky. Several bombers were blown to bits by direct hits, and another two or three, which had been damaged, tried to crash into the carrier. One officer was so excited he emptied his .45-caliber pistol at the enemy aircraft.

Captain Arthur C. Davis, the carrier's skipper, noted that the attack was carried out with precision, the Vals diving at seven-second intervals. In little more than four minutes, it was over. *Enterprise* was hit by three bombs and whipped about "like a musical saw." One bomb crashed through her flight deck to explode in the crew's quarters, and another fell on the starboard gun gallery, wiping out seventy-four men. Two of the elevators on the "Big E" were knocked out and she was on fire, but her damage-control and firefighting crews performed magnificently. Within an hour, she was steaming at twenty-four knots and had resumed flight operations. Only a few of the attacking aircraft survived.

Poor weather prevented American dive-bombers and torpedo planes from finding *Shokaku* and *Zuikaku*, while a second wave of Japanese bombers was also unable to locate their targets, because of unsatisfactory flight direction. Two *Saratoga* SBDs, which became separated from the main strike force, attacked the seaplane carrier *Chitose*, thinking she was a battleship, and put her out of action. The following morning, eight SBDs from Henderson Field found the Tokyo Express itself. They pummeled the escorting cruiser *Jintsu* and set a large transport ablaze. Eight B-17s appeared as the destroyer *Mutsuki* stood by to take off the stricken vessel's troops and crew. But her captain, Commander K. Hatano, disdainful of the level of accuracy heretofore exhibited by the high-level bombers, proceeded with his work. Three bombs quickly sank his ship. "Even the B-17s could make a hit once in a while," he grumbled after being pulled from the sea.

The Battle of the Eastern Solomons was an American victory—the Japanese had lost *Ryujo* and sixty planes with their irreplaceable crews, and had been prevented from landing reinforcements. "Our plan to capture Guadalcanal came unavoidably to a standstill," a Japanese officer commented. Nevertheless, there were serious defects in the U.S. Navy's operations. Search planes failed to find the two large enemy carriers, and only luck prevented the Japanese from making another strike that might have been fatal to *Enterprise* or *Saratoga*.

Over the next several weeks, Japanese submarines were the greatest hazard for the American fleet, and the eastern approaches to the Coral Sea became known as Torpedo Junction. On August 30, *Saratoga* was torpedoed by *I-26*. Rivets popped from the force of the explosion; leaks were started and a fireroom was flooded, reducing the carrier's speed to thirteen knots. Twelve men were slightly wounded, including Admiral Fletcher. Pearl Harbor was so crowded with damaged ships that *Saratoga* had to limp all the way to the West Coast for repairs; there Fletcher was relieved. "Two or three of these fights are enough for any man," said his friend Admiral McCain. "A rest will do him good." Fletcher's decision to withdraw the *Wasp* for refueling before the Battle of the Eastern Solomons was obviously the last straw as far as Admiral King was concerned, and Fletcher never again held a carrier command. He was exiled to the North Pacific, where he finished out the war.

Two weeks later, *Wasp* was escorting a convoy of six transports with reinforcements for Guadalcanal when was she struck by a spread of three torpedoes from *I-19*, under Commander Takachi Kinashi, the top Japanese submariner of the war. Fiery blasts ripped through the forward part of the ship. Planes on the flight deck were tossed about as if they were toys. The heat detonated the ready ammunition at the anti-aircraft guns, and fragments of hot metal showered the ship. Water mains were broken, and with the flames roaring out of control, *Wasp* had to be abandoned. *North Carolina* sustained a thirty-two-foot rip in her hull from another torpedo. The entire operational carrier strength of the U.S. Navy in the Pacific now consisted of the recently arrived *Hornet* and her sixty-three planes.

The intrepid Admiral Tanaka stepped up the nightly runs of the Tokyo Express, and nothing the Americans could do seemed to be able to derail it. Radar was of little use with so much land background; the thick tropical night and unpredictable weather made his ships hard to spot with the naked eye. By early September, the Japanese force on the island had grown to six thousand men. On the nights of September 12 and 13, they launched an all-out attack against American positions on a low ridge about a thousand yards from Henderson Field. The Japanese hurled themselves twelve times against Bloody Ridge, as it was appropriately dubbed, only to be thrown back by the marines. Less than half the attacking force survived to stagger back into the jungle. The Americans were too exhausted to pursue them.

Having decided to make a full-scale effort to conquer Guadalcanal, the Japanese poured in men and equipment from New Guinea, the Dutch East Indies, and China. On the moonless night of October 11, fresh troops were sent down the Slot on a pair of seaplane carriers and six destroyers, shielded by three cruisers and two destroyers, all under the command of Admiral Aritomo Goto. Lying in wait was Task Force 64—four cruisers and five destroyers—led by Rear Admiral Norman Scott. Long-range reconnaissance had provided him with an accurate picture of enemy movements, and he was patrolling Ironbottom Sound between Cape Esperance and Florida.

Scott's ships were steaming in line ahead with three destroyers in the van when, toward midnight, he ordered a reversal in course to take the column back across the passage. During this maneuver, the cruiser *Helena* picked up the enemy formation on her radar at a distance of fourteen miles. Uncertain of what the "blip" meant, her captain delayed for fifteen minutes before passing the sighting to Scott. By this time, the admiral's neat line was in confusion, for the three lead destroyers, which had delayed in executing the column maneuver, had lost their position and were trying to recover it. They swung wide of the cruisers and were moving at flank speed along the starboard of the larger ships to regain the head of the line—placing themselves between the cruisers and the enemy.

Fortunately for Scott, the Japanese, who lacked radar, failed to sight his ships, and the American cruisers passed across the head of Goto's column—the classic crossing of the enemy's "T." Orange and yellow flashes leaped from the guns of Scott's vessels, shattering and sinking a Japanese destroyer and damaging the cruisers *Furutaka* and *Aoba*. Goto was mortally wounded on the bridge of the latter. In the ensuing melee, both sides fired on their own ships. The Japanese beat a hasty retreat. A U.S. destroyer was sunk during the chase and the cruiser *Boise* was heavily damaged by a Japanese shell that exploded in a forward magazine. She was saved by *Salt Lake City*, the next ship in line, which deliberately interposed herself between the burning *Boise* and the enemy. On the Japanese side, the shattered *Furutaka* sank not far from Savo.

Although the outcome of the Battle of Cape Esperance was somewhat murky, the U.S. Navy hailed it as a clear-cut victory, the first in a night surface action with the Japanese. No one mentioned that the Tokyo Express had landed its reinforcements on Guadalcanal without interference. American morale was further buoyed by the arrival, on October 13, of twenty-eight hundred army troops from 164th Infantry Regiment of the Americal Division of MacArthur's command, along with jeeps, trucks, ammunition, and supplies for seventy days.* The convoy was covered by *Hornet* and the new battleship *Washington*. There were now about twenty-three thousand American troops on Guadalcanal, plus another forty-five hundred on Tulagi; the Japanese force had grown to about twenty thousand men.

The new arrivals received a rude welcome to the island. Enemy bombers from Rabaul plastered Henderson Field that afternoon, and the battleships *Haruna* and *Kongo* steamed into Ironbottom Sound that night to shell the airstrip. They pumped in about nine hundred fourteen-inch shells of a new thin-skinned antipersonnel type. "The

---

*The supplies included several hundred cartons of Hershey bars, and the marines were soon engaged in a brisk exchange of chocolate for war souvenirs. "A Samurai sword went for three dozen large Hershey bars; a 'meat ball' flag—which Marines were now adept at manufacturing when supplies of originals ran low—was worth about a dozen" (Griffith, *The Battle for Guadalcanal*, pp. 151–52).

night's pitch dark was transformed by fire into the brightness of day," said a Japanese naval officer. Forty-eight planes were destroyed, fuel dumps were set afire, and the runway smashed. Every remaining plane needed repair. "It is almost beyond belief that we are still here, still alive," declared a war correspondent who emerged shaken from a foxhole. The following night, two cruisers gave the field another pasting as the Tokyo Express landed two thousand more men.

Gloom settled in on the Americans. General Vandegrift angrily told Admiral Ghormley that it was "urgently necessary" for the troops to receive air-and-surface support if Guadalcanal was to be held. Nimitz was equally grim. "It now appears that we are unable to control the sea in the Guadalcanal area," he reported. "Thus our supply of the positions will only be done at great expense to us. The situation is not hopeless, but it is certainly critical." In Washington, President Roosevelt, worried that the crisis in the Southwest Pacific might adversely affect the midterm congressional elections, was badgered by Admiral King into diverting resources to Guadalcanal from Torch, the impending North African invasion.

Hoping to avoid new disasters in the Southwest Pacific, Nimitz relieved Ghormley on October 17. The cloud hanging over Kelly Turner's head from Savo Island precluded him from being named to the top command, and the aggressive Admiral Halsey, now recovered from his illness and eager for action, was chosen as Ghormley's successor. Halsey's appointment had an electrifying effect upon his new command. "I'll never forget it," said one officer. "One minute we were too limp with malaria to crawl out of our foxholes; the next we were running around whooping like kids." Halsey immediately summoned his commanders to Nouméa for a strategy session.

"Are we going to evacuate or hold?" he asked Vandegrift.

"I can hold," the marine commander replied, "but I've got to have more active support than I've been getting."

"All right," the admiral replied. "Go on back. I'll promise you everything I've got."

Living up to his word, Halsey ordered *Washington* to take up station in Ironbottom Sound to prevent a repetition of the Japanese nighttime bombardments of Henderson Field. Rear Admiral Thomas C. Kinkaid, who had succeeded Fletcher as carrier commander, was ordered to place task forces built around *Hornet* and the hastily repaired *Enterprise* to the north of the Santa Cruz Islands. Once on station, they were to be ready to ambush any Japanese naval forces that appeared to the northeast of Guadalcanal.

The Japanese struck first, however. Admiral Yamamoto, convinced the Americans were now on the ropes, gathered his forces for a knockout blow. A massive land attack was launched against the battered American positions around Henderson Field on October 22, while Vice-Admiral Nobutake Kondo, with a striking force of four battleships and four carriers—*Shokaku, Zuikaku, Zuiho*, and *Junyo*— as well as fourteen cruisers and thirty-plus destroyers, waited impatiently to the northeast of Guadalcanal, ready to fly in aircraft as soon as Henderson Field had been captured. The Japanese confidently expected that the airstrip would be in their hands by October 25.

Japanese troops attacked out of pitch darkness and in pouring rain, but the well-entrenched marines and soldiers were no pushovers. Savage fighting developed all along the perimeter, and one of the most vicious struggles of the Pacific war ensued. On one occasion, the Japanese came within yards of overrunning the last American defensive position on the airfield, held by the First Battalion, Seventh Marines, commanded by Lieutenant Colonel Lewis "Chesty" Puller, with the newly arrived soldiers to their left. When morning came, there were more than a thousand dead Japanese piled up before them. American losses totaled fewer than two hundred men. The Japanese army told the navy on three successive occasions to ready its planes to land at Henderson, only to postpone a final go-ahead each time. Eventually convinced of the army's inability to capture the strip, Yamamoto ordered his ships to annihilate the enemy naval forces supporting Guadalcanal.

Shortly before dawn on October 26, a prowling PBY sighted the Japanese steaming south toward the island. Halsey, consulting his charts, determined that Kinkaid's carriers—with the added bonus of the new battleship *South Dakota*, fitted with dozens of fast-firing Bofors forty-millimeter anti-aircraft guns—were in range of the enemy. Shipboard radio-intelligence units with access to an air code taken from a Japanese plane downed on Guadalcanal also provided Kinkaid with an advantage. "Attack—Repeat—Attack!" Halsey ordered.

Kinkaid launched sixteen SBDs from *Enterprise* on a search-and-attack mission, and they scoured the sea near the Santa Cruz Islands in pairs. Two of the dive-bombers found *Zuiho* and planted a pair of five-hundred-pound bombs on her. One opened a gaping hole in her flight deck and set the vessel afire. Unable to recover her planes, she limped away to Truk. By this time, the Japanese had pinpointed the American carriers, and 135 bombers and fighters sped toward the target. They passed seventy-three American aircraft heading in the opposite direction and shot down eight.

Since *Enterprise* was hidden by a rain squall, the Japanese concentrated on *Hornet*. Coming in at seventeen thousand feet, they were too high for the CAP, but twenty-five of the attacking planes were shot down by the heavy barrage of anti-aircraft fire thrown up by the carrier and her screen. *Hornet* was hit several times, however. A Val dived into her superstructure, slammed off the signal bridge, and penetrated the flight deck before exploding. Two torpedoes also smashed into her engineering spaces, and she stopped dead in the water. The carrier's chances of survival dropped in direct proportion to her speed. Attempts were made to tow her out of the battle zone, but she was struck again and again by enemy planes. With darkness falling, the blazing flattop was finally abandoned, and was sunk by Japanese destroyers.

The Japanese had already turned their attention to *Enterprise*, which had emerged from the protective mist. Because of the effectiveness of her defensive fire, they scored only two hits. *South Dakota*, demonstrating the venomous effectiveness of her armament, was credited with shooting down twenty-six enemy planes, although, along with several other vessels of the screen, she was hit, too. The destroyer *Porter* was scuttled after a bizarre accident in which she was hit by a torpedo "ditched" by a disabled TBF.

In the meantime, *Hornet*'s planes had reached *Shokaku*. With Zeros on their tails, the SBDs nosed into their dives and hit the carrier with four thousand-pound bombs. Unfortunately, the accompanying TBFs had become separated and failed to locate the crippled vessel. A well-placed torpedo or two might have finished her off; it ended up taking nine months to make her operational again. The cruiser *Chikuma* was also battered. *Enterprise*'s strike force, disorganized by the Zeros that had attacked them on their way to their targets, were almost out of fuel by the time they found the enemy ships, and the attack was ineffectual. Both sides, having suffered heavy losses among their air groups, decided to withdraw.

The Battle of the Santa Cruz Islands was a tactical victory for the Japanese. They had sunk a carrier and damaged a battleship while sustaining damage to two carriers. Once again, American carrier strength in the Solomons had been reduced to a single ship. Kinkaid had also lost eighty-one planes. Nevertheless, Yamamoto was unable to exploit his advantage. Ninety-seven Japanese planes had been shot down, many by the deadly fire of the new anti-aircraft guns carried by the American ships, and his corps of experienced airmen, already greatly reduced, was further depleted. Although an American officer noted "no diminution in the courage of the individual [Japanese] pilot," he detected "a most marked decrease in skill." Admiral Nimitz supplied the best assessment of the battle: "Despite the loss of about three carrier air groups and damage to a number of ships, the enemy retired with all his ships. We nevertheless turned back the Japanese again in their offensive to regain Guadalcanal and shattered their carrier air strength on the eve of the critical days of mid-November."

Both sides stiffened their positions on Guadalcanal in the wake of the Santa Cruz battle. The Americans brought in troops by day and shelled Japanese positions ashore; the Tokyo Express ran down the Slot at night and then bombarded Henderson Field. Savage little nighttime battles between Tanaka's destroyers and American PT-boats were commonplace. Simultaneously, reports from coast watchers, aerial reconnaissance, and especially signals intelligence filtering in to Halsey provided unmistakable evidence that the Japanese were planning a grand-scale offensive against the island.[*] By November 8, his staff had prepared a nearly complete outline of Yamamoto's plans for the operation, which was also to be led by Admiral Kondo.

Tanaka was to run eleven fast transports that would be escorted by an equal number of destroyers carrying some ten thousand fresh troops to be put ashore at Tassafaronga on Savo Sound during the

---

[*] Full justice can only be done to the radio-intelligence analysts when it is understood that the Imperial Navy had on October 1 changed its entire communications system in an effort to maintain security. A month later, it made another call-sign change, which further complicated the task of the analysts.

night of November 14–15. To distract attention from these vessels, and to paralyze the Cactus Air Force, a bombardment group of two battleships, *Hiei* and *Kirishima*, and other vessels under Vice-Admiral Hiroaki Abe were to shell Henderson Field on the nights of November 12–13 and 13–14. The carrier *Junyo* would provide air cover while remaining well to the north of the Solomons. For his part, Halsey swept up an additional six thousand marines and soldiers and sent them to Guadalcanal in Kelly Turner's transports. *Enterprise* was ordered up from Nouméa with repair crews still on board under the protection of *Washington* and *South Dakota*. Turner beat Tanaka to Guadalcanal, arriving off Lunga Point on November 12 to unload his transports and AKAs, despite heavy Japanese air attacks. Upon being informed by a patrol plane of the approach of Abe's bombardment group, Turner, who had unloaded 90 percent of his cargo, withdrew to the southeast. Unable to count on *Enterprise*, still a day's steaming away, he boldly denuded the screening force of five cruisers and eight destroyers, hoping they would upset the Japanese attack.

Rear Admiral Daniel Callaghan, the commander of this force, accepted the seemingly impossible task. Until only a few weeks before, he had been Ghormley's deputy, and, based upon experience if not seniority, Norman Scott, who supported him with five additional cruisers, should have been in command. Callaghan steamed into Ironbottom Sound in line ahead, which meant his destroyers would be unable to launch massed torpedo attacks against the enemy. In fact, he seemed to have little in the way of battle plans except to exploit his radar—which the Japanese lacked—with the aim of surprising the enemy, to make up for the inferiority of his ships.

The Battle of Guadalcanal began at 0124 on November 13—a Friday—when *Helena*, serving as Callaghan's eyes, picked up the oncoming Japanese on her radar at a range of nearly fourteen miles and flashed a warning to *San Francisco*, the flagship. Abe had not yet discovered the American ships, and the squadrons raced toward each other at a combined speed of forty knots. Callaghan ordered a turn to starboard, with the apparent intention of crossing the enemy's "T," as Scott had done off Cape Esperance.

Suddenly, the destroyer *Cushing* spotted a pair of Japanese destroyers only fifteen hundred yards ahead, and to avoid a collision swung out of line, throwing the entire American force into disarray. Fearing that he might hit his own ships, Callaghan held his fire, which gave Abe time to overcome his initial surprise. Callaghan was not helped in reorganizing his ships by the U.S. Navy's continuing sin—useless chatter on the TBS (Talk Between Ships) voice radio net.[*]

The Americans did not open fire until 1050, when the anti-aircraft cruiser *Atlanta*, flying Scott's flag, aimed at an enemy destroyer's searchlight a scant sixteen hundred yards away. *Atlanta* was promptly overwhelmed by the fourteen-inch shells of the battleships, as well as by Long Lance torpedoes. Scott was killed, his vessel engulfed in flames. A disorganized melee followed that was almost unparalleled in naval history. It was, said one American officer, "a barroom brawl after the lights had been shot out." Fortunately for the Americans, the magazines of the Japanese battleships were loaded with high-explosive shells for bombardment of shore targets rather than armor-piercing ordnance, so their big guns could not be used to full effectiveness.

San Francisco traded salvos with *Hiei*, Abe's flagship, until Callaghan was killed and she was forced out of action. *Portland* also tangled with the battleship, and had her stern almost blown off. *Cushing* and another destroyer, *Laffey*, joined in the attack, and when they were wrecked, *O'Bannon*, *Sterett*, and *Monssen* continued the fight. The action—which lasted exactly twenty-four minutes—was fought at ranges so close that some of the larger ships could not depress their guns enough to hit their opponents. Admiral King later described it as "one of the most furious sea battles ever fought."

Two Japanese destroyers were sunk, and Abe was so unnerved by the unexpected resistance that he ordered a withdrawal. At daylight, *Hiei*, which had been hit at least thirty times, was discovered to the northeast of Savo, impotent and turning in circles. She was finished off by planes from Henderson Field—the first Japanese battleship lost in the war. American losses were heavy. *Atlanta* and four destroyers were sunk; *Portland*, *San Francisco*, and *Juneau* (*Atlanta*'s sister ship) were damaged. Following the battle, *Juneau* was torpedoed by a Japanese submarine, *I-26*, and exploded, with the loss of seven hun-

---

[*]Nearly a half-century later, on July 3, 1988, ill-disciplined jabber in the Combat Information Center of the cruiser *Vincennes* was said to have been a contributing factor in the accidental shooting down of an Iranian airliner over the Persian Gulf, with the loss of all 290 passengers and crew.

dred men, including five brothers of the Sullivan family.* Although the battle had been sloppily handled, Callaghan's courageous decision to take on a vastly superior enemy force prevented the battleships from both shelling Henderson Field and landing additional troops.

Brushing off Abe's defeat—for which he was relieved from command—Yamamoto pressed ahead with his plans to dislodge the Americans from Guadalcanal. Three cruisers slipped in past Savo in the darkness of November 14 and shelled the airfield—doing far less damage than the fourteen-inch guns of the battleships might have accomplished. With the coming of daylight, planes from Henderson Field and *Enterprise*, which was now within range, caught up with them and their screen, sinking one cruiser and damaging two others.

Tanaka's eleven transports, each carrying about a thousand men, were also discovered heading down the Slot to make their delivery that night. Fighters sent in from Rabaul were unable to protect the convoy from attack by waves of dive-bombers and torpedo planes from Henderson and from *Enterprise*, and later B-17s from Espiritu Santo. By nightfall, all but four of the transports had been sunk, although the troops were taken off by the accompanying destroyers. Nevertheless, as a protective darkness descended, "Tenacious" Tanaka pressed ahead with the remnant. He was supported by *Kirishima* (the surviving battleship of Abe's force), four cruisers, and nine destroyers. All the ships were under the command of Admiral Kondo, who was determined to redeem his failure of two nights before by blasting the airfield.

Washington, South Dakota, and four destroyers flying the flag of Rear Admiral Willis A. Lee, a gunnery expert, lay waiting for them in Savo Sound. Unaware of the presence of two American battleships, Kondo thought he would have to deal only with cruisers and destroyers. *Kirishima* and two heavy cruisers remained to the west of Savo

---

*It was believed that no one had survived the explosion, so no effort was made to rescue survivors. In fact, about 140 men from *Juneau* did survive, most of them wounded. Because of several mishaps, the men were not picked up for a week. By then, exposure, thirst, delirium, and savage shark attacks had reduced the number of survivors to ten. See Dan Kurzman, *Left to Die*.

while, shortly before 2300, his light cruisers and destroyers swept around the island and attacked the four destroyers at the head of Lee's column. Land echoes on the Americans' radar screens momentarily confused them. Japanese gunfire and torpedoes sank two of the U.S. vessels and crippled a third, in exchange for the loss of one Japanese destroyer.

Kondo's heavy ships concentrated their fire on *South Dakota*, which suffered an electrical failure that knocked out her radar, lights, and turrets for a critical three minutes. Enemy searchlights held her fast, and she absorbed hit after hit. Reacting quickly, Lee locked *Washington*'s nine radar-directed sixteen-inch guns on *Kirishima*. Inside her turrets, massive machinery silkily thrust huge shells and their cordite charges into the breeches of the guns. Breech blocks snapped shut. The long, dully gleaming gun barrels rose, checked, and steadied as they followed the movements of the director sights. "Gun-ready" lights flicked on. At 2316, "Ching" Lee gave the order: "Commence firing when ready."

With a blinding flash, the guns opened up. In seven minutes, *Kirishima* was reduced to a blazing wreck—the second battleship lost by the Japanese in as many days. Three cruisers were seriously damaged. Kondo canceled the planned bombardment of Henderson Field and, making smoke, withdrew to the northeast, leaving Tanaka's four remaining transports to a bloody fate. They arrived at first light off Tassafaronga, perfect targets for American planes and shore-based artillery. Hit repeatedly and in flames, they were beached. In all, just about two thousand of the some ten thousand Japanese troops originally embarked made it ashore, with only a small quantity of food and ammunition. Taken as a whole, the Battle of Guadalcanal was a decisive victory for the U.S. Navy, and decided the fate of the island.

The Imperial General Staff, however, undeterred by this disaster, refused to give up Guadalcanal, although Admiral Yamamoto no longer wished to risk major elements of the Combined Fleet against the "land carrier" of Henderson Field or the ever-expanding naval forces mustered by Halsey. The task of supplying a trickle of ammunition and food to beleaguered troops on "Starvation Island," as Guadalcanal was now known to the Japanese, was left to the Tokyo Express. In many respects, the Japanese were in a position like that of the German Sixth Army half a world away, at Stalingrad—pinned down, their supply line cut and doomed to wither on the vine.

On the night of November 30, Tanaka raced down the Slot with eight destroyers that had about fifteen hundred steel drums containing provisions and ammunition lashed to their decks. These were to be cut loose off Tassafaronga to drift ashore or be brought in by swimming Japanese soldiers. Five cruisers and six destroyers, under Rear Admiral Carleton H. Wright, met him, but fumbling tactics turned the Battle of Tassafaronga into another American debacle. The cruiser *Northampton* was sunk by torpedoes, and three other cruisers were put out of action, at the cost of only a single Japanese destroyer. It was almost as devastating as Savo. "For an enemy force of eight destroyers . . . to inflict such damage on a more powerful force at so little cost is something less than a credit to our command," noted an angry Halsey.

Tassafaronga was, however, an empty victory. Further Japanese attempts to land men and supplies were blocked, and in the last Tanaka was wounded.* And even as the Americans were absorbing the bitter lessons of war, their strength was increasing, while that of the Japanese was waning. On December 9, fifty thousand U.S. Army troops and marines relieved the malaria-ridden veterans who had been in action almost incessantly since landing on Guadalcanal seventeen weeks before. Army Major General Alexander M. Patch, who took over from Vandegrift, immediately began cleaning out enemy positions on the high ground overlooking Henderson Field. By then, the Japanese were reduced to bringing in supplies by submarine.

As the new year began, U.S. intelligence analysts were convinced that the Japanese had only two alternatives, either to send in new reinforcements or to surrender—and surrender would be out of character. The Imperial General Staff chose a third alternative: to evacuate their troops from Guadalcanal. Battleships, carriers, destroyers, and transports were sent to the Rabaul area to cover the withdrawal. U.S. patrol planes and coast watchers quickly spotted these ships, but intelligence analysts interpreted the buildup as a sign that the Japanese were about to send in fresh reinforcements. Hoping to lure

---

*The Japanese could not have held out so long at Guadalcanal had it not been for Admiral Tanaka, but his extraordinary contribution to the campaign went unrecognized. He finished out the war with desk jobs in Singapore and Burma.

them into another major battle, Halsey sent four transports to Lunga Point as bait. They were covered by Rear Admiral Robert C. Giffen, who had three heavy and three light cruisers, eight destroyers, and, for the first time in the Pacific, two of the new escort carriers.

Impatient with the slow speed of the carriers, Giffen left them behind so he could rendezvous with the transports as soon as possible, and thus was without fighter cover when Japanese torpedo planes attacked his formation off Rennell Island at twilight on January 29, 1943. Flares dropped by scout planes fixed the location of the American ships, and the unlucky *Chicago* was hit twice and eventually sunk. The four U.S. transports arrived at Guadalcanal unmolested, as did five more on February 4. By this time, however, only a handful of Japanese still remained on the island.

In a truly amazing feat, the Japanese had extricated the eleven thousand exhausted and nearly starving men who remained of the some thirty thousand who had been landed on Guadalcanal, without the Americans' having the slightest inkling of what was going on. No one at Halsey's headquarters in Nouméa, no one in Pearl Harbor, no one in Washington raised the question of a possible Japanese evacuation of the island until it was almost over. This was one of the biggest intelligence failures of the war. Even so, the Japanese achievement did not alter the fact that Guadalcanal had been lost, along with some twenty thousand troops, about a thousand aircraft, and fifteen warships. MacArthur had in the meantime repulsed the Japanese overland thrust toward Port Moresby, on the Papuan peninsula of New Guinea, despite heavy Australian and American battle casualties. On February 9, 1943, Patch radioed an anticlimactic message to Halsey: "Tokyo Express no longer has a terminus on Guadalcanal."

The most important results of Guadalcanal were pyschological. The U.S. Navy had experienced failures in command, weaponry, tactics, and training, and the campaign had underscored the tenacity of the individual Japanese soldier and sailor. Nevertheless, it was the Japanese who gave way. The spear blunted at Midway had been broken at Guadalcanal. The Japanese defense perimeter was penetrated for the first time—and over the next two years would be steadily eroded.

CHAPTER 10

"Off Hatteras the Tankers Sink"

The British steamer *Cyclops*, splotches of rust showing on her weatherbeaten hull, wallowed along about three hundred miles east of Cape Cod on the morning of January 12, 1942. Germany had declared war on the United States a month before and, although no U-boats had appeared off American shores, the merchantman's captain was anxious about being at sea alone. Suddenly, a torpedo slammed into the vessel's starboard side. A yellow-tinged explosion cloud leaped as high as her funnel, and she began sinking by the bow. Operation Paukenschlag (Roll of the Drums), Admiral Dönitz's offensive against American coastal shipping, had begun.

Although Dönitz was as surprised as the Americans by the Japanese attack on Pearl Harbor, he welcomed Hitler's decision to go to war with the United States. Two days before the German declaration of war on December 11, he began preparing to open a new front in the Battle of the Atlantic, on the very doorstep of the United States. Pearl Harbor would force the U.S. Navy to divert ships from the Atlantic to the Pacific, Dönitz reasoned, leaving his submarines almost a clear field off the East Coast, where about 8.5 million tons of shipping were concentrated. The Americans also lacked the experience in antisubmarine warfare accumulated by the Royal Navy at heavy cost, which would permit a return to the attacks by individual boats against ships sailing independently that had been so successful earlier in the war. "Attempts must be made as quickly as possible to utilize these advantages, which will disappear shortly, and to 'beat the drum' along the American coast," Dönitz wrote in his war diary.

For the admiral, the attack on America's coastal shipping had the additional advantage of getting his U-boats back into the Atlantic. At the start of 1942, he had ninety-one operational submarines, but twenty-five had been diverted, at Hitler's orders, to operations off Gibraltar and in the Mediterranean.* Another twenty boats were in the Arctic and off Norway—in the Führer's words, the "zone of destiny"—where his famous intuition led him to expect a British invasion. In consequence, "operations in the Atlantic . . . have been at a standstill," Dönitz noted. The toll of shipping sunk in that theater had dropped from 200,000 tons in September 1941, to 156,000 tons in October, and then to a scant 62,000 tons in November, the lowest since May 1940. An attack on Convoy HG 76 in December 1941 had been particularly costly, with only two merchantmen sunk against four U-boats lost.

One hundred boats represented Dönitz's operational ideal for Paukenschlag, but, taking a realistic view, he asked the Naval High Command to release twelve long-range Type IX boats for operations along the American coast, and a number of shorter-range Type VIICs to operate off Newfoundland, which was a thousand miles closer to their Bay of Biscay bases. If the larger boats carefully husbanded their fuel, they would be able to remain in the target area for two or three weeks. Much to the admiral's chagrin, he was permitted to deploy only six Type IX boats, and one of these did not make the trans-Atlantic voyage, because of mechanical difficulties. Seven smaller Type VIICs were assigned to Canadian waters.

Experience had shown that the shock value of the unexpected appearance of U-boats in new areas was highly effective, so Dönitz wished to have the attack on American shipping come like a thunderclap. U-boat captains were instructed to take up positions between Halifax and Cape Hatteras and to remain unobserved until the prearranged time for launching the attack was reached—January 13, 1942. Each boat carried fourteen torpedoes, reserved for large

---

*There were another 158 boats in training or undergoing trials.

ships, with tankers having the highest priority. Other vessels were to be disposed of by gunfire.

Kapitänleutnant Reinhard Hardegen of *U-123* found the 9,076-ton *Cyclops* too tempting a target to be passed up, and jumped the gun on Paukenschlag by sinking the hapless freighter the day before. Farther north, Kapitänleutnant Ernst Kals of *U-130* sank two steamers off Halifax early the next morning. On January 14, Hardegen sank a large tanker within sight of the Nantucket lightship. By the end of the month, the five U-boats had sunk thirty-five ships, totaling more than 200,000 tons. In contrast, just ten vessels, of 63,000 tons, were sunk on the North Atlantic route during the same period, of which only three were in convoy.

Moving down the coast in search of targets of opportunity, Hardegen sank a tanker off New York City. Taking his boat close into the harbor entrance, he saw the lights atop the Ferris wheel at Coney Island. Like the other U-boat skippers, Hardegen was amazed to find New York and other coastal cities a blaze of bright lights. Three months passed before a coastal blackout became effective because officials from Atlantic City to Miami resisted—it would be bad for the tourist business. Merchantmen steamed along fully lighted and transmitted routine messages in plain English, which the U-boats picked up. Off Cape Hatteras, Hardegen reported:

> Our operation has been most successful: eight ships, including three tankers totaling 53,860 tons within twelve hours. It is a pity that there was not a couple of large minelaying submarines with me the other night off New York, or ten or twelve here last night instead of one. I am sure all would have found ample targets. Altogether I saw about twenty steamships, some un-darkened; also a few small tramp-steamers all hugging the coast. Buoys and beacons in the area had dimmed lights which, however, were visible up to two or three miles.

The U-boats usually lay submerged during the day and surfaced at dusk to dispatch their victims with torpedoes and gunfire. Ships were sunk only thirty miles off the Jersey coast and the Virginia Capes. Three or more vessels were sometimes sunk in a single day, often within sight of spectators ashore. By day they could see the columns of smoke rising from burning freighters; by night they saw the red glow of blazing tankers. Residents of the sea islands off the Carolina coast could hear the diesel engnes of the U-boats as they cruised close inshore at night. Panic raced up and down the Atlantic coast, and Nazi spies were rumored to be directing the U-boats to their targets. Thick black oil from blasted tankers and debris from wrecked ships fouled the Atlantic beaches. Tankers remained in port, because their crews feared being sunk. Insurance companies refused to provide coverage. The loss of tankers eventually led to the building of pipelines to carry oil from the fields and ports of Texas and Louisiana to the East Coast. The most important, called the "Big Inch," was built in just under a year, from August 1942 to July 1943.

In February, fresh U-boats were sent out to relieve the first wave, which was growing short of fuel.[*] U-123 had exactly twenty-one gallons of fuel in her tanks when she reached Lorient. Several Type VIIC boats made the crossing by cramming provisions into every possible location, including the head, filling auxiliary tanks with fuel oil, and running on the surface at only seven knots, on one of the two diesel engines. When staples such as bread and sausage ran out, the crews subsisted on canned food and hardtack. Constipation, skin diseases, and other symptoms of dietary deficiency appeared, although canned fruits and vegetables prevented scurvy, the age-old curse of mariners.

For the first—and indeed the only—time during the war, Dönitz and his U-boats came within appreciable distance of sinking the seven hundred thousand tons of shipping a month he had set as a goal. In all, some 2.5 million tons of shipping were sunk from January to July 1942, in what the U.S. Navy called the Eastern, Gulf, and Caribbean Sea Frontiers. Only eight U-boats were destroyed. Tanker losses imperiled future military operations, and dozens of merchant seamen lost their lives as their ships were sunk under them. It was the worst defeat ever suffered by the U.S. Navy, because, unlike Pearl Harbor, it was not a surprise attack.

The British and Canadians were dismayed and angered to see ships that had been shepherded across the Atlantic at great risk, sunk by predators once they had reached the supposed safety of the Amer-

---

[*]Hitler congratulated Dönitz on the spectacular success of Paukenschlag—promoting him to full admiral in March 1942—and then ordered him to send more submarines to defend Norway against an invasion.

ican coast. "The trouble is, Admiral," Commander Rodger Winn, the head of the OIC Submarine Tracking Room bitingly told a member of Admiral King's staff early in 1942, "it's not only your bloody ships you are losing; a lot of them are ours." Nor were responsible American officers any more complacent. "The Battle of the Atlantic is being lost," declared Captain Wilder D. Baker, the navy's chief antisubmarine-warfare expert.

U-boat skippers jubilantly hailed this period as the "Second Happy Time"—the first having occurred in the summer of 1940—and the "American Shooting Season." Their task was abetted by "clumsy handling of ships and unpracticed sea and air patrols," according to Dönitz. Reporting his success to headquarters by radio, one captain, Jochen Mohr of *U-124*, resorted to doggerel:

> The new moon–night is as black as ink.
> Off Hatteras the tankers sink.
> While sadly Roosevelt counts the score.
> Some fifty thousand tons
> —by Mohr

Large shipping losses had been expected when the United States entered the war, but no one had envisioned a disaster of the magnitude occurring off the American coast. Ultra had alerted the Americans to the approach of the German submarines but other problems had a higher priority. The attention of the U.S. Navy was fixed on the disasters unfolding in the Pacific, and on providing escort groups for troopships crossing the North Atlantic. Converted liners like the *Queen Mary* and *Queen Elizabeth*, which could race across the Atlantic at twenty-six knots, far faster than a U-boat, did not require escorts, but most of the American troops being sent to Europe shipped out on smaller and slower vessels. Also, the U.S. Navy was fighting a two-ocean war. It had to protect major troop movements in the Pacific, and there were distinct fears in early 1942 that the Japanese might invade Hawaii, or even the West Coast of the United States.

The basic problem was a shortage of escorts. Like the Royal Navy, the U.S. Navy had in the interwar years almost totally ignored antisubmarine warfare. Most of its limited funds had been spent on

upgrading the now nearly useless battleships. President Roosevelt
had prodded the navy to build small craft such as submarine chasers,
though to no avail. "The navy couldn't see any vessel under a thousand tons," he declared. In case of war, the navy expected to fall back
upon the destroyers left over from World War I while additional
escorts were being constructed, but this reserve had been depleted
by the destroyers-for-bases deal with Britain. Besides, escorts had a
lower priority than landing craft—also in short supply.

Once transocean and troopship escort requirements were met,
Vice-Admiral Adolphus E. Andrews, commander of the Eastern Sea
Frontier, received what was left to deal with the U-boat onslaught.
The Royal Canadian Navy took over responsibility for convoys north
of Maine, but Andrews still had to cover the three-thousand-mile
sweep of coast from Maine to Key West. He had a ragtag force of
about twenty Coast Guard cutters, outmoded patrol craft, and gunboats left over from World War I, none of which could outrun a surfaced U-boat, and 108 aircraft, most of them unfit for antisubmarine
warfare and manned by untrained and inexperienced crews. Guns,
sonar, and depth charges were also in short supply. "Should the
enemy submarines operate off this coast, this command has no force
available to take action against them, either offensively or defensively," Andrews told King.

Though agreeing that "the submarine situation on the east coast
approaches the 'desperate,' " King rejected a staff proposal on February 3 to start coastal convoys. Contemporaries and historians have
united in faulting him for this decision. "I still do not understand the
long delay in making all ships sail under escort," complained the
president. And Jürgen Rohwer, the German naval historian, has said
that the American delay in adopting East Coast convoys "was without doubt one of the greatest mistakes in the Allied conduct of the
Battle of the Atlantic."

Some observers contend that King resisted Atlantic convoys
because he was interested only in the Pacific war; others say he was
opposed to convoys in general; and there are those who claim that
Anglophobia ruled, and he opposed convoys merely because the
British recommended such efforts. All paint a false picture. King
understood and appreciated the importance of convoys, noting at one
point that "escort is not just *one* way of handling the submarine men-

ace, it is the *only* way that gives any promise of success." But he was opposed to weakly defended convoys. "Inadequately escorted convoys are worse than none," he declared. Ill-defended convoys would, in his view, merely mass unprotected targets for the U-boats.

King's real mistake lay in not learning from the experience of the British—from Churchill down—which proved that even weakly defended convoys were better than no convoys. The presence of escorts forced the enemy to adopt tactics that reduced his effectiveness. Two years of bitter struggle had taught the Royal Navy that in dealing with U-boats the best form of attack is defense—and the only form of defense against the submarine is the convoy. Numbers had nothing to do with calculating what constituted an effective escort; a trained escort group of four ships was better than an untrained one of eight.

To add to the problem, Ultra was of little use in dealing with the U-boat menace, inasmuch as the handful of boats operating off the East Coast did not form wolf packs. This also reduced the effectiveness of rerouting. And, beginning in February 1942, the traffic between Dönitz and his submarines could not be read by Bletchley Park, for the Atlantic boats began using a complex new cipher known as Triton.

Open warfare also broke out between the U.S. Navy and the Army Air Force, which had responsibility for land-based aircraft and coastal defense. Admiral King urged that planes be provided to protect coastal shipping, but the Air Force commanders refused to be diverted from the strategic-bombing campaign against Germany to what they considered a secondary operation. King saw no option but to accept high losses of merchantmen for several months, until crash building programs produced enough escorts—particularly, highly effective destroyer escorts—and patrol bombers to begin a fully protected system of convoys.[*]

---

[*]Although designed by an American, the twelve-hundred-ton destroyer-escort was a larger and more powerful offshoot of the small *Hunt*-class British destroyer. Fifty of these craft were ordered in mid-1941, but construction was slowed when it was believed the program would interfere with the building of general-purpose destroyers. The British saved the program, however, by ordering 250 destroyer-escorts under Lend-Lease. Once the U.S. Navy discovered the value of these ships—they could not only be mass produced but proved to be excellent U-boat hunters as well as convoy escorts—some 550 of various configurations were completed.

President Roosevelt had an even simpler solution for the crisis—build ships faster than the Germans could sink them. Summoning America's industrial might, he proposed, on February 19, the largest merchant-ship construction program in history. Twenty-four million tons of shipping were to be built before the end of 1942, and twice that in 1943. This meant that the rate of construction would be increased from one ship a day to three, more than double the rate of sinkings during the height of the U-boat onslaught.

The slaughter off the American coast took place against a background of disasters that battered the Allied cause in the first half of 1942. Japan was unchecked in the Pacific until the Battle of the Coral Sea, early in May. In April, the Germans launched a new offensive against the Red Army in southern Russia and were sweeping toward the oil fields of the Caucasus. Behind the smoke screen of war, the Nazis were going about the grisly business of the Final Solution. In North Africa, Rommel's victorious Afrika Korps was advancing on Cairo, while furious sea and air battles raged around Malta as the Axis tried to starve and bomb the island bastion into surrender. Nearer to home, in the English Channel, the Royal Navy suffered one of its greatest humiliations of the war. Under its very nose, *Scharnhorst*, *Gneisenau*, and *Prinz Eugen* escaped from Brest on February 12, 1942, and raced up the Channel in broad daylight to arrive in Germany virtually unharmed.

The Channel Dash was born of Hitler's anxiety about the security of Norway. He believed an Allied attack was imminent, an obsession unwittingly fueled by the British with a series of lightning commando attacks on the Norwegian coast. *Scharnhort* and *Gneisenau* had been lying at Brest since March 1941, when they had returned from a successful raid against Allied shipping, and were joined by *Prinz Eugen* following her ill-fated sortie with *Bismarck*. There they remained, blockaded by sea and vulnerable to enemy bombing, but still an ever-present threat to Britain's lifeline. Churchill ordered Bomber Command to concentrate on the ships at the expense of other targets, and the Brest squadron absorbed three-quarters of all the bomb tonnage dropped by the British during 1941—a validation of the doctrine of "the fleet-in-being."

With the approach of 1942, Grand Admiral Raeder planned to send the ships, which were nearing the completion of repairs, out on a fresh foray into the North Atlantic. The pocket battleship *Admiral Scheer*, which was in the Baltic, was to use Japanese bases and strike at enemy commerce in the South Atlantic and Indian Ocean. Dönitz argued, however, that the heavy ships had outlived their usefulness. "These ships no longer play a vital role in the present war, and consequently should no longer have a call on repair facilities urgently needed by the U-boat Arm," he declared. Although there is no evidence that Hitler saw this memorandum, his attitude was very much in agreement with that of Dönitz. With plenty to worry him on the Eastern Front, he had no wish to get involved in another Atlantic foray.

On November 13, 1941, the Führer asked Raeder about the possibility of bringing the ships back to Germany by "a surprise withdrawal" through the English Channel and thence to Norway. *Tirpitz*, sister ship of *Bismarck*, had already been sent to Trondheim to act as a deterrent to British activity off Norway. Flustered by this upsetting request, Raeder thought it impossible. The Naval High Command dragged its feet, but Hitler insisted that the ships be concentrated in northern Norway. If not, they would be decommissioned and their crews and guns transferred to Norway. Faced with this bleak prospect, the admirals caved in to the Führer's demands.

Vice-Admiral Otto Ciliax, commander of the Brest squadron, laid careful plans for the breakout. Ciliax reasoned that the British expected his ships to make a run through the Channel, but he thought they would assume that the Germans would use the cover of darkness for the passage through the Straits of Dover, the most dangerous part of the operation, and thus would sail in daylight. Ciliax decided to sail at night in foul weather and run through the Channel in daylight under strong air cover. Rumors were spread that the ships were preparing for a sortie into the Atlantic while minesweeping operations directed by Commodore Friedrich Ruge took place at night. The ships were to be escorted by a screen of destroyers and S-boats, and Ciliax was promised cover by some 250 fighters led by Colonel Adolf Galland, one of the Luftwaffe's leading aces.

As darkness fell on the moonless night of February 11, 1942, the destroyers headed for sea with *Scharnhorst*, Ciliax's flagship; *Gneisenau* and *Prinz Eugen* were preparing to follow. The secret of their route and destination had been kept so well that the crews believed they were taking part in another drill. Just as the big ships were about to get under way, RAF bombers attacked Brest, and the ships remained at their berths. When the last plane had droned away, they renewed their preparations for sea. Shortly before 2300—two hours behind schedule—the squadron was on its way, unscathed and undetected.

Although Ultra had provided scraps of information indicating that the Brest squadron was preparing a run through the Channel, the time of departure was unknown. Preparations to deal with a breakout were also haphazard. No capital ships were sent into the area, because of the danger of attack from the Luftwaffe, so the RAF was given the major role in dealing with the threat. Early in February, three hundred bombers were placed on two hours' readiness. But when the Germans failed to come, two-thirds of these planes were reassigned and the remainder were placed on four hours' readiness—without informing the Admiralty of the change in plan.

As a result of foul weather and operational mishaps, the German ships were at sea for nearly twelve hours before the British became aware of it. The alarm was not given until after 1100, when a pair of Spitfires in hot pursuit of two German fighters flew directly over the ships, which were steaming up the Channel at thirty knots. They were covered by a large air flotilla plus numerous destroyers and S-boats and, having covered nearly two-thirds of their escape route, were almost off Dover.

There was no question of a coordinated attack in such an emergency. Only six hours of daylight remained, and most of the British sea and air units assigned to deal with the enemy ships were out of range or unprepared to launch a strike. The available forces were thrown piecemeal into the battle: first a handful of motor-torpedo boats, which were brushed aside, and then six torpedo-carrying Swordfish led by Lieutenant Commander Eugene Esmonde.* Esmonde and his seventeen pilots, observers, and gunners had volunteered for what they expected to be a night attack on the German ships—a forlorn hope even under the best of circumstances. Now they were being asked to do the impossible. Under no illusions about the chance for success, Esmonde agreed to a daylight attack after the RAF promised an escort of five squadrons of fighters. "For the love of

---

*Esmonde had led the first torpedo-plane attack on *Bismarck*.

God," he pleaded with his superiors, "get the fighters to us on time."

Buffeted by strong winds, the Swordfish slowly circled over the English Channel shortly after midday as Esmonde scanned the sky for the promised escort of Spitfires and Hurricanes. Fifteen hundred feet below, *Scharnhorst, Gneisenau,* and *Prinz Eugen* were drawing farther away, to the safety of a German port. Even when a flock of Spitfires finally appeared, Esmonde's feeling of relief was brief, for he counted only ten British fighters. Without adequate cover, the chance of a successful attack against the ships was nil, but there was no time to wait for more. The German vessels were now off Ramsgate, an ideal place for an attack.

The Swordfish pointed their noses down toward the sea while the ten available Spitfires weaved back and forth above them. Swarms of German fighters tied up the Spitfires in dogfights, while others jumped the Swordfish. But the clumsy old biplanes proved to be surprisingly elusive targets. Time and again, the far faster Messerschmitts and Focke-Wulfs misjudged their speed and overshot them. Some of the German fighters dropped their wheels and flaps in an attempt to slow down to the speed of the Swordfish. When tracer bullets set Esmonde's plane afire, his gunner, Leading Seaman W. J. Clinton, climbed out of the cockpit and, sitting astride the fuselage, beat out the flames with his gloved hands. He then calmly climbed back behind his gun.

All the Swordfish were shot down, however, without any of their torpedoes' striking the speeding warships. The German vessels, having run the gauntlet of attacks by the RAF and the Royal Navy, reached the safety of the Elbe, although *Scharnhorst* and *Gneisenau* were damaged by mines. Emergency repairs were made to both ships, and they made port in the early hours of February 13. All the airmen were decorated, with fifteen of the awards being made posthumously. Esmonde, whose body washed up on the Kentish coast two months later, was awarded the Victoria Cross.

In Germany, the Channel Dash was hailed as a triumph over the Royal Navy, and the British were furious at their humiliation. For nearly twelve hours, a German squadron had been at large in the English Channel without even being spotted. When Admiral Pound telephoned Churchill to tell him the enemy ships had escaped, there was a long silence before the prime minister barked, "Why?" and slammed down the receiver. "Nothing more mortifying to the pride of our sea power has happened in home waters since the seventeenth century," growled *The Times*.*

Yet, as Admiral Raeder later acknowledged, the Channel Dash, although appearing at the time to be a tactical success, was in reality a defeat. Once they were in Germany, the Kriegsmarine's large surface ships were no longer a threat to Allied shipping in the Atlantic, and the British were henceforth relieved of the necessity of diverting bombers to the "fleet-in-being" on the French coast. Only *Scharnhorst* got to Norway. *Gneisenau* was caught by British bombers on the night of February 26 while undergoing repair at Kiel and sustained several serious hits. Over the next year, she fell victim to the same stop-and-go treatment that had kept the aircraft carrier *Graf Zeppelin* in limbo since 1940. In 1943, she was decommissioned and her guns were mounted ashore. The final ignominy came in March 1945, when *Gneisenau's* rusting hulk was towed to Gdynia and sunk as a blockship. *Prinz Eugen* spent the rest of the war in the Baltic, finally ending as a target at the postwar Bikini atomic tests.

In the meantime, Dönitz had extended his U-boat offensive into the Caribbean with Operation Neuland. The Germans sank seventeen ships in this area during the last two weeks of February and shelled a refinery on Aruba. The intensity of this offensive increased in March. "The U-boats ravaged American waters almost uncontrolled, and in fact almost brought us to the disaster of an indefinite prolongation of the war," according to Churchill. He exploited the situation in an effort to persuade Roosevelt to approve the appointment of a British admiral to exercise control over the Battle of the Atlantic. Admiral King firmly resisted. Pointing to the Channel Dash fiasco, he argued that the British were in no position to hand out advice, and the president rejected the proposal. The Admiralty also suggested that a mine barrier be constructed along the Eastern Seaboard to protect shipping—but the few antisubmarine minefields laid resulted in the sinking of or damage to more than a dozen American ships.

Roosevelt himself bombarded King with gratuitous suggestions on

*In June 1667, the Dutch Admiral Michiel A. de Ruyter sailed up the Thames River to within twenty miles of London, sinking and burning both merchant ships and men-of-war and bringing out the British flagship as a prize.

how to deal with the U-boat menace. An enthusiastic yachtsman, he directed the navy chief in February 1942 to organize hundreds of civilian yachts and fishing boats into a coastal picket line. This "Hooligan Navy" boosted the morale of the civilians involved, but was useless except in fair weather, and contributed little—if any-thing—to stopping the U-boats.[*]

Also at Churchill's urging, the president forced King to convert four merchant vessels into decoys or Q-ships—including an old trading schooner—which were intended to lure unsuspecting U-boats into range of their hidden guns. One of these ships, the *Atik*, was torpedoed by *U-123* on March 26, 1942, with the loss of all 141 members of her crew. Measured by the number of casualties, it was the U.S. Navy's single most self-destructive operation of the war. Furious, King insisted this wasteful and dangerous project be abandoned.

In an effort to help, the already overextended Canadian Navy ran convoys from Halifax to Boston. Admiral Andrews, while waiting for enough escorts to begin full-scale convoys, took the first steps to halt the hemorrhaging of shipping in the Eastern Sea Frontier by hammering together a jerry-built defense. Choke points, such as the entrances to Chesapeake, Delaware, and Narragansett bays, where shipping congregated, were defended, and limited antisubmarine sweeps were carried out in the main shipping channels. Using the temporary diversion of destroyers[†] from the seventy-five allotted to the North Atlantic, Andrews improvised a rudimentary convoy system that provided a semblance of protection for some coastal shipping.

Known as the Bucket Brigade because the convoys were passed from one escort group to another, they hugged the coast during the day and anchored at night in protected inlets and harbors. To make up for the lack of aircraft, blimps were stationed at Lakehurst, near the Jersey shore, to cover shipping. Andrews had no illusions that these makeshift arrangements would eliminate the U-boat menace but hoped "such measures would reduce the dimension of that attack

---

[*]Ernest Hemingway was among its most enthusiastic members. He combed the seas off Cuba in his yacht *Pilar*, armed with a machine gun, a hunting rifle, and hand grenades. Later, he used the experience in his posthumously published novel *Islands in the Stream*.

[†]One of these ships, the four-piper *Jacob Jones*, was torpedoed by *U-578* off the entrance to Delaware Bay on February 28, with the loss of all eleven of her crew.

to bearable proportions until such time [as] sufficient ships and planes were assigned to the Frontier." On March 1, the Americans scored their first "kill" of the war when a navy Hudson, based in Newfoundland sank *U-556*.

Late in March, reverse Lend-Lease—the arrival of twenty-four British coal-burning trawlers that had been converted to antisubmarine warfare (ASW)—plus additional escorts obtained by slowing down the Atlantic convoy cycle, allowed Andrews to organize an Interlocking Convoy System that provided day-and-night protection for shipping between Halifax and New York. It was extended in mid-May from Hampton Roads to Key West. In contrast to April, when at least one ship a day had been lost, reported the Eastern Sea Frontier War Diary, during "the first seventeen days of May not one ship was lost in the Eastern Sea Frontier," and only fourteen were sunk during the rest of the month.

The might of American industry was also being turned against the U-boats. With the battle cry "Sixty Ships in Sixty Days," a massive program for the production of patrol craft and subchasers was launched. A training school for antisubmarine warfare was opened in Miami under the direction of Lieutenant Commander E. F. Mac-Daniel—soon known as "MacDaniel's Academy"—and over the next two years some fifty thousand eager young officers and crewmen passed through his not-so-gentle hands. A sonar school was established at Key West. At the same time, an Anti-Submarine Warfare Unit was opened at the Boston Navy Yard bringing together experienced naval officers and civilian scientists, who applied the principles of operations research, learned from the British, to convoy actions and sinking U-boats.*

But if shipping losses dropped in the Eastern Sea Frontier, they soared in the Gulf of Mexico and the Caribbean. Dönitz, whose policy was to seek out zones of least resistance, ordered most of the eigh-

---

*Scientists working in operations research advised the navy on the most effective way of using existing weapons. For example, they determined how deep depth charges should be set to explode for maximum effect. It was also demonstrated that the size of a convoy could be doubled without doubling the size of its perimeter. The perimeter of an eighty-ship convoy was only one-seventh greater than that of a convoy of forty ships. Bigger convoys meant more efficient use of escorts. Moreover, average losses decreased from 2.6 percent to 1.7 percent when convoys comprised more than forty-five ships.

teen boats operating to the west, into those waters, when things got too hot for them off the East Coast. Concentrating off the mouth of the Mississippi and about Aruba and Trinidad, they met considerable success. Some ventured as far south as the Brazilian coast in search of prey, and provided the Brazilians an excuse to enter the war against Germany and Italy.

To replenish and refuel these boats, Dönitz sent out large Type XIV submarines that had been converted to tankers—called "milch cows"—which extended their time on patrol for extra weeks.* In May, forty-one ships, totaling 219,867 tons, were sunk in the Gulf alone. Over half were tankers; most of the rest were carrying bauxite, the raw material of aluminum, vital for aircraft production.

Sixteen Coast Guard cutters, five new subchasers, and other craft, as well as a squadron of patrol bombers, were shifted to the Gulf and Caribbean Sea Frontiers to deal with this new menace. For the crews of the escorts used to the cold, bleak North Atlantic, the Caribbean seemed like a holiday cruise, but they were soon brought face to face with the nasty ordeal of abandoning ship in tropical waters. Captain Donald Blythe, whose tanker, the *San Gaspar*, was turned into a flaming inferno by a torpedo from *U-575* off Curaçao on July 18, reported:

> I gave the order "Jump for it!" and we all jumped overboard and swam for dear life away from the ship. One young sailor unfortunately got caught by the flames, but the rest of us managed to swim clear. . . . While swimming we were attacked by barracuda which tried to bite us, and as I had no clothes and the others very little, we made an attractive bait for them. Shoals of small dogfish also attacked us, but we managed to keep swimming through the night. At daybreak we saw a Catalina aircraft which flew over us, but took no notice. . . . Tiger sharks appeared and joined in the attack. . . . By kicking vigorously I was able to keep the sharks away temporarily, but they became bolder as the day went on. Towards noon we were nearly exhausted, when two bombers dropped a rubber dinghy within twenty feet of us. When in the dinghy the sharks became bolder and we had to stab at them with the aluminum paddles to keep them away.

*Type XIV boats carried seven hundred tons of fuel, which meant that one of them could supply twelve type VIIs with enough fuel for an extra four weeks, or five Type IXs for an extra eight weeks at sea.

Alarmed by the magnitude of the catastrophe, General George Marshall, the army's chief of staff, warned Admiral King that "the losses
by submarines off our Atlantic seaboard and in the Caribbean now
threaten our entire war effort. . . . We are all aware of the limited
number of escort craft available, but has every conceivable improvised means been brought to bear on this situation? I am fearful that
another month or two of this will so cripple our means of transport
that we will be unable to bring sufficient men and planes to bear
against the enemy in critical theaters to exercise a determining influence on the war."

Stung, King immediately replied that he had "long been aware . . .
of the implications of the submarine situation. . . .I have employed—
and will continue to employ—not only regular forces but also such
improvised means as give any promise of usefulness. . . ."

Gradually, the number of escorts available for the Gulf and
Caribbean increased and a comprehensive convoy system was established. It was linked to the Eastern Sea Frontier's Interlocking Convoy
System, and the first escorted convoy sailed from Key West to Panama
on July 6. Within a month, feeder convoys were sailing from various
ports as far south as Brazil. By the end of the summer of 1942, this network was operating with the efficiency of a railroad timetable. Of the
fourteen hundred ships sailing under convoy over the next three
months, only eleven were sunk. The loss of two U-boats and damage
to others in the first half of July indicated to Dönitz that the "Second
Happy Time" was over. He again concentrated his boats in the six-
hundred-mile-wide "Black Pit" air gap to the south of Greenland.

In retrospect, it is now clear that July 1942 was the high tide of
Axis success. In Russia, the Germans had captured Rostov on the
Don; Rommel had reached El Alamein, just sixty miles from Alexandria; the Japanese defense perimeter was unbreached despite Midway. And for the first time, Dönitz had the three hundred boats he
had wanted when the war began, with the building rate far in excess
of the kill rate achieved by the Allies.* But that month also marked
another historic turning point. For the first time since the war began,
the worldwide monthly loss of Allied shipping—still a monumental
618,000 tons, but down 25 percent from June—was marginally sur-

---

*Of which 140 were operational, with the rest on training missions or trial runs.

passed by new construction. Although Dönitz did not know it, he had lost the tonnage war.

Beginning in 1942, the question of a Second Front in Europe dominated relations between the Allies. Many Americans—President Roosevelt, General Marshall, and Admiral King among them— believed that the best way to end the U-boat threat was to invade Europe as soon as possible and capture German bases on the Biscay coast. Stalin, desperately in need of relief from the latest German assault, pressed for an immediate invasion of Western Europe to divert enemy troops from the Eastern Front. Both Roosevelt and Churchill were worried that, if such support were not forthcoming, the Russians might make a separate peace with Hitler. But Churchill, haunted by the bloodletting of World War I, resisted a major landing in France as risky at best, and a venture that might result in tremendous casualties. Instead, he pressed a peripheral strategy designed to wear down the Germans by attacks in Norway and the Mediterranean while massive bombing raids were conducted against German industry. Stalin contemptuously dismissed these proposals, and his conspiratorial mind seethed with suspicion that the Soviet Union and Germany were being encouraged to destroy each other so that capitalism could dominate Western Europe.

Two weeks after Pearl Harbor, Churchill flew to Washington to confer with the president. Instead of a cross-Channel invasion of France, he pressed for a landing in French North Africa, to trap the Afrika Korps between two Allied armies and to reopen the Mediterranean to Allied shipping. Besides taking pressure off the Russians, such a landing might also knock Italy out of the war and give Allied morale a tremendous boost. American strategists regarded Churchill's proposal as fundamentally irrelevant. "The American way of war," as the historian Russell Weigley has noted, is to seek out and confront an enemy at his principal source of strength. Nazi Germany was the center of enemy resistance, and General Marshall urged a cross-Channel assault on Europe as soon as enough men, shipping, and aircraft were available. Brigadier General Dwight D. Eisenhower, chief of the army's War Plans Division, put the matter bluntly: "We've got to go to Europe and fight—and we've got to quit wasting resources all over the world, and still worse, wasting time."

In the spring of 1942, Marshall produced a plan for Operation Sledgehammer, an invasion of France that autumn. Three American and two British divisions were to capture the Cherbourg Peninsula and hold it over the winter. This would force the Germans to transfer troops from the Eastern Front and relieve the pressure upon the Russians. Worried even then by the prospect of Soviet domination of central Europe, Marshall proposed to follow up Sledgehammer in 1943 with Operation Roundup, the landing of at least another thirty Allied divisions, which would occupy central Europe before the Russians could get there. King joined in championing the cross-channel operation in order to seize the U-boat bases in western France.

The British opposed Sledgehammer, pointing out that even if the troops were ready for action at that moment—which everyone agreed they weren't—weather conditions in the Channel were too unsettled at that time of year for a landing. Where were the landing craft required? And how would the troops be supplied throughout the winter while they were under German attack? Since British troops would participate in Sledgehammer, Churchill's veto was absolute.

Unable to produce a Second Front immediately, Roosevelt and Churchill attempted to placate Stalin's anger by sending him huge quantities of supplies and equipment despite the drain on Anglo-American shipping. Convoys making the two-thousand-mile voyage from Iceland, around North Cape, and through the Barents Sea faced nightmarish conditions. Lashed by subzero winds that sometimes reached hurricane force from off the polar icecap, the ships faced waves seventy feet high. Spray froze immediately, forming an icy shroud that had to be chipped away immediately from superstructures, guns, and decks before the top-heavy ships rolled over. And in summer there was permanent daylight—a nightmare for ships and men trying to remain concealed from a vigilant enemy.

Until the spring of 1942, the Germans had not seriously attempted to interfere with the Russian convoys, but with the arrival of *Tirpitz*, *Scheer*, *Lützow*, and *Hipper* and more aircraft in northern Norway, the convoys came under severe attack. Some convoys lost as many as 20 percent of the vessels that had originally sailed. In May, Convoy PQ 16 lost seven of thirty-four ships as well as the cruisers *Edinburgh* and *Trinidad*. *Tirpitz* was a special thorn in the side of the British, who worried she might break out into the North Atlantic and wreak havoc on merchant shipping.

One of the best ways to discourage such a sortie was to make it impossible for the battleship to make for the French coast upon her return from a raid. There was only one drydock large enough to accommodate the huge vessel—the *Normandie* dock at St.-Nazaire, where the famous liner had been built—and the British determined to put it out of commission. In the early hours of March 28, the explosive-crammed old four-piper *Campbeltown*, having made her way up the five-mile-long Loire estuary without being discovered, rammed the gate of the dock and was abandoned by her crew. She exploded the next day, destroying her objective, inflicting heavy casualties upon the Germans, and eliminating any future possibility of *Tirpitz*'s docking in western France. Some of the luster lost in the Channel Dash was restored to the Royal Navy.

Professional naval officers opposed continuation of the "Murmansk Run" as the Arctic day lengthened and the ships were silhouetted against the ice pack by the eerie pallor of the midnight sun. But these objections were brushed aside, because the convoys were designed more to appease Stalin than to meet military requirements. "These Russian Convoys are becoming a regular millstone round our necks and cause a steady attrition in both cruisers and destroyers," Admiral Pound complained to Admiral King. The American was sympathetic. Although the defense of the Russian convoys was the responsibility of the Royal Navy, King assigned Task Force 39, built around the carrier *Wasp* and the battleship *Washington*, to support the British and replace some heavy ships assigned to the seizure of Madagascar in the Indian Ocean.[*]

Convoy PQ 17, bound for Archangel with thirty-three merchantmen—twenty-two flying the American flag—left Hvalfjord, Iceland, on June 27, 1942.[†] They were escorted by six destroyers, two flak ships, two submarines, and eleven corvettes, minesweepers, and

---

[*]On May 5, 1942, British troops, covered by the carriers *Indomitable* and *Illustrious*, landed on Madagascar to seize the port of Diego-Suarez from the Vichy French. This was done to prevent the Japanese from obtaining control of the island and cutting the supply line around the Cape of Good Hope to the Suez Canal, the main route for supplies for British forces in the Middle East.

[†]There were thirty-five ships originally, but two turned back.

armed trawlers, all under Commander John E. Broome in the destroyer *Keppel*. Four British and American cruisers lent close support, and the battleships *Duke of York* and *Washington* as well as the carrier *Victorious* were on call. Unknown to Broome, Admiral Pound, who was skittish about the possibility of an attack upon the convoy by *Tirpitz*, had informed Admiral Tovey, commander of the Home Fleet, that if the German battleship sortied, he intended to order PQ 17 to scatter. If that happened, "it would be sheer bloody murder," Tovey angrily replied.

The Germans planned a warm welcome for PQ 17. As soon as U-boats and aircraft spotted the convoy off Jan Mayen Island on July 1, Operation Rosselsprung (Knight's Move) was put into effect. *Tirpitz* was ordered north to join *Scheer* and *Hipper* in Altenfjord, where she strained at the leash while awaiting Hitler's permission to strike. Over the next three days, the Luftwaffe launched repeated attacks on the convoy, sinking two ships and damaging a Soviet tanker. Several planes were shot down by the escort's concentrated fire, and the rest now kept a respectful distance. Broome reported that the convoy's "tails were well up" and "provided the ammunition lasted, PQ17 could go anywhere."

And then, on July 4, came a shocking string of messages from the Admiralty to Rear Admiral L. H. K. Hamilton, commander of the cruiser force, that sounded the death knell of PQ 17:

> 2111. Most Immediate. Cruiser force withdraw to west at high speed.
> 2123. Immediate. Owing to threat of surface ships convoy is to disperse and proceed to Russian ports.
> 2136. Most Immediate. My 9.23 of the 4th. Convoy is to scatter.[*]

Admiral Pound knew that *Tirpitz* and the other German heavy ships were in position to strike PQ 17, but he did not know if they were at sea. Tovey's heavy ships were too far away to lend support if they were. Unfortunately, OIC could not supply the First Sea Lord with a definite answer as to the status of *Tirpitz* and her sisters, because

---

[*]In naval jargon, the words "disperse" and "scatter" are not synonomous. The former implies an orderly breakup of a convoy with each vessel making for its destination at its best speed. The latter means an immediate flight on all points of the compass—a nautical "run for your lives" (Van der Vat, *The Battle of the Atlantic*, p. 285).

Bletchley Park had not yet broken the Enigma rotor setting for that day. Pound faced a serious dilemma. If the German heavy ships were operational, they would be in a position to attack the convoy from the early hours of July 5. The convoy's only defense was to stay together under the protection of the escort, yet the classic response to an attack by superior surface forces was to scatter.

Pound's signal to scatter caused consternation in the convoy. A destroyer captain signaled Broome: "What part of the bloody War Plan is this?" One of the cruiser *Norfolk*'s officers wrote: "At 26 knots the four cruisers and all the destroyers swept close past the convoy. Our last sight of the merchantmen showed them slowly opening out and separating. The effect on the ship's company was devastating. . . . The ship was in a turmoil; everyone was boiling, and the Master at Arms told me he had never seen such strong feelings before. . . . It was the blackest day we ever knew—sheer bloody murder."

And it was. Within hours, U-boats and the Luftwaffe ruthlessly hunted down the fleeing merchantmen, some of which vainly raced north to take cover in the ice pack. One by one, they were picked off. Only eleven merchantmen and two rescue ships reached the safety of a Russian port. More than three thousand vehicles, 430 tanks, 210 planes, and nearly a hundred thousand tons of general cargo were lost—sufficient, as one authority said, "to have equipped an army." One hundred and fifty-three merchant seamen died in the lifeboats and rafts that littered the frigid Arctic waters. Later, it was learned that *Tirpitz*, *Hipper*, and *Scheer* did not put to sea until the afternoon of July 5, twelve hours *after* the dispersal of PQ 17, and were soon recalled, because the Luftwaffe and the submarines had already decimated the convoy. Once again, Admiralty interference with tactical decisions that should have been left to the commander on the spot had proved to be fatal.*

The slaughter of PQ 17 had widespread repercussions. The Russian convoys were suspended for the rest of the summer, until suffi-

---

*In mid-August 1942, *Admiral Scheer* sailed on a raiding voyage to the north of Siberia in search of merchantmen trying to pass from the Atlantic to the Pacific across the roof of the world. The raid was called off after two weeks when the pocket battleship's float plane was accidentally damaged, and her captain believed it too risky to continue with inadequate reconnaissance. The Soviet icebreaker *Sibiryakov* was sunk in a hopeless fight that reminded some of *Scheer*'s crew of her encounter with *Jervis Bay* in 1940.

cient air cover could be provided. Admiral King, furious at Pound's bungling and the loss of American ships, immediately withdrew TF 39 and sent it to the Pacific. From this time on, he looked with disfavor upon conducting joint operations with the British. Fresh ammunition was also furnished to the increasingly vocal lobby in Washington that urged concentration on the war against Japan.

PQ 18, a forty-ship convoy that sailed from Iceland in September, included the escort carrier *Avenger*. German morale was high after the ravaging of PQ 17, and as soon as the ships approached North Cape, they were attacked by Ju-88s, which were driven off by the flattop's dozen Hurricanes. Forty torpedo bombers eluded the fighters, however, and sank eight merchantmen in eight minutes. The convoy sailed on, leaving a trail of debris floating behind it. "I have not slept longer than two hours a night for the last three nights," reported Lieutenant Wesley N. Miller, commander of the Armed Guard on the American freighter Saint Olaf. "My food is brought to the bridge. I do not leave even to visit the head. . . . It was twenty-one hours duty out of every twenty-four if one wanted to live."

Several attacks over the next few days were broken up, with the fighters and the escort's guns accounting for forty-one bombers—vindicating the wisdom of keeping convoys together. U-boats also attacked the convoy, accounting for three freighters against the loss of four submarines. PQ 18 lost thirteen ships, but its defenders imposed such losses on the enemy that it was the turning point in the battle of the Russian convoys. Over the next few months, however, the British were unable to send convoys to the Soviet Union, because the attention of the antagonists had been diverted to the Mediterranean.

•

CHAPTER 11

"We Are Fighting Back"

Winston Churchill was meeting at the White House with President Roosevelt on June 17, 1942, when General Marshall entered the room and without a word passed a cable to Roosevelt. After taking a glance at it, the president handed it to the prime minister. Churchill was shaken by the message: "Tobruk has surrendered with 25,000 men taken prisoner." It was, he said later, one of the heaviest blows he received during the war. Little stood between Rommel's Afrika Korps and the Suez Canal and the oil fields of the Middle East.* Roosevelt quickly offered the British three hundred new Sherman tanks to replace their heavy losses, even though the U.S. Army had not yet received its first shipment of these weapons.

The fall of Tobruk focused attention on the Middle East and allowed Churchill to bring a fresh urgency to his earlier plan for an invasion of western North Africa. At first, Roosevelt opposed the proposal, but, eager to have American troops in action before the end of 1942, he finally gave his approval on July 25—despite the objections of the Joint Chiefs of Staff, who knew that it meant no invasion of Europe in 1943. It was one of the very few times the president ignored Marshall's advice on strategy. Torch, as the North African operation was known, was scheduled for late October or early November. The bloody failure of the British to bring off a large-scale

---

*Hitler awarded Rommel a field marshal's baton for the capture of Tobruk and its garrison. "I would rather he had given me one more division," Rommel told his wife.

raid on the French coastal town of Dieppe on August 19 made it clear that Churchill was on firm ground in arguing that the Allies were not ready for a cross-Channel invasion.[*]

In addition to the defeat suffered by the Eighth Army (the new designation of the Army of the Nile), the Mediterranean Fleet was enduring its own skein of catastrophes. Unable to exercise command of the Mediterranean, it tried to interdict the flow of men and supplies intended for the Afrika Korps. Malta, which sat squarely astride the sea route between Italy and Libya, was central to these operations. There was a deadly parallel between the state of Malta's fortunes and the land campaign in North Africa. When Malta was well supplied, air and naval forces based there disrupted Rommel's supply line; when Malta was tightly besieged, his army was on the move.

The Germans considered an airborne invasion of this thorn in their sides, but Hitler rejected it in light of the casualties suffered during the landing on Crete. And if Malta were captured, he realized, it would be difficult to supply it. The Führer preferred to allow the British to make these sacrifices. Malta and the adjacent seas became a killing ground where both sides lost heavily in the ensuing war of attrition.

---

[*]Some six thousand Allied troops—the bulk of them Canadians along with some British commandos and fifty American Rangers—took part in the Dieppe raid. The objective of Operation Jubilee, as it was designated, was to test the strength of the German defenses on the French coast and to practice techniques for a full-scale invasion. Attempts to surprise the Germans failed, and the raiders, who had attacked enemy emplacements without a heavy naval bombardment and air supremacy, were met with a withering fire. Two dozen tanks were landed, but most were destroyed. Both sides also suffered heavy losses in a massive air battle over the beachhead.

As a military operation, Dieppe was a failure. The Allies lost more than half the attacking force, with 3,379 men killed, wounded, or captured in the nine hours of fighting, and all their vehicles and equipment were left behind on the beach. "This is the first time," mocked Hitler, "that the British have had the courtesy to cross the sea to offer the enemy a complete sample of their weapons." It was claimed that the lessons learned at Dieppe were invaluable to both the Allies and the Germans, but Admiral Sir Bertram Ramsay, who had conducted the Dunkirk evacuation, wrote, "Dieppe was a tragedy and the cause may be attributed to the fact that it was planned by inexperienced enthusiasts." In Canada, Dieppe has, like Gallipoli for Australia and New Zealand, become a symbol of Britain's readiness to sacrifice Dominion troops for its own ends. See Robertson, *Dieppe: The Shame and Glory.* Ramsay's comment is in W. J. R. Gardner, "Sir Bertram Ramsay," in Howarth, ed., *Men of War*, p. 360.

U-81 torpedoed *Ark Royal* to the east of Gibraltar on November 13, 1941, and she sank under tow, leaving the British without a carrier in the Mediterranean. Twelve days later, the old battleship *Barham* was struck by three torpedoes from *U-331* south of Crete. She was "completely hidden in a great cloud of yellowish-black smoke, which went wreathing and eddying high up into the sky," reported Admiral Cunningham. "When it cleared away, the *Barham* had disappeared. There was nothing but a bubbling, oily-looking patch on the calm surface of the sea. It was ghastly to look at, a horrible and awe-inspiring spectacle. . . ." Nearly nine hundred members of her crew died with their ship.

On December 14, a cruiser was torpedoed and sunk off Alexandria. Five days later, a force of three cruisers and four destroyers which had sailed from Malta to intercept an Axis convoy off Tripoli, ran into an Italian minefield.* One of the cruisers and a destroyer were sunk, two other cruisers were damaged, and the Axis convoy got through. That same day, Cunningham's fleet suffered the culminating disaster of 1941. The flagship *Queen Elizabeth* and *Valiant* were sunk at their moorings at Alexandria by Italian frogmen.

The Italians, who were riding a trio of human torpedoes, penetrated the base and attached charges to the ships' bottoms timed to go off later. Although the frogmen were captured, they refused to disclose the nature of their mission. At just about 0620, there was a violent explosion right under *Valiant's* foreturret, Cunningham reported. "Four minutes after that, when I was right aft in the *Queen Elizabeth* by the ensign staff, I felt a dull thud and was tossed about five feet into the air by the whip of the ship and was lucky not to come down sprawling. I saw a great cloud of black smoke shoot up the funnel and immediately in front of it, and knew at once that the ship was badly damaged. *Valiant* was down by the bows. *Queen Elizabeth* took a heavy list to starboard."

Fortunately for the British, the two stricken battleships settled straight to the shallow bottom with their decks above water, and the enemy was deceived into believing they were still operational. In

---

*On December 17, this squadron had encountered a convoy defended by two Italian battleships supported by light forces in the Gulf of Sirte. The Italians withdrew after a brief and indecisive engagement that was called the First Battle of Sirte.

fact, they were out of action for nearly a year. With no replacements readily available, the Mediterranean Fleet—now without aircraft carriers or battleships—had ceased to exist except for a handful of light cruisers and destroyers. Had the Germans and Italians realized it, they were in a position to command the Mediterranean.

As 1942 began, the British could run convoys through to Malta only with considerable difficulty, while Rommel, reinforced and resupplied by two successful convoys in January, embarked on the offensive that led to the capture of Tobruk and the near collapse of the British position in the Middle East. The loss of forward airfields in the desert boded ill for Cunningham's efforts to supply Malta, for the convoys would now have to run the gantlet of enemy sea and air bases on both flanks of the route.

By March 1942, Malta's situation was desperate, and Cunningham concentrated every effort on getting a supply convoy of four fast merchant ships through to the island. Three light cruisers and ten destroyers under the command of Rear Admiral Sir Philip Vian—everything that was available—covered the convoy on its passage from Alexandria. As they neared the island, they were joined by a light cruiser and six destroyers. On March 22, an Italian fleet led by the battleship *Littorio*, accompanied by two heavy and one light cruiser and eight destroyers, intercepted the British force.

Four separate actions took place that afternoon in heavy seas—known as the Second Battle of Sirte*—in which Vian, through brilliant tactics and skillful use of smoke, succeeded in preventing the Italians from getting through to the convoy. Three of his destroyers were hit by fifteen-inch shells as they delivered a torpedo attack, but a pair of cruisers briefly engaged *Littorio* at thirteen thousand yards and took the pressure off them. Two of the freighters survived German bombing to reach the Grand Harbor of Malta, only to be sunk a few days later, having only partially unloaded their cargoes.

On July 27, 1942, the German people heard a radio broadcast they thought one of the most extraordinary of the war. Admiral Dönitz, basking in the propaganda glory of Paukenschlag, declared that, despite the "exaggerated hopes" raised by the U-boat campaign, "the

*This is the action described by C. S. Forester in his wartime novel, *The Ship*.

harsh realities of the submarine war" meant that "more difficult times lay ahead of us." What did this mean? British intelligence surmised that these remarks were intended as a warning that the high rate of sinkings achieved off the American coast could not be maintained, and saw it as a tip-off that the U-boats were returning to grapple with escorted convoys where casualties could be expected.

With Allied resources diverted to the protection of American coastal traffic, Dönitz sent his boats into the North Atlantic, where the convoys were thinly defended. Patrols were established on either side of the six-hundred-mile-wide mid-Atlantic air gap—called the Devil's Gorge by U-boat skippers—where his wolf packs could attack east- and westbound convoys without fear of Allied aircraft. They had invaluable support from B-Dienst. The British had finally realized the Germans were reading the Merchant Navy Code and had introduced a new one. Within four weeks, B-Dienst penetrated it and could follow the movements of Allied convoys. "Never forget that you are the only reconnaissance on which I can rely," Dönitz told the code breakers.

The return of the U-boats to the main convoy routes was signaled by an attack by Convoy SC 94 by eighteen U-boats on August 5 that lasted several days. Eleven ships were lost, while two submarines were sunk and another two were damaged. The U-boats gained the upper hand in a battle the following month with ON 127, which lost nine ships, and the Canadian destroyer *Ottawa*, without the loss of any U-boats. In all, between June and November 1942, an average monthly total of over five hundred thousand tons of shipping was sunk, with the highest toll recorded in November, when nearly seven hundred thousand tons were sent to the bottom.

Convoys under escort by the Royal Canadian Navy experienced markedly heavier losses than those shepherded by the British. This was the result of the mushroom growth of the RCN, to four hundred ships and ninety thousand men in little more than three years. Whatever experience they gained was diluted by the constant need to provide officers and crews for new ships. Moreover, Canadian corvettes had hardly been improved from the original design and sometimes lacked radar and other modern technology. Yet these vessels were assigned to escort slow convoys, where the U-boat threat was greatest. As a result, ships and crews were overworked and morale was low. One British escort commander was appalled when he saw a Canadian corvette with the words "We Want Leave" painted in large letters on her rust-streaked sides.

Admiral Sir Max Horton, the aggressive newly appointed commander of the Western Approaches, immediately took the RCN in hand. Brushing aside Ottawa's objections, he reshuffled the ocean escorts. Four Canadian groups were assigned to the Gibraltar run, and Royal Navy ships replaced them in the North Atlantic. The Canadians regarded this as a slap in the face, but resistance collapsed after ONS 154 lost fourteen ships while under RCN protection. Following rigorous training between voyages on the Gibraltar route, the Canadian ships were returned to the North Atlantic run.

There were also several other far-reaching developments in the war against the U-boats. Hard-won experience had revealed that, the longer an escort had time to hunt a U-boat that had been sighted, the better the chances of destroying it. But the primary task of the escort was to remain with the convoy. In September 1942, there were finally enough ships available to organize the first independent escort group, which could hunt enemy submarines to the death once they had been located in the vicinity of a convoy. The first such unit, the Twentieth Escort Group, sailed with ONS 132 and proved its worth by driving down two trailing U-boats, causing them to lose contact with the convoy. The group accounted for nine U-boats before being withdrawn to take part in the North African invasion.

The Allies were also winning the technology race. Shortwave radar that made it possible to pick up surfaced submarines, and high-frequency direction finders (HF/DF, known as "Huff-Duff"), which enabled the escorts to home in on a U-boat's radio traffic, were introduced. The Germans never caught on to the secret and credited the Allies' ability to locate U-boats running on the surface entirely to radar rather than their own radio emissions. Forward-firing "Hedgehogs"—a mortarlike apparatus which could simultaneously fire sixteen small depth charges—were being fitted to escort vessels. German scientists had been unable to provide the U-boats with radar of their own, and the "Metox" receiver, which was designed to pick up enemy radar, was useless against the newest Allied radar technology.

Dönitz's increasing uneasiness caused him to send his boats farther afield, to the Freetown route and as far away as the Cape of Good Hope. Four Type IX boats, accompanied by a milch cow, were just south of the Equator, where, on the night of September 12, *U-156* torpedoed the British troopship *Laconia*, about five hundred miles north of Ascension Island. From survivors, Kapitänleuntant Werner Hartenstein learned that she had been crammed with some eighteen hundred Italian prisoners of war captured in North Africa and their Polish guards, as well as some British soldiers and a sizable contingent of women and children.

Hartenstein immediately began picking up survivors regardless of nationality and radioed U-boat headquarters requesting instructions. Placing his boat at risk, he repeatedly transmitted a message in English on the international emergency wavelength:

> If any ship will assist the shipwrecked *Laconia* crew I will not attack her, provided I am not attacked by ship or air force. I picked up 193 men 04.53 S 11.26 W. German submarine.

Worried about the effect of the sinking on Germany's already strained relations with Italy, Dönitz ordered three other boats of the group to join in the rescue operation and asked the Vichy French in West Africa to send ships. Even after Hitler ordered Dönitz not to place his boats in jeopardy, the rescue effort continued. Over the next two days, *U-156*, towing four lifeboats and with two hundred survivors packed on deck and below, steered through calm seas toward a rendezvous with the French vessels. All seemed to be going well until about noon on September 15, when this bizarre entourage was sighted by a U.S. Air Force B-24 bomber based on Ascension Island.

The pilot notified his base of what he had seen and asked for orders. He was told to destroy the submarine, although Hartenstein had draped a large Red Cross flag over his bridge "as proof of my peaceful intentions." With the first fall of bombs, he cleared his boat of survivors by cramming them into the lifeboats or leaving them in the water hanging on to lines along the sides of the boats. *U-156* managed to dive without being seriously damaged, but one of the bombs sank a boat crowded with Italian prisoners. Several hours later, the French picked up the survivors. Some eight hundred Britons and Poles were saved, but only 450 Italians, because, it was charged, their captors had closed the watertight doors on them before *Laconia* sank.

In the wake of the *Laconia* affair, on September 17, Dönitz issued the following orders to all U-boat captains:

1. All attempts at rescuing members of ships that have sunk, including attempts to pick up persons swimming, or to place them in lifeboats, or attempts to upright capsized boats, or supply provisions or water, are to cease. The rescue of survivors contradicts the elementary necessity of war for the destruction of enemy ships and crews.

2. The order for the seizure of commanding officers and chief engineers remains in force.

3. Survivors are only to be picked up in cases where their interrogations would be of value to the boat.

4. Be severe. Remember that in his bombing attacks on German cities the enemy has no regard for women and children.[*]

In the Mediterranean, Malta, bombed every day by Axis aircraft, was on the brink of starvation and surrender. In July 1942, not a single convoy was able to fight its way through to the beleaguered island, and many of its installations had been destroyed. On August 10, fourteen hastily gathered merchantmen—including the tanker *Ohio*, with fifteen thousand tons of oil—passed through the Straits of Gibraltar in a desperate attempt to relieve Malta. The value of this convoy—known as Pedestal—can be gauged by the strength of the escort. It included the large carriers *Victorious* and *Indomitable* as well as the old *Eagle*, the battleships *Nelson* and *Rodney*, and a strong cruiser-destroyer screen. *Furious* was also to accompany the convoy to a point 550 miles west of Malta and fly off thirty-eight Spitfires that

---

[*]Prosecutors at the Nuremberg war-crimes trial charged that the "*Laconia* order," as it was known, was a veiled attempt to encourage U-boat commanders to kill survivors. Dönitz was saved from a certain death sentence, if convicted, by a deposition by Admiral Nimitz, who acknowledged that American submarines made no effort to rescue survivors. Dönitz was found guilty of waging aggressive war and complicity in unstated war crimes and sentenced to ten years' imprisonment—the lightest sentence imposed upon anyone in the Nazi leadership by the tribunal.

One U-boat captain, Kapitänleutnant Heinz-Wilhelm Eck of *U-852*, was convicted by a British court-martial of machine-gunning the survivors of a Greek ship in March 1944, and shot. It should be pointed out that neither the Kriegsmarine in general nor the submarine service in particular was condemned at Nuremberg for its conduct of the war at sea.

were badly needed by the RAF. The Germans and Italians massed nearly eight hundred aircraft in Sardinia and Italy, and threw a sizable force of surface ships and submarines across Pedestal's course.

Several enemy reconnaissance aircraft were sighted by the escort, which shot some of them down, but all was comparatively quiet until midafternoon on August 11. Suddenly the convoy was rocked by a series of dull explosions. "Oh Christ! look at the *Eagle*," someone cried out. Four torpedoes fired by *U-73* had nearly blown the old ship apart, and she sank within eight minutes, with the loss of her aircraft and more than two hundred of her crew. There were no further attacks, and shortly after sunset *Furious* launched her deck load of Spitfires and returned to Gibraltar.

An ominous silence descended upon the convoy, soon broken by the command "Fighters stand-to!" Thirty-five dive-bombers and torpedo planes attacked the ships, but they were driven off by Hurricanes and heavy anti-aircraft fire. "The sight took our breath away," said Lieutenant Hugh Popham, one of the fighter pilots. "The light was slowly dying, and the ships were no more than a pattern on the great steel plate of the sea. . . . Every gun in the fleet was firing and the darkling air was laced with threads and beads of fire."

The enemy launched a major effort against the convoy as it neared Sardinia the following morning. More than a hundred aircraft of various types were thrown into the attack. A freighter was damaged so badly it had to be left behind, and *Indomitable*'s flight deck was hit. But by nightfall the last raiders had been beaten off. As previously planned, the two remaining carriers withdrew and returned to Gibraltar as the convoy pressed on into "Bomb Alley," the narrow passage between Sicily and the North African coast.

The RAF could provide little cover, and the convoy was attacked by wave after wave of bombers and torpedo planes as well as by submarines and S-boats. Two of the escorting cruisers were sunk and another pair damaged. Only five of the merchantmen survived the savage onslaught, to pass between the arms of the breakwater at Valletta amid the frenzied cheers of the population and the garrison. The badly damaged *Ohio* with her precious cargo was among them—oil without which Malta could not survive.

Pedestal was the last major encounter between the opposing naval forces in the Mediterranean. Partially resupplied and refueled,

British submarines and strike aircraft based on Malta played havoc with Rommel's supply line. In August, 25 percent of his supplies were lost on passage across the Mediterranean; by October, 44 percent of the total tonnage was being sunk. Not long after, the Afrika Korps was reeling back across the North African desert in full retreat from El Alamein with the Eighth Army in hot pursuit.

On November 8, 1942, a Sunday, President Roosevelt was at Shangri-La, his Catoctin Mountain retreat in western Maryland (now known as Camp David). He seemed on edge—as though awaiting important news. Finally, a telephone call came through from the War Department in Washington. An aide noted that Roosevelt's hand shook as he took the receiver. He listened intently until he heard the message through and then burst out: "Thank God! Thank God! That sounds grand. Congratulations."

The president hung up the phone and turned to his guests with a broad smile.

"We have landed in North Africa," he told them. "Casualties are below expectations. We are fighting back."

Operation Torch was the largest amphibious invasion in history up to that time. Simultaneous landings were made by more than a hundred thousand troops—three-quarters of them American—at Casablanca, on the Atlantic coast, and at Oran and Algiers, inside the Mediterranean. Some 370 merchant ships and more than three hundred warships were involved. Because of Vichy French bias against the British, Churchill thought the invasion should be under the command of an American, so Lieutenant General Eisenhower, who led the American troops in Britain, was given the post. Admiral Sir Andrew Cunningham was in charge of the naval side of the operation.

A Western Naval Task Force transported thirty-five thousand troops directly from the United States for the assault on Casablanca. A Center Naval Task Force, carrying thirty-nine thousand American troops, sailed from the United Kingdom under British naval cover to attack Oran. A third contingent, the Eastern Naval Task Force, staged from Britain with twenty-three thousand British and ten thousand American troops, was assigned to capture Algiers. Follow-up convoys would pour in reinforcements once the ports were taken, and planes from Gibraltar would make use of the airfields. Cunningham urged the capture of Bizerte or Bône to prevent the Axis from making a stand in Tunisia, but the proposal was turned down—one of the major Allied blunders of the war.

Success hinged as much on political as on naval and military factors, for no one knew whether the French would welcome or resist an Allied invasion. The senior officers had sworn a personal oath of allegiance to the aged Marshal Pétain, the head of the Vichy regime; to renounce it would, in their eyes, be an act of treason. Allied diplomats and secret agents had some success in persuading junior army officers not to contest the landings. But the navy, which manned the vital coastal-defense batteries and controlled the fleet, was loyal to Admiral Darlan, the real leader of the Vichy regime. Of particular concern was the uncompleted battleship *Jean Bart* at Casablanca. Although she was immobilized, her single operational turret with its four fifteen-inch guns constituted a formidable battery. The light cruiser *Primaguet* and several destroyers and submarines were also question marks.

The operation was plagued by the limited time available for training in amphibious techniques and by shortages of equipment, especially large landing craft capable of handling tanks. Nevertheless, the Western Task Force, composed of 102 warships, transports, and auxiliaries under the command of Rear Admiral H. Kent Hewitt, sailed as scheduled from Hampton Roads on October 23. It was joined at sea by the new battleship *Massachusetts*, two heavy cruisers, the light carrier *Ranger*, four escort carriers, and a light-cruiser–destroyer screen. In the meantime, the convoys carrying the troops for the assaults against Algiers and Oran proceeded southward from Britain, rounded Cape Trafalgar, and anchored under the gray loom of Gibraltar's rock. To prevent the Italians or the French fleet at Toulon from interfering, these units were covered by the Royal Navy's Force H— three battleships, a battle cruiser, and two fleet carriers.

For ten days, the Western Task Force steamed through perfect autumn weather at fourteen knots, zigzagging by day and sailing a direct course at night. German submarine activity increased as the enemy became aware of the large number of ships gathering in American and English ports, but the Naval Staff believed the Allies were preparing an attack against Dakar, and Dönitz massed his U-boats around Madeira and the Azores. In consequence, a large convoy, SL 125, homeward bound from Freetown and proceeding to the north and east of the invasion fleet, was attacked by ten U-boats. Thirteen ships were lost and not a single submarine sunk, but the unlucky convoy drew the U-boats away from the troop convoys converging on North Africa.[*]

Hewitt arrived off the Moroccan coast early on November 7, to find weather conditions deteriorating; forecasts supplied by the army called for waves fifteen feet high, which would cause the operation to be scrubbed. On being advised by his own meteorological officer that there would be a temporary moderation of conditions locally, Hewitt decided to go ahead with the invasion the next morning as planned. Three landings were to be made—one at Safi, to the south of Casablanca, and two to the north: at Mehdia, to capture the airfield at nearby Port Lyautey, and at Fedhala, about fifteen miles from the city. The naval commanders advocated prelanding bombardments to pave the way for the troops, but the generals, hoping for a surprise, insisted on going in without naval-gunfire support.

Torch began as dawn broke over Safi on November 8, when two four-pipers, *Cole* and *Benadou*, charged into the harbor amid shelling by the shore batteries. Each landed about two hundred Rangers who seized the harbor installations. Standing offshore, the old battleship *New York* and the cruiser *Philadelphia* suppressed the French guns as planes from the escort carriers shot up airfields before the bulk of the troops came in. Sherman tanks were landed from the *Lakehurst*, a former Havana ferry that Hewitt pressed into service because tank-landing craft were unavailable. Within hours, the tanks were on their way by coastal road to Casablanca, shadowed by six landing craft carrying gasoline.

Confusion and mistakes dogged the landing at Mehdia. Faulty landfalls on the flat, featureless coastline caused some troops to be put ashore on the wrong beaches, and the opportunity to take the fortifications blocking the approaches to Port Lyautey, eight miles upriver from the coast, was lost. When bad weather set in, the rapidly rising surf made it difficult to land reinforcements. Old Seagull observation biplanes catapulted off the veteran battleship *Texas* and

---

[*]The convoy commodore sardonically told Captain Roskill, the British official naval historian, that it was the only time he was ever congratulated for losing ships.

the cruiser *Savannah* made a unique contribution to the battle by bombing—and halting—a French tank column with depth charges fitted with impact fuses.

Casablanca, by far the strongest and most important target, was fraught with the most danger. Wildcats from *Ranger* swept in over the city at daylight to strafe airfields and shore batteries and shot down several planes that challenged them. The command "Play Ball!"—the signal to begin landing operations—was given at 0620. Some transports were late in taking position to land their troops, however, and there were delays in getting the landing craft away, because the army insisted that the men carry full packs. Since most of the boats were only partially filled, the first wave to land at Fedhala was only half the planned strength. Landing craft collided with each other, and boats were wrecked or broached in the heavy seas. Some men, overburdened with equipment, were drowned. In spite of these mishaps, thirty-five hundred troops were landed, enough to secure the beachhead.

Admiral François Michelier, the French naval commander in Morocco, ordered the shore batteries to fire on the landing craft and the troops on the beaches. Fire was returned by destroyers operating close inshore, with the cruisers *Brooklyn* and *Augusta* in backup. *Jean Bart* opened up on *Massachusetts*, but the battleship's sixteen-inch guns silenced the French vessel's single turret on the fifth salvo. Shortly after 0800, Michelier dispatched seven destroyers and eight submarines to attack the transports under cover of a smoke screen. They were intercepted by *Augusta* and *Brooklyn*, which broke up the sortie. Not long after, these ships returned, now led by the cruiser *Primaguet*. A confused battle ensued in which the French were bombed and strafed by *Ranger*'s planes while French submarines only narrowly missed several of the American ships. All the French vessels were sunk or severely damaged by noon without serious consequence to the invaders.

The landing forces that attacked Algiers and Oran met much less spirited resistance. The worst casualties were suffered by several small vessels that forced the harbor booms; two former U.S. Coast Guard cutters that had been turned over to the British, *Walney* and *Hartland*, received the heaviest fire. A cease-fire was quickly arranged at Algiers; at Oran, sporadic fighting took place and the French did not capitulate until November 10.

In response to the Allied landings, the Germans took over the unoccupied sections of France and attempted to seize the ships at Toulon. Instead of bringing them out to join the Allies, the admiral in command of the base scuttled them. German submarines finally arrived off the North African coast on November 10 and sank four transports, but it was too late to affect the situation.

Fighting continued in the Casablanca sector until November 9. An armored column moving south from Fedala was shelled by French ships. They were driven off by *Augusta*, but the cruiser came under fire from *Jean Bart's* turret, which had been repaired. Nine SBD dive-bombers from *Ranger*, each carrying a thousand-pound bomb, were ordered to the attack. Three hits were scored on the battleship, putting her out of action. "No more *Jean Bart!*" radioed one of the jubilant pilots. That evening, Admiral Hewitt planned an all-out bombardment to begin at 0715 the next morning. Fifteen minutes before the ships were to open fire, a cease-fire was announced. By coincidence, Admiral Darlan had been visiting Algiers, and in exchange for Allied recognition of his political authority in North Africa, he agreed to order an end to all resistance. "It was in the nick of time," said Hewitt, "for fingers were already on firing keys and bomb releases."

Within three months of the decision to invade North Africa—and three days after the landing—the Allies, by skillful application of maritime power, had achieved all their objectives. U.S. casualties totaled 1,469 killed, wounded, and missing; those of the French were estimated at about forty-five hundred. As in any military undertaking, there had been mishaps and failures. Both the troops and the boat crews needed more training and better equipment, especially large landing craft. Naval-gunfire support had been ineffective, because the ships fired at long range, and the army was yet to be convinced of the importance of heavy gunfire from ships in amphibious operations. But as Admiral Cunningham observed, "We could not afford to wait, and the risk of embarking on these large-scale operations with inadequate training was deliberately accepted in order to strike when the time was ripe."

The big question now was, what was to be done next?

•

CHAPTER 12

"We Had Lost the Battle of the Atlantic"

In the night shadows of January 9, 1943, a small cavalcade of limousines glided away from the South Portico of the White House and hurried through the empty streets of Washington to a little-known railroad siding near the Bureau of Engraving and Printing. The president's train was waiting. Franklin Roosevelt was joined in his private car, the *Ferdinand Magellan,* by his civilian advisers and a glittering array of generals and admirals. At Miami, a four-engine Pan American flying boat stood by to fly the presidential party across the Atlantic to Casablanca in North Africa.[*]

The tide of battle was turning against the Axis in all theaters of war, and the time had come for the Allies to settle upon a future strategy. Stalin was urged to join Roosevelt and Churchill at Casablanca, but he refused to leave Russia while his troops had the German Sixth Army surrounded in the ruins of Stalingrad. In the Mediterranean, what remained of the Afrika Korps was in the process of being ground up in Tunisia between the advancing American and British armies.

[*]This was the first airplane flight by an American president. Roosevelt had surprised the American people by flying to the Democratic convention in Chicago to give his acceptance speech in 1932, but he had not taken to the air since becoming chief executive. Theodore Roosevelt, who went to Panama in 1906 to inspect work on the Panama Canal, was the first president to leave the country while in office. FDR was the first in wartime.

And the Japanese had been thrown on the defensive by the bloody conclusion of the Guadalcanal and Papuan campaigns.

Roosevelt and Churchill and the Combined Chiefs of Staff arrived at the conference, which lasted from January 14 to 23, with differing agendas. The Americans were pushing for a cross-Channel invasion of France later that year and were unwilling to become bogged down in a Mediterranean sideshow. On the other hand, the British extolled the virtues of continuing operations against what they called the "soft underbelly" of the Nazi empire. With some logic, they argued that the Anglo-American armies were not yet strong enough to breach Hitler's Fortress Europe. For example, the Germans could have forty divisions in France in mid-1943 to oppose a landing by at most twenty-five divisions. Moreover, there were not enough landing craft and other shipping available to support an invasion. While the Allied buildup continued, Churchill urged that North Africa be used as a springboard for an attack on Sicily, which would reopen the Mediterranean, drive Italy from the war, and encourage Turkey to enter the struggle on the side of the Allies.

General Marshall, applying the Clausewitzian principle of concentration of force at the decisive point, vehemently objected that "periphery pecking" would drain off resources from the main offensive against Germany. Admiral King also supported a European invasion in 1943 as the best way to end the U-boat scourge, but acknowledged its impossibility because of the shipping shortage. Essentially, his main goal at Casablanca was to prevent the emphasis on Europe from diverting resources from the Pacific. Only about 15 percent of Allied resources were being used against Japan. If the share going to the Pacific were doubled, he argued, Admiral Halsey and General MacArthur could strike northward from the Solomons toward the Philippines while Admiral Nimitz drove westward across the Central Pacific along the lines of the old Orange Plan. If the Japanese were left undisturbed, they would have time to strengthen their defenses. For their part, the British suspected King of seeking to overturn the "Germany First" agreement and devote the full attention of the U.S. Navy to victory over Japan.

American war planners were unable to produce a valid alternative to the Mediterranean strategy, so Roosevelt accepted it. The cross-Channel invasion was postponed until 1944; Sicily was to be invaded as soon as Rommel was defeated in Tunisia. As Marshall put it, the Sicilian operation, code-named Husky, was approved simply "because we will have in North Africa a large number of troops available" with nothing better to do. In the meantime, planning began for the invasion of France in 1944.

To placate Stalin for the further delay of the repeatedly postponed "Second Front," the flow of supplies to Russia was to be increased and the strategic bombing of Germany stepped up. King's plan for an intensified campaign against Japan through a series of limited offensives was also approved, with the Marshalls and Carolines being targeted for attack as soon as enough ships and men were available. As King told Nimitz, the Americans insisted on "recognition of the fact that there is a war going on in the Pacific and that it had to be adequately implemented even though the major operation continues in Europe." The question of an invasion of Italy was left dangling, with the Americans firm in opposing any further operations in the Mediterranean after Husky. The leaders agreed that "the defeat of the U-boat must remain a first charge" on Allied resources and ordered a staff conference to be held to reorganize the antisubmarine effort. In the final analysis, the Casablanca summit produced no firm program for defeating Germany or Japan, but all the parties pretty well got what they wanted.

Roosevelt ended the conference with something of a bombshell. "Unconditional surrender," he told a news conference, rather than the negotiated armistice of World War I, was the sole condition for ending the war. Churchill reluctantly went along. The president insisted upon unconditional surrender to prevent a recurrence of post–World War I German claims that they had not been defeated in the field but were "stabbed in the back" by radicals and Jews. This time they must be forced to admit they were beaten. And he wished to reassure the ever-suspicious Stalin that the United States and Britain were in this fight to the death and would make no separate peace with Hitler or the Japanese.

On New Year's Eve 1942, Hitler had entertained guests at the Wolfsschanze (Wolf's Lair), his headquarters in East Prussia. Aides had not seen him so cheerful for some time as he informed each new arrival of the good news. A Russian-bound convoy had been destroyed by the pocket battleship *Lützow* and the heavy cruiser *Admiral Hipper* in the Barents Sea, and he was only awaiting the details; the Naval High Command was preparing a special communiqué. It was indeed propitious that this feat of German arms should be announced to the world at the start of a new year. Vice-Admiral Theodor Krancke, Grand Admiral Raeder's representative at the Führer's headquarters, was instructed to keep him informed of every detail as soon as information came in.[*] Krancke begged the impatient Hitler to understand that Vice-Admiral Oskar Kummetz, who commanded the squadron, had to keep radio silence to avoid betraying the position of his ships. As soon as he reached Altenfjord, a full report would become available.

"When will that be?" Hitler asked. "When will I get my report?"

"Probably during the course of the evening—unless Admiral Kummetz is unforeseeably held up. . . ."

Midnight arrived, heralding the new year, but there was no news. Pacing restlessly, Hitler refused to go to bed, and periodically ordered Krancke to telephone Berlin. Slowly, his mood changed to one of repressed fury. Not long after dawn, he was given a copy of a news flash issued by the British press agency Reuters: The Royal Navy had fought off an attack by a superior force of German ships on a convoy in the Barents Sea. A German destroyer had been sunk and a cruiser badly damaged. The British had lost a destroyer.

Mad with rage and suspecting a conspiracy by the admirals to hide the disaster from him, Hitler subjected Krancke to a tirade against the navy. In World War I, the High Seas Fleet had made little contribution to the German war effort, and its idle ships had been a breeding ground for Bolshevism and revolution. In this war, the surface fleet had never been worth its keep; the admirals were cowardly and overcautious—he ignored the effects on naval strategy of his reluctance to risk the heavy ships—and, given a last chance to prove itself, the navy had produced another humiliating failure. It was his "irrevocable decision" to scrap the entire fleet, down to the last destroyer; men, armor, and guns were to be put to profitable use as part of the Atlantic coastal defenses. Admiral Raeder was immediately summoned to the Wolfsschanze to receive these orders.

---

[*]Krancke had commanded *Admiral Scheer* during its highly successful raiding voyage in 1940–41.

Paradoxically, the attack on the convoy had been launched as an effort by Raeder to court the Führer's favor. In December, once the protective winter darkness had again descended upon the Arctic and the success of Torch made more escorts available, the British had resumed the Russian convoys. Worried that continued inaction and lack of success would drain morale and imperil future construction programs, Raeder saw an opportunity to obtain Hitler's support for the navy by a successful attack on these convoys, called Operation Regenbogen (Rainbow).

In resuming the Russian convoys, the Royal Navy had made several changes in the arrangements. Rather than sail in a massive group of thirty or forty ships, outward-bound convoys were divided into two smaller units, one sailing a few days after the other. A separate cruiser force was also assigned to each, while heavier units of the Home Fleet stood by on call. Limited air cover was provided on the outward leg, from Iceland and Scotland. Their designation was also changed, probably to erase unhappy memories, from "PQ" to "JW," and as a security measure they were to commence at "51."

Convoy JW 51A departed Scotland on December 15, fourteen merchantmen under escort by seven destroyers and five smaller vessels. Cover was provided by the six-inch-gun cruisers *Jamaica* and *Sheffield* of Force R, flying the flag of Rear Admiral Robert L. Burnett. The convoy arrived at Murmansk without loss on Christmas Day. Having refueled, Burnett put about to protect JW 51B, also of fourteen merchantmen—nine American, four British, and one Panamanian—which had left Scotland on December 22. These ships carried 202 tanks, 2,046 vehicles, 120 aircraft, 24,000 tons of oil and aviation gasoline, and 54,321 tons of general cargo, testimony to the massive aid being supplied the Russians. Six destroyers and five smaller vessels under the command of Captain Robert St. V. Sherbrooke in the destroyer *Onslow* provided a close escort.

JW 51B was less fortunate than its predecessor, and five merchant ships lost touch with the convoy in a gale. The minesweeper *Bramble* was detached to search for them. On December 30, the remaining ships were sighted south of Bear Island by *U-354*, which made an unsuccessful attack. Raeder, sensing an ideal opportunity for an easy victory for the surface navy, ordered Regenbogen into action. With luck, *Lützow*, *Hipper*, and a half-dozen large destroyers which had been waiting in Altenfjord would provide the Führer with a resounding triumph at sea as a New Year's gift.

Flying his flag in *Hipper*, Vice-Admiral Kummetz sortied at 1800, with orders to destroy the convoy while avoiding a superior force. Within an hour of putting to sea, he received further orders symbolic of Hitler's refusal to put his ships at risk: "Contrary to the operational order . . . use caution even against enemy of equal strength, because it is undesirable for the cruisers to take any great risks." These instructions were hardly likely to inspire aggressive action.

In the early hours of December 31, Kummetz divided his force into two elements: *Hipper* would circle to the north and draw off the escort while *Lützow* was to come in from the south with the now defenseless convoy at her mercy. The plan was sound but went awry because poor weather made it difficult to distinguish friend from foe, the resoluteness of the outgunned escort, and the reluctance of the Germans to press home the attack considering Hitler's refusal to risk the ships. Kummetz was particularly concerned that a torpedo attack by enemy destroyers might cripple one of his heavy vessels.

The action began at about 0915, when *Obdurate*, one of the British destroyers, sighted three strange ships shadowing the convoy and challenged them. The vessels, German destroyers, quickly revealed their identity by opening fire. Captain Sherbrooke, the escort commander, immediately steered his ship, *Osborne*, and three other destroyers to support *Obdurate*, even though some of their guns had frozen up. The remaining destroyer, *Achates*, laid down a smoke screen to protect the convoy. *Hipper* unexpectedly loomed out of the mist and opened fire on *Achates*. Near misses riddled the destroyer with shell splinters, cutting her steam lines and reducing her speed to fifteen knots.

Suddenly, Kummetz confronted the unsettling sight of *Onslow* charging straight at his ship and then wheeling as if she were launching torpedoes. It was a mock attack, but exactly the threat the German admiral most feared. Breaking off the action, he vanished into a snow squall. Sherbrooke now ordered two of his smaller ships to run south to rejoin the convoy—where, unknown to the British, *Lützow* and her three destroyers were getting into position. The situation was desperate, and efforts to raise Force R by radio failed. *Onslow*'s navigator estimated that the cruisers were from one to four hours' steaming away. Periodically, *Hipper* emerged from the snow squall to fire at the three remaining enemy destroyers. Two of *Onslow*'s guns were now so badly frozen the breeches could only be closed by hammering on them.

At 1018, Kummetz tried to smash his way through the destroyers to the convoy. *Hipper*'s eight-inch guns landed two hits on *Onslow*, shattering her bridge and setting her on fire. Forty men were killed or wounded, including Sherbooke—the left side of his face was ripped away by splinters, and an eye hung out of its socket. Nevertheless, he continued to give orders in a calm voice. Instead of seizing the advantage and pressing on toward the convoy, Kummetz turned northeast, into another snow squall, leaving the burning *Onslow* to limp back to the convoy. This turn brought *Hipper* within range of *Bramble*, which was searching for stragglers; the minesweeper was quickly sunk, alone and unseen in the frigid Arctic.

To the south, *Lützow* and her destroyers were closing in fast on the convoy, with only a few corvettes and minesweepers to challenge them. Kummetz's plan had worked beautifully, and the defenseless convoy was at the mercy of the pocket battleship and her eleven-inch guns. Inexplicably, at 1050, Captain Rudolf Stang let the opportunity slip through his fingers when the snow obscured his target. "Impossible . . . to ascertain whether dealing with friend or foe because of the poor light, and the smoke and mist on the horizon," he wrote in his log. When *Lützow* emerged from the squall at 1115, the convoy was nowhere in sight.

In the meantime, *Hipper* made another attempt to close with the convoy. German shells ripped open the side of the crippled *Achates*, which was endeavoring to defend her charges. "We tried to block the gap with a bookcase but it fell right through," reported Ordinary Seaman Ted Cutler. "When it occurred to most of us that it was time to seek pastures new, we made for the deck. There was chaffing and singing until the end. . . ." About a hundred officers and men were lost with their ship. Kummetz shifted his guns to the other destroyers and, in an effort to get *Lützow* into the battle, signaled Stang that there were no cruisers with the convoy. Only minutes later, as if to belie his report, six-inch shells from *Sheffield* and *Jamaica*, which had arrived at last, straddled *Hipper*. Uncertain of the location of the convoy, Admiral Burnett had steered for the flashes of heavy guns.

Taken completely by surprise, Kummetz now found himself sandwiched between the British cruisers and the escort. As his ship heeled over in a turn toward this new enemy force, a British shell penetrated under her side armor and flooded a boiler room, cutting the cruiser's speed to twenty-three knots. Another set a blaze in her hangar. *Hipper*'s own fire was ineffective, because ice obscured her rangefinders, and she made off into a smoke screen laid down by her destroyers. In the melee, one of these ships, *Friedrich Eckholdt*, was sunk with all hands. *Lützow*, which had again caught sight of the convoy, opened fire at long range, slightly damaging one merchantman—the only vessel in the convoy to be hurt. In light of the "no-unnecessary-risks" order, the flagship's reduced speed, and the worsening visibility, Kummetz ordered his ships to withdraw at 1137—having snatched defeat from the jaws of victory.

The Battle of the Barents Sea was a well-earned triumph for the Royal Navy. Gallantry, dash, and initiative had paid off, and JW 51B reached Murmansk unscathed on January 3, 1943. The battered *Onslow* returned to Scapa Flow, to the cheers of the entire Home Fleet. Sherbrooke survived his wounds and was awarded the Victoria Cross.* On the other side, Kummetz maintained radio silence as his ships returned to Altenfjord, with *Hipper*'s crew fighting desperately to secure the remaining engine room as the sea poured in. Admiral Tovey noted "[t]hat an enemy force of at least one pocket battleship, one heavy cruiser and six destroyers, with all the advantages of surprise and concentration, should be held off for four hours by five destroyers and driven from the area by two 6-inch cruisers is most creditable and satisfactory."

With the hope that the Führer's anger would cool, Krancke and Captain von Puttkamer, Hitler's naval aide, arranged a five-day delay for Raeder's appearance. Göring gleefully seized upon the navy's embarrassment to point out how many of the Luftwaffe's squadrons were tied up guarding the worthless big ships. Raeder came to the meeting on January 6, 1943, with carefully prepared reports and arguments, but had no chance to use them. For more than an hour, the Führer delivered another tirade on the uselessness of the surface

---

*Remembering Nelson's blind eye, the Admiralty in due time promoted Sherbrooke to rear admiral.

navy in contrast to the U-boats, which descended upon the unhappy Grand Admiral like a hailstorm. Once again, Hitler expressed his intention of demobilizing the surface fleet.

When Hitler had finally exhausted himself, Raeder requested a private meeting. Rather than preside over the emasculation of his fleet, he tendered his resignation. Hitler changed his tone at once, but nearing sixty-seven the Grand Admiral was weary after years of battling for his service and was adamant. Raeder said he would step down on January 30—the tenth anniversary of the beginning of his service to Hitler—so that he would appear to be retiring in the normal course of events.

In a last-ditch effort to save the fleet he had brought into existence, seen plunged into war before it was ready, and never been allowed to use to its full potential, Raeder prepared a lengthy memorandum for Hitler's education and future guidance. Rather than being a drag on the war effort, he argued, the surface navy had served as both a deterrent and a threat to Britain's sea communications. It had forced the enemy to deploy resources from protection of its trade, which assisted the U-boats. The Luftwaffe's deficiencies in supporting naval operations were pointed out, and Hitler's own interference was tactfully touched upon. Raedar saved his heaviest salvo for last: in exchange for a total of fifteen coastal batteries and a token force of men, the Führer was handing the Allies their biggest naval victory of the war without even making them fight for it.

Unmoved by the logic of Raeder's appeal, Hitler promoted Karl Dönitz to Grand Admiral with instructions to liquidate the large surface ships. At fifty-one, Dönitz was at the height of his powers, and his thoughts were filled with the prospect of turning the war around for the Fatherland—virtually on his own. With Germany on the defensive everywhere, the U-boat service, which he kept under his own control, was the only military unit capable of producing victory.[*] Now that he had the power to do what he believed needed to be done, Dönitz intended to increase submarine production and fill the North Atlantic with so many U-boats that Allied shipping would be unable to avoid them.

---

[*]Eberhard Godt, his longtime chief of staff, took over day-to-day operations of the U-boat command with the rank of rear admiral.

Having won Hitler's confidence, Dönitz was determined to culti-
vate the relationship. Raeder's aloofness from the Führer and his
entourage had handicapped the Kriegsmarine in the bureaucratic
infighting with the army and Luftwaffe for resources. Dönitz met frequently with Hitler to put forward the navy's viewpoint on policy
matters and to protect it from the interference of Göring. His optimism, his concentration on achieving goals rather than harping on
the difficulties the enemy might place in his way, his commitment
and devotion, all appealed to Hitler, and he became a trusted member of the inner circle of the Third Reich.

Yet, for all his mastery of the Byzantine intricacies of Nazi politics,
Dönitz remained a naval professional. When he took up his new post,
he was convinced Hitler was right about the surface fleet, but once
he had examined the question of scrapping the ships, he concluded
this would add nothing to the war effort. As long as the big ships were
afloat, they constituted a threat to the Allies. Although he agreed to
decommission two old training ships, two light cruisers, and the damaged *Hipper*, he suggested, to Hitler's surprise, that *Tirpitz*, *Scharnhorst*, *Lützow*, *Scheer*, and *Prinz Eugen* remain in commission.
Scharnhorst would be sent to Norway to join *Lützow* and *Tirpitz* in
defending against an invasion and to be ready to attack the Russian
convoys. Hitler reluctantly approved this plan only after a bitter
argument in which Dönitz stuck to his guns. "We shall see who is
right," the Führer finally snapped. "I will give you six months to
prove that the big ships can still achieve something."

As Grand Admiral, Dönitz now had duties that extended beyond
the "tonnage war." He was responsible for the defense of thousands
of miles of coastline, from Scandinavia to the Aegean and Black seas.
Iron-ore shipments from Sweeden, troop transports and supplies for
the army in Russia, blockade runners from Japan—all had to be protected. In the Mediterranean, the navy was struggling to keep open
the supply line from Italy to the Afrika Korps, now squeezed into a
corner of Tunisia. But his eye was firmly fixed on the Battle of the
Atlantic. He quickly reached agreements with Armaments Minister
Albert Speer for increased submarine production, giving priority to
the development of new designs. "The sea war is now the U-boat war
. . ." Dönitz told his staff upon taking over his office in Berlin. "All has
to be subordinated to this main goal."

Dönitz saw much that perturbed him. Following the outstanding success of the U-boats during November 1942, in which nearly 700,000 tons of shipping had been sunk, the toll dropped to less than 350,000 tons in December, and to 261,000 tons in January 1943, the lowest monthly total since November 1941.* Even though Dönitz had more U-boats at sea than ever before, the average kill per boat had fallen, and many boats were returning to base without having sighted potential targets. Dönitz sensed something wrong. Repeatedly, B-Dienst picked up the sailing directions for convoys, but wolf packs sent to intercept them found that the ships had been rerouted away from danger. U-boat losses were also edging upward, from five each in December and January to eighteen in February.

In fact, in the second week of December, Bletchley Park, using huge computerlike calculators called *bombes*, had broken the Atlantic U-boat's Triton cipher—called the "Shark" key—after nearly a year-long blackout, and was reading it with short delays. By Christmas, OIC had detailed information on all boats at large in the North Atlantic. As Dönitz put it, "my opposite number . . . was able to take a look at my cards without my being able to take a look at his." Was improved enemy radar the culprit? New direction finders? Or was there a spy at work in U-boat headquarters? Dönitz was assured that Enigma was impregnable, and everyone except himself and Admiral Godt was placed under surveillance by Naval Intelligence. "Now it can only be me or you," the Grand Admiral joked to Godt when the inquiry ended without having found a traitor.†

In its Monthly Anti-Submarine Warfare Report for January 1943, the Admiralty warned that "the tempo is quickening, and the critical phase of the U-boat war in the Atlantic cannot be long postponed."

---

*The U-boats' greatest success in January was against Convoy TM 1, in which they sank seven of nine tankers bound from Trinidad to Gibraltar with fuel for Allied operations in the Mediterranean. The troopship *Dorchester* was also sunk, in the North Atlantic, with the loss of 605 American lives.

†In an effort to rattle submarine crews, the British established a radio transmitter which broadcast inside information about the U-boat service. Upon one occasion, the station provided the results of a soccer game between teams representing two flotillas, held that very afternoon in Bordeaux, including the names of those who scored goals. This highly effective stunt was the work of Commander Ian Fleming of naval intelligence, later the creator of James Bond.

OIC detected a steady buildup of U-boats in the "Black Pit" to the southeast of Greenland—the one area where convoys did not enjoy some form of air protection. The chief reason for the persistence of this gap was inept use of the available long-range B-24 Liberator bombers, the only planes with the "legs" to operate in mid-Atlantic. Coastal Command had only fifteen of these planes, of which about eight were operational at any given time.

The British and American air forces refused to divert Liberators from the bombing campaign against Germany. Convoy defense was left to old Hudson and Wellington bombers, with a range of six hundred miles, flying out of airfields in the United Kingdom and Iceland. Sunderland and Catalina flying boats had a longer range but carried only a limited load of depth charges. The situation was even worse on the western side of the air gap, where neither the Americans nor the Canadians had aircraft based in Newfoundland with a range of more than six hundred miles. Escort vessels had also been diverted from the North Atlantic convoys to protect ships bound for North Africa.

The pace of attacks in the "Black Pit" picked up in February as the number of U-boats in the North and Central Atlantic reached a hundred. Early in the month, HX 224 was attacked by a small wolf pack which sank two ships but lost a submarine in exchange. A following boat, U-632, sank a straggler and rescued the only survivor. Probably in a state of shock from his ordeal, he revealed that another convoy, SC 118, was following in the wake of the first. This information was flashed to headquarters, and Dönitz hastily assembled a fresh pack of twenty boats.

Over the next five days, a bitter battle raged about the convoy. In the beginning, the escorts held off the U-boats, but in the pitch blackness of February 7, the Germans managed to get in among the convoy. Kapitänleutnant Siegfried Baron von Forstner in U-402 sank six ships. Once the convoy emerged from the air gap, patrol planes from Iceland provided protection and repeatedly forced the U-boats under. But thirteen merchantmen were lost in all, while three submarines were sunk and two severely damaged. Among the vessels sunk was the troopship *Henry Mallory*, with heavy loss of life among 384 U.S. Army troops and marines bound for Iceland. One was a young soldier who had been writing to his wife of only a few weeks: "There have been a lot of explosions and firing tonight, and we don't know what is going on. We are all pretty frightened." The unfinished letter was taken from his floating corpse a few hours later.

With sufficient boats available, Dönitz had little trouble in replacing those lost, and the level of operations was maintained. Two milch cows operating north of the Azores refueled no fewer than twenty-seven U-boats, enabling them to remain on patrol. The next attacks fell on three successive outward-bound convoys, which suffered heavily. Thus, total losses for February in the North Atlantic were up substantially over the previous month, to nearly three hundred thousand tons. While it was certain that Britain would not starve nor her factories be forced to shut down, severe shortages of food and goods existed. Each individual was now entitled to only two ounces of tea per week and four ounces of bacon, the cheese ration was halved to four ounces—and all evidence indicated that March would be even worse.

The month began with the Atlantic Convoy Conference, planned at Casablanca. Admiral King opened the meeting on March 1 with the rejection of a British proposal for a single commander of the entire air-and-sea campaign in the Atlantic. Unhappy with escorts of mixed nationality, he announced, in keeping with Canadian demands for greater responsibility, that he was turning over defense of the North Atlantic convoys to the British and Canadians. The U.S. Navy would assume responsibility for the protection of convoys on the Central and South Atlantic routes, including the vital tanker traffic between the Caribbean and Britain.[*]

The North Atlantic was divided into British and Canadian operational areas, with the CHOP (Change of Operational Control) Line set at forty-seven degrees west longitude. Ships to the east of this line were controlled by Western Approaches Command; those to the west were the responsibility of the RCN, which regained the escorts sent to the Gibraltar run for training. This made Canada a senior partner in the conduct of the war and led to the creation of Canadian North-

---

[*]King's announcement, although it came as a surprise to the British and Canadians, was hardly as dire as some writers—especially on the British side—have made it sound. The American contribution to the defense of the North Atlantic convoys at this time was minimal. The Royal Navy furnished 50 percent of the escorts, the Canadians 46 percent, and the U.S. Navy only 4 percent (Figures from Morison, *History*, vol. X, p. 20, n. 10).

west Atlantic Command, Canada's first independent operational command in either world war.

To lessen the blow of this announcement, King agreed to assign a support group, consisting of the escort carrier *Bogue* and five destroyers, to join the five support groups being organized by the Royal Navy for convoy defense in the North Atlantic. And, following direct intervention by President Roosevelt, steps were taken to close the last great loophole in the Allied defenses against the U-boats. The U.S. Navy and Air Force and RAF Bomber Command finally agreed to divert Liberators to North Atlantic operations. But they would not become available until the latter part of the month—even though a harrowing U-boat blitz was already well under way.

SC 121, a slow eastbound convoy of fifty ships, was struck on March 6 by seventeen U-boats as it struggled through heavy seas and gale winds. The convoy was defended by a mixed U.S., British, and Canadian escort group that was exhausted by previous battles and in a poor state of repair. Soon, the convoy was scattered over miles of ocean. The U-boats hung on to its flanks for three days despite blustery weather, picking off stragglers one by one. Others got through the disorganized defense to sink ships in the main body. In all, thirteen vessels were lost, a quarter of the total, a victory rendered even more complete by the absence of any U-boat loses.

In contrast, HX 228, which came under fierce attack by eighteen U-boats from March 10 to 14, was protected by a better-organized defense led by Commander A. A. Tait in the destroyer *Harvester*. A shadowing U-boat was driven off when its sighting signal was picked up by HF/DF, but Kapitänleutnant Hans Trojer of *U-228* managed to penetrate the convoy. "Fired two torpedoes at two large overlapping merchant ships," he reported. "First torpedo hit. Ship disintegrated completely in flames and a vast cloud of smoke. Hundreds of steel plates flew like sheets of paper through the air. A great deal of ammunition exploded. . . ."

Following a lull, *Harvester*'s radar picked up *U-444* as she was running in to make an attack. Depth charges forced the submarine to the surface, and Commander Tait rammed and sank her. *Harvester* was badly damaged, however, and as she limped after the convoy on one engine, she was torpedoed by *U-432* and broke in half. The French corvette *Aconit* raced to the rescue and, detecting the U-boat on her sonar, blew it to the surface and ran it down. In the meantime, *Harvester* had sunk with most of her crew and a number of survivors from other ships. The battle of HX 228 ended as the convoy steamed out of the "Black Pit" and air cover forced the rest of the U-boats under. The Germans had sunk four ships plus *Harvester* and had lost two submarines.

As the convoy battle heightened, the Operations Room of Western Approaches Command, at Derby House in Liverpool, became as stormy as the Atlantic. Most of the battles were fought at night, and Admiral Sir Max Horton, the commander-in-chief since November 1942, who had his quarters in the building, often presided over the Operations Room in well-worn bathrobe and pajamas. His words were always direct. " 'Where is . . .?' 'What is?' and sometimes 'Why not?' or 'Why the Hell not?' " recalled one officer. Horton had been a submariner and was said to have a sixth sense about what a U-boat skipper would do next.[*] He regarded Admiral Dönitz, who had a similar background, as a personal adversary. For his part, Dönitz, despite his other duties, spent long hours at the large chart of the North Atlantic in his makeshift operations room in a converted hotel in the Charlottenberg district of Berlin, moving the pins that represented his boats into position for what was to become one of the greatest convoy battles of the war.

Two eastward-bound convoys had sailed from New York—SC 122, a slow convoy of sixty ships which departed on March 5, and a faster one, HX 229, of forty ships, which followed three days later.[†] B-Dienst promptly supplied Dönitz with the details on the sailing of SC 122, and he threw four wolf packs, with a total of forty-four U-boats, across its path. At the moment, the British were handicapped by a temporary blackout of Enigma as the Germans switched from a three-rotor to a four-rotor machine effective at midnight on March 8. Stormy weather permitted SC 122 to pass the first patrol line unscathed, but a homeward-bound submarine stumbled over HX 229, steaming almost in its

---

[*]As a young submarine captain in World War I, Horton torpedoed the German cruiser *Hela* in Heligoland Bight in September 1914, the first enemy ship to be sunk by a British submarine.

[†]In actuality, there were three convoys, because HX 229 had two sections.

wake south of Iceland. Unaware that he was actually dealing with two convoys, and believing these ships to be part of SC 122, Dönitz ordered the boats that had been stationed some hundred miles north, awaiting that convoy, to come south to join the assault. As luck would have it, they sighted SC 122, and both convoys came under savage attack.

HX 229 was escorted by only two destroyers and two corvettes, because numerous escort vessels were undergoing repairs of damage suffered during the brutal January and February storms. Three merchantmen were sunk on the night of March 16 as U-boats slipped through the wide gaps in the screen. The first, a Norwegian freighter, sank in only four minutes, and the explosions so lit the sky there was no need to illuminate the scene with flares. Another five ships were torpedoed the following morning. No rescue ships had been assigned to the convoy, and the escorts were faced with the bitter choice of leaving survivors to their fate or further weakening the already inadequate escort by falling behind to pick them up.

The escort accompanying SC 122 was stronger, and the attackers were beaten off at first. But rough seas reduced the usefulness of radar and sonar, and on March 17, the U-boats sank four ships. By now, the two disorganized convoys had blended together into a single large mass of ships spread out over fifty miles of ocean, surrounded by U-boats. The Germans attacked around the clock, ripping away at the convoys again and again. Reinforcements for the escort were ordered from Reykjavik, but there was some question whether they would arrive in time to make any difference.

As the U-boats assembled for the final kill, they were startled by the unexpected appearance of a Coastal Command Liberator overhead. Flying Officer Cyril Burcher had taken off from a base in Northern Ireland, some nine hundred miles away, and by stretching his fuel to the utmost had managed to reach the embattled ships. Burcher was able to remain with the convoy only a brief time, but he temporarily forced the U-boats down. That night the Germans resumed the attack, but with the coming of daylight, other planes appeared to spread their protective wings over the convoys, and Dönitz called off his wolf packs.

"This is the greatest success ever achieved in a convoy battle," the U-Boat Command jubilantly announced, claiming that thirty-two merchantmen of 187,560 tons and a destroyer had been sunk. Twenty-one ships of 141,000 tons were actually lost, none of them escorts, and a submarine was sunk in exchange—a dangerously high level of carnage. Both sides read these results erroneously. Dönitz saw them as proof of the soundness of the tonnage war and his tactics, because half the successes were scored by crews on their first operations. But he failed to note that his boats had been forced under as soon as air cover appeared. Nor did he take steps to restrict the chatter between the U-boats and headquarters, which permitted HF/DF ashore and on shipboard to get a bearing on every boat that used its radio.

For the Allies, the picture was bleak. "The Germans never came so near to disrupting communication between the New World and the Old as in the first twenty days of March 1943," observed an Admiralty staff review at the end of that fateful year. "It appeared possible that we should not be able to continue [to regard] convoy as an effective system of defense." In this brief period, ninety-seven ships totaling more than a half-million tons were sunk, mostly in the "Black Pit." Bad weather and the U-boats' need to return to base for repairs and replenishment reduced some of the pressure, but the proportion of convoyed ships lost was up 68 percent over February. There was a shortage of tankers, and oil stocks in Britain and in North Africa were falling. Some high-ranking Naval Staff officers were thinking about the unthinkable: perhaps fewer vessels would be lost if convoys were abandoned and ships were routed independently.

Yet Max Horton, on whose shoulders a considerable portion of the burden of the Atlantic battle lay, was undismayed. He felt the setbacks were being unnecessarily magnified into a herald of general defeat. Support groups and escort carriers that would close the air gap and provide reinforcements for escorts under attack by wolf packs were at last becoming available.* Now the immediate need was for additional destroyers. Upon being asked by Churchill at a meeting of the prime minister's Anti–U-Boat Warfare Committee what he

---

*Part of the delay had resulted from the Admiralty's insistence on extensive modifications to the American-built escort carriers. The advisability of some of these modifications was confirmed when the British escort carrier *Dasher* was destroyed by an explosion of aviation-gasoline vapor because of careless smoking while at anchor in the Clyde on March 27, 1943. See Roskill, *The War at Sea*, vol. III, pt. I, pp. 34–36.

was going to do about the critical situation in the Atlantic, Horton replied: "Give me fifteen destroyers and we shall beat the U-boats."

"You admirals are always asking for more and more ships," growled the prime minister, angrily banging the table, "and when you get them things get no better."

Having come fully prepared for such an encounter, Horton produced a study worked up by his staff showing what could be accomplished if the ships were made available. Churchill glanced over it, and he and Admiral Harold Stark, commander of U.S. Navy Forces in Europe, conferred briefly. Finally, he turned to Horton and said: "You can have your fifteen destroyers; we shall have to stop the Russian convoys for the present."*

By the end of March, five support groups were either formed or forming, with two built around the British escort carriers *Biter* and *Archer*. They were joined by a sixth group, centered on the U.S. escort carrier *Bogue* and the five destroyers that had been promised by Admiral King at the Washington conference. These ships were the first installment of continuous air cover for trans-Atlantic convoys. SC 123 and HX 230, which were protected by *Bogue* and its group, lost only a single straggler. Admiral Dönitz took note of this development. "On March 26 an aircraft carrier was observed inside the screen of a westbound convoy. Its aircraft foiled the attempts of the U-boats to close the convoy."

Both sides regarded April and May as the crisis of the Atlantic battle. There was little argument among the British that a repetition of the horrendous losses of March would be a clear-cut signal that the campaign had been lost—that convoys were not the answer to attacks by modern submarines. On the other side, Dönitz pressed every effort to get more boats to sea and prodded his commanders to even more aggressive action. The number of submarines at sea reached a peak, with 128 boats operational. But the tonnage sunk was well down from

---

*Stalin objected vehemently to the suspension of Russian convoys, but Churchill was able to take this politically volatile step because the Russian victory at Stalingrad had reduced German pressure and a new and less dangerous overland supply route to the Soviet Union had been opened through Iran. In any event, the coming of summer and perpetual daylight in the Arctic seas would have led to a stand-down.

February's total. The Germans sank thirty-nine merchantmen total-ing 235,000 tons in March, and lost fifteen submarines. And, despite Dönitz's exhortations, there were signs of a decline in the efficiency and morale of his crews. Inexperienced commanders now outnum-bered veterans, and some betrayed signs of timidity, particularly fear of air attack, as well as a tendency to overestimate the number of their kills.

The pattern for the future was set by HX 231, a convoy of sixty-one ships under the protection of a six-ship escort led by Commander Peter Gretton, an experienced escort leader. The convoy was sighted on April 4 to the south of Greenland, and Dönitz deployed a wolf pack of twenty boats against it. Heavy weather made it impossible to provide more than intermittent air cover, and over the next two days a battle raged about the convoy. Repeated attacks by the U-boats were beaten off as the escort's HF/DF zeroed in on their radio trans-missions. The Germans sank only two ships from the convoy and picked off four stragglers. Two U-boats were sunk and several were damaged, a rate of exchange the Germans could not afford. In the seven following convoys, the ratio was one merchantman sunk for each U-boat destroyed. Such statistics inspired an Admiralty report in the first week of May which prophetically stated:

> Historians of this war are likely to single out the months of April and May 1943 as the critical period during which strength began to ebb away from the German U-boat offensive—not because of lower figures of shipping or higher numbers of U-boats sunk, but because for the first time U-boats failed to press home their attacks on convoys. . . .

The decline of German fortunes in the North Atlantic was brutally confirmed by a week-long battle raging at that very moment about ONS 5, a westbound convoy of forty-three ships. On April 29, a week after it sailed from Liverpool shepherded by Gretton in the old destroyer *Duncan*, along with another destroyer, the frigate *Tay*, four corvettes, and two rescue trawlers, the convoy was sighted by a U-boat about five hundred miles southeast of Greenland. Bad weather grounded air patrols, and Dönitz ordered fourteen boats to the area. They made repeated night assaults on the convoy. Five attacks were driven off by the escort, and two submarines were damaged, but a freighter was torpedoed in a daylight submerged attack the following day. The situation was being closely watched by Admiral Horton and a support group of five destroyers was dispatched from St. John's, Newfoundland, to reinforce the ocean escort. They joined the convoy on May 2.

Judging chances for success in such poor weather to be small, Dönitz called off the attack on ONS 5 and ordered his boats to the southwest to join another pack, which was gathering for an assault on SC 128. Unable to refuel the short-legged *Duncan* from an accompanying tanker because of foul weather, Gretton was forced to leave the convoy along with another fuel-short destroyer and head directly into St. John's. He handed over command to Lieutenant Commander R. E. Sherwood in *Tay*. The following day, three more escort vessels had to run into port to refill their tanks. To replace them, Horton dispatched another support group, composed of a sloop, three frigates, and a former U.S. Coast Guard cutter, but it would take several days to arrive. That same day, the weather began to moderate, and RCAF flying boats sighted and attacked several U-boats closing in on the convoy, sinking one.

After SC 128 passed through the German patrol lines without being detected, an angry Dönitz mobilized forty U-boats and sent them against ONS 5. The escort was now reduced to *Tay*, two destroyers, and four corvettes—odds of six to one. With the coming of darkness on May 4, the Germans launched their onslaught and sank five vessels during a night of attack and counterattack. Next day, the corvette *Pink* rounded up a half-dozen stragglers into a little convoy of its own and sank a U-boat for good measure. Even so, the crews of the escorts were worn out by day after day of frightful weather followed by sleepless nights as they tried to defend their charges.

The U-boats went on the attack again on the evening of May 5. "Make haste, as there are forty of you there will be nothing of the convoy left," Dönitz radioed. Fortunately for the convoy, it was joined that night by the support group dispatched from St. John's. Thick fog also drifted in, shrouding the ships from sight and giving the radar-equipped escorts an advantage. "About twenty-four attacks took place from every direction except dead ahead," Commander Sherwood, the escort leader, reported, and added with understatement, "[T]he situation was confused." Not only were these attacks repulsed, but four U-boats were sunk. The following day, ONS 5 came within range of an air umbrella flying from Newfoundland, and a frustrated Dönitz broke off the battle.

Twelve merchant ships had been sunk but, far more important, the Germans lost nine U-boats, including two that collided with each other—more than in any convoy battle of the w⌐r. Another five had been badly damaged by relentless surface and air attacks. Admiral Dönitz attributed these substantial losses to the efficiency of enemy radar, which could not be picked up by the U- boats' search receivers; such new weapons as the Hedgehog and heavier depth charges; the increasing presence of very-long-range aircraft over the convoys; and the vulnerability of the ponderous Type IX boats as compared to the older, more maneuverable Type VIIC class. He failed to grasp the tactical importance of HF/DF and Ultra signals intelligence in the defeat of his wolf packs.

Events were to prove that the triumph of ONS 5's escort was no fluke. Four days later, a wolf pack of thirty-six U-boats sank only five ships from Convoys HX 237 and SC 129 against the loss of four submarines. Six boats were lost by a pack that attacked SC 130 without sinking a single merchantman.* This was the last North Atlantic convoy to be seriously menaced. U-boats were now being sunk at an average rate of more than one a day, with the number failing to return from patrol in May reaching a staggering forty-one—a figure as shocking to the U-Boat Command as it was unprecedented. Dönitz had already conceded defeat. "The overwhelming superiority achieved by the enemy defense was finally proved beyond dispute . . . ," he declared. On May 24 he called off the offensive against the Atlantic convoys. "We had lost the Battle of the Atlantic," the admiral later acknowledged.

Could the Germans have won the Battle of the Atlantic?

In the final analysis, Dönitz was battling the productive capacity of American shipyards rather than the convoy escorts. The Allied victory was won as much on the building ways as on the stormy waters

---

*U-954 was lost with all hands, including Leutnant zur See Peter Dönitz, the admiral's twenty-year-old younger son. Dönitz showed no emotion in public when informed of his son's death.

of the Atlantic—by the simple fact that, after July 1942, American workers produced merchant ships faster than Dönitz's U-boats could sink them.* Germany's only chance to bring Britain to her knees by severing her maritime lifelines had been in the early years of the war, when antisubmarine-warfare techniques were still primitive, and before America's prodigious industrial prowess had come into play—not later than mid-1941. After that, the demands of the Russian war made it impossible for Germany to allocate enough resources to win the U-boat campaign.

This window of opportunity was missed by the failure to have enough submarines in commission when the war began. The Germans never managed to get more than twenty U-boats into the Atlantic at any one time in the first fifteen months of the conflict. Given this feeble effort, plus Hitler's halfhearted support of the submarine-construction program, the inadequate number of surface ships and aircraft available to reinforce the U-boats, and Britain's early adoption of convoys, Dönitz had no real hope of eliminating British merchant shipping. By the time the Führer finally put his full support behind the U-boat campaign, Allied air and naval forces—and shipbuilders—had already reached high levels of efficiency. Hitler made numerous mistakes during the war, but none was more grievous than his failure to start with an adequate submarine program.

"One shudders to think what would have happened if the Germans before the war had not been so foolish as to build up a third-rate heavy ship force at the expense of their really decisive arm, the U-boat service," observed Air Marshal Sir John Slessor, chief of Coastal Command. And Churchill noted: "The submarine boat attack was our worst evil. It would have been wise for the Germans to stake all on it."

Dönitz was a fine tactician, but once the United States had entered the conflict, his vaunted "tonnage war" was essentially irrelevant. One need consider only a single set of statistics to gauge the truth of this statement. In the years between 1942 and 1945, the Allies lost 12,590,000 tons of shipping. But during the same period, their mer-

---

*One of the by-products of this enormous shipbuilding campaign was a break in the color barrier. The need for crews led to the hiring of large numbers of African Americans, and the National Maritime Union insisted they not be segregated.

chant fleet rose from thirty-two million tons to fifty-four million. The effort required to make headway against such a margin was far beyond the capabilities and resources of the U-boat command.

This is not to deny that the Atlantic battle was a bitter, hard-fought struggle. Hindsight makes it clear that an Allied victory was inevitable, but those on both sides doing the fighting—and dying— were unaware of this, and there were moments when the submarine offensive came close to isolating Britain. As Churchill noted, "The Battle of the Atlantic was the dominating factor all through the war. Never for one moment could we forget that everything happening elsewhere, on land, at sea, or in the air, depended ultimately on its outcome. . . ."

Dönitz's withdrawal of his boats from the North Atlantic hardly meant the end of the U-boat war, however. "Again and again," the admiral wrote, "we debated whether a continuation of the campaign was justified in the face of these heavy losses. But in view of the vast enemy forces which our U-boat boats were tying down, we came always to the same conclusion. The U-boat campaign must be continued with the forces available. Losses which bear no relation to the success achieved must be accepted, bitter though they are." So Dönitz shifted his sights to the Central Atlantic, where the sea was teeming with supply ships and transports destined for the invasion of Sicily and there was another air gap. The U.S. Navy, which had the responsibility for the defense of these ships, was ready for him, however.

Admiral King may have been too much the nationalist, and ill-suited by prejudice and personality to conduct coalition war, but he understood the basic strategy, tactics, and technology needed to win the struggle against the U-boats. Immediately after the Atlantic Convoy Conference in March 1943, he unified the navy's haphazardly organized ocean-escort and antisubmarine-warfare activities into a central command designated the Tenth Fleet. King took personal command, but daily operations were run by Rear Admiral Francis S. Low, his chief of staff. The Tenth Fleet, with no ships of its own, directed the operations of the hunter-killer groups composed of escort carriers, destroyers, and destroyer escorts assigned to the Atlantic Fleet.

One of the Tenth Fleet's key elements was a strong intelligence unit, OP-20G, headed by Commander Kenneth A. Knowles, an American version of OIC that had its own Submarine Tracking Room, with ready access to Ultra and HF/DF "fixes." The battle between the U.S. Navy and Army over control of land-based long-range aircraft was also resolved by a simple "horse trade" brokered by President Roosevelt in which the army got out of ASW by exchanging its old Liberators for an equal number of navy B-24s that had just come off the production line and were as yet unmodified to hunt submarines.

The Germans began the mid-Atlantic campaign on June 4, 1943 when a seventeen-boat wolf pack attacked Convoy GUS 7A. Fore-warned by Ultra, the escort carrier *Bogue* was on the prowl, and its Avengers sank one U-boat while keeping the rest at bay. Over the next three weeks, these boats attacked successive convoys, but the carriers always seemed to be on hand to thwart them. With his patrol lines constantly disrupted, a frustrated Dönitz withdrew the U-boats after they had succeeded in picking off only a single ship at the cost of two submarines—one of them a milch cow.

Over the next three months, escort carriers *Bogue*, *Santee*, *Card*, and *Core* and their supporting destroyers ranged over the Central Atlantic, their target the milch cows which sustained U-boat operations. While their primary role was to protect convoys, carriers were permitted to operate independently against wolf packs as long as they were able get back to the convoy before the Germans could strike. Having access to Ultra, these hunter-killer groups were able to pinpoint the milch cows with deadly accuracy. Within a span of little more than three months, sixteen attack U-boats and eight submarine tankers were destroyed while only one ship in a convoy defended by escort carriers was lost.

Some of these battles recalled the ship-to-ship duels of an earlier age. In one of the most bizarre actions of the war, a blimp fought it out with a surfaced U-boat. Lighter-than-air enthusiasts boasted of the excellent record of the blimp as a deterrent—none of the ships escorted by airships fell victim to a direct submarine attack—but no blimp had made an unassisted kill of a U-boat. Lieutenant N. K. Grills of the airship *K-34* decided to fill this blank when he sighted *U-134* off the Florida keys on June 18, 1943.

Before the blimp could get into position to drop her depth charges, however, the Germans unlimbered their guns and poured hot lead into her. Grills proceeded with the attack, even though his craft was lurching crazily from the impact of enemy fire. Shells passed through the airship's envelope without exploding but sliced it open, and as the helium drained out, it lost altitude. Suddenly, a change of wind blew *K-34* over the U-boat, and Grills tried to drop his depth charges. Nothing happened: the releasing gear had jammed. The blimp slowly settled into the sea, and *U-134* sailed away, to be sunk later by British aircraft.

On the night of November 1, the four-piper *Borie*, part of a hunter-killer group working with the escort carrier *Block Island*, was dispatched to search out a submarine that had attacked a Gibraltar-bound convoy. Sonar contact was made, and *U-405* was blown to the surface by a heavy pattern of depth charges. Lieutenant Charles H. Hutchins, the destroyer's captain, rammed the U-boat and ran *Borie*'s bow right up on her foredeck, locking the two vessels together in a deadly embrace. Unable to depress their four-inch guns enough to hit the enemy craft, *Borie*'s crew resorted to anything they could get their hands on: machine guns, rifles, shotguns, and Very pistols. Someone threw a sheath knife, which caught a German sailor in the stomach; others dropped empty shell cases on the heads of the enemy. The pounding and grinding of the two steel hulls opened up the old destroyer's plates, and she began taking on water.

After ten minutes of fury, the U-boat managed to wrench free. Too battered to submerge, she tried to make a getaway on the surface. Hutchins signaled for flank speed, and the engine-room gang, working in water up to their chests, responded. Like tomcats in the dark, the two vessels circled each other, trying to ram. By skillful maneuvering, Hutchins got into position to straddle *U-405* with a brace of depth charges, which damaged her so badly the crew abandoned ship. *Borie* was in bad shape, too, and went down in heavy seas with a loss of twenty-seven men.

Severe losses were also suffered by the U-boats in the Bay of Biscay, where Coastal Command launched an offensive against submarines passing to and from their bases. Previous efforts to choke off this traffic had produced meager results, because the U-boats' Metox receivers detected Allied planes using radar in time for them to crash-dive. But the patrol planes were now being fitted with new radar that could not be detected by Metox. It was used in conjunction with the Leigh Light, an eighty-million-candlepower searchlight, to make sudden, blinding night attacks from the air on U-boats that had surfaced to recharge their batteries. Shaken, Dönitz committed a tactical blunder. Boats transiting the Bay of Biscay were ordered to surface and recharge batteries in daylight. If surprised and unable to dive, they were to fight back with newly installed flak batteries.

These "stay-up-and-fight" tactics were briefly effective against lone Allied aircraft. Encouraged, Dönitz ordered his boats to cross the bay in groups for mutual support. Reviving the Q-ship, he sent out heavily armed U-boats to try to decoy unsuspecting planes into attacking. But they were met with simultaneous attacks from both sea and air, and the Bay of Biscay soon became the U-boats' own "Black Pit." In one six-day period, nine U-boats were sunk by a combination of British, American, and Australian planes and a support group of five sloops commanded by Captain Frederick J. Walker, the ace submarine-killer. Dönitz was forced to rescind his "stay-up-and-fight" order, and with the Bay of Biscay all but closed by Allied blockade, departures from the Biscay bases were suspended. Later, he resumed sailings by routing the U-boats through Spanish waters. In all, the escorts accounted for twenty-eight U-boats in the Bay of Biscay offensive, reducing the effectiveness and morale of Dönitz's crews.

Grand Admiral Erich Raeder, commander-in-chief
of the Kriegsmarine, during an inspection trip to
Norway in 1942.   (Naval Historical Center)

Admiral of the Fleet Sir Dudley Pound, the First
Sea Lord and operational chief of the Royal Navy.
(Naval Historical Center)

The last Führer. Grand Admiral Karl
Dönitz, commander of German U-boats,
and Adolf Hitler's successor as head of
the Nazi state. (National Archives)

The German pocket battleship
Admiral Graf Spee. This view shows
her stern torpedo tubes. The pocket
battleships were really large cruisers.
(Naval Historical Center)

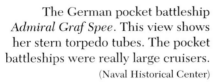

"Stringbags." Although
the Fairey Swordfish
torpedo plane was already
obsolescent when World
War II broke out, it
played a major role in
British naval operations.
(U.S. Naval Institute)

Sea Wolves. Type VIIC U-boats returning to base at Narvik, Norway, following
the devastating attack upon Convoy PQ 17. The Type VIIC boats were the most
widely used German submarine.
(Naval Historical Center)

Kapitänleutnant Günther Prien being greeted by Admiral Alfred Saalwachter,
commander of Navy Group West (center) and Grand Admiral Erich Raeder after sinking
the British battleship *Royal Oak* in the supposedly impenetrable base at Scapa Flow.
(U.S. Naval Institute)

Into captivity. Fregattenkapitan Otto Kretschmer, Germany's leading U-boat ace of World War II, leaving the British destroyer *Walker* after his capture in March 1941. Kretschmer spent the rest of the war in a prison camp in Canada. He rose to admiral in the West German navy.
(U.S. Naval Institute)

"Cheap and nasty." The Flower-class corvette *Lotus*. Note the "acoustic hammer" fitted to the bow for exploding mines at a safe distance using sound waves.
(Naval Historical Center)

Admiral Alexander B. Cunningham, commander-in-chief of the Royal Navy's Mediterranean Fleet.
(National Archives)

Italian battleships *Littorio* (foreground) and *Vittorio Veneto* at gunnery practice in 1940.
(Naval Historical Center)

OTENCIA MARÍTIMA ALEMANA

The German battleship
Bismarck. This picture,
published in a Spanish
magazine, shows the vessel's
immense bulk, which made
her a steady gun platform.
(Naval Historical Center)

Admiral Ernest J. King,
U.S. chief of naval operations.
(Naval Historical Center)

Admiral Isoroku Yamamoto, who planned
the surprise attack on Pearl Harbor and
was commander-in-chief of the Imperial
Japanese Navy's Combined Fleet.
(Naval Historical Center)

Japanese photograph of Battleship Row during the Pearl Harbor attack.
Left to right in foreground, *Nevada*, repair ship *Vestal* alongside *Arizona*, *West Virginia* alongside *Tennessee*, *Oklahoma* alongside *Maryland*, oiler *Neosho* and *California* on the far right. Note shock waves in the water and torpedo tracks.
(Naval Historical Center)

President Roosevelt and his Pacific commanders, General Douglas MacArthur (left) and Admiral Chester W. Nimitz, during a presidential visit to Pearl Harbor in July 1944.
(Naval Historical Center)

Admiral Raymond A. Spruance.
(National Archives)

Admiral William F. Halsey in deep meditation on the bridge of his flagship, *New Jersey*.
(National Archives)

Vice-Admiral Marc A. Mitscher, commander of the fast carriers, in a pensive moment
during the Battle of the Philippine Sea in June 1944.
(Naval Historical Center)

Admiral Jisaburo Ozawa, the ablest of the
Imperial Navy's carrier admirals.
(Naval Historical Center)

Vice-Admiral Takeo Kurita,
commander of the Japanese "center force"
at the Battle of Leyte Gulf.
(Naval Historical Center)

Zero. A captured A6M5, an improved model of the famous Zero fighter,
photographed in September 1944. The U.S. insignia, which had been painted
over the original Japanese markings, has also been painted over.

(National Archives)

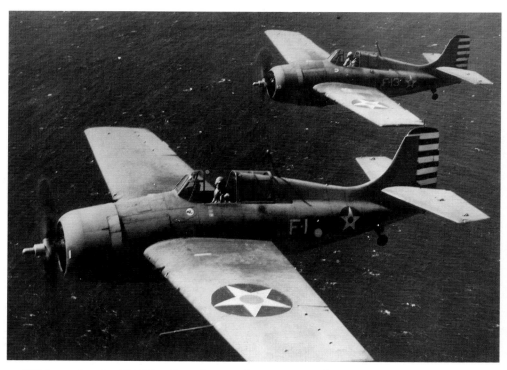

Wildcats. A pair of F4F3s, flown by two famous navy pilots, Lieutenant Commander
John H. Thach (in F-1) and Lieutenant Edward H. O'Hare (F-13), in April 1942.
Although inferior to the Zero in rate of climb and maneuverability,
the F4F managed to hold its own in air battles.

(National Archives)

SBD Dauntless over Wake Island in October 1943. The Dauntless was
the best carrier dive-bomber of the war.
(National Archives)

Hellcat. An F6F fighter
is readied for take off from
Yorktown late in 1943.
Note the auxiliary fuel tank
to extend the plane's range.
The Hellcat was the finest
navy fighter of the war.
(National Archives)

The fleet submarine
Tang, one of the
most successful U.S.
submarines. *Tang*
was lost after being
hit by one of her
own torpedoes.
(Naval Historical Center)

Commander Richard
H. O'Kane, *Tang*'s
commanding officer.
(National Archives)

Vice-Admiral Charles A. Lockwood, commander of U.S. submarines in the Pacific. Lockwood's boats all but wiped out Japan's maritime trade.
(Naval Historical Center)

To the sands of Iwo Jima. U.S. marines inch up the beach after landing on Iwo on February 19, 1945. Digging in was almost impossible in the loose volcanic sand. Mount Suribachi looms in the background.

(National Archives)

Franklin burning and listing after being hit by a Japanese air attack while operating off the coast of Japan on March 19, 1945. Despite heavy damage and casualties—724 officers and men were killed—the carrier survived.
(National Archives)

The Japanese frigate *Kaibokan* capsizes after being hit by U.S. Air Force B-25s off Amoy, China, on April 6, 1945. Note the men clambering down the ship's side and into the water.
(U.S. Air Force Photo)

The Japanese superbattleship *Yamato* under attack by U.S. Navy planes in the East China Sea on April 7, 1945. She sank after being hit by ten torpedoes and five bombs.

(National Archives)

A marine Corsair fires a salvo of eight rockets at a Japanese position on Okinawa early in June 1944. The plane from which this photograph was taken was knocked out of control by rocket blast and almost crashed.

(Marine Corps Photo)

Part of the fleet that came to stay. The destroyer *Hazelwood* after being struck
by a kamikaze off Okinawa on April 29, 1945. Forty-five officers and men
were killed, but the ship survived.

(National Archives)

•

CHAPTER 13

"A Most
God-Almighty Bang"

Tossing seas made visibility difficult, as the American destroyer *Bristol* edged carefully toward the southern tip of Sicily in the evening darkness on July 9, 1943. Commander J. A. Glick, her skipper, spotted a dark shape in the water only a few hundred yards off and bore down on it. Forbidden to use his radio or blinker, he hailed "Hello!" An English voice replied with a cheery, "Hel-lo!" It was the Royal Navy submarine *Safari*. Glick took a bearing on the craft, and *Bristol* assumed her designated position, as zero hour approached for Operation Husky, the invasion of Sicily, which was to begin at 0245 the next morning.

The invasion had been pushed ahead following the Axis surrender in North Africa on May 11. Despite valiant efforts by the Italian navy to supply the troops penned into a corner of Tunisia, the remnants of the Afrika Korps were gradually chewed up by the Allied armies. Between November 1942 and May 1943, the Italians lost twenty-eight destroyers and motor-torpedo boats in defending their African convoys. Hitler was urged to evacuate the 250,000 troops—three-quarters of them German—before it was too late, but he insisted on fighting to the bitter end. Reinforcing failure, he sent in some of the German army's finest units to be destroyed. Only a few days before the final curtain fell in Africa, a destroyer was sunk as it tried to land elements of the crack Hermann Göring Division.

Husky was an even more massive operation than Torch. Early in July, the jampacked harbors of North Africa emptied as an armada of about 2,600 ships and landing craft stood out into the Mediterranean and headed for Sicily with some 170,000 American, British, and Canadian troops on board. The island was defended by 300,000 Italian troops stiffened by 50,000 Germans. Once again, General Eisenhower was in supreme command, with Admiral Cunningham designated naval chief. A Western Naval Task Force commanded by Vice-Admiral Hewitt was to put the American Seventh Army (Lieutenant General George S. Patton) ashore on the southeast coast of the island. The British Eighth Army (Lieutenant General Bernard L. Montgomery) was to be landed on the American right flank by an Eastern Naval Task Force led by Vice-Admiral Sir Bertram Ramsay of Dunkirk fame. Force H, six British battleships and two fleet carriers under Vice-Admiral Sir Algernon V. Willis, was to prevent interference by the Italian fleet.

Planning for Husky and cooperation among the various services left something to be desired, however. The top commanders turned over most of the detailed planning to their staffs. Too often they executed decisions without adequate knowledge of the situation. Eisenhower failed to object when the air commander, Lieutenant General Carl A. Spaatz of the U.S. Army Air Force, decided to fight his own war. Wedded to the concept of strategic air operations, he planned to "seal off the battlefield" by saturation bombing of targets in Italy rather than supplying close air support for the landing. And, despite objections from the naval commanders, the generals, as in North Africa, rejected preparatory naval bombardments and insisted on making the landings in darkness with the hope of achieving surprise. There was to be no shelling unless the enemy opened up first. Moreover, no efforts were made to seal the Strait of Messina—only 2.5 miles wide at its narrowest part—to cut the main Axis supply line and escape route to the mainland. It was held to be beyond the range of Allied fighters, and no escort carriers were available.

On the Axis side, there was some question whether the Allied objective was Sicily or Greece. To confuse the enemy further, British intelligence adopted a macabre subtefuge. The corpse of a "Major William Martin" of the Royal Marines washed ashore on the Spanish coast with faked secret documents indicating that the main assault would come in Greece, with a secondary landing in Sardinia. These were permitted to fall into the hands of German agents. Hitler and the High Command fell for the ruse and ordered valuable troops and torpedo boats to Greece and Sardinia.

Unlike in Torch, the Allied troops had received adequate training, and for the first time large landing craft such as the Landing Ship Tank (LST), Landing Craft Tank (LCT), and Landing Craft Infantry (LCI) were available in numbers, which permitted new landing techniques to be introduced. The largest of these craft was the diesel-powered LST, a three-hundred-foot seagoing vessel that could carry over two thousand tons of cargo in its cavernous interior. It was run right up on the beach, and troops and equipment were discharged through the large doors in the bow. The LCI, smaller than the LST, discharged its troops down gangways lowered from the bow. The LCT was a barge-like craft with a ramp. Previously, troops were carried to the scene of action in transports and then transferred to landing craft, a technique called "ship-to-shore assault." For Husky, they were now brought directly to the beaches from ports of embarkation, a process known as "shore-to-shore assault," which was considerably less dangerous.

The Allied armada took a severe buffeting from the turbulent sea and high winds as it approached Sicily, and there were fears that the landings might have to be called off. But conditions moderated after midnight, and Hewitt and Ramsay decided to proceed as planned. In fact, the foul weather contributed to the success of the assault. The defenders relaxed their precautions in the belief that, as Cunningham said, "tonight at any rate, they can't come. But they were wrong: for, in spite of all that the sea and wind could do, they came." A drop of airborne troops, some of them carried out to sea by the high winds, spoiled any attempt at tactical surprise, however.

Searchlights flashed across the black water, picking out landing craft as they neared the shore, and machine guns crackled from the darkness. As falling shells raised geysers in the water about the boats, the supporting cruisers, destroyers, and rocket-firing landing craft opened up on enemy gun emplacements. By daylight, the Allied troops were firmly established ashore. Several airfields were over-run, and Syracuse was captured on D+1, before the port facilities could be destroyed. Because of the lack of tactical air support, the ships were called upon repeatedly to bombard shore positions and deal with enemy tank columns trying to crash through to the beaches.

It should have been convincing evidence to skeptical generals of the effectiveness of naval gunfire.

Upon one occasion, General Patton watched through field glasses from a command post as sixty Axis tanks rolled across a flat plain toward his bridgehead at Gela. He had no antitank guns to halt them, but there was a shore-based naval gunfire-control party nearby. "If you can connect with your Goddamn Navy, tell them for God's sake to drop some shell fire on the road," he ordered. Within minutes, salvos from the six-inch guns of the cruiser *Boise* were exploding among the tanks, halting their advance.

Although the Italian fleet made no attempt to interfere with operations, wave after wave of German dive-bombers attacked the invasion fleet. The ships were practically without air support, and a destroyer and several freighters were sunk. An ammunition ship exploded late in the afternoon of D+1 with a shattering roar and burned for hours afterward. That evening, General Spaatz chose to send in 144 C-47 transports carrying reinforcements for the 82nd Airborne Division. Admiral Hewitt tried to alert the ships of the incoming flight, but it was already too late. The planes arrived over the fleet while a German air attack was in progress. Tracers and smoke from the burning ammunition ship covered everything. Recognition signals were useless and the excited gunners shot down twenty-two of the transports before firing ceased.

Although the campaign for Sicily was expected to be brief and decisive, the Germans fought hard—the Italians, having had their fill of the war, offered token resistance—and it took thirty-eight days to bring the operation to a conclusion. After some initial delays, Patton broke out of the beachhead and captured Palermo on July 22 following a spectacular advance. Thrusting eastward, he skillfully used Allied naval superiority to leapfrog enemy positions as he headed for the Strait of Messina. Warships were kept busy answering calls for shore bombardment and anti-aircraft cover, opening up ports, and dealing with enemy submarines, eleven of which were sunk.

The Eighth Army met more stubborn resistance in the mountainous country along the east coast, where the enemy fought a delaying action to cover the escape of their forces from the island. Although ships stood by ready to lift off Montgomery's troops and land them behind the enemy, Admiral Cunningham bitterly noted that the general had failed to learn from Patton's example. The failure of the Eighth Army to get to the strait on time allowed a hundred thousand Axis troops to withdraw in good order across the waterway to the tip of the Italian boot with their tanks, guns, and equipment. Force H made no attempt to reduce the batteries on both sides of the passage until the evacuation was well under way. Apparently, the British admirals could not shake the memory of the loss of the heavy ships sent to bombard the batteries in the Dardanelles in 1915. Thus, Sicily was a hollow victory.

In May, Churchill and Roosevelt had met in Washington, where the British pressed for an invasion of Italy after the conquest of Sicily. Both General Marshall and Admiral King again warned against being "sucked" into a Mediterranean quagmire that would delay Operation Overlord, as the cross-Channel invasion of Europe was now designated. The worst fears of the Americans appeared confirmed when the British took the position that Overlord could not take place until 1945 or 1946. If the invasion of France was delayed, Marshall pointedly warned Churchill, the United States would redeploy its main military-and-naval strength to the Pacific. A rupture was avoided when the British accepted May 1, 1944, as a target date for Overlord and the Americans agreed to allow circumstances to determine whether or not there should be an invasion of Italy.

Events in Italy forced the Allies' hand. The Italians were heartily sick of the war into which Mussolini had forced them, and on July 25 King Victor Emmanuel III and the Fascist Grand Council screwed up their courage and deposed him.* The new regime began secret negotiations with the Allies for an armistice while promising the Germans to continue fighting. But their erstwhile ally distrusted these promises, and rushed in troops to occupy the country. The Allies countered with a double-pronged invasion of the mainland—and thus, without having a clear idea of their objectives, committed themselves to a campaign in Italy.

---

*Mussolini, though placed under arrest and imprisoned in the Abruzzi mountains, was freed by German commandos. He set up a puppet Fascist regime in northern Italy, but when German defenses in the area collapsed, he was captured by communist partisans and shot on April 28, 1945, along with his mistress.

On September 3, the Eighth Army crossed over from Messina, supported by a heavy bombardment by the battleships of Force H. Meeting only weak opposition because the bulk of the German forces were redeploying about Naples, Montgomery headed northward through rugged country. Six days later, on September 9, the newly organized half-American, half-British Fifth Army, under the command of an American general, Mark Clark, followed up with an assault on the Gulf of Salerno, approximately twenty miles south of Naples.* Naples, with its valuable port, was the goal of the operation, but Salerno was chosen for the landing because it was just within the range of fighters based in Sicily. Even so, the planes would be able to remain over the battle zone for only twenty minutes, so four British escort carriers were assigned to provide air cover until airfields could be captured. En route to the landing, Eisenhower broadcast the news that Italy had surrendered, and all hands expected a walkover at Salerno.

They were in for an unpleasant surprise. Repeating the error of the North African invasion, Clark elected to forgo a preliminary naval bombardment with the hope of attaining surprise, despite the vehement protests of Admiral Hewitt, the amphibious commander. "Any officer with a pair of dividers could figure out that the Gulf of Salerno was the northernmost practicable landing place for the Allies," he declared.

The Germans fiercely resisted the landing; beachheads were established only with difficulty and precariously held. Withering fire prevented some LSTs from unloading their tanks, and some vessels were blown up by mines and blasted out of the water by the dreaded German eighty-eight millimeter guns. Marauding fighters strafed and bombed the invaders, and radio-directed glide bombs controlled by accompanying aircraft were launched against the fleet. Two American cruisers, *Savannah* and *Philadelphia*, and the British *Uganda* were hit by these devices. The carrier planes suffered heavy losses; by the time engineers carved out a rough emergency airstrip for land-based fighters on D+2, only about a quarter were still operational.

---

*Admiral Cunningham pressed for a landing closer to Rome, and the German Admiral Ruge has said the Allies were overcautious in not making such a landing in view of the disorganized state of Axis forces (Ruge, *Der Seekrieg*, p. 336).

The crisis came on September 13, and for a time it appeared as if the Fifth Army would be thrown back into the sea. There was a five-mile gap between the British and American forces, and the Germans mounted a series of furious counterattacks designed to exploit it. Clark asked Hewitt to prepare plans for evacuating troops from one sector of the bridgehead to another—a reversal of the first magnitude. The admiral called in his cruisers and destroyers and, supported by the British battleships *Warspite* and *Valiant*, with *Nelson* and *Rodney* in the offing, unleashed a heavy bombardment against German gun batteries, troop concentrations, and tanks, which succeeded in halting the enemy thrusts. One German officer reported:

> The advancing troops had to endure the most severe heavy fire that had yet been experienced—the naval gunfire from at least 16 to 18 battleships, cruisers and large destroyers lying in the roadstead. With astonishing precision and freedom of maneuver these ships shot with very overwhelming effect at every target spotted.

Not long after, the Eighth Army plodded up from the south to link up with the beachhead, and the enemy withdrew northward. On October 1, three weeks after the Salerno landing, Allied troops entered Naples. Naval salvage teams quickly went to work clearing the port and waterfront of the destruction left behind by the Germans. They did their work so well that by the end of the year more tonnage was being discharged at Naples than in peace time.

One of the benefits of the Italian surrender was the passing of much of the Italian fleet into Allied hands, despite German efforts to prevent it. The new battleship *Roma* was sunk by a guided bomb on its way to give itself up, with the loss of fourteen hundred crewmen, but most of these vessels arrived at their destinations unharmed. In all, five battleships, eight cruisers, seven destroyers, forty submarines, and a hundred merchantmen were turned over to the Allies. With a fine Nelsonian flourish, Admiral Cunningham signaled the Admiralty: "Be pleased to inform Their Lordships that the Italian Battle Fleet now lies under the guns of the fortress of Malta."

The frozen silence of Altenfjord was ruptured on the afternoon of Christmas Day 1943 by the rattle of anchor chains as *Scharnhorst* emerged from a cocoon of antitorpedo nets. Holiday decorations and

Christmas trees thrown over the side, she stood out to sea at 1900 in company with five destroyers. "The long slender shadow of the handsomely proportioned ship glided past and slowly gathered speed, without light, without sound," said one observer. "Beautiful and lethal, she came speeding from her mountain lair to hunt in the open."

Nearly a year had passed since the Barents Sea battle, and at Stalin's urging, the British had resumed the Russian convoys the previous month. *Scharnhorst* was the only big ship available when Grand Admiral Dönitz decided to strike these convoys and revenge the humiliation at the Barents Sea debacle. The rapidly deteriorating situation in Russia contributed to the descision. The Germans had suffered a gigantic defeat in a great tank battle at Kursk in the summer of 1943, and Dönitz thought the Kriegsmarine had to do something to help the army in its time of peril. With each twenty-ship convoy carrying some four hundred aircraft, over four thousand tanks and other vehicles, plus guns, ammunition, and other supplies, the destruction of one or two could make a difference on the Eastern Front.

In September, *Scharnhorst* and *Tirpitz* had sortied from their hideaways in the fjord on a morale-boosting attack on the Allied weather station on Spitsbergen, in which the latter ship fired her fifteen-inch guns "in anger" for the only time. By the time the Home Fleet, now commanded by Admiral Sir Bruce Fraser, arrived on the scene, the German ships had returned to their berths. Captain Friederich Huffmeier was dissatsified with the marksmanship of *Scharnhorst*'s gunners, however, and on September 21 took the battle cruiser to sea for target practice, leaving *Tirpitz* alone.

The evening passed quietly. The men guarding the nets covering the entrance to the anchorage failed to observe a dark shape that trailed behind a coaster as it passed through the gates of the boom at 0500. Unaware that *Scharnhorst* was out of her berth, the British had launched six midget submarines, known as X-craft, with the hope of destroying or disabling the remaining major elements of the German surface navy. Only two, *X-6* and *X-7*, managed to penetrate the anchorage, where they placed limpet mines on *Tirpitz*'s hull before being forced to the surface. The crews were captured and were being interrogated when the ship shuddered with "a most God-Almighty bang." Two of her turrets were jammed, her main engines and rudders so severely damaged that it would take months to repair her.

Dönitz allowed several Russian convoys to pass unhindered to lull the British into a sense of security. Then on December 19 he decided to unleash *Scharnhorst* against JW 55B, outward bound with nineteen British and American merchantmen and an escort of ten destroyers. The German squadron flew the flag of Rear Admiral Erich Bey, who had led the destroyers at the Second Battle of Narvik during the Norwegian campaign. Bey's orders were more aggressive than usual, and he was exhorted to cause as much damage as possible. "Exploit the tactical situation skillfully and boldly," ordered Dönitz.

Bey headed northward from Altenfjord, calculating that he would be in a position to attack JW 55B at dawn on December 26—about 1000 hours in that latitude. The weather was appallingly bad, which deprived him of help from the Luftwaffe and reduced the operational effectiveness of the German destroyers, whose larger-than-usual 5.9-inch guns made them bad sea-keepers. German intelligence also failed to warn Bey that the course he was steering would bring him into contact with two British covering forces. Force 1, consisting of the heavy cruiser *Norfolk* and the light cruisers *Sheffield* and *Belfast*, was led by Vice-Admiral Robert L. Burnett, who had commanded the cruisers in the Barents Sea fight, and was covering the homeward bound convoy RA 55A. Admiral Fraser, convinced that *Scharnhorst* would come out this time, was shadowing JW 55B with Force 2, consisting of his flagship, the battleship *Duke of York*, the light cruiser *Jamaica*, and four destroyers.

Having reached the convoy's presumed position, Bey ordered his destroyers to spread out and search ahead while he followed them. Unfortunately for him, a signaling error caused these vessels to lose contact with *Scharnhorst* in the dense snow squalls. Nevertheless, Bey was in a good position, his ship between Burnett's cruisers and the convoy, which was only about thirty miles away. The Battle of North Cape, which followed, was unusual in that it was a prolonged old-style gun duel between surface forces in which aircraft and submarines were not involved.

The action began at 0834, when *Norfolk*'s radar picked up an unidentified target at twenty-five thousand yards. Burnett rapidly closed with it; at 0924, *Belfast* obtained a visual contact at thirteen thousand yards and fired star shell in an attempt to illuminate *Scharnhorst*. Bey was taken by surprise—apparently because he was not using his radar, out of fear that it might be detected by the British. The cruisers opened fire at 0929, with *Norfolk*'s eight-inch guns scoring two unimportant hits. The Germans retaliated with a few harmless broadsides before turning away to the southeast. In the meantime, Fraser, coming up from the west with Force 2, ordered the convoy-escort commander to send four of his destroyers to join Burnett.

Though Burnett gave chase, the much heavier *Scharnhorst* was able to make better way in the high seas than his cruisers. Shrewdly accepting a temporary loss of contact with the enemy, he steered a shorter, more direct course that would keep him between the convoy and *Scharnhorst* should Bey try to approach again. Fraser was in a quandary. Burnett's cruisers had lost contact with the enemy, and his destroyers were running short of fuel, which meant he would soon have to break off the search. If *Scharnhorst* were heading homeward, he would be unable to catch her. And what if she were actually heading west, toward the open Atlantic?

Burnett's judgment proved sound, however. Shortly after noon, *Scharnhorst* was again sighted trying to close in on the convoy, and the cruisers exchanged salvos with her at eleven thousand yards. The four destroyers that had joined Force 1 tried to launch torpedo attacks, but the Germans shied away. *Norfolk* was severely knocked about by the enemy's eleven-inch shells—one turret was wrecked—and *Sheffield* suffered splinter damage. Then, even though *Scharnhorst* emerged unscathed from the twenty-minute-long encounter, Bey decided he would be unable to get at the convoy and broke off the action, intending to return home.

Scharnhorst's run to the south, however, was a fatal mistake; it placed her on a perfect course for Fraser to intercept her. German reconnaissance aircraft sighted Force 2, but the report was garbled, and Bey had no idea of the peril he faced until 1647, when his ship was unexpectedly bathed in the silver-gray light of star shells. Suddenly, she was obliterated by a wall of water thrown up by *Duke of York*'s fourteen-inch shells. Lieutenant B. B. Ramsden of *Jamaica* reported:

> I think we fired two or three broadsides before the reply came. . . . I saw the angry wink of her first 11-inch broadside. There was a vague flash off the port bow then—crack, crack, crack, and the drone and whine of splinters passing somewhere near. Another 6-inch broadside, and a few

seconds later the same angry wink on the horizon. This time I saw her shells burst, the splashes, mast-high and unpleasantly near the *Duke of York*, who was steadily crashing away with her full broadsides.

Scharnhorst's two forward eleven-inch turrets were quickly put out of action by British shells. Unable to discern much more than gun flashes on the horizon, both sides fired "blind," relying upon radar to aim their guns. Some of *Duke of York*'s guns constantly misfired, repeating the experience of her sistership *Prince of Wales* in her fight with *Bismarck*. With her superior speed, the German vessel began to pull away, and Fraser resigned himself to *Scharnhorst*'s escape. But at 1820, a lucky hit penetrated one of the battle cruiser's boiler rooms and severed a steam line. *Scharnhorst*'s speed fell to eight knots, and Fraser sent in his destroyers for a torpedo attack. All hope of escape cut off, Bey radioed the Führer: "We shall fight to the last shell."

Scharnhorst attempted to hold off the enemy destroyers with her secondary batteries, but her fire was now ragged and poorly controlled. Although one of the destroyers was severely damaged, they put four torpedoes into *Scharnhorst*, which led to flooding and another sharp reduction in speed. Her fate was sealed. Fifteen minutes of relentless pounding by *Duke of York*'s guns knocked out her last remaining turret, and British cruisers and destroyers crowded in to finish her off. She "must have been a hell on earth," noted Lieutenant Ramsden. "Great flashes rent the night and the sound of gunfire was continuous, and yet, she replied, but only occasionally now with what armament she had left."

At 1945, *Scharnhorst* blew up. When the smoke had cleared, she had vanished, leaving only thirty-six survivors of her crew of 1,986 officers and men. She had fought bravely but was a victim of poor communications and intelligence as well as a lack of resolution on the part of Bey, whereas the British had conducted the battle with daring and flexibility. The Kriegsmarine's last battle cruiser and her crew had been thrown away uselessly. With the destruction of *Scharnhorst*, the German surface fleet had, except for the damaged *Tirpitz* and a few other ships, ceased to exist. The full strength of the Allied navies could now be turned to the struggle in the Pacific.

•

CHAPTER 14

"Keep Pushing the Japs Around"

The New Zealand ASW trawlers *Kiwi* and *Moa* were operating in Kamimbo Bay, on the western tip of Guadalcanal, on the night of January 29, 1943, when they made a firm Asdic contact on a Japanese submarine. They had been alerted through decrypts of Japanese radio traffic of scheduled supply runs being made by enemy submarines. Two depth-charge attacks blew *I-1* to the surface, and *Kiwi* opened fire with her four-inch gun. Lieutenant Commander George Bridson, her captain, altered course to ram, and ordered full speed ahead. Unaware of the situation, *Kiwi*'s engineer protested, and Bridson shouted into the voice tube, "Shut up! There's a weekend's leave in Auckland dead ahead of us!"

The 600-ton trawler caught *I-1* on the port side, recoiled, and rammed again. "That'll be a *week's* leave!" bellowed Bridson. Landing barges could be seen on the submarine's deck, and soldiers in full pack were leaping over the side. "Once more for a *fortnight!*" cried Bridson as his vessel smashed into the submarine a third time. Badly damaged, *I-1* finally ran aground on a reef, and the remnants of her crew escaped ashore. A boarding party found the submarine's codebooks and other secret papers, which were forwarded to FRUPAC, the Fleet Radio Unit Pacific at Pearl Harbor.* This haul of crypto material proved valuable

*Formerly Station Hypo.

as both sides consolidated and regrouped in preparation for new operations following the Japanese defeat in Papua and Guadalcanal.

Having successfully completed the first part of the strategic plan for the Southwest Pacific drafted the previous year, the Allies now undertook the remainder: the advance up the Solomons and reduction of Rabaul on New Britain, with its hundred thousand troops, airfields, and naval base the keystone of the Japanese defense perimeter. Planning for this operation was entangled, however, in a larger struggle about overall strategy for the Pacific war. Throughout the conflict, it often seemed as if the U.S. Army and Navy were more interested in battling each other than the Japanese, with credit for the victory and a larger share of postwar budgets at stake.

Once Rabaul was taken or neutralized, General MacArthur argued for an advance upon Japan via New Guinea and the Philippines—what he called the New Guinea–Mindanao Axis. With the fighting moving out of the navy-dominated South Pacific across the "Pope's Line" just west of Guadalcanal, into his Southwest Pacific area, he insisted that the entire weight of the Pacific Fleet and its amphibious forces should be concentrated under his command. This strategy would, he said, maintain a defensive shield between Australia and the Japanese-occupied Central Pacific islands while his forces climbed the ladder to the Philippines. American power would be concentrated in a united thrust against Japan, while cutting her off from her southern conquests.

Admirals King and Nimitz were in no mood to turn the fleet over to MacArthur. While they professed to see some merit in his plan, they considered the Southwest Pacific a sideshow and argued that this route was too roundabout and subject to enemy flank attacks. In keeping with the old Orange Plan and Rainbow Five, the navy insisted that the major line of attack should come across the Central Pacific. A Central Pacific offensive would force the Japanese to fragment their forces, in the face of attacks coming from two directions, according to the navy. The Central Pacific offered a better climate than the rain-soaked Southwest Pacific jungles, and shorter lines of communication and supply. Once American forces had driven through the Central Pacific, they could leapfrog to the Philippines to join MacArthur's simultaneous but subsidiary advance. Following the liberation of the islands, bases would be established on Formosa and the Chinese coast for the final onslaught against Japan, which would include a tight commercial blockade, heavy bombing, and possibly an invasion.*

Only President Roosevelt could have settled the argument between MacArthur and the navy, but he preferred to defer a final decision, as he often did, and in the end he never made it. The Joint Chiefs debated the issue until May 1943, when a double-pronged advance along both routes was approved. But the Central Pacific offensive demanded at least parity with the Japanese in carriers, and only *Enterprise* and *Saratoga* were available. The Big E's hull was tender, because of battle damage, and she would shortly depart for repairs.† As a result, the campaign in the Central Pacific was delayed until enough ships and landing craft became available—probably until late 1943 at the earliest. In the meantime, a green light was given for a limited offensive in the Southwest Pacific.

In preparation for the Southwest Pacific campaign, Admiral King reorganized his forces. Admiral Halsey's South Pacific Force was designated the Third Fleet, with Kelly Turner's amphibious team part of it as the III Amphibious Force. Although Halsey looked to MacArthur for general strategy, he depended upon Nimitz for men, ships, and aircraft to carry them out, which created something of a bureaucratic nightmare. King also created the Seventh Fleet under Vice-Admiral Arthur S. Carpenter, a ragtag force of American, Australian, Dutch, and New Zealand ships that became known as "MacArthur's Navy" and was designed to keep the general's hands off the Pacific Fleet. It included the VII Amphibious Force led by Rear Admiral Daniel E. Barbey. Everyone expected MacArthur and Halsey, supreme egoists both, to clash, yet they got along well when they met in March 1943 to plan a two-pronged advance upon Fortress Rabaul.

---

*There was a third alternative—a British comeback led by Admiral Lord Mountbatten through the Indian Ocean and Straits of Malacca to recover Burma and Singapore and to move into the South China Sea. Nothing ever came of it, because Mountbatten's forces were constantly cannibalized to feed the ever-hungry maw of the Mediterranean. His operation, designated the Southeast Asia Command (SEAC), soon became known to cynical Americans as "Save England's Asiatic Colonies."

†The British carrier *Victorious* was sent to the Pacific, but some time was required to refit her to operate with the U.S. Navy, and she did not arrive in the combat zone until May 1943. She then worked well with the American units, but was withdrawn when new American carriers became available.

Operation Cartwheel, as it was called, required MacArthur to capture Lae and Salamaua on New Guinea's Huon Peninsula, the western anchor of the defenses of Rabaul, which would outflank the base.
Simultaneously, Halsey's amphibious forces were to leapfrog up the
Solomons from Guadalcanal to Bougainville, bypassing and isolating
Japanese strongholds along the way and constructing airfields to
cover the next landing. The plan, said Halsey, was to "keep pushing
the Japs around."

The Japanese, notwithstanding their defeat at Guadalcanal, drew
comfort from the fact that the conquest of the island had cost the
Allies six months' time as well as heavy casualties. Even after more
than a year of fighting, the enemy was thousands of miles from the
source of the oil and other raw materials which fueled the Japanese
war machine. And the Japanese still held their spiderweb of strategically located "unsinkable aircraft carriers" in the Central Pacific.
With the Allies heavily engaged in the Atlantic and the Mediterranean, the Japanese were confident they could keep their defense
perimeter intact.

Japanese strategy was flawed in several respects, however. Following Midway and Guadalcanal, the strategic initiative had passed to
the Allies, which meant they could decide which Japanese strongholds to bypass and which to attack. By mid-1943, American yards
were turning out more warships annually than the Imperial Navy had
before the war. And though the Japanese made good their aircraft
losses—producing ten thousand planes in a single year—they were
unable to replace the experienced airmen lost in the various campaigns. There was no effective program to train replacements, and
the quality of Japanese pilots was deteriorating.

"We were told to rush the men through, to forget the fine points,
just to teach them to fly and shoot," reported Saburo Sakai, the crack
navy fighter pilot, recuperating from wounds suffered at Guadalcanal. "For long and tedious months I tried to build fighter pilots
from the men they thrust upon us. It was a hopeless task." The survivors of this haphazard program were then thrown into combat—
without the skills to defend themselves.

Both sides refused to risk their few available carriers in the narrow
and treacherous waters of the Solomons, so naval aircraft were

shifted ashore. The Japanese enlarged the airfield at Munda Point, on New Georgia, and built new strips at Vila, on the southern tip of Kolombangara, and on Bougainville and Buka. Some two hundred planes were added to the hundred land-based aircraft of the Eleventh Air Fleet at Rabaul, making it one of the largest Japanese air concentrations of the war.

The Americans took the first step up the Solomons ladder less than two weeks after the Japanese evacuation of Guadalcanal. On February 21, 1943, U.S. troops landed unopposed in the Russells, a small group of islands lying between Guadalcanal and New Georgia, about sixty miles northwest of Henderson Field. As dogfights raged overhead, the Seabees carved a two-thousand-foot airstrip out of the jungle ooze and muck. Alarmed, Admiral Yamamoto ordered the army commander at Rabaul to send reinforcements to Lae on New Guinea, preparatory to moving them south.

On the morning of March 2, a convoy of eight transports carrying some seven thousand troops, under escort by an equal number of destroyers, was sighted as it entered the Bismarck Sea. Repeated attacks were launched by bombers belonging to the Fifth Air Force, commanded by Lieutenant General George C. Kenney. Having realized that high-level bombing at sea was usually a waste of time, Kenney resorted to a new technique known as "skip bombing." Flying at mast-top levels, his B-25 Mitchells dropped five-hundred-pound bombs fitted with delayed-action fuses, which ricocheted off the water into the sides of the enemy ships.

Over the next two days, all the transports and four destroyers fell victim to swarms of American and Australian aircraft. Only five Allied planes were lost. Planes and PT-boats followed up by strafing the survivors. These atrocities were justified on the grounds that the enemy did the same thing. The episode was called the Battle of the Bismarck Sea, but it was little more than target practice with live ammunition and bombs.

Japanese airfields on New Georgia and Kolombangara were repeatedly shelled and bombed. On the night of March 6, three light cruisers and three destroyers under Rear Admiral Aaron S. Merrill were heading up the Slot to bombard Kolombangara when the "blips" on their radar scopes pinpointed a pair of Japanese destroyers that had been running in supplies to the garrison. The Americans now showed they had learned from the bitter night fighting at Guadalcanal. Radar-controlled gunfire and torpedoes accounted for both enemy ships. Not long afterward, mines laid across the favored routes of the Tokyo Express sank three enemy destroyers and damaged a fourth. The Imperial Navy could ill afford such losses. It had started the war with 110 destroyers, and by July 1943 had added only fourteen against thirty-five lost.

Admiral Yamamoto had seen all his warnings about American resilience, energy and resources confirmed. To some observers he now seemed less decisive, less aggressive—as if he knew the war was lost. "I do not know what to do next," he had written a friend after Guadalcanal. In the end, he decided to fight the Allied air offensive with one of his own, moving his headquarters from Truk to Rabaul to direct operations personally. On April 7, the admiral launched Operation I-Go with air attacks on shipping and bases in the central Solomons and New Guinea. He was on hand as nearly two hundred bombers and fighters took off for a sweep down the Slot for a raid on Guadalcanal.

The largely inexperienced pilots claimed no fewer than twenty-five enemy transports sunk and 175 planes shot down in this and similar raids—claims that Yamamoto seems to have accepted without question. In reality, only the destroyer *Aaron Ward* and four auxiliary vessels were sunk, in exchange for the loss of forty planes and more irreplaceable air crews. Believing the Americans now unable to take the offensive because they had lost so much shipping, Yamamoto called off further attacks.

Four days later, the admiral decided, against the advice of his staff, to inspect Japanese naval and air bases in the upper Solomons as a morale-boosting gesture. FRUPAC had been monitoring the Rabaul radio circuits, and this vigilance paid off when it picked up a signal that had been carelessly dispatched in a low-level cipher detailing Yamamoto's entire itinerary. The times of his arrivals and departures were given to the minute for each location. It was the admiral's death warrant.

A glance at the map showed Admiral Nimitz that the initial leg of the tour would bring Yamamoto within range of American fighters on Guadalcanal. Should an attempt be made to intercept him? Intense discussions took place at Pacific Fleet headquarters. Paradoxically, in a war in which millions died, there was initial reluctance to consider the assassination of an enemy military leader, but this quickly gave way to more pragmatic considerations. Nimitz asked Commander Edwin Layton, his intelligence chief, if the Japanese could replace Yamamoto with a more effective fleet commander. Layton, who had known the admiral while he was a language student in Japan, assured Nimitz there was only one Yamamoto. Moreover, his loss would be a serious blow to Japanese morale, because in the public mind he was the reincarnation of the legendary Admiral Togo, the victor of Tsushima.

The ambush was assigned to sixteen U.S. Army P-38 Lightning fighters based on Henderson Field, because they had the range to reach the target area. To keep the enemy from learning that their code had been penetrated, the intelligence about Yamamoto's movements was credited to coast watchers. There was a succinct one-line addition to the cable sending the P-38s to the attack: "Talley Ho. Let's get the bastard."

The interception was flawless. Two Bettys were droning over the Pacific toward Bougainville on the morning of April 18, 1943, when the Lightnings suddenly dropped out of the sun with guns blazing. While most of them kept the escort of a half-dozen Zeros busy, a pair of the twin-tailed fighters concentrated on the bombers. Captain Thomas G. Lanphier caught one broadside on and riddled it with a long burst. Flames erupted from an engine, a wing broke off, and the plane smashed into the jungle below. The other Betty crashed into the sea. Admiral Yamamoto and most of his staff had been wiped out—victims of the carelessness of their own forces and the alertness of the American code breakers. He was replaced as commander-in-chief of the Combined Fleet by the less imaginative and more conservative Admiral Mineichi Koga.

While the Japanese people mourned Yamamoto, the U.S. dealt with some unfinished business in the Aleutians. The Japanese had captured Attu and Kiska during the attack on Midway, the only part of the operation that had gone according to plan, thanks to the bumbling of Rear Admiral Robert A. Theobald. Some strategists thought the Japanese intended to use these bleak islands as jumping-off points for an invasion of either Siberia or the West Coast of the

United States, but Washington soon decided the Aleutians were a road that led nowhere. Operations by both sides were precluded by a common enemy—high winds, fog, snow, drizzle, and more fog— some of the most abominable weather in the world.* Theobald had retained his post as commander of the North Pacific Area through his friendship with Admiral King, but his relations with Major General Simon Bolivar Buckner, Jr.,† chief of the Alaska Defense Command, quickly soured.

Although Theobald sent a small task force to shell Kiska, it was unable to find the island in fog. On the second try, the navy gunners missed the Japanese installations and churned up impressive holes in the tundra. Buckner, who thought Theobald not aggressive enough, complained that he was "as tender of his [ship's] bottoms as a teen-age girl." Theobald replied just as sharply. King finally replaced Theobald with Rear Admiral Thomas Kinkaid, who had done yeoman service in the fighting around Guadalcanal.

Kinkaid and Buckner tried to persuade the Joint Chiefs to allow them to evict the Japanese from Attu and Kiska, but General Marshall ordered only a holding action. In the meantime, the islands were subjected to repeated bombing attacks—when the pilots could find their targets in the cold fog or the gales of blinding snow. Expecting an American attempt to push them off the islands, the Japanese tried to reinforce their garrisons, but Kinkaid was determined to block these efforts. Late in March 1943, FRUPAC deciphered messages revealing that the Japanese were about to reinforce Attu with a polar version of the Tokyo Express, and Kinkaid dispatched a task group led by Rear Admiral Charles H. McMorris to intercept the convoy.

---

*The Aleutians produced a surprise dividend for the United States, however. A late-model Zero was damaged while attacking Dutch Harbor on June 4, 1942, and flipped over when it tried to make an emergency landing on the soft ground. Although the pilot was killed, the plane was relatively undamaged. Previous Zeros that had been recovered were in such poor condition that they were of little value to American technicians, but this craft was restored and tested and revealed the Zero's strengths and weaknesses. Though it has been stated that these tests influenced the development of the F6F Hellcat fighter, the replacement for the F4F, this is untrue, for the latter was almost ready for action. See Lundstrum, *The First Team and the Guadalcanal Campaign*, app. I.

†Buckner was the son of the Confederate general who, as commander of Fort Donelson (on the Tennessee River, in 1862), received General U. S. Grant's famous demand for "unconditional surrender," to which he acceded.

McMorris flew his flag in the light cruiser *Richmond*, and had the heavy cruiser *Salt Lake City*—the "Swayback Maru" to her sailors— and four destroyers under his command. The crews were standing to for predawn general quarters at 0730 on March 26 when a destroyer radar picked up the two Japanese transports about a hundred miles south of the Russian-held Komandorski Islands, which lie between Attu and the Kamchatka Peninsula. Unaware that the transports were being escorted by Admiral Boshiro Hosogaya's two heavy and two light cruisers and four destroyers, McMorris surged ahead, expecting as he later confessed, "a Roman holiday."

Surprised by Hosogaya's ships, McMorris, although outnumbered and outgunned, decided to attack the transports. The Japanese admiral interposed his squadron between the onrushing enemy task group and the transports, and the situation was radically altered. McMorris tried to make a getaway and radioed Kinkaid for air support. He was told that air-force bombers would not be able to reach him for five hours. Running eastward at high speed, *Salt Lake City* dueled at long range with *Nachi* and *Maya*, the two leading Japanese heavy cruisers, for three hours. *Nachi* was hit at least twice. Though the Japanese had the advantage of speed, Hosogaya lost it by zigzagging so his ships could bring their after turrets to bear. The Japanese also fired forty-two torpedoes at the fleeing U.S. vessels without scoring a hit.

Just as it appeared McMorris's ships might escape, *Salt Lake City*'s steering gear failed. Before it could be repaired, a Japanese shell exploded in her after engine room. Water poured in, and she took on a five-degree list to port. In an attempt to correct for it, a damage-control party inadvertently put out her boilers' fires, and she lay dead in the water. McMorris ordered one of his destroyers to make smoke to conceal the plight of the stricken *Salt Lake City* as the three others launched a suicide torpedo attack against the two onrushing heavy cruisers. Eight-inch shells kicked up gray waterspouts among the destroyers as they swept in at flank speed. "I do not know how the ships could live through the concentration of fire we directed at them," said a Japanese officer.

Suddenly, to the surprise of the Americans, the Japanese column turned away. Unaware of the damage to *Salt Lake City*, and expecting enemy bombers to appear overhead at any moment, Hosogaya had broken off the action. He contended he was short of ammunition and fuel, but was accused of forfeiting a certain victory and summarily retired. *Salt Lake City* got up steam again, and the task group returned to Dutch Harbor. Though McMorris had shown more courage than judgment, he saved his ships from an enemy force twice his size and firepower and prevented reinforcements from reaching Attu.

The Battle of the Komandorski Islands, as it was called, convinced Kinkaid that Kiska and Attu must be retaken before Japanese reinforcements got through. The Joint Chiefs reluctantly approved a landing on Attu, thought to be the most weakly defended of the pair, with Kinkaid in overall command. The army's Seventh Division was plucked from the Nevada desert and shipped off to Alaska without proper equipment or training for the operation scheduled for early May 1943. Three old battleships, *Pennsylvania*, *Idaho*, and *Nevada*, emerging from their post–Pearl Harbor refits, and an escort carrier, all under the command of Rear Admiral Francis Rockwell, supplied naval support.

Bad weather delayed the invasion until May 11, when eleven thousand troops commanded by Major General Albert E. Brown were put ashore at two widely separated points without meeting any opposition. Vastly outnumbered, the Japanese withdrew to prepared positions on the crests of Attu's rugged hills. American progress was slow in the face of heavy Japanese machine-gun and mortar fire. Air and naval gunfire support was inadequate because of the fog and Rockwell's decision to protect his battleships from enemy artillery by holding them seven miles offshore, too far to help the troops. Unhappy with the army's slow progress, Kinkaid precipitously relieved Brown—a move hardly likely to improve cooperation among the services.

Ironically, Brown was sacked just as his troops were pushing the enemy into the extreme northeast tip of Attu. Without food, ammunition, or hope of relief after seventeen days of fierce fighting, the Japanese chose to attack and die. On the night of May 28, some eight hundred men launched a surprise *banzai* charge. Wild, hysterical screaming pierced the night as the Japanese, some armed only with bayonets fixed to empty rifles, swarmed over the American outposts. They broke through an infantry company, overran a medical station, slaughtering the wounded and the medical staff, and were finally halted at a ridge held by a hastily thrown-together force of engineers, medics, and other rear-echelon personnel. When the bloodbath was over, only twenty-nine of the some twenty-three hundred Japanese on the island remained alive to be taken prisoner. The capture of Attu cost six hundred American dead and twenty-seven hundred other casualties—one of the bloodiest island campaigns of the Pacific war in proportion to the forces engaged. It was a heavy price for an island of no strategic significance.

Eleven weeks later, on August 15, Admiral Kinkaid dispatched an armada of nearly a hundred ships to Kiska with thirty-five thousand troops, including fifty-three hundred Canadians. The island had been subjected to steady bombing for a month, and its radio had gone off the air on July 27, which was thought to be the work of a lucky bomb. Unknown to the Americans, a Japanese relief force had evaded their patrols in the fog and evacuated the fifty-two-hundred-man garrison, repeating their successful evacuation of Guadalcanal. Admiral King was visiting Navy Secretary Frank Knox when Kinkaid reported the Japanese were gone, leaving only some dogs and hot coffee.

"What does this mean?" asked the mystified Knox.

"The Japanese are very clever," responded King. "Their dogs can brew coffee."

In the meantime, the American buildup for the march up the Solomons to Rabaul continued. Henderson Field was expanded into a full-scale bomber base surrounded by three fighter strips. Five miles to the east, Carney Field, an even bigger bomber base than Henderson, became operational in April 1943. Some three hundred navy, army, marine, and New Zealand aircraft were integrated into Air Command Solomons—Airsols for short—under the command of Rear Admiral Marc A. Mitscher, a grizzled pioneer naval aviator. The army's 43rd Division, a New England National Guard unit, and several marine raider battalions were preparing for the invasion of New Georgia and the seizure of the Japanese airfield at Munda Point.

Admiral Koga, the new commander-in-chief of the Combined Fleet, launched a series of bombing raids on Guadalcanal to disrupt this buildup, with little success. One of the most spectacular air battles took place on June 7, when a force of upward of fifty Zeros was intercepted over the Russell Islands. The Americans downed twenty-three planes and lost seven. Marine Lieutenant Gilbert Percy had a particularly harrowing experience. He bailed out of his badly damaged plane at three thousand feet—but his parachute failed to open. Percy put his arms straight down at his sides and kept his feet together as he hit the water. He was knocked unconscious, but was kept afloat by his life jacket and recovered sufficiently to make his way ashore, with a broken pelvis and broken ankles—and a distinction no one cared to contest.

Airsols' fighters and bombers knocked out the air bases at Munda and Vila on Kolombangara as a preliminary to the New Georgia operation, and Japanese flyers were forced back upon Bougainville and Rabaul. Rear Admiral Aaron Merrill's cruiser-destroyer force also shelled Kolombangara and Bougainville in an effort to create a diversion. MacArthur added to the confusion of the Japanese by launching an attack on the Trobriand Islands, off the north coast of New Guinea. The newly created VII Amphibious Force, part of "MacArthur's Navy" and led by Rear Admiral Barbey, landed troops at Nassau Bay, seventeen miles south of Salamaua, thus cutting it and Lae off from further help. The Japanese also found they could not hold the port of Finschhafen, at the end of the Huon Peninsula. By war's end, VII Amphibious Force had made over fifty landings despite persistent shortages of landing craft, and its commander was tagged as "Uncle Dan the Amphibious Man."

Lulled into a false sense of security by the exaggerated claims of his pilots, Koga was taken by surprise when, on June 30, a submarine sighted the troop-laden transports of Kelly Turner's III Amphibious Force plodding northwestward. Before the Japanese could react, some six thousand American troops were ashore on Rendova and four other points in the New Georgia group. Once enemy resistance was wiped out, the troops were ferried over to New Georgia itself, to begin the drive to the Munda airfield through a morass of rain-soaked jungle. By the time the Japanese mounted an air attack, the invasion of New Georgia was all but complete. Turner's command ship, *McCawley*, was the only vessel seriously damaged. Hit by a torpedo, she was abandoned and later sunk by an American PT-boat.

If Munda fell, the Japanese reasoned, the entire Solomons chain would be open to American air-and-naval attack. New Georgia became a carbon copy of Guadalcanal—on a lesser scale—as a new version of the Tokyo Express began slipping in nightly shipments of reinforcements, food, and ammunition for the forty-five hundred Japanese troops on the island. Naval guns, artillery, and air attacks expended mountains of ammunition, and thirty-five thousand U.S. Army troops and marines needed a month to root out the well-dug-in Japanese and capture the airfield. Mopping-up operations were not completed until late September.

The first of six naval battles fought in the waters of the central Solomons over the next five months, the Battle of Kula Gulf occurred on the night of July 5–6. Ten destroyers under the command of Rear Admiral Teruo Akiyama—seven crammed with twenty-six hundred troops and supplies for New Georgia—raced down the Kula Gulf, which runs between that island and Kolombangara. Akiyama planned to detach the transports in two groups and make his getaway. Admiral Halsey, alerted by decrypts of Japanese radio traffic, sent three light cruisers and four destroyers under Rear Admiral Walden L. Ainsworth, flying his flag in *Honolulu*, to intercept the intruders.

Luckily for Akiyama, the radar-equipped PBYs which prowled the area at night—known as Black Cats—missed his force. Having successfully detached three transports at the bottom of Kula Gulf, he had reversed course and was heading north when Ainsworth detected his ships at 0140 at a range of twelve miles. Ainsworth believed he had the element of surprise, but, unlike most small Japanese ships, *Niizuki*, Akiyama's flagship, was also fitted with radar, so he was aware of the presence of the Americans. Akiyama detached his second transport group of four ships and continued northward. When he realized the strength of the opposition, he ordered these ships to put about and rejoin him as he attacked with his three unencumbered destroyers.

Ainsworth made several mistakes. Following the usual American practice, he tied his destroyers to his cruiser line, delayed orders to open fire until the range was down to seven thousand yards, and instructed his captains to use their guns first and then their torpedoes.* The Japanese, realizing that gun flashes were a giveaway, preferred to launch their deadly Long Lance torpedoes first. Flames

---

*Incredibly, even though a recovered Long Lance had been examined by the Bureau of Ordnance, its findings regarding the weapon's capabilities had not been disseminated. Had Ainsworth known of them, he would probably never have ventured so close to the Japanese.

leaped from the guns of the American vessels; the three Japanese destroyers were shrouded in darkness. The radar-controlled American guns locked on *Niizuki*. Hit heavily and hard, she quickly sank, taking most of her crew, including Admiral Akiyama, with her. The two remaining destroyers fired a shoal of torpedoes before speeding away.

"Suddenly . . . I was flung into the air by a loud roar," recalled Lieutenant G. C. Morris, radio officer of the cruiser *Helena*. "We had caught a Jap torpedo. In a heap on the deck of the [radio] shack I looked about in total bewilderment, unable to believe we had been hit. . . . The ship was trembling—a curious, fluttering trembling, almost dainty, like that of a young girl frightened in the dark."

The Long Lance had severed *Helena*'s bow back to her No. 2 turret. Two more torpedoes slashed into her, and the stern section sank while the bow remained afloat. The Japanese escaped with slight damage. Ainsworth now turned his attention to the four destroyer-transports just coming within range. He neatly capped their "T," and three of them were hit, one so badly she was run aground and blasted the next morning by American planes. Though sporadic firing and skirmishing went on until dawn, the remaining Japanese ships escaped up the Slot. In all, about 850 troops were safely put ashore. The exchange of two destroyers for a light cruiser seemed a fair trade, but in view of the overwhelming firepower of the American ships, Ainsworth should have done better. Instead, superior Japanese tactics, torpedoes, and night-fighting skills paid off.

The Japanese again exhibited superior night-fighting skills a week later, on July 13, at the Battle of Kolombangara. Another Tokyo Express, this one led by Rear Admiral Shunji Izaki and consisting of four destroyer-transports escorted by five other destroyers and the light cruiser *Jintsu*, a veteran of action in the Solomons. The Japanese were sighted by a Black Cat, which alerted Ainsworth to their presence. The New Zealand cruiser *Leander* had joined his two remaining cruisers and nine destroyers. Izaki had already sent in his four transports to unload off the western coast of Kolombangara when his ships appeared on the radar screens of the American vessels. Ainsworth held his fire as the two squadrons hurtled toward each other at a combined speed of fifty-seven knots.

The Japanese fired their Long Lances at 0108, and the American destroyers launched their torpedoes a minute later. As at Kula Gulf,

all the radar-directed guns of Ainsworth's ships locked on a single target—*Jintsu*, Izaki's flagship—smashing her into a hulk. Both sides
wheeled away, but one of the Long Lances crashed into *Leander* and
damaged her so severely she dropped out of the fight. Ainsworth pursued the Japanese, who reloaded their torpedo tubes under cover of
a rain squall in a phenomenal eighteen minutes and fired a second
spread.

Honolulu and *St. Louis*, the two remaining cruisers, were both
damaged (the former lost a large chunk of her bow), the destroyer *Gwin*
exploded and sank, and two others collided in the melee. Ainsworth
believed he had sunk several enemy ships, but the Japanese retired
unscathed, having safely delivered their troops, damaged three U.S.
cruisers, and sunk a destroyer. Both Kula Gulf and Kolombangara
were Pyrrhic victories for the Imperial Navy, however. It could not go
on losing ships while the American fleet grew larger and larger.

In addition to Ainsworth's battered cruisers and destroyers, about
fifty PT-boats based on Rendova tried to derail the Tokyo Express.
Low, squat, and seventy-seven feet long, these high-speed craft were
armed with four torpedo tubes and four .50-caliber machine guns and
were commanded by young Reserve officers with a carefully culti-
vated reputation for derring-do. Night after night, in moonlight or
squall, they patrolled the black waters off New Georgia, breaking up
attempts to reinforce the garrison by trains of armed motor barges, or
daihatsu. Torpedoes were useless in such fighting, and when machine
guns proved ineffective against the barges, the PT skippers obtained
thirty-seven-millimeter cannon. The Japanese added more guns and
armor to the barges. The Americans raised the ante in this miniature
arms race by mounting three-inch guns on large landing craft and
taking them along on barge-busting expeditions.

On the night of August 1–2, fifteen boats—including *PT-109*, commanded by Lieutenant (j.g.) John F. Kennedy—were assigned to prevent a Tokyo Express from passing through Blackett Strait, south of
Kolombangara. Visibility was good, and they had ample warning of
the presence of Japanese ships, yet *PT-109* was rammed and sunk by
the destroyer *Amagiri*. Kennedy and his crew of twelve were flung
into water ablaze with flaming gasoline. Two men were lost, but the
young officer, despite injuries, led the survivors to safety while tow-

ing an injured man by a lifebelt strap gripped between his teeth. Once they had landed, Kennedy swam for help. He was rescued by islanders in a war canoe and, after being smuggled to a PT-boat base, came back for his men. Kennedy was awarded the Navy and Marine Corps Medal, as it was carefully noted, for the "survival phase" of the episode.*

Well before the debacles of Kula Gulf and Kolombangara, U.S. Navy destroyer men had been demanding that they be cut loose from protecting the cruisers so they could fight the Japanese on equal terms. New faces brought new ideas, and two aggressive officers, Captain Arleigh A. Burke and Commander Frederick Moosbrugger, set to work completely revising night-fighting tactics for destroyers.† Essentially, they argued that destroyers should lead surprise attacks, not be held in reserve. They should be routinely stationed ahead of the cruisers at night with permission to attack as soon as the enemy was sighted. These attacks should be made in two mutually supporting columns. Under cover of darkness, one would rapidly slip in toward the Japanese while withholding fire to mask its approach. Once in range, these ships would launch torpedoes and make their getaway. When the enemy started shooting at the first group, the second would open up from another direction. As the rattled enemy dealt with this new threat, the first column would whipsaw him with another attack.

Moosbrugger got the first chance to test these tactics. Admiral

---

*Kennedy was originally recommended for the Silver Star, but this recommendation was turned down; he received the Navy and Marine Corps Medal after the intervention of Assistant Navy Secretary James V. Forrestal, a Wall Street friend of his father, Joseph P. Kennedy. The loss of *PT-109* was regarded as "something of a scandal within the navy." Despite the warnings of the presence of enemy destroyers in the vicinity, two of Kennedy's crew were asleep and two were lying on the deck when the collision occurred. "Kennedy had the most maneuverable vessel in the world," recalled one PT-squadron leader. "All that power and yet this knight in white armor managed to have his boat rammed by a destroyer. Everybody in the fleet laughed about that" (quoted in Isenberg, *Shield of the Republic*, p. 751).

†The navy was also receiving numbers of a new class of destroyers, the twenty-one-hundred-ton *Fletcher* class, which mounted five five-inch guns and numerous anti-aircraft weapons. The best vessel of its type produced during the war, the *Fletchers*, could be configured for ASW, as an anti-aircraft escort, or as a radar picket ship.

Halsey, learning through radio intelligence that the Japanese were sending four destroyers to resupply Kolombangara on the night of August 6, assigned Moosbrugger with six destroyers to break it up. The squadron was steaming up Vella Gulf in two divisions while hugging the west coast of the island to prevent detection when the enemy vessels were spotted at 2233. The first inkling the Japanese had of the presence of American ships was the sight of white water boiling under the fantails of Moosbrugger's destroyers as they turned away after firing their torpedoes at four thousand yards.

Three of the Japanese destroyers were torn apart by the tin fish, then finished off by gunfire. The carnage was appalling. The vessels exploded with such violence that men thirty miles away thought the volcano on Kolombangara had erupted. The Japanese lost some twelve hundred soldiers and sailors, while Moosbrugger's squadron was untouched. This defeat was a serious blow to Japanese morale, and it showed that U.S. destroyers could win night battles, too.

The Japanese expected that Kolombangara would be Halsey's next objective, now that the fighting for New Georgia was winding down, but he refused to play their game. Instead, he decided to outflank the island and, on August 15, invaded less heavily defended Vella Lavella, which lay fourteen miles to the northwest. Though Japanese planes from Rabaul tried to interfere with the landing, they were beaten off by Airsols with heavy losses. The Japanese had not lost their skill in evacuation, however. While fighting was under way on Vella Lavella, nearly twelve thousand bypassed troops were lifted off from Kolombangara under cover of darkness, over the five nights between September 30 and October 4.

By October 1, the last remaining troops on Vella Lavella, about six hundred men, were penned in on the northwest coast of the island. Radio intelligence revealed that the Japanese were planning to evacuate them on the night of October 6–7, but the only ships Halsey had readily available were three destroyers under the command of Captain Frank R. Walker.* Walker was ordered to rendezvous off Vella Lavella with Captain Harold Larson's three destroyers, which were steaming at full speed to join him, and break up the evacuation.

---

*As captain of the destroyer *Patterson*, Walker had issued the warning that the Japanese were entering Savo Sound before the start of the battle on August 9, 1942.

Walker made radar contact with the Japanese at about 2230—three destroyer-transports and several barges and other small craft, under escort by six destroyers—and decided to attack without waiting for Larson. Sweeping in at flank speed, he got off his torpedoes first and sank one of the Japanese destroyers. Before he could make his getaway, however, one of his ships was sunk by enemy torpedoes and another was damaged in a collision with the sinking vessel. The arrival of Larson's destroyers caused the Japanese to withdraw, but only after the troops were evacuated from Vella Lavella.

This was the last sea battle won by the Japanese in World War II.

Halsey's next target was Bougainville, the largest of the Solomons and the final link in the ring of steel being forged around Rabaul. The Japanese were determined to hold the island as long as possible, and Admiral Koga transferred most of his carrier-based planes to Rabaul so they could participate in the Bougainville campaign. A series of fierce air battles followed rivaling in intensity those being fought in the skies of Western Europe. Both sides claimed to have inflicted great damage, but the Japanese suffered the most. Allied raids took a heavy toll of Koga's carrier planes, badly damaged Rabaul's port facilities, and diverted Japanese attention from the Bougainville operation.

Bougainville was no pushover, however. The Japanese had thirty-three thousand troops there and on the adjacent Shortland Islands, Buka, and the Treasury Islands, as well as five military airfields at the island's northern and southern tips. Halsey decided to land at Cape Torokina, on Empress Augusta Bay, halfway up the weakly defended western shore. Rather than capture an airfield, as at Munda, he planned to build one and allow the Japanese to exhaust themselves trying to capture it. Although strategists held that an expeditionary force required a three-to-one ratio of superiority, he had only thirty-four thousand marines, U.S. Army, and New Zealand troops. Naval forces were also in short supply, because of the concurrent demands of the Mediterranean campaign while, to the north, Nimitz was about to begin the "Atoll War" in the Central Pacific.

The Bougainville campaign began on October 27, as Americans and New Zealanders seized the tiny Treasury Islands, and a marine raider team shot up a base on Choiseul, across the Slot, to distract the Japanese. Four days later, on November 1, Rear Admiral Theodore S.

Wilkinson, Kelly Turner's successor[*] as head of III Amphibious Force, put some fourteen thousand men of the Third Marine Division ashore against light opposition at Empress Augusta Bay. Both the navy and marines had learned much about amphibious landings since Guadalcanal, and most of the troops and considerable equipment were ashore by nightfall.

That night, Vice-Admiral Sentaro Omori raced south from Rabaul with two heavy and two light cruisers and six destroyers, in an attempt to duplicate Admiral Mikawa's feat off Savo Island. Radio intelligence and Allied aerial reconnaissance gave him away, despite a sheltering rain squall, as he sped down from Rabaul at thirty-two knots. Halsey sent his only available ships to protect the beachhead: TF 39, composed of four new light cruisers under the command of Admiral Merrill along with the eight destroyers of Arleigh Burke's Destroyer Squadron 23—the "Little Beavers."[†]

Merrill deployed his cruisers in a line across the entrance to Empress Augusta Bay, with four destroyers under Burke ahead and four astern under Commander Bernard L. Austin. Aware that his ships constituted the principal Allied surface force in the Southwest Pacific, Merrill intended no Nelsonian battle of annihilation. The two destroyer divisions would cut loose to attack the Japanese in accord with the Burke-Moosbrugger tactical doctrine, but the cruisers were to remain on the defensive. The radar of his flagship, *Montpelier*, detected the Japanese at eighteen miles at 0227 on November 2.

Without waiting for orders to attack, Burke's destroyer division dashed in to launch torpedoes, but the American ships were unexpectedly illuminated by flares dropped by Omori's floatplanes. With his position revealed, Merrill ordered his cruisers to open fire. Once again, the radar-directed guns all locked on a single target—the light cruiser *Sendai*—which allowed the others to avoid American fire. Hit repeatedly, she steamed in circles with her rudder jammed. Two Japanese destroyers collided as they tried to avoid the crippled vessel.

Barking orders through his TBS radio, Merrill skillfully maneu-

---

[*]Nimitz had named Turner Commander, Amphibious Forces, Pacific Fleet, with headquarters at Pearl Harbor.

[†]Each of Desron 23's ships had a painting on its bridge of a cartoon character known as Little Beaver, who wore only moccasins, a headband with a feather, and an outsized G-string while firing an arrow into the rear end of a figure labeled "Tojo."

vered his cruisers through an elaborate sequence of course changes, sidestepping and turning and weaving to avoid the enemy's Long Lances, while pouring a torrent of six-inch shells down upon the Japanese. Swinging out of line to evade them, the destroyer *Hatsukaze* was rammed by Omori's flagship, the heavy cruiser *Myoko*, which sliced off a large part of her bow. Next, a firefight broke out between the four American light cruisers and the two Japanese heavy cruisers, in which both sides scored hits. By 0837, Omori had enough and retired to the northwest.

The American destroyers regrouped, and in the melee Burke's vessels fired twenty-five torpedoes, none of which hit a Japanese ship. "My God, how do you like that!" moaned Burke. One of Austin's vessels blundered into a tin fish and lost its stern. Two of his ships collided, and he came under fire from Burke.

"Cease firing! Cease firing!" yelled the irate Austin into the TBS. "Goddammit, that's me!"

"Were you hit?" asked Burke.

"Negative."

"Sorry," Burke responded, "but you'll have to excuse the next four salvos. They are already on the way."

Merrill had won a complete victory. Despite being outgunned and the failure of the torpedo attacks, he had sunk a light cruiser and a destroyer and damaged several other enemy ships. Moreover, he had prevented the Japanese from interfering with the landing. With dawn coming, he ordered his destroyers to break off the chase and to close up to provide a tighter defense for the inevitable air attack. "It was an organized hell in which it was impossible to speak, hear, or even think," Merrill said later of the assault upon his vessels by about a hundred planes. Firing briskly, the ships accounted for seventeen enemy aircraft and suffered only inconsequential hits.

Incensed at Omori's failure, Admiral Koga removed him from command and shifted more planes and seven heavy cruisers from Truk to Rabaul in preparation for another strike at the American forces in Empress Augusta Bay. Halsey had no heavy ships to match this fleet but obtained temporary loan from Nimitz of a carrier task force under Rear Admiral Frederick Sherman[*] that included

---

[*]Sherman had been captain of *Lexington* when she was lost in the Battle of the Coral Sea.

Saratoga and the new eleven-thousand-ton light carrier, *Princeton*. Having built his reputation on calculated risks, Halsey decided to attack Rabaul—no easy task, because it was the most strongly defended position in the Pacific. Sending carriers against such a bastion was thought in some quarters to be near suicidal for the air crews, and perhaps for the carriers themselves. "I never expected to see those carriers again," Halsey later confessed. Once he had given the order, he tried to forget that his son was serving on *Saratoga*.

On November 5, TF 38 launched ninety-seven planes from the northern end of the Solomons, about 230 miles southeast of the target. It was a "maximum effort," with no planes left behind to defend the carriers—that job was left to Airsols. Rain and overcast hid the carriers, but the sky was clear over Rabaul Harbor, which was crammed with some fifty ships. As the dive-bombers and torpedo planes bore in through a steel curtain of anti-aircrft fire, new F6F Hellcat fighters tangled with the seventy-five Japanese planes that rose to meet them. About twenty-five enemy aircraft were shot down, and an equal number were listed as "probables," whereas the strike force lost ten planes. No ships were sunk, although Koga's cruisers were so badly damaged that he canceled plans for a surface attack on the amphibious force off Bougainville.

Elated by the success of this operation, Halsey resolved to repeat it on an even larger scale. Nimitz supplied him with the new twenty-seven-thousand-ton fleet carriers *Essex* and *Bunker Hill* and the light carrier *Independence*, all commanded by Rear Admiral Alfred E. Montgomery. This force struck Rabaul again on November 11, damaging another heavy cruiser and sinking a destroyer. Of the 173 carrier planes that Admiral Koga had shifted from Truk to Rabaul, 121 were destroyed in the ensuing air battles.

These raids had results ranging well beyond the ships damaged and the planes shot down. They marked the beginning of the end of Rabaul's usefulness as a base. The long-debated question whether carriers could be risked against strongly defended land bases had also been settled once and for all. And the losses suffered by the Japanese resulted in further erosion of the Imperial Navy's air arm on the eve of the American drive across the Central Pacific.

As the marines extended their perimeter on Bougainville—including the building of an airfield by Seabees and army engineers, which would give Airsols a springboard to Rabaul—the Japanese feared an

Allied landing on Buka, just off the northern tip of the island. In the last week of November, Halsey received intelligence indicating that they were planning to evacuate some seven hundred aviation personnel from Buka—the airfield was no longer usable, because of constant bombing—and to run in a convoy of some nine hundred soldiers to defend it. Three destroyer-transports, screened by two large destroyers, were assigned to the mission.

On November 24, Captain Burke received a crisply worded signal from the admiral: "Thirty-One Knot Burke, get this. Put your squadron athwart the Buka-Rabaul evacuation line about thirty-five miles west of Buka. If no enemy contact . . . come south to refuel. . . . If enemy contact you know what to do."[*]

Burke certainly knew what to do. He divided the five destroyers of Desron 23 into two divisions—one of three ships, commanded by himself, and the other by Commander Austin—and took up station at the western end of St. George Channel. If the enemy was sighted, he would make a torpedo attack while covered by Austin; then they would reverse roles. Radar contact was made with the Japanese escort at 0141 on November 25, as the Japanese ships were heading home after having completed their mission. Burke led his Little Beavers into the attack, launching fifteen torpedoes at a range of forty-five hundred yards.

The two destroyers were hit. *Onami* suddenly disintegrated in a ball of flame, and *Makanami* stopped dead in the water, its back broken. Alarmed by the explosions, the three transport destroyers fled at flank speed with Burke in hot pursuit, having left Austin to deal with the crippled *Makanami*. *Yugiri*, the largest of the fleeing vessels, launched torpedoes at its pursuers, to no avail. The Americans opened up with their forward guns, and the Japanese returned fire. To shake off their pursuers, the Japanese destroyers separated, each veering off on its own course.

Resisting the temptation to divide his force, Burke pursued *Yugiri*,

---

[*] Burke had become known as "Thirty-One Knot Burke" as a result of his practice of reporting that he was "making thirty-one knots" with a force he had previously stated was incapable of sustained speeds in excess of thirty knots. When the press heard the nickname, they assumed it meant he was a hell-for-leather destroyer sailor, but in actuality it was an inside joke. Even the old four-pipers were designed to make better speed than thirty-one knots.

which was headed due north. A native of Colorado, he informed Halsey that he was "riding herd on the Japs" and emitted an occasional "Come a Ki-Yi-Yippee!" Hit several times by the concentrated gunfire of the three American destroyers, *Yugiri* began turning in circles and slowly to sink. Burke and Austin now took up a pursuit of the remaining two vessels, until they were within sixty miles of Rabaul.

"I don't think we can go much longer without refueling," Austin reported on the TBS.

"Maybe we can refuel in Rabaul," replied Burke.

"Okay," Austin shot back, "but we might have trouble with the fuel-hose connections."

The Battle of Cape St. George was completely one-sided—three Japanese destroyers sunk, no American ships hit. "An almost perfect action," observed Admiral William S. Pye, president of the Naval War College. It was the last of the fifteen surface battles that had been fought in the Solomons that had begun with Savo Island in August 1942. The Imperial Navy, no longer able to replace its losses as the U.S. Navy was increasing at an incredible rate, withdrew from the Southwest Pacific. "The nature of the war at sea changed after November 25," observes Paul S. Dull in his history of the Imperial Navy. "The Japanese Navy now surely faced ultimate defeat, short of a miraculous victory in a decisive battle—which never occurred."

Under constant air assault, once-mighty Rabaul was no longer of value as a naval base, but the nearly one hundred thousand Japanese troops there were digging in to meet an attack. Going underground, they built bunkers, concealed gun positions, and subterranean supply depots despite constant air attacks. And even though all carrier planes had been withdrawn to Truk, the Japanese still had three hundred serviceable aircraft in the Bismarcks. Admiral King sensibly concluded that a direct assault on Rabaul was no longer worth the casualties it would cost. Seeadler Harbor—in the Admiralties, to the north of New Guinea—was a finer anchorage than Rabaul's Simpson Harbor, and there was ample level ground for these airfields. In August 1943, the Combined Chiefs, meeting at Quebec, supported King's plan to bypass Rabaul. General MacArthur vehemently objected, but as Samuel Eliot Morison has observed: "Tarawa, Iwo Jima and Okinawa would have faded to pale pink in comparison with the blood which would have flowed if the Allies had attempted an assault on Fortress Rabaul."

Nevertheless, MacArthur, concerned about leaving such a strong enemy base in his rear, chose to tighten the screws on Rabaul. On December 26, the First Marine Division—rested and re-equipped after Guadalcanal—crossed the Dampier Strait from New Guinea and, supported by air strikes and Admiral Barbey's VII Amphibious Force, went ashore at Cape Gloucester, at the opposite end of New Britain from Rabaul. For the first time, the troops were supported by rocket-firing LCIs, which blasted great, gaping holes in the jungle. This experiment worked so well that Admiral King ordered a hundred of these craft.

The operation was a waste of effort, however—the result, it has been suggested, of MacArthur's erroneous belief that he had to occupy both sides of the strait to control it, "an idea that never struck the British as necessary at Gibraltar, or even in the English Channel."* Once ashore, the marines found that Cape Gloucester unpleasantly resembled Guadalcanal at its worst. Torrential monsoon rains, waist-deep swamps, and high, sharp kunai grass were almost greater handicaps than the some five thousand Japanese troops facing them. Boots rotted, weapons rusted and fouled, and "the rain made slop of the food," recalled one veteran. Giant trees, their roots loosened by gunfire, fell without warning, crushing unwary men beneath them. Nearly three weeks were needed to drive the Japanese from the uncompleted airfield and the hills overlooking it.

While these landings and air strikes were in progress, PT-boats were carrying on their own nightly war against Japanese supply barges along the dark coasts of New Guinea and New Britain. From November 1943 to January 1944, they sank a total of 147 such craft, and the advancing Allied ground forces sometimes found the enemy near starvation. Some resorted to cannibalism to survive. With barge traffic disrupted, the Japanese tried to supply their troops by submarine, and dumped watertight boxes of foodstuffs over the side to float ashore.

On the morning of December 27, 1943, as *PT-190* and *PT-191* were returning from patrol, a lookout on one boat swept the sky to the north. "Jee-suz! Jap planes!" he shouted, pointing upward.

---

*Van der Vat, *The Pacific Campaign*, p. 289.

Almost immediately, a Val dive-bomber peeled out of its V formation and came screeching down on the boats. One bomb exploded in the wake of *PT-191*, another off the bow of *PT-190*. They shied apart as suddenly as two startled fillies and at full speed zigzagged toward low-hanging squall clouds about a dozen miles away. Soon, they were under attack by upward of thirty planes, both fighters and bombers. As they raced through the waterspouts blown up by near misses, both boats sent out frantic calls for assistance, but the radio circuits were busy. Finally, they got through, and were promised immediate fighter cover.

Ensign Rumsey Ewing, captain of *PT-191*, was hit in the stomach, and Ensign Fred Calhoun, although painfully wounded in the thigh, took over command. Bomb fragments wounded two more men, and bullets penetrated the boat's engine compartment. She was kept running only through the skill of Motor Machinist's Mate 1/c V. A. Bloom. *PT-190*, commanded by Lieutenant Edward I. Farley, shot down two Vals, and tracers from *PT-191* dug into another plane. It spiraled upward and then went into a steep dive, crashing into the sea. By the time help arrived, *PT-191* had shot down another Japanese plane, bringing the total to two for each boat, and both were comfortably hidden in the rainstorm.

Barbey and his VII PhibFor—as the navy referred to it—were already on the move again. On January 2, 1944, a U.S. Army combat team was landed at Saidor, on the north coast of New Guinea, to tighten the Allied grip on the waters between New Guinea and New Britain. A month later, New Zealand and American troops took the Green Islands, only 115 miles east of Rabaul. The seizure of the Admiralty Islands was the next order of business, not only to complete the encirclement of Rabaul, but to secure Seeadler Harbor. Los Negros, easternmost of the islands, was taken at the end of February, and Manus, the main island of the group, was overrun a month later. Task Two had been fulfilled with a vengeance, and Rabaul was completely boxed in.

As 1943 drew to a close, the strategic situation was roughly as follows: In the North Pacific, the Japanese had been ousted from their footholds in the Aleutians. After bitter fighting ashore and at sea, they had been cleared out of the Solomons. In the Southwest Pacific, MacArthur was gearing up for a four-hundred-mile jump to the west, along the New Guinea coast, to Hollandia, and then to leapfrog on to the Philippines. Finally, as the U.S. Navy had planned since the inception of Plan Orange, the main tide of battle was shifting to the coral atolls of the Central Pacific.

•

CHAPTER 15

"Something . . . Quite New in Naval Warfare"

> I was up on the bridge. I was just standing there looking out to sea. . . . All of a sudden I noticed something. Like little black spots on the horizon. I looked through the glasses and it was a formation of our ships that stretched for miles! Carriers and battleships and cans—a whole task force . . . They came on and passed within a half a mile. . . . Carriers so big they blacked out half the sky! And battlewagons sliding along—dead quiet . . . riding west across the Pacific.

This is the way Mr. Roberts, the hero of Thomas Heggen's now classic play about the wartime U.S. Navy, described the passage of a fast-carrier task force—a sight becoming increasingly familiar in late 1943, as the navy began its thrust across the Central Pacific toward the heart of Japan. This campaign became possible because of the massive expansion of the Pacific Fleet. *Essex*-class carriers, each capable of carrying from ninety to a hundred aircraft, and *Independence*-class light carriers, which could handle thirty-five planes, were arriving in the Pacific in increasing numbers. It was a far cry from the grim days of 1942, when the Pacific Fleet's carrier strength consisted only of the bomb-battered *Saratoga* and *Enterprise*.

Organized by Admiral Nimitz into the Fifth Fleet under the command of Vice-Admiral Raymond Spruance, the victor of Midway, this armada initially included six fleet carriers and five light carriers, five fast battleships, and a sizable screen of cruisers and destroyers, all bristling with five-inch, forty-millimeter, and twenty-millimeter anti-aircraft guns, and new and improved radar.* TF 58, the Fast Carrier Task Force, commanded by Rear Admiral Charles A. Pownall, was the spearhead.

There was also a corresponding improvement in the quality of U.S. Navy aircraft. The new F6F Hellcat and the F4U Corsair fighters were superior to the legendary Zero. Although less maneuverable than the Zero because of the weight of their armor and self-sealing tanks, they topped it in speed, ruggedness, ceiling, and firepower. The huge gull-wing Corsair, which could fly faster than four hundred miles an hour, proved to be less satisfactory than the F6F as a carrier fighter because of its high landing speed, but in the hands of shore-based marine pilots it achieved remarkable success.† The lumbering TBD Devastator torpedo plane had been replaced by the infinitely superior TBF Avenger which proved to be an effective torpedo plane and strike bomber. Some of these planes were fitted with radar and were used in night attacks. Not all the new planes were improvements, however. Dive-bomber pilots still swore by the reliable old SBD Dauntless and heartily disliked its replacement, the unstable SB2C Helldiver, which they dubbed "the Beast."

The Central Pacific thrust required a shift to a new kind of naval warfare. U.S. forces would no longer have the tactical advantage of being able to choose from multiple landing sites on the relatively undefended beaches of comparatively large islands, as in the Southwest Pacific. Landings in the Gilberts and Marshalls would be on coral atolls separated by vast expanses of open sea, characteristics favorable to the defense.‡ To deal with the absence of advanced staging areas and nearby airfields for land-based air support, U.S. naval tacticians developed new operational doctrines for the fast-carrier task forces. The tactics were tried out in the fall of 1943 as the carriers

---

*The five-inch guns fired shells with a new VT or proximity fuse, which automatically detonated them within seventy feet of a target, with deadly results.

†Major Gregory "Pappy" Boyington, the marines' top-scoring ace, won most of his twenty-eight victories in a Corsair. His "bag" also included six Japanese planes shot down while flying with the American Volunteer Group (the Flying Tigers) in China.

‡The battles of the Atoll War were short and intense. The Fourth Marine Division fought four complete battles and suffered nearly 75-percent casualties—yet was in action a total of sixty-one days during the entire war.

raided Marcus and Wake islands and Tarawa in the Gilberts.

TF 58 was deployed in four task groups, each consisting of a mixture of large and light carriers with its own screen. These ships operated individually or together, as circumstances required. Improved communications and fighter-direction techniques and concentrated anti-aircraft fire allowed them to maneuver and defend themselves to a degree undreamed of in earlier carrier operations. High above the flight decks, carrier superstructures sprouted the antennas of new and improved radar which sent "blips" down to the Combat Information Centers, to be evaluated as friend or foe—and, if foe, promptly dealt with by fighters vectored out by the CIC. On the other hand, Japanese radar was still primitive by American standards.

These powerful task forces were accompanied by a uniquely American contribution to the art of war—a floating fleet train of oilers, repair, and store ships ready to refuel combat vessels at sea while under way, or to turn a remote atoll into a major base complete with floating drydock and shops. Support came from cargo ships like Mr. Roberts's sluggish old *Reluctant*, which plowed the backwaters of the Pacific with "food and trucks and dungarees and toothpaste and toilet paper . . . [steaming] from Tedium to Apathy [with] . . . an occasional trip to Monotony."

While American naval power was expanding, Japanese strength was ebbing. Following the futile defense of the approaches to Rabaul and the loss of the Solomons, Imperial General Headquarters drew up a new strategic plan for the war. A reduced perimeter was established—"the absolute national defense sphere"—a line that ran from Burma and Indochina though the East Indies, across western New Guinea and the Carolines, on to the Marshalls. In effect, the some three hundred thousand troops who could not be rescued from Rabaul, the Solomons, and eastern New Guinea were abandoned to their fates. Japanese strategy was now based on the premise of inflicting casualties on the enemy, not on achieving victories. The strategic advantage had passed to the Americans.

Though Japanese lines of communication and transport needs were reduced by this decision, the Imperial Navy was in no condition to resist the Central Pacific thrust. About fifteen hundred naval aircraft had been lost in the New Guinea–Solomons campaigns, and the army's air losses are estimated to have been as nearly great. Between April 1943 and February 1944, thirty-three ships were lost—twenty-five destroyers, five light cruisers, one escort carrier, one seaplane carrier, and the battleship *Mutsu*, which was sunk in June 1943 by an explosion possibly caused by spontaneous combustion in a magazine. Japanese shipyards were also crowded with damaged vessels.

The heyday of Admiral Nagumo's crack carrier fleet, which had carried all before it in 1941–42, was by now the remotest of memories. There were nine carriers left, including the new thirty-three-thousand-ton *Taiho*, which had an armored flight deck like the British flattops. But most of the ships were small and, though they had a combined potential air strength of 525 aircraft, never carried deck loads anywhere near these figures. New planes had also been developed, including an upgraded Zero fighter, the B6N1 Jill torpedo plane, and the new D4V Judy dive-bomber, which was nearly as fast as the Hellcat. These aircraft were formidable foes in the hands of skilled pilots, but skilled pilots were growing scarcer.

In the early morning of November 19, 1943, three Japanese scout planes were winging home to Tarawa in the Gilberts from a patrol when they caught a glimpse of an American armada spread out over a wide expanse of sea. Lieutenant Kichi Yoshuyo nervously tuned his high-frequency transmitter: "Enemy contact report . . . fleet sighted . . . several carriers and other types too numerous to mention . . ." And this vast fleet was on a course that would bring it within range of Tarawa within twenty-four hours.

Rear Admiral Keiji Shibasaki passed on the grim news to Kwajalein, in the Marshalls, and to the main base of the Combined Fleet, at Truk, in the Carolines. Japanese plans for the defense of the Gilberts called for an attack upon the invasion fleet by aircraft and warships staged through Truk. But the air-and-sea umbrella earmarked for this task had been blown to tatters in the fruitless defense of the Solomons and the Bismarck Archipelago. The only alternative left to Shibasaki and the forty-six hundred crack troops of the Naval Special Landing Force on Tarawa—the Japanese version of marines—was to fight to the death.*

---

*There were another twenty-two hundred construction troops and Korean laborers at Tarawa.

Originally, Admiral Nimitz had planned to begin the American offensive in the Central Pacific by leaping over the Gilberts to Kwajalein and Wotje, in the Marshalls. He changed his mind after reconnaissance revealed that the Japanese had built an airfield on Tarawa and a seaplane base at Makin. Planes based upon those atolls could harry the flanks of forces attacking the Marshalls. The Gilberts operation, dubbed "Galvanic," was under the overall control of Kelly Turner, who had returned from Pearl Harbor to become commander of V Amphibious Force, with the troops under Major General Holland M. Smith of the marines. Major General Julian C. Smith's battle-hardened Second Marine Division, of eighteen thousand men, was assigned to capture Tarawa, while some sixty-five hundred troops of the army's 27th Infantry Division were to land on Makin. Turner himself commanded TF 52, which would cover the Makin landing; Rear Admiral Harry W. Hill, his deputy, led TF 53, deployed against Tarawa. Almost as an afterthought, a company of marines would also go ashore, from the large submarine *Nautilus*, to capture tiny Abemama Atoll.

Tarawa—or, more accurately Betio, the largest islet of the atoll, where the Japanese had constructed the airfield—was the primary objective of the assault. Only about two and a half miles long and six hundred yards wide, it was triangular and although smaller than Central Park, was honeycombed with blockhouses, pillboxes, and artillery emplacements covered with concrete, sand, steel plates, and coconut logs, each one supporting another, and impervious to all but direct hits by heavy shells. Eight-inch coast-defense guns purchased from the British at the time of the Russo-Janpanese War, mortars, and machine guns had been sighted in on expected landing places. Betio was also ringed by a coral reef that formed a natural barrier to landing craft. To it the Japanese had added mines, barbed wire, and underwater obstacles. Inside the reef lay a shallow lagoon.

Holland Smith, known as "Howlin' Mad" in the Marine Corps because of his short fuse, wanted the navy to shell Betio for three days in preparation for the landing. Admiral Spruance, commander of the Fifth Fleet, and Turner wanted to hit hard and hit fast and be gone before their ships could be attacked by the Japanese, and offered only a few hours of bombardment. Following a bitter argument, Smith accepted the Navy's timetable.

Julian Smith, commander of the Second Division, saw the reef as the major hazard. Newly developed amphibious tractors, or LVTs, could cross such obstacles, but there were only 125 such craft on hand. The bulk of the marines would have to go ashore in the usual LCVPs. Fully loaded, these craft drew four feet of water; it was uncertain whether the water over the reef, even at high tide, would be deep enough to permit passage. If not, the marines would have to wade the last six hundred yards to shore through the lagoon without cover.

Major Frank Holland, a New Zealander who had kept the tidal records at Tarawa, warned Julian Smith that the tide could be low at this time of the year. The safest course was to delay the assault for a month, until late December, when a full moon would bring a higher tide. Having hunted waterfowl in the Chesapeake Bay marshes, Smith was familiar with such "neap" tides, and sought a postponement. But Admiral Nimitz was under pressure from Admiral King to get the Central Pacific offensive under way immediately. King's reasoning was purely political—he wanted the U.S. to be so committed to the Central Pacific that the ships and other forces could not be withdrawn to the Atlantic or the Mediterranean.

Smith took Holland to meet with Admiral Hill on the flagship, the battleship *Maryland*, where he repeated his warnings. One of Hill's officers produced a chart showing that four and a half feet of water could be expected over the reef. "You won't have three feet!" Holland snapped. Hill asked a group of Australian and New Zealand merchant-marine officers, who were to act as pilots for the invasion, whether they had ever been at Tarawa when boats could not cross the reef. No one had. Yet, though Hill was satisfied, Holland was adamant. "You won't be able to cross the reef," he predicted. General Smith grimly warned his marines to be prepared to wade ashore under enemy fire.

The attack on Tarawa began at 0505 on November 20, with a preinvasion bombardment by TF 53. Three old battleships, four cruisers, and several destroyers pounded Betio with about three hundred tons of high explosives over the next two and a half hours. Salvos from *Maryland*'s sixteen-inch guns quickly silenced a pair of eight-inch guns that fired at the ships. Bright fires glowed through the dark haze of smoke and dust that curtained the island, and the sky at times glowed brighter than noonday on the equator. Gun emplacements, observation towers, radio installations—anything that showed above ground was bombed and strafed. "Surely, we all thought, no mortal man could live through such destroying power," observed *Time* correspondent Robert Sherrod.

But there were several miscalculations. Although many of the Japanese were killed by the bombardment, others, protected by several thicknesses of coconut logs and concrete, survived. The bombardment should have been at least three times as intensive, but Admiral Hill was faced with the possibility that the Japanese fleet might interfere, so at least forty projectiles per gun were held in reserve in case of a fleet action. This reduced the number of shells available for the shore bombardment by about 37 percent, he later acknowledged. Not only should there have been a heavier and more sustained bombardment, but close-range naval gunfire has a flat trajectory—better results would have been achieved against the enemy defenses if it had been supplemented by heavy bombers carrying two-thousand-pound bombs.

The invaders had a choice of landing areas: on the narrow beaches on the southern and western ends of Betio, or on the northern side, where a pier stuck out 750 yards across the lagoon and over the reef to deep water. Expecting a landing on the first two positions because they required a shorter approach, the Japanese had established their strongest defenses there. The Americans decided to attack from the lagoon side, where the marines could land on a broad front, and where, as it turned out, the Japanese had not entirely completed their defenses.

Two minesweepers went in first. Screened by heavy smoke, *Pursuit* and *Requisite* swept a channel into the lagoon while the bombardment was still under way. One vessel remained behind to mark the line of departure for the assault waves as the other turned back to escort the destroyers *Ringgold* and *Dashiell* into position to duel with guns ashore. *Ringgold* was hit twice, but both shells were duds. Amphtracs (LVTs) followed at 0830, with Lieutenant William D. Hawkins's scout-and-sniper platoon leading the way. They landed on the pier, and Hawkins, followed by Lieutenant Alan G. Leslie with a flamethrower, advanced methodically up it, spouting blazing death at the Japanese machine-gun nests.[*]

---

[*]Hawkins died of wounds sustained later in the battle, and he was awarded the Medal of Honor posthumously. The airfield on Betio was named for him.

"Bullets pinged off that tractor like hailstones off a tin roof," related Private N. M. Baird, who landed with the first wave. "Two shells hit the water twenty yards off the port side and sent up regular geysers. I swept the beach [with an LVT's machine gun] just to keep the bastards down as much as possible. . . . We were 100 yards in now and the enemy fire was awfully damn intense and gettin' worse. They were knockin' boats out left and right. A tractor'd get hit, stop, and burst into flames, with men jumpin' out like torches. . . ."

The Japanese were initially stunned by the air-and-sea bombardment, but because of a communications breakdown (these occurred repeatedly during the operation) the shelling was halted well before the marines landed. Shaking their dazed minds free of the shock of the avalanche of shells, the defenders dug new strongpoints in the rubble produced by the bombardment. The first three battalions of marines, carried over the reef in amphtracs, got ashore without serious losses, despite low water. But they had advanced only a hundred feet up the beach before being halted by a coconut-log-and-coral seawall and deadly enemy fire. Colonel David M. Shoup, who commanded the troops ashore, directed the battle while standing waist-deep in the water along with a sergeant carrying a radio on his back.*

The situation was even worse out on the reef. The LCVPs that were bringing in the later waves of troops were hung up because of shallow water, so the men had to clamber over the side to be scythed down by hidden machine guns as they waded ashore. This is where the marines took most of their casualties. "I could swear that it took me twenty-four hours to walk across that reef," recalled one man. Horrifying images tumbled over each other: landing craft full of dead and wounded overturned, stuck on the reef or in flames; bodies bobbing on the waters of the lagoon; the wounded drowning; men screaming for help; withering machine-gun fire.

There was no established beachhead, only the tiny, fire-swept head of the pier at the reef's edge and a few toeholds ashore. By noon, most of the amphtracs had been knocked out after making repeated trips to the beach in place of the LCVPs. Everything was stalled, the assault

---

*Shoup, also awarded the Medal of Honor, was the only recipient to survive the battle. He was commandant of the Marine Corps during the Kennedy administration.

had lost its momentum, reinforcements and ammunition could not be brought ashore, and some fifteen hundred marines who had already landed were pinned down on the narrow beach in front of the seawall, unable to advance or retreat. Eight hours after the launching of the attack, General Smith radioed Holland Smith, who was with Admiral Turner off Makin: "Issue in doubt."

No mass Japanese attack developed during the night, but the marines remained on the alert. Periodically, they were fired upon from the rear by enemy soldiers who had swum out in the darkness to the wrecked boats and amphtracs to turn their machine guns upon the men on the beach. Water was running low. The situation was even worse on the Japanese side. Half the garrison had been killed, and their communications were broken. They were under constant bombardment by *Ringgold* and *Dashiell*, which lay close in to the beach, providing gunfire support on call from navy fire-control parties ashore.

The tide of battle began to turn on the second day, when reinforcements fought their way to the crowded, corpse-strewn beach. Supported by light tanks, the marines captured the airfield, drove across Betio, splitting the Japanese defenders in two, then set to work rooting them out. Techniques for dealing with enemy strongpoints were improvised on the spot. Teams of riflemen and combat engineers attacked fortified positions with satchel charges and flamethrowers. Sherrod described one such assault:

> A Marine jumped over the seawall and began throwing blocks of TNT into a coconut-log pillbox. . . . Two more Marines scaled the seawall, one of them carrying a twin-cylindered tank strapped to his shoulders, the other holding the nozzle of the flame thrower. As another charge of TNT boomed inside the pillbox, causing dust and smoke to billow out, a khaki-clad figure ran out the side entrance. The flame thrower, waiting for him, caught him in its withering stream of intense fire. As soon as it touched him, the Jap flared up like a piece of celluloid. . . .

In the meantime, the long-overdue high tide finally rolled over the reef, and reinforcements, guns, and tanks were now pouring ashore. Sherrod, seeing a pair of jeeps rolling along the pier towing thirty-seven-millimeter guns, observed that, "if a sign of certain victory was needed, this is it." Early the next morning, November 22, Tarawa radio broadcast its final message: "Our weapons have been destroyed and from now on everyone is attempting a final charge. . . . May Japan exist for ten thousand years!"

The marines made substantial, if hard-won, progress throughout the day, driving the enemy into the island's narrow eastern tip. The survivors launched a *banzai* charge just after darkness closed in. Wave after wave of Japanese troops, stupefied with *sake* and armed with rifles, swords, bayonets, grenades, and knives, hurled themselves upon a section of line held by a company of the Sixth Marines. Naval gunfire and automatic weapons took a heavy toll of the enemy, yet the impetus of the charge carried them into the American position, where the fight turned into a savage business of bayonets, knives, and clubbed rifles. Repulsed, the Japanese came back again and again.

With the coming of daylight, the grimy, stubble-bearded marines stumbled from their foxholes. Deep lines were etched into their young-old faces, and they had the "thousand-yard stare" of battle shock in their eyes. They counted the mangled bodies of some 325 Japanese around their defense perimeter. For all practical purposes, the Battle for Tarawa was over.

Tarawa came at a high price—1,009 marines and navy medical corpsmen killed and another 2,101 wounded. The seventy-six hours of battle had exacted a greater toll than had Guadalcanal in six months. Except for 146 prisoners, mostly Korean laborers, the entire Japanese garrison was wiped out. On the home front, criticism and controversy greeted the shocking casualty lists. Newspaper and magazine photos of dead marines floating on the tide, and of burned-out LTVs impaled on the seawall, created the indelible impression of a tragic blunder, with comparisons made to the Charge of the Light Brigade. Some observers questioned whether marine generals should be permitted to conduct future operations, particularly since General MacArthur seemed to be winning easy victories in his drive along the northern coast of New Guinea. Alarmed Americans looked with foreboding to forthcoming assaults against other heavily defended Japanese-held atolls in the Central Pacific.

The marines were still mopping up Tarawa's adjacent islands when Admiral Nimitz ordered every aspect of the campaign analyzed in detail to prevent errors from being repeated. The inquiry called for future naval bombardments and air strikes to be heavier and more sustained, the time lag between lifting fire and landing to be reduced, better close air support during the assault, and improved communications between ship and shore. In the final analysis, however, the real reason for the slaughter was the haste in which the operation was carried out. Had there been a delay for a full moon and a higher tide, there would have been sufficient water to pass over the reef with far fewer casualties.

While desperate fighting was taking place on Betio, another battle was being fought on Makin, about a hundred miles to the north. No one had thought Tarawa would be easy, but Makin was not expected to be a problem for the sixty-five hundred army troops commanded by Major General Ralph C. Smith. The atoll was defended by about six hundred Japanese, of whom only 250 were combat troops, yet Makin turned out to be almost as frustrating in its own way as Betio— and, for the U.S. Navy, almost as costly.

The troops met little resistance in landing, but progress was slow, because the men, mostly green New York National Guardsmen, were pinned down by a handful of Japanese snipers, real and imagined. Fire discipline was poor, and units repeatedly panicked and fired at each other. The pace of the advance was so infuriatingly slow to "Howlin' Mad" Smith that he charged ashore on the second day in an unsuccessful effort to speed it up. Three days were required to secure the island, rather than the single day allotted. Sixty-six men were killed and 185 wounded—with half the casualties attributed to "friendly fire." Abemama fell without difficulty to marines come ashore from *Nautilus* in rubber boats.

As a result of the slow advance on Makin and the bitter resistance on Tarawa, Admiral Spruance was forced to hold his carriers off the Gilberts, even though the risk to them grew every day. Thanks to this delay, the Japanese were able to mount a counterattack. Eighteen Betty torpedo bombers from Kwajalein evaded radar detection and badly damaged *Independence* off Tarawa. On November 24, the escort carrier *Lipscombe Bay* was torpedoed twenty miles off Makin by the submarine *I-175*. She exploded in a huge column of orange flames that engulfed her superstructure. The battleship *New Mexico*, fifteen hundred yards away, was showered with flaming debris. The carrier sank twenty minutes after being hit, and nearly 650 men, two-thirds of her crew, were lost.

The sinking of *Lipscombe Bay* marked the end of the Gilberts campaign. In less than a week, the U.S. had captured three firm footholds in the archipelago and controlled the island group. Seabees and army engineers were already at work clearing up the debris of battle and preparing the atolls for their role in the next strike—in the Marshalls, lying just short of halfway between Pearl Harbor and the Philippines.

An assault on the Marshalls, which provided cover for the Japanese base at Truk, had been part of the navy's Pacific strategy since the Orange Plan, but resistance to the idea had developed on several levels. While the fighting was under way at Tarawa, Allied leaders were meeting in Cairo,* where Winston Churchill made a renewed pitch for expanded operations in the Mediterranean at the expense of the Pacific war. In response, Admiral King, who had accompanied President Roosevelt to Cairo and had pushed the attack on Tarawa to prevent Churchill from creating such a diversion, forcefully pointed out that the Central Pacific campaign was already proceeding at too rapid a pace to be reined in.

On another front, Douglas MacArthur used the high casualties of Tarawa to try to divert resources from the Central Pacific to his operations. "Give me central direction of the war in the Pacific and I will be in the Philippines in ten months," he wrote Secretary of War Stimson in an effort to bypass the Joint Chiefs. "Don't let the Navy's pride of position and ignorance continue this tragedy. . . ."

MacArthur was outflanked, however, when the navy received support for its Central Pacific thrust from an unexpected quarter. The air force wanted bases for its new, long-range B-29 Superfortresses just coming off the production lines. These planes could carry a heavy bombload fifteen hundred miles to a target and return. Flying from airfields in the Marianas, the next target after the Marshalls, they would be within easy reach of the Japanese home islands. To the wry amusement of the admirals, the air force now became the most vociferous advocate of a Central Pacific drive.

Spruance, Turner, and Holland Smith planned to begin the Mar-

---

*President Roosevelt secretly crossed the Atlantic in the newly commissioned forty-five-thousand-ton battleship *Iowa*. One of the escorting destroyers accidentally fired a torpedo at her, which narrowly passed astern.

shalls campaign with simultaneous attacks on Wotje and Maloelap atolls, on the eastern fringe of the island group. Once these atolls were taken, they would be used as bases for an assault on Kwajalein, the Japanese headquarters, at the geographic center of the chain. But Nimitz decided to bypass the outlying atolls and strike directly at Kwajalein. Shocked, his commanders objected that Kwajalein was surrounded by Japanese airbases and the assault force would be subjected to continuous air strikes. "If you don't want to do it, the [Navy] Department will find someone else to do it," Nimitz told them at a stormy meeting on December 14, 1943. "Do you want to do it or not?" They decided they wanted to do it.

The Japanese were as surprised by Nimitz's decision to go the heart of the Marshalls as were his commanders. "There was divided opinion as to whether you would land at Jaluit or Mili," a Japanese staff officer later told his interrogators. "Some thought you would land at Wotje, but few thought you would go right to the heart of the Marshalls and take Kwajalein." As a result, the outer atolls were given priority for troop reinforcements. Kwajalein, although garrisoned by eight thousand plus men, of whom twenty-two hundred were combat troops, was, as Nimitz suspected, not so heavily fortified as Betio had been.

Turner's V Amphibious Force, now numbering three hundred ships and eighty-four thousand marines and army troops, had three major targets in the Marshalls: the twin islands of Roi and Namur, which were connected by a causeway; Kwajalein itself, about forty miles to the south; and Majuro, 250 miles southeast, which had been selected by Spruance because it had an excellent harbor and was lightly defended. Eniwetok, at the western perimeter of the atoll, would be next. Once the Marshalls had been neutralized, the Mariannas, part of the inner ring of Japan's defenses, would be taken.

The newly activated Fourth Marine Division was assigned to capture Roi-Namur; the army's Seventh Infantry Division targeted Kwajalein; Majuro was to be taken by elements of the 27th Division, which had performed poorly at Makin. Turner commanded the attacking force at Kwajalein, and Rear Admiral Richard L. Conolly, who had distinguished himself as commander of amphibious forces in the Mediterranean, was in charge of the landing at Roi-Namur. As at Makin, Holland Smith would be in overall command of the troops when they were ashore. D-Day for all three landings was set for January 31, 1944.

Preparatory to the landings, the Marshalls were hammered by air attacks launched by land-based aircraft coming from the new fields in the Gilberts and by TF 58, now under Rear Admiral Marc Mitscher, the former commander of Airsols. "The American attacks are becoming more furious," a Japanese soldier noted in his diary. "Planes come over day after day. Can we stand up under the strain?" This was the first time the fast carriers had a chance to demonstrate what they could do to assist an amphibious operation. In the Gilberts, they had mainly been used defensively, to ward off Japanese air attacks. Mitscher, however, intended to annihilate enemy air strength in the area before the landings. This task was performed so well that, after two days of strikes, there were virtually no Japanese aircraft left in the Marshalls capable of flying. Japan's "unsinkable carriers" were now useless.

Having learned a bitter lesson at Tarawa, the American commanders took no chances at Roi-Namur and Kwajalein. The islands were pounded by three days of naval gunfire and aerial bombing before the troops were sent in. Conolly won the eternal gratitude of the marines and the nickname "Close-in Conolly" by insisting that the old battleships attached to his force come in so close to shore to shell enemy defenses that their keels were almost scraping coral. Adjacent islands were taken as sites for artillery support before the major landings. Destroyers moved in close to the beach and continued firing almost until the troops had landed. Landing craft mounting rockets and forty-millimeter guns preceded the assault waves, taking up where the destroyers left off.

Roi-Namur was captured in little more than a day, with marine medium tanks advancing so rapidly they had to be called back so a coordinated attack could be organized. The Americans suffered their worst casualties when they mistook a concrete magazine full of Japanese torpedo warheads and heavy ammunition for a bunker and attacked it with satchel charges. "Great God Almighty!" radioed a pilot overhead. "The whole damn island has blown up!" Advancing slowly and methodically, and holding casualties to a minimum, the army took five days to capture Kwajalein, but in the euphoria of a smashing victory, only "Howlin' Mad" Smith complained about the delay. A Royal Navy officer who witnessed the landings at both Salerno and Kwajalein observed: "[It was] the most brilliant success I have ever taken part in. . . . Nothing could have lived through that sea and air bombardment. . . . It is something that is quite new in naval warfare . . . an absolute treat to watch. . . ."

Eniwetok was next. The capture of the archipelago would deprive the Japanese of the major outposts guarding Truk, only 750 miles away in the Carolines and less than a thousand miles from the Marianas. Nimitz had scheduled the invasion for May 1, but Spruance and Turner noted that this would give the Japanese time to improve their defenses. Why not attack now? Nimitz set February 17 as a target date and ordered Mitscher and TF 58 to neutralize Truk to prevent the enemy from interfering with the invasion of Eniwetok. Lean and taciturn, "Pete" Mitscher had little of the color of Halsey and Kelly Turner, and did not match the intellectual brilliance of Spruance, but thirty years of naval aviation service had uniquely fitted him for carrier command. He intended to prove once and for all that carriers could knock out enemy bases without the support of land-based aircraft.

The strike at Truk was timed to coincide with an assault on Eniwetok Atoll by a mixed army-marine expeditionary force under the command of Admiral Hill. The troops were to capture the northern island of Engebi, and then Parry and Eniwetok islands. As they prepared to go ashore, TF 58 was ninety miles northeast of Truk, and at 0635 on February 17, Mitscher launched his aircraft. Within a few minutes, seventy fighters were airborne.

Truk was hit first. More than thirty of the Japanese planes "scrambled" to meet them were shot down, and others were destroyed on the ground. Worried by the loss of Kwajalein and anticipating an attack on Truk, Admiral Koga had ordered most of the Combined Fleet to the Palaus, but a large number of merchantmen had been left behind in the broad lagoon. Radar-fitted TBFs and dive-bombers accounted for nearly two hundred thousand tons of merchant tonnage during the two-day strike, along with three light cruisers and four destroyers. The Japanese also lost 275 planes. TF 58 lost twenty-five planes, and the carrier *Intrepid* was damaged by a torpedo attack. The air strike against Truk was one of the most successful carrier operations of the war. The island was finished as an important base, and the Combined Fleet retreated all the way to Lingga Roads, near Singapore.

While Mitscher was dealing with the Japanese ashore, the battleships *New Jersey* and *Iowa*, a carrier, two heavy cruisers, and four destroyers, all under Spruance's command, swept the seas around the island to catch any ships trying to escape. Shortly after noon, *New Jersey*'s spotter planes reported enemy ships dead ahead at a distance of twenty-five miles. They were the light cruiser *Katori* and a pair of destroyers, making a getaway from Truk. Spruance sent his two heavy cruisers, *Minneapolis* and *New Orleans*, to deal with them. *Katori* fought until she rolled over and plunged to the bottom; one of the destroyers was also sunk.

The invasion of Eniwetok began with a landing by the 22nd Marines on Engebi, which was captured in a single day after being hammered by a massive air-and-sea bombardment. On neighboring Parry and Eniwetok, however, the plan went awry. The Japanese had also learned from the previous battles, and were so well dug in that it was believed the islands were unoccupied. Intelligence discovered on Engebi revealed the truth, but it was too late to mount a full-scale bombardment. Although Parry was taken by the marines after a day-long struggle, two battalions of the 106th Infantry (of the 27th Division) needed two and a half days of bitter fighting to secure Eniwetok.

Nimitz was already looking a thousand miles west, to the Marianas. Quickly shifting targets, TF 58 paused only to refuel and replenish, before a February 21, 1944, strike against airfields on Saipan and Tinian, which lay four miles apart, and Guam, where a large force of aircraft had recently been deployed. Japanese torpedo planes attacked one group of carriers, but heavy anti-aircraft fire accounted for ten "bogies" and drove off the rest. Mitscher countered with a sunrise sweep by his F6Fs, which shot down most of the seventy-five attacking Zeros. Before withdrawing, TF 58 had sunk forty-five thousand tons of shipping and destroyed 168 aircraft.

While Mitscher and TF 58 were striking repeatedly at the Marianas as part of a softening-up process before an invasion, the other prong of the American offensive was snaking its way closer to the Philippines. General MacArthur, unwilling to play second fiddle to the navy, broached a daring plan to bypass the string of Japanese garrisons and airfields that blocked the road to his cherished Philippines. Exploiting the freedom of movement conferred by control of the sea and the air, he intended to avoid enemy troop concentrations by pivoting from one island or coastal base to another.

MacArthur proposed to begin this campaign by leapfrogging four hundred miles west along the northern coast of New Guinea to Humboldt Bay—or Hollandia, as it was called by the Americans—in what had been Dutch New Guinea. Once the three airfields there were captured, he would jump another 550 miles to the western tip of the giant island and use it as the springboard for an invasion of the southern Philippines. Following considerable discussion, the Joint Chiefs gave the green light for this plan in early March. At the same time they approved Admiral Nimitz's proposal to bypass Truk, capture the Marianas in June, and then target either Formosa or Amoy on the Chinese coast.

The Hollandia invasion was ready in little more than a month—a remarkably short time considering the perennial shortage of shipping and equipment in the Southwest Pacific. Admiral Kinkaid, recently transferred from the Aleutians to command the Seventh Fleet, and Admiral Barbey, the VII Amphibious Force chief, gathered some 215 vessels, ranging from landing craft to cruisers, to carry the eighty-four thousand American and Australian troops to their beachheads. It was the largest amphibious force yet seen in that theater. MacArthur also had been promised carriers from TF 58, to provide cover and keep the Japanese from interfering. The enemy suspected a movement along the north coast of New Guinea, possibly to Wewak, and prepared for it by reinforcing the Hollandia airfields with some 350 aircraft.

The great leap forward could not get under way until these fields had been taken out. In late March, eighty B-24s from General Kenney's Fifth Air Force with a strong fighter escort struck the Hollandia fields. The Japanese were taken unaware, and the bulk of their planes were caught on the ground. Successive raids followed over the next three weeks, decimating Japanese air strength in the area. Later, it was determined that 340 enemy planes had been wrecked on the ground and another fifty shot down.

On April 21, Barbey's TF 77 began the voyage to Hollandia with eight escort carriers on loan from TF 58 providing support.* The var-

---

Saratoga and four destroyers had also been sent to join the British Pacific Fleet, now commanded by Admiral James Somerville and based on Trincomalee, in Ceylon. The fleet provided a diversion for the Hollandia operation by launching carrier strikes against Japanese bases at Sabang, on the northeast tip of Sumatra, and later Surabaja, in Java. The French battleship *Richelieu* and the Dutch cruiser *Tromp* also participated in the strike. Oil tanks, harbor facilities, two small merchantmen, and twenty-four enemy aircraft were destroyed. Only one Allied fighter was lost.

ious units rendezvoused west of the Admiralties and headed north toward the Palaus to deceive Japanese scout planes. Shortly after the tropical sunset, the convoy veered to the southwest and divided into three attack groups. While Wewak was being pounded to convince the Japanese it was the American objective, the easternmost group of ships headed for Aitape, about 125 miles southeast of Hollandia, where a regiment landed on April 22. The surprised Japanese fled into the jungle. Australian engineers immediately began work on an airstrip, and fighters were using it within two days.

Simultaneously, two divisions landed twenty miles apart on Humboldt Bay and Tanahmerah Bay, bracketing the airfields, after the beaches had been plastered by naval gunfire and aircraft. But Kenney's bombers had already done such outstanding work that the navy found few targets. "The amphibious ships ran up on the beaches and simply opened their front doors," observed Dan Barbey. The dazed Japanese, with no time to organize a defense, faded into the jungle. "The allied invasion of Hollandia and Aitape was a complete surprise to us," related a Japanese officer. Four days later, the three airfields were in American hands. Of the eleven thousand Japanese in the area, 650 were taken prisoner—the first large batch to surrender, a sign of deteriorating morale. All but a handful of the rest died of starvation or disease in the jungle before reaching the nearest Japanese base.

With his magazines still filled with bombs unused at Hollandia, Mitscher launched another strike at Truk on April 30. The planes, concentrating on repair shops, warehouses, and oil-storage tanks, left towering columns of flames and smoke behind them. Ninety-three Japanese planes were destroyed in exchange for a loss of twenty-seven American planes—most to anti-aircraft fire—but many of the American airmen were rescued. Nine downed fliers were picked up by a single-engine Kingfisher floatplane. With several men sitting on the wing, it taxied along the surface of the ocean until making contact with *Tang*, one of the submarines placed in position for this purpose. In all, *Tang*, commanded by Lieutenant Richard H. O'Kane, picked up twenty-two downed airmen.

The Imperial Navy, driven west from its anchorage at Truk, finally settled on a base at Tawitawi, an island off the northeast coast of Borneo, where it would be close to its fuel supplies. American submarines were reaping a rich harvest of tankers, reducing the Japanese fleet's supply of refined oil, so the ships were forced to use unprocessed oil, which was volatile and contained impurities that damaged their boilers. Following the loss of the Gilberts and Marshalls, a new defense line was drawn through the Marianas, the Palaus, northern New Guinea, and the Dutch East Indies. The Combined Fleet could not hope to match the U.S. Navy in battleships and carriers, but Admiral Koga was unwilling to abandon hope for the long-sought Mahanian decisive surface battle, so dear to the admirals on both sides.

Koga hoped to tempt the Americans into the western Carolines, where they would be within reach of the Imperial Navy's fuel-short carriers and land-based aircraft. In evident imitation of TF 58, Koga also reorganized the Combined Fleet, placing its carriers and best units in the newly created First Mobile Fleet, under the command of Vice-Admiral Jisaburo Ozawa, the Imperial Navy's foremost carrier expert.

Koga never had the opportunity to execute his plan. On March 31, the admiral's plane disappeared in a severe storm between the Palaus and the Philippines. Admiral Shiguru Fukudome, his chief of staff, went down in the same storm off Cebu, and was fished out of the sea by Filipino guerrillas. They relieved him of a briefcase that contained a copy of the Japanese plan. Fukudome was released, but the secret documents made their way to Pearl Harbor. Admiral Soetake Toyoda, the new top naval commander, rapidly prepared a modified plan, A-GO, a combined operation by the First Mobile Fleet and land-based aircraft, to deal with an American thrust.

A fresh surge by MacArthur necessitated changes in this plan. He advanced some three hundred miles to Biak, a large island near the tip of New Guinea, where there were three airfields. As a result of faulty intelligence, Biak was thought to be lightly defended, so only twelve thousand troops were assigned to capture it. Actually, Colonel Naoyuki Kuzumi, the Japanese commander, had eleven thousand men, five times the estimate, and many of them were trained combat troops. Rather than try to repel the enemy assault on the beach, Kuzumi held back as the enemy landed on May 27—thirty-ninth anniversary of the Battle of Tsushima—and had his men hole up in the cave-pocked hills. As the battle raged, MacArthur feared that Biak might become another Guadalcanal; it took until early August to secure the airfields and burn and blast the enemy from their caves, despite several communiqués announcing the end of all resistance.

Furious arguments raged among Japanese planners over the next American move. Would it be against the southern Philippines? The Palaus? Or the Marianas? In contrast to the methodical way in which Admiral Nimitz had deduced that Midway was the next enemy objective in June 1942, the Japanese engaged in guessing games. MacArthur's offensive was finally—and mistakenly—designated the main Yankee thrust. Toyoda produced Operation Kon, designed to reinforce the Japanese units holding out on Biak and to lure Admiral Spruance's Fifth Fleet into the hoped-for decisive battle in waters chosen by the Japanese.

Japanese air strength in the Central Pacific was drained away southward to the defense of Biak. Two successive Tokyo Expresses tried to deliver the first of some twenty-two thousand troops earmarked for Biak but failed, with the loss of a destroyer and damage to several others. Several submarines sent into the area also accomplished little. The destroyer-escort *England*, under Lieutenant Commander W. P. Pendleton, wiped out an entire patrol line, sinking no fewer than six boats in a twelve-day period in May, a record unmatched by any ship in any theater of operations. This feat was heightened by the fact that *England*'s crew had just ten weeks' sea experience.*

Next, Admiral Ozawa dispatched a powerful force under Rear Admiral Matome Ugaki that included the super battleships *Yamato* and *Musashi* and several cruisers and destroyers with a fresh shipment of troops for Biak. But on June 11, just as this armada was preparing to sail from Batjan, in the Moluccas, the entire strategic situation was suddenly altered by events a thousand miles away. TF 58 launched another series of raids on airfields on Saipan, Tinian, and Guam, which the Japanese believed was preliminary to an invasion. Toyoda activated A-GO, and Ozawa promptly sped north to counter this new threat. The decisive battle of the Pacific war was about to begin—not in southern waters, however, as hoped for by the Japanese, but in the Philippine Sea.

---

*"There'll always be an *England* in the United States Navy," Admiral King signaled the ship in congratulations. Otherwise, reports Morison, no particular attention was paid to this extraordinary exploit (*History*, vol. VIII, p. 228, n. 18).

•

CHAPTER 16

"The Far Shore"

Major Werner Pluskat tracked the horizon with his field glasses as the first streaks of dawn lightened the sky along the Normandy coast on the morning of June 6, 1944. He commanded four batteries—twenty guns in all—stationed on the cliffs overlooking what later became known as Omaha Beach. With a long-awaited Allied invasion looming, his unit had been alerted during the night by reports that enemy paratroops were dropping behind the coast. But as Pluskat repeatedly scanned the sea, he saw only the white tops of the waves, nothing more. Was it another false alarm? Wearily, he swung his glasses to the left again, picked up the dark mass of the Cotentin Peninsula, and slowly tracked to the right. Suddenly, Pluskat stopped and stared hard in frozen disbelief. A ghostly armada had suddenly appeared from nowhere!

In the murky gray light, the horizon was magically filling with ships—ships of every size and description. There appeared to be thousands of them, casually moving back and forth as if they had been out there for some time. Almost in a daze, Pluskat telephoned Major Block, an intelligence officer at the 352nd Infantry Division's headquarters. "Block," he declared, "it's the invasion. There must be ten thousand ships out there."

"Get hold of yourself, Pluskat!" snapped Block. "The Americans and the British together don't have that many ships. Nobody has that many ships!"

"If you don't believe me come up here and see for yourself!" shouted Pluskat. "It's fantastic! It's unbelievable!"

"What way are these ships heading?" Block asked after a slight pause.

"Right for me!" cried Pluskat.

Even as the American and Japanese carrier fleets were approaching a deadly rendezvous off the Marianas, Operation Overlord, the invasion of Hitler's Fortress Europe, was under way, after a series of postponements, false starts, delays, and foot-dragging. A half-dozen American and British battleships and thousands of fighters and bombers were soon pounding the Normandy coast preparatory to a landing. The ability of the British and the Americans to mount massive military operations in both the Atlantic and the Pacific at the same time was clear evidence of the unstoppable power of the Allied war machine.

From the moment that the last British soldier had been plucked from the beaches of Dunkirk, it was clear to both sides that, if the war lasted long enough, Britain and her allies would someday have to return. Serious planning for an invasion began after the Casablanca Conference in January 1943, when Lieutenant General Sir Frederick Morgan was appointed chief of staff to the yet-to-be-chosen Supreme Allied Commander, or COSSAC. The Germans had spent several years fortifying the thirty-five hundred miles of coastline from Norway to Spain, and Morgan's first task was to survey possible landing sites where this Atlantic Wall could be breached. Special attention was paid to the English Channel area, which provided the shortest invasion route and the quickest turnaround for shipping involved in the assault. COSSAC also launched planning for a simultaneous invasion of southern France, called "Anvil."

By the time of the Teheran Conference in November 1943, COSSAC had accomplished all it could without the appointment of an actual commander. Roosevelt, Churchill, and Stalin set May 1, 1944, as the date for the invasion and agreed that, inasmuch as the United States would provide the largest number of troops involved in the operation, an American should be named Supreme Allied Commander.* Roosevelt wanted to appoint General Marshall to the post, but Admiral King and others argued that Marshall was too valuable as a

---

*Also at Teheran, Stalin agreed to enter the war against Japan within ninety days of Germany's defeat.

member of the Joint Chiefs. The job went instead to General Eisenhower, who was recalled from the Mediterranean.

"You will enter the Continent of Europe, and in conjunction with the other United Nations, undertake operations aimed at the heart of Germany and the destruction of her armed forces," Eisenhower was told. Significantly, unlike the previous landings in North Africa, Sicily, and Italy, which had only limited objectives, the invasion of Europe was intended to end the war with an Allied victory. With an American in overall charge, British officers were named to head the ground, air, and sea forces: General Montgomery, Air Chief Marshal Sir Trafford Leigh-Mallory, and Admiral Sir Bertram Ramsay. In January 1944, Air Chief Marshal Sir Arthur Tedder became Eisenhower's deputy.

No one was better suited than Ramsay for the task of organizing Operation Neptune, the naval side of Overlord. Since he had been in charge of the invasions of North Africa and Sicily, and had organized the Dunkirk evacuation, it was only fitting that he should guide the return of Allied forces to the Continent almost exactly four years later. The task facing him was without precedent. The success of the invasion rested first and foremost on the Allied navies' ability to get the troops across the English Channel, with all its unpredictability of wind, sea, and tide. Sea, land, and air operations had to be efficiently dovetailed if the gamble was to pay off.*

The naval forces also had to act as floating artillery until sufficient guns could be put ashore. They had to keep German forces out of the Channel, sweep lanes through the dense minefields, and clear the beaches of obstacles designed to impede the landings. Nor would Ramsay's problems end with the actual invasion of what the D-Day commanders called the "Far Shore." The Allied armies would depend upon an uninterrupted flow of seaborne reinforcements, stores, ammunition, and fuel until they could break out of the Normandy beachheads. Yet there was little prospect of the immediate capture of a port to handle this traffic, because the Germans had heavily forti-

---

*Curiously, these stupendous problems are often ignored by historians of the D-Day invasion, who begin their accounts with the arrival of the troops on the beaches, as if the marshaling of men and ships and stores and the crossing of the Channel were matters of minor importance.

fied all such harbors. Opening headquarters in Norfolk House, the London mansion of the duke of Norfolk, Ramsay and his staff began to deal with these problems.

Where was the landing to take place? The obvious choice was the Pas de Calais, just twenty miles across the Channel from Dover, within range of fighter bases in Britain and easy reach of Paris and the Ruhr, Germany's industrial heart. But the beaches were narrow and bounded by high cliffs, which would limit the first assault wave to only two divisions, and the location of airfields and roads would facilitate a German counterattack. Moreover, intelligence reports indicated it was exactly where the enemy expected an attack and was heavily defended. The Brittany coast was unsuitable for other reasons. It offered five major ports, but it was too far from Paris and the German frontier.

So, almost by default, the Allies decided to land three infantry divisions and two airborne divisions supported by two follow-up divisions on the Normandy coast, between the Cotentin Peninsula and the Orne River, on the Bay of the Seine. This fifty-mile stretch of sandy beach was somewhat sheltered, and although the terrain behind it favored the defense—the difficult *bocage* of small fields separated by hedgerows—there were good exit routes leading inland, and the German defenses were less robust than in the Pas de Calais.

Later, under prodding by General Montgomery, the first wave of the Allied force was increased to five seaborne and three airborne divisions. He also insisted that the initial assault should include a landing at the base of the Cotentin Peninsula as a preliminary to the capture of Cherbourg. The invasion date was pushed back a month, to early June, to find another thousand landing craft for the additional troops. Anvil, the invasion of southern France, was put on hold.

The success of the landings depended upon Allied air superiority to keep German reinforcements from reaching the beach. Three months before D-Day, General Eisenhower ordered the start of a massive air attack upon the French railway system and the bridges across the Seine and other rivers, but the British and American air commanders resisted, preferring to concentrate on the strategic bombing of Germany's cities and industrial base. Eisenhower, determined to head off a repetition of the lack of cooperation from the flyers that had bedeviled the Mediterranean campaign, threatened to resign, and won Roosevelt's support for his "Transportation Plan."

Southern England was transformed, over the next several months, into a massive arsenal and staging area. It was sinking under the weight of the load, went the joke, and the only thing holding it up was the barrage balloons intended to snare low-flying enemy aircraft. The Allies gathered 6,939 ships and landing craft for Overlord.* They built 163 airfields, from which twelve thousand planes were to fly in support of the invasion. Two million tons of weapons and supplies and mountains of food and fuel were stockpiled.

The British came up with a daring and ingenious solution to the problem of the lack of an adequate port to unload reinforcements and cargo. Two prefabricated artificial harbors known as "Mulberries," made from concrete-filled pontoons and old ships, would be towed across to the French coast in sections and installed off the invasion beaches. To make up for lack of a fuel terminal, an underwater oil pipeline (code-named Pluto) was laid across the Channel. As D-Day neared, an army of 2.5 million men coiled across the English countryside, awaiting the signal to spring across the Channel.

In the meantime, amphibious forces were called upon to make one final landing in the Italian theater. Following the capture of Naples, Field Marshal Albert Kesselring, the German commander, had conducted a masterful foot-by-foot retreat up the Italian boot, and the Allies found themselves hopelessly bogged down in a major land campaign in an area now considered a backwater. In an effort to bypass the German-held Gustav Line blocking the road to Rome, Churchill urged a landing near the Italian capital. Landing craft were in short supply and there were misgivings among the generals, but the prime minister pressed ahead. On January 22, 1944, some fifty thousand Allied troops were put ashore at Anzio, about thirty-three miles south of Rome.

The Germans were caught by surprise by this end run, and the road to Rome lay wide open, unguarded by the enemy. But Major

---

*The breakdown was as follows:

Naval Combatant Vessels	1,213
Landing Ships and Craft	4,126
Ancillary Ships and Craft	736
Merchant Ships	864

Seventy-nine percent of these vessels were British or Canadian.

General John P. Lucas, the American commander, was unable to exploit his advantage because he lacked the combat force to hold inland objectives, and Kesselring was given time to regroup. Within a few days, several German divisions were dug in on the heights overlooking the beachhead, and the troops were under constant fire by the deadly German 88s, pinned down and unable to move. The beachhead was the front line. Hundreds of men were needlessly lost at Anzio as they huddled in soggy foxholes and dugouts in wretched weather. "I had hoped that we were hurling a wildcat onto the shore," Churchill later explained, "but all we got was a stranded whale." Radio correspondent Eric Sevareid was even blunter in his summation. "Anzio," he said, was "a stupid mistake."

Grand Admiral Dönitz, grimly surveying the Kriegsmarine's prospects as 1944 began, offered nothing in his New Year's Order of the Day except increased fervor and faith in Adolf Hitler. "An iron year lies behind us," he declared. "Whatever fate may demand from us in the coming year, we will endure, united in will, steady in loyalty, fanatical in belief in our victory. . . . The Führer shows us the way and the goal. We follow him with body and soul to a great German future!"

Others were more realistic. "The smell of death was everywhere," observed Korvettenkapitän Herbert A. Werner, skipper of U-230. The morale of the U-boat crews was strained to the breaking point as twenty-seven boats failed to return in the last two months of 1943. Upon his arrival in the bomb-proof pens of Brest after a nightmarish crossing of the Bay of Biscay, now known as "Death Valley," Werner declared that "only then, with seven metres of reinforced concrete over our heads were we safe. . . . I took a deep breath, heaved a great sigh of relief. That was all I could do about our sinking fortunes. . . . I noticed many empty berths in the bunker. . . ."

Observing the Allied buildup in Britain, the German High Command now realized that the failure of the U-boats to disrupt the North Atlantic convoys after mid-1943 was an even greater disaster than it had appeared at the time. In the following twelve months, vast numbers of troops and stocks of equipment, weapons, and ammunition had been ferried almost unmolested across the Atlantic, making the assault on Fortress Europe possible.

Faced with these bleak prospects, Dönitz, like Hitler, looked to a new generation of "wonder" weapons to turn the tide against the Allies. First were the acoustic torpedo, which homed in on a ship's propeller noise,* and the snorkel (Schnorchel) or nose, a mast that could be raised and lowered like a periscope and contained both fresh-air and exhaust shafts. These allowed U-boats to use their diesel engines to charge their electrical batteries and replenish their air supplies underwater. They could remain submerged longer, hiding from prowling aircraft and increasing their chances of survival.

The first snorkel boats became operational in February 1944, but the U-boat crews were not at all enthusiastic. The snorkel head created a large wake and could be spotted by an alert observer. Thus, the snorkel was safe only at night; during the day, the crews had to lie still and silent on their bunks to conserve oxygen until the breathing tube could be floated to the surface.

Dönitz was convinced that the only real solution to continued U-boat losses was a completely new type of vessel—a "true submarine," with high underwater speed and long endurance. Before the war, an engineer named Helmuth Walter had proposed a propulsion plant for submarines that combined a gas turbine and a non-oxygen-using fuel such as hydrogen peroxide. The idea had been brushed aside, but in the summer of 1942 Dönitz pressed Hitler to authorize development of two experimental Walter submarines.

As the Atlantic crisis deepened, the construction of twenty-four small and two large boats was given high priority. The first of the small boats had a phenomenal submerged speed of twenty-five knots, well above that of most escorts, and was extremely maneuverable, able to change depth and speed rapidly to confuse U-boat hunters. To maintain their streamlined shape, the Walter boats dispensed with the familiar deck gun. There were numerous defects in the early models—high-test peroxide was extremely volatile, for instance— and it was estimated that the first operational boat would not be ready for delivery until 1945.

---

*Acoustic torpedoes were used primarily against escorts. The British developed a countermeasure—a noise-making machine called a Foxer, which was towed a safe distance behind a ship to attract the torpedo. They claimed that no ship towing a Foxer was struck by an acoustic torpedo. But Jürgen Rohwer, the German naval historian, states that, of the seventy-seven hits by acoustic torpedoes, eight were made against ships with their Foxers streamed—or 10.4 percent (Terraine, *The U-Boat Wars*, p. 640).

To meet immediate requirements, and to bridge the gap between the old and the new, Dr. Walter suggested the development of large snorkel boats with the streamlined form of the high-speed submarine and enormous battery capacity. Two types of craft, known as "Electro-boats," were developed: the Type XXI, a large boat of 1,621 tons, capable of short bursts of submerged speed of eighteen knots, and the smaller, 230-ton Type XXIII, which could do thirteen knots underwater for inshore operations. Type XXI had six torpedo tubes and twenty torpedoes; Type XXIII, two tubes and torpedoes.

Unhappy with the navy's submarine-production schedules, Dönitz turned to his friend Albert Speer, the highly efficient armaments minister, whose experts suggested that the boats be built in eight prefabricated sections and put together like automobiles on a production line. The target date for delivery of the first was April–May 1944, with production to reach thirty per month by September 1944. Because of heavy Allied bombing, the subsections were built at widely dispersed factories and then assembled at shipyards in Hamburg, Bremen, and Danzig.

Eight Electro-boats were completed and delivered to the Kriegsmarine by August 1944. The Allies had no ready technical or operational answers to the formidable Type XXI, with its high speed and ability to remain submerged for long periods. The early Walter boats had several defects, however, and were placed on training status in the Baltic. This hurried effort to build hundreds of new submarines had a trade-off, however. Submarine construction dug deeply into the available supply of high-grade steel and skilled workers desperately needed for the production of tanks and other weapons for the massive land battles being fought on both the Eastern and Western fronts.

With the tide running inexorably against him, Dönitz tried to keep the U-boat campaign going until the Electro-boats were ready. If the Allied invasion of France was repelled, he believed the enemy would lose heart and recognize Fortress Europe as impregnable. German forces could be released for a counterattack on the Eastern Front, and the Führer could present terms to the Western Allies to be negotiated from a strong position. There was also the possibility that they might wake up to what a communist victory would mean and join Germany in an anti-Bolshevik crusade.

As for the U-boat fleet, Dönitz had 449 boats in commission in May

1944, of which 162 were operational. But a large number of these were undergoing refits and repairs, and only forty-three were available to attack enemy shipping on any given day. Trying to repeat his successes of the early part of the war, Dönitz concentrated on convoys as they neared their home ports. Surprise was achieved to some extent, but the massing of U-boats in the Western Approaches played into the hands of the escorts. For example Captain "Johnny" Walker's Second Escort Group sank six U-boats in a twenty-seven-day patrol.*

Toward the end of March, Dönitz began collecting a group of some forty U-boats to attack the invasion fleet when it appeared. Their one goal, he told his captains, was: "Attack—close-in—sink!" This was followed up by another order, with overtones of an exhortation to suicide: "Every vessel taking part in the landing, even if it has but a handful of men or a solitary tank aboard, is a target of the utmost importance which must be attacked regardless of risk. . . . Every boat that inflicts losses on the enemy while he is landing has fulfilled its primary function even though it perishes in doing so."†

In the meantime, the German navy lent what support it could the army on the Eastern Front, including keeping supply lines open to units of the German army under attack in the Crimea and along the Baltic coast. When the Crimea was finally evacuated, the navy succeeded in lifting off over thirty thousand troops, including some wounded, from Odessa, but another seventy-five thousand had to be left behind. The Kriegsmarine's remaining surface ships—the pocket battleships *Lützow* and *Scheer*, the heavy cruisers *Prinz Eugen* and *Hipper*, and four light cruisers—were stationed in the Baltic and Norway to protect the flow of iron ore from Sweden and Norway. These tasks were performed with some success and proved, ironically, the correctness of those who had supported a navy attuned to

---

*In one such case, *U-505* was blown to the surface by a U.S. Navy escort group headed by Captain Daniel V. Gallery and captured by a boarding party before her crew could scuttle her. It was the first vessel taken by the navy by boarding since the War of 1812. *U-505* is now on display at the Chicago Museum of Science and Industry.

†On April 28, 1944, a trio of German S-boats got in among a convoy of nine American LSTs that had been rehearsing landings at Slapton Sands, west of Dartmouth. Two of the LSTs were sunk and a third was damaged, with the loss of nearly eight hundred men—equal to nearly a third of those killed in action on D-Day itself. Oberleutnant zur See Klaus Dönitz, the admiral's surviving son, was killed on May 14, 1944, in another S-boat raid in the Channel.

coastal defense as better suited to Germany's needs than a high-seas fleet.

Early in 1944, Ultra intelligence reported that the damage sustained by *Tirpitz* in the X-craft attack had been repaired and she would again be seaworthy by mid-March. Russian bombers attacked the ship in February but failed to score any hits. Worried that she might get out again and try to break up convoys carrying supplies for Overlord, the Home Fleet kept a substantial force of battleships and carriers on the alert at Scapa Flow to deal with such an eventuality. Admiral King was unhappy with the insistence of the Royal Navy upon keeping such valuable ships tied down at Scapa, believing this placed an extra burden on the U.S. Navy, which had to move ships from the Pacific to fill their places in Neptune.

Late in April, two Fleet Air Arm strike forces, each consisting of twenty-one Barracuda bombers, were embarked on *Victorious* and *Furious*, accompanied by two escort carriers carrying a fighter screen, and they steamed toward *Tirpitz*'s lair in the Altenfjord. The fjord was too shallow for a torpedo attack, so ten of the planes carried sixteen-hundred-pound bombs, which, it was believed, could penetrate the battleship's thick deck armor if dropped from higher than three thousand feet. The first wave of Barracudas was launched at 0430 on April 30, about 120 miles from the Norwegian coast.

The fighters screamed down on the surprised *Tirpitz* to suppress her anti-aircraft batteries; the Barracudas followed up, and disregarding orders dived to below three thousand feet to ensure hits on the target. Flames leaped from the vessel's superstructure, and fountains of white water erupted about her. An hour later, another wave of fighters and bombers flew to the attack. In all, *Tirpitz* was hit fourteen times, but the heavy bombs failed to pierce her armor because they had been dropped from too low an altitude. Even so, she was a shambles topside, her fire-control system had been wrecked, she was flooded, and 438 of her crew were killed or wounded. Two British bombers were lost.

Although the Germans were constructing formidable defenses on the French coast, a confusing chain of command, unresolved strategic conflicts, and Allied deception efforts hampered their plans for dealing with an invasion. Field Marshal Gerd von Rundstedt, commander-in-chief of Army Group West and overall commander in France, wanted to defend the French coast with a powerful mobile reserve of tanks and infantry, to be rushed to the scene of action as needed to meet Allied threats. Having studied the Salerno assault, he concluded that a static defense could not stand up to the pounding of a heavy naval bombardment. But Marshal Rommel, who had direct responsibility for the defense of the Atlantic Wall, believed that the invaders had to be stopped on the beaches, because, with the Allies in complete control of the air, a mobile reserve would be slaughtered before it could get into action. Unless the Allies were thrown back into the sea within twenty-four hours, Rommel argued, Germany faced certain defeat.

Hitler was called upon to decide the issue but made it worse. Though Rommel was given control of some of the tanks, the Führer himself retained personal control over more than half the armored forces in Normandy. By equivocating between the two plans, the Germans had the advantages of neither. Further confusion was caused by Operation Fortitude, a British-initiated deception scheme designed to convince the enemy that the main Allied landing would come somewhere other than Normandy. Fake radio traffic, false troop movements, phony docks, and cardboard mock-ups of combat vehicles persuaded the Germans that the swashbuckling General Patton commanded an army group that was supposedly poised to strike Calais, or even Norway.*

Falling for the Allied feints, Hitler refused Rommel's requests to bring heavy guns down from the Norwegian coast to France. The approaches to Bergen were protected by thirty-four batteries of heavy guns, and Narvik had eighty batteries. On the other hand, there were only thirty heavy guns on the entire French coast between the Somme and the Loire. Making the best of what he had, Rommel laced the shoreline with pillboxes, artillery emplacements, thousands of mines, and obstacles—steel stakes, barbed wire, booby traps, and automatic flamethrowers—designed to halt the landing craft and trap the invaders under the fire of German guns. Behind the beaches, the lowlands were flooded and stakes were driven into open fields to pre-

---

*Operation Fortitude succeeded so well that Hitler kept the Fifteenth Army Group uselessly tied down in the Pas de Calais for three weeks after D-Day while awaiting the "main" Allied landing.

vent use by paratroops and gliders. Manpower and materiel shortages prevented Rommel from completing the Atlantic Wall, but it was
nevertheless a formidable barrier to a successful invasion.

On May 25, the Supreme Commander set D-Day for June 5.
Because of weather and tidal conditions and the need for moonlight
to drop paratroops, Eisenhower's choice was limited to between
June 5 and 7 or June 18 to 20. He selected the earlier period.* The
ships began their movements from points as widely separated as the
Thames estuary and Northern Ireland to the bases and ports from
which they would embark for France. Very strict security was
imposed, and the troops and crews were cut off from outside communication. By June 3, there were some 170,000 assault troops on
the transports and large landing craft.

The naval forces were divided into a predominantly British Eastern Naval Task Force under command of the ubiquitous Rear Admiral Sir Philip Vian, and a mainly American Western Naval Task Force
under Rear Admiral Alan G. Kirk, a veteran of amphibious operations
in the Mediterranean. The Eastern group was divided into Forces G,
J, and S, which were to land two British and one Canadian division
on Gold, Juno, and Sword beaches, running from the Orne to Port-
en-Bessin. The Western group was divided into two forces that were
to put one U.S. Army division ashore at Utah Beach, adjacent to the
Contentin Peninsula, and two at Omaha Beach, which abutted the
British landing beaches. In addition, one British and two American
airborne divisions were to drop inland and cover the right and left
flanks of the beachheads.

As the first assault convoys set out, the weather became gusty and
the sea rose. Low clouds scudded across the sky, and it was apparent
that a violent storm was brewing. Most of the troops, cooped up in the
tossing landing craft, were soon desperately seasick. In the early
hours of June 4,† Eisenhower, informed by meteorologists that the

---

*Eisenhower's choice for D-Day was fortunate. Had the invasion been scheduled for
June 18–20, it would have run into one of the worst storms in forty years. Thus, the fleet
would probably have suffered the same fate as the Spanish Armada in 1588.

†That same day, Allied troops, having launched an attack against the Gustav Line in
Italy a month before, entered Rome, after relieving the Anzio beachhead. Kesselring
made a skillful retreat and survived to fight another day.

situation was full of menace, decided to postpone the invasion for twenty-four hours, until June 6. Though this signal was transmitted to the fleet, one American convoy of 138 vessels and four escorts failed to get the message and pressed on toward France. Two destroyers raced out to head it off, but farce nearly turned to tragedy. The convoy turned back, but the destroyers blundered into a German minefield, from which they escaped with difficulty.

On the morning of June 5, the wind rattled the windows of the British naval headquarters, near Portsmouth, as the Allied chiefs gravely considered the situation. The rain, as Eisenhower later recalled, was blowing horizontally. But an RAF meteorologist predicted clearing skies for the next day. The Supreme Commander conferred briefly with his admirals and generals and then stood up. "O.K.," he said. "We'll go."

Within a half hour of sunset on June 5, the leading ships of the seaborne assault moved into the main staging area, known as "Piccadilly Circus," southeast of the Isle of Wight. They proceeded down "The Spout" of five mine-swept channels toward France, a channel for each task force. Ramsay came out in a torpedo boat to see them off. About halfway across the Channel, these lanes converged into two, one for fast, the other for slow convoys. A westerly wind blowing at fifteen knots whipped the choppy sea into waves three feet high. Thousands of men—seasick, wet, and wrapped in cocoons of anxiety—shivered on deck or huddled in the great caverns of the LSTs or in the cramped LSIs, in the yellow glow of electric lights and the stench of vomit.

Overhead, they could hear the rumble of the transports carrying the airborne troops into battle. The drop itself was chaotic. Only two of the six U.S. parachute regiments landed near their objectives. Some men drifted to earth as far as thirty-five miles from their targets; others were machine-gunned during the seemingly eternal forty-three seconds it took to float to the ground from seven hundred feet. Eighteen gliders crashed on landing, within a few minutes of each other. Yet British troops seized the key bridges over the Orne River east of Caen, and to the west the Americans captured the important crossroads of Ste.-Mère-Eglise. The very disarray of the airborne landing confused the Germans, who were unable to tell from where the main attack was coming.

In spite of the foul weather, the Channel crossing was made in good order and almost on schedule. Some of the smaller craft strayed off course, but none foundered. With the impatience of sheepdogs chivvying a dim-witted flock, sleek destroyers and patrol boats darted about, keeping order. Paradoxically, the weather worked to the advantage of the Allies. Believing a landing unlikely in such conditions, Rommel had gone home to Germany for his wife's birthday. Vice-Admiral Krancke, commander of Naval Group West, noted in his war diary that the tides were "not right" for an invasion. Routine air patrols and planned sweeps of the Channel by torpedo boat were canceled. And when the German radar malfunctioned, it was attributed to the weather rather than enemy interference.

As they watched the passage of the invasion fleet, those of a literary turn of mind might have recalled Shakespeare's portrayal of Henry V's cross-Channel operation of 1415:

> . . . behold
> A city on th' inconstant billows dancing;
> For so appears this fleet majestical,
> Holding due course to Harfleur. Follow, follow. . .

Shortly after dawn on June 6, the transports, which had anchored off the Normandy beaches at 0200, began debarking the assault troops. Ramsay had ordered them to take up positions seven miles offshore, but Kirk placed his ships eleven miles out, beyond the range of the German coastal batteries. As a result, the American troops were forced to travel farther to reach the beaches than the British units, and were in poorer shape when they arrived. LCVs and LCMs shuddered and banged against the steel sides of the transports as the heavily laden men waited their turn to climb down slippery ladders or nets into the heaving boats. Once loaded, they advanced along designated lanes to the line of departure and circled until ordered to run in to the beaches through lanes cleared by the minesweepers.

Between the transports and the beach the bombardment groups lay at anchor, ready to open up. Fire support for the American sectors included the venerable battleships *Nevada, Texas,* and *Arkansas,* which were to engage the heavy batteries with their twelve- and fourteen-inch guns. The heavy cruisers *Tuscaloosa, Quincy,* and

Augusta, five British and two French light cruisers, and twenty-two destroyers were to operate closer in. *Rodney, Warspite,* and *Ramillies* provided the big guns in the British areas and were supported by a fifteen-inch-gun monitor, twelve cruisers, and thirty-seven destroyers. Low clouds interfered with the aim of the Allied heavy bombers assigned to take out the German batteries, and the pilots were ordered to drop their bombs inland so they would not accidentally fall on the approaching troops. Unfortunately, the naval commanders were not informed of the change in plan.

"It seemed like we were out there forever circling," recalled Sergeant John R. Slaughter of the 116th Infantry, 29th Division. "I was trying to keep warm, trying to stay dry and trying to keep from throwing up. In the end I was throwing up into my own helmet, rinsing it in the bottom of the boat and throwing up again. . . . When we formed our wave and started in, the motion and the spray got worse. Then . . . the bombardment started. BOOM-BA-BA-BOOM! BOOM-BA-BA-BOOM! The noise was incredible. The battleship *Texas* was on our starboard side, and each time she fired a salvo from her 14-inch guns the recoil squatted her down in the water, setting up a shock wave that would nearly swamp us. We were all sick, wet, miserable, bailing with our helmets, deaf from the guns, chilled from the wind and all I could think was 'Just get us in there. Nothing could be worse than this'. . . ."

The battleships fired methodically at targets spotted by Spitfire fighters, an innovation introduced during the Sicilian campaign. Closer inshore, the cruisers fired at such a rapid rate that the muzzle flashes looked like summer lightning; destroyers shouldered their way among the landing craft, searching out targets of opportunity for their five-inch guns. Bank after bank of rockets shrieked toward the beaches, trailing streams of orange-red flame. The curtain of fire was lifted as the first wave of landing craft neared the beach.

The assault on Utah Beach was timed for low tide, to expose as many of the underwater obstacles as possible. At 0631, only one minute behind schedule, landing craft dropped their ramps, and troops of the U.S. Fourth Infantry Division waded a hundred yards to shore. Resistance was surprisingly light. Confusion and a strong current had pushed the invaders more than a mile from the intended landing zone, which proved to be a fortunate error, for the new area was only

lightly defended. Naval gunfire contributed to the swift and successful landings at Utah. A direct hit by *Nevada*'s gun silenced three powerful ten-inch guns, and the heavy cruisers suppressed other batteries.

The destroyer *Corry* stood into shore to provide support. She was
soon firing so rapidly that water had to be played on her overheated
gun barrels. As the sea about his ship began to boil with near misses,
Lieutenant Commander George D. Hoffman decided to increase the
range. Before his ship could make its getaway, however, she struck a
mine and, back broken, began to sink. The gun crews continued to fire
until water lapped over *Corry*'s decks, and she was abandoned—one
of the major losses suffered by the U.S. Navy on D-Day. By the end of
the day, the invaders had cleared a six-mile beachhead and had moved
inland to link up with the paratroopers around Ste.-Mère-Eglise.

Ten miles to the east, at Omaha Beach, where the forty thousand
men of the First and 29th divisions were to land, the German shore
batteries opened fire on *Arkansas* at 0530. Twenty minutes later, the
bombardment group replied on schedule. But the shelling lasted only
thirty-five minutes—far too short to be effective, considering the
strength of the enemy defenses and the fact that most of the bombs
dropped earlier had gone astray. The Germans had established twelve
strongpoints along the seven-thousand yard expanse of shore, which
provided a withering field of fire. Moreover, undetected by Allied
intelligence, the veteran 352nd Infantry Division had been shifted into
the area and was awaiting the invaders. Unlike Utah Beach, which
consisted of sand dunes, Omaha was overlooked by steep cliffs as
much as two hundred feet high, which were ideal for the defense.

Texas's big guns concentrated on a supposed battery of six long-
range guns on the cliffs of Pointe-du-Hoc,* at the western end of the
beach, while *Arkansas* took station off the Port-en-Bessin battery, on
the eastern side, between the American and British beachheads.
Navy demolition teams were the first ashore and went to work blasting a path through the obstacles. They were decimated by German

---

*U.S. Army Rangers scaled Pointe-du-Hoc with ropes and ladders in the face of stiff
German resistance, supported by naval gunfire, only to find wooden telephone poles
mounted where the guns should have been. The enemy had dismounted them and was
building new casements, but Allied intelligence had failed to detect the ruse. Searching
inland, the Rangers found the guns and destroyed them.

fire, and although the survivors managed to blow a total of six gaps, they were unmarked. Many of the mined obstacles were still intact when the first landing craft approached the shore.

The boat carrying Sergeant Slaughter's company was almost swamped by a near miss from a German shell. Panicking, the British coxswain shouted that he was going to drop the ramp immediately— which meant the troops would have been dropped off in water over their heads. One man calmly put a .45 pistol to the sailor's head and said: " '*All* the way in!' " recalls Slaughter. "And the coxswain took us in. . . . We could hear the machine guns and bullets were everywhere. There were dead men floating in the water and others acting dead, both coming in on the tide. Men were screaming. The water was turning red. . . ."

Enemy machine guns and mortars raked the narrow, crescent-shaped beach, inflicting heavy casualties on the first waves as they came ashore, half paralyzed by seasickness, exhaustion, and terror. Some landing craft were swamped in the choppy sea before they even reached the beach. The boats carrying amphibious tanks and artillery were sunk, and the engineers lost their equipment in the surf. Wrecked landing craft, disabled tanks, dead and wounded—all piled up along the shoreline. For the first several hours, the invaders held only a few yards of beach, and leaderless groups of men huddled under a seawall from the intense fire. Fifty landing craft turned in circles offshore, trying to locate gaps in the beach obstacles. At 0900, Lieutenant General Omar N. Bradley, commander of the First Army, concluded that "our troops had suffered an irreversible catastrophe" and considered shutting down Omaha and shifting the follow-up troops to Utah or the British sectors.

A catastrophe it was, but not irreversible. Individual acts of courage helped turn the tide. LCT-30 closed the beach, but Lieutenant Sidney W. Brinker saw other landing craft holding back. Brinker drove at full speed at the obstacles at the end of a cleared channel, rode over them, and silenced all the enemy guns in the area. Surviving noncoms and junior officers were organizing small groups of men into fighting units. Machine guns were set up to answer the German fire. Tanks finally started arriving ashore. Engineers blew gaps in the wire and minefields, and patrols began to move forward. "Two kinds of people are staying on this beach," yelled Colonel

George Taylor of the Sixteenth Regimental Combat Team, "the dead and those who are going to die. Let's get the hell out of here!"

With the loss of most of the artillery sent ashore, naval-gunfire support played a key role in clearing the way for the breakout from the beach areas. *Texas, Arkansas*, and two British and two French cruisers created a ring of fire around the beachhead, cutting it off from the interior and preventing the Germans from either shifting their forces or bringing up reinforcements. With her fire directed by survivors of the naval fire-control parties, *Texas* blasted the casemated Pointe-de-la-Percée battery, at the western end of the Omaha cliffs, and sent the guns tumbling down the cliff into the sea.

Nine U.S. and three British destroyers closed to within four hundred yards of the beach, so close their gunners could select targets of opportunity with the naked eye. "They had their bows on the bottom," reported Admiral Kirk. *Carmick* turned enemy emplacements at Les Moulins that had pinned down some American troops into rubble. A battery on the bluffs was pounded so hard by *McCook* that it tried to surrender to the destroyer. When reports were received that the Germans were spotting from a church tower behind the beach, *Emmons* neatly clipped off the top. One of the ships, *Baldwin*, was hit by enemy shellfire but was only superficially damaged. Supported by the destroyers, the troops captured the bluffs, seized the ravines leading away from the beach, and established a line a mile inland. "The fire curtain provided by the guns of the Navy . . . proved to be one of the best trump cards of the Anglo–United States invasion armies," according to an assessment of the breaching of Fortress Europe made by the German army.

The Luftwaffe and the German navy offered only minor resistance to the invasion. Heavy fighter and bomber attacks on German airfields reduced the latter to impotence, and the Sword Beach transport group was the only naval unit to come under attack by enemy surface vessels. Four S-boats from Le Havre slipped in among them and struck just as the ships reached lowering position. The Norwegian destroyer *Svenner* was hit and sank, and several other ships narrowly escaped being torpedoed in this daring raid. The Germans withdrew at high speed, covered by a smoke screen that had been laid by the British to mask the assault force. Fifteen boats also sortied from Cherbourg, but when their crews were confronted with the awesome power of the Allies they withdrew.

The landings on Gold, Juno, and Sword—the British and Canadian beaches—were easy compared with Omaha. The obstructions were less thickly sown, the defenses not so formidable. Admiral Vian's battleships, guided into position by signals from two midget submarines, provided the British assault forces with a larger prelanding bombardment than the Americans had. This shelling was highly accurate. To the amazement of the Germans, *Rodney* planted her sixteen-inch shells squarely on enemy tanks massing for a counterattack seventeen miles behind Gold.

Hitler also made a contribution to the Allied success. The Führer had gone to bed early that morning at Berchtesgaden, his Bavarian retreat, and was allowed to slumber on by his coterie of sycophants despite frantic pleas from the army commanders in Normandy for release of the armored forces under his personal control. Even when informed of the Allied landings, Hitler believed it a feint. The real attack was coming later in the Pas de Calais, he claimed, and delayed releasing the tanks until it was too late. "If I was commander of the Allied forces right now," observed Rommel, who reached his headquarters that night, "I could finish off the war in fourteen days."

Although not all objectives were gained, by nightfall of D-Day the Allied navies had put 132,000 troops ashore, at a cost of 10,000 casualties, of whom a quarter were killed—far fewer than anticipated. The number of German deaths was somewhere between 4,000 and 8,000. Within a week, some 250,000 men had been landed in France. "Overlord," Stalin cabled Churchill, "is a joy to all."

Only part of Neptune had been completed, however. As the assault brigades expanded their beachheads, unloading facilities were urgently needed for the massive reinforcements and supplies on the way. On the night of D-Day, one of the strangest armadas in history wallowed across the Channel—old warships and merchantmen on their last voyage, huge concrete caissons and steel frameworks under tow by tugs—the first sections of the Mulberry artificial harbors to be erected off Omaha and Gold beaches. Although only partially completed, they were in use by June 17.

Two days later, a violent gale swept the area. Unloading ceased as the crews of warships and merchant vessels struggled to save their ships. Heavy seas battered the half-completed breakwaters, wrecking the Mulberry off Omaha Beach and driving eight hundred landing craft ashore. Admiral Ramsay immediately shifted operations to the other Mulberry, which, although damaged, had survived the storm. Luckily, several small harbors had already been pressed into service, and it had been determined that, because of the flatness of the Normandy beaches, LSTs could run themselves ashore to be unloaded. In the face of severe handicaps, 920,000 men, 586,000 tons of supplies, and 177,000 vehicles of all types were landed in France in the first month following D-Day.

With as many as sixteen convoys a day on continuous passage across the Channel, German surface forces and U-boats had plenty of targets—if they could penetrate the Allied defense. Several S-boat attacks on the flanks of the assault were beaten off, after the loss of a few landing craft. Four destroyers put out from Brest on June 8, but, forewarned by Ultra, the Allies were ready for them. In the largest purely naval action of Neptune, one of the German vessels was sunk in a sharp firefight off Cherbourg, another was driven ashore, and a third was badly damaged; one British destroyer was damaged. At Ramsay's urging, Bomber Command unleashed raids on the S-boat pens at Le Havre and Boulogne on the nights of June 14 and 15. Some of the heavy bombs created a tidal wave that crushed the boats, and most of the German surface navy in the Channel area was eliminated at a single blow.

Thirty-six U-boats of various types that had been placed on anti-invasion duty also sortied, but they had little success against the massive Allied air-and-surface cover, reinforced by Ultra decrypts. Six nonsnorkel boats were promptly sunk, and after that, the rest were withdrawn from operations. Two British frigates and a few landing craft were lost, but no major amphibious or merchant ship was sunk by a U-boat in the first three weeks of Neptune. Later sorties by snorkel-fitted boats scored some successes; *U-984* damaged a frigate and four Liberty ships in a Channel convoy.[*]

---

[*]*U-763* had one of the most extraordinary experiences of the war. She attacked a convoy, was depth-charged for nearly thirty hours, and in dodging her pursuers lost her bearings. Kapitänleutnant Ernst Cordes concluded that he was off the Channel Island of Alderney, but when he came up to periscope depth, he was surprised to see he was enclosed on three sides by land, with numerous ships anchored nearby. After consulting his charts, the shocked Cordes discovered he was in Spithead, the great naval anchorage off Portsmouth, one of the most heavily defended harbors in the world. He lay silent on the bottom until nightfall and finally slipped away in the wake of a convoy. The British did not learn of this episode until after the war.

"Special Attack Units"—various types of manned torpedoes—were also employed by the Germans in the Channel, but they proved more dangerous to their crews than to Allied shipping. Mines were a greater danger, especially the "oyster" type, which were detonated by changes in water pressure as a ship passed over them. Since they could not be swept, attempts were made to deal with them by ordering merchant skippers to reduce speed in mine-infested waters, but the "oyster" mine was never completely mastered.

The great mid-June storm had made it obvious that the Allied hold on Normandy was still precarious. Unless Cherbourg, the nearest major port, could be captured, the invaders were hostage to the tricky Channel weather. The U.S. Army had already driven across the Cotentin Peninsula, sealing off some forty thousand German troops and laying strongly fortified Cherbourg under siege. The defenses seemed impervious to air attack, so the army called upon the navy to knock out the heavy coastal batteries flanking the city. Some mounted eleven-inch guns with a range of almost twenty-five miles. Naval doctrine held that ships should not expose themselves to coast-defense guns nearly equal in size to their own weapons, but Rear Admiral Morton L. Deyo accepted the challenge.

Because of the storm, Deyo's ships—*Arkansas, Texas*, and *Nevada*, four cruisers, and eleven destroyers—could not take up station off Cherbourg until June 25. The bombardment began at noon and lasted for three hours. While the ships pounded the fortifications from the sea, troops attacked from the landward side. With their guns directed by spotter planes and shore fire-control parties, the ships put several batteries, including one of the eleven-inch guns, out of commission and played an important role in the capture of Cherbourg, which fell next day. *Texas* took a shell on the bridge, which killed the helmsman, and two destroyers were hit. "Heavy fire from the sea" was cited by the enemy commander as one of the factors that made resistance useless. The Germans did their best to destroy the port facilities, yet Cherbourg was in use within two weeks of its capture.

By then, Allied troops had broken out of the hedgerows of Normandy, Patton's Third Army leading the way, and German resistance was crumbling. Brest and the other Biscay ports were under attack, and the remaining submarines were withdrawn to Norway. Of the twenty-six U-boats that got away, all but four safely made the two-thousand-mile voyage around the British Isles, together with nine that had been operating in the Channel. The escape of so many boats must be credited to the snorkel, for most of this dangerous journey was made submerged.

Once the Russians opened a promised summer offensive on the Byelorussian front, squeezing Germany between east and west, both Rommel and von Rundstedt were convinced that further resistance would only lead to the destruction of the Fatherland. Hitler angrily rejected all suggestions for surrender, however. One of the Führer's entourage telephoned von Rundstedt after the Allied breakthrough in Normandy and cried despairingly, "What shall we do? What shall we do?"

"Make peace, you fools!" snapped von Rundstedt. "What else can you do!"*

With the shipping shortage overcome, Eisenhower now turned his attention to the postponed invasion of southern France. Operation Dragoon, as it was now dubbed, called for transports and landing craft to be brought around from the English Channel to pick up three American and two French divisions redeployed from Italy and land them on a thirty-mile front from Toulon to Cannes. Once Marseilles and other ports were taken, these units, plus reinforcements, were to advance up the Rhone River Valley to join Patton's army in the vicinity of Dijon and take over the right flank of the Allied advance into Germany.

---

*Hitler relieved von Rundstedt after this outburst; Rommel was wounded by Allied gunfire. Both were probably aware of the plot to assassinate Hitler on July 20 but were not participants. The conspirators, who hoped that the Western Allies would make a separate peace with Germany after Hitler was deposed, planned to name Rommel head of state. This sealed his fate. After the plot failed, he was offered the choice of committing suicide with a promise of safety for his family, or disgrace for himself and imprisonment for his family. He chose death by poison on October 14, 1944. In a typically cruel twist, Hitler chose von Rundstedt to give the eulogy at his funeral.

Dönitz, on the other hand, was one of the first to race to Hitler's side after the attempted assassination, and issued a proclamation to the Kriegsmarine violently condemning the conspirators and expressing "holy wrath and bitter rage toward our criminal enemies and their hirelings. . . . In the miraculous escape of our Führer we see additional proof of the righteousness of our cause" (Padfield, *Dönitz*, p. 370).

Churchill had other plans, however. Inspired more by speculation about the political character of postwar Europe than by military strategy, he wanted the Allied armies to continue pressing up the Italian boot into the Po Valley and to land near Trieste, at the head of the Adriatic, with the idea of beating the Russians to Vienna and the Balkans. Marshall and King opposed this plan. Disillusioned with the Italian campaign, and unwilling to become involved in the Balkans, they wished to occupy as much of industrial northwestern Europe as possible before the war ended, and vetoed Churchill's proposal. The proper choice of action remains a matter of controversy.

On August 15, U.S. Vice-Admiral Kent Hewitt, making use of everything he had learned at Casablanca, Sicily, and Salerno, executed a textbook-perfect landing along the beaches of the Côte d'Azur. Land-based bombers knocked out enemy airfields; a nighttime drop of some five thousand British and American paratroops sealed off the beachhead, and an intensive two-hour bombardment by the heavy ships that had participated in the Normandy landings stunned the defenders with its ferocity. The troops, including Free French units, landed without serious resistance, and by nightfall all objectives had been taken.

Once Marseilles and Toulon were captured, the Seventh Army stormed north up the Rhône Valley, linking up with the Allied armies that had taken Paris and were advancing on Germany on a broad front extending from the Channel to the Swiss frontier. Antwerp was taken, providing an undamaged port—essential for an invasion of Germany.* In the east, the Russian offensive had carried the Red Army to the gates of Warsaw; Romania had been overrun, and with it the precious Ploesti oil fields; Bulgaria had withdrawn from the war; and Finland had signed an armistice with the Russians. The navies, by carrying the troops to battle, putting them ashore, and keeping them supplied, had played a fundamental role in winning this victory. The best summary of Neptune's success appeared in the war diary of Naval Group West:

---

*There was a snag in the capture of Antwerp. The port lay eighty miles up the Scheldt River from the North Sea, and the Germans held Walcheren, an island which dominated the estuary. Royal Marine commandos captured Walcheren after a bitter fight in what turned out to be the last sizable amphibious operation in the European war.

The amounts [of men, equipment, and supplies unloaded in France] represent many times the reserves of materiel and men moved up to the front by us, and present a clear picture of the enemy's superiority, and of the advantages of seaborne supplies, given sea and air superiority.

CHAPTER 17

•

"Get the Carriers!"

In the Pacific, news of the Allied landing in France was greeted with grim satisfaction. On the evening of June 6, 1944 reported Robert Sherrod, a crowd of marines and sailors were clustered under the palms on Eniwetok waiting for a movie to begin. A navy lieutenant mounted a wooden platform before the screen and gestured for silence. "Here is a piece of news that has just come in," he declared. "The invasion of Europe has just been announced." The crowd leaped to its feet and gave out a single great cheer, recalled Sherrod. To them, the beginning of the end of the European conflict meant a step forward in winning their own war against Japan—and going home.

Nine days later, many of these men were taking part in Operation Forager, a massive assault on the Marianas. Marc Mitscher's Fast Carrier Force—four task groups, consisting of fifteen carriers, seven battleships, twenty-one cruisers, and sixty-nine destroyers—was already plowing westward in cruising formation. The destroyers were screening the "big boys," anti-aircraft guns alert, sonars "pinging," radars searching . . . searching . . . for the tiny points of greenish light that signified the presence of the enemy.

They were to prepare the way for the 775 ships carrying and escorting some 127,500 troops, two-thirds of them marines. Admiral Spruance was in charge of all sea, land, and air forces. Kelly Turner, participating in his fifth landing, commanded the V Amphibious Force. "Howlin' Mad" Smith was in overall command of the troops and led the Northern Attack Force, which included the Second and Fourth Marine Divisions. On June 15 it was to assault Saipan and Tinian, a small island five miles away. The Southern Attack Force, the Third Marine Division, destined for Guam, about a hundred miles to the south, was under "Close-in" Conolly, while Major General Roy H. Geiger of the marines commanded the troops. Major General Ralph Smith commanded the floating reserve, the army's 27th Division, whose tardy tactics had aroused bitter criticism from "Howlin' Mad" Smith.

As in most joint army-navy ventures, bickering and interservice rivalries arose during the planning sessions. Admiral Nimitz quieted one such dispute with a story. "This all reminds me of the first amphibious operation—conducted by Noah," he said. "When they were unloading from the Ark, he saw a pair of cats come out, followed by six kittens. 'What's this?' he asked. 'Ha, ha,' said the tabby cat, 'and all the time you thought we were fighting.' "

The Marianas operation marked a new phase of the Pacific war. Saipan and Guam were large islands which could not be bombarded into submission. They were within Japan's inner defense perimeter—although Guam had been a U.S. possession—and the Japanese could be expected to fight even more fiercely than usual for them, because if they were lost Japan itself would be laid open to attack by long-range bombers and submarines. Prime Minister Hideki Tojo[*] personally guaranteed that Lieutenant General Yoshitsugo Saito and his thirty-two thousand troops and sailors would successfully defend Saipan. The naval forces were commanded by Admiral Nagumo, once Japan's foremost carrier commander. He had been relegated to Saipan following his defeat at Midway.

As the assault force steamed steadily toward the Marianas, life was regulated by the ever-present sounds of warships at sea: the hiss of spray along the bow . . . the steady hum of the turbines . . . the shrillness of the bo'sun's pipe . . . the repeated calls for working parties to turn to. Destroyers insouciantly raced about, as if kicking up their heels before the plodding transports. "We are through with flat atolls now," Smith confided to Sherrod. "We learned to pulverize atolls, but we are up against mountains and caves where Japs can dig in." Then

---

[*]Tojo was also army minister and chief of the army's General Staff.

he added slowly, "[A] week from now there will be a lot of dead Marines."

Mitscher, flying his flag in the carrier *Lexington*, began the operation on June 11, sending in two hundred Hellcats to blast airfields in the Marianas. Over the next forty-eight hours, his planes made repeated strikes against these targets. Thirty-six Japanese planes were destroyed in the air and on the ground. Eleven U.S. fighters were lost, mostly to anti-aircraft fire. To prevent the enemy from shuttling planes from the home islands via Iwo Jima and Chichi Jima in the Bonins to the Marianas, Spruance sent Rear Admiral Joseph J. Clark racing 650 miles to the north with two carrier task groups to knock out these airfields. The seven battleships, under Vice-Admiral Willis Lee, who had saved the day off Guadalcanal, moved in with their sixteen-inch guns to pound the defenses of Saipan with a heavier rain of fire than had poured down on the Normandy beaches. Ninety-six frogmen—a new addition, prompted by the Tarawa experience, and led by Lieutenant Commander Draper L. Kauffman— slipped in under the bombardment to blow up underwater obstacles and reconnoiter the approaches to the beaches on the island's flat southeast coast.*

At 0542 on June 15, Turner made the signal "Land the Landing Force." Chaplains offered a last prayer and blessing over the loudspeakers, and the marines clambered down the nets into boats and amphtracs that had been disgorged from the maws of the LSTs. Mountainous Saipan could be seen rising from the sea like some prehistoric beast, roughly five miles wide and fifteen miles long. Rocket-firing TBFs and close-in destroyers delivered a carefully timed final pounding to the enemy's positions as, like a horde of water beetles, six hundred amphtracs rolled in on a nearly four-mile-long front. Unlike the situation at Tarawa, there were enough to take everybody ashore. There were no collisions or confusion among the landing craft, and within twenty minutes eight thousand marines were ashore, despite stiff enemy artillery and mortar fire.

Throughout the day, the defenders held out on the edge of the uncompleted Charan-Kanoa airstrip, supported by heavy mortar and machine-gun fire and well-sited batteries on Hill 500 and Mount

---

*Sixteen of the frogmen were killed or wounded in the assault.

Tapotchau, at 1,550 feet the highest point on the island. By nightfall, more than twenty thousand marines had landed with their artillery, ready to begin the drive inland the next day. That night, in a vain effort to push the Americans into the sea, a thousand screaming Japanese troops supported by thirty-six light tanks poured down from the hills in a *banzai* charge. This attack was beaten back with the assistance of close-in destroyers, and twenty-nine tanks were accounted for. General Saito now dug in on the slopes of Tapotchau to await relief by the Imperial Navy.

"The Japs are coming after us," Admiral Spruance told his commanders during a conference on his flagship, the cruiser *Indianapolis*, on the afternoon of June 16. He had been alerted to the enemy's movements by radio intercepts, coast watchers, and U.S. submarines following the course of the Mobile Fleet. Admiral Ozawa had sortied from Tawitawi with his ships flying Admiral Togo's signal at Tsushima: "The fate of the Empire rests on this one battle. Every man is expected to do his utmost."* Once Ozawa had joined up with Admiral Ugaki's battleships, which were returning from the aborted Biak operation, the fleet passed through San Bernardino Strait, in the Philippines, heading toward the Central Pacific. The Japanese did not emerge unscathed: U.S. submarines sank four of Ozawa's destroyers in the Sulu Sea.

Spruance's nimble mind calculated the distances and weighed the possibilities. Turner's forces were fully committed to the assault on Saipan and would be vulnerable to attack, so he dared not move too far to the west to challenge Ozawa, not wanting to give the Japanese the opportunity to outflank him during the night and fall upon the transports. The reserve 27th Division was landed on Saipan, but the invasions of Tinian and Guam were postponed, and the transports assigned to those operations were directed to lie a safe distance away from the action. The Japanese could not reach the area until June 19, Spruance estimated, so Clark was allowed to complete his strikes on the Bonins and to rendezvous with the fleet on the night of June 18.

Saburo Sakai, the one-eyed Japanese ace, was one of the defend-

---

*This was borrowed from Lord Nelson's signal at Trafalgar: "England expects that every man will do his duty."

ers of Iwo Jima. Many of the American pilots were as green as his own flyers, which, he explained, permitted him not only to survive combat missions but to run his bag to sixty enemy planes. Describing one of these kills over Iwo, he related:

> I snapped into a tight loop and rolled out on the tail of a Hellcat, squeezing out a burst as soon as the plane came into the gun sight. He rolled away and my bullets met only empty air. I went into a left vertical spiral, and kept closing the distance, trying for a clear shot at the plane's belly. The Grumman tried to match the turn with me; for just that moment I needed, his underside filled the gun sight and I squeezed out a second burst. The cannon shells exploded along the fuselage. The next second thick clouds of black smoke poured back from the airplane and it went into a wild, uncontrolled dive for the sea.

Ozawa had nine carriers divided into three groups. The van included the light carriers *Zuiho*, *Chitose*, and *Chiyoda*, supported by the superbattleships *Yamato* and *Musashi* and the old battleships *Haruna* and *Kongo*. Force A included *Taiho* (Ozawa's flagship), the *Shokaku*, and *Zuikaku*; Force B included *Hiyo*, *Junyo*, and the smaller *Ryujo* and *Nagato*, another battleship. In all, the Japanese had about 475 aircraft piloted by a mixture of veterans and fledglings. Ozawa got an insight into the size of the force opposing him when the Japanese on Saipan picked up a downed American flyer who had on him a list of call signs for the U.S. ships.

Mitscher had 956 planes, double the Japanese strength, but Ozawa felt he had a fighting chance. He planned to fight within range of the some four hundred Japanese aircraft based on Guam and the adjacent islands,[*] and his planes had two hundred miles' greater range than those of the Americans. Thus, he intended to stay out of reach of U.S. carriers while his planes could shuttle between their carriers and island bases. And, unlike Spruance, he did not have the responsibility of protecting a beachhead. Ozawa was limited, however, by a shortage of fuel. His ships had only enough fuel to come straight at the Americans, which deprived him of the ability to manuever.

---

[*]The number of planes available was whittled away by the American air attacks, and only 156 of these aircraft were available at the time the battle began—a fact unknown to Ozawa.

Spruance positioned TF 58's carrier groups to the west of Saipan, on a line perpendicular to the wind, so they could turn in and out of it to launch and recover planes without interfering with each other. Willis Lee's Battle Line took up position between the carriers and the approaching Japanese. Even such a brilliant employer of air power as Spruance evidently still had a vestigial belief in the big gun as the ultimate arbiter of war at sea, as shown by his battle plan, issued on June 17 to his commanders:

> Our air will first knock out enemy carriers, then will attack enemy battleships and cruisers to slow or disable them. Lee's battle line will destroy enemy fleet by fleet action if the enemy elects to fight or by sinking slowed or crippled ships if enemy retreats. Action against the enemy must be pushed vigorously by all hands to complete destruction of his fleet.

Late on June 18, the Japanese fleet was sighted about 350 miles to the west in the Philippine Sea. The aggressive Mitscher wanted to close with the enemy during the night so he would be able to launch his planes at dawn, within two hundred miles of the enemy carriers, but Spruance refused permission. He was concerned that a Japanese carrier group might make an end run and destroy the Saipan beachhead while Mitscher was diverted by the others. But this explanation did little to salve the bitter disappointment of Mitscher and his flyers, who felt they were being denied the opportunity to strike the first blow.

Throughout the night, there was activity on both sides. Planes were fueled, and bombs and torpedoes loaded. Mechanics carefully checked their charges. Lookouts searched the sky for the dark blob that might mean an enemy scout plane, and the sea for the telltale ripple of a periscope. On the bridges, positions were worked out again and again on charts and radar plots. Below decks, pilots, air crew, officers, and seamen tossed fitfully in their bunks and awaited the coming of a day of battle.

The Battle of the Philippine Sea began soon after dawn on June 19. The morning was fair and clear, but from the direction of Guam appeared a tiny thunderhead in the form of a few Japanese aircraft. Hellcats darted after them, and one soon reported: "Tallyhoed two

Judys; splash one." More Japanese planes were reported to be taking off from Orote Field on Guam, so Mitscher sent in thirty-three Hellcats to deal with them. About thirty enemy fighters and bombers were shot down or destroyed on the ground. Shortly before 1000, the Hellcats received the signal from *Lexington* to return: "Hey Rube!"—the cry used by circus workers who needed help. Japanese carrier planes had been picked up on radar while they were still 140 miles to the west.

Ozawa had launched sixty-nine planes at 0830; a second strike of 128 planes followed about a half-hour later. Just after taking off, Warrant Officer Sakio Komatsu sighted a torpedo that had been fired by the American submarine *Albacore* streaking toward *Taiho*. He nosed his plane over into a suicide dive that exploded the torpedo before it struck home. But another torpedo smashed into the carrier's side. The damage appeared moderate—a jammed forward elevator and some fuel lines weakened—and the flagship continued operations.

Mitscher ordered every available Hellcat into the air to meet the incoming Japanese. Flight decks exploded into a carefully controlled, multicolored frenzy. Plane handlers in blue shirts and helmets, plane directors in yellow, hookmen in green, chockmen in purple, and firefighters in red scurried about, readying the planes for launching. Pilots hoisted themselves into their cockpits, and with a howl and a rush, the big Hellcats hurtled into the sky, to be vectored out to their targets by the fighter-director officers (FDOs) in the Combat Information Centers, deep in the bowels of the ships.*

Within minutes, 140 fighters were put into the air to join the eighty already airborne. To provide room for them to land, refuel, and rearm

---

*Fighter-director officers were the long-range eyes of the fighter pilots. They observed the flight paths of incoming "bogies" and passed range and bearing information to plotters, who put the targets on a Plexiglas screen where the positions of friendly fighters were also marked. FDOs determined the size, altitude, course, and speed of the incoming force and vectored their standing combat air patrols (CAPs) out to intercept it.

When the flight commander made visual contact, he advised the FDO about its actual course, speed, and composition and then attacked. Another CAP would immediately be put in place to replace the one in action. This system allowed enemy raiders to be engaged when they were still well away from the fleet. Most FDOs were reservists chosen for their ability to think clearly and make decisions even under tremendous pressure. The FDO in *Essex* was Lieutenant (j.g.) John Connally, later secretary of the navy, governor of Texas, and secretary of the Treasury.

upon their return, all dive- and torpedo bombers were ordered into the air to orbit on the eastern—or unengaged—side of the task force until Ozawa's fleet was within range. Besides the CICs and radar, Mitscher had an ace in the hole. Lieutenant (j.g.) Charles A. Sims, a Japanese-language officer, monitored the radio chatter of the enemy flyers, and picked up information about their missions.

The two forces collided about ninety miles from the American carriers. Pushing the charging handles of their six .50-caliber guns and checking their sights, the Hellcat pilots nosed down from twenty-five thousand feet on the sixty-nine Japanese planes spread out below them. Commander Charles W. Brewer reported that his initial burst of gunfire literally ripped a Zero to pieces. Before the debris had hit the sea, Brewer was already on the tail of another fighter. He accounted for two more Zeros during the brief battle.

Japanese planes were "falling like leaves," said one pilot, and those that escaped got only as far as the line of battleships protecting the carriers before they were shot down by anti-aircraft guns firing shells with VT fuses. Some cartwheeled along the surface of the sea in flaming arcs and exploded in black geysers of smoke and seawater. The only hit was on *South Dakota*, which lost twenty-seven men—without a reduction in her fighting capacity. In all, forty-two Japanese planes were shot down by the Hellcats and the surface-ship screen. No enemy aircraft reached the carriers, and only one American plane was lost.

Hellcats tore into the second, larger wave of enemy aircraft a half-hour later. Commander David McCampbell, head of the *Essex* air group, repeatedly dived into a formation of Judy dive-bombers, shooting down four and claiming a probable. Later in the day, he accounted for three more Japanese planes, and by the end of the war was the U.S. Navy's leading ace, with thirty-four victories and the Medal of Honor.

Radio circuits crackled with a riotous mixture of shouts, curses, warnings, and cries of encouragement. "Hell, this is like an old time turkey shoot!" yelled one pilot—and thus the battle became known as "The Great Marianas Turkey Shoot." About twenty enemy planes broke through the Hellcats; most were disposed of by the battleships' guns. Six Judys reached *Wasp* and *Bunker Hill*, but did little damage. Only fifteen of the 109 aircraft that had attacked TF 58 survived.

Mitscher also struck Orote Field on Guam. The Helldivers and Avengers that had been slowly orbiting the carriers were ordered to bomb the field to make it unusable for the straggling Japanese survivors. Enemy anti-aircraft fire was heavy, but the runway was cratered with five-hundred- and thousand-pound bombs, and several planes were destroyed on the ground.

Lieutenant (j.g.) Alexander Vraciu had one of the most exciting experiences of the day. Shortly after he took off from *Lexington*, the engine of his Hellcat began to leak oil, and he was ordered to orbit the carrier along with five other cripples. Vraciu, who already had thirteen victories to his credit, spotted a flock of Judys heading for *Lexington*. With a couple of wingmen, he dived in among them, pushing his plane to within two hundred feet of a Judy's tail before opening fire. "Scratch one Judy!" Vraciu shouted into his radio as the Japanese plane exploded into fragments.

Two more enemy planes fell before his guns, and the Japanese "began to separate like a bunch of disorderly cattle," he recalled. "Every time one of the Japs would try to lead a string of others out of the formation, the Hellcat pilots turned into 'cowboys' and herded them back into the group. If they had been able to scatter, we wouldn't have shot down as many as we did." Vraciu ran his bag to six and was chasing another Judy when it was shot down by anti-aircraft fire. Suddenly, the sky was empty of enemy planes, and the Hellcats returned to their carriers. Vraciu had expended only 360 rounds of ammunition in winning his half-dozen victories. Mitscher personally congratulated him and asked the photographers to take a picture of them. "Not for publication," said the admiral. "To keep for myself."

Unaware of the magnitude of Japanese losses, Admiral Ozawa continued to feed planes into the meat grinder. A third strike, of forty-nine aircraft, was flown off his carriers, but half failed to find the American fleet and returned to their ships. The others were ambushed by Hellcats, and several were shot down. A fourth wave, of eighty-two planes, followed. Those that were not accounted for by the CAPs or the fierce flak were bagged trying to land on Guam. Only nine survived.

The Mobile Fleet was also being harassed by U.S. submarines. Shortly before noon, *Cavalla* got in among Force A and fired a full spread of four torpedoes into *Shokaku*. The carrier caught fire and blew up about three hours later, and only a few of her 1,263 officers and men were picked up. *Taiho* suffered a similar fate when the fumes from the fuel lines weakened by *Albacore*'s earlier torpedo suddenly ignited and her armored flight deck was ripped open by a tremendous blast. Ozawa transferred his flag to a cruiser and then the carrier *Zuikaku*. Only a quarter of *Taiho*'s crew of 2,150 were rescued before she sank.

The sky over TF 58 had been swept clear of enemy aircraft by late afternoon. Two Japanese carriers had been sunk by submarines, and a phenomenal 373 planes were shot down. Mitscher had lost only twenty-three aircraft through enemy action, and not one of his ships had been seriously damaged. Ozawa had only about a hundred planes left, but because of highly colored reports from his flyers, he believed that many of the missing aircraft had landed at Guam and that the enemy had suffered even worse losses than his own. As a result, he planned to offer battle again the next day, after retiring to the northwest for refueling. Both sides groped for each other during most of the next day, July 20, until American scout planes sighted the enemy fleet toward 1600, lying just within range.

Freed at last of his concern that the Japanese might outflank TF 58 and attack the Saipan beachhead, Spruance now gave Mitscher permission to go after the seven remaining enemy carriers. Mitscher faced a dilemma. If he launched his planes, they would return in the dark with nearly empty fuel tanks, and few of his pilots had experience in night carrier landings. But if he waited until daylight, he might loose his last opportunity to destroy the Japanese fleet. "Launch 'em," the taciturn Mitscher declared. In six-inch-high letters, his orders were chalked on the ready room blackboards: "Get the carriers!"

Within ten minutes, 216 aircraft—seventy-seven dive-bombers, fifty-three torpedo planes, and eighty-six fighters—lifted off the decks of the ten American carriers and headed into the setting sun. Once the attack force had been launched, Mitscher resumed course toward the enemy to reduce the distance the returning planes would have to cover. And then came a shock. One of the scout planes that had discovered the Japanese fleet reported that it had made an error in the position of the Japanese: they were sixty miles farther away than originally reported, which meant some of the planes would be flying three hundred miles to make the strike—well beyond their ranges. Mitscher considered recalling his planes, but after restudying the charts, he allowed the mission to continue.

Flying carefully to conserve fuel, the strike force found part of the Japanese fleet just before sundown. Ozawa managed to put about seventy-five planes into the air, but these were not enough to halt the strike. Two tankers trailing the fleet were hit and so badly damaged they were abandoned by their crews. Several TBFs, including one piloted by Lieutenant (j.g.) George B. Brown, caught up with the carrier *Hiyo* and began runs on her in the face of heavy flak. Brown was badly wounded, his plane was on fire, and part of a wing was shot away. The rear gunner and radioman bailed out. Nevertheless, when the flames burned themselves out, Brown pressed home the attack, skimming past the winking gun flashes of the screening destroyers and apparently put a torpedo into *Hiyo*. A wingmate tried to lead his plane back toward TF 58, but Brown disappeared into a cloud and was never seen again.

Hiyo, struck by another torpedo, caught fire and sank. *Zuikaku*, *Junyo*, and *Chiyoda*, as well as the cruiser *Maya*, were all badly damaged by dive-bombers, and sixty-five more Japanese aircraft were shot down. As he withdrew to the west, Ozawa had only three dozen or so planes left of the more than four hundred spotted on the flight decks of his carriers the previous morning.

Bombs and torpedoes expended, the American planes began the flights back to their carriers in ones and twos, many with their fuel gauges below the halfway mark and bucking a fourteen-knot headwind. Night closed in, and only a few of the more skilled pilots—or the luckier ones—managed to land on the darkened flight decks. Returning pilots could make out the ships' wakes, yet were unable to distinguish the carriers from other large ships. On the carriers, planes were heard circling overhead, some flashing red and green recognition lights. Engines coughed and sputtered as they ran out of fuel. There were heavy splashes as some "ditched" in the black sea.

The voices on the radio told the story.

"I've got ten minutes of gas left. Think I'll put her down in the water while I've still got power. So long Joe!"

"This is Forty-six Inkwell. Where am I please? Somebody tell me where I am!"

Every eye was on Mitscher as he sat slumped in his chair in *Lex-*

ington's flag plot, long-billed cap pulled down over his gnomelike face. He was torn between identification with his pilots and concern that the fleet might attract enemy submarines if its landing lights were turned on. Finally, decision made, he turned to Arleigh Burke, his chief of staff, and quietly gave an order: "Turn on the lights."

The carriers switched on their red masthead lights, glow lights outlined flight decks, searchlights lit up the sky, and ships fired star shell. One pilot said it was like "a Hollywood premiere, Chinese New Year's and the Fourth of July rolled into one." Planes landed on any flattop they could find, and some crashed into planes that had landed. One, mistaking the main-truck light of a destroyer for the signal of a landing-control officer, made a perfect landing in the sea beside her. By 2200, every plane had either landed or "ditched," and the carriers steamed away, leaving destroyers and floatplanes behind to search for downed airmen. Although about a hundred planes were lost, almost 90 percent of the flyers were saved.

With the end of the Battle of the Philippine Sea, Spruance sent Lee's battleships in pursuit of the fleeing Japanese, but Ozawa had too much of a head start and left no cripples behind to be snapped up. Following a long day's search on June 21, the hunt was called off, and Spruance resumed direct support of the Saipan operation. This encounter, the last classic carrier battle of the war, was a clear-cut, decisive victory for the Americans, won with the loss of only 130 aircraft and seventy-six air crewmen. Swept clean of planes and left a defenseless husk, the Japanese carriers would never be able to fight another such battle. Ozawa submitted his resignation in the wake of this defeat, but Admiral Toyoda refused to accept it.

The Japanese blamed their defeat on the defensive power of the U.S. Navy's carrier task forces. The air-search radars on board American ships gave them ample warning of an impending attack; the large number of fighters and the use of FDOs to direct them to where they were most needed were also critical advantages; and the VT fuses fitted to U.S. anti-aircraft shells had a devastating effect upon attacking aircraft that managed to run the fighter gantlet. "The widely held view that carriers were vulnerable became obsolete as soon as the U.S. fast carrier forces appeared in the Pacific," noted a Japanese analyst.

Yet the battle ended in a cloud of controversy. Mitscher was unhappy about Spruance's decision to hold him back on the night of June 18–19. "The enemy has escaped," he declared. "His fleet was not sunk." Naval aviators scoffed at Spruance's fear that the Japanese might have slipped around TF 58 and mauled Turner's transports and the beachhead had the carriers been turned loose. This is what comes of placing a nonavaitor in command over avaitors, they complained. King and Nimitz backed Spruance. Spruance had not unnecessarily risked his own carriers, and had shielded the landing on Saipan—the strategic objective of the operation. "Going after the Japanese and knocking their carriers out would have been much better and more satisfactory than waiting for them to attack us," he stated later, "but we were at the start of a very important and large amphibious operation and we could not afford to gamble and place it in jeopardy." It is hard not to agree. By reining in Mitscher, he had positioned TF 58 so that its fighters were airborne and waiting to pounce on the incoming Japanese planes. The result was the permanent maiming of the Imperial Navy's most potent weapon—its air power.

The Japanese defeat at sea sealed the fate of the Marianas, although the Saipan garrison fought on with customary tenacity. By the time Mitscher's flyers were making their twilight attack on the Japanese carriers, the marines and army troops had cut the island in half, and the Japanese, who had endured terrible losses, were retreating to the northern half. In the struggle for Mount Tapotchau, the 27th Division was forced back by the enemy while the two marine divisions on either flank pushed forward, causing a dangerous sag in the American line. "Howlin' Mad" Smith was alarmed. Unhappy with the division's lack of offensive spirit and poor leadership, he ordered General Ralph Smith relieved of command on June 20. The case of "Smith versus Smith" turned into a long-running row between the army and the marines, with each service accusing the other of incompetence—and worse.

Two days later, a *banzai* charge by three thousand Japanese troops broke through a gap in the 27th's lines, and was not halted until the enemy had surged a mile into the American position and run up against marine artillery. When the massacre was over, the mounds of enemy dead was greater than at Tarawa, according to Robert Sherrod. Smith angrily ordered the entire 27th division into reserve and declared he would never employ it in combat again. Organized resistance on Saipan ended on July 9, yet with Japanese troops holed up in caves and ravines, the island was not declared secure for another month. The capture of Saipan cost 3,426 American dead, most killed in the early fighting, and another 13,099 wounded. Burial parties counted 23,811 Japanese dead, including General Saito and Admiral Nagumo; 921 were taken prisoner.

There was a macabre aftermath to the battle. Believing the propaganda that they would be subjected to savage atrocities by the Americans, nearly eight thousand Japanese civilians, some with children in their arms, committed mass suicide by plunging off the cliffs on the northern end of the island into the shark-infested waters.

"Part of the area is so congested with floating bodies we simply can't avoid running them down," Lieutenant Emery Cleaves of the minesweeper *Chief* told Sherrod. "There was . . . one, nude, who had drowned herself while giving birth to a baby. The baby's head had entered this world, but that was all of him. A small boy of four or five had drowned with his arm firmly clenched around the neck of a Jap soldier; the two bodies rocked crazily in the waves. I've seen literally hundreds in the water."

The Third Marine Division, the First Provisional Marine Brigade, and the army's 77th Division landed on Guam on July 21. Three days later, the same forces that had captured Saipan went ashore on Tinian, at a beach so narrow the Japanese did not believe a landing there was possible. "We had the bastards surrounded before they knew where we were," said one marine officer. Using heavy artillery barrages and air drops of deadly napalm for the first time, the marines captured the island after nine days with only light casualties. Holland Smith called Tinian "the perfect amphibious operation of the war."

Guam, larger and more heavily garrisoned than Tinian, took longer. Thirteen days of sustained bombardment demoralized the defenders, and the landing was only lightly opposed. Orote Field and Apra Harbor were quickly taken, but fighting in the mountains was more arduous. Guam was declared secure on August 10, after some 18,500 Japanese had been wiped out, leaving only a few hundred hiding in the hills and thick underbrush. Some refused to surrender until years after the war. In all, the Marianas cost the lives of about six thousand marines and soldiers; Japanese losses were nearly sixty thousand men.

*   *   *

"Hell is on us," remarked a Japanese official following the loss of the Marianas, and many knowledgeable Japanese now agreed the war could not be won. The emperor indicated his desire for early peace negotiations, and the Tojo Cabinet, faced with the collapse of the vast ambitions with which it had begun the war, resigned. A new government was formed under General Kuniaki Koiso, who, realizing the inevitability of ultimate defeat, would have welcomed peace but did not know how to bring it about. Nor would he propose it in the face of the Japanese inability to contemplate surrender. The fall of Saipan had, nevertheless, allowed a peace party to take root and slowly gain strength in the inner circles of the Japanese government.

On the other hand, the Imperial Naval Staff produced a desperate plan to recapture Saipan by slipping in a large number of troops in a grander version of the Tokyo Express. Ozawa's severely depleted air groups were to be filled out for this mission by army pilots and fresh graduates of the flight schools. The army's General Staff quickly shot down the plan, saying it had no planes to spare for such a dubious operation.

A few days after the fall of the Tojo Cabinet, Admiral Toyoda called upon the new navy minister, Admiral Mitsumasa Yonai. "Can we hold out until the end of the year?" Yonai asked.

"It will probably be extremely difficult to do so," Toyoda replied.

"This," says Morison, "was equivalent to an American's asking 'Is the war already lost?' and a reply, 'It is, and you had better hurry up and make peace.' "

In the Marianas, engineers were already at work on expanding and improving the airfields, which within a few months would bring the B-29s and their cargoes of fiery death within range of Japan's vulnerable cities. Meanwhile, MacArthur completed the conquest of Biak, and the north coast of New Guinea was captured without difficulty. On September 15, the Southwest Pacific campaign came to an end with the landing of the 31st Division on undefended Morotai, in the Moluccas, only three hundred miles from Mindanao. Supported by the Seventh Fleet and VII PhibFor, MacArthur had in three months advanced fourteen hundred miles with minimal casualties, one of the great feats of World War II.

Once on Morotai, the general went to the point nearest the Philippines "and gazed toward the northwest, almost as though he could already see through the mist the rugged lines of Bataan and Corregidor," recalled an aide. " 'They are waiting for me there,' " he murmured. " 'They have been waiting a long time.' "

·

CHAPTER 18

"We'll Stand by You!"

Sputtering and coughing, the engines of the Wildcats and Avengers flown by Escort Carrier Group Three—"Taffy 3"—roared into life as the sun rose on October 25, 1944.[*] Lifting off from a half-dozen "jeep" carriers that lay off Samar, in the central Philippines, the planes headed for Leyte to support the U.S. Army troops landed five days before as General MacArthur fulfilled his pledge to return to the islands. Operations were proceeding routinely when an urgent warning was received from a patrol plane piloted by Ensign Hans Jensen: four enemy battleships and a flock of cruisers and destroyers were approaching from the northwest at high speed.

"Air pilot, tell him to check his identification," replied an irritated Rear Admiral Clifton A. F. Sprague. He was certain the pilot had misidentified some American ships.

"Identification of enemy force confirmed," Jensen answered. "They have pagoda masts!"

Sprague's unsuspecting vessels had been catapulted by a series of mishaps into the center of the greatest surface-air-undersea battle in history—the Battle of Leyte Gulf. Taking a desperate gamble, Japan risked the remnants of the Imperial Navy in a final throw aimed at safeguarding her supply lines and retaining her most important conquests. By the time the encounter ended, she had lost more tonnage

---

[*]The F4Fs had been replaced on the fleet carriers by the F6F Hellcat, but they continued to be used by escort carriers.

than both sides at Jutland, and the Japanese navy ceased to exist as an organized fighting force.

Following the Battle of the Philippine Sea and the capture of the Marianas, high-level debates erupted among strategists on both sides over what to do next. Unable to offer much more than a stubborn defense because of their losses, the Japanese tried to determine where the next Allied thrust would come. Three alternative "SHO" or "Victory" plans for another decisive battle—SHO-1, SHO-2, and SHO-3—were prepared by Admiral Toyoda, the commander of the Combined Fleet, to deal with an assault on the Philippines, Formosa, and Okinawa, or the home islands. The Supreme War Direction Council, meeting in August 1944 in the presence of the emperor, decided an assault on the Philippines was most likely, and maximum strength should be deployed there.

American strategists were also uncertain about their next moves. Moments such as this underscored the need for a supreme commander in the Pacific to play a role similar to that of Eisenhower in Europe. General Marshall was still supporting MacArthur's plan to leapfrog from Morotai to Mindanao, at the southernmost tip of the Philippines, then to Leyte, a sizable island in the center of the archipelago, and finally on to Luzon. But Admiral King, and Admiral Nimitz to a lesser extent, objected that the plan to retake the Philippines from basement to attic would be too slow and too costly. They thought the islands should be bypassed in favor of a landing on Formosa, 375 miles closer to Japan than Luzon, and possibly at Amoy, on the Chinese coast. "A direct attack on Formosa, without reference to the Philippine Islands," argued King, "would dominate the sea lanes by which Japan received essential supplies of oil, rice and other commodities from her recently conquered empire."

MacArthur, as was to be expected, objected strenuously. He pointed to the May 1943 agreement for a joint thrust to the Philippines and across the Central Pacific, and emphasized that he had made a promise to the Filipino people to return. To do otherwise would compound the loss of face suffered by the United States when the islands had fallen to the Japanese. He demanded that the Joint Chiefs allow him to come to Washington to present his views personally. With MacArthur being touted as potential rival to President Roosevelt as he prepared to run for a fourth term, this was the last thing the administration wanted. The president, who planned an inspection tour of Pacific bases following the Democratic convention, had a better idea. He would meet in Hawaii in July 1944 with Nimitz and MacArthur to iron out differences between them.

Overawed by no one, MacArthur arrived a half-hour late in a large open car preceded by a shrieking motorcycle escort to greet the cruiser *Baltimore*, which had brought the president to Pearl Harbor.[*] Roosevelt was sympathetic to the general's impassioned pleas, but a final decision was delayed until a meeting in Quebec with Churchill in September. The timetable worked out by the Joint Chiefs called for MacArthur to land on Mindanao on November 15 and Leyte on December 20. Nimitz's Central Pacific force was to capture support bases for the invasion of the Philippines in the western Carolines— Peleliu in the Palaus, Yap, and Ulithi. The latter had a huge enclosed lagoon that would make an excellent fleet anchorage now that Eniwetok was considered too far in the rear. The Luzon-versus-Formosa question was not resolved until the end of September when the Joint Chiefs gave the nod to Luzon.[†]

The decision to permit MacArthur to proceed with his Philippine offensive was strategically unnecessary and a mistake that proved costly in American lives. Earlier, there had been some validity in MacArthur's emphasis upon the Philippines as the logical point from which to strike at Japan. But the capture of the Marianas had completely altered the situation. With the B-29s almost ready to attack the Japanese heartland directly, a campaign for the Philippines was unnecessary. Rather than being bogged down in bloody diversions in the Philippines, the Palaus, the Bonins, and the Ryukyus, the U.S. should have applied its full energies—the unstoppable fast carriers, devastating B-29s, and blockading submarines—to a knockout blow against Japan. Had this been done, Japan might have been brought to its knees without using the atomic bomb.

*   *   *

[*]Resplendent in white uniforms, a line of admirals from Nimitz's headquarters turned out to pay respects to the president. When they were ordered to "Right Face!," two faced left, evoking a gleeful cheer from *Baltimore's* crew.

[†]A landing on the Chinese coast lost its appeal to King and Nimitz after the Japanese launched an offensive that overran most of the air bases in eastern China from which the aerial assault upon Japan was to have been launched.

Admiral Halsey upset the timetable established by the Joint Chiefs. After the Marianas campaign, Admiral Spruance and his team of senior officers—except Admiral Mitscher, who remained with his Fast Carrier Task Force, now designated TF 38—returned to Hawaii to plan the next campaign; the Fifth Fleet was christened the Third Fleet and placed under Halsey's command. The change in designation confused the Japanese, who believed they were now dealing with two massive American fleets in the Central Pacific.

As soon as his flagship, the battleship *New Jersey*, joined Mitscher's carriers, Halsey ordered a series of softening-up strikes, in late August and early September, against Japanese airfields on Mindanao, the central Philippines, and the Bonins, in preparation for the landings at Peleliu and Yap. TF 38 included nine fleet carriers and eight light carriers organized in four task groups, each with its encircling screen of battleships, cruisers, and destroyers.

As part of these raids, four TBFs from the light carrier *San Jacinto*, plus eight Helldivers and a dozen F6Fs from *Enterprise*, struck the radio station at Chichi Jima in the Bonins on September 2. Enemy defensive fire was intense. Twenty-year-old Lieutenant (j.g.) George H. W. Bush's Avenger had nosed over to make its bombing run when "all hell broke loose," he later recalled. "You could see all this stuff all around, these black explosions." Suddenly, he felt a heavy jolt; the engine of his plane had been hit.

"Smoke started pouring out of the damned thing," Bush remembered. "I looked at the instruments, and we were going down fast. I pulled out over the island and realized I was in trouble." Smoke was pouring out of the engine, and flames were sweeping back across his wings, but Bush pressed home the attack. Having made his bomb run, he headed out to sea and leveled the plane to give his radioman and gunner time to bail out. When Bush himself plunged over the side, he struck his head on the tail and, stunned, jerked his ripcord too soon. The chute caught the plane's tail, dragging him down with it, but he yanked it free.

For two hours, Bush paddled his life raft away from the enemy-held island with his hands, bleeding from a head wound, exhausted and sick from ingesting saltwater. His crew had disappeared. "It seemed . . . just the end of the world," he recalled. Suddenly, from out of the sea, barely a hundred yards away, poked a periscope and then the gray conning tower of an American submarine, the *Finback*. Within minutes, the future president of the United States was hustled on board the boat and it slipped back into the depths.

Halsey's report on his foray electrified the Joint Chiefs. In two days, 173 enemy plans had been shot down, another 305 were destroyed on the ground, and fifty-nine ships of various types were sunk, at the cost of only eight aircraft. Proclaiming the islands a "hollow shell"—a claim that proved wildly overoptimistic—Halsey urged that the attack on Peleliu be abandoned and that Yap and Mindanao be bypassed in favor of an immediate invasion of Leyte. The Joint Chiefs agreed and MacArthur was given the target date of October 20 for the invasion of the island. The invasion of Luzon was set for December, despite Admiral King's objections. Nimitz agreed to bypass Yap but held that an airfield on Peleliu would assist the Leyte operation—and the assault went ahead as planned.

Rear Admiral Theodore Wilkinson's III Amphibious Force put the First Marine Division ashore on Peleliu on September 15. Three days of air and naval bombardment blew away the scrubby jungle growth on the ridges behind the beaches, revealing numerous caves, but no one gave them much thought. Rear Admiral Jesse B. Oldendorf, in charge of the bombardment, exuberantly declared, "We have run out of targets." Major General William Rupertus, the division commander, confidently told correspondents that Peleliu would be secured in four days.

The marines met only light resistance and seized the airfield on the first day. But that soon changed. Having abandoned the costly tactics of resisting on the beaches in the face of massive battleship gunfire support, the Japanese aimed not to win victories but to create as many enemy casualties as possible. Colonel Kunio Nakawaga, who with his ten thousand men had dug into the natural caves in the jagged limestone ridges above the airfield, let the invaders come to him. These caves had been developed into an interlocking, mutually supporting labyrinth of underground strongpoints that were almost impervious to naval gunfire and aerial bombing and were well supplied with food, water, and ammunition. The struggle for Peleliu became one of the bloodiest and most vicious battles of the Pacific war and set the pattern for what the Americans would face at Iwo Jima and Okinawa.

The Japanese had to be rooted out of the caves or buried in them with close assaults, demolition charges, and long-range flamethrowers mounted on Sherman tanks. The heat rose to 115 degrees, water was short, and casualties were heavy. Black marines of the segregated Sixteenth Field Depot, whose job it was to unload cargo on the beach, served as stretcher-bearers under heavy fire. Many also volunteered as riflemen to fill gaps in the line companies.

"Our body filth from sweat, rain, and dust made us miserable," relates Eugene B. Sledge. The smell of rotting bodies and excrement from thousands of men in a small area was nauseating. "The Japs fought like demons, and shot our stretcher teams—the corpsmen and the wounded," according to Sledge. "We hated them with a passion known to few antagonists. . . . We never took prisoners, even when some few tried to give up. They often tried to throw a grenade at us. . . ."

The island was declared secure on September 22, although scattered pockets of resistance held out until February 1945. "Bloody Peleliu" cost nearly two thousand American lives and eight thousand wounded. Some units were nearly wiped out. Almost the entire Japanese garrison was killed or committed suicide. Peleliu proved only of marginal strategic importance at best, and ended up as a backwater fuel depot. It was Nimitz's major mistake of the war. Angaur, six miles to the southwest, was assaulted on September 17 by two regiments of the army's 81st Division, and taken without great difficulty. Two six-thousand-foot runways were ready for use by October 17. Ulithi had been abandoned by the Japanese, and its splendid natural harbor promptly became the Third Fleet's major forward base.

To prevent Japan's remaining air strength from interfering with the impending invasion of the Philippines, and to sever communications between the archipelago and Japan, Halsey and TF 38 struck at Luzon, the Ryukyus, and Formosa on October 10–14. Admiral Shigeru Fukudome put all 230 fighters of his Sixth Base Air Force into the air to oppose the strike, and, as Halsey put it, there was "a knock-down drag-out fight between carrier air and shore-based air." Watching one stage of the battle, Admiral Fukudome reported:

> Our planes appeared to do so well that I thought I could desire no better performance. In a matter of moments, one after the other, planes were seen falling down enveloped in flames. "Well done! Well done! A tremendous success!" I clapped my hands. Alas! To my severe

disappointment, a closer watch revealed that all those shot down were *our* fighters, and all those proudly circling our heads were enemy planes! Our fighters were nothing but so many eggs thrown at the stone wall of the indomitable enemy formation. In a brief one-sided encounter, the combat terminated in our total defeat.

Over the next two days, the Japanese attacked the fleet with all the planes that had been accumulated to replace the carrier air groups lost in the Philippine Sea, and between 550 and 600 aircraft were destroyed. These losses nearly matched those of the RAF during the Battle of Britain. Seventy-six American planes were lost in combat, and the heavy cruiser *Canberra* and light cruiser *Houston* were badly damaged. A notable epic in the annals of naval salvage followed.

Canberra, named for the Australian cruiser sunk off Savo, had taken a torpedo amidships which blew a huge jagged hole in her hull. Damage-control parties kept her afloat, although she was dead in the water. Normal procedure would have been to scuttle the vessel, but Halsey made the bold decision to tow her out of harm's way. *Wichita* took her under tow until two fleet tugs, *Munsee* and *Pawnee*, assumed the job. Not long after, *Houston* was damaged even more severely than *Canberra*. Halsey now faced a dilemma. Should he try to save the ships—at the expense of further raids on the Japanese bases, because the carriers would have to divert part of their air groups to cover them?

The admiral's staff quickly determined that the cripples could be protected without hampering offensive operations. *Munsee* remained with *Canberra*, *Pawnee* took up the tow of *Houston*, and the two ships crept along within a mile of each other at 3.5 knots. Halsey now hoped "Cripdiv 1,"* as it was jokingly called, would be bait to lure the Japanese fleet to destruction. Japanese planes repeatedly attacked "Cripdiv 1," and everyone asked, Would they *ever* get out of enemy air range? These attacks were beaten off, but one plane got through and nearly blew off *Houston*'s stern with a torpedo. Immediately after this hit, the signal lamps of *Pawnee* blinked a message to the stricken cruiser: "We'll stand by you!"

And stand by she did. Even when *Houston* took on sixty-five hundred tons of water, more than any other ship had absorbed without sinking,

---

*A play on the usual navy abbreviation "Crudiv" for "Cruiser Division."

Pawnee maintained her tow. Slowly, the crippled cruisers drew out of range of the Japanese, and were handed over to fresh tugs and a salvage ship, off Cape Engaño, at the northern tip of the Philippines. They were towed to Ulithi for temporary repairs before proceeding to Pearl Harbor and then to shipyards in the United States. Inexperienced and overexcited, the Japanese airmen claimed to have sunk eleven carriers and battleships. The emperor issued a special rescript hailing the "Victory of Taiwan." Halsey, in a fine stroke of public relations, sardonically reported he was "retiring toward the enemy following the salvage of the Third Fleet ships recently reported sunk by Radio Tokyo."

"I have returned."

With these portentous words, Douglas MacArthur proclaimed his arrival in the Philippines on the afternoon of October 20, 1944. Wearing his ever-present Philippine field marshal's cap and sunglasses and freshly pressed khakis, he waded ashore at Leyte as a host of newsreel cameras recorded the event. The liberation of the islands had begun. Following a bombardment by Rear Admiral Jesse Oldendorf's half-dozen old battleships, six U.S. Army divisions were put ashore on the northwestern side of Leyte by Admiral Kinkaid's Seventh Fleet, reinforced by units of Halsey's Third Fleet, which had been stripped down to TF 38. By World War II standards, it was an easy operation: perfect weather, no surf, no mines, and no underwater obstacles. Close air support was provided by Task Group 77.4, which consisted of three task units of six escort carriers each, plus their screens of destroyers and destroyer escorts.

Initial enemy resistance was surprisingly light. The single Japanese division on the island—the Sixteenth, of about twenty thousand men—had retreated to prepared positions in the hills, in keeping with the new Japanese tactics, and it appeared that the reconquest of Letye would be comparatively easy. Japanese air attacks were desultory, although the light cruiser *Honolulu* was badly damaged by a torpedo dropped by a plane that slipped in under cloud cover. The Australian cruiser *Australia* was knocked about by one that deliberately flew into her foremast with its full bomb load. By nightfall of D+1, some hundred thousand American troops were ashore, and a nearby airstrip had been taken.

Although the Leyte invasion had brought the Southwest and Cen-

tral Pacific forces together, there was no provision for a supreme commander. Admiral Kinkaid, commander of the augmented Seventh
Fleet, answered to General MacArthur; Halsey, whose Third Fleet
was now essentially TF 38, answered to Admiral Nimitz. The fleet
commanders were expected to cooperate and coordinate their efforts,
yet the situation was made to order for misunderstanding, and no one
had the authority to impose order. While Kinkaid was to provide
close support for the assault, there was some confusion about Halsey's
role. Inasmuch as Nimitz had instructed him to "cover and support"
the invasion, Kinkaid believed that it was Halsey's job to protect the
amphibious forces. But Halsey took as his main mission that part of his
orders stating: "In case opportunity for destruction of major portion of
the enemy fleet offers, or can be created, such destruction becomes
primary task." Having little patience with the cautious tactics adopted
by Raymond Spruance in the Marianas, the admiral made it plain that,
if a similar opportunity presented itself, he would go after the enemy
fleet. The Japanese were well aware of Halsey's aggressive state of
mind—and tailored their own plans to take full advantage of it.

SHO-1 was activated on October 17. A daring and desperate mixture
of stealth and ruse, it depended for success upon a mixture of surprise, Japanese superiority in night operations—and Halsey's
impetuosity. Two fleets were to converge like a giant pincers upon
Leyte Gulf, slash through to Kinkaid's transports and supply ships,
cut off the American beachheads, and, if possible, destroy major com-
ponents of the American fleet, especially carriers. Whether the
Japanese had any faith in this plan is an open question. Even as a war
game, SHO-1 was unrealistic, in view of the massive sea-and-air
power mustered by the U.S. Navy. Moreover, there was no contingency plan to allow for reversals. In reality, SHO-1 was "a kind of
banzai charge," says one historian, and the Samurai tradition of fighting to the bitter end had as much to do with it as sound military logic.
    Vice-Admiral Takeo Kurita commanded the strongest of the Japa-
nese forces, the Center Group. Although he came from a family of
scholars—his father had written a history of Japan—he was a man of
action, having originally served on destroyers. As with Halsey, "the
destruction of enemy carriers was a kind of obsession" with him.
Kurita's fleet was a powerful one—five battleships, including the fear-

some *Yamato* and *Musashi*—and was to pass through San Bernardino Strait, to the north of Leyte. But it lacked air cover; even the scout planes usually carried by the battleships and cruisers had been sent to the Philippines.

The Southern Group, which included two old battleships flying the flag of Vice-Admiral Shoji Nishimura, was to transit Surigao Strait, to the south of the island, and be followed by Vice-Admiral Kiyohide Shima's three cruisers and four destroyers.* The Northern Group, Admiral Ozawa's four carriers—the veteran fleet carrier *Zuikaku* and three light carriers, with only 116 planes among them—were the key to the operation. They were to trail their cloaks to the north of Luzon and lure Halsey and his ships away from Leyte, so Kurita and Nishimura could accomplish their tasks. To sweeten the pot, the hybrid carrier-battleships *Ise* and *Hyuga* were proffered as additional bait.†

While the Japanese fleet was gathering—it took almost a week for them to reach the vicinity of Leyte—the American ships were deployed at several points off the beachhead. Kinkaid, his transports and supply ships, and Oldendorf's battleships were in Leyte Gulf. To the east were eighteen escort carriers under the command of Rear Admiral Thomas L. Sprague. Halsey and TF 38 were to the east of Luzon. Halsey decided it was an opportune time to detach his carrier groups in rotation for rest and replenishment. Intelligence reports minimized the possibility of a Japanese naval attack, and his ships had operated in tropical seas without cessation for almost ten months, during which most of their crews had never set foot on shore. TG 38.1 was sent to Ulithi on October 22, and TG 38.4 was to follow the next day.

A line of submarines had been thrown out to the west of the Philippines to observe enemy movements. Early in the morning of October 23, *Darter* and *Dace* were cruising on the surface together at five knots in the reef-studded Palawan Passage when their radars picked

---

*It would have been more efficient to merge Shima's and Nishimura's ships, but the forces were kept separate, because the two admirals loathed each other. Nishimura, a seagoing sailor, considered Shima, who had risen through staff jobs, a politician and wire-puller. Had the fleets joined together, Shima, who was slightly senior but less experienced, would have been in command.

†Six carriers of various sizes were left behind in home waters because of a lack of planes and trained air crew. *Ise* and *Hyuga* had flight decks and hangars where their two after fourteen-inch gun turrets had been. There were no aircraft available for these ships, however, and they had been crammed with over a hundred light anti-aircraft guns and six anti-aircraft rockets to support the carriers.

up the glowing pinpoints of a number of ships at a range of fifteen miles. "Let's go!" Commander David H. McClintock of *Darter* shouted over to *Dace* by megaphone. The submarines gave chase at flank speed. As the radar picture became clearer, they could make out a large formation of heavy ships with a flanking screen of destroyers. *Darter* flashed an enemy-in-sight report to Halsey. Let Commander McClintock tell what occurred next:

> The gray ships kept getting larger. We were a little to the east of the column and would pass on parallel courses. At 0525 the first target could be identified as a heavy cruiser with huge bow waves. . . . At 0527 all tubes were ready . . . range under 3,000 yards. The column zigged west to give a perfect torpedo range of just under 1,000 yards. . . . Now the angle on the bow was getting bigger . . . range under a thousand . . . shooting bearing . . . mark . . . fire one! As the next five forward fish left us, the Jap flagship turned on a searchlight to signal to the east. Did she see our torpedoes? She was going by now. No she wasn't zigging! Shift targets to the second cruiser . . . bearing mark . . . fire seven! The first stern torpedo is on its way.

As the torpedo sped from its tube, explosions were heard and someone shouted "Depth charges!" But McClintock quickly observed, "Depth charges hell . . . torpedoes!"

"I swung the periscope back to the first cruiser and will never forget that sight," he added. "She was belching flames from the base of the forward turret to the stern. Five torpedoes had hit. Dense black smoke of burning oil covered her and she was going down by the bow. She was still going ahead but her number one turret was cutting through the water. She was finished."

The stricken vessel was *Atago*, Admiral Kurita's flagship. She went to the bottom, with the loss of 359 men, although Kurita and his staff were picked up by a destroyer. Kurita was recovering from dengue fever, and the dunking did nothing to improve his physical condition. *Takao*, the cruiser struck by two of McClintock's stern torpedoes, was badly damaged. *Maya*, hit by three torpedoes from *Dace*, exploded and sank within four minutes, leaving only a mass of floating debris.*

**Darter's luck soon ran out. On the night of October 24, while she and *Dace* were trying to close in on the crippled *Takao*, she ran aground on an uncharted reef and was abandoned. The crew were taken off by *Dace*, which returned safely to base in Australia.

Panic swept the Japanese fleet. Repeated alarms were sounded, and destroyers raced about, blindly dropping depth charges on nonexistent submarines. Kurita, who had transferred his flag to *Yamato*, finally got a grip on the fleet, and it pressed on toward Leyte. Its passage, however, was observed by two more American submarines on the evening of October 23, as it steered east toward the Mindoro Strait, in the Philippines. To add to Kurita's unease, he received an alarming situation report from Admiral Toyoda. The enemy, said the chief of the Combined Fleet, was fully alert to the approach of the several Japanese forces, and Kurita could expect air attacks the following day. This report was unduly pessimistic. Only Kurita had been located—Nishimura's and Shima's forces were not discovered until the following day—and the Americans were still unaware of their approach.

Upon receiving *Darter*'s sighting report, Halsey immediately prepared for a major fleet action. Three of TF 38's four task groups—TF 38.1, was on its way to Ulithi to replenish—were concentrated during the night closer to the east coast of the Philippines to be in better position to launch early-morning searches. TF 38.3 took up station off the Polillo Islands; TF 38.2 stood off the exit from the San Bernardino Strait; and TF 38.4 was off Leyte Gulf. At dawn on October 24, each group sent out planes to scout the surrounding islands. Kurita's force was sighted at 0822. Halsey, exercising direct tactical command, immediately ordered the task groups to launch an attack. TF 38.1, en route to Ulithi, was recalled at top speed.

Before Halsey's strike order could be executed, the Japanese hit first, as they had in the Battle of the Philippine Sea. Admiral Fukudome launched some 180 aircraft he had laboriously massed ashore in three waves of about sixty planes each against TG 38.3, commanded by Rear Admiral Frederick C. Sherman. The first wave was met by seven Hellcats from *Essex*, led by the navy's leading ace, Commander David McCampbell. In a half-hour, McCampbell and his wingman, Lieutenant Roy W. Rushing, shot down fifteen planes; McCampbell established a record for a single mission by destroying nine planes. Undoubtedly, the decline in the quality of Japanese flyers contributed to this success. "After following the decimated formation nearly all the way to Manila, we returned . . . near exhausted of ammunition and near fuel exhaustion," McCampbell reported.

Upon landing, his plane had "barely sufficient gas to taxi out of the arresting gear."

Another group of Japanese aircraft attacked the light carrier *Princeton*. "We held off eighty planes for fifty minutes . . . shooting down twenty-eight," reported Lieutenant Carl Brown. "Ordinarily, we would not have tackled eighty planes with eight Hellcats, but it was get them before they got our ships. . . . We went after them with all guns and throttles wide open." Nevertheless, a Judy slipped through the net and dropped a pair of five-hundred-pound bombs on the carrier's flight deck.

The blast touched off fierce fires in *Princeton*'s hangar deck. Six Avengers loaded with torpedoes exploded, feeding the inferno. All men not needed to fight the flames were taken off by the cruiser *Birmingham* and several destroyers which came alongside the stricken carrier at considerable danger to themselves. Tons of water were poured into Princeton while Hellcats drove off enemy planes that were trying to finish her off. By midafternoon, all the fires had been extinguished except a blaze near the stern. Just after *Birmingham* came alongside to help prepare *Princeton* for towing, the carrier's after magazine blew up, raining flaming debris down on the cruiser.

"The spectacle which greeted the human eye was horrible to behold," said one of *Birmingham*'s officers. "Dead, dying and wounded, many of them badly and horribly, covered the decks. . . . Blood ran freely down our waterways, and continued to run for some time." The cruiser was severely damaged, and 229 of her crew were killed, and 420 wounded. *Princeton*, now beyond salvage, was torpedoed—the first American carrier to be lost since the old *Hornet* had been sunk in the Solomons two years earlier.

The U.S. Navy soon exacted its revenge. Some 250 planes from TG 38.2 and TG 38.3 flew across Leyte to attack Kurita's ships in the Sibuyan Sea. Even though they lacked air cover—Fukudome's fighters were to have provided it—*Yamato* and *Musashi* each mounted 120 guns, and their anti-aircraft fire was intense.* *Musashi* bore the brunt of the assault. She was hit by eight torpedoes and four bombs,

*Lacking the deadly VT shells of the Americans, *Musashi* fired special eighteen-inch shells that were designed to explode among the clouds of attacking aircraft like giant shotgun shells. They proved to be ineffective, and damaged the bores of the big guns.

which merely slowed the huge vessel. Ten more torpedoes and a half-dozen direct bomb hits finally stopped *Musashi* dead in the water. *Yamato*, the veteran battleship *Nagato*, and several other ships were damaged during the attack. In an effort to get out of range of the implacable American planes and deceive them as to his intentions, Kurita turned back in the direction from which he had come. But as darkness fell, he put about again, and his fleet passed the gloomy sight of *Musashi* dying in the last rays of the setting sun. At about 1930, she plunged to the bottom stern-first, with half her twenty-four hundred officers and men. Kurita pressed on toward the San Bernardino Strait and the Leyte beachheads.

In the meantime, Admiral Kinkaid had been warned of the approach of Admiral Nishimura's Southern Force. The Japanese were attacked from the air on the morning of October 24, and the battleship *Fuso* was damaged, but Nishimura kept coming. He relished the idea of a night battle and made no effort to communicate with Admiral Shima's force, which was following some thirty miles astern. Correctly assuming that the Japanese were heading for Surigao Strait, Kinkaid directed Rear Admiral Oldendorf to place the six old battleships of his bombardment group—*West Virginia, Tennessee, California, Maryland, Pennsylvania*, and *Mississippi*—across the northern end of the strait to provide "a welcoming committee." All except *Mississippi* had risen from the mud of Pearl Harbor.

Entering the twelve-mile-wide passage late on the night of October 24, Nishimura was only fifty miles south of his target, Kinkaid's transports. In the lead were two destroyers, and a mile behind came the flagship, *Yamashiro*, flanked by two destroyers. *Fuso* and the cruiser *Mogami*, six hundred yards apart, brought up the rear. The moon had set, and there were occasional flashes of lightning. PT-boats launched several torpedo attacks against Nishimura's vessels, which created some confusion but scored no hits.

Just after 0200 on October 25, the five destroyers of Captain Jesse G. Coward's Desron 54 stormed in at high speed to port and starboard of the enemy line in a classic scissors attack. They fired twenty-seven torpedoes at a range of eight- to nine thousand yards and sped away. Yet, instead of taking evasive action, Nishimura maintained course—and paid for it. Hit by several torpedoes at 0207, *Fuso* was engulfed in a huge fireball, and ripped apart by explosions. Nishimura, apparently unaware of the catastrophe—perhaps his staff dared not tell him—continued to run the gantlet of torpedo attacks. Two Japanese destroyers were sunk, and a third was damaged. Next it was the turn of the nine destroyers of Captain Roland Smoot's Desron 24. They scored a hit on *Yamashiro*.

Oldendorf's battleships, which had held their fire during the destroyer phase of the action, now carried out the dream of every admiral throughout history—crossing the "T" of an enemy battle line. The old ships opened fire at 0353 at a range of twenty-three thousand yards. Salvo after salvo of radar-directed fourteen- and sixteen-inch armor-piercing shells plunged down upon Nishimura's remaining ships, while cruisers flanking the battle line added their shells to the inferno. *Yamashiro* bore the brunt of this punishing fire. Blazing like a furnace, she sank at 0419 with almost her entire complement. The cruiser *Mogami*, burning and crippled, limped away to the south, escorted by a destroyer. The only American casualties were in the destroyer *Grant*, which was severely mauled after being caught in the crossfire between the two fleets.

Admiral Shima's force arrived in the strait several hours after Nishimura, having already suffered damage to the light cruiser *Abukama* from a torpedo fired by *PT-137*, commanded by Lieutenant (j.g.) Isadore M. Kovar. *Nachi*, Shima's flagship, was rammed by the hapless *Mogami* as she wallowed down the passage, rudder gone and steering with her engines. Appalled by the carnage, Shima retired, but he was followed by Oldendorf's cruisers and destroyers, which finished off a damaged destroyer. *Mogami* and *Abukama* were sunk by bombers the next morning, leaving two cruisers and five destroyers as the Southern Group's only survivors.

The U.S. Navy had won what was probably the last naval battle ever fought in a formal line. Oldendorf's veteran battleships had, in Morison's words, fired "a funeral salute to a finished era of naval warfare. One can imagine the ghosts of all the great admirals from Raleigh to Jellicoe standing at attention as [the] Battle Line went into oblivion. . . ."

Misunderstandings are inherent in a divided command, and with Halsey responsible to Nimitz, and Kinkaid to MacArthur, they soon occurred—and were compounded by communications foul-ups. Throughout the maneuvering that preceded the actions against Kurita's and Nishimura's forces, Halsey had wondered where the Japanese carriers were, "the one piece missing in the puzzle." It seemed incredible that the enemy could have mounted such a massive operation without making use of their carriers. While awaiting developments, Halsey produced a "Battle Plan" in which he earmarked four battleships, five cruisers, and nineteen destroyers for a new TF 34 under Vice-Admiral Willis Lee, which was to cover the eastern exit of San Bernardino Strait. King and Nimitz were the addressees of this signal, but it was read by Kinkaid as well. All thought TF 34 had actually been formed, and Kinkaid later said this was "exactly what I would do."

In reality, however, it was merely a contingency plan, not an order to be immediately carried out. Halsey later sent a clarifying signal that said: "If the enemy sorties [through the strait] TF 34 *will be** formed when directed by me." Unfortunately, this second message was passed only among Halsey's ships, not on radio as the first had been, and was not picked up by King, Nimitz, or Kinkaid. The lives of hundreds of men were to turn on this point.

Ozawa's four carriers and two hybrids were finally discovered to the northeast of Luzon, on a southward heading, on the afternoon of October 24, after the Japanese admiral had all but broadcast his position in his eagerness to be discovered. To announce his presence, he had dispatched seventy-six planes to join in Fukudome's strike against TG 38.3, but they were mistaken as land-based planes. Most were shot down. Only when he sent *Ise* and *Hyuga* well ahead of the rest of his ships were they located by American scout planes.

Unaware that they were "paper tigers" almost devoid of aircraft, Halsey regarded the flattops as his most important target—just as the Japanese intended. "I cannot understand how the enemy, with his highly developed intelligence system, so badly overestimated Ozawa's force," Rear Admiral Tomiji Koyanagi, Kurita's chief of staff, later observed. In his eagerness to be off in pursuit of Ozawa's carriers, Halsey convinced himself that Kurita's Central Force was no longer a threat, because of the pummeling it had received, and that Kinkaid

*My italics.

could deal with it. "I went into the flag plot" of *New Jersey*, he wrote in his memoirs, "put my finger on the Northern Force's charted position, 300 miles away, and said, 'Here's where we're going. . . . [S]tart them north.' " He took sixty-seven ships with him, including those designated for TF 34. At the least, he should have queried Kinkaid about his ability to handle the oncoming Japanese.

At 2024, Halsey signaled Nimitz and Kinkaid: "Strike reports indicate enemy [Kurita's force] heavily damaged. Am proceeding north with 3 groups to attack enemy carrier force at dawn." The message was poorly worded; had it been clearer, the Battle of Leyte Gulf would have been even more costly for the Japanese than it was. Both Kinkaid and Nimitz, believing Halsey had four task groups with him, and having read his directives regarding TF 34, assumed he was leaving Lee's battleships to bar San Bernardino Strait to the Japanese. "Had he used the word *all* instead of the number 3 to describe what he was taking with him on his trek north, Kinkaid would have realized that San Bernardino Strait was being left unguarded," observes one historian.

Halsey, for his part, believed Kinkaid was maintaining surveillance of the passage, but the latter failed to order aerial reconnaissance of the strait. In fact, he made no effort to determine if TF 34 was actually guarding the strait until 0400 on October 25—when he sent such a query to Halsey. Unfortunately, it was delayed in transit because of communications complications resulting from the fact that the two admirals answered to different commanders. Thus, not one ship, not even a destroyer, was guarding the passage—and Kurita steamed through undetected during the night. Despite heavy losses, SHO-1 seemed to be working. Nothing stood in the way of a still-powerful Japanese fleet and the Leyte beachheads except the fragile escort carriers of TF 77.4.

These vessels were deployed in three groups of six along a north-south line, a short distance seaward of Leyte Gulf, each with a mixed screen of six destroyers and destroyer escorts. The southernmost, "Taffy 1," commanded by Rear Admiral Thomas Sprague in *Sangamon*, lay off Mindanao; then came "Taffy 2," under Rear Admiral Felix Stump in *Natoma Bay*, which was off the entrance to Leyte Gulf; Rear Admiral Clifton Sprague's "Taffy 3" was off Samar, and closest to the advancing Japanese. No relation to the other Sprague, he flew his flag in *Fanshaw Bay*; his other ships were *St. Lo, White Plains, Kalinin Bay, Kitkun Bay*, and *Gambier Bay*. Each vessel carried a mixed bag of fourteen to eighteen Wildcat fighter-bombers and a dozen Avengers.

Kurita, with four battleships, six heavy cruisers, two light cruisers, and eleven destroyers, steamed out of San Bernardino Strait and turned south just as dawn was breaking on October 25. Clouds hung low, occasional gusts of rain swept the ships, and the sea was choppy. Unaware that Halsey was pursuing Ozawa's carriers, Kurita was amazed that no enemy ships or submarines were blocking his way. "This was indeed a miracle," said Admiral Koyanagi. It was not until 0649 that a Japanese lookout spotted masts about twenty miles to the southeast, just about the time Ensign Jensen sighted the oncoming enemy fleet. The younger officers on *Yamato*'s bridge cheered. Kurita closed at twenty-four knots, convinced he was facing four or five of Halsey's fleet carriers screened by two battleships and at least ten heavy cruisers. The Japanese opened fire at 0653.

One minute later, Clifton Sprague of Taffy 3 was startled by the fall of monstrous 3,220-pound eighteen-inch shells about his ships, raising enormous geysers of purple-and-yellow seawater. The Japanese used various-colored dyes to spot the fall of shells. "Hey, they're shooting at us in technicolor!" cried one sailor. This was the first time—and the last—that *Yamato*'s giant guns were fired at an enemy ship. No one had ever expected escort carriers to fight the main Japanese fleet, but Sprague reacted as if he had planned for it. Hastily launching his Wildcats and Avengers, which were armed with any weapon available—heavy bombs, fragmentation bombs, torpedoes, even depth charges—he laid down a smoke screen and fled south, filling the airwaves with frantic calls for help.

Rather than leaving a few cruisers behind to dispose of the jeeps quickly and plunging ahead with his fleet to wreak havoc on MacArthur's beachheads, only a hundred miles to the south, Kurita diverted his entire force to an attack on Clifton Sprague's ships. Admiral Koyanagi later explained that, although Kinkaid's transports were the supposed target of SHO-1, Japanese doctrine, like that of the U.S. Navy, gave the highest priority to attacking enemy carriers. Kurita ordered a "general attack," which in effect transformed his fleet from a unified command to a collection of individual ships racing ahead pell-mell to get at the enemy. Weakened by fever, exhaustion, and the traumatic experience of having one flagship sunk under him and another bombed, his judgment may have been clouded.

"I didn't think we'd last fifteen minutes," Sprague said, "but I thought we might as well give them all we've got before we go down." Two cruisers were hit by the American planes: *Suzuya* was damaged and slowed by a near miss, and *Haguro* lost one of her eight-inch turrets. Sprague's ships dodged in and out of a rain squall, which providentially concealed them from the enemy guns. When his motley collection of planes ran out of bombs and torpedoes, they strafed the Japanese ships with machine guns. And when they ran out of ammunition, they made passes at the ships in hopes of distracting the gunners. These dummy runs forced the Japanese ships to make frequent changes in course, so they were unable to use their superior speed to catch the fleeing carriers. One pilot, Lieutenant Paul B. Garrison, made twenty strafing runs, ten with empty guns.

Angrily damning Halsey for leaving the strait open, Kinkaid tried to get help to Taffy 3. Oldendorf's half-dozen battleships were ordered north at flank speed, but they were more than 130 miles from the scene of action. Taffy 2 and 3 sent their planes to Sprague's assistance. "The enemy was closing with disconcerting rapidity and the volume of fire was increasing," Sprague reported. "At this point it did not appear that any of our ships could survive another five minutes of the heavy caliber fire being received." Faced with "the ultimate in desperate circumstances," he ordered the destroyer screen to launch a torpedo attack. "Small boys . . . intercept!" he radioed.

"We need a bugler to sound the charge," declared Commander Amos T. Hathaway, as his ships—*Heerman, Hoel,* and *Johnson*—dashed to within point-blank range of the enemy before firing their torpedoes. They were supported by the three destroyer-escorts. Five tin fish from *Hoel* forced *Yamato* and *Nagato* to veer temporarily out of the fight, and one from *Johnson* blew the bow off the cruiser *Kumano.* Having expended their torpedoes, the destroyers peppered the heavily armored Japanese ships with five-inch shells. They put up such a stiff fight that the Japanese believed the destroyers were cruisers and the destroyer-escorts were destroyers—confirming their conviction that they were in contact with the main American fleet.

The enemy's big guns soon found their target, and *Johnson* was sunk by a salvo of fourteen-inch shells. "It was like a puppy being smacked by a truck," said one of her officers. *Hoel* was hit and dead in the water. *Heerman* engaged four of the biggest Japanese ships. To confuse the enemy gunners, Hathaway zigzagged and chased splashes, believing the Japanese would not fire twice at the same place. A shell struck a locker full of dried navy beans, reducing them to a pulp, which was sucked up through an intake and dumped on an officer on the bridge. "He lost his taste for beans right there," Hathaway observed.

By now the carriers had emerged from the protection of the rain squall, and several were hit, *Gambier Bay* the most seriously. Ablaze and losing speed, she dropped behind her consorts. The destroyer-escorts *Roberts* and *Dennis* gallantly tried to draw off the enemy, and the former was sunk in the attempt. *Gambier Bay* capsized at 0907. *Kalinin Bay* was hit sixteen times. As Sprague reported:

> The shells created a shambles below decks, her officers told me later, and only the heroic efforts of her crew kept the little ship going. Bos'ns crews wrestled under five feet of water to plug up big holes in the hull; engineers worked knee-deep in oil, choking in the stench of burned rubber; quartermasters steered the ship for hours from an emergency wheel below, as fire scorched the deck on which they stood; and all hands risked their lives to save mates in flooded or burning compartments. . . .

What was Halsey doing while this drama was unfolding off Samar?

As frantic messages from Sprague and Kinkaid poured in, TF 38 was launching 180 planes for the first of six attacks against Ozawa's decoy carriers. During the night of October 24, some intelligence officers expressed mounting concern about the wisdom of abandoning San Bernardino Strait, doubts strengthened by a report from a night-flying patrol plane that Kurita had put about and was making for the passage again. Yet, when Rear Admiral Gerald F. Bogan of TF 38.2 tried to pass this report on to *New Jersey*, a staff officer curtly replied: "Yes, yes, we have that information." Willis Lee twice signaled Halsey that he was certain the Japanese were coming through San Bernardino, but received only a "Roger" in reply. Arleigh Burke awakened Mitscher and asked him to do something. "Does Admiral Halsey have this report?" Mitscher asked. When the answer was affirmative, he said, "If he wants my advice, he'll ask for it." Then he turned over and went back to sleep.*

With single-minded intensity, Halsey concentrated on the Japanese carriers, which had been found about two hundred miles east of Cape Engaño, at the northeastern tip of Luzon. At 0648, he was surprised to receive the delayed message from Kinkaid asking if TF 34 was guarding San Bernardino Strait. This was the first indication he had that Kinkaid was even aware of TF 34, because he had not been included in the traffic regarding the creation of this force. On the other hand, Halsey had included Kinkaid among those signaled he was "proceeding north with 3 groups."

The puzzled Halsey immediately radioed Kinkaid that TF 34 "is with our carriers now engaging enemy carriers." And with that he turned his attention to the strikes against Ozawa's ships. The handful of planes still left on the Japanese carriers were quickly brushed aside by the first wave of American planes, but the hybrids *Ise* and *Hyuga* threw up a heavy curtain of anti-aircraft fire that saved them. *Chitose* was bombed and sunk, and the flagship *Zuikaku* was so badly damaged by a torpedo that Ozawa transferred to a cruiser. *Zuiho* was also damaged during this strike. One young Helldiver pilot was so excited that, upon landing on *Lexington*, he raced to Mitscher on the flag bridge, shouting: "I gotta hit on a carrier! I gotta hit on a carrier!"

A second wave of American planes disabled *Chiyoda*, the only undamaged Japanese flattop. The crippled *Zuikaku* was hit by three more torpedoes in a third attack, and the last of the carriers that had struck Pearl Harbor rolled over and sank. Before abandoning ship, her crew gathered on the flight deck to salute the flag as it was lowered. The fourth strike concentrated on the damaged *Zuiho*, and she, too, went under. The last two strikes of the day inflicted little additional damage on the fleeing Japanese. In all, TF 38 had sunk three carriers and damaged a fourth.

In the meantime, messages from Kinkaid requesting help poured in upon *New Jersey*'s bridge. "WHERE IS LEE X SEND LEE," said one in plain text. Although annoyed by these pleas, and having his own bat-

---

*Mitscher may have been miffed that Halsey had assumed tactical command of TF 38, making him little more than a passenger in his own flagship. Then again, he may have felt that pressing information upon a commander that he already possessed in a combat situation would be distracting.

tle to fight, Halsey ordered TG 38.1, which was en route from Ulithi to rejoin the fleet, to proceed "at best possible speed" to Leyte Gulf to aid Kinkaid. Meanwhile, he continued to pound ahead in Ozawa's wake with the intention of bringing Lee's battleships into range of the survivors. And then he received a message from Admiral Nimitz that brought him up sharply.

At Pearl Harbor, Nimitz, who was following the trials of Taffy 3 and receiving only disjointed reports of the calamitous events taking place off Samar, fired off a message to Halsey with copies to Admiral King and Kinkaid: "WHERE IS TASK FORCE 34." The communications officer who encoded the message repeated the key words to prevent garbling, then added the usual padding at the beginning and end to confuse enemy cryptographers. It began "TURKEY TROTS TO WATER" and ended "THE WORLD WONDERS."* When the message was received on board Halsey's flagship, the final phrase seemed part of the message, and it reached the admiral in the following form: "WHERE IS RPT WHERE IS TASK FORCE THIRTY FOUR RR THE WORLD WONDERS."

Halsey was furious. "I was stunned as if I had been struck in the face," he wrote later. "The paper rattled in my hands. I snatched off my cap [and] threw it on the deck." Regarding the message as an open humiliation, he delayed for an hour—saying he was refueling—before putting about with his two fastest battleships, *New Jersey* and *Iowa*, along with three light cruisers and eight destroyers. He picked up carrier support from Bogan's TF 38.2 as he sped south. Ozawa's ships were only forty-two miles away when he turned back, Halsey claimed. Later, he declared the greatest error he had made during the battle was "bowing to pressure and turning south."

In any event, it was too late to catch Kurita. Although Ozawa had

---

*E. B. Potter, in his biography of Nimitz, speculates that, inasmuch as October 25 was the anniversary of the Charge of the Light Brigade at Balaklava in the Crimea in 1854, the communications officer may have unconsciously echoed Tennyson's famous poem:

> *When can their glory fade?*
> *O the wild charge they made!*
> *All the world wonder'd.*

Potter observes that "it would not be too surprising if he did, for English professors and students of literature tend to be attracted, or assigned, to communications" (*Nimitz*, pp. 339–40).

accomplished his mission of luring TF 38 away to the north, Kurita, fearing that the enemy now had time to concentrate against him, had retired. At 0911, he signaled his ships: "Cease action, come north with me, 20 knots," and escaped back through San Bernardino Strait. He later considered putting about for Leyte Gulf again, but dropped the idea. The transports had undoubtedly unloaded and dispersed, he reasoned; no help could be expected from Nishimura, and he was uncertain of the whereabouts of both Halsey's fleet and Ozawa's carriers.

By failing to press on to Leyte Gulf, Kurita has been criticized for throwing away a victory that was within his grasp, but as Winston Churchill aptly remarked, only "those who have endured a similar ordeal may judge him." To the north, Mitscher's carriers, dispatched by Halsey in pursuit of Ozawa's cripples, sank *Chiyoda*, the remaining Japanese carrier, and a destroyer before the chase was called off. The retreating Kurita also lost a cruiser to U.S. planes.

Even though Kurita had retreated, the ordeal of the escort carriers was far from over. The final blows of the battle were delivered by a new and terrifying weapon, especially to the Western mind—the Divine Wind, or Kamikaze Corps, which had sworn to crash their bomb-laden aircraft into enemy ships.* American sailors now faced the harrowing experience of having whining streaks of death fall upon them from the sky, sparking a stomach-tightening, paralyzing flash of fear. Release came only *after* the shattering crash, when a man either found himself unhurt and thankful—or was dead or wounded.

Taffy 1, the southernmost of the groups, sustained the first attack when a Zero descended upon *Santee* like an angry wasp and crashed into her, setting the ship afire. The crew had just extinguished the flames when she was struck by a torpedo fired by a Japanese submarine, but she did not sink—a remarkable tribute to her design and her

---

*The kamikazes took their name from a typhoon supposedly sent by the Sun Goddess that had shattered the great invasion fleet of the Mongol Emperor Kublai Khan in 1281. The first suicide attack units were created by Vice-Admiral Takijiro Onishi, commander of Japanese air operations in the Philippines. With most of Japan's experienced pilots dead, he concluded that conventional air attacks stood little chance of success, but even inexperienced young pilots with minimal training could dive their planes into enemy ships and achieve a glorious death for the emperor. Though Onishi had hoped to coordinate the first kamikaze attack with the SHO-1 plan, Kurita had retreated before any missions could be flown.

crew. *Suwannee* also survived a direct hit from a kamikaze, and Kitkun Bay, of Taffy 3, was severely damaged by a near miss. *St. Lo*, also of Taffy 3, was still less fortunate. A suicide plane crashed through her flight deck and exploded among a store of bombs and torpedoes, tearing the ship apart. She was the first vessel to be sunk by a kamikaze—and a preview of things to come.

Leaving the remnants of his screen to pick up survivors, Admiral Sprague withdrew his remaining vessels. "We had been through so much by then," he said with considerable understatement, "that it didn't seem to matter whether we had escorts with us or not." With the kamikazes gone, the sky and the sea looked serene, and it all seemed but a bad dream. Unfortunately, like other bad dreams, this one was to recur, again and again.

So ended the three-day Battle of Leyte Gulf—in reality four separate actions that occurred largely outside that body of water. The Japanese had gotten the decisive fleet engagement with the U.S. Navy for which they had yearned, and lost one fleet carrier, three light carriers, three battleships, ten cruisers, and eleven destroyers—three hundred thousand tons in all, more than a quarter of all Japanese losses since Pearl Harbor. The Americans lost a light carrier, two escort carriers, a pair of destroyers, and a destroyer-escort. But the results of Leyte Gulf cannot be measured merely in tonnage sunk. Although substantial units of the Imperial Navy had survived, including six battleships, Leyte was the last occasion on which the Japanese fleet operated as a unified fighting force. Never again would it be a real threat.

The guns had barely fallen silent before arguments erupted over who was to blame for leaving San Bernardino Strait open. Both King and Nimitz concluded that Halsey had made a crucial error of judgment and tactical leadership in swallowing the bait dangled before him by Ozawa. Anyone else would probably have been relieved, but Halsey kept his post, because removing him would have shaken morale.* Naval historian Kenneth Hagan also contends Nimitz could not have relieved Halsey had he wanted to, because Halsey had

---

*It is worth noting that following the war, Halsey was promoted to the five-star rank of fleet admiral, an honor not accorded to the less colorful but more deserving Spruance, the victor of Midway and the Philippine Sea.

fought precisely as decades of training and doctrine had prepared him. Halsey's partisans, on the other hand, blamed Kinkaid for failing to conduct air searches of the northern approaches to the strait and not inquiring whether it was covered until too late. Kinkaid also erred, they claimed, in assuming, based upon an intercepted signal not intended for him, that Halsey had detached TF 34.

None of these errors would have occurred had operations off Leyte been in the hands of a single supreme commander, or if adequate communications had existed between the various elements of the American fleet. Yet, despite the arguments over how the battle had been fought, Leyte Gulf was a decisive victory, and the way was now clear for the final American advance upon Japan.

•

CHAPTER 19

"Execute Unrestricted . . . Submarine Warfare"

From the start, the patrol had gone badly. *Sealion II* had failed to make contact with a Shanghai-bound convoy that should have been easy pickings. Then the submarine suffered a series of mishaps that put a stern torpedo tube out of commission. So, when three large "blips" appeared on her radar screen as *Sealion* cruised the Formosa Strait shortly after midnight on November 21, 1944, Commander Eli T. Reich hoped her luck was about to change. Making twenty knots on the surface, she closed on the targets. Reich was excited to learn they were battleships, the old *Haruna* and *Kongo*, screened by several destroyers. *Kongo* had been part of Admiral Kurita's Central Force in the Battle of Leyte Gulf a month before.

Three hours passed before Reich could get into position to attack. Firing at long range on the surface, he targeted the lead battleship with a spread of six torpedoes and launched his three remaining stern tubes at the other. *Kongo* was hit by three torpedoes of the first salvo, and one of the destroyers ran into the second spread and blew up. To Reich's consternation, however, the battleships steamed on at sixteen knots, as if nothing had happened. *Sealion* gave chase and torpedomen reloaded the boat's nine usable tubes in preparation for another attack. Toward morning, *Kongo*'s speed dropped to eleven knots, and, along with two escorting destroyers, she fell behind the rest of the squadron. Reich maneuvered for another shot, but, before he could get into position, he reported:

> 0524 Tremendous explosion dead ahead—sky brilliantly illuminated, it looked like a sunset at midnight. Radar reports battleship getting smaller—that it has disappeared—leaving only the two smaller pips of the destroyers. Destroyers seem to be milling around vicinity of target. Battleship sunk—the sun set.
> 0525 Total darkness.

Sealion was the first American submarine to sink a battleship, and had done so at long range with only three torpedoes. Reich now laid chase to *Haruna*, but she outdistanced the submarine in a heavy sea. Returning to the scene of his kill, he searched for survivors or evidence to support his claim to have sunk a battleship, finding only an oil slick and circling planes.

Six days later, on November 27, another American submarine struck an even heavier blow against the Imperial Navy. B-29 bombers flying from the Marianas had launched their first raids on the Japanese home islands, and *Archerfish* and several other boats were ordered to take up positions off Honshu to pick up any downed aviators. She was not called upon to make rescues, however, and was released to conduct an antishipping patrol. Commander Joseph F. Enright, who had once asked to be relieved of a submarine command because he lacked confidence in his abilities, edged up to the outer entrance of Tokyo Bay. At 2048, a large blip appeared on *Archerfish*'s radar.

Enright was soon certain he was tracking a big aircraft carrier. She was, in fact, *Shinano*, sister ship of *Yamato* and the lost *Musashi* and, at fifty-nine thousand tons, one of the largest warships in the world. Originally planned as a third superbattleship, she had been converted into a carrier while still on the ways and had a heavily armored flight deck reinforced with a thick layer of concrete. *Shinano* was conceived as a giant, unsinkable depot ship and, although she carried only forty-seven planes, was to be stocked with bombs, torpedoes, and fuel to service other carriers. Rushed to completion after the Battle of the Philippine Sea, she was undergoing trials in Tokyo Bay when the B-29 raids began, and was ordered to complete shaping up her untrained crew of nineteen hundred men in the safe waters of the Inland Sea. Her watertight integrity had not been proved, pumps had not been installed, and the crewmen didn't know their battle or damage-control stations.

Under escort by three destroyers, *Shinano* was making over twenty knots, faster than the submarine's best speed, but Enright, operating on the surface, laid a course designed to intercept her. "From here on," he reported, "it was a mad race for a possible firing position." After six hours, it appeared as if *Archerfish* were losing the race, but at about 0300 the carrier unexpectedly changed course and headed directly toward the boat. Enright dived and maneuvered into a favorable firing position.

"Up periscope!" he ordered. "Looks perfect! Bearing—mark!"

"Zero zero one!

"Set!"

At 0316, four torpedoes were fired from *Archerfish*'s bow tubes at fifteen hundred yards and two from the stern tubes.

Forty-seven seconds after the first torpedo had been fired, Enright took a look around through his periscope and saw a hit on the carrier's stern. "Large ball of fire climbed her side," he observed. Ten seconds later, he saw a second hit, about fifty yards forward of the first. With a destroyer pounding down on him, Enright went deep. Before *Archerfish* was rocked by depth charges, he heard four more properly timed hits, indicating that all six of his torpedoes had struck *Shinano*. Sonar also picked up the sound of a ship breaking up. Enright rode out the Japanese attack, and at 0610 returned to periscope depth to look around. "Nothing in sight," he reported, but he was certain he had sunk the carrier.

Shinano had actually been hit by four torpedoes, which ripped open a wide gash below her waterline. Captain Toshio Abe was not unduly concerned. Leyte Gulf had shown that the *Yamato*-class hulls could absorb an astonishing amount of punishment. Abe decided to maintain his course at twenty knots. Gradually, *Shinano* began to take on a list, but no effort was made to counterflood. Some of the watertight doors failed to work, and the green crew was too panicked to conduct effective damage control. Eight hours after being struck by *Archerfish*'s torpedoes, the huge vessel heeled over and went to the bottom with five hundred of her men.

The sinking of *Kongo* and *Shinano* within a week constituted two of the most spectacular triumphs scored by American submarines during the Pacific war. But the major contribution of the U.S. Navy's undersea forces to victory was a campaign of attrition against Japan's seaborne trade. As an island nation, Japan, like Britain, was dependent upon maritime commerce for the oil and raw materials that fueled her war machine, and for which she had launched the war. U.S. submarines cut this lifeline—and accomplished what Grand Admiral Dönitz and his fleet of U-boats were never able to do in the Atlantic.

"Execute Unrestricted Air and Submarine Warfare Against Japan."

This signal was immediately flashed to all U.S. naval forces by Admiral Harold Stark, then chief of naval operations, following Pearl Harbor. Before entering both world wars, the United States had denounced unrestricted submarine warfare as contrary to international law, but these objections went by the board after the Japanese attack. Any vessel flying the Japanese flag—warship or *maru*[*]—was fair game. "We set as a primary task of the war in the Pacific day-by-day and week-by-week destruction of more Japanese war material than Japanese industry could replace," President Roosevelt acknowledged in a State of the Union Address a year later. "A large part of this task has been accomplished by the gallant crews of our American submarines who strike on the other side of the Pacific at Japanese ships—right at the very mouth of the harbor of Yokohama."

The U.S. and Imperial Japanese navies were roughly equal in submarine strength at the outset of the war. On both sides the boats were manned by volunteer crews of fiercely dedicated, highly trained officers and men. The Americans had fifty-one operational submarines in the Pacific—twenty-two assigned to the Pacific Fleet at Pearl Harbor, and twenty-nine to the Asiatic Fleet based on Manila. Some of these boats were of the old S-class of about eight hundred tons, similar to the German Type VIIC, but the standard boat was the *Tambor*-class fifteen-hundred-ton fleet submarine.

The finest submarine of the war, the fleet boat had a cruising range of ten thousand miles and carried sufficient fuel and stores for fifty-five days at sea—for the U.S. Navy had nothing resembling the German milch cows. Fleet boats could do almost twenty-one knots on

---

[*]*Maru*, the Japanese term for "merchantman," was usually included in a vessel's name.

the surface and nine knots submerged, and crash-dived to periscope depth in thirty-five seconds. Armament included ten torpedo tubes and twenty-four torpedoes as well as a three-inch (later two five-inch) deck gun. A crew of about eighty officers and men enjoyed living conditions far superior to those on other boats; they were even air-conditioned, a boon in seas where temperatures on long dives reached 120 degrees.*

The Japanese had sixty submarines, forty-seven of the I-class fleet boat and thirteen of the smaller R-O type. The I-class submarines were of some two thousand tons and had a surface speed of twenty-four knots, a submerged speed of eight knots, and a cruising range from 10,000 to 17,500 miles. They were armed with six to eight torpedo tubes and twenty-four torpedoes, and one or two 4.7-inch guns. But the I-boats were crowded, slow in diving, and difficult to handle when submerged, and they had the fatal flaw of being noisy under the surface.† Until late in the war, they lacked radar. The sixteen Japanese submarines deployed during the Battle of Leyte Gulf managed to sink only a single destroyer-escort. One advantage held by the Japanese was the quality of their forty-knot long-range torpedoes, which had twice the explosive charge of the American tin fish.

Unquestionably, the best strategic use the Japanese could have made of their undersea fleet was a determined effort to cut the supply lines from Pearl Harbor to the Southwest Pacific and Australia. But, transfixed by the Mahanian belief that the enemy's capital ships should be their primary target, they never launched such an effort. Although submarine officers repeatedly made such requests, they were ignored, and no campaign was ever launched against American shipping remotely comparable to the German U-boat effort in the Atlantic. Five

---

*The British and Dutch also sent submarines to the Far East, but their boats, designed for Atlantic operations, proved to be unsuited for the Pacific. They were too small to carry sufficient fuel and supplies for long-range patrols, and less habitable than American fleet submarines. The crew of one un-air-conditioned British boat suffered five cases of heat stroke on a single patrol. These boats operated close to their bases on Ceylon, primarily in the Java Sea and the Gulf of Siam, and their targets were usually small merchant vessels and junks in the interisland trade, most of which were sunk by gunfire.

†German experts examined Japan's submarines and found major shortcomings. Hitler made a gift of two Type IX U-boats to the Imperial Navy, but only one arrived in Japan, and it was never put into service.

large boats were dispatched to the West Coast of the United States in late December 1941 and early January 1942 to attack shipping, but nothing came of the operation. Japanese submarine captains reported that they had difficulty navagating in the cold, swift ocean currents off the West Coast. They also complained that their periscopes could rise only twenty feet above their conning towers, which did not give them enough water to evade American destroyers and aircraft.

For the first months of the war, Japanese submarines had considerable success in sinking U.S. warships, especially in "Torpedo Junction," off the Solomons, during the summer of 1942. The Japanese had, however, a fatal tendency to divert their boats into exotic sideshows that drained away their strength. Submarines were used to carry midget submarines, usually to no tactical purpose, or to rendezvous with flying boats to refuel them or to carry out pinprick surface bombardments, such as those on Vancouver and the coast of Oregon in 1943. One, *I-25*, launched a small plane loaded with incendiaries, with the intention of setting forest fires in the Pacific Northwest. As the war progressed, more and more Japanese submarines were taken off patrols and used to carry men, ammunition, and food to beleaguered island garrisons. Although the U.S. Navy began Pacific convoys immediately after the beginning of the war, there was so little enemy submarine activity that by the end of 1943 single U.S. ships were sailing across the Pacific without escort.

U.S. Navy submarines drew their first blood on December 16, 1941, when *Swordfish* torpedoed and sank an 8,662-ton Japanese freighter in the South China Sea. *Gudgeon* accounted for the first enemy warship to be sunk by an American submarine. On January 27, 1942, she was led by radio intelligence to *I-173*, a Japanese submarine that had shelled Midway. *Gudgeon* was submerged when her sonar operator picked up the enemy boat making fifteen knots on the surface. Only ten minutes later, in a textbook exercise, the American boat fired three torpedoes that blew *I-173* out of the water.

These exploits were hardly typical, however. Early American submarine operations—especially in the Philippines—were marked by failed strategic doctrine, tactical conservatism, and very poor torpedoes. As previously related, the Asiatic Fleet's submarines utterly failed to impede the Japanese landings on Luzon. "We had the greatest concentration of submarines in the world there," noted *New York Times* military analyst Hanson W. Baldwin, "but we didn't do a thing!" In some cases, the torpedoes were at fault; in others, the submarine skippers were overly cautious and unaggressive. One-third of them were relieved during the first year of the war and replaced by younger officers.

Prewar training had much to do with these failures. Submarines were mainly used in fleet exercises to scout ahead of the battle fleet, reporting the enemy's movements and slowing down his ships with torpedo attacks. For safety's sake, submarine skippers were instructed to avoid periscope-depth attacks in favor of far less effective "sound" or sonar attacks, made at long range at a depth of one hundred feet or more. Submarine captains who charged toward the battle fleet for close-in attacks were dismissed as "reckless" violators of tactical doctrine, and their fitness reports so marked. Although the Germans were making effective use of surface attacks at night, the U.S. Navy regarded night-battle practice as dangerous, and few experiments were made with such operations until shortly before the United States entered the war.

Following the defeat of Allied forces in the Dutch East Indies, U.S. submarines operated mostly out of Pearl Harbor and bases at Brisbane and Fremantle in Australia. The shortage of other vessels made it necessary for submarines to be diverted to rescue missions and supplying guerrillas in the Philippines. As a result, only about thirteen boats were on patrol at any given period. Because of the huge distances to be covered in the Pacific, half their time at sea was spent on the passage to and from the theater of war. The Australian-based boats covered the entire Malay Barrier, and the Pearl Harbor boats roamed the Pacific. Too few boats patrolled too much ocean.

Taking a leaf out of Admiral Dönitz's book, American submarine admirals thought in terms of tonnage sunk, and little consideration was given to the type of tonnage being sent to the bottom. Not until 1944 were the tankers en route between the East Indies and Japan singled out as the Achilles' heel of both Japan's industry and its navy. The lifeline of the Japanese Empire could have been cut as early as 1943 had U.S. submarines "concentrated more effectively in the areas where tankers were in more predominate use," the U.S. Strategic Bombing Survey later concluded. Some 750,000 tons of shipping was sunk in 1942, but Japanese shipyards replaced all but ninety thousand tons. Tanker tonnage actually increased, and imports from overseas were unimpaired.

U.S. submarines would have been more effective had they carried adequate torpedoes. Time after time, submarines made perfect shots without results. The steam-driven Mark XIVs often ran deeper than they had been set, sometimes so far below a target's hull that the magnetic detonator failed to explode. Even a zero depth setting was sometimes not shallow enough to destroy an enemy ship. The Mark VI contact detonators were equally faulty, and jammed upon direct impact. The major reason for these disasters was the failure to test the torpedoes in peacetime—torpedoes cost $10,000 each, and it was regarded as wasteful to expend them in target practice.

Yet, despite the repeated complaints of submarine captains, the Bureau of Ordnance, responsible for the design and testing of torpedoes, refused to heed them. Such failures, it said, were the fault of the men firing the torpedoes, not the torpedoes themselves. "The torpedo situation during the first half of the war was a national disgrace," says Captain Edward L. Beach, the submariner-historian, "and the negligent perpetrators responsible should have been severely punished."[*]

The frustrating experience of Lieutenant Commander Lawrence R. Daspit of *Tinosa* was typical. Daspit encountered the nineteen-thousand-ton tanker *Tonan Maru No. 3*, one of Japan's largest merchant ships, off Truk, and fired a spread of four of his sixteen torpedoes at her. Two hit near the vessel's stern but did not explode, and she kept moving. Daspit fired two more torpedoes, which damaged the big *maru*'s propellers, forcing her to stop. "There she lay, dead in the water," Daspit later related, "but with guns which considerably outranged our small 3-inch gun. She was unescorted and the chances that she could hit us with gunfire when her only target was a periscope, infrequently exposed, were small. We, therefore, took the time deliberately to fire all but one of our remaining torpedoes. They were all good, solid hits, and all duds!" Fifteen torpedoes were fired, thirteen had hit the target, and only *two* had detonated. And this occurred in July 1943— more than a year and a half into the war!

---

[*]When the magnetic detonators on German torpedoes proved defective, Dönitz had those responsible court-martialed. In contrast, those who refused to deal with the complaints about torpedo failures in the U.S. Navy escaped any reckoning.

Rear Admiral Charles A. Lockwood, Jr., commander of U.S. Submarine Forces, Southwest Pacific, which operated from Fremantle, was impressed by the reports of repeated torpedo deficiencies. Such a large proportion of failures convinced him that more than ineffective performance by his crews must be involved. When the Bureau of Ordnance refused to conduct tests of the Mark XIVs, he decided to run his own. Torpedoes were fired at varying depths through nets that clearly demonstrated they ran at least ten to fifteen feet deeper than set. But instead of speedily acting upon this information, the bureau smugly dismissed Lockwood's observations as unscientific.

Enraged, Lockwood sarcastically suggested that since the torpedoes didn't work the bureau should supply his submarines with special boathooks, so the crews could rip off the sides of Japanese vessels. And he took his complaints to Admiral King, a onetime submariner, who lost no time in applying his famous blowtorch to the bureaucrats of the Bureau of Ordnance. They finally tested the Mark XIV torpedo and confirmed that its depth-control mechanism was indeed defective. The problem of the Mark VI contact exploders was less esoteric: the firing pins were replaced by sounder ones. Performance improved slightly, but flaws still plagued the torpedoes, including premature explosions; some went off hundreds of yards from their targets.

In January 1943, King assigned Lockwood to command of the Pearl Harbor submarines. He quickly moved the base of Pacific Fleet submarines to Midway, thereby trimming twenty-four hundred miles off each patrol. And he tackled the problem of torpedo failures. The premature explosions were traced to defective magnetic pistols that were to be set off under the target by its magnetic field. But the shape of a ship's magnetic field varied depending upon its position on the earth's surface. Near the equator, the magnetic field of a ship was quite different from that off Newport, Rhode Island, where the magnetic exploders had been developed. The magnetic pistols were deactivated, and the improved Mark VI contact pistols used instead.

By the end of 1943, the increased efficiency of American submarines was clear. They accounted for 231,000 tons of Japanese shipping in November alone. For the year as a whole, twenty-two Japanese warships and 296 *marus* were sunk, with the loss in merchant shipping totaling 1,335,240 tons. Japanese shipyards produced a little over a half-million tons and captured and salvaged shipping provided another hundred thousand tons, for a net loss of 718,000 tons. Fifteen U.S. boats were lost, as against twenty-three Japanese submarines that failed to return.

The experience of *Sculpin* demonstrated the dangers to be encountered in submarine operations. On the night of November 18–19, 1943, during the Gilberts operation, she was stationed between Truk and Ponape to observe Japanese fleet movements. Commander Fred Connaway sighted an enemy convoy and submerged to make an attack, but his boat was detected and forced down. An hour after the convoy passed on, Connaway surfaced and found that the Japanese had left a sleeper behind, the destroyer *Yamagumo*. *Sculpin* crash-dived and was showered with depth charges, which caused some damage.

Some time later, Connaway came up to periscope depth to look around, but *Sculpin*'s depth gauge stuck at 125 feet, and the submarine accidentally surfaced. *Yamagumo* charged in and dropped eighteen depth charges. *Sculpin* was hurt badly before she could get deep. Water poured in from several leaks, and her diving planes and rudder were jammed. Clocks, gauges, and other detachable objects hurtled about like missiles. "Blow all ballast!" ordered Connaway. Hoping to fight his way clear, he gave the order for a gunfight, "Battle surface!"

One of *Yamagumo*'s five-inch shells destroyed the boat's conning tower, killing Connaway and his executive and gunnery officers. The senior surviving officer decided to scuttle and ordered "Abandon Ship!" after all vents had been opened. Commander John P. Cromwell, a staff officer on board as an observer, decided to go down with her: familiar with the plans for the Gilberts operation, he feared the Japanese would torture him until he talked. Cromwell was posthumously awarded the Medal of Honor. Forty-two survivors were picked up by *Yamagumo* and, except for a wounded man who was thrown overboard, taken to Truk, where they were transferred to two escort carriers. One, *Chuyo* was torpedoed by *Sailfish*, another U.S. submarine on her way to Japan, and only one of this group of prisoners survived.[*]

*   *   *

---

[*]Submarine captains were sometimes aware through Ultra intelligence that potential target ships were carrying American prisoners, which created a moral dilemma. In most cases, they decided to attack the ships, convinced that the Japanese would place American POWs on all the ships if they realized the vessels would be spared.

At the beginning of 1944, Lockwood was at last ready to draw the noose tight about Japan. U.S. submarines had been fitted with surface-search radar, enabling them to detect targets at night and in fog, and air-search radar, to protect themselves against prowling enemy aircraft. Op 20-G, the navy's code breakers, had cracked the *maru* code used by the Japanese to transmit the routing of their merchant shipping, which meant submarines could be sent to attack an enemy convoy rather than ranging over the Pacific in long fuel-consuming searches for prey. A new electric-powered torpedo, the Mark XVIII, which made no wake to be detected by enemy lookouts, was also introduced.*

With about 140 boats available for patrols, wolf packs of U.S. submarines operating from new forward bases in New Guinea, the Admiralties, and the Marianas saturated the trade routes from the East Indies to the Japanese home islands. Unlike Dönitz, Lockwood and the other U.S. submarine commanders exercised only limited operational command of the boats, to give the skippers maximum initiative. Ultra intelligence was transmitted to the boats in a special code to prevent it from being picked up by the enemy.

Japan still had three hundred thousand more tons of tankers than at the beginning of the war, so Lockwood ordered his boats to concentrate on tankers. *Jack*, known as "Jack the Tanker Killer," sank four out of five tankers in one convoy. Packs of three or four boats, such as "Hydeman's Hellcats," "Blair's Blasters," and "Wilkins' Wildcats," took their toll. Twenty-seven tankers were sunk by U.S. submarines in the final six months of 1944. In October, the sixty-eight boats on patrol sent 320,900 tons of Japanese shipping to the bottom—a third of it tankers—the highest U.S. monthly score of the war.

That same month, *Tang*, on her fifth patrol under Commander Richard H. O'Kane, had threaded her way through a minefield into the Formosa Strait and began sinking everything in sight. O'Kane was the U.S. Navy's top submarine "ace," with 93,824 tons to his credit. A Philippines-bound convoy of five *marus* loaded with crated aircraft was sighted on the night of October 23, and *Tang* surfaced among them, firing her torpedoes in quick succession. Three of the

---

*The Mark XVIIIs had their own set of bugs to be worked out. Some submarine skippers had the unnerving experience of having their own tin fish double back on them, because of defective gyroscopes.

freighters were hit, and the others tried to ram the submarine, but it slipped between them, and they collided with each other.

Twenty-four hours later, *Tang* found a convoy of tankers and transports. O'Kane again surfaced among the enemy ships, and sank two large tankers. The submarine was illuminated against the burning vessels, and the escorts tried to ram her, but O'Kane maneuvered out of reach and got off another torpedo to score a hit on one of them. With only two torpedoes left, O'Kane fired at a damaged transport. The first ran hot and true. As the second left the tube, there was a cheer from the crew—a highly successful patrol had been completed—and they could now return to base. On the bridge, O'Kane was horrified to see the last torpedo suddenly broach, porpoise, and circle back toward *Tang*. He rang up full speed and threw the rudder hand over, but the torpedo exploded against the submarine's stern.

O'Kane and eight other men on the bridge were thrown into the sea as *Tang* sank stern-first. The shattered hulk came to rest on the bottom, at 180 feet. Thirty men reached an escape hatch in the forward torpedo room. As they waited for the Japanese patrols topside to leave, electrical fires were ignited. Paint melted on the bulkheads, and the remaining oxygen was being rapidly consumed. Thirteen men escaped with Momsen lung-breathing devices, of whom five survived. Altogether, nine of *Tang's* crew, including O'Kane, were picked up by a Japanese escort vessel. O'Kane was awarded the Medal of Honor after his release from a prison camp at the end of the war.

Japan's logistical situation soon became desperate under the submarine assault. Merchant vessels were restricted to short voyages in the Sea of Japan, which they transited by night, taking shelter in port by day. Rice imports dropped off. A crash program was launched to distill aviation fuel from potatoes to replace the blockaded supply of oil from the East Indies, but it was inadequate. Industrial production plummeted as supplies of bauxite, iron ore, and coke from the Asian mainland were cut off. Even the quality of ammunition deteriorated. Because of the fuel shortage, warships had to remain in port, and when they ventured out they faced a high risk of being sunk by lurking U.S. Navy submarines. On December 9, 1944, the veteran carrier *Junyo* was torpedoed and damaged; ten days later, the light carrier *Unyo* was sunk.

The American attack on Japan's lifeline was aided by the almost complete failure of the Imperial Navy to safeguard its own surface ships against submarines. Obsessed with the idea of an "offensive war," the Japanese regarded convoys as "defensive," and therefore somewhat demeaning and unworthy of the samurai spirit. Like Admiral King during the devastating attacks on shipping off the American coast in 1942, the Japanese had failed to learn from the British experience.

Even limited convoys were not introduced until April 1942, and when a First Convoy Escort Fleet was organized later that year, it had only eight old destroyers assigned to it. No escort-building program was undertaken until March 1943, and these forces never attained the standard of professionalism and efficiency achieved by the Allies in the Atlantic. No aircraft were assigned exclusively to convoy protection and ASW until nearly the end of that year.

One of the wildest night melees of submarine warfare in the Pacific took place in the predawn hours of July 31, 1944, when *Steelhead* and *Parche* sighted a Japanese convoy off Formosa. Attacking on the surface, *Steelhead* opened the action with a spread of six torpedoes aimed at a tanker and a large freighter. Both vessels were hit, and the tanker erupted in brilliant flames that illuminated a wide area. *Parche* was guided in by the spectacular fireworks, but the escort had formed a tight ring about the undamaged ships. Commander Lawson P. Ramage outmaneuvered a trio of escorts that tried to head him off and gained a position between them and the convoy. At that moment, the convoy zigged and headed directly for his boat. Firing three down-the-throat bow shots at the oncoming vessels, Ramage scored a crippling hit on a freighter, which later sank.

Parche, lit up by burning ships and flares, made a good target herself, and the *marus* opened up with five-inch deck guns and machine guns. Tracers arched toward the boat, and shell splashes plumed the sea about her. Ramage ordered the bridge cleared. With a volunteer to man the target-bearing transmitter, he remained topside to con *Parche*. For forty-six minutes, he swept through the disorganized convoy at high speed, dodging attempts to ram, and fired nineteen torpedoes in blazing succession as the sweating torpedo crews labored to keep the tubes loaded. *Parche* escaped unscathed, having sunk two freighters and two tankers and severely damaged a fifth ship. The exploit earned Ramage the Medal of Honor.

The heightened tempo of the U.S. Navy's antishipping campaign in 1944 accounted for more than six hundred ships, a total of about 2.7 million tons—well over the 2.2 million tons sunk in the previous two years together. Japan's tanker tonnage was slashed from nine hundred thousand to two hundred thousand tons—a massacre that created an oil shortage so severe that the Strategic Bombing Survey concluded it caused "the collapse of the fleet, the air arm, merchant shipping and all other activities dependent upon oil fuel." As a result, the survey's authors stated that "certainly prior to 31 December 1945 . . . Japan would have surrendered even if the atomic bombs had not been dropped, even if Russia had not entered the [Pacific] war, and even if no invasion had been planned or contemplated."*

With the exception of wooden-hulled coasters and fishing boats, the Japanese merchant marine had virtually ceased to exist by the end of the war. In all, 288 American submarines accounted for 4,861,000 tons of Japanese merchant shipping, or 1,150 vessels, not including small craft.† Thus, a force containing less than 2 percent of the U.S. Navy's personnel accounted for 55 percent of Japan's losses at sea. Submarines sank 276 warships, including a battleship, eight carriers, and eleven cruisers. They also rescued some five hundred downed U.S. airmen. Fifty-two submarines failed to return and are memorialized on a plaque on the seawall at the U.S. Naval Academy as "still on patrol."

Wars are won by a combination of ground, naval, and air forces, each of which carries a share of the common burden. The submarine force was but one component of the massive American naval armada, yet its accomplishments were all out of proportion to its size. But the submarine campaign against Japanese commerce was one of the most important factors in the defeat of Japan. The unrestricted campaign against sea communications weakened Japan to such an extent that it enabled the amphibious drive supported by carrier-borne air power to succeed.

---

*It should be noted, however, that others disagree with this assessment, and argue that the fanaticism of the Japanese was such that they would have fought on long after logic dictated a surrender.

†Additionally, mines planted by submarines, surface minelayers, and aircraft sank or damaged 1,075 ships, or a total of 2,250,000 tons of shipping—a significant part of it in Japanese home waters.

CHAPTER 20

•

"Have Rolled Two Sevens"

"Leyte and then Luzon."

So said General MacArthur as he outlined his future strategy in his talks with President Roosevelt prior to the invasion of the Philippines. Following the Battle of Leyte Gulf, no one expected much trouble with Leyte itself. With Japanese troops on the island outnumbered and isolated, MacArthur was already planning the liberation of the main island of Luzon and the rest of the Philippines. Admiral Nimitz was preparing landings on Iwo Jima and Okinawa, to the north, the stepping-stones to Japan. But the Japanese High Command decided the decisive battle for the archipelago should be fought on Leyte.

Reinforcements poured in from Luzon, Panay, and Mindanao, even from China. Weaving in and out of narrow waterways and straits, transports, fishing boats, and barges slipped men and supplies ashore at Ormoc, on the west coast of Leyte. By early December 1944, the number of Japanese troops on the island had grown from twenty thousand to seventy thousand. Even though the U.S. Sixth Army was double the Japanese strength, it met fierce resistance as it tried to push across Leyte.

The Americans were unable to stem this remarkable effort because of a temporary weakness in air power. The Seventh Fleet's escort carriers were in poor shape after being knocked about off Samar and suffering the continuing attention of the kamikazes. TF 38, the Third Fleet's Fast Carrier Task Force, at sea for weeks, was low on fuel and supplies. Land-based air-force planes were to have taken over the job of providing support for the army, but they were mired down by monsoon rains that turned the dirt runways of Leyte into seas of mud. Of thirty-four P-38 fighters assigned to the rain-lashed field at Tacloban, only twenty were operational after five days. Using planes ferried in from Luzon, Japan, and Formosa, the Japanese vigorously contested control of the air on a scale not seen since the Solomons campaign.

"Nip planes seemed all over the sky," reported Commander Arthur M. Purdy of the destroyer *Abner Reed* during one attack.

> Our barrage of fire ripped off [the wings of a kamikaze] but he still kept coming. He apparently dropped his bomb about 100 yards from the ship and it went down the after stack, exploding in our steaming boiler. The plane itself practically swept away the whole midship section and within a matter of seconds the entire after deck house was one tremendous fire fanned by the wind. Seven or eight minutes later a tremendous explosion, undoubtedly a five-inch magazine going up, shook us. The ship immediately sagged by the stern and ten minutes later sank.

Worried by the Japanese buildup, MacArthur asked that TF 38 halt the flow of troops to Ormoc. Admiral Halsey wished to launch attacks on Tokyo and other Japanese cities as soon as he had refueled and replenished at Ulithi,* but Admiral Nimitz sent him back to the Philippines. Halsey struck at Manila early in November, destroying some two hundred enemy planes in two days of raids. Although these strikes reduced Japanese air strength in the Philippines, the kamikazes continued to come. One crashed into *Lexington*, killing and wounding over 180 crewmen. *Franklin* and *Belleau Wood* were also hit.

On November 11, a Japanese convoy of five or six transports, seven destroyers, a minesweeper, and a submarine, together carrying ten thousand troops, was sighted in the Camotes Sea, approaching Ormoc Bay. TF 38 immediately dispatched 347 planes, which sank

---

*Mogmog, the largest island in Ulithi Atoll, had nothing to offer sailors who had spent weeks at sea except a few hours on land, several softball diamonds, and a beach where they could swim and drink the two cans of warm beer allotted each man. Sometimes there were as many as twenty thousand men milling about ashore.

four destroyers and all the transports before a single man, pound of rice, or round of ammunition had been landed. Two more destroyers were bagged after the remnant turned back for Manila. Except for a handful who managed to swim ashore, all the Japanese troops drowned. Only nine U.S. planes were shot down.

Two weeks later, planes from *Ticonderoga* sank a heavy cruiser off Luzon and disrupted several other convoys steaming down to Ormoc. The kamikazes wasted no time in launching counterattacks. The skies over the carriers were freckled with anti-aircraft bursts; the air was filled with the hysterical chatter of the twenty-millimeter Oerlikons, the spaced coughs of the forty-millimeter Bofors duals and quads, and the sharp thunderclaps of five-inch guns. The only defense against a suicide plane was concentrated, accurate, and rapid gunfire. Sometimes even that was not enough, as the impetus of the plane carried it to its target, even with the pilot dead at the controls. *Hancock, Intrepid, Cabot*, and *Essex* were all damaged and withdrawn. "We got our tail feathers burned . . . and, frankly, we had to get out in a hurry," said Rear Admiral Robert B. Carney, Halsey's chief of staff. *Colorado* and *Maryland* were hit by kamikazes in Leyte Gulf.

Land-based planes, including marine night fighters, finally established control of the air over Leyte, but as at Guadalcanal, the flow of enemy men and supplies was never completely halted. Nevertheless, General Tomoyuki Yamashita, the redoubtable conqueror of Malaya, who now commanded the Fourteenth Army in the Philippines, believed Leyte was the wrong place to fight. He argued that the Japanese should execute only a delaying action on the island, while building up strength on Luzon to meet the inevitable American invasion. Yamashita was overruled by higher authority, and the flow of elite troops to Leyte continued.

The battle settled into a prolonged struggle in the rugged mountains protecting Ormoc from attack from the east. Repeated assaults on Japanese gun emplacements and dugouts the enemy had established along a natural defense line on what the troops called "Breakneck Ridge" developed into the bloodiest fighting of the campaign. MacArthur had dealt with such problems in New Guinea by making sweeping amphibious end runs around enemy strongholds. But shipping was in short supply, because he insisted upon immediately carrying out planned landings on Mindoro, 250 miles to the northwest of Leyte, and on Luzon, which lay just beyond it. Mindoro itself was of little importance, although its airfields were coveted for the Luzon invasion.

Admiral Kinkaid, although subordinate to MacArthur, was unwilling to risk his ships in a move northward until air supremacy over the central Philippines was assured. He told the general he was willing to chance being relieved by going over his head to Admiral King with his protests. Halsey backed up Kinkaid, saying his carriers could not return to the Philippines in full strength for ten days. Under pressure from the navy, MacArthur gave way. The Mindoro landing was postponed to December 15, and the invasion of Luzon to January 9, 1945.

With shipping and naval support freed up, the 77th Division was landed by Rear Admiral Arthur D. Struble's Amphibious Group 9 at Ormoc Bay, in the enemy rear. With the attention of the Japanese fixed on a series of determined but fumbling attacks on American bases in eastern Leyte, including parachute drops and commando raids, the troops got ashore unopposed. "Have rolled two sevens in Ormoc," radioed Major General Andrew D. Bruce, the jubilant divisional commander. The 77th quickly joined with other advancing American units to encircle and divide the Japanese. Once the troops were safely ashore, however, the kamikazes came out in full force against Struble's ships. The defending air-force fighters were outnumbered and overwhelmed.

"Jap planes were falling like rockets all over the place," said one officer. "Falling isn't really correct because they were coming in under full power to pile into our ships." The destroyer *Mahan* and the destroyer-transport *Ward* were damaged so badly they had to be abandoned. Two other destroyers were hit as well but survived. Kamikazes also struck a supply convoy as it neared Ormoc and sank the destroyer *Reid*. One gunner had the harrowing experience of being knocked down by the bloody upper half of a Japanese pilot's torso as it hurtled through the air after the plane exploded.

Ashore, the Japanese were now squeezed between two American forces, and although they continued fighting tenaciously for several more weeks, the real struggle for Leyte was over. The campaign was much tougher and proceeded far slower than MacArthur had anticipated, but for the Japanese it was devastating. The Battle of Leyte Gulf destroyed the Imperial Navy as an offensive fighting force; the battle for the island itself resulted in such losses in troops and planes that defeat on Luzon and the loss of the Philippines were inevitable.

With Admiral John McCain in command—"Pete" Mitscher was taking a well-earned rest—the fast carriers of TF 38 returned to the Philippines in mid-December to shield the Mindoro landing. McCain intended not only to stem the flow of Japanese planes from Formosa and the home islands to Luzon, but to take the sting out of the kamikazes by imposing an around-the-clock "air blanket" over the island's fields. If the Japanese tried to lift "even one corner of the blanket," said Admiral Carney, Hellcats pounced upon them. "At night we maintained night fighters over the enemy airfields and every time one of the so-and-sos tried to move, he was shot down." To beef up protection against suicide attackers, McCain surrounded his fleet with radar picket destroyers, which had their own combat air patrols, and strengthened the regular CAP.*

Kamikazes from the central Philippines struck Admiral Struble's Mindoro invasion fleet as it neared the island—McCain's "air blanket" having kept the Luzon fields covered. None of the big carriers was hit although the flagship *Nashville* and a destroyer were severely damaged. The invasion on December 15 took the Japanese by surprise, and some twenty-seven thousand troops went ashore without opposition. U.S. Army and Australian engineers immediately went to work to prepare the airfields for the Luzon invasion. One fighter strip was ready in five days, another in thirteen.

Halsey, in the meantime, had withdrawn the Third Fleet into the Philippine Sea to refuel his destroyers in preparation for massive raids against Luzon. On December 18, the ships were struck by an even more fearsome enemy than the kamikazes: a savage typhoon.† Navy aerologists misread the storm's track and Halsey sailed his fleet straight into its path. Rising seas and hammering winds prevented the destroyers *Hull*, *Spence*, and *Monaghan* from topping their tanks, leaving them badly out of trim. Hoping to refuel later, they failed to

---

*The number of fighters in each carrier air group was increased from fifty-four to seventy-three at the expense of the number of bombers. To make up for this reduction in bomber strength, some Hellcats were modified to carry 2,000 pounds of bombs and six 5-inch rockets, which gave them the same punch as an SB2C Helldiver dive-bomber.

†This typhoon is the centerpiece of Herman Wouk's novel *The Caine Mutiny*.

reballast with seawater, and were riding light and high, yawing and rolling even more then usual, as the typhoon increased in intensity. Barometers dropped, rain squalls and spray reduced visibility, station-keeping was difficult—if not impossible. Watertender 2/c Joseph C. McCrane of *Monaghan* reported:

> The storm broke in all its fury. We started to roll heavy to the star-board and everyone was holding onto something and praying as hard as he could. . . . One of the fellows was praying aloud. Every time the ship would take about a 70-degree roll starboard he would cry out 'Please bring her back, dear Lord. Don't let us down now!' . . . Soon a few other guys would join in. Then when we came back we'd chant: 'Thanks, dear Lord!' . . . We must have taken about seven or eight rolls to the starboard before she went over on her side. . . . The next thing I knew I was in the water trying to keep from being pounded against the side of the ship. . . .

McCrane was one of only six men to survive the sinking of *Monaghan*. Twenty-nine men from *Spence* and sixty-two from *Hull* were also pulled from the shark-infested sea after being adrift on life rafts for several days. In all, nearly eight hundred sailors fell victim to the wrath of the wind and sea. Several other ships narrowly escaped a similar fate, seven were seriously damaged, and nearly two hundred planes were wrecked as the mountainous sea tossed even the heavy carriers about like rowboats. A court of inquiry sitting in Ulithi at year's end blamed Halsey for the storm damage and losses but imputed no negligence to him. The admiral's mistakes, said the court, "were errors in judgment committed under the stress of war operations."

While the Third Fleet rounded up its widely scattered elements from across hundred of miles of ocean and repaired damage in preparation for the assault on Luzon, Japanese surface units and kamikazes lashed the Mindoro beachhead. A cruiser-destroyer force slipped across the South China Sea from Camranh Bay, in Indochina, under cover of foul weather, and shelled the airfield on the night of December 26–27. They were driven off, however, and a retreating destroyer was torpedoed and sunk by *PT-223*. Repeated kamikaze attacks over the next several days took out several supply vessels, including a pair of ammunition ships, both of which exploded and sank with all hands. The Japanese ended their attacks on Mindoro at the beginning of

1945 as they shifted to a new target, a massive Allied invasion force heading for Lingayen Gulf, on Luzon, where Japanese troops had landed four years before.

Flying his flag on *California*, newly promoted Vice-Admiral Olden-dorf led a bombardment group of some 160 ships, including his six old battleships, a dozen escort carriers, and assorted cruisers and destroyers that departed Leyte Gulf on January 2 and steamed toward Luzon. Two days later, transports and amphibious craft carrying some 175,000 Sixth Army troops and their protective screen followed. Repeated American attacks on airfields in the Philippines and on Formosa had reduced the number of Japanese planes available to about two hundred, but foul weather made "blanketing" impossible. Oldendorf's ships served as a magnet for a kamikaze blitz, and the voyage north was an ordeal.

The armada was plowing through the Sulu Sea just west of Panay on January 4 when, without warning, the escort carrier *Ommaney Bay* suddenly lurched to port and was engulfed in flames. A kamikaze had dived out of the sun, crashed into her island, and cartwheeled across the flight deck before exploding. Wracked by internal explosions, she was abandoned and sunk. The following day, kamikazes damaged two heavy cruisers, *Louisville* and *Australia*, a destroyer, and the escort carrier *Manila Bay*.

The rain of death was merely beginning. On the morning of January 6, Oldendorf entered Lingayen Gulf to sweep for mines and begin the preliminary bombardment of suspected enemy positions. Shortly before noon, lookouts sighted several shining specks in the sky, which turned out to be suicide planes. From then until sunset, the fleet was under almost continuous attack. To avoid radar detection, the kamikazes hugged the hills and valleys surrounding Lingayen Gulf, and planes came in from several directions at the same time to confuse the CAPs and the ships' gunners. Many were destroyed, but some got through. *California* and *New Mexico** suffered hits, as did the light cruiser *Columbia*. *Australia* and *Louisville*,

---

*Admiral Sir Bruce Fraser, who was preparing to take over the Royal Navy's new Pacific Fleet, was an observer on *New Mexico*'s bridge when the suicide plane hit. Fraser was unhurt, but some members of his staff were killed or wounded.

were struck, both for the second time; a destroyer-minesweeper was sunk, and several smaller ships were damaged.

With a heavy cloud of smoke from the damaged ships hanging over his fleet, Oldendorf was alarmed about the possibility of fresh attacks the next day. The outnumbered planes operating from his escort carriers were inadequate to deal with swarms of kamikazes, so he sent Admiral Kinkaid an urgent call for help from the air force and TF 38. "Consider need of additional air power urgent and vital. . . . Should suicide bombers attack transports, the results might be disastrous." Halsey had planned another attack on the Formosan air bases, but as soon as he received a plea from Kinkaid, he sent in his planes to plaster the Luzon airfields again. The cost was high—twenty-eight planes, more than in any recent operation.

The kamikaze onslaught eased off over the next few days, although ships continued to fall victim to random suicide attacks. As Admiral Barbey's VII Amphibious Force neared Luzon, where General Yamashita and some 250,000 troops awaited it, the fleet came under attack by both kamikazes and midget submarines. One sub aimed two torpedoes at the light cruiser *Boise*, which was carrying General MacArthur and his staff, but they missed. Two escort carriers, *Kadashan Bay* and *Kitkun Bay*, were put out of action by suicide planes, and a troop-laden attack transport was hit. In Lingayen Gulf, the unlucky *Australia* took two more hits, one of which blew a fourteen-foot-wide hole in her hull. Oldendorf offered to relieve her, but the Australians declined and remained on station after making repairs.

By the time the Japanese ran out of planes, around mid-January, the kamikazes had sunk twenty-four ships off Luzon and damaged sixty-seven. Nearly eight hundred sailors were killed, and another fourteen hundred wounded, many of them badly burned or mangled. It was the worst battering taken by an Allied fleet since the Solomons, and in proportion to the magnitude of the Japanese effort, was even more devastating than the massed kamikaze attacks that were to be met off Okinawa a few months later.

Over a thousand ships crowded Lingayen Gulf as the sun rose on the morning of January 9. Opposition was light to nonexistent as the landing craft swarmed in after prolonged shelling by Oldendorf's big ships. The worst threat to the invasion came from a flotilla of suicide boats—eighteen-foot plywood motorboats each crammed with five hundred pounds of explosives—which tried to ram American ships. An LCI was sunk, and eight transports were damaged. By evening, some fifty thousand troops were ashore and had linked up to form a continuous beachhead four miles deep. Rather than wasting his men in a vain attempt to hurl the enemy back into the sea, General Yamashita withdrew. He planned, after causing as much trouble as possible, to retreat to prepared positions in the mountains of northern Luzon and draw the American troops into a protracted struggle.

Once the bulk of the Sixth Army was ashore, the liberation of Luzon became primarily an army campaign, but the Seventh Fleet and Halsey's carriers continued to provide support. Kinkaid kept the vital three-hundred-mile Mindoro–Lingayen Gulf supply line open in the face of a presumed threat from the battleship-carriers *Ise* and *Hyuga* and other heavy enemy ships reportedly at Camranh Bay. Barbey's amphibious units also repeatedly landed troops at various points on Luzon, isolating the defenders, pinning them down, and blocking them from organizing a united front.

For his part, Halsey, still spoiling for a fight, plunged through Luzon Strait into the South China Sea in mid-January in search of the remnants of the Japanese fleet. TF 38 launched nearly fifteen hundred sorties over the Indochinese coast, but the Japanese had wisely departed for Lingga Roads. Nevertheless, fifteen combat ships including a light cruiser, twelve tankers, and seventeen other *marus* were sunk, a total of 132,700 tons. Over a hundred Japanese planes were reportedly destroyed on the ground. Japanese shipping in Indochinese waters was all but halted. Strikes were also launched against Formosa and, for the first time, Japanese-occupied Hong Kong, but the latter raids were ineffective, because of deteriorating weather. As Radio Tokyo trumpeted that the Third Fleet was bottled up in the South China Sea and facing disaster, Halsey insouciantly slipped back into the Pacific the way he had come. "Superlatively well done," he signaled his fleet upon its arrival at Ulithi.

While TF 38 was making these raids, American troops swept across Luzon's central plain toward Manila. Bataan, of painful memory, was sealed off, and Clark Field captured. Yamashita ordered Manila evacuated—as the Americans had done in 1942—and MacArthur hoped to make a triumphant entry into the city on January 26, his sixty-fifth birthday. Rear Admiral Sanji Iwabachi, the local commander, disobeyed orders and conducted a fanatic block-by-block, house-by-house defense of the city. Three American divisions needed a month to clear the Philippine capital, at a cost of eleven hundred dead. The entire Japanese garrison of twenty thousand sailors and soldiers died in the rubble, as did a hundred thousand Filipinos, many massacred by the Japanese. Manila, once the "Pearl of the Orient," was in ruins, mute testimony to the ferocity of the battle. Of all Allied cities, only Warsaw suffered more. Manila again demonstrated that the Japanese, although doomed by Western standards, would continue to fight in hopes that their very ferocity would demoralize the enemy—which had much to do with the eventual Allied decision to use the atom bomb.

The liberation of Manila hardly meant the end of the war in the Philippines, however. Yamashita was holed up in his mountain redoubt, where he managed a skillful and stubborn delaying action that was still continuing at war's end. Also, MacArthur decided to embark on a wasteful campaign to clear all the Japanese out of every nook and cranny of the Philippines. Ironically, this decision, which drained men from operations in Luzon, made Yamashita's resistance possible. Every strategically relevant objective in the archipelago had already been captured, and a proper sense of priorities would have left the mopping up of the outlying Japanese garrisons to Filipino guerrillas. But the Joint Chiefs failed to rein in MacArthur.[*] Indeed, between late February and mid-April 1945, Admiral Barbey was ordered to stage no fewer than thirty-eight separate landings in the central and southern Philippines.

Australian troops were given the messy task of clearing and mopping up Borneo, which was to be a stepping-stone to the oil fields of the Dutch East Indies. By this time, however, the oil of both Borneo and the East Indies was of no strategic value to the Japanese, because they no longer had the means to transport it to the home islands. The Joint Chiefs allowed the Borneo campaign to proceed, but blocked

---

[*]Two of MacArthur's biographers, William Manchester and D. Clayton James, believe that the failure of the Joint Chiefs to halt these operations led directly to MacArthur's repeated insubordinations of the Korean War, which ultimately resulted in his dismissal by President Truman in 1951 (Manchester, *American Caesar*, pp. 428–30; James, *The Years of MacArthur*, vol. I, p. 738).

MacArthur's plans for the invasion of Java. With the launching of the attacks on Iwo Jima and Okinawa, the main focus of operations shifted to the north, and MacArthur's campaign played itself out among the scattered islands of the Philippines like an exhausted tropical storm.

"No more let us falter! From Malta to Yalta! Let nobody alter!"

So wrote a jocular Winston Churchill as the all-but-victorious Allied Big Three—Roosevelt, Stalin, and Churchill—journeyed in February 1945 for a summit meeting at Yalta, a former tsarist resort on the Black Sea. There were compelling reasons for such a meeting. The last, desperate German offensive in the West had just been beaten back in the Battle of the Bulge. Allied bombers were reducing German cities to spectral ruins. The Red Army had overrun Poland and Eastern Europe and was closing in on Germany itself. The Japanese had been driven back to their home islands, and the B-29s were battering Japan's cities.

But the military professionals believed that nothing short of the invasion of Japan would end the war in the Pacific. Yalta was intended to settle the future of Eastern Europe and ensure the entry of the Soviet Union into the war against Japan as soon as Hitler was defeated. Stalin agreed to declare war on the Japanese within two to three months after the end of the war in Europe, in exchange for the return of booty lost to the Japanese after the Russo-Japanese War.

The Third Reich was in its death throes. Casualties were staggering. Pathetic columns of refugees fleeing the Red Army clogged the roads. But Germany was like a punch-drunk boxer, blind and stupid with pain, but still fighting. Even some members of the Nazi hierarchy, such as Goebbels, Ribbentrop, and the odious SS chief Heinrich Himmler, had come to terms with reality and were extending peace feelers to the Western Allies, hoping to stave off the Russians. Only Admiral Dönitz totally identified himself with the Nazi state and expressed unshaken faith in the strategic genius of Adolf Hitler.

Germany, he told interrogators following the war, was goaded into continued resistance in the face of impossible odds because the Allies offered only unconditional surrender, and "enemy propaganda painted a gloomy picture of the intended treatment of Germany after defeat." This explanation, made while Dönitz awaited trial for war crimes, hardly squares with a speech he made to his flag officers on August 24,

1944, in which he insisted that the Kriegsmarine must remain obedi-
ent to the will of the Führer: "Our duty and our fate is to fight fanatically . . . for each of us to stand fanatically behind the National Socialist
State. . . . Each deviation from this is a laxness and a crime. . . ."

Albert Speer recalled drawing the admiral aside following a brief-
ing on the latest disasters and saying something had to be done to
avoid the catastrophe facing Germany. "I am here to represent the
Navy," Dönitz replied curtly. "All the rest is not my business. The
Führer knows what he is doing."

Thus, the final scenes of the war at sea in European waters had
more in common with the worst excesses of Wagnerian opera than
with logical military operations. Like the Japanese kamikazes, Dönitz
tried to do as much damage as possible before Germany's collapse.
He was convinced that victory might still be snatched from the Allies
by the Type XXI and XXIII Electro-boats and pressed forward with
their construction. As a result, the early months of 1945 were an anxious period for Allied naval officials, who feared a renewal of the Battle of the Atlantic; this might jeopardize the land campaign in
Western Europe before Germany could be pounded into defeat. The
new U-boats, warned A. V. Alexander, the First Lord of the Admiralty,
could produce "losses of a level we suffered in spring 1943."

The Allies had a ringside seat for the building of these craft. Vice-
Admiral Katsuo Abe, the chief of the Japanese naval mission in Berlin,
closely followed their progress, and his dispatches to Tokyo were
avidly read by American code breakers. The new boats were fitted with
antiradar-coated snorkel heads, radar-search receivers, sensitive
hydrophones able to pick up a ship fifty miles away, and new acoustic
torpedoes. "It would seem at first glance that the Type XXI is an
epoch-making U-boat," Abe reported. By mid-December 1944, British
naval intelligence estimated that ninety-five of the large Type XXI
oceangoing boats were being assembled or fitted out, and thirty-five had
been commissioned and were training in the Baltic. Forty-nine smaller
Type XXIII boats were thought to be approaching readiness.

To meet this threat, the Allies launched a massive bombing campaign designed to cripple Electro-boat construction. Bombers raided
the scattered plants where the prefabricated sections were made and
the network of canals over which they were brought to the coastal
shipyards for final assembly, as well as the shipyards themselves.

Training areas in the Baltic were heavily mined. Following the war, Dönitz credited the fatal delay in getting his new boats into action to "the ever-increasing weight of Allied air-raids on Germany."

S-boats and the midget submarines and manned torpedoes of the "Special Battle Units" made desperate sorties against shipping, taking fearful punishment, scoring only isolated successes—mostly the result of mining, which did not affect the Allied advance. Snorkel submarines operating from Norway were more effective. For the first time since 1941, there was a dramatic rise in sinkings in British coastal waters as the boats used the swift currents and unfavorable sound conditions in shallow waters to elude ASW vessels. By February, there were at least twenty-five snorkel boats operating in the narrow seas, and between January and April 1945, they sank fifty-one ships totaling 253,000 tons.

Kapitänleutnant Harmut Graf von Matuschka of *U-482* shocked the British by sinking a corvette and four merchant ships in the approaches to Liverpool. Of the nearly three thousand nautical miles logged by his boat, only about 250 were made on the surface. *U-486* torpedoed the troopship *Leopoldville* in the Channel on Christmas Eve 1944, with the loss of 819 American soldiers. On February 25, *U-2322*, the first of the small Type XXIII boats to get to sea, sank a small freighter off the east coast of Scotland—a portent of the future. The British were amazed at the speed with which it made its getaway. "Ideal boat for short operations near coast, fast, maneuverable, simple depth-control, small surface to locate and attack," Oberleutnant Fridjof Heckel, her commander, reported. Dönitz brought the news to Hitler personally, and assured him that "the mighty sea-power of the Anglo-Saxons is essentially powerless."

Five more Type XXIII boats saw action in British coastal waters and sunk a total of seven ships, a pair of them accounted for by *U-2326* on the last night of the war. Making good use of their elusiveness, they baffled prowling aircraft, HF/DF radio detection, and radar, and all returned to harbor safely. If the tiny Type XXIIIs could perform so well, what could be expected of the oceangoing Type XXI boats if and when they became operational? "If and when" was the key issue. At the end of April, twelve XXIs were ready for sea and ninety-nine were on their acceptance trials.

The Allies took energetic steps to deal with the snorkel blitz. They held back some three hundred escorts that were earmarked for the Far East and introduced new tactics. Support groups trailed convoys ready to leap instantly on any U-boat that revealed its presence. In March 1945, when there were fifty-three U-boats at sea, fifteen were sunk, eleven by escorts, four by aircraft. Twenty-four others were destroyed in German harbors.

Dönitz also sent his boats out on a last death ride to the American coast. Late in March 1945, six Type IX snorkel boats put to sea and were then ordered to form a small wolf pack. To add to the urgency of the situation, rumors were spread that the boats carried a marine version of the V-2 rockets which had been raining down on London.* Well warned by Ultra, the U.S. Navy prepared a lively welcome for them in the form of a large "Barrier Force" of escort carriers and destroyers. Four boats were quickly sunk, and the remaining two gave themselves up when Germany surrendered. Their only success was the sinking of the destroyer-escort *Frederick C. Davis*, with the loss of two-thirds of her crew.

The main task of the Kriegsmarine in the last months of the war was to rescue as many as possible of the troops and civilians fleeing the ruin and horror of the Baltic provinces and East Prussia before they were overrun by the Russians. Every merchant vessel that could float and the handful of serviceable warships were pressed into these operations. Only the pocket battleships *Scheer* and *Lützow* and a few cruisers and destroyers were left. *Tirpitz*, reduced to a floating battery because of all the previous damage, had been finally sunk in her Norwegian hideout on November 12, 1944, along with nine hundred of her crew, by RAF Lancaster bombers using specially designed six-ton "Tall Boy" bombs.

The remaining surface ships supported the German army's vain attempt to hold back the Russian advance along the Baltic coast by bombarding enemy positions ashore and serving as transports themselves. In all, more than two million soldiers and refugees were rescued and brought to the West before war's end—the greatest

---

*The Germans had designed a large canister in which a V-2 was to be towed submerged behind a U-boat to the coast of the United States, where the missile was to be launched from the surface, but this was rejected as impracticable.

seaborne evacuation in history. This operation was not executed without loss, as Russian submarines, aircraft, small craft, and mines, as well as the RAF, all took their toll.

On the night of January 30–31, 1945, the 25,484-ton liner *Wilhelm Gustloff*, packed with as many as eight thousand refugees, wounded, and soldiers, was torpedoed by the Soviet submarine *S-13*, under Commander Alexander I. Marinesko. Fewer than a thousand survivors were pulled from the black, freezing waters of the Baltic.* Ten days later, Marinesko torpedoed the 17,500-ton liner *Steuben*, which was being used as hospital ship. She sank only seven minutes after being hit, and witnesses heard a great scream from the estimated three thousand wounded and refugees trapped on board. The five-thousand-ton motorship *Goya* was torpedoed by *L-3*, another Russian submarine, with the loss of all but 183 of the estimated seven thousand people crammed in her.

As the Russians closed in on the Baltic bases, the remaining U-boats were ordered to Norway. Operating unopposed over the western Baltic and the Kattegat, rocket-firing Typhoon fighter-bombers pounced gleefully upon these targets, destroying twenty-seven German submarines in a last, bloody massacre. *Scheer, Lützow, Köln*, and *Emden* were all sunk in bombing attacks. *Leipzig* and *Hipper* were total wrecks. Only *Prinz Eugen* and *Nürnberg* survived the holocaust.

On the last day of April, Hitler, after gloating over the news of Franklin Roosevelt's death on April 12, committed suicide in his bunker beneath the shattered streets of Berlin, now almost totally overrun by the Red Army. In his final testament, he rewarded Karl Dönitz for his faith and loyalty by naming him as his heir. The once relatively obscure flag officer commanding U-boats of 1939 became the second—and last—Führer of the Third Reich. That same day, Korvettenkapitän Adalbert Schnee and a crack crew departed Bergen, Norway, in *U-2511*, the first Type XXI boat to embark on a war patrol. Picked up by a corvette's sonar in the North Sea, the submarine raced away at a submerged speed of sixteen knots, leaving the baffled corvette well behind.

---

*The sinking of the *Wilhelm Gustloff* is the worst maritime disaster in history. In contrast, 1,503 people lost their lives when the *Titanic* went down after striking an iceberg in 1912; in 1915, *Lusitania* was torpedoed, killing 1,198 passengers and crew.

Dönitz was at Flensburg, on the north coast, directing the rescue of troops and civilians from East Prussia—when he received the stunning news of his appointment and Hitler's death. Aware that the war was now lost, he played for time to permit more Germans to escape the clutches of the Russians by attempting to capitulate to the Western Allies alone. He hoped to avoid unconditional surrender, which would freeze all German movements and end the rescue operation. On May 4, the British accepted the proffered surrender of German forces in northwestern Germany, Denmark, western Holland, and Norway, and Dönitz ordered all U-boats to cease offensive operations and return to base.

Schnee had a British cruiser squarely in the crosshairs of *U-2511*'s periscope when he received the cease-fire message. Angrily, he went through the complete drill for preparing to unleash a spread of torpedoes and then, without doing so, dived deep and effortlessly made away. The cruiser continued on course, oblivious to the fate it had so narrowly escaped.

Dönitz's efforts to strike a deal with the Western Allies failed when General Eisenhower insisted upon unconditional surrender to all three Allies, and the final German capitulation became effective on May 8, 1945—VE-Day. So ended the orgy of death and destruction in Europe and its surrounding seas. No one is certain how many men died as their ships were sunk, or planes shot down, or submarines depth-charged, but, as Kipling said, "if blood be the price of admiralty," it was paid in full many times over. No fewer than 2,603 Allied merchant ships had been sunk, as well as 175 naval vessels. On the German side, of the 1,162 U-boats built, 830 took part in operations and 784 were lost. With few exceptions, the entire surface navy was wiped out.

Not long after the surrender, Grand Admiral Dönitz was arrested. "Words at this moment would be superfluous," he declared.

•

CHAPTER 21

"Uncommon Valor Was a Common Virtue"

"Run, run, run. Get off the beach. Get off the beach." These frenzied thoughts flashed through the mind of Private Allen R. Matthews, a rifleman in the first wave of marines to land on Iwo Jima. ". . . They are sighting in on the beach and they'll get you as sure as hell. . . . [G]et off the beach and run." To Matthews's surprise, his legs sank into brown volcanic ash up to his calves. It was as loose as sugar. "I said to myself *run* but I could only shuffle. . . ." Men were staggering and falling all around him, and "the beach sand spouted up like black water from a geyser. . . . A shell had fallen close by. . . ."

It was shortly after 0900 on February 19, 1945. Only moments before, sixty-nine armored amphtracs, each carrying twenty marines and navy medical corpsmen, had waddled out of the Pacific onto the beach and crawled forward behind a creeping barrage from the warships lying offshore. The vehicles churned vigorously through the volcanic ash, yet only a few were able to breast a fifteen-foot-high terrace lying just behind the beach. The others disgorged their men at its base, from where the heavily laden troops struggled upward through the loose sand.

Initially, the marines met only sporadic rifle fire and a few mortar shells. Perhaps it was going to be easy; maybe the preinvasion air-and-naval bombardment had knocked out the Japanese defenders. But once they heaved themselves up onto the crumbling terrace, they were cut down by heavy machine-gun and mortar fire from concealed pillboxes, blockhouses, and caves that had withstood three days of intensive bombardment. Automatic fire spat from apertures only a few inches above ground. Land mines, sown like wheat in a field, exploded in sickening blasts.

Shells fell among the landing craft following in the wakes of the amphtracs. Troops and equipment piled up on the beach as men inched forward on their stomachs. From Mount Suribachi, an inactive volcano that at 556 feet was the highest point on the island, hidden Japanese artillery blanketed the beaches. Huge 320-millimeter mortars lobbed seven-hundred-pound shells down onto the marines. Tanks churned helplessly in the volcanic ash and became easy marks for enemy gunners they couldn't see. Battered boats and burning tanks littered the area, and the living and dead lay side by side on the hellish beach. Wounded men were hit again or killed as they awaited evacuation. Casualties were running as high as 30 percent in some units.*

But the marines moved forward, inspired by their corps's traditions and examples of individual valor. First one man lunged into the maelstrom of enemy fire, then twos and threes, then fire teams and squads, then larger units. More and more landing craft survived to put additional tanks and artillery on the beach. Men pulled themselves up the terraces onto the plateau and reached the edge of one of the island's two airfields. Still others rammed across the narrow neck of the island at Suribachi's base and isolated it from the rest of Iwo. "They crept and crawled, dodged and ducked, slithered and staggered—but they moved forward," said Bill Ross, a marine combat correspondent.

Iwo Jima was selected by Admiral Spruance as the next target in the U.S. Navy's relentless march toward Japan because the island's airfields were deemed necessary to support the B-29 bombing campaign against the home islands. Okinawa itself, only 375 miles from Japan, would follow. When Spruance relieved Admiral Halsey as commander of the Third Fleet at the end of January, the world's most powerful naval force once more became the Fifth Fleet; the fast carriers of TF 38 were now designated TF 58, with Admiral Mitscher

---

*Gunnery Sergeant John Basilone, who had won the Medal of Honor on Guadalcanal, was among them.

again in command. "Without Iwo Jima I couldn't bomb Japan effectively," General Curtis E. LeMay—commander of the 21st Bombing
Command, based in the Marianas—had told Spruance.

Sustained B-29 raids on Japanese cities had begun the previous
November with only mixed success. Japanese fighters based on Iwo,
halfway between the Marianas and Tokyo, lay in wait for the bombers
disrupting their formations, and radar stations on the island gave
Tokyo early warning of their approach. To avoid Iwo, the planes had
to make a fuel-consuming dog-leg that reduced their margin for error
in the return flight. In American hands, Iwo would be a perfect
halfway house for crippled B-29s. They could land there in emer-
gencies, and fighters based on the island could accompany the
bombers over the targets.

From the air, Iwo looks like a pork chop. It is four and a half miles
long and two and a half miles wide at its meatier, northeastern end,
with a total area of eight square miles, a third of that of Manhattan.
Suribachi is the most dominant feature, rising solitary and menacing
at the extreme tip of the small end. Just to the north, where the island
is at its narrowest—scarcely a mile across—are the beaches. They
run northeastward for about thirty-five hundred yards, until the
ground gradually widens and rises in rugged terraces to a bleak
plateau that the Japanese had leveled for the two airfields. A third
strip was under construction. Rain was the only source of water, and
cockroaches crawled everywhere.

The initial target date for the Iwo operation was January 20, but it
was twice set back because of the spirited Japanese resistance on
Luzon, first to February 3 and then to February 19. The invasion of
Okinawa was to follow in six weeks. To tamp down enemy interference, Mitscher attacked targets in the home islands for the first time.
Sixteen carriers escorted by over a hundred other warships attacked
aircraft plants and airfields near Tokyo. Three hundred forty Japanese planes were claimed as shot down and another 190 destroyed on
the ground; sixty U.S. planes were lost.

Seventy-two days of aerial bombardment by B-24s and B-25s from
the Marianas preceded the invasion of Iwo—the longest and most
intensive preassault aerial bombardment of the Pacific war—but this
only drove the Japanese deeper underground. They had been
preparing for an invasion since the Marianas campaign in July 1944.
Fully aware that there would be no help from the outside, Lieutenant

General Tadamichi Kuribayashi had put his twenty-one thousand troops and sailors to building gun emplacements and tunneling deep into Iwo's porous volcanic rock. There would be no attempts to shell the ships of the bombardment group, no stand on the beaches, no *banzai* charges, not even a large-scale counterattack—instead a stubborn, sustained defense in depth that would cost the enemy as many casualties as possible.

Numerous caves were dug into the slope of Suribachi facing the beaches, and the rest of the island was studded with successive defense lines of concrete pillboxes. The northern sector was a rabbit warren of tunnels and redoubts, some seventy-five feet deep, with a dozen entrances. Big naval guns, artillery pieces, anti-aircraft and machine guns, and even twenty-four dug-in tanks were emplaced with supporting fields of fire, in locations where a direct hit would be needed to knock them out. "Every man will resist until the end, making his position his tomb," Kuribayashi told his troops "Every man will do his best to kill ten enemy soldiers."

Three marine divisions totaling seventy-five thousand men were assigned to the capture of Iwo—the veteran Fourth and the new Fifth Division were to lead the assault, with the battle-hardened Third Division in support. The V Amphibious Corps, under Major General Harry Schmidt, was the largest force of marines assembled under one command during the war. The top commands were held by the team of Kelly Turner and "Howlin' Mad" Smith.

The full extent of the Japanese defenses was unknown to the American commanders. Nevertheless, what they learned from aerial photographs of the island made clear that its capture would be difficult. Five days were allotted to the capture of the island, but Smith predicted Iwo would be "the toughest place we have had to take." The use of poison gas was discussed but rejected, because American policy called for no first use; gas was to be resorted to only in retaliation, if an enemy used it initially. The marines wanted a ten-day preliminary bombardment of the island, but Spruance allowed only three days, because of the speeded-up timetable, the difficulty in resupplying ammunition, and the diversion of TF 58 to Mitscher's raid on Tokyo.

Turner promised to deliver an intensive bombardment which, he said, would pump as many shells onto Iwo as a ten-day bombardment. The marines replied that the tonnage of shells was not what counted. Previous naval attacks against well-built defenses in both Europe and the Pacific had made clear that only deliberate point-blank shelling of well-defined targets, using a variety of shells and trajectories over a long period of time, was effective. Unfortunately, the marine commanders turned out to be correct. "No previous target in the Central Pacific . . . received such a volume of preparatory shelling per square yard of terrain—nor had any other gone into the assault phase with so many of its defenses unscathed," according to an authoritative study of amphibious warfare in the Pacific.

Six battleships, including *Nevada, Texas*, and *Arkansas*—all veterans of the Normandy invasion—and five cruisers opened the bombardment of Iwo at 0707 on February 16. The island had been divided into squares, with each square assigned to a specific ship. Known targets were marked and numbered. There were over seven hundred of these, each entered on a card index on *Wake Island*, flagship of Rear Admiral William P. Blandy, who was in charge of naval-gunfire support. The shelling was "a slow, careful probing for almost invisible targets, with long dull intervals between the firing," reported John P. Marquand, the novelist, who witnessed it from *Tennessee*. Overcast and rain squalls soon settled in over the island like a protective cloak, however, and only few of the targets were destroyed by the end of the first day.

The highlight came when Lieutenant (j.g.) D. W. Gandy, the pilot of one of the cruiser *Pensacola*'s Kingfisher spotter planes, radioed that there was a Zero on his tail. A split second later, Gandy reported, "I got him! I got him!" and the victim was seen falling into the sea. It was unheard of for a slow, ungainly float plane to shoot down a Zero.

The weather improved the next day, and Blandy's ships closed to within three thousand yards of Iwo to send heavy direct fire onto their targets. Minesweepers and a line of LCI gunboats bringing in underwater demolition teams worked even closer inshore and came under scattered fire from the Japanese. *Pensacola* moved in to help. She proved too inviting a target for one battery commander and, disobeying orders, he opened fire. Hit six times, the cruiser retired with seventeen dead and 120 wounded. Destroyers closed in to cover the LCIs.

General Kuribayashi, apparently believing that the presence of minesweepers meant the invasion was at hand, directed the big guns hidden at the foot of Suribachi and the northern end of the island to open up on the gunboats. Ten of the twelve were hit. "There was blood on the main deck, making widening pools as she rolled in the sea," Marquand reported as one of the LCIs came alongside *Tennessee* to transfer casualties. "The decks were littered with wounded. . . ." The second day of bombardment ended with the Japanese convinced they had repulsed a landing.

Two days of shelling had blasted away the camouflage from batteries and bunkers covering the beach not previously known to exist, and on D–1 Blandy closed to 2,500 yards for the heaviest bombardment of the operation. Pillboxes and blockhouses were literally blasted out of the ground. This day-long shelling was more effective than all the previous "softening" attacks from both air and sea. But as the ships withdrew for the night, many enemy installations were intact.

Blandy notified Turner that, although the beaches were sufficiently clear for the landing scheduled for February 19 (D-Day), he had enough ammunition to add another day of bombardment, plus a reserve to cover the assault. Turner's decision was governed by the weather. Forecasters said the next day would be fair but predicted conditions would deteriorate on February 20; Turner ordered the operation to proceed as scheduled. If the marines had not landed on the 19th, observes Ronald Spector, the assault would probably have been postponed until February 21—providing two extra days of much-needed naval-gunfire support. It was a Sunday, and a chaplain on one transport passed out a small blue card to all hands, carrying the words of Sir Jacob Astley's prayer before the Battle of Edgehill in 1642, during England's bloody civil war:

> Oh Lord! Thou knowest how busy I must be this day:
> If I forget Thee, do not Thou forget me.

"Whether the dead were Japs or Americans, they had one thing in common: they had died with the greatest possible violence," reported Robert Sherrod, who came ashore on the afternoon of D-Day. "Nowhere in the Pacific war had I seen such badly mangled bodies.

Many were cut squarely in half. Legs and arms lay fifty feet from any body. . . . Only legs were easy to identify; they were Jap if wrapped in khaki puttees, American if covered by canvas leggings. The smell of burning flesh was heavy in some areas."

By nightfall, despite heavy casualties, thirty thousand marines were ashore, plus artillery and tanks. Iwo's fate was sealed, even though the reduction of the island took almost another month, rather than the estimated five days. The next day, D+1, the campaign began to compress the Japanese into the rugged northeastern end of the island, and to tighten the noose about Suribachi. Pushing forward with little cover, the marines were shelled and machine-gunned from hidden caves and bunkers. In one small area, the Japanese had constructed more than three hundred gun emplacements and other defenses." To add to the general misery, a cold, drizzling rain began to fall, jelling with the coarse volcanic ash to clog weapons.

Flamethrowers spearheaded the attack, and the marines fought with hand grenades and demolition charges. Concrete blockhouses had to be blasted again and again before the troops inside were finally silenced. Naval-gunfire and close-air support played an important role in wearing the Japanese down. Each marine battalion had a navy fire-control party attached, which could call in ships and planes to deal with targets as they were found. The caves on the side of Suribachi that covered the beaches were shelled by *Washington*'s sixteen-inch guns. Three salvos precipitated landslides that sealed off some.

On D+2, kamikazes got through TF 58's defenses. *Saratoga*, the oldest carrier in the fleet, and several escort carriers were steaming to the east of Iwo shortly before 1700 and were preparing to launch rocket-equipped fighters for an attack on the island. Several approaching aircraft were picked up by radar, but were misidentified as "friendlies." Before the mistake could be rectified, five Japanese planes dropped out of the clouds, weaving and bobbing crazily. Four were shot down clear of the carrier, but one struck near the bow, and the whole forward section of *Saratoga* exploded into flames. Within two hours, however, damage-control parties had the blaze under control.

The Japanese were hardly through with the "Sara," and as darkness fell, they marked the wounded vessel with flares and resumed the attack. Five kamikazes were accounted for by the carrier's guns, and the screening destroyers shot down another four, but one slipped through and planted a sixteen-hundred-pound bomb squarely on her flight deck. A jagged hole thirty feet in diameter was blasted through five decks, and the ship was shaken violently—but she lived. With only half a flight deck, she was landing her orbiting aircraft two hours later. One hundred twenty-three men had been killed; another 192 wounded.

The escort carrier *Bismarck Sea* was not so lucky. She was heading into the wind to recover her own planes and some temporarily roost-less aircraft from *Saratoga* when a kamikaze came boring in. Even though the plane was hit, it crashed into the ship abreast of the after elevator, which dropped into the hangar deck. Wracked by repeated explosions of gasoline and ammunition, *Bismarck Sea* was hit by another kamikaze that wiped out the firefighting party. She was now a shambles, and was abandoned. Blazing from stem to stern, she turned over and sank. Of her crew of 943 men, 218 were lost.

Suribachi was a symbol to the men fighting for Iwo. The mountain fortress was code-named "Hot Rocks," but the marines had a more telling name for it—"Mount Plasma." Gunnery-support ships poured salvo after salvo into the crumbling crags and defiles, yet the Japan-ese kept returning to their guns, keeping up an incessant rain of death. The 28th Marines, Fifth Division, inched up Suribachi's slopes, slowly clearing it of defenders, foxhole by foxhole, cave by cave. On the morning of February 23, they were ordered to rush the top. First Lieutenant Harold G. Schrier was handed a small Ameri-can flag by Lieutenant Colonel Chandler Johnson, his battalion com-mander, and told: "Take a platoon up the hill and put this on top."

Moving in single file, the forty-man patrol clambered up the north-east side of the dormant volcano, sometimes on their hands and knees. They passed several threatening cave openings, but there was no fire from the enemy. In fact, no living Japanese were seen. Once the summit was crested, there was a brief firefight that ended as quickly as it began. The marines found a seven-foot length of iron pipe, attached the flag and raised it.

From the beach area below, the flag could barely be seen, but men in the foxholes cheered and pounded each other's backs. Ship's whis-tles and horns wailed and screeched. The visiting James V. Forrestal, who had become secretary of the navy after the death of Frank Knox in 1944, turned to "Howlin' Mad" Smith and said gravely: "Holland, the rising of that flag on Suribachi means a Marine Corps for the next five hundred years." The old warrior nodded and his eyes filled with tears.

"Some son of a bitch is going to want that flag but he's not going to get it," Colonel Johnson, who had sent the flag up, told his adjutant. He ordered the original brought down, and a larger one, obtained from *LST-799*, put in its place. Joe Rosenthal, an Associated Press photographer who had landed on D-Day, missed the first flag-raising and almost missed the second as he piled up rocks for a better vantage point for taking a picture. He hurriedly snapped a picture as five marines and a corpsman raised the new flag over Suribachi.* A masterpiece of informal composition and lighting, it is the most famous photograph of World War II.

The capture of Suribachi gave the Americans control of the southern third of Iwo, but the struggle went on. Over the next three weeks, the marines advanced behind a rolling barrage of naval gunfire through a moonscape of volcanic rock, gullies, and ridges aptly named "Meat Grinder" and "Bloody Gorge." The northern plateau concealed the bulk of the Japanese defenses, and gains were measured in yards. Marine combat engineers used bulldozers to clear avenues through the minefields for flamethrowing tanks and infantry. Some Japanese positions were bypassed and sealed up, burying the defenders alive, but most were forced out with flamethrowers, grenades, and demolition charges. Huge bluebottle flies swarmed from the mangled corpses of the dead onto the marines' C-rations.

While the Japanese were slowly being ground down in the north, Seabees labored to put the airfields into service, even though intensive fighting raged nearby. The first of many B-29s to land on Iwo made an emergency landing on March 4, after being damaged in a raid on Japan. Finally, a battalion of marines fought their way through the Japanese defense lines to the sea, splitting the island in two. Mopping up began, and on March 16 General Schmidt called Iwo secure, although isolated pockets of Japanese continued to resist for several more weeks. The final *banzai* attack, on March 25, was beaten back.

On the American side, 5,931 marines, 881 sailors, and nine army soldiers were killed in action or died of wounds, and nearly twenty thousand were wounded. Battle casualties totaled 30 percent of the landing force, and 75 percent in the infantry regiments of the Fourth

---

*Three of the six-man flag-raising team were later killed in action, and another was wounded.

and Fifth Divisions. When informed of the casualties, President Roosevelt shuddered in horror. For the Japanese, the entire garrison of twenty-one thousand men was wiped out except 216 prisoners, mostly wounded. General Kuribayashi, who committed suicide, and his command were enshrined as heroes in Japan. Twenty-seven marines and corpsmen were awarded the Medal of Honor, thirteen posthumously. "Uncommon valor was a common virtue" among those who fought on Iwo Jima, observed Admiral Nimitz.

Was Iwo Jima worth the sacrifice? The loss of life renewed the controversy that followed Tarawa, with some newspapers railing against the heavy casualties in such assaults. The marines blamed the losses on the navy's failure to supply the requested ten-day preliminary bombardment, to which the navy rejoined that the targets remaining after the third day of shelling were too deep underground to have been taken out by bombardment. Some analysts contend the island was worth the price because more than twenty-four thousand crewmen might have been lost in crippled planes that landed safely on Iwo before the war ended. Fighters flying from the island also flew cover missions for the bombers. One wounded marine best summed it up, saying: "I hope to God that we don't have to go on any more of those screwy islands."

But there was one more—Okinawa.

Lizard-shaped Okinawa lies on the doorstep of Japan, only 350 miles from Kyushu, the southernmost of the home islands. Admiral Spruance chose it as the next Allied objective because it could provide airfields and a fleet anchorage for the invasion of Japan. Unlike previous objectives in the Central Pacific, Okinawa was large—sixty miles long, and from two to eighteen miles wide—and was densely populated, with about a half-million people. Sizable numbers of troops would be required for a successful invasion, the supply problem was formidable, and the island was in range of kamikazes flying from China and Formosa as well as Japan. Okinawa—Operation Iceberg—exceeded the Normandy invasion in tonnage and manpower involved. British observers called it "the most audacious and complex enterprise yet undertaken by American amphibious forces."

Admiral Spruance, as commander of the Fifth Fleet, was in overall command of the operation, which was scheduled to begin on April 1, and Kelly Turner was in charge of the amphibious phase, but there was a change in the familiar command structure. At the insistence of the War Department, which refused to allow army troops to serve under a marine general after Saipan, Lieutenant General Simon B. Buckner, Jr., who had been in charge in the Aleutians, replaced Holland Smith as commander of the combined army-marine Tenth Army. Totaling some 180,000 troops, it consisted of III Marine Amphibious Corps, composed of the First and Sixth Divisions, and the XXIV Army Corps, comprising the Seventh and 96th Infantry Divisions. Three more army divisions—the 27th, 81st, and 77th—were held in reserve. Another 115,000 service troops supported the operation.

In the meantime, General LeMay had altered the aerial campaign against Japan. Forced to the reluctant conclusion that daylight high-level bombing was ineffective, he switched to night area bombing with incendiaries. The effect was devastating against Japan's crowded cities. On the night of March 9, 1945, more than three hundred B-29s dumped thousands of incendiaries on Tokyo, creating a wind-whipped inferno that destroyed one-quarter of the city. "I watched people, adults and children, running for their lives, dashing madly about like rats," reported one survivor. "The flames raced after them like living things, striking them down." As many as a hundred thousand people died in the holocaust and some 267,000 dwellings were destroyed.

The Tokyo raid set the pattern for the American bombing offensive. Nagoya, Kobe, Osaka, Yokohama, and Kawasaki followed as targets for the implacable B-29s. Japanese civil defenses were ill-prepared to counter such an onslaught, and the core of the nation's industrial heartland was consumed in flames. Ranging almost at will, the bombers next struck half a hundred smaller cities and manufacturing centers, leaving huge pyres of smoke and ash towering behind them. Immense civilian casualties resulted, but American strategists viewed the firebombing campaign as a way of overcoming fanatic Japanese resistance and making an invasion unnecessary, thereby saving thousands of American lives.

The Okinawa campaign began on March 17, with a massive strike by TF 58, ten heavy and six light carriers divided into four task groups, against airfields on Kyushu and shipping in the Inland Sea. They claimed some five hundred Japanese planes as destroyed, which prevented the enemy from marshaling an attack against the

Okinawa invasion force. *Wasp, Enterprise, Yorktown*, and *Franklin* were all damaged—*Franklin* worst of all. Two 550-pound bombs ignited planes being fueled and armed on her flight deck, and the carrier was ripped by explosions fed by her own bombs and gasoline stocks. "I saw a sheet of flame come out from under the starboard side of the flight deck and envelop the starboard batteries and catwalks and spread aft," reported Captain Leslie H. Gehres.

But Gehres refused to abandon ship. Several hundred men were trapped below, and as he later related, "I had promised those kids I'd get them out." Some three hundred men were on the blazing hangar deck, where they were in utter darkness in the suffocating heat, the sole air supply coming through a baseball-sized hole in the ship's side. Lieutenant (j.g.) Donald Gary groped through a maze of compartments to lead them out. Gary was awarded the Medal of Honor, as was Father Joseph T. O'Callahan, one of *Franklin*'s chaplains. He seemed to be everywhere, praying for the dying, comforting the wounded, fighting fires, jettisoning ammunition, and lending encouragement. No other ship in World War II suffered such extensive damage and remained afloat. But the carrier was saved through the superhuman efforts of her crew, using new firefighting equipment and techniques. Even so, 724 of *Franklin*'s crew were dead, and 256 wounded. None of these setbacks interfered with the invasion timetable set for Okinawa.

Eight days of preliminary bombardment began on March 23, with Normandy veteran Admiral Morton Deyo's old battleships leading the way. They were joined by the battleships and carriers of the Fifth Fleet, including the newly constituted British Pacific Fleet, which was designated TF 57. As the end of the war in Europe approached, the British were eager to restore their prestige in the Far East, and Roosevelt and Churchill had agreed in September that the Royal Navy should take part in the naval war against Japan. Admiral King objected, on the grounds that the British carriers were unable to remain at sea as long as their American counterparts, but his complaints were brushed aside.

Admiral Sir Bruce Fraser, based at Sydney, was in overall command, and Vice-Admiral Sir Bernard Rawlings flew his flag in *King George V*. He had four carriers—later increased to five—and eleven destroyers. The carriers, under Philip Vian, had about 240 aircraft, mostly of American make. In fact, the British had more success with the powerful F4U Corsair as a carrier fighter than did the U.S. Navy.

The Pacific Fleet began operations in January 1945, with an attack against the oil refineries at Palembang in southern Sumatra, source of much of Japan's aviation fuel, and other facilities.

While Okinawa was getting a workout from the American and British fleets, Turner surprised the Japanese by landing the 77th Division in the Kerama Retto, a cluster of islets fifteen miles west of Okinawa. Lightly held, they were taken without difficulty, and the roadstead was transformed into an emergency base for refueling and repairs. The seizure of these islands proved to be one of Turner's wisest decisions. A shadow of the terror to come had already touched the invasion fleet, and Spruance's flagship, *Indianapolis*, was among Kerama's first customers. On March 31, while the cruiser was taking part in the final pounding of the beaches, she was hit by a kamikaze, and Spruance transferred his flag to *New Mexico*. Nevertheless, at the end of the day Admiral Blandy announced that the preparation was "sufficient for a successful landing."

Easter Sunday, April 1, 1945, was a time of prayer and hope for a world sensing the approaching end of a global war; to the American commanders off Okinawa, it was a fine day for an amphibious operation. The wind rippled the East China Sea, the weather was cool, visibility was good, and the brown escarpments and hills of the island were clearly outlined on the horizon. Ranging off Okinawa's western side was the greatest armada of the Pacific war—more than forty carriers, eighteen battleships, two hundred destroyers, hundreds of transports, cruisers, and landing craft—about thirteen hundred vessels in all. L [for Love]-Day, as D-Day for Okinawa was called, was at hand.

Shortly before 0830, under cover of a massive bombardment from the sea and air, the first wave of landing craft passed over the coral reefs surrounding Okinawa and headed through swept channels toward the beaches. "Maybe Nimitz, Spruance, and Turner learned something from Iwo Jima," "Howlin' Mad" Smith said of the intensive bombardment of Okinawa. Two landings were made on a five- to six-mile strip of beach. Simultaneously, other units feigned a landing on the island's southern tip to confuse the Japanese. Little was known about the enemy's defenses, but after Iwo Jima everyone expected the worst. In the distance, the guns of the battleships thundered, while overhead planes wheeled and dipped and dropped their bombs.

But when the amphtracs churned up onto the beach, they met no opposition. Swarming from the vehicles, the troops advanced standing up. There was no withering machine-gun fire, no deadly 320-millimeter mortar rounds. Veterans of the fury at Guam, Saipan, Peleliu, and other landings were shocked. Was this some sort of April Fool's Day joke? The two airfields behind the beaches were quickly captured, and the only enemy encountered were a few snipers, who were quickly dealt with. By evening, there were fifty thousand U.S. troops ashore. "Where were the Japs?" asked an incredulous Robert Sherrod.

Lieutenant General Mitsuru Ushijima, following the example of the defenders of Iwo Jima, had elected not to resist the American landings. Instead, he deployed his hundred thousand troops in a maze of artillery, mortar, and machine-gun emplacements concealed by natural and man-made caves in the mountainous lower third of Okinawa, which included the port of Naha. As long as he held out, Ushijima reasoned, the Americans could not use the island as an "England" for invading Japan. If the troops were tied down, the enemy would be forced to keep his fleet offshore to provide support, where it would be a target for the kamikazes. Ushijima knew the Americans would ultimately take Okinawa, but intended to make them pay dearly for every foot of soil and coral rock.

In the days following the landing, the marines, supported by naval gunfire, moved north while the army plunged across the narrow center of the island and turned south. "I may be crazy but it looks like the Japanese have quit the war, at least in this sector," Turner radioed Admiral Nimitz. "Delete all after 'crazy,'" was Nimitz's sardonic reply. Events soon proved him correct. The marines continued to meet only light opposition, but after a few days the army troops began to encounter stiffening resistance as they ran up against the enemy's fortified Shuri Line. The honeymoon on Okinawa was ending.

"Raid One. Bogies closing from northwest, fifty miles north of Bolo. This is Delegate, out."

Thus, during the mid-watch on April 6, the Fifth Fleet's epic ordeal off Okinawa began.

"Delegate" was the central fighter director in Turner's command ship, *Eldorado*. He had just warned all ships lying off the island of the approach of a large flight of enemy aircraft. "Bolo" was the code word for Zampa Point, the reference point for air-raid warnings.

General quarters sounded, and guns were manned. Radars scanned the skies, and operators fine-tuned their sets to clarify the flickering points of light on their screens. A CAP of fifty fighters was vectored out to intercept the raiders—the first of several flights, totaling some seven hundred planes, which struck the fleet that day. Of these, 355 were kamikazes, the rest conventional bombers. Each was intent on sinking a Yankee ship. The Japanese gave them the name *kikusui*, or "floating chrysanthemums." Only sporadic kamikazes had appeared in the early days of the invasion, because of the heavy attacks on Japanese airfields in Kyushu and other points by American and British carriers. But a full-scale attack was expected as soon as the enemy could assemble enough planes.

While Mitscher's big carriers were operating about a hundred miles to the northeast, Spruance had spread his armada in a great wide sweep around Okinawa. To the southeast lay seventeen escort carriers, their planes providing CAPs and air support for the ground troops. Battleships steamed back and forth within easy range of the island, shelling Japanese positions. Transports and cargo vessels huddled offshore, keeping the flow of men and supplies moving to the beach. Radar picket destroyers were disposed on sixteen different stations around the fleet fifty miles apart to provide early warning of an attack.

The Japanese concentrated on the outlying picket vessels, believing that once they were knocked out the rest of the fleet would be easy targets. Radar Picket Stations 1, 2, and 3, on an arc twelve miles to the north of Okinawa, were the hottest spots. Forty aircraft milled about the destroyer *Bush*, which shot down two planes and drove off a pair, but another plane crashed between her two stacks. Flooded, the vessel took on a list. *Colhoun* closed to render assistance and tried to interpose herself between the sinking ship and a flight of fifteen Japanese planes. Three were shot down, but a fourth struck *Colhoun*, killing the crews of a pair of forty-millimeter guns. Three more planes attacked her; one was shot down by *Colhoun*, *Bush*'s gunners got another, and the third crashed into the forward fireroom. Even as both destroyers were sinking, they continued to fight, accounting for two more kamikazes.

Air-surface battles occurred all around Okinawa on that bloody afternoon. The Combat Information Centers of the picket destroyers were a Babel of radioed reports and warnings:

"Pedantic, this is Riverside. I see bogey one eight zero. Do you concur? Over."

"This is Pedantic. Affirmative. That makes three raids. . . . "

Leutze and *Newcomb*, providing cover for the transports, bore the brunt of another attack. Within minutes, a kamikaze crashed into *Newcomb*'s after stack, a second was shot down, and a third, carrying either a bomb or a torpedo, struck her amidships, turning her engine rooms into a shambles. A fourth smashed into the forward stack, spraying the ship with burning gasoline and searing some of the gunners. Flames were shooting hundreds of feet into the air. *Leutze* came alongside and passed hose lines to the stricken vessel. There was no letup in the aerial attack, and a plane crashed into *Leutze*. In danger of sinking, she was towed to the refuge at Kerama by the minelayer *Defense*, already damaged herself, by two kamikaze hits. Both *Leutze* and *Newcomb* were so badly damaged that they were scrapped.

Sometimes a direct hit was not enough to stop a plunging kamikaze, related Commander Albert O. Momm, of the destroyer *Mullany*:

> The plane crashed into the ship at the after deckhouse between the two high 5-inch gun mounts, and exploding with a spray of gasoline started huge fires, leaving the deckhouse, gun mounts, and gun directors a mass of torn wreckage. We lost steering control and communications abaft the after deckhouse. Attempts to sprinkle the after magazines and ammunition handling rooms were useless; the mains had been pierced and sprinkler valves destroyed by the crash and explosions that followed it.

Mullany's guns shot down three more attackers and she survived.[*] Three other destroyers, an LST, and two ships carrying ammunition—which the troops ashore would soon need—were sunk in these raids. Another ten vessels, including eight destroyers, suffered major damage. Nearly a thousand sailors were killed or wounded, many horribly burned. In the process, a large part of the Japanese attacking force was destroyed. Over the next three months, the Allied fleet was struck by ten similar massed kamikaze attacks, and the anchor-

---

[*]The destroyer's gunnery officer was Lieutenant Oliver Hazard Perry, Jr., a distant relation of the hero of the Battle of Lake Erie in 1813, and a direct descendant of Commodore Matthew Calbraith Perry, who had opened Japan to the West less than a century before.

age in the Keramas was crowded with crippled ships. But unlike Guadalcanal, where the navy was charged with abandoning the marines after Savo, the Fifth Fleet had come to stay—and it remained off Okinawa despite the most concentrated attack ever sustained by any naval force.

Alerted by reports from prowling submarines that the giant battleship *Yamato*, the light cruiser *Yahagi*, and eight destroyers had been sighted leaving the Inland Sea, Mitscher deployed three carrier groups to the north of Okinawa to head them off. Without enough fuel to return, *Yamato* and her consorts had been thrown into the battle on a one-way death ride in which she was to do as much damage to the invasion fleet with her eighteen-inch guns as possible before meeting inevitable destruction. The battle group was sighted in the East China Sea early on April 7, and at 1000 Mitscher launched every available aircraft—TBFs carrying torpedoes, Helldivers with armor-piercing bombs, and Hellcat and Corsair fighters carrying five-hundred-pound bombs—a total of 386 planes.

"But," said a bewildered British observer in *Bunker Hill*, the flagship, "you have launched before you can possibly be sure of their location."

"We are taking a chance," replied Arleigh Burke, Mitscher's chief of staff. "We are launching against the spot where we would be if we were the *Yamato*."

Low cloud cover hindered the search for the Japanese ships. "Rain and more rain. Clouds and more clouds," related Lieutenant Thaddeus T. Coleman, a dive-bomber pilot. "Where are the Japs?" Suddenly there was an "eruption of AA close ahead. Then we knew we had found them and, because of their bursts, we knew we knew where they were. . . . Our training instructions, to dive steeply from 10,000 feet or higher, proved useless. Here the ceiling was only 3,000 feet, with rain squalls all around. Bomber pilots pushed over in all sorts of crazy dives, fighter pilots used every maneuver in the book, torpedo pilots stuck their necks all the way out, dropped right down on the surface, and delivered their parcels so near the ships that many of them missed the ships' superstructures by inches. The Japanese ships squirmed like a nest of snakes. . . ."

Yamato, with her 146 anti-aircraft guns, and the other vessels threw up a curtain of anti-aircraft fire, but wave after wave of planes bore in to the attack. Hit by ten torpedoes and at least six bombs, the battleship took on a strong list to port. The starboard engine and boiler rooms were ordered counterflooded. Ensign Mitsuru Yoshiba, on the bridge, telephoned the occupants to warn them to abandon their stations, but it was too late. "Water, both from torpedo hits and the flood valves, rushed into these compartments and snuffed out the lives of the men at their posts, several hundred in all."

At 1420, less than two hours after the attack began, *Yamato*'s deck was nearly vertical. "Shells of the big guns skidded and bumped across the deck of the ammunition room, crashing against the bulkhead and kindling the first of a series of explosions," Yoshiba reported. The ship "slid under completely," followed by "the blast, rumble, and shock of compartments bursting from air pressure and exploding magazines." Only 269 men of her crew of twenty-five hundred survived. *Yahagi* and four of the destroyers were also sunk, with the loss of another 1,167 sailors, and the remaining four ships were damaged. Only ten U.S. planes were lost. While *Yamato* was under attack, a lone kamikaze crashed into the carrier *Hancock*, killing eighty-four Americans.

The Japanese sent in 185 kamikazes together with 195 fighters and torpedo planes on April 12—the day President Roosevelt died. "Don't let any return," Kelly Turner told his crews. As usual, the radar picket destroyers caught it first. *Cassin Young* shot down four kamikazes but took a suicider in the forward engine room. *Purdy* was also damaged. *Abele* was hit by one of the new, manned twenty-six-hundred-pound *baka* bombs and sank. *Tennessee* was damaged, and a gunner, blown overboard, had one of the strangest experiences of the battle. He came to the surface near the life raft from a downed enemy plane and climbed in—to find his companion was the headless body of a Japanese flyer.

Four days later, *Pringle* was sunk, the carrier *Intrepid* was damaged, and *Laffey* made naval history.* In less than eighty minutes, the destroyer was attacked by twenty-two planes, six of which crashed into her, and she was hit by four bombs. When the fight ended, the

---

*During the Normandy operation, *Laffey* was hit by a 240-millimeter German shell, but luckily it did not explode.

destroyer had only four twenty-millimeter guns still firing, but had shot down nine kamikazes. Thirty-one of *Laffey*'s crew were killed or missing, and seventy-two were wounded. When the ship's ensign was shot to pieces, Signalman 2/c Thomas McCarthy grabbed another from the flag locker, shinnied up the mast, and tied it in place. "Probably no ship has ever survived an attack of the intensity that she experienced," Morison observed.

Worried about the mounting losses, Spruance told Nimitz that "the skill and effectiveness of enemy suicide attacks and the rate of loss and damage to ships are such that all available means should be employed to prevent further attacks." He urged stepped-up air attacks, including those by B-29s, on the Kyushu and Formosa airfields. Nimitz asked LeMay for help, but the airman objected to using his bombers for "tactical" missions. He said their best use was to continue the fire raids on Japanese cities. Admiral King, at his bluntest, let it be known that, if the Air Force refused to cooperate with the navy, the navy would refuse to continue to supply Air Force bases in the Marianas. The Kyushu airfields were bombed, but the B-29s succeeded only in cratering the runways, which were quickly repaired. Raids by MacArthur's Fifth Air Force on Formosa were equally unsuccessful. The kamikazes kept coming.

The ground campaign on Okinawa also settled down to a savage war of attrition. Buckner pressed ahead with an attack by six army and two marine divisions on the Shuri Line. Rain and mud hindered maneuver and daily progress was measured in yards. Frequently, there was no advance at all. Hundreds of men died on both sides as seesaw battles raged along the island's muddy ridges. "I doubt if the Army's slow, methodical method of fighting really saves any lives in the long run," Spruance observed. "It merely spreads the casualties over a long period of time. The longer period greatly increases the naval casualties. . . . There are times when I get impatient for some of Holland Smith's drive." Later, Buckner was criticized for not using Allied control of the sea to make a flank amphibious landing on Japanese positions.

For forty consecutive days and nights—until foul weather brought a brief relief—the Fifth Fleet was under steady attack by both small and large groups of suicide planes. The ships remained in Readiness Condition One, a step removed from general quarters, which kept two-thirds of the crews at battle stations. Gunners and loaders remained at their guns. Superheated steam was kept at the ready to make full speed at a moment's notice, raising temperatures in the boiler and engineering spaces to over a hundred degrees. Sleep was a luxury. Nerves frazzled and tempers frayed under the strain of waiting for the insistent "bong, bong, bong" of general quarters—and the terror of a kamikaze attack.

Somehow, through it all, the crews of the radar pickets managed to keep their sense of humor. One gunboat crew, weary of being under almost constant attack while larger ships were ignored, rigged up a large sign with a pointing arrow and the words: "To Jap Pilot—This Way to Task Force 58."

Although the pickets were the primary Japanese target, the fast carriers took their share of hits. Mitscher's flagship, *Bunker Hill*, her deck jammed with planes ready to take off, was hit by two suiciders in quick succession. She lost 396 men and was put out of commission. She was the second-worst hit carrier of World War II to survive— *Franklin* being the worst. The admiral transferred his flag to *Enterprise*, only to have her take a hit by a kamikaze. "Any more of this and there will be hair growing on this old bald head," Mitscher said as he shifted to *Randolph*. *Formidable*, *Victorious*, and *Indomitable* also sustained hits; unlike the American flattops, they suffered only minor damage, thanks to their armored flight decks. "When a kamikaze hits a U.S. carrier, it's six months' repair in Pearl," observed an American liaison officer. "In a Limey carrier, it's 'Sweepers, man your brooms.' "

On May 27, Spruance and Mitscher were relieved by Halsey and McCain, and once again, for the last time, the Fifth Fleet became the Third Fleet, and the fast carriers were renumbered TF 38. By then, improved American fighting techniques, combined with heavy Japanese losses, round-the-clock pounding of the airfields from which the kamikazes came, and shortages of volunteers and fuel, resulted in a steady reduction in the tempo of attacks. Ashore, fire from the ships played a leading role in supporting the ground troops. "Naval gunfire," states the official army history, "was employed longer and in greater quantities in the battle of Okinawa than in any other in history."

One by one, the successive Japanese lines of defense were broken. U.S. troops reached the southern extremity of Okinawa on June 21, and the island was declared secure. Mopping up continued for another month. There was not much celebration for a victory that had involved the bloodiest slaughter of the Pacific war. The U.S. Navy lost 34 ships sunk, and 364 were damaged, some beyond repair. The battle claimed the lives of 4,900 sailors, and another 4,800 were wounded. Ashore, some 7,600 soldiers and marines were killed—including General Buckner—and 31,000 were wounded. Of the 100,000-man Japanese garrison, 11,000 were taken prisoner. An estimated 80,000 Okinawan civilians caught in the fighting also became casualties. Some 2,800 kamikaze and supporting aircraft were shot down, while 763 U.S. carrier planes were lost. Within days, Seabees and army engineers were turning Okinawa into a springboard for the forthcoming invasion of Japan.

Well before Okinawa, the Joint Chiefs had set November 1, 1945, as the date for Operation Olympic, the invasion of Kyushu. This was to be followed by Coronet, a landing on Honshu. As Allied forces were deployed from Europe to the Pacific for the final campaign of the war, American and British carrier planes and B-29s ranged over Japan at will. Impotent at sea and in the air, there was little the Japanese could do as enemy aircraft raked airfields and struck at rail yards and other facilities and mined the Inland Sea. The last ships of the Imperial Navy—including the battleships *Haruna, Ise*, and *Hyuga*—were sunk at their moorings in Kobe and Kure. Allied battleships began a series of bombardments of targets ashore, beginning with the steelworks at Kamaishi.

The navy and air force were unenthusiastic about an invasion of Japan, however. Neither the Orange nor the Rainbow plans had called for an invasion, because of the heavy casualties entailed. Both services believed the Japanese could be forced to surrender by continued and unremitting blockade and bombing. In June 1945 Admiral Lockwood launched Operation Barney, sending the nine submarines of "Hydeman's Hellcats" into the Sea of Japan, the only part of the Pacific where Japanese shipping still moved freely.* Between June 8 and 20, these boats sank twenty-seven vessels for a total of about fifty-seven

---

*En route, *Tinosa*, one of the Hydeman boats, picked up ten survivors from a downed B-29. When the airmen learned of the submarine's mission, they wanted to be put back on their raft.

thousand tons, plus a submarine, and cut Japan off from Manchuria and Korea. Famine loomed in Japan. One boat, *Bonefish*, failed to return.

Prompted by this success, Lockwood dispatched six more boats into those waters. By then, most of the large Japanese trading vessels had already been sunk. *Barb* put a demolition crew ashore on Kara-futo in the Sakhalin Islands to the north of Japan, which blew up a train. The last surface battle of the war was fought by six Royal Navy destroyers which caught the heavy cruiser *Haguro* in the South China Sea and, following a close-range melee, torpedoed her.

Admiral Spruance openly expressed what many navy officers thought. "Landings in Japan proper, such as the planned Kyushu landings . . . were not necessary and would have been extremely costly," he later declared. "From our island positions around Japan, we had enough airfields for bombing objectives in Japan if further bombing attacks were needed. We controlled the sea approaches to Japan. . . . Time was decidedly on our side. Japan was cut off and could well have been permitted to 'die on the vine.'" Nimitz and Admiral William D. Leahy, chairman of the JCS, agreed.

Generals Marshall and MacArthur, the latter anointed as supreme commander for the invasion, justified a landing as the only way to win the war quickly. The army argued that the bombing and blockade strategy would require another year before it forced Japan to accept unconditional surrender—more time than it was believed the war-weary American public would accept. Moreover, there was no guar-antee that such a campaign would be successful. And there were the uncertain consequences of Soviet entry into the Pacific war. Admiral King went along with the invasion, he later explained, more as an obligatory show of unanimity among the Joint Chiefs than in belief in the necessity of an invasion.

Once he had committed the navy to the project, King pulled no punches. The number of vessels gathered for the invasion by August was staggering: 1,137 combat ships, 14,847 planes, 2,783 large land-ing craft, and thousands of smaller craft—all supported by 400 advance bases and hundreds of supply vessels. Some 155,000 soldiers had been sent directly from Europe to Pacific staging areas and another half-million were designated to follow.

This force was not used. The awful cost of capturing Iwo Jima and Okinawa—total casualties for the two operations exceeded those suffered during the previous three years of the Pacific war—forced President Harry S Truman, Roosevelt's successor, and the Joint Chiefs to have second thoughts about an invasion of Japan. Heavy American casualties were feared and losses among the Japanese military and civilians were expected to far exceed them. Marshall was also worried that the huge Japanese forces in China and Southeast Asia might continue to fight on even if the government in Tokyo were to give up. Later, it was learned that the Japanese had hoarded some 5,000 planes plus fuel and armaments for use as kamikazes, plus another 5,000 for conventional missions, and were fortifying the landing beaches for a fight to the death. The alternative was to use the atom bomb, which had been developed to be used against Nazi Germany, against Japan. An experimental bomb had been successfully tested on July 16, and within hours *Indianapolis* had departed San Francisco for Tinian with the detonation device of the deadly weapon that was to be dropped from a B-29.[*]

On the Japanese side, Baron Kantaro Suzuki—the head of the new government that had come to power in April—wished to make peace, as did Emperor Hirohito, but Suzuki was afraid to cross hard-line

---

[*]With its supersecret mission completed, *Indianapolis* sailed for Guam and then Leyte on July 28, where she was due at 1100 on July 31. The port director at Guam sent this information to the Philippine Sea Frontier's port director at Tacloban and to Rear Admiral Lynde D. McCormick, to whom the cruiser was to report. The message was received on board *Idaho*, McCormick's flagship, in a garbled form which could not be deciphered, but her communications officer did not ask for a repeat. As a result, the most important addressee, who was to have expected the ship by a certain date, was not looking for her.

Submarines had been reported in the area, and Captain Charles B. McVay 3d had orders to zigzag "at discretion," which he did by day but not at night, when it was overcast. On the evening of July 30, *Indianapolis* was sighted by the Japanese submarine *I-58*, which fired a spread of six torpedoes at her; two of these ripped the bottom out of her. Of the 1,199 men on board, between 800 and 850 men survived the sinking, but because of blunders ashore the ship's failure to arrive was not noted, and a report by an air-force pilot of seeing Very lights at sea and an Ultra decrypt of the Japanese captain's contact report were also ignored. The *Indianapolis*'s survivors were not discovered for eighty-four hours. Only 316 were still alive after a harrowing battle with sharks and exposure.

In a public-relations gesture to the families of those lost, McVay was court-martialed for endagering his ship by failing to zig-zag. He was found guilty and was ordered to lose a hundred numbers in seniority within his grade. With the court's recommendation, the sentence was remitted and he was restored to duty. McVay retired in 1949 with a "gravestone" promotion to rear admiral. He committed suicide in 1968. Many naval officers saw him as a scapegoat for the mistakes of others. See Newcomb, *Abandon Ship!*; Kurzman, *Fatal Voyage*.

segments of the military determined to continue the war. Confused efforts were made to persuade the Russians to intercede with the other Allies, but nothing came of these moves because Stalin was planning to enter the fighting. On July 26, the Allied leaders, meeting in Potsdam, outside Berlin, presented Japan with an ultimatum: unconditional surrender, relinquishment of all conquests since 1895, and Allied occupation until the establishment of a "peacefully inclined and responsible government." The alternative was "prompt and utter destruction." Suzuki, more frightened of the Japanese militarists than of the Allied powers, rejected the Potsdam Declaration.

The fearful consequences came soon after. Hiroshima and Nagasaki, with both military bases and war industries, were selected as targets for the atom bomb. The civilian populations were showered with leaflets warning them to leave the cities. There may have been reasons for resorting to the bomb other than forcing Japan to surrender. It may have been intended to overawe the Soviets. And then, simply possessing the bomb may have been its own imperative.

On August 6, a B-29 dropped an atom bomb on Hiroshima, and three days later, another was exploded over Nagasaki, with horrifying results. The bombs killed upward of 140,000 people, not to mention those who died over the years from radiation sickness, and razed both cities. The Soviet Union hurled its armies into Japanese-occupied Manchuria. Even then, some diehards wished to fight on. General Korechiki Anami, the war minister, implored the Supreme Council for one last great battle on Japanese soil—as demanded by the national honor. But the catastrophes convinced the emperor of the futility of further resistance, and he announced Japan's surrender on August 14. Every man in the Pacific war zone or bound there breathed a prayer of thanks. It meant they would live.[*]

TF 38 had completed a carrier strike over the Tokyo area and had just launched another when it received orders from Admiral Nimitz to "cease fire."

---

[*]The U.S. Navy lost 57,595 men killed and missing in World War II and 94,165 wounded. Marine casualties totaled 27,267 men killed and another 62,207 wounded. The Coast Guard lost 1,917 killed and 955 wounded. Eight hundred and eighty-one merchant seamen were killed and another 4,780 were reported missing. A total of 502 navy ships of various types were sunk, including 156 combat vessels (Baer, *One Hundred Years of Sea Power*, p. 272).

Epilogue

Wreathed in the acrid white smoke of salutes, *Missouri* lay at anchor in Tokyo Bay on Sunday, September 2, 1945. Hundreds of warships swarmed about the battleship's massive gray bulk as she loomed out of the overcast. From her flagstaff rippled the flag that had flown over the U.S. Capitol on December 7, 1941. Representatives of all the Allied nations were taking their places on *Missouri*'s quarterdeck for the formal surrender of the Japanese Empire. It was one day short of six years since Britain and France had declared war on Nazi Germany. The fast carriers that had played a key role in bringing Japan to her knees rode over the horizon. Admiral Halsey had kept them at sea, ready to launch aircraft in case the Japanese surrender turned out to be a sham. Stern ranks of Allied officers, none wearing decorations or sidearms, silently greeted the Japanese as they came on board from a destroyer, eleven impassive figures in black morning coats and military drab.

"We are gathered here, representatives of the major warring powers, to conclude a solemn agreement whereby peace may be restored," intoned General MacArthur into a battery of five microphones. Although he was stiffly erect, close observers noted that his hands were trembling. He called upon the nations of the world, both victors and vanquished, to rise above past hatreds "to the higher dignity which alone benefits the sacred purposes we are about to serve.

. . . It is my earnest hope—indeed the hope of all mankind—that from this solemn occasion a better world shall emerge. . . ."

Almost as if on cue, the clouds dissolved and *Missouri's* deck sparkled in the sunshine. Amid profound silence, the signing of the instruments of surrender began, the defeated going first. The documents were placed on one of the battleship's mess tables, which was covered by a green baize cloth. Using six pens, MacArthur signed as Supreme Commander for the Allied Powers. Admiral Nimitz signed for the United States and Admiral Fraser for Britain, followed by representatives of all the other Allies. Once the last signature had been affixed, MacArthur declared the proceedings closed at 0918. It was 1,364 days since the Japanese attack on Pearl Harbor.

MacArthur walked over to Halsey and, putting his arm around the admiral's shoulders said, "Start 'em up now!"

"Aye, aye, sir!" replied Halsey with a broad grin.

The sky above rumbled as a mass flight of B-29s and hundreds of carrier planes swept over the battleship. All the great names evocative of aerial combat above the sea were there—Hellcats . . . Corsairs . . . Avengers . . . Helldivers—wings seeming to stretch from horizon to horizon. Following a long, sweeping turn over the fleet, they flew away into the sunlight, streaming from the snow-crowned tip of Fujiyama.

Appendix I

TABLE OF EQUIVALENT RANKS

U.S. NAVY	ROYAL NAVY	KRIEGSMARINE
Fleet Admiral	Admiral of the Fleet	Grossadmiral
Admiral	Admiral	Admiral
Vice-Admiral	Vice-Admiral	Vizeadmiral
Rear Admiral	Rear Admiral	Konteradmiral
Commodore	Commodore	Kommodore
Captain	Captain	Kapitän zur See
—	—	Fregattenkapitän
Commander	Commander	Korvettenkapitän
Lieutenant Commander	Lieutenant Commander	Kapitänleutnant
Lieutenant	Lieutenant	Oberleutnant zur See
Lieutenant Junior Grade (j.g.)	—	—
Ensign	Sub-Lieutenant	Leutnant zur See

Appendix II

BATTLE OF THE ATLANTIC

Allied Ship and Axis Submarine Losses*

	TOTAL	SHIPS SUNK BY SUBMARINE	SUBMARINES LOST
1939	222	114	9
1940	1,059	471	22
1941	1,299	432	35
1942	1,664	1,160	85
1943	597	377	237
1944	205	132	241
1945	105	56	153

PACIFIC OCEAN

U.S. Submarine Campaign Statistics*

	JAPANESE WARSHIP LOSSES NUMBER	TONNAGE	JAPANESE MERCHANTMAN LOSSES NUMBER	TONNAGE	U.S. SUBMARINE PATROLS	U.S. SUBMARINES LOST
1941–42	2	11.0	180.0	725	350	8
1943	22	29.1	335.0	1,500	350	17
1944	104	405.7	603.0	2,700	520	19
1945	60	66.1	186.5	415	330	8

*Approximate figures.

534

Maps

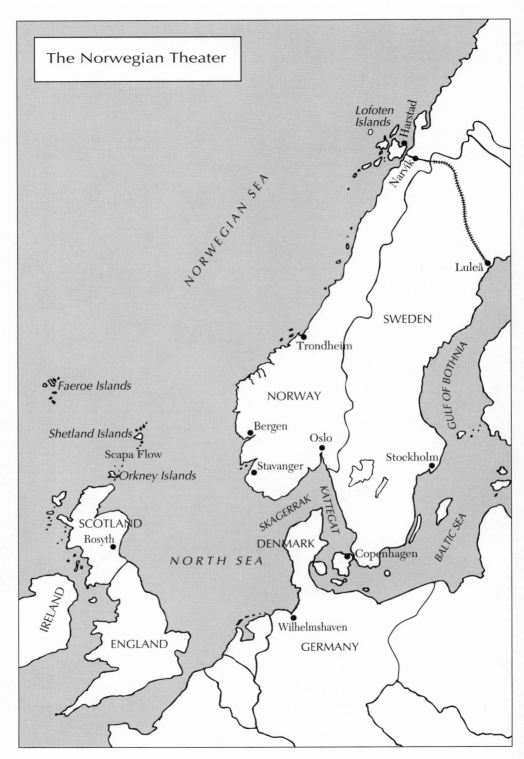

The Norwegian Theater

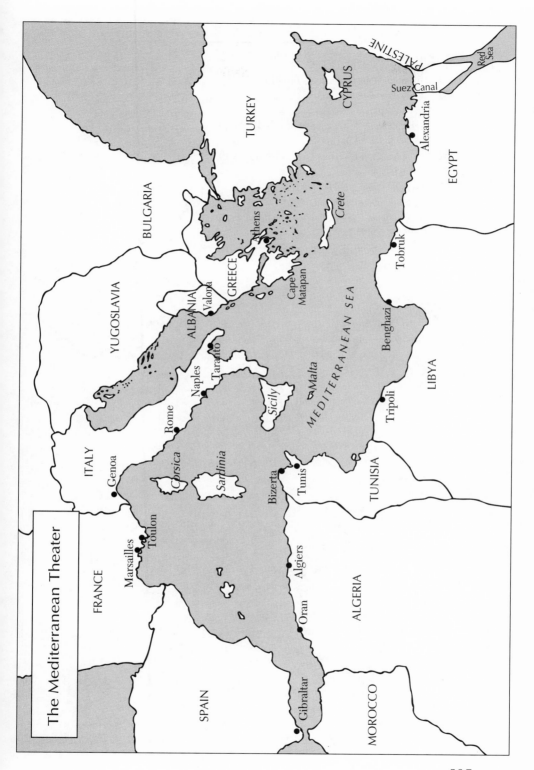

The Mediterranean Theater

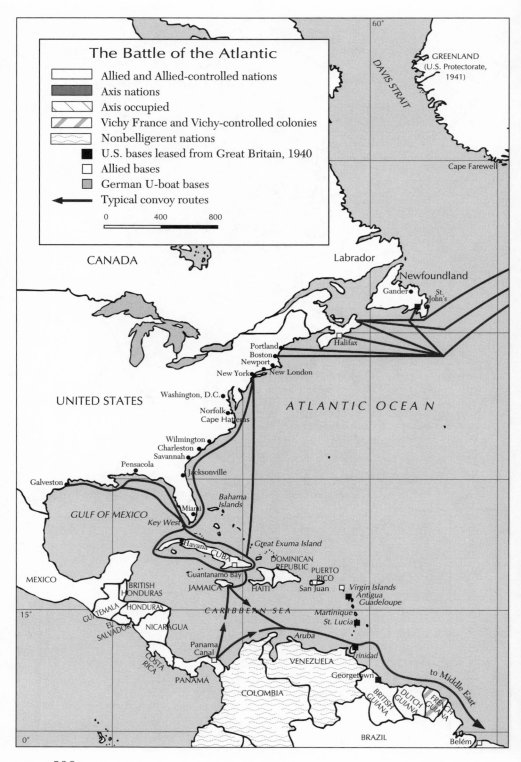

The Battle of the Atlantic

- Allied and Allied-controlled nations
- Axis nations
- Axis occupied
- Vichy France and Vichy-controlled colonies
- Nonbelligerent nations
- U.S. bases leased from Great Britain, 1940
- Allied bases
- German U-boat bases
- Typical convoy routes

0   400   800

GREENLAND
(U.S. Protectorate,
1941)

DAVIS STRAIT

60°

Cape Farewell

CANADA

Labrador

Newfoundland

Gander   St. John's

Halifax

Portland
Boston
Newport
New York   New London

Washington, D.C.

UNITED STATES

Norfolk
Cape Hatteras

ATLANTIC OCEAN

Wilmington
Charleston
Savannah

Pensacola

Jacksonville

Galveston

Bahama
Islands

GULF OF MEXICO

Miami

Key West

Great Exuma Island

Havana   CUBA

DOMINICAN
REPUBLIC

MEXICO

Guantanamo Bay

PUERTO
RICO

San Juan

Virgin Islands
Antigua
Guadeloupe

BRITISH
HONDURAS

JAMAICA

HAITI

GUATEMALA

HONDURAS

Martinique
St. Lucia

EL
SALVADOR

NICARAGUA

15°

CARIBBEAN SEA

Aruba

Panama
Canal

VENEZUELA

Trinidad

to Middle East

COSTA
RICA

PANAMÁ

Georgetown

COLOMBIA

BRITISH
GUIANA

DUTCH
GUIANA

FRENCH
GUIANA

0°

BRAZIL

Belém

538

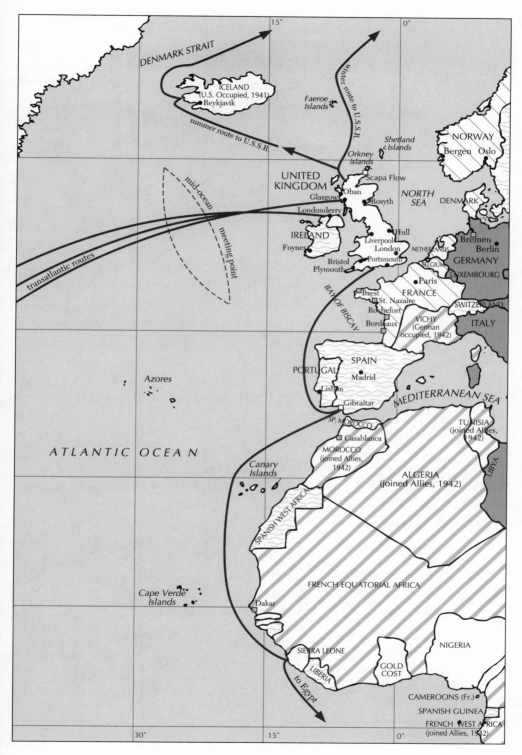

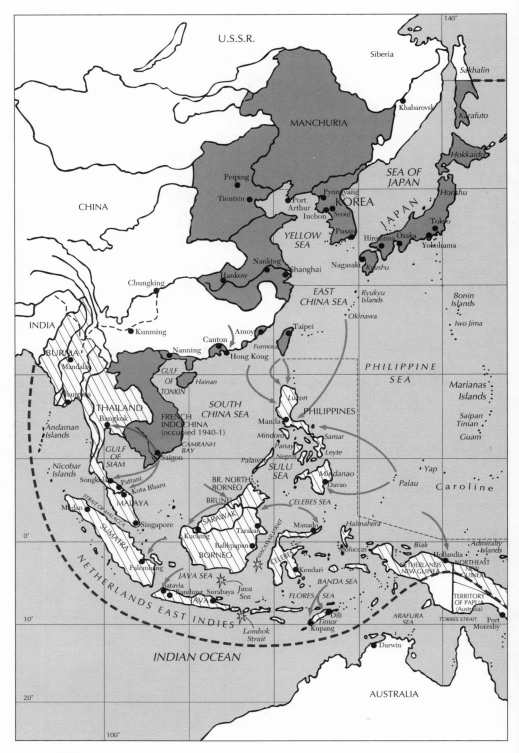

U.S.S.R.

Siberia

Sakhalin

MANCHURIA

Khabarovsk

Karafuto

CHINA

Peiping

Tientsin

SEA OF
JAPAN

Hokkaido

Honshu

Port
Arthur
Inchon

Pyongyang

KOREA

Seoul

JAPAN

Tokyo

Pusan

Hiroshima Osaka

Yokohama

YELLOW
SEA

Nanking

Shanghai

Nagasaki Kyushu

Chungking

Hankow

EAST
CHINA SEA

Ryukyu
Islands

Bonin
Islands

Kunming

Canton Amoy

Okinawa

Iwo Jima

Nanning

Hong Kong

Taipei

PHILIPPINE
SEA

INDIA

BURMA

Mandalay

GULF
OF
TONKIN

Formosa

Hainan

Marianas
Islands

Rangoon

THAILAND

SOUTH
CHINA SEA

Luzon

PHILIPPINES

Saipan
Tinian

Andaman
Islands

Bangkok

FRENCH
INDOCHINA
(occupied 1940-1)

Manila

Mindoro

Samar

Guam

CAMRANH
BAY

Palawan

Panay
Negros Leyte

Nicobar
Islands

GULF
OF
SIAM

Saigon

SULU
SEA

Mindanao

Yap

Songkhla
Pattani
Kota Bharu

STRAIT OF MALACCA

Davao

Palau

Caroline

Medan

MALAYA

BR. NORTH
BORNEO

CELEBES SEA

Singapore

SARAWAK

Kuching

BRUNEI

Tarakan

Manado

Halmahera

Biak

Admiralty
Islands

Hollandia

SUMATRA

Balikpapan

BORNEO

MACASSAR STRAIT

CELEBES

Moluccas

NETHERLANDS
NEW GUINEA

NORTHEAST
NEW GUINEA

Palembang

JAVA SEA

Kendari

BANDA SEA

Batavia
Bandung Surabaya

Java
Sea

TERRITORY
OF PAPUA
(Australia)

JAVA

FLORES   SEA

NETHERLANDS EAST INDIES

Dili
Timor
Kupang

ARAFURA
SEA

TORRES STRAIT

Port
Moresby

Lombok
Strait

Darwin

INDIAN OCEAN

AUSTRALIA

140°

100°

0°

10°

20°

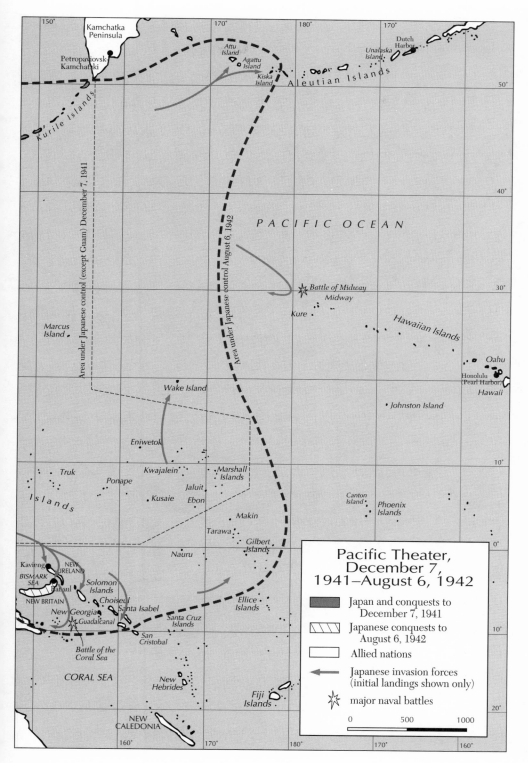

Pacific Theater,
December 7,
1941–August 6, 1942

Japan and conquests to
December 7, 1941

Japanese conquests to
August 6, 1942

Allied nations

Japanese invasion forces
(initial landings shown only)

major naval battles

0   500   1000

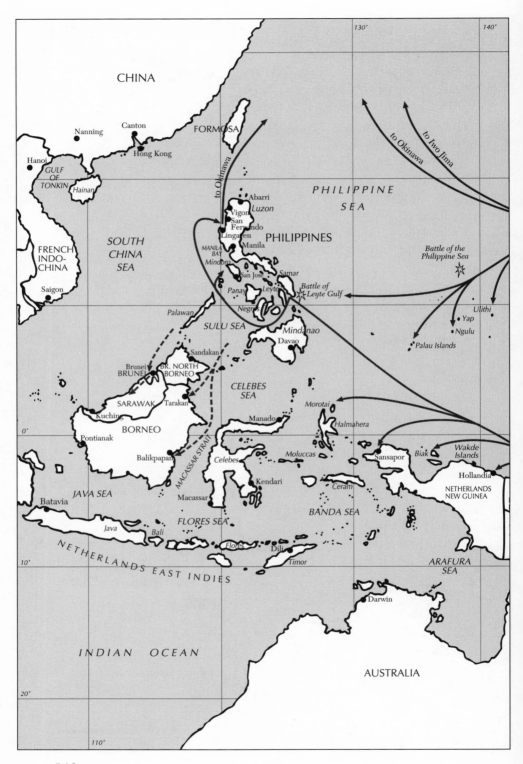

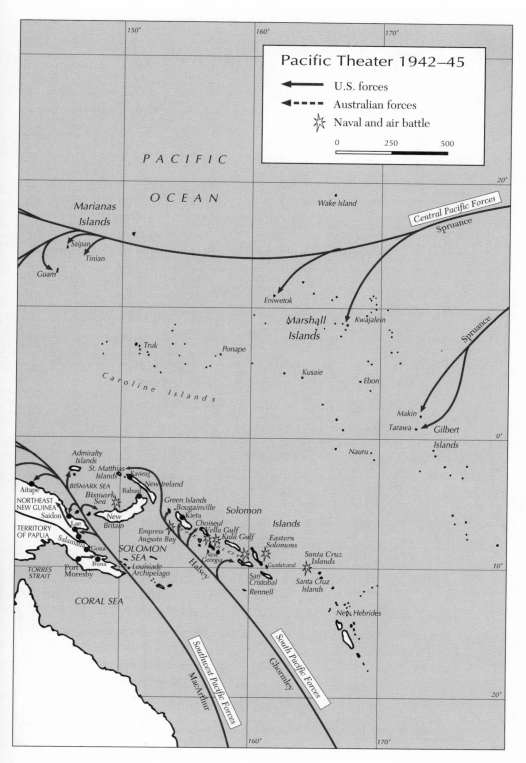

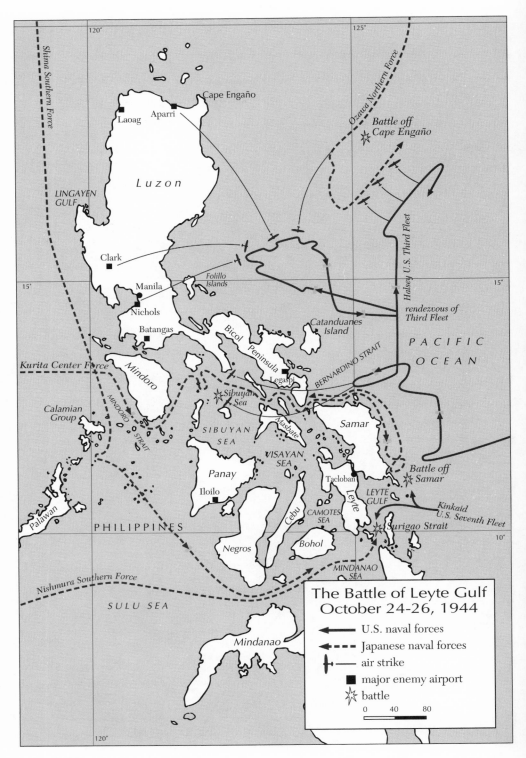

The Battle of Leyte Gulf
October 24–26, 1944

U.S. naval forces
Japanese naval forces
air strike
major enemy airport
battle

0   40   80

Notes

PROLOGUE

For life on a U-boat, see Buchheim, *The U-Boat War*. For the sinking of the *Athenia*, see ADM 199/140; Caulfield, *Tomorrow Never Came*; Showell, ed., *Fuehrer Conferences on Naval Affairs*, pp. 1–2; Padfield, *Dönitz*, pp. 191–94; Hughes and Costello, *The Battle of the Atlantic*, pp. 5–7; *The Trial of the Major War Criminals*, vol. V, pp. 264–71; and Rohwer and Hummelchen, *Chronology of the War at Sea*, p. 1.

CHAPTER 1

Churchill's own account of his arrival at the Admiralty is in Churchill, *The Second World War*, vol. I, p. 410; also see Manchester, *Last Lion*, vol. II, p. 547. Royal Navy reaction to Churchill's return is in Gretton, *Former Naval Person*, p. 253. "daily prayers" is in Roskill, *Churchill and the Admirals*, p. 93; Gretton, *Former Naval Person*, pp. 259, 283. "A quarter of a century" is in Churchill, *The Second World War*, vol. I, p. 410. "It was as if" is in R. Hough, *The Longest Battle*, p. 3. Statistics on cargoes are in Ellis, *Brute Force*, p. 133. "A realistic policy" is in Dönitz, *The Conduct of the War at Sea*, p. 33. "The German flag" is in Marder, *From the Dreadnaught to Scapa Flow*, vol. V, pp. 190–91. For World War I at sea, see Bennett, *Naval Battles of the First World War*. For the run-up to the Washington Conference, the conference itself, and the aftermath, see N. Miller, *The U.S. Navy*, pp. 193–98; Kaufman, *Arms Control During the Pre-Nuclear Era*. "a major defeat" is in Morison, *The Two-Ocean War*, p. 9. For the state of the Fleet Air Arm, see Miller, *The Naval Air War*, pp. 15–16. "Not one exercise" is in Roskill, *Naval Policy Between the Wars*, vol. I, p. 536. For British attitude toward convoys, see ADM 234/241. For the German navy between the wars, see Ruge, *Der Seekrieg*; Von der Porten, *Pictorial History of the German Navy*. For the clandestine building of submarines, see Van der Vat, *The Atlantic Campaign*, pp. 43–68. For the ideology of the German navy, see C. S. Thomas, *The German Navy in the Nazi Era*; Rust, *Naval Officers Under Hitler*. "the eerie" is quoted in Von der Porten, *Pictorial History*, p. 14. "the submarine should never again" is in Roskill, *The War at Sea*, vol. I, p. 34. Germany's producing only four submarines a month is in Dönitz, *Conduct*, p. 3. For the German navy and the Luftwaffe, see Ruge, *Der Seekrieg*, pp. 46–49. For the Z-Plan, see ibid.; Von der Porten, *Pictorial History*. "In no circumstances" is in Dönitz, *Memoirs*. p. 42. "My God!" is in Padfield, *Dönitz*, p. 188. For the state of the German navy in 1939, see Ruge, *Der Seekrieg*, p. 46; Dönitz, *Conduct*, p. 3. "As far as the Kriegsmarine" is in C. S. Thomas, *German Navy*, p. 187. For Raeder's war strategy, see Ruge, *Der Seekrieg*, pp. 44–50; Von der Porten, *Pictorial History*, pp. 40–43. For the American reaction, see N. Miller, *F.D.R.*, pp. 438–41. Convoy in the Place de la Concorde is in Hughes and Costello, *Battle*, p. 48. Torpedo troubles and Dönitz reaction are in Terraine, *The U-Boat Wars*, pp. 231–41. "to Mr. Churchill" is in W. Frank, *The Sea Wolves*, p. 29. For mining operations, see Ruge, *Der Seekrieg*, pp. 67–68; Griffiths, *The Hidden Menace*, pp. 70–102. For Churchill and the misuse of "hunter" groups of carriers, see Churchill, *The Second World War*, vol. I, pp. 362–63; Roskill, *War at Sea*, vol. I, pp. 134–35; Roskill, *White Ensign*, p. 41; Gretton, *Former Naval Person*, pp. 263–64. For the downing of two Skuas, see Price, *Aircraft Versus Submarine*, p. 44. For attack on *Ark Royal*, see Pearce, *Great Naval Battles*, pp. 24–25. For loss of *Courageous*, see ADM 199/157. For the sinking of *Royal Oak*, see ADM 199/158; Weaver, *Nightmare at Scapa Flow*; Snyder, *The Royal Oak Disaster*; Prien's ghost-written account, *I Sank the Royal Oak*, is unreliable on many points. For the defects in the defenses of Scapa Flow, see Churchill, *The Second World War*, vol. I, p. 383. For Dönitz and the attack, see Padfield, *Dönitz*, pp. 201–2. Herrmann's comments are in Weaver, *Nightmare*, p. 24. *U-47*'s log is in Showell, ed., *Fuehrer Conferences on Naval Affairs*, p. 50. "Don't go Daisy" is in Weaver, *Nightmare*, p. 70. "No threat by other countries" is in Hughes and Costello, *Battle*, p. 42. "Rescue no one" is in Padfield, *Dönitz*, p. 206. Recall of the *Deutschland* is in Showell, ed., *Fuehrer Conferences*, p. 54. "On land I am" is in Von der Porten, *Pictorial History*, p. 61. For cruise of *Scharnhorst* and *Gneisenau* and sinking of *Rawalpindi*, see Bekker, *Hitler's Navy*, pp. 41–55. For the *Graf Spee*, see ADM 186/794; Pope, *Graf Spee*. Briefer accounts of the Battle of the River Plate are in Stephen, *Sea Battles in Close-Up*, pp. 10–29; Von der Porten, *Pictorial History*, pp. 67–77; Roskill, *War at Sea*, vol. I, pp. 118–21. "sickening feeling" is in Pope, *Graf Spee*, p. 153. "Prospects of continuing" is in ADM 186/794. For the diplomatic maneuvering, see Millington-Drake, *The Drama of the Graf Spee*. "No internment" is in Showell, ed., *Fuehrer Conferences*, pp. 68–69. "He should have" is in Van der Vat, *The Atlantic Campaign*, p. 96. Churchill's comment is in Bennett, *Naval Battles of World World II*, p. 16.

CHAPTER 2

The *Altmark* affair is covered in ADM 199/280; Vian, *Action This Day*, pp. 24–31; Cant, *The War at Sea*, p. 63; Frischauer and Jackson, *The Navy's Here!* McNeill's comments are in Cant, *The War at Sea*, p. 63. "Any British" is in Frischauer and Jackson, p. 237. For background to Norwegian operations, see Moulton, *A Study of Warfare in Three Dimensions*. For Churchill's views on Norway, see Churchill, *The Second World War*, vol. I, pp. 479–92. For Operation Catherine, see Churchill, *The Second World War*, vol. I, pp. 626–28; Marder, *From the Dardanelles to Oran*, pp. 140–47. For the mining, see Roskill, *The War at Sea*, vol. I, pp. 157–59. For the German view, see Ruge, *Der Seekrieg*, pp. 78–83; Assmann, "The Invasion of Norway"; Fuehrer Conference of Oct. 10, 1939, in Showell, ed., *Fuehrer Conferences on Naval Affairs*, p. 47. For meetings with Quisling and planning for Norwegian operations, see Showell, ed., *Fuehrer Conferences*, pp. 63–67. "I went out" is quoted in Humble, *Hitler's High Seas Fleet*, p. 49. Specific plans for Norwegian operation are in Ruge, *Der Seekrieg*, pp. 84–85. "The operation in itself" is in Showell, ed., *Fuehrer Conferences*, pp. 84–87. "All these reports" is in Roskill, *War at Sea*, vol. I, p. 159. Moulton's account is in his *Study of Warfare*, p. 296. For the voyage of the German destroyers, see Dickens, *Narvik*, pp. 22–24. For the *Glowworm* epic, see ibid.; Macintyre, *Narvik*, pp. 30–31. For a discussion of Forbes's difficulties, see Roskill, *Churchill and the Admirals*, pp. 99–100. For the Home Fleet's movements, see Roskill, *War at Sea*, vol. I, pp. 160–61; ADM 186/798. For Churchill and Plan R-4, see Roskill, *War at Sea*, vol. I, pp. 161–62. "Look, Sir!" is in Dickens, *Narvik*, p. 34. For the battle-cruiser action, see ibid., pp. 31–35; Roskill, *War at Sea*, vol. I, pp. 165–66. For the German landings, see Von der Porten, *Pictorial History of the German Navy in World War II*, pp. 91–94; Moulton, *Study of Warfare*, pp. 74–99. For the British reaction, see ibid, pp. 104–9. Prien's comment is in Dönitz, *Memoirs*, p. 89. The air attack on *Königsberg* is in Cameron, *Wings of the Morning*. For the two Battles of Narvik, see ADM 199/473, 474, 475, 476, 478. For Warburton-Lee's attack on Narvik, see Dickens, *Narvik*, pp. 48–96. For the Second Battle of Narvik, see ibid., pp. 112–55; Roskill, *H.M.S. Warspite*, pp. 202–8. For Whitworth at Narvik and Roskill's observations, see Roskill, *War at Sea*, vol. I, p. 178. For the Trondheim operation, see Moulton, *Study of Warfare*, pp. 199–213. "The whole place" is quoted in Winton, *Carrier Glorious*, p. 114. "Our Fleet Air Arm air-craft" is quoted in ibid., p. 156. "In the course of" is quoted in Roskill, *War at Sea*, vol. I, p. 190. For Narvik operations, see Moulton, *Study of Warfare*, pp. 214–60; Roskill, *War at Sea*, vol. I, pp. 190–93. For German operations, see Von der Porten, *Pictorial History*, pp. 103–9; Bekker, *Hitler's Naval War*, pp. 141–66. "Thick funnel" is quoted in Bekker, *Hitler's Naval War*, p. 155. For the loss of *Glorious*, see Winton, *Carrier Glorious*, pp. 164–82. "like the lid" is quoted in Von der Porten, *Pictorial History*, p. 107. "Slowly the giant" is quoted in Winton, *Carrier Glorious*, p. 217. For Roskill's comments, see Roskill, *War at Sea*, vol. I, p. 196.

CHAPTER 3

"We have been defeated" is in Churchill, *The Second World War*, vol. II, p. 42. "The small countries" is in ibid., p. 24. For the technique and weapons of the blitzkrieg, see Deighton, *Bliztkrieg*. For a concise discussion of the reasons for the French collapse, see Cohen and Gooch, *Military Misfortunes*, ch. VIII. For limited role of the German navy in the offensive, see Ruge, *Der Seekrieg*, pp. 97–100. For the Royal Navy, see Roskill, *The War at Sea*, vol. I, pp. 205–15. "in readiness" is in Churchill, *The Second World War*, vol. II, pp. 58–59. For Channel operations during 1940, see ADM 199/360, ADM 234/360. The best general account of the naval side of Dunkirk is Divine, *The Nine Days of Dunkirk*; also see Gelb, *Dunkirk*; Harman, *Dunkirk*; Roskill, *War at Sea*, vol. I, pp. 216–28; for a French account, see Auphan, *The French Navy in World War II*, pp. 68–82. "Should prepare" is in Churchill, *The Second World War*, vol. II, p. 99. "Let's hope" is in Harman, *Dunkirk*, p. 127. "Immediately" is in ibid., p. 128. "like some mighty" is in Gelb, *Dunkirk*, p. 203. Lightoller's account is in Harman, *Dunkirk*, pp. 203–4. For FDR and the situation in Europe, see Miller, *F.D.R.*, pp. 441–55; Heinrichs, *Threshold of War*. "Dollars cannot" is in Morison, *The History of U.S. Naval Operations During World War II*, vol. I, p. 28. "Hitler is now" is in *The Ciano Diaries*, p. 266. For reading the Luftwaffe version of Enigma, see Kahn, *Seizing the Enigma*, pp. 114–15. For the invasion of Britain, see Ansel, *Hitler Confronts England*; Fleming, *Operation Sea Lion*. For the British attack on the French fleet, see ADM 186/797, "Battle Summary No. 1," Tate, *The Deadly Stroke*, Churchill, *The Second World War*, vol. II, pp. 235–41; Marder, *From the Dardanelles to Oran*, pp. 179–288; for the French version, see Auphan, *French Navy*, pp. 122–39; "one of the most disagreeable" is in Churchill, *The Second World War*, vol. II, p. 235. For Directive No. 16, see Showell, ed., *Fuehrer Conferences on Naval Affairs*, pp. 116–17. "Tell me your opinion" is in Bekker, *Hitler's Naval War*, pp. 169–70. For the "Happy Time," see Padfield, *Dönitz*, pp. 219–26; Ministry of Defence, *The U-Boat War in the Atlantic*, ch. II; Macintyre, *The Battle of the Atlantic*, ch. III. "We all felt" is in

Hughes and Costello, *The Battle of the Atlantic*, p. 89. "Obtain a" is in Bekker, *Hitler's Naval War*, p. 190. "The high tonnage losses" is in Rohwer, "The U-Boat War" in *Decisive Battles of World War II*, p. 263. "As darkness came" is in Hughes and Costello, *The Battle of the Atlantic*, p. 106. For the corvette, see Preston and Raven, *The Flower Class Corvette*. For the destroyer transfer, see Goodhart, *Fifty Ships That Changed the World*; Churchill, *The Second World War*, vol. II, pp. 398–416. For the Battle of Britain, see Churchill, *The Second World War*, vol. II, pp. 319–80; Townsend, *Duel of Eagles*; Deighton, *Fighter*; for the German side, see Murray, *Luftwaffe*, pp. 43–61. For the final preparation for Sea Lion, see Fleming, *Operation Sea Lion*, pp. 287–90.

CHAPTER 4

For a general account of the naval war in the Mediterranean from June 1940 to June 1941, see Macintyre, *The Battle for the Mediterranean*; Roskill, *The War at Sea*, vol. I, chh. XV, XX. "You may be sure" is in Pack, *Cunningham*, p. 86. For a look at the status of the Italian navy at the start of the war, see Bragadin, *The Italian Navy in World War II*, ch. I; Sadkovich, *The Italian Navy in World War II*. Comments on its inferiority complex are in Ruge, *Der Seekrieg*, p. 134. "try out the Italian air" is in Macintyre, *The Battle of the Mediterranean*, p. 19. For the *Espero* fight, see Bragadin, *Italian Navy*, pp. 20–21; Cant, *The War at Sea*, pp. 166–68. "How a ship shakes" is in in Bradford, *The Mighty Hood*, pp. 139–40. The most complete account of the action off Calabria is in Smith, *Action Imminent*, pp. 34–105. "ABC felt that" is in Bennett, *Naval Battles of World War II*, p. 114. "The Italians' shooting" is in ibid. "I saw the great" is in Cunningham, *A Sailor's Odyssey*, p. 262. "At times a ship" is in ibid. "Bombs, bombs" is in Smith, *Action Imminent*, p. 98. For Dakar, see Marder, *Operation Menace*; Roskill, *War at Sea*, vol. I, pp. 308–19; Auphan, *The French Navy in World War II*, pp. 183–93. For the Cape Spada encounter, see Bragadin, *Italian Navy*, pp. 30–31. "Our principal trouble" is in Pack, *Cunningham*, p. 100. For the Taranto attack, see ADM 234/325; *London Gazette*, suppl., July 14, 1947; Schofield, *Taranto*. "That's Taranto" is in Cameron, *Wings of the Morning*, p. 49. "She saw us" is in ibid., p. 53. For Cape Spartivento, see Smith, *Action Imminent*, pp. 259–334; Bragadin, *Italian Navy*, pp. 49–54. "The Army owes" is in Pack, *Cunningham*, p. 119. "attack the British navy" is in Roskill, *War at Sea*, vol. I, p. 420. For the attack on *Illustrious*, see Smith, *The History of Dive Bombing*, pp. 108–15. For Matapan, see ADM 186/797, "Battle Summary No. 44"; Pack, *The Battle of Matapan*; shorter versions are in Roskill, *War at Sea*, vol. I, pp. 427–31; Pack, *Cunningham*, ch. XI; Bennett, *Naval Battles*, pp. 118–34; for the Italian view, see Bragadin, *Italian Navy*, pp. 85–98; the intelligence background of the battle is in Hinsley, *British Intelligence in the Second World War*, vol. I, pp. 403–6. Cunningham's subterfuges are in Cunningham, *Sailor's Odyssey*, pp. 325–26. "I felt" is in Bennett, *Naval Battles*, p. 134, n. 10. "We were shot at" is in Pack, *Matapan*, p. 52. "with his mouth full" is in ibid., p. 75. "a caged tiger" is in ibid., p. 39. "No prudent staff officer" is in ibid., p. 93. "You're a pack" is in ibid., p. 115. "One heard" is in Cunningham, *Sailor's Odyssey*, p. 332. For the destroyer action off Tripoli, see Macintyre, *Battle for the Mediterranean*, pp. 58–59. For the attack on Tripoli, see Roskill, *Churchill and the Admirals*, pp. 182–85; Pack, *Cunningham*, pp. 156–58. For the Greek and Cretan campaigns and their aftermath, see D. A. Thomas, *Nazi Victory*. For Cunningham's account see Pack, *Cunningham*, pp. 155–83; *London Gazette*, suppl., May 24, 1948; German comments are in Ruge, *Der Seekrieg*, pp. 190–95. "With a torch" is in Roskill, *War at Sea*, vol. I, pp. 446–47. "I feel the episode" is in Cunningham, *Sailor's Odyssey*, p. 357. Mountbatten's comments are in R. Hough, *The Longest Battle*, p. 224. "I shall never forget" is in Cunningham, *Sailor's Odyssey*, p. 384. "It takes three years" is Pack, *Cunningham*, p. 177.

CHAPTER 5

The cruise of *Admiral Scheer* is covered in Krancke's own account (written with H. J. Brenneke), *Battleship Scheer*. "exceptionally favorable" is in Bekker, *Hitler's Naval War*, p. 202. British reaction to *Scheer*'s cruise is in Roskill, *The War at Sea*, vol. I, pp. 289–92. The most complete account of the German auxiliary cruisers is D. Woodward, *The Secret Raiders*; also see Rogge and Frank, *The German Raider Atlantis*; Detmers, *The Raider Kormoran*; ADM 234/324. For logistic problems, see Stratton, "Germany's Secret Navy Supply Service." "a cut flower" is in Churchill, *The World Crisis*, p. 185. "We hit with our" is in Woodward, *Secret Raiders*, p. 151. For *Hipper*'s cruise, see Bekker, *Hitler's Naval War*, pp. 207–8; Roskill, *War at Sea*, vol. I, pp. 291–92. For *Scharnhorst* and *Gneisenau*, see Handel-Mazzetti article; Von der Porten, *Pictorial History of the German Navy in World War II*, pp. 202–4; Bekker, *Hitler's Naval War*, pp. 209–15; Roskill, *War at Sea*, vol. I, pp. 373–78. For the *Bismarck* episode, see ADM 234/322; Kennedy, *Pursuit*; Grenfell; *The Bismarck Episode*; Ballard, *The Discovery of the Bismarck*; for a German survivor's account, see Müllenheim-Rechberg, *Battleship Bismarck*; there are succinct accounts in Roskill, *War at Sea*, vol. I, pp. 395–418; Bennett, *Naval Battles of World War II*, pp. 135–49. "seen it coming" is in Bekker, *Hitler's Naval War*, p. 220. For *Bismarck* leaving port, see Müllenheim-Rechberg, *Battleship Bismarck*, p. 100. Lütjen's orders are in ibid., app. B. "I'd like to" is in ibid., p. 86. Hitler's visit to *Bismarck* is in ibid., pp. 96–98. Informing Hitler of the sortie is in *Fuehrer Conferences on Naval Affairs*, p. 197. "lively misgivings" is in Raeder, *My Life*, p. 354. "Ship bearing" is in Ballard, *Discovery of the Bismarck*, p. 70. "The enemy ships" is in Bennett, *Naval Battles*, p. 137. "The *Hood!*" is in Müllenheim-Rechberg, *Battleship Bismarck*, p. 139. "The clock showed" is in ibid., p. 138–39. "We started turning" is in Hughes and Costello, *The Battle of the Atlantic*, p. 147. "She's blowing up!" is in Müllenheim-Rechberg, *Battleship Bismarck*, p. 142. "there had been a rushing sound" is in Ballard, *Discovery of the Bismarck*, p. 84. "Overwhelmed with joy" is in Müllenheim-Rechberg, *Battleship Bismarck*, p. 144. For the clash between Lindemann and Lütjens, see ibid., pp. 147–49. "For most Englishmen" is in Kennedy, *Pursuit*, p. 90. Churchill's observations are in *The Second World War*, vol. III, pp. 312–320. "It was incredible" is in Kennedy, *Pursuit*, p. 119. For the intelligence background to the pursuit of *Bismarck*, see Hinsley, *British Intelligence in the Second World War*, vol. I, pp. 339–46. For the French officer, see Kennedy, *Pursuit*, pp. 133–36. "Never been so scared" is in ibid., pp. 153–54; Lütjens's messages are in *Fuehrer Conferences*, pp. 209–13. "Sorry about" is in Kennedy, *Pursuit*, p. 165. "The enemy" is in ibid., p. 469. For *Bismarck*'s final fight, see the above sources plus Tovey's report in *London Gazette*, suppl., Oct. 14, 1947; also see ADM 234/322. "The sun appeared" is in Kennedy, *Pursuit*, p. 205. "Get closer" is in ibid. "Some men were trapped" is in Müllenheim-Rechberg, *Battleship Bismarck*, p. 274. For Enigma and the rounding up of the German supply network, see Hinsley, *British Intelligence*, vol. I, p. 245. For the end of the raiders, see Woodward, *Secret Raiders*; Roskill, *War at Sea*, vol. I, *passim*. "The loss of the *Bismarck*" is in Raeder, *My Life*, p. 214.

CHAPTER 6

For the return of *U-38*, see W. Frank, *The Sea Wolves*, pp. 85–86. "Dönitz seldom 'ordered' " is in Padfield, *Dönitz*, p. 227. Shirer's comment is in Shirer, *Berlin Diary*, p. 190. For the status of the U-boat war at beginning of 1941, see ADM 234/578, p. 66. "I am not at all certain" is in Ministry of Defence, *The U-Boat War in the Atlantic*, pp. 61–62. For Dönitz and KG 40, see ibid., pp. 62–64. "How willingly" is in Gilbert, *Churchill*, p. 691. Text of "Battle of the Atlantic directive" is in Roskill, *The War at Sea*, vol. I, app. O. For the loss of the "aces," see Van der Vat, *The Atlantic Campaign*, pp.

166–71; Terraine, *The U-Boat Wars*, pp. 313–16. Macintyre's account is in Macintyre, *U-Boat Killer*, pp. 101–5; also see Macintyre, *The Battle of the Atlantic*, pp. 79–85. For Dönitz's operations in early 1941, see Ministry of Defence, *U-Boat War*, pp. 71–76. For the Royal Navy's defense of the convoys, see ADM 234/578, pp. 70–78. For statistics on British imports, see Tarrant, *The U-Boat Offensive*, p. 100. For the problems of the Royal Canadian Navy, see Milner, *North Atlantic Run*; Lamb, *The Corvette Navy*. "The mess decks" is in Lamb, *Corvette Navy*, p. 24. For the Russian side of the sea war, see Achkasov and Pavlovich, *Soviet Naval Operations in the Great Patriotic War*. For the German side, see Ruge, *The Soviets as Naval Opponents*; Mitchell, *A History of Russian and Soviet Sea Power*, pp. 377–92; D. Woodward, *The Russians at Sea*, pp. 209–229. Directive No. 21 is in Showell, ed., *Fuehrer Conferences on Naval Affairs*, p. 159. For Enigma and Ultra, see McLachlan, *Room 39*; Kahn, *Seizing the Enigma*; Lewin, *Ultra Goes to War*. For the capture of *U-110*, see Roskill, *The Secret Capture*. "Coincidence" is in Padfield, *Dönitz*, p. 229. For operations off West Africa, see W. Frank, *Sea Wolves*, pp. 109–10; Ministry of Defence, *U-Boat War*, pp. 92–97. "Their sorties" is in Roskill, *War at Sea*, vol. I, p. 477. For Roosevelt and the road to war, see Miller, *F.D.R.*, pp. 459–76; Heinrichs, *Threshold of War*. "The days ground you" is quoted in Abbazia, *Mr. Roosevelt's Navy*, p. 318. "Every word" is in Churchill, *The Second World War*, vol. III, p. 432. For the *Greer* incident, see Abazzia, *Roosevelt's Navy*, chs. 20, 23, 25; Morison, *The History of U.S. Naval Operations During World War II*, Vol I, pp. 79–81, 92–98; German account of *Greer* incident is in *Fuehrer Conferences*, pp. 230–31; Churchill's reaction is in Churchill, *The Second World War*, vol. III, p. 517. "German forces must" is in *Fuehrer Conferences*, p. 232. For the *Kearny* affair, see Morison, *History*, Vol I, pp. 92–93. For *Reuben James*, see ibid.; *Washington Post*, Oct. 5, 1991. For Japan's reasons for fighting and the planning for Pearl Harbor, see Prange, *At Dawn We Slept*; Agawa, *The Reluctant Admiral*. "If I am told" is in Howarth, "Yamamoto," in *Men of War*, p. 114 "Pearl Harbor was still" is in Morison, *The History of U.S. Naval Operations During the Second World War*, vol. III, p. 94. Richardson discussed his dispute with Roosevelt in Richardson, *On the Treadmill to Pearl Harbor*, pp. 223–26. For Friedman and MAGIC, see N. Miller, *Spying for America*, pp. 263–67; Lewin, *The American Magic*. "Gentlemen, are they" is in Toland, *The Rising Sun*, p. 192.

CHAPTER 7

For Pearl Harbor, see Prange, *At Dawn We Slept*; Lord, *Day of Infamy*; Morison, *The History of U.S. Naval Operations During the Second World War*, vol. III, pp. 80–146; Okumiya and Horikoshi, *Zero!*; Fuchida and Okumiya, *Midway*, pp. 25–36; Dull, *A Battle History of the Imperial Japanese Navy*, pp. 3–20; Slackman, *Target: Pearl Harbor*; Okumiya, "Pearl Harbor: The Japanese Perspective." "Air Raid!" is in Lord, *Day of Infamy*, p. 71. "Powder!" is in ibid., p. 90. "bounce as if" is in Fuchida and Okumiya, *Midway*, p. 28. "Those of us" is in Young, *Trapped at Pearl Harbor*, p. 77. For discussion of conspiracy theories, see Prange, *At Dawn*, pp. 725–38, 839–50; Wohlstetter, *Pearl Harbor*, pp. 386–401; Lewin, *The American Magic*; Beach, "Who's to Blame?"; D. C. Richardson, "You Decide"; Layton, *"And I Was There"* and *Oral History* for his comments. U.S. Department of Defense, *The MAGIC Background to Pearl Harbor*. For post–Pearl Harbor events, see Lundstrom, *The First South Pacific Campaign*. For Wake Island see Heinl, *The Defense of Wake*; and Morison, *The History of U.S. Naval Operations During the Second World War*, vol. III, pp. 223–54; for MacArthur, see Manchester, *American Caesar*, pp. 205–12. For the Asiatic Fleet, see Leutze, *A Different Kind of Victory*, pp. 231–51; Winslow, *The Fleet the Gods Forgot*. "Instead of encountering" is in Sakai, *Samurai!* "The entire yard" is in Morison, *History*, vol. III, p. 173. For submarine failures, see Blair, *Silent Victory*, pp. 135–51. "Prime Minister, I" and "In all the war" is in Churchill, *The Second World War*, vol. III, p. 620. For the loss of Force Z, see ADM 234/330; Middlebrook, *Battleship*; Grenfell, *Main Fleet to Singapore*; Roskill, *The War at Sea*, vol. I, pp. 553–70. "Tom, when the first" is in Marder, *From the Dardanelles to Oran*, p. 167, n. 127. "Everyone was busy" is in Okumiya and Horikoshi, *Zero!*, p. 68. "What is the matter" is in ibid., p. 74. "nervous and shaky" is in ibid., pp. 76–77. "The air was filled" is in ibid., p. 79. For the Dutch East Indies campaign, see Van Oosten, *The Battle of the Java Sea*; Leutze, *Different Victory*, pp. 252–82; Winslow, *Fleet the Gods Forgot*; Morison, *History*, vol. III, pp. 271–380; Dull, *Battle History*, pp. 49–93. "The sound of our guns" is in Winslow, "Galloping Ghost." "A torpedo penetrated" is in ibid. For the Indian Ocean campaign, see Dull, *Battle History*, pp. 103–11; Roskill, *War at Sea*, vol. II, pp. 21–33. "Sighted enemy vessels" is in Okumiya and Horikoshi, *Zero!*, p. 92.

CHAPTER 8

For Tokyo raid, see Morison, *The History of U.S. Naval Operations During the Second World War*, vol. III, pp. 389–98. "hold what you've got" is in Lundstrom, *The First South Pacific Campaign*, n.p. Morison's comments on Nimitz are in Morison, *History*, vol. III, p. 256. For King's strategic thinking, see Buell, *Master of Sea Power*, p. 576. Brooke's comment is in Bryant, *The Turn of the Tide*, p. 446n. For comparison of Zero and Wildcat, see Lundstrom, *The First Team*, pp. 12–14, 185–86. For Imperial Japanese Navy training, see Parillo, "The Imperial Japanese Navy," in Sadkovich, ed., *Reevaluating Major Naval Combatants of World War II*, p. 62. "An eye" is in Lundstrom, *First Team*, p. 63. For the flight over the Owen Stanley Range, see ibid., pp. 127–28. "At this pace" is quoted in Layton, "Early Carrier Raids." "The wind and sea" is in Halsey and Bryan, *Admiral Halsey's Story*, p. 103. For Japanese planning of the Coral Sea offensive, see Dull, *A Battle History of the Imperial Japanese Navy*, pp. 113–20; Fuchida and Okumiya, *Midway*, pp. 48–63; Morison, *History*, vol. IV, pp. 3–20. For the intelligence background, see Holmes, *Double-Edged Secrets*; the Rochefort and Layton oral histories; Pineau, "Rochefort," in Howarth, ed., *Men of War*. For the battle, see Bates, "The Battle of the Coral Sea"; Millot, *The Battle of the Coral Sea*; Dull, *Battle History*, pp. 121–43; Morison, *History*, vol. IV, pp. 21–64. "Scratch one flattop!" is in ibid., p. 42. "The area on the port side" is in Lindley, *Carrier Victory*, pp. 38–39. "Never in all" is in ibid., p. 41. "We have stopped" is in ibid., pp. 43–44. For Midway, see Bates, "The Battle of Midway"; Barde, *The Battle of Midway*; Lord, *Incredible Victory*; Morison, *History*, vol. IV; Prange, *Miracle at Midway*; Dull, *Battle History*, pp. 133–71. "Do you see" is in Lord, *Incredible Victory*, p. 66. "Bright, white smile" is in Potter, *Nimitz*, p. 91. "lacked the will" is in Spector, *Eagle Against the Sun*, p. 166. "As we steamed" is in Fuchida and Okumiya, *Midway*, p. 3. For Spruance, see Wukovits, "Spruance," in Howarth, ed., *Men of War*; Buell, *The Quiet Warrior*. "You will be governed" is in Morison, *History*, vol. IV, p. 84. "A Zero fighter" is in Fuchida and Okumiya, *Midway*, p. 151. "I want each of us" is in Lord, *Incredible Victory*, p. 86. "As I put my nose down" is in Dickinson and Sparks, "The Target Was Utterly Satisfying." "The terrifying scream" is in Fuchida and Okumiya, *Midway*, p. 177; "Bogey" is in Lord, *Incredible Victory*, p. 193. "Well, I've" is in ibid., p. 196. For Japanese reactions to the loss of Nagumo's carriers, see Fuchida and Okumiya, *Midway*, pp. 216–17; Morison, *History*, vol. IV, p. 138.

CHAPTER 9

For Guadalcanal, see R. B. Frank, *Guadalcanal*; Morison, *The History of U.S. Naval Operations During the Second World War*, vol. IV, p. 245–96, and vol. V; Griffith, *The Battle of Guadalcanal*; Shaw, *First Offensive*; Freeman, *Requiem for a Fleet*. "It gave you" is in Morison, *History*, vol. IV, p. 283. "Since the Japanese have" is in King and White-hill, *Fleet Admiral King*, p. 381. Japanese planning for Guadalcanal is in Dull, *A Battle History of the Imperial Japanese Navy*, pp. 175–86. "Seldom has" is quoted in R. B. Frank, *Guadalcanal*, p. 57. Peyton's comments are in Dyer, *The Amphibians Came to Conquer*, vol. I, p. 301. Vandegrift's comments are in *Once A Marine*, p. 120. Turner reading Liddell Hart is in Dyer, *Amphibians*, p. 318. "Instead of" is in Morison, *History*, vol. IV, p. 25. For situation on the beaches, see Morison, *History*, vol. IV, pp. 285–86; Dyer, *Amphibians*, pp. 350–52. "one of the worst" is in Morison, *History*, vol. V, p. 17. The most complete account of Savo action is Bates, "The Battle of Savo Island"; also see New-comb, *Savo*; Morison, *History*, vol. V, pp. 17–64; Dull, *Battle History*, pp. 187–96. "Total fighter strength" is in Bates, "Savo Island," p. 92. "running away" is in Vandegrift, *Once a Marine*, p. 129. "knew the situation" is quoted in Newcomb, *Savo*, p. 172. Morison's comments on Fletcher's actions are in Morison, *History*, vol. V, p. 28. "such a precipitous" is in Bates, "Savo Island," p. 94. Sighting of Mikawa's force is in ibid., pp. 83–84. "When I reached the bridge" is in Morison, *History*, vol. V, p. 46. For Henderson Field, see T. G. Miller, *The Cactus Air Force*; Mersky, *Time of the Aces*. For the Thach Weave, see Lundstrom, *The First Team*, pp. 477–85. For eastern Solomons, see Dull, *Battle History*, pp. 197–207; Morison, *History*, vol. V, pp. 79–107; R. B. Frank, *Guadalcanal*, pp. 159–93. For attack on *Enterprise*, see Stafford, *The Big E*, pp. 128–31. "Even the B-17s" is in Morison, *History*, vol. V, p. 105. "Our plan to capture" is in ibid., p. 107. For Cape Esperance, see Dull, *Battle History*, pp. 209–21; Morison, *History*, vol. V, pp. 147–71, 292–312; Cook, *Cape Esperance*. "It is almost" is quoted in Spector, *Eagle Against the Sun*, p. 206. "It now appears" is in Potter, *Nimitz*, p. 195. "I'll never forget" is in Griffith, *The Battle of Guadalcanal*, p. 163. "Are we going" is in Halsey and Bryan, *Admiral Halsey's Story*, p. 117. For Santa Cruz, see Dull, *Battle History*, pp. 227–35; Morison, *History*, vol. V, pp. 199–224; R. B. Frank, *Guadalcanal*, pp. 366–403. "Attack" is in Morison, *History*, vol. V, p. 204. *Porter* accident is in ibid., pp. 388–89. "no diminution" is in ibid., p. 401. For the Naval Battle of Guadalcanal, see Dull, *Battle History*, pp. 237–49; Morison, *History*, vol. V, pp. 225–87; R. B. Frank, *Guadalcanal*, pp. 428–92. "a barroom brawl" is in R. B. Frank, *Guadalcanal*, p. 441. For Tassafaronga, see Dull, *Battle History*, pp. 253–60; Morison, *History*, vol. V, pp. 288–315; R. B. Frank, *Guadalcanal*, pp. 493–518.

CHAPTER 10

For Operation Paukenschlag, see Freeman, ed., *Eastern Sea Frontier War Diary*; Van der Vat, *The Atlantic Campaign*; Morison, *The History of U.S. Naval Operations During the Second World War*, vol. I; Terraine, *The U-Boat Wars*; Ministry of Defence, *The U-Boat War in the Atlantic*. For U.S. coastal trade, see Morison, *History*, vol. I, p. 255. "Attempts must be made" is in Padfield, *Dönitz*, p. 236. "operations in the Atlantic" is in Dönitz, *Memoirs*, pp. 200–201. For Hardegen's operations, see Gannon, *Operation Drumbeat*. "Our operation" is in Ministry of Defence, *U-Boat War*, ch. IV, p. 5. "The trouble is" is in Cohen and Gooch, *Military Misfortunes*, p. 60. "clumsy handling" is in Padfield, *Dönitz*, p. 237. "The navy couldn't" is in Morison, *History*, vol. I, p. 201. "Should the enemy submarines" is in Freeman, ed., *War Diary*, p. 19. "the submarine situation" is in Buell, *Master of Sea Power*, p. 187. "I still do not" is in ibid., p. 189. Rohwer is quoted in Ellis, *Brute Force*, p. 579, n. 20. "escort is not just one" is in Van der Vat, *Atlantic Campaign*, p. 267. "Inadequately escorted" is in ibid., p. 242. For the Channel Dash, see John Potter, *Fiasco*; Roskill, *The War at Sea*, vol. II, pp. 149–52; Bekker, *Hitler's Naval War*, pp. 229–35. "These ships no longer" is in Bekker, *Hitler's Naval War*, p. 229. "a surprise withdrawal" is in Showell, ed., *Fuehrer Conferences on Naval Affairs*, pp. 237–38. For intelligence and the breakout, see Hinsley, *British Intelligence in the Second World War*, vol. II, pp. 179–88. "The U-boats ravaged" is in Churchill, *The Second World War*, vol. IV, p. 109. For Andrews' activities, see Freeman, ed., *War Diary*, pp. 166–200. "I gave the order" is in Hughes and Costello, *The Battle of the Atlantic*, pp. 206–7. Marshall's letter and King's reply are in King and Whitehill, *Fleet Admiral King*, pp. 455–56. For Weigley's comment, see Weigley, *The American Way of War*, pp. 312–19. "We've got to go" is in Hughes and Costello, *Battle*, p. 210. For Sledgehammer/Roundup, see Buell, *Master*, pp. 205–7. For the St.-Nazaire raid, see D. Mason, *Raid on St. Nazaire*; Irving, *The Destruction of Convoy PQ 17* is a controversial account of this incident; also see Roskill, *White Ensign*, pp. 204–9; Barnett, *Engage the Enemy More Closely*, pp. 718–22. "I have not slept longer" is in Hughes and Costello, *Battle*, p. 227. For the intelligence background, see Hinsley, *British Intelligence*, vol. II, pp. 214–23.

CHAPTER 11

"Tobruk had surrendered" is in Churchill, *The Second World War*, vol. IV, p. 382. For the preliminaries to the North African invasion, see Morison, *The History of Naval Operations During the Second World War*, vol. II, pp. 11–15. For Mediterranean operations, see Macintyre, *The Battle for the Mediterranean*. "completely hidden" is in Cunningham, *A Sailor's Odyssey*, p. 424. "Four minutes after that" is in ibid., p. 433. For the Sirte action, see Grove, *Sea Battles in Close-Up*, vol. II, ch. V. For Dönitz's return to the North Atlantic, see Van der Vat, *The Atlantic Campaign*, pp. 289–91; ADM 234/578, p. 88. For support groups, see ADM 234/578, pp. 88–89. For *Laconia* sinking and its aftermath, see Peillard, *The Laconia Affair*. For Pedestal, see Macintyre, *Battle*, pp. 167–84. "Oh Christ!" is in Jackson, *Strike from the Sea*, p. 110. "Fighters stand to" and "The sight took" are in Popham, *Sea Flight*, p. 128. For the North African landings, see ADM 234/359; Morison, *History*, vol. II, chs. I–X; Pack, *Invasion North Africa 1942*; Hinsley, *British Intelligence in the Second World War*, vol. II, ch. 24.

CHAPTER 12

For Casablanca, see Buell, *Master of Sea Power*, pp. 264–81; Spector, *Eagle Against the Sun*, pp. 220–23. For Barents Sea battle and its aftermath, see Pope, *73 North* and Stephen, *Sea Battles in Close-Up*, vol. I, ch. 9; Bekker, *Hitler's Naval War*, ch. 5. For cargo carried by JW 51B, see Pope, *73 North*, app. I. For Cutler's remarks, see Bennett, *Naval Battles of World War II*, p. 156. For Dönitz as Grand Admiral, see Padfield, *Dönitz*, pp. 266–74. For the Battle of the Atlantic, see Ministry of Defence, *The U-Boat War in the Atlantic*, ch. VI; ADM 234/578, ch. 13; Roskill, *The War at Sea*, vol. II, ch. 14; Van der Vat, *The Atlantic Campaign*, pp. 312–34. "Now it can only" is in Hughes and Costello, *The Battle of the Atlantic*, p. 243. "the tempo is quickening" is in ADM 234/578, p. 91. For Convoy SC 118, see Waters, *Bloody Winter*, pp. 135–77. For the Atlantic Convoy Conference, see Buell, *Master*, pp. 292–93. For the convoy battles of March and April 1943, see Rohwer, *The Critical Convoy Battles of March 1943*; ADM 234/578; Waters, *Bloody Winter*, pp. 178–238; Middlebrook, *Convoy*. "Fired two torpedoes" is in ibid., p. 205. "Where is" is in *Sir Max Horton*, p. 151. "The Germans never came" is in Roskill, *War at Sea*, vol. II, p. 367. Horton's exchange with Churchill is in Middlebrook, *Convoy*, p. 317. "On March 26" is in Dönitz, *Memoirs*, p. 330. For decline in U-boat morale, see ADM 234/578, p. 93; Beesly, *Very Special Intelligence*, pp. 175–76. For HX 231, see Gretton, *Crisis Convoy*. "Historians of this war" is in ADM 234/578, p. 92. For ONS 5, see Seth, *The Fiercest Battle*. "The overwhelming" is in Dönitz, *Memoirs*, pp. 340–41; see also Ministry of Defence, *The U-Boat War in the Atlantic*, pp. 111–13. For Allied shipping losses compared with ship construction, see Ellis, *Brute Force*, p. 161.

"Again and Again" is in Dönitz, *Memoirs*, p. 420. For the Tenth Fleet, see Morison, *The History of U.S. Naval Operations During the Second World War*, vol. X, pp. 21–26; Van der Vat, *Atlantic Campaign*, pp. 335–36; also see Knowles, "Ultra and the Battle of the Atlantic." For the effectiveness of the escort carriers, see Y'Blood, *Hunter-Killer*; Morison, *History*, vol. X. *K-34* incident is in Morison, *History*, vol. X, p. 194. For *Borie*, see ibid.. pp. 162–68; Maher and Wise, "Stand By for a Ram!" For the Bay of Biscay offensive, see ADM 234/578, pp. 106–14; Morison, *History*, vol. VII; Roskill, *War at Sea*, vol. III, pt. I, ch. II.

CHAPTER 13

For the planning and execution of the invasion of Sicily, see Morison, *The History of U.S. Naval Operations During the Second World War*, vol. IX; D'Este, *Bitter Victory*. For the British view, see ADM 234/356; Roskill, *The War at Sea*, vol. III, part I, ch. VI. "tonight at any rate" is in ibid., p. 129. "If you can connect" is in D'Este, *Victory*, p. 296. For Cunningham's criticism of Montgomery, see Morison, *History*, vol. IX, pp. 206–7. For Salerno, see ibid., pp. 227–314; Roskill, *War at Sea*, vol. III, part I, ch. VII. "Any officer with" is in D'Este, *Fatal Decision*, p. 38. "The advancing troops" is in Liddell Hart, *History of the Second World War*, p. 464. "Be pleased" is in Pack, *Cunningham*, p. 270; the full tally of Italian ships turned over to the Allies is in Roskill, *War at Sea*, vol. III, app. F. For *Scharnhorst*'s last battle, see Stephen, *Sea Battles in Close-Up*, vol. 1, ch. X; Roskill, *War at Sea*, vol. III, part I, pp. 78–89; pp. 80–89. For the X-craft attack on *Tirpitz*, see Kennedy, *Menace*, pp. 119–31. Ramsden's comments are in Bennett, *Naval Battles of World War II*, pp. 165, 166.

CHAPTER 14

Sinking of *I-1* is in Winton, *Ultra in the Pacific*, pp. 97–98. For strategic discussion, see Morison, *The History of U.S. Naval Operations During the Second World War*, vol. VI, pp. 89–97. "keep pushing" is in Morison, *History*, vol. VI, p. 89. For the Japanese view, see Van der Vat, *The Pacific Campaign*, pp. 257–58; Morison, *History*, vol. VI, pp. 22–26. "We were told" is in Sakai, *Samurai!*, p. 252. For the Bismarck Sea battle, see Morison, *History*, vol. VI, pp. 54–65; Dull, *A Battle History of the Japanese Navy*, pp. 268–70. Japanese losses are in Dull, *Battle History*, p. 273. "I do not know" is in Howarth, "Isoroku Yamamoto," in Howarth, ed., *Men of War*, p. 127. Operation I-Go is in Dull, *Battle History*, pp. 272–73. For Yamamoto's ambush, see Layton, "Oral History"; Winton, *Ultra*, pp. 106–113. For the Aleutians, see Dull, *Battle History*, pp. 260–65; Morison, *History*, vol. VII, pp. 3–65; McIntyre, "War in the Illusions." "What does this mean?" is in Love, *A History of the U.S. Navy*, vol. II, p. 141. Percy's adventure is in Buchanan, *The Navy's Air War*, pp. 176–77; Barbey provided his own account of his operations in *MacArthur's Amphibious Navy*; also see Melson, *Up the Slot*. For Kula Gulf and Kolombangara, see Dull, *Battle History*, pp. 274–77; Morison, *History*, vol. VI, ch. XI. "Suddenly . . . I was" is in Morris and Cave, "Kula Gulf" in S. F. Smith, *The United States Navy in World War II*, p. 454. For PT-boat operations, see Morison, *History*, vol. VI, pp. 209–12. For Burke's destroyer tactics, see Potter, *Admiral Arleigh Burke*, pp. 83–84. For Vella Gulf, see Morison, *History*, vol. VI, pp. 212–22; Dull, *Battle History*, vol. VI, pp. 278–79. Walker's operations are discussed in Morison, *History*, vol. VI, pp. 241–52; Dull, *Battle History*, p. 284. For Empress Augusta Bay, see Morison, *History*, vol. VI, ch. XVII; Dull, *Battle History*, pp. 288–90; Potter, *Burke*, pp. 95–98. "I never expected" is in Karig, *Battle Report*, vol. IV, p. 39. For carrier strikes against Rabaul, see Morison, *History*, vol. VI, ch. XVIII; Dull, *Battle History*, pp. 290–95. For the Battle of

Cape St. George, see Morison, *History*, vol. VI, pp. 352–59; Dull, *Battle History*, pp. 294–95; Potter, *Burke*, pp. 102–7. "Tarawa, Iwo Jima" is in Morison, *History*, vol. VI, p. 409. For Cape Gloucester, see Spector, *Eagle Against the Sun*, pp. 246–47; Barbey, *MacArthur's Navy*, pp. 109–25; Morison, *History*, vol. VI, pp. 378–89. Use of rocket-firing LCIs is in Love, *History*, vol. II, pp. 150–51. "an idea that never" is in Van der Vat, *Pacific Campaign*, p. 289. For the PT-boat episode, see Karig, *Battle Report*, vol. IV, pp. 61–62. For MacArthur and naval gunfire, see Morison, *History*, vol. VI, p. 438, n. 4.

CHAPTER 15

"I was up on the bridge" is in the Heggan and Logan play, *Mr. Roberts*. For new carriers and aircraft, see Reynolds, *The Fast Carriers*, ch. three. Japanese aircraft losses are in Potter and Nimitz, eds., *Sea Power*, p. 733. Japanese ship losses are in Dull, *A Battle History of the Imperial Japanese Navy*, pp. 299–300. Yoshuyo's report is in Karig, *Battle Report*, vol. IV, p. 78. For Tarawa, see Alexander, *Across the Reef*; Sherrod, *Tarawa*; Isley and Crowl, *The U.S. Marines and Amphibious War*, ch. VI; Morison, *The History of U.S. Naval Operations During the Second World War*, vol. VII; Spector, *Eagle Against the Sun*, ch. 12. "You won't have" is in J. Smith, "Oral History," p. 285. "Surely, we all" is in Sherrod, *Tarawa*, p. 62. Naval gunfire is discussed in Alexander, *Across the Reef*. "Bullets pinged" is in Morison, *History*, vol. VII, p. 162. "I could swear" is in Karig, *Battle Report*, vol. IV, p. 88. "A Marine jumped" is in Sherrod, *Tarawa*, p. 74. "if a sign" is in ibid., p. 101. "Give me central" is in Hagan, *This People's Navy*, p. 322. For Kwajalein, Roi-Namur, and Eniwetok, see Isley and Crowl, *U.S. Marines*, ch. VII; Chapin, *Breaking the Outer Ring*, Morison, *History*, vol. VII, chs. XV–XVI. "There was divided" is in Karig, *Battle Report*, vol. IV, p. 108. "The American attacks" is in Morison, *History*, vol. VII, pp. 214–15. "Close-in Conelly" is in Isley and Crowl, *U.S. Marines*, p. 272. "Great God" is in Morison, *History*, vol. VII, p. 248. "the most brilliant" is in Van der Vat, *The Pacific Campaign*, p. 306. For Barbey's operations, see *MacArthur's Amphibious Navy*. "The amphibious ships" is in Karig, *Battle Report*, vol. IV, p. 192. "The allied invasion" is in Manchester, *American Caesar*, p. 346. Rescues by *Tang* are in Karig, *Battle Report*, vol. IV, pp. 195–96. For discussion of Japanese strategy, see Dull, *Battle History*, pp. 303–5.

CHAPTER 16

Pluskat's adventures are in Ryan, *The Longest Day*, pp. 185–86. For D-Day planning, see Morison, *The History of U.S. Naval Operations During the Second World War*, vol. XI; Roskill, *The War at Sea*, vol. III, p. II. D'Este, *Decision in Nomandy*. For Anzio, see Morison, *History*, vol. IX; D'Este, *Fatal Decision*. "An iron year" is in Padfield, *Dönitz*, p. 347. "The smell of death" is in Werner, *Iron Coffins*, p. 172. For the development of the snorkel and advanced submarines, see Tarrant, *The Last Year of the Kriegsmarine*. For Dönitz's strategic view in 1944, see Padfield, *Dönitz*, p. 363. "Every vessel taking part" is in Terraine, *The U-Boat Wars*, p. 644. For the attacks on *Tirpitz*, see Kennedy, *Menace*, pp. 134–49. For German preparations to counter the Allied landings, see Ruge, *Der Seekrieg*, pp. 358–66; D'Este, *Decision in Normandy*, pp. 115–19. "O.K." is in Morison, *History*, vol. XI, pp. 82–83. Slaughter's account is in *Washington Post*, May 22, 1994. *Corry's* sinking is based upon conversations with George D. Hoffman. For the destroyer action, see Morison, *History*, vol. XI, pp. 142–49. For the German reaction to the invasion, see Tarrant, *Last Year*, pp. 55–70. "If I was commander" is in Ryan, *Longest Day*, p. 297. For Mulberry and the gale, see Roskill, *War at Sea*, vol. III, pt. II, pp. 61–66. For firefight off Cherbourg, see Morison, *History*, vol. XI, pp. 195–212. "What shall we do" is in Churchill, *The Second World War*, vol. V, p. 23. For Dragoon, see Morison, *History*, vol. XI, pp. 221–92. "The fire curtain" is in ibid., pp. 168–69.

CHAPTER 17

"Here is a piece" is in Sherrod, *On to Westward*, p. 33. For the planning for the Marianas operation, see Morison, *The History of U.S. Naval Operations During the Second World War*, vol. VIII, pp. 149–69; Isley and Crowl, *The U.S. Marines and Amphibious War*, pp. 310–19. "We are through" is in Sherrod, *Westward*, pp. 37–38. For the landing on Saipan, see Chapin, *Breaching the Marianas*; Morison, *History*, vol. VIII, chh. XII, XIII; Isley and Crowl, *U.S. Marines*, pp. 319–42. For the Battle of the Philippine Sea, see Y'Blood, *Red Sun Setting*; Morison, *History*, vol. VIII, chh. XIV–XVI; Grove, *Sea Battles in Close-Up*, vol. II, ch. eight; Dull, *A Battle History of the Imperial Japanese Navy*, pp. 303–311; Buell, *The Quiet Warrior*, pp. 257–280. "The Japs are" is in Buell, *The Quiet Warrior*, p. 262. "I snapped into" is in Sakai, *Samurai!*, p. 265. For Vraciu's adventures, see Vraciu, "Hellcat at the Turkey Shoot." "The widely held view" is in Minoru Nomura, "Ozawa in the Pacific," in Evans, ed., *The Japanese Navy in World War II*. "Going after" is is in Grove, *Sea Battles*, p. 196. For Smith vs. Smith, see Isley and Crowl, *U.S. Marines*, pp. 342–47. "Part of the area" is in Sherrod, *Westward*, p. 147. For Guam, see O'Brien, *Liberation*. "We had the bastards" is in Sherrod, *Westward*, p. 150. The Japanese plan to recapture Saipan is in Nomura, "Ozawa in the Pacific," pp. 330–32. " 'This,' says Morison" is in Morison, *History*, vol. XII, p. 66. "and gazed toward" is in James, *The Years of MacArthur*, vol. II, p. 64.

CHAPTER 18

For the Leyte campaign, see Morison, *The History of U.S. Naval Operations During the Second World War*, vol. XII; Bates, "The Battle for Leyte Gulf"; Cutler, *The Battle of Leyte Gulf*; Field, *The Japanese at Leyte Gulf*; C. V. Woodward, *The Battle for Leyte Gulf*; Dull, *A Battle History of the Imperial Japanese Navy*, ch. XII; Spector, *Eagle Against the Sun*, ch. 19; Grove, *Sea Battles in Close-Up*, vol. II, ch. 9. "Air plot" is in Sprague and Gustafson, "They Had Us on the Ropes." "A direct attack" is in Love, *A History of the U.S. Navy*, p. 228. For Bush's adventures, see Furgurson, "Bush's War." For Peleliu, see Gailey, *Peleliu 1944*. For the Sixteenth Field Depot, see F. Hough, *The Island War*, p. 312. "our body filth" is in Sledge, "Peleliu 1944." "a knock-down" is in Spector, *Eagle*, p. 424. "Our planes appeared" is in Polmar, *Aircraft Carriers*, p. 380. For "Cripdiv 1," see Morison, *History*, vol. XII, pp. 95–109. "a kind of banzai charge" is in Dull, *Battle History*, p. 331. "In case of opportunity" is in Morison, *History*, vol. XII, p. 58. "The gray ships" is in Karig, *Battle Report*, vol. IV, pp. 340–41; see also Roscoe, *On the Seas and in the Skies*, p. 438. "We held off" is in Karig, *Battle Report*, vol. IV, p. 370. "The spectacle" is in Morison, *History*, vol. XII, p. 181. "a funeral salute" is in ibid., p. 241. "I went into" is in Halsey and Bryan, *Admiral Halsey's Story*, p. 217. "Had he used" is in Cutler, *Leyte Gulf*, p. 171. "Hey" is in Morison, *History*, vol. XII, p. 253. "I didn't think" is in Sprague and Gustafson, "On the Ropes." "The enemy was closing" is in ibid. "We need" is in Hathaway, "Small Boys—Intercept!" "It was like" is in Morison, *History*, vol. XII, p. 257. "He lost his taste" is in Hathaway, "Small Boys." "The shells created" is in Sprague and Gustafson, "On the Ropes." For Bogan and Lee warnings, see Cutler, *Leyte Gulf*, pp. 210–12. "I gotta hit" is in Morison, *History*, vol. XII, p. 327. "I was stunned" is in Halsey and Bryan, *Halsey's Story*, p. 220. "bowing to pressure" is in Halsey's notes to Baldwin, "The Sho-Plan—The Battle for Leyte Gulf," in Baldwin, *Sea Fights and Shipwrecks*, p. 181. "We had been" is in Potter and Nimitz, *Sea Power*, p. 793. Hagan's comments are in "History as Self-Fulfilling Prophecy."

CHAPTER 19

"U.S. Submarine War Patrol Reports" is basic to the study of the submarine war. For the sinking of *Kongo*, see Blair, *Silent Victory*, pp. 775–76. For the sinking of *Shinano*, see Enright, *Shinano!* "We set as" is in Zevin, ed., *Nothing to Fear*, p. 353. For a comparison of U.S. and Japanese submarines and tactics, see Spector, *Eagle Against the Sun*, p. 481; Ito, *The End of the Imperial Japanese Navy*, p. 183. For a summary of the submarine war in the Pacific, see Hezlett, *The Submarine and Sea Power*, chs. XI, XII. For a report on Japanese submarine activity off the West Coast see Washington *Post*, Jan. 1, 1982. "We had the greatest" is in Spector, *Eagle*, p. 483. Comments from the Strategic Bombing Survey are in its final reports. For a summary of the torpedo problem, see Beach, "Culpable Negligence"; Blair, *Victory*, pp. 273–81. Daspit's account is in Blair, *Victory*, pp. 435–37. For loss of *Sculpin*, see ibid., pp. 524–25. For breaking of *maru* code, see Holmes, *Double-Edged Secrets*. For *Tang*'s last patrol, see Blair, *Victory*, pp. 767–69. For the Japanese failure at ASW, see Oi, "Why Japan's Anti-Submarine Warfare Failed." *Parche*'s coup is in Holmes, *Undersea Victory*, pp. 355–56.

CHAPTER 20

"Leyte and then Luzon" is in Morison, *The History of U.S. Naval Operations During the Second World War*, vol. XIII, p. 3. For the Philippines campaign, see ibid. (vol. XIII); Barbey, *MacArthur's Amphibious Navy*; Spector, *Eagle Against the Sun*, ch. twenty-two. "Nip planes" is in Karig, *Battle Report*, vol. V, pp. 31–32. "We got our" is in ibid., pp. 46–47. For the text of Kinkaid's statement to MacArthur, see ibid., pp. 64–65. "Have rolled" is in Spector, *Eagle*, p. 517. "Jap planes were falling" is in Karig, *Battle Report*, vol. V, p. 79. "even one corner" is in ibid., pp. 87–88. For the typhoon, see Morison, *History*, vol. XIII, pp. 59–84. "The storm broke" is in Karig, *Battle Report*, vol. V, pp. 95–97. "Consider need" is in ibid., p. 174. For Yamashita's campaign, see Toland, *The Rising Sun*, pp. 629–30. For Yalta, see Dallek, *Franklin D. Roosevelt and American Foreign Policy*, pp. 506–25. "Our duty and our fate" is in Padfield, *Dönitz*, p. 378. Speer and Dönitz's exchange is in Speer, *Inside the Third Reich*, p. 426. "losses of a level" is in Van der Vat, *The Atlantic Campaign*, p. 378. "It would seem" is in Hinsley, *British Intelligence in the Second World War*, vol. III, pt. 2, pp. 474–87. "the ever-increasing weight" is in Dönitz, *Memoirs*, p. 428. "Ideal boat" is in Van der Vat, *Atlantic Campaign*, p. 379. "the mighty sea-power" is in Padfield, *Dönitz*, p. 382. For an assessment of the future effectiveness of the Type XXIII boat, see Hezlet, *The Submarine and Sea Power*, p. 236. For the final attack on the American coast, see Morison, *History*, vol. X, pp. 344–56. For sinking of *Tirpitz*, see Kennedy, *Menace*, ch. X. For sinkings in the Baltic, see Dobson, *The Cruelest Night*. For voyage of *U-2511*, see Tarrant, *The Last Year of the Kriegsmarine*, pp. 206–7. "words at this moment" is in Padfield, *Dönitz*, p. 435.

CHAPTER 21

"Run, run" is in Matthews, *The Assault*, p. 36. For Iwo Jima, see Bartley, *Iwo Jima*; B. D. Ross, *Iwo Jima*; Morison, *The History of U.S. Naval Operations During the Second World War*, vol. XIV. "They crept and crawled" is in Ross, *Iwo Jima*, p. 69. "Without Iwo Jima" is in Costello, *The Pacific War*, p. 540. For Japanese preparations, see Toland, *The Rising Sun*, ch. 26. Use of poison gas is discussed in Sprietsma, *Analysis of the Battle of Iwo Jima*, p. 7. "No previous target" is in Isley and Crowl, *The U.S. Marines and Amphibious War*, p. 465. Marquand's account is in S. E. Smith, *The United States Navy in World War II*. "I got him" is in Morison, *History*, vol. XIV, p. 27. For discussion of Turner's decision to land, see Spector, *The Eagle and the Sun*, p. 499; Isley and Crowl, *U.S. Marines*, p. 474. "Whether the dead" is in Sherrod, *On to Westward*, p. 180. For *Saratoga*'s ordeal, see Karig, *Battle Report*, vol. V, pp. 309–10. For sinking of *Bismarck Sea*, see ibid., pp. 310–12; Morison, *History*, vol. XIV, pp. 54–55. For the flag-raising see Toland, *Rising Sun*, pp. 656–57. For discussions of the importance of Iwo Jima, see Isley and Crowl, *U.S. Marines*, p. 529; Morison, *History*, vol. XIV, pp. 73–75; Spector, *Eagle*, pp. 502–3. "I hope to God" is in Marquand, in S. E. Smith, *United States Navy*. "Uncommon valor" is in Isley and Crowl, *U.S. Marines*, p. 501. For Okinawa, see Morison, *History*, vol. XIV; Feifer, *Tennozan*; B. M. Frank, *Okinawa*; Belote and Belote, *Typhoon of Steel*; for the Japanese side, see Huber, *Japan's Battle of Okinawa*. "Maybe Nimitz" is in Ross, *Iwo Jima*, pp. 348–49. "the most audacious" is in Morison, *History*, vol. XIV, p. 86. "I watched people" is in Costello, *Pacific War*, pp. 550–51. For *Franklin*'s ordeal, see Belote and Belote, *Typhoon*, pp. 39–42. For the British fleet, see Winton, *The Forgotten Fleet*; Roskill, *The War at Sea*, vol. III, pt. II, ch. XXVI. "Where were" is in Sherrod, *Westward*, p. 277. "I may be crazy" is in Potter, *Nimitz*, p. 372. For the kamikaze attacks, see Belote and Belote, *Typhoon*; Morison, *History*, vol. XIV, pp. 181–282. "The plane crashed" is in Belote and Belote, *Typhoon*, p. 102. For *Yamato*, see Yoshiba, "The End of *Yamato*"; Morison, *History*, vol. XIV, pp. 205–9; Spurr, *A Glorious Way to Die*. "But you have" is in Karig, *Battle Report*, vol. V, p. 396. "Rain and more rain" is in ibid., pp. 396–97. "Water, both from" is in Yoshiba, "End of *Yamato*." "Probably no ship" is in Morison, *History*, vol. XIV, p. 235. "Any more of this" is in ibid., p. 439. Spruance's comments are in Buell, *The Quiet Warrior*, pp. 356–57. "When a kamikaze" is in Winton, *Forgotten Fleet*, p. 122. "Naval gunfire" is in Appleman et al., *Okinawa*, p. 253. Operation Barney is in Blair, *Silent Victory*, pp. 858–65. Spruance on landings in Japan is in Forrestal, *Spruance*, pp. 209–10. For the invasion of Japan, see Spector, *Eagle*, pp. 540–43. For the decision to use the atomic bomb and Japan's decision to surrender, see Craig, *The Fall of Japan*; Miller, *War Plan Orange*, pp. 365–69; Baer, *One Hundred Years of Sea Power*, pp. 268–72. Statistics on ships involved in proposed invasions are in Baer, *One Hundred Years*.

Bibliography

UNPUBLISHED SOURCES

ADM 186/794. "The Chase and Destruction of the *Graf Spee*." Public Records Office, Kew, U.K.

ADM 186/797. "Battle Summaries." Public Records Office, Kew, U.K.

ADM 186/798. "Naval Operations in the Campaign in Norway." Public Records Office, Kew, U.K.

ADM 186/799. "Naval Operations in Home Waters and the Atlantic, Sept. 1939–April 1940." Public Records Office, Kew, U.K.

ADM 199/140. "Sinking of S.S. *Athenia*." Public Records Office, Kew, U.K.

ADM 199/157. "Report on the Sinking of H.M.S. *Courageous*." Public Records Office, Kew, U.K.

ADM 199/158. "Loss of H.M.S. *Royal Oak*." Public Records Office, Kew, U.K.

ADM 199/280. "Interception and Boarding of German Auxiliary *Altmark*." Public Records Office, Kew, U.K.

ADM 199/360. "War Diaries, Dover Command, 1st February–1st December 1940." Public Records Office, Kew, U.K.

ADM 199/473, 474, 475, 476, 478. "First and Second Battles of Narvik." Public Records Office, Kew, U.K.

ADM 223/8, 15, 16, 18, 19. "Naval Intelligence Papers Concerning the Battle of the Atlantic." Public Records Office, Kew, U.K.

ADM 234/241. "Anti-Uboat Operations." Public Records Office, Kew, U.K.

ADM 234/322. "The Chase and Sinking of the German Battleship *Bismarck*." Public Records Office, Kew, U.K.

ADM 234/324. "Actions with Enemy Disguised Raiders." Public Records Office, Kew, U.K.

ADM 234/325. "Air Attack on Taranto." Public Records Office, Kew, U.K.

ADM 234/330. "Loss of H.M. Ships *Prince of Wales* and *Repulse*." Public Records Office, Kew, U.K.

ADM 234/356. "Invasion of Sicily." Public Records Office, Kew, U.K.

ADM 234/358. "Invasion of Italy." Public Records Office, Kew, U.K.

ADM 234/359. "Invasion of North Africa." Public Records Office, Kew, U.K.

ADM 234/360. "The Evacuation from Dunkirk." Public Records Office, Kew, U.K.
ADM 234/578. "The Defeat of the Enemy Attack on Shipping: 1939–1945." Public Records Office, Kew, U.K.
Allard, Dean C. "The Battle of the Atlantic: A United States Overview." Paper delivered at the International Historical Conference on the Battle of the Atlantic, Liverpool, England, May 28, 1993.
Barde, Robert E. *The Battle of Midway: A Study in Command.* Ph.D. Thesis, University of Maryland, 1971.
Bates, Richard W. "The Battle for Leyte Gulf. Strategical and Tactical Analysis." 3 vols. Naval War College, Newport, R.I. 1953.
———. "The Battle of the Coral Sea. Strategical and Tactical Analysis." Naval War College, Newport, R.I., 1947.
———. "The Battle of Midway: Strategical and Tactical Analysis." Naval War College, Newport, R.I., 1949.
———. "The Battle of Savo Island: Strategical and Tactical Analysis." Naval War College, Newport, R.I., 1950.
Bellinger, Patrick N. L. "The Gooney Bird." MSS Autobiography, Naval Historical Center, Washington, D.C.
Boyd, Carl. "Ultra and U.S. Submarine Operations in the Pacific, 1942–1945." Address Before the U.S. Commission on Military History, November 19, 1994.
German Naval Staff. *War Diary.* Naval Historical Center, Washington, D.C. (Microfilm of English translation.)
Hagan, Kenneth J. "History as Self-Fulfilling Prophesy." Paper delivered at the Cantigny Conference, Wheaton, Ill, March 1, 1995.
Layton, Edwin T. "Oral History." Nimitz Library, U.S. Naval Academy, Annapolis, Md.
Lundeberg, Philip K. *American Anti-Submarine Operations in the Atlantic, May 1943–May 1945.* Ph.D. Thesis, Harvard University, 1954.
OP-20 G. "Final Report." National Archives, Washington, D.C.
Rochefort, Joseph J. "Oral History." Nimitz Library, U.S. Naval Academy, Annapolis, Md.
Smith, Julian. "Oral History." Marine Corps Historical Center, Washington, D.C.
"U.S. Submarine War Patrol Reports and Related Documents." Naval Historical Center, Washington, D.C.

BIBLIOGRAPHIES AND REFERENCE WORKS

Colleta, Paolo E., ed. *A Selected and Annotated Bibliography of American Naval History.* University Press of America, Lanham Md, 1988.
Dupuy, R. Ernest, and Trevor N. Dupuy. *The Encyclopedia of Military History.* New York: Harper & Row, 1986.
Jane's Fighting Ships of World War II. New York: Military Press, 1970.
Law, Derek G. *The Royal Navy in World War II: An Annotated Bibliography.* London: Greenhill Books, 1988.
Rohwer, Jürgen and S. Hummelchen. *Chronology of the War at Sea.* Annapolis, Md.: Naval Institute Press, 1992.
Smith, Myron J. *World War II at Sea.* 3 vols. Metuchen, N.J.: Scarecrow, 1976.
Snyder, Louis L. *Historical Guide to World War II.* Westport, Conn.: Greenwood, 1982.

PRINTED DOCUMENTS

Eastern Sea Frontier War Diary. Robert H. Freeman, ed. Ventnor, N.J.: Shellback Press, 1987.

King, Ernest J. *The U.S. Navy at War, 1941–1945: Official Report to the Secretary of the Navy*. Washington, D.C.: Navy Department, 1946.

The Trial of the Major War Criminals. Vol. V. Nuremberg, 1946.

The London Gazette. Suppl., July 14, 1947.

The London Gazette. Suppl., Oct. 14, 1947.

Millington-Drake, Eugen. *The Drama of the Graf Spee*. London: Davies, 1965.

Ministry of Defence (Navy). *The U-Boat War in the Atlantic: 1939–1945*. London: Her Majesty's Stationery Office, 1989.

Showell, Jak P. Mallman, ed. *Fuehrer Conferences on Naval Affairs*. Annapolis, Md.: Naval Institute Press, 1990.

U.S. Department of Defense. *The MAGIC Background of Pearl Harbor*. 8 vols. Washington, D.C.: U.S. Government Printing Office, 1977.

U.S. Strategic Bombing Survey. *Campaigns of the Pacific War*. Washington, D.C.: U.S. Government Printing Office, 1946.

———. *Summary Report (Pacific War)*. Washington, D.C.: U.S. Government Printing Office, 1946.

BOOKS AND ARTICLES

Abbazia, Patrick. *Mr. Roosevelt's Navy*. Annapolis, Md.: Naval Institute Press, 1975.

Achkasov, V. I., and N. B. Pavlovich. *Soviet Naval Operations in the Great Patriotic War*. Annapolis, Md.: Naval Institute Press, 1981.

Alexander, Joseph H. *Across the Reef: The Marine Assault on Tarawa*. Washington, D.C.: Marine Corps Historical Center, 1993.

———. "Bloody Tarawa." *Naval History*, November–December 1993.

Ansel, Walter. *Hitler Confronts England*. Durham, N.C.: Duke University Press, 1960.

Appleman, Roy E., et al. *Okinawa: The Last Battle*. Rutland, Vt.: Tuttle, 1960.

Assmann, Kurt. "The Invasion of Norway." *U.S. Naval Institute Proceedings*, April 1952.

Auphan, Paul. *The French Navy in World War II*. Annapolis, Md.: United States Naval Institute, 1959.

Baer, George W. *One Hundred Years of Sea Power*. Stanford, Cal.: Stanford University Press, 1994.

Baldwin, Hanson W. *Sea Fights and Shipwrecks*. Garden City, N.Y.: Hanover House, 1955.

Ballantine, Duncan S. *U.S. Naval Logistics in the Second World War*. Princeton, N.J.: Princeton University Press, 1947.

Ballard, Robert D. *The Discovery of the Bismarck*. New York: Warner/Madison Press, 1990.

Barbey, Daniel. *MacArthur's Amphibious Navy*. Annapolis, Md.: Naval Institute Press, 1969.

Barlow, Jeffrey G. "The U.S. Navy's Fight Against the Kamikazes." In Jack Sweetman, ed., *New Interpretations of Naval History*. Annapolis, Md.: Naval Institute Press, 1993.

Barnett, Corelli. *Engage the Enemy More Closely*. New York: Norton, 1991.

Bartley, Whitman S. *Iwo Jima: Amphibious Epic*. Washington, D.C.: U.S. Government Printing Office, 1954.

Beach, Edward L. "Culpable Negligence: A Submarine Commander Tells Why We Almost Lost the Pacific War." *American Heritage*, December 1981.

———. "Down by Subs." *U.S. Naval Institute Proceedings*, April 1991.

———. "Who's to Blame?" *U.S. Naval Institute Proceedings*, December 1991.

Beesly, Patrick. "Special Intelligence and the Battle of the Atlantic." In Robert W. Love, ed., *Changing Interpretations and New Sources in Naval History*. New York: Garland, 1980.

————. *Very Special Intelligence*. Garden City, N.Y.: Doubleday, 1978.

Bekker, Claus. *Hitler's Naval War*. Garden City, N.Y.: Doubleday, 1974.

Belke, T. J. "Roll of Drums." *U.S. Naval Institute Proceedings*, April 1983.

Belote, James H., and William M. Belote. *Titans of the Sea*. New York: Harper & Row, 1975.

————. *Typhoon of Steel*. New York: Harper & Row, 1970.

Bennett, Geoffrey. *Naval Battles of World War II*. New York: McKay, 1975.

————. *Naval Battles of the First World War*, New York: Scribner's, 1968.

Blair, Clay, Jr. *Silent Victory: The United States Submarine War Against Japan*. Philadelphia: Lippincott, 1973.

Bonnett, Stanley. *The Price of Admiralty*. London: Robert Hale, 1968.

Borg, Dorothy, and Shumpei Okamoto. *Pearl Harbor as History*. New York: Columbia University Press, 1973.

Bradford, Ernle. *The Mighty Hood*. Cleveland, Ohio: World, 1959.

Bragadin, M. A. *The Italian Navy in World War II*. Annapolis, Md.: United States Naval Institute, 1957.

Brice, Martin. *Axis Blockade Runners of World War II*. Annapolis, Md.: Naval Institute Press, 1981.

Brown, David. *Carrier Operations in World War II*. 2 vols. Annapolis, Md.: Naval Institute Press, 1968, 1974.

Bryant, Arthur, *The Turn of the Tide*. Garden City, N.Y.: Doubleday, 1957.

Buchanan, A. R. *The Navy's Air War*. New York: Harper, n.d.

Buchheim, Lothar-Gunther. *The U-Boat War*. New York: Knopf, 1978.

Buell, Thomas B. *Master of Sea Power: A Biography of Fleet Admiral Ernest J. King*. Boston: Little, Brown, 1980.

————. *The Quiet Warrior: Raymond Spruance*. Boston: Little, Brown, 1974.

Calvocoressi, Peter, Guy Wint, and John Pritchard. *Total War*. New York: Pantheon, 1989.

Cameron, Ian. *Wings of the Morning*. New York: Morrow, 1963.

Cant, Gilbert. *The War at Sea*. New York: Day, 1942.

Caulfied, Max. *Tomorrow Never Came: The Story of the S.S. Athenia*. New York: Norton, 1958.

Chalmers, W. S. *Max Horton and the Western Approaches*. London: Hodder & Stoughton, 1954.

Chapin, John C. *Breaching the Marianas: The Battle for Saipan*. Washington, D.C.: Marine Corps Historical Center, 1994.

————. *Breaking the Outer Ring: Marine Landings in the Marshall Islands*. Washington, D.C.: Marine Corps Historical Center, 1994.

Churchill, Winston S. *The Second World War*, 6 vols. Boston: Houghton Mifflin, 1948–53.

————. *The World Crisis*. New York: Scribner's, 1949.

Ciano, C. *The Ciano Diaries 1939-1943*. Garden City, N.Y.: Doubleday, 1946.

Cohen, Eliott A., and John Gooch. *Military Misfortunes*. New York: Free Press, 1990.

Cook, Charles. *The Battle of Cape Esperance*. New York: Crowell, 1968.

Costello, John. *The Pacific War*. New York: Rawson, Wade, 1981.

Craig, Walter. *The Fall of Japan*. New York: Dial, 1967.

Creswell, John. *Sea Warfare, 1939–1945*. Berkeley, Calif., University of California Press, 1967.

Colleta, Paolo E. "Rear Admiral Patrick N. L. Bellinger, Commander Patrol Wing Two, and General Frederick L. Martin, Air Commander Hawaii." In William B. Cogan, ed., *New Interpretations in Naval History*. Annapolis, Md.: Naval Institute Press, 1989.

Cunningham, Viscount. *Sailor's Odyssey*. London: Hutchinson, 1951.

Cutler, Thomas J. *The Battle of Leyte Gulf*. New York: HarperCollins, 1994.

Dallek, Robert. *Franklin D. Roosevelt and American Foreign Policy: 1932–1945*. New York: Oxford University Press, 1979.

Deighton, Len. *Blitzkrieg*. New York: Knopf, 1980.

———. *Fighter*. New York: Knopf, 1978.

D'Este, Carlo. *Bitter Victory*. New York: Dutton, 1988.

———. *Decision in Normandy*. New York: Dutton, 1983.

———. *Fatal Decision*. New York: HarperCollins, 1991.

Detmers, Theodor. *The Raider Kormoran*. London: William Kimber, 1959.

Dickens, Peter. *Narvik*. Annapolis, Md.: Naval Institute Press, 1974.

Dickinson, Clarence E., and Boyden Sparks. "The Target Was Utterly Satisfying," in S. E. Smith. *The United States Navy in World War II*. New York: Morrow, 1966.

Divine, David. *The Nine Days of Dunkirk*. New York: Norton, 1959.

Dobson, Christopher. *The Cruelest Night*. Boston: Little, Brown, 1979.

Dönitz, Karl. *Conduct of the War at Sea*. Washington, D.C.: Office of U.S. Naval Intelligence, 1946.

———. *Memoirs: Ten Years and Twenty Days*. London: Weidenfeld and Nicholson, 1959.

Dull, Paul. *A Battle History of the Imperial Japanese Navy*. Annapolis, Md.: Naval Institute Press, 1978

Dunn, R. J. *Niagara Gold*. Wellington, N.Z.: A. H. Reed, 1942.

Dyer, George. *The Amphibians Came to Conquer*. 2 vols. Washington, D.C.: Department of the Navy, 1969.

Edwards, Kenneth. *Operation Neptune*. London: Collins, 1946.

Ellis, John. *Brute Force*. New York: Viking, 1990.

Enright, Joseph F., with James W. Ryan. *Shinano!* New York: St. Martin's, 1987.

Evans, David, C., ed. *The Japanese Navy in World War II*. Annapolis, Md.: Naval Institute Press, 1986.

Feifer, George, *Tennozan: The Battle of Okinawa and the Atomic Bomb*. New York: Ticknor & Fields, 1992.

Field, James. *The Japanese at Leyte Gulf*. Princeton, N.J.: Princeton University Press, 1947.

Fleming, Peter. *Operation Sea Lion*. New York: Simon and Schuster, 1957.

Forester, C. S. *The Ship*. London: Michael Joseph, 1943.

Forrestal, E. P. *Admiral Raymond A. Spruance, U.S.N.*, Washington, D.C.: Government Printing Office, 1966.

Frank, Benis M. *Okinawa: The Last Great Island Battle*. New York: Elsevier-Dutton, 1978.

Frank, Richard B. *Guadalcanal*. New York: Random House, 1990.

Frank, Wolfgang. *The Sea Wolves*. New York: Rinehart, 1955.

Freeman, Robert H. *Requiem for a Fleet*. Ventnor, N.J.: Shellback Press, 1984.

Frischauer, Willi, and Robert Jackson. *The Navy's Here!* London: Gollancz, 1955.

Fuchida, Mitsuo, and Masatake Okumiya. *Midway: The Battle That Doomed Japan*. Annapolis, Md.: Naval Institute Press, 1953.

Furgurson, Ernest B. "Bush's War." *Washingtonian*, August 1985.

Gailey, Harry A. *Peleliu 1944*. Annapolis, Md.: Nautical and Aviation, 1983.

Gannon, Michael. *Operation Drumbeat*. New York: Harper & Row, 1980.

Gelb, Norman. *Dunkirk*. New York: Morrow, 1989.

Gilbert, Martin. *Churchill*. New York: Holt, 1991.

———. *The Second World War*. New York: Holt, 1989.

Goodhart, Philip. *Fifty Ships That Changed the World*. Garden City, N.Y.: Doubleday, 1965.

Gray, Colin S. *The Leverage of Sea Power*. New York: Free Press, 1992.

Greenfield, Kent R. *American Strategy in World War II*. Baltimore, Md.: Johns Hopkins University Press, 1943.

Grenfell, Russell. *The Bismarck Episode*. New York: Macmillan, 1962.
———. *Main Fleet to Singapore*. London: Faber and Faber, 1951.
Gretton, Peter. *Crisis Convoy*. Annapolis, Md.: Naval Institute Press, 1974.
———. *Former Naval Person: Winston Churchill and the Royal Navy*. London: Cassell, 1968.
Griffith, Samuel. *The Battle of Guadalcanal*. Annapolis, Md.: Nautical and Aviation, 1979.
Griffiths, Maurice. *The Hidden Menace*. Greenwich, U.K.: Conway Maritime Press, 1981.
Grove, Eric. *Sea Battles in Close-Up*. vol. II. Annapolis, Md.: Naval Institute Press, 1993.
Hagan, Kenneth, ed. *In Peace and War: Interpretations of American Naval History, 1775–1978*. Westport, Conn.: Greenwood, 1977.
———. *This People's Navy*. New York: Free Press, 1991.
Halsey, William F., and J. Bryan III. *Admiral Halsey's Story*. New York: Whittlesey House, 1947.
Hammel, Eric. *Munda Trail: The New Georgia Campaign*. New York: Orion, 1989.
Handel-Mazetti, Peter. "The *Scharnhorst-Gneisenau* Team at Its Peak." *U.S. Naval Institute Proceedings*, August 1956.
Hara, Tameichi, Fred Saito, and Roger Pineau. *Japanese Destroyer Captain*. New York: Ballantine, 1961.
Harman, Nicholas. *Dunkirk: The Patriotic Myth*. New York: Simon and Schuster, 1980.
Hathaway, Amos T. "Small Boys—Intercept!" In S. E. Smith, ed. *The United States Navy in World War II*. New York: Morrow, 1966.
Heggan, Thomas, and Joshua Logan. *Mr. Roberts*. New York: Random House, 1948.
Heinl, Robert D. *The Defense of Wake*. Washington, D.C.: U.S. Marine Corps Historical Section, 1947.
Heinrichs, Waldo. *Threshold of War*. New York: Oxford University Press, 1988.
Hezlet, Sir Arthur. *Aircraft and Sea Power*. New York: Stein and Day, 1970.
———. *Electronics and Sea Power*. New York: Stein & Day, 1973.
———. *The Submarine and Sea Power*. London: Davies, 1967.
Hickam, Homer H., Jr. *Torpedo Junction: U-Boat War off America's East Coast*. Annapolis, Md.: Naval Institute Press, 1989.
Hinsley, F. H. *British Intelligence in the Second World War*. 5 vols. London: Her Majesty's Stationery Office, 1979–1990.
Holmes, W. J. *Double-Edged Secrets*. Annapolis, Md.: Naval Institute Press, 1981.
———. "Naval Intelligence in the War Against Japan, 1941–1945." In Craig L. Symonds, ed., *New Aspects of Naval History*. Annapolis, Md.: Naval Institute Press, 1981.
———. *Undersea Victory*. Garden City, N.Y.: Doubleday, 1966.
Horton, D. C. *New Georgia*. New York: Ballantine, 1971.
Hough, Frank. *The Island War*. Philadelphia: Lippincott, 1947.
Hough, Richard. *The Longest Battle*. New York: Morrow, 1986.
Howard, Michael. *The Mediterranean Strategy in the Second World War*. New York: Praeger, 1968.
Howarth, Stephen, ed. *Men of War*. New York: St. Martin's, 1993.
Hoyt, Edwin P. *Japan's War*. New York: McGraw-Hill, 1986.
———. *MacArthur's Navy*. New York: Orion, 1989.
Huber, Thomas M. *Japan's Battle of Okinawa, April–June 1945*. Fort Leavenworth, Kan.: Combat Studies Institute, U.S. Army Command and General Staff College, 1990.
Hughes, Terry, and John Costello. *The Battle of the Atlantic*. New York: Dial/James Wade, 1977.
Humble, Richard. *Hitler's High Seas Fleet*. New York: Ballantine, 1971.
———. *Japan's High Seas Fleet*. New York: Ballantine, 1973.

Inoguchi, Rakihei, Tadashi Narajima, and Roger Pineau. *The Divine Wind.* New York: Ballantine, 1968.

Irving, David. *The Destruction of Convoy PQ 17.* London: Cassell, 1968.

Isenberg, Michael T. *Shield of the Republic.* New York: St. Martin's, 1993.

Isley, Jeter A., and Philip A. Crowl. *The U.S. Marines and Amphibious War.* Princeton, N.J.: Princeton University Press, 1951.

Ito, Masanori. *The End of the Imperial Japanese Navy.* New York: Norton, 1962.

Jackson, Robert. *Strike From the Sea.* London: Arthur Barker, 1920.

Jacobsen, H. A., and Jürgen Rohwer, eds. *Decisive Battles of World War II: The German View.* London: André Deutsch, 1965.

James, D. Clayton. *The Years of MacArthur.* Vol. II. New York: Houghton Mifflin, 1972.

Jensen, Oliver. *Carrier War.* New York: Simon and Schuster, 1945.

Jesse, F. Tennyson. *The Saga of the San Demetrio.* London: His Majesty's Stationery Office, 1942.

Jordan, Vause. *U-Boat Ace.* Annapolis, Md.: Naval Institute Press, 1990.

Kahn, David. *The Codebreakers.* London: Weidenfeld and Nicolson, 1967.

————. *Seizing the Enigma.* Boston: Houghton Mifflin, 1991.

Karig, Walter. *Battle Report.* 5 vols. New York: Farrar & Rinehart, 1944–49.

Kaufman, Robert G. *Arms Control During the Pre-Nuclear Era: The United States and Naval Limitation Between the Two World Wars.* New York: Columbia University Press, 1990.

Keegan, John. *The Price of Admiralty.* New York: Viking, 1989.

Kemp, Peter K. *Decision at Sea: The Convoy Escorts.* New York: Elsevier-Dutton, 1978.

————. *Key to Victory.* Boston: Little, Brown, 1957.

Kennedy, Ludovic. *Menace: The Life and Death of the Tirpitz.* London: Sidgwick & Jackson, 1979.

————. *Pursuit: The Chase and Sinking of the Battleship Bismarck.* New York: Viking, 1974.

King, Ernest J., and Walter Muir Whitehill. *Fleet Admiral King: A Naval Record.* New York: Norton, 1952.

Knott, Richard C. *Black Cat Raiders of WWII.* Annapolis, Md.: Nautical and Aviation, 1981.

Knowles, Kenneth A. "Ultra and the Battle of the Atlantic: The American View." In Robert W. Love, ed., *Changing Interpretations and New Sources in Naval History.* New York: Garland, 1980.

Krancke, Theodor, and H. J. Brennecke. *Battleship Scheer.* London: William Kimber, 1956.

Kurzman, Dan. *Fatal Voyage: The Sinking of the U.S.S. Indianapolis.* New York: Atheneum, 1990.

————. *Left to Die: The Tragedy of the U.S.S. Juneau.* New York: Pocket Books, 1993.

Lamb, James B. *The Corvette Navy.* Toronto: Macmillan of Canada, n.d.

Layton, Edwin T. *"And I Was There."* New York: Morrow, 1985.

Leutze, James. *A Different Kind of Victory.* Annapolis, Md.: Naval Institute Press, 1981.

Lewin, Ronald. *The American Magic.* New York: Farrar, Straus & Giroux, 1982.

————. *Ultra Goes to War.* New York: McGraw-Hill, 1979.

Liddell Hart, Basil H. *History of the Second World War.* London: Cassell, 1970.

Lindley, John M. *Carrier Victory.* New York: Dutton, 1978.

Lockwood, Charles A., Jr. *Sink 'Em All.* New York: Dutton, 1951.

Lord, Walter. *Day of Infamy.* New York: Holt, 1957.

————. *Incredible Victory.* New York: Harper & Row, 1967.

Love, Robert W., Jr. *A History of the U.S. Navy.* Vol. II. Harrisburg, Pa.: Stackpole Books, 1992.

Lundstrom, John. *The First South Pacific Campaign.* Annapolis, Md.: Naval Institute Press, 1976.

————. *The First Team*. Annapolis, Md.: Naval Institute Press, 1984.

————. *The First Team and the Guadalcanal Campaign*. Annapolis, Md.: Naval Institute Press, 1994.

————. "Frank Jack Fletcher Got a Bum Rap." *Naval History*, Summer and Fall, 1992.

Macintyre, Donald. *The Battle for the Mediterranean*. London: Batsford, 1964.

————. *The Battle of the Atlantic*. New York: Macmillan, 1961.

————. *The Battle of the Pacific*. London: Batsford, 1966.

————. *Narvik*. London: Pan Books, 1973.

————. *The Naval War Against Hitler*. New York: Scribner, 1971.

————. *U-Boat Killer*. New York: Norton, 1956.

McLachlan, Donald. *Room 39*. New York: Atheneum, 1968.

Maher, Robert A., and James E. Wise, Jr. "Stand By for a Ram!" *Naval History*, Summer 1993.

Manchester, William. *American Caesar*. Boston: Little, Brown, 1978.

————. *The Last Lion: Winston Spencer Churchill*. Vol. II. Boston: Little, Brown, 1988.

Marder, Arthur J. *From the Dardanelles to Oran*. London: Oxford University Press, 1974.

————. *From the Dreadnaught to Scapa Flow*. Vol V. London: Oxford University Press, 1970.

————. *Old Friends, New Enemies: The Royal Navy and the Imperial Japanese Navy*. London: Oxford University Press, 1981.

————. *Operation Menace: The Dakar Expedition and the Dudley North Affair*. London: Oxford University Press, 1976.

Mason, David. *Raid on St. Nazaire*. New York: Ballantine, 1970.

Mason, John T. *The Atlantic War Remembered: An Oral History Collection*. Annapolis, Md.: Naval Institute Press, 1990.

————. *The Pacific War Remembered: An Oral History Collection*. Annapolis, Md.: Naval Institute Press, 1986.

Matthews, Allen R. *The Assault*. New York: Simon and Schuster, 1947.

McIntyre, Larry. "War in the Illusions." *Naval History*, Summer 1993.

Melson, Charles D. *Up the Slot: Marines in the Central Solomons*. Washington, D.C.: Marine Corps Historical Center, 1994.

Mersky, Peter B. *Time of the Aces: Marine Pilots in the Solomons, 1942–1944*. Washington, D.C.: Marine Corps Historical Center, 1993.

Middlebrook, Martin. *Battleship*. London: Penguin, 1979.

————. *Convoy*. New York: Morrow, 1977.

Miller, Edward S. *War Plan Orange*. Annapolis, Md.: Naval Institute Press, 1991.

Miller, Nathan. *F.D.R.: An Intimate History*. Garden City, N.Y.: Doubleday, 1983.

————. *The Naval Air War: 1939–1945*. Annapolis, Md.: Naval Institute Press, 1991.

————. *Spying for America: The Hidden History of U.S. Intelligence*. New York: Dell, 1990.

————. *The U.S. Navy: A History*. New York: Morrow, 1990.

Miller, Thomas G. *The Cactus Air Force*. New York: Harper & Row, 1969.

Millot, Bernard. *The Battle of the Coral Sea*. Annapolis, Md.: Naval Institute Press, 1974.

Milner, Marc. *North American Run*. Annapolis, MD.: Naval Institute Press, 1985.

Mitchell, Donald W. *A History of Russian and Soviet Sea Power*. New York: Atheneum, 1974.

Monis, C. E. and Hugh B. Cave, "Kula Gulf" in S.E. Smith, *The United States Navy in World War II*. New York: Morrow, 1966.

Monserrat, Nicholas. *The Cruel Sea*. New York: Knopf, 1951.

Morison, Samuel Eliot. *The History of U.S. Naval Operations During the Second World War*. 15 vols. Boston: Little, Brown, 1947–62.

————. *Strategy and Compromise*. Boston: Little, Brown, 1958.

————. *The Two-Ocean War*. Boston: Little, Brown, 1963.

Moulton, J. L. *A Study of Warfare in Three Dimensions*. Athens, Ohio: Ohio University Press, 1967.

Müllenheim-Rechberg, Burkard Baron von. *Battleship Bismarck*. Annapolis, Md.: Naval Institute Press, 1990.

Murray, Williamson. *Luftwaffe*. Baltimore, Md.: Nautical and Aviation, 1985.

Newcomb, Richard E. *Abandon Ship! Death of the U.S. Indianapolis*. New York: Holt, 1958.

————. *Savo*. New York: Holt, Rinehart and Winston, 1961.

O'Brien, Cyril J. *Liberation: Marines in the Capture of Guam*. Washington, D.C.: Marine Corps Historical Center, 1994.

Office of the Chief of Naval Operations. *Amphibious Operations: Capture of Okinawa Ryukyus Operation*. Washington, D.C.: Navy Department, 1946.

————. *Battle Experience: Radar Pickets and Methods of Combatting Suicide Attacks off Okinawa*. Washington: Navy Department, 1945.

Oi, Atshushi. "Why Japan's Anti-Submarine Warfare Failed." *U.S. Naval Institute Proceedings*, June 1952.

Okumiya, Masatake. "Pearl Harbor: The Japanese Perspective." *Naval History*, Winter 1991.

———— and Jiro Horikoshi with Martin Caidin. *Zero!* New York: Ballantine, 1956.

Pack, S. W. C. *The Battle of Matapan*. London: Macmillan, 1961.

————. *Cunningham*. London: Batsford, 1974.

————. *Invasion North Africa 1942*. New York: Scribner, 1978.

Padfield, Peter. *Dönitz: The Last Führer*. New York: Harper & Row, 1984.

Parillo, John. "The Imperial Japanese Navy," in James Sadkovich, ed. *Reevaluating Naval Combatants of World War II*. Westport, Conn.: Greenwood, 1990.

Pearce, Frank. *Great Naval Battles of World War II*. London: Robert Hale, 1990.

Peillard, Leonce. *The Laconia Affair*. New York: Bantam, 1983.

Pineau, Roger. "Rochefort," in Howarth, ed. *Men of War*. New York: St Martin's Press, 1992.

Polmar, Norman. *Aircraft Carriers*. Garden City, N.Y.: Doubleday, 1969.

————. *The American Submarine*. Annapolis, Md.: Nautical and Aviation, 1981.

Pope, Dudley. *Graf Spee: The Life and Death of a Raider*. Philadelphia: Lippincott, 1957.

————. *73 North: The Battle of the Barents Sea*. Philadelphia: Lippincott, 1958.

Popham, Hugh. *Sea Flight*. London: William Kimber, 1954.

Potter, E. A. *Admiral Arleigh Burke*. New York: Random House, 1990.

————. *Nimitz*. Annapolis, Md.: Naval Institute Press, 1976.

————, and Chester W. Nimitz, eds. *Sea Power*. Annapolis, Md.: Naval Institite Press, 1960.

Potter, John. *Fiasco*. New York: Stein and Day, 1970.

Prange, Gordon W. *At Dawn We Slept*. New York: McGraw-Hill, 1981.

————. *Miracle at Midway*. New York: McGraw-Hill, 1982.

Preston, Antony, and Alan Raven. *Flower Class Corvettes*. London: Bivouac Books, 1973.

Price, Alfred. *Aircraft Versus Submarine*. Annapolis, Md.: Naval Institute Press, 1975.

Prien, Gunther. *I Sank the Royal Oak*. London: Gray Inn, 1954.

Pugh, Philip. *The Cost of Seapower*. London: Conway, 1986.

Puleston, William D. *The Influence of Sea Power in World War II*. Westport, Conn.: Greenwood, 1970.

Raeder, Erich. *My Life*. Annapolis, Md.: Naval Institute Press, 1960.

Reynolds, Clark. *The Fast Carriers*. New York: McGraw-Hill, 1968.

Rhys-Jones, Graham. "The Loss of the *Bismarck*." *Naval War College Review*, Spring, 1993.

Richardson, David C. "You Decide." *U.S. Naval Institute Proceedings*, December 1991.

Richardson, James O. *On the Treadmill to Pearl Harbor: The Memoirs of Admiral James*

O. Richardson USN (Ret.). Washington, D.C.: U.S. Government Printing Office, 1973.

Ringle, Ken. "Remembering the *Reuben James." Washington Post,* October 5, 1991.

Robertson, Terence. *Dieppe: The Shame and Glory.* London: Pan, 1962.

———. *Escort Commander: The Story of Captain Frederick John Walker.* New York: Bantam, 1979.

Rogge, Bernhard, and Wolfgang Frank. *The German Raider Atlantis.* New York: Ballantine, 1956.

Rohwer, Jürgen. "Convoy—The View From the Other Side," in Craig L. Symonds, ed., *New Aspects of Naval History.* Annapolis, Md.: Naval Institute Press, 1991.

———. *The Critical Convoy Battles of March 1943.* Annapolis, Md.: Naval Institute Press, 1977.

———. "Ultra and the Battle of the Atlantic: The German View." In Robert W. Love, Jr., ed., *Changing Interpretations and New Sources in Naval History.* New York: Garland, 1980.

Roscoe, Theodore. *On the Seas and in the Skies.* New York: Hawthorne, 1970.

———. *U.S. Destroyer Operations in World War II.* Annapolis, Md.: Naval Institute Press, 1953.

———. *U.S. Submarine Operations in World War II.* Annapolis, Md.: Naval Institute Press, 1949.

Roskill, Stephen. *Churchill and the Admirals.* New York: Morrow, 1977.

———. *H.M.S. Warspite.* London: Futura, 1974.

———. *Naval Policy Between the Wars.* 2 vols. Annapolis, Md.: Naval Institute Press, 1968, 1976.

———. *The Secret Capture.* London: Collins, 1959.

———. *The War at Sea.* 3 vols. London: Her Majesty's Stationery Office, 1954–1961.

———. *White Ensign.* Annapolis, Md.: Naval Institute Press, 1960.

Ross, Al. *The Destroyer Campbeltown.* Annapolis, Md.: Naval Institute Press, 1990.

Ross, Bill D. *Iwo Jima: Legacy of Valor.* New York: Vanguard, 1985.

Ross, Tweed W., Jr. *The Best Way to Destroy a Ship.* Manhattan, Kan.: MA/AH Publishing, 1980.

Ruge, Friedrich. *Der Seekrieg: The German Navy's Story, 1939–1945.* Annapolis, Md.: U.S. Naval Institute, 1957.

———, ed. *The Soviets as Naval Opponents.* Annapolis, Md.: Naval Institute Press, 1979.

Runyon, Timothy J., and Jan M. Cooper, eds. *To Die Gallantly: The Battle of the Atlantic.* Boulder, Col.: Westview Press, 1994.

Rust, Eric. *Naval Officers Under Hitler: The Story of Crew 34.* New York: Praeger, 1991.

Ryan, Cornelius. *The Longest Day: June 6, 1944.* New York: Simon and Schuster, 1959.

Sadkovich, James J. *The Italian Navy in World War II.* Westport, Conn.: Greenwood, 1994.

———, ed. *Reevaluating the Major Naval Combatants of World War II.* Westport, Conn.: Greenwood, 1990.

Sakai, Saburo, with Martin Caidin and Fred Saito. *Samurai!* New York: Dutton, 1958.

Salewski, Michael. "The Submarine War: A Historical Essay" in Lothar-Gunther Bucheim. *U-Boat at War.* New York: Knopf, 1978.

Schofield, Bernard B. *The Russian Convoys.* London: Barsford, 1964.

———. *Taranto.* Annapolis, Md.: Naval Institute Press, 1973.

Schull, Joseph. *The Far Distant Ships.* Annapolis, Md.: Naval Institute Press, 1952.

Seth, Ronald. *The Fiercest Battle.* New York: Norton, 1962.

Shaw, Henry I. *First Offensive: The Marine Campaign for Guadalcanal.* Washington, D.C.: Marine Corps Historical Center, 1992.

Sherrod, Robert. *History of Marine Corps Aviation in World War II.* Washington, D.C.: Combat Forces Press, 1952.

———. *On to Westward.* New York: Duell, Sloan and Pearce, 1945.

————. *Tarawa*. New York: Duell, Sloan and Pearce, 1944.

Shirer, William L. *Berlin Diary*. New York: Knopf, 1941.

Showell, Jak P. Mallman. *The German Navy in World War Two*. Annapolis, Md.: Naval Institute Press, 1979.

————. *U-Boat Command and the Battle of the Atlantic*. St. Catherines, Ont.: Vanwell Publishing, 1989.

————. *U-Boats Under the Swastika*. Annapolis, Md.: Naval Institute Press, 1988.

Slackman, Michael. *Target: Pearl Harbor*. Honolulu: University of Hawaii Press, 1990.

Sledge, Eugene B. "Peleliu 1944: Why Did We Go There?" *U.S. Naval Institute Proceedings*, September 1994.

————. *With the Old Breed at Peleliu and Okinawa*. Novato, Calif.: Presidio, 1981.

Slessor, John. *The Central Blue*. New York: Praeger, 1957.

Smith, Peter C. *Action Imminent*. London: William Kimber, 1980.

————. *The Great Ships Pass*. Annapolis, Md.: Naval Institute Press, 1977.

————. *The History of Dive Bombing*. Annapolis, Md.: Nautical and Aviation, 1981.

Smith, S. E. ed., *The United States Navy in World War II*. New York: Morrow, 1966.

Snyder, Gerald S. *The Royal Oak Disaster*. San Rafael, Calif.: Presidio, 1978.

Spector, Ronald. *Eagle Against the Sun*. New York: Free Press, 1985.

Speer, Albert. *Inside the Third Reich*. New York: Macmillan, 1970.

Sprague, C. A. F., and Philip H. Gustafson. "They Had Us on the Ropes." in S. E. Smith, *The United States Navy in World War II*. New York: Morrow, 1966.

Sprietsma, Charles F. *Analysis of the Battle of Iwo Jima*. Maxwell Field, Ala.: Air Command and Staff College, 1984.

Spurr, Russell. *A Glorious Way to Die: The Kamikaze Mission of the Battleship Yamato*. New York: New Market, 1981.

Stafford, Edward P. *The Big E*. New York: Random House, 1962.

Stephen, Martin, *Sea Battles in Close-Up*, Vol. I. Annapolis, Md.: Naval Institute Press, 1988.

Sternhill, Charles M., and Alan M. Thorndike. *Antisubmarine Warfare in World War II*. Washington, D.C.: Office of Chief of Naval Operations, 1946.

Stillwell, Paul. *Air Raid Pearl Harbor*. Annapolis, Md.: Naval Institute Press, 1991.

Stratton, Roy O. "Germany's Secret Naval Supply Service." *Naval Institute Proceedings*, October 1953.

Sweetman, Jack. "Battle at North Cape." *U.S. Naval Institute Proceedings*, December 1993.

————. "Leyte Gulf." *U.S. Naval Institute Proceedings*, October 1994.

————. "Midway." *U.S. Naval Institute Proceedings*, June 1992.

Syrett, David. *The Defeat of the German U-Boats*. Columbia, S.C.: University of South Carolina Press, 1994.

Tarrant, V. E. *The Last Year of the Kriegsmarine*. Annapolis, Md.: Naval Institute Press, 1994.

————. *The U-Boat Offensive: 1914–1945*. Annapolis, Md.: Naval Institute Press, 1989.

Taylor, Thodore. *The Magnificent Mitscher*. New York: Norton, 1954.

Terraine, John. *The U-Boat Wars: 1916–1945*. New York: Putnam's, 1989.

Thomas, Charles S. *The German Navy in the Nazi Era*. Annapolis, Md.: Naval Institute Press, 1991.

Thomas, David A. *Nazi Victory: Crete, 1941*. New York: Stein and Day, 1972.

Tillman, Barrett. *Avenger at War*. New York: Scribner, 1980.

————. *The Dauntless Dive Bomber of World War Two*. Annapolis, Md.: Naval Institute Press, 1976.

————. *Hellcat: The F6F in World War Two*. Annapolis, Md.: Naval Institute Press, 1979.

————. *Wildcat: The F4F in World War Two*. Annapolis, Md.: Nautical and Aviation, 1983.

Toland, John. *The Rising Sun*. New York: Random House, 1970.

Townsend, Peter. *Duel of Eagles*. New York: Simon and Schuster, 1970.
Tuleja, Thaddeus V. *Twilight of the Sea Gods*. Westport, Conn.: Greenwood, 1975.
Tute, Warren. *The Deadly Stroke*. New York: Coward, McCann & Geoghegan, 1973.
Utley, Jonathan. *Going to War with Japan*. Knoxville, Tenn.: University of Tennessee Press, 1985.
Vandegrift, Archibald. *Once a Marine*. New York: Norton, 1964.
Van der Vat, Dan. *The Atlantic Campaign*. New York: Harper & Row, 1988.
————. *The Pacific Campaign*. New York: Simon and Schuster, 1991.
Van Oosten, F. C. *The Battle of the Java Sea*. Annapolis, Md.: Naval Institute Press, 1976.
Vian, Philip. *Action This Day*. London: Frederick Muller, 1960.
Von der Porten, Edward P. *Pictorial History of the German Navy in World War II*. New York: Crowell, 1976.
Vraciu, Alexander, with Edward Sims. "Hellcat at the Turkey Shoot." In S. E. Smith. *The United States Navy in World War II*. New York: Morrow, 1966.
Waters, John M., Jr. *Bloody Winter*. Annapolis, Md.: Naval Institute Press, 1984.
Waters, S. D. *The Royal New Zealand Navy*. Wellington, N.Z.: Department of Internal Affairs, 1956.
Watt, Donald C. *How War Came*. New York: Pantheon, 1989.
Weaver, H. J. *Nightmare at Scapa Flow*. Henly-on-Thames: Cressrelles, 1980.
Weigley, Russell. *The American Way of War*. Bloomington, Ind.: Indiana University Press, 1973.
Weinberg, Gerhard L. *A World at Arms: A Global History of World War II*. New York: Cambridge University Press, 1994.
Werner, Herbert A. *Iron Coffins*. New York: Holt, Rinehart and Winston, 1969.
Wheatley, Ronald. *Operation Sea Lion*. Oxford: Clarendon Press, 1958.
Williamson, John A., and William D. Lanier. "The Twelve Days of the *England*." *U.S. Naval Institute Proceedings*, March 1980.
Willmott, H. P. *The Barrier and the Javlin*. Annapolis, Md.: Naval Institute Press, 1983.
————. *Empires in the Balance*. Annapolis, Md.: Naval Institute Press, 1982.
Winslow, Walter G. *The Fleet the Gods Forgot*. Annapolis, Md.: Naval Institute Press, 1982.
————. *The Ghost That Died in the Sunda Strait*. Annapolis, Md.: Naval Institute Press, 1984.
Winton, John. *Carrier Glorious*. London: Seeven & Warburg, 1986.
————. *The Forgotten Fleet*. New York: Coward-McCann, 1967.
————. *Ultra at Sea*. New York: Morrow, 1988.
————. *Ultra in the Pacific*. Annapolis, Md.: Naval Institute Press, 1994.
Wohstetter, Roberta. *Pearl Harbor: Warning and Decision*. Stanford, Cal.: Stanford University Press, 1962.
Woodward, C. Vann. *The Battle for Leyte Gulf*. New York: Macmillan, 1947.
Woodward, David. *The Russians at Sea*. London: William Kimber, 1966.
————. *The Secret Raiders*. New York: Norton, 1955.
Wouk, Herman. *The Caine Mutiny*. Garden City, N.Y.: Doubleday, 1950.
Wukovits, John. "Spruance," in Howarth, ed. *Men of War*. New York: St. Martins Press, 1992.
Y'Blood, William T. *Hunter-Killer: U.S. Escort Carriers in the Battle of the Atlantic*. Annapolis, Md.: Naval Institute Press, 1983.
————. *The Little Giants*. Annapolis, Md.: Naval Institute Press, 1968.
————. *Red Sun Setting*. Annapolis, Md.: Naval Institute Press, 1981.
Yoshiba, Mitsuru. "The End of *Yamato*." *U.S. Naval Institute Proceedings*, February 1952.
Young, Stephen B. *Trapped at Pearl Harbor*. Annapolis, Md.: Naval Institute Press, 1991.
Zevin, Ben. ed. *Nothing to Fear: The Selected Addresses of Franklin D. Roosevelt*. New York: Popular Library, 1946.

Index